CAMBRIDGE

TALENT

Student's Book & Workbook 2
with eBook, virtual classroom and online expansion

Audrey Cowan and Alun Phillips
with Ciaran Ward and Teresa Ting

Vivere Better Learning

Welcome to Talent
your new course from Cambridge University Press

GRAMMAR

Starter Unit for revision of the basic structures.

Grammar Guide boxes and practice activities.

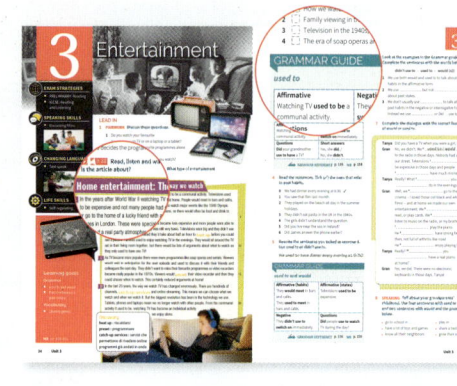

Presentation spreads introduce key language through topical and thought-provoking texts.

Grammar boxes with clear and succinct rules.

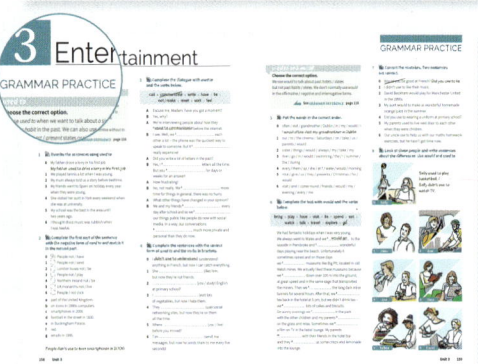

Workbook contains three pages of extra grammar practice along with cumulative practice and concept checking activities in every unit.

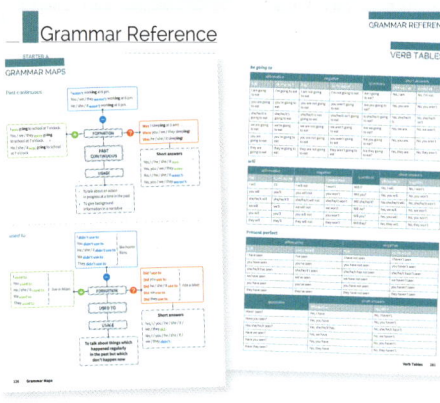

Grammar Reference with explanation of main language. Grammar maps, verb tables and irregular verb list provide a complete reference section.

SKILLS

Reading Skills to promote critical thinking and stimulate class debate.
Strategy boxes give practice in task types for Cambridge exams: **Preliminary** and **IGCSE**.

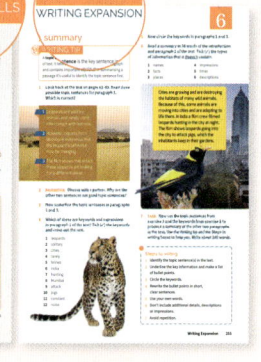

Writing Skills and **Writing Expansion** with model texts and guided practice.

Speaking Skills with functional dialogues on film and **Strategy** boxes to develop your confidence.
Sounds English section to improve your pronunciation.

Listening Skills lessons with a variety of text types, voices and accents.

VIDEOS

Documentary-style **presentation videos** with onscreen activities provide a dynamic start to the unit.

Functional language videos present language in fun and memorable contexts.

Changing Language videos use the latest findings from Corpus research and on street interviews to show how English is really spoken today!

EXAMS

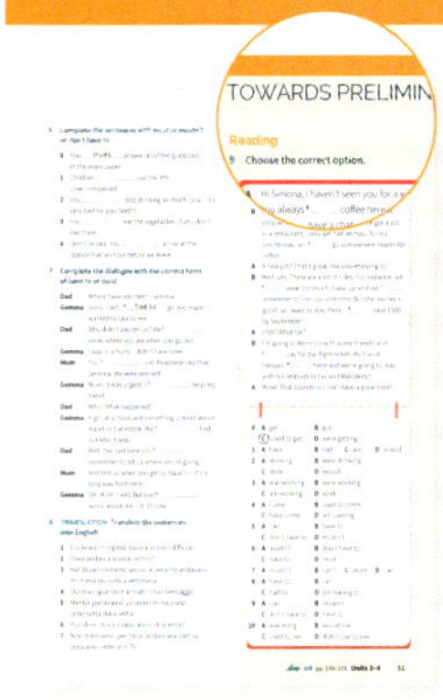

Exam Skills sections in the Workbook provide practice of the Cambridge Preliminary exam.

Exam revision every two units providing exam-style practice of unit language.

ACADEMIC SKILLS

Academic Skills sections prepare you for further study and academic success!

IELTS exam development is clearly highlighted.

VOCABULARY

Vocabulary pages present words in realistic contexts. Practice and production activities help you memorise new words.

Vocabulary Extension lessons using infographics and maps help you to organise new words and expand your vocabulary.

LIFE SKILLS

Like Skills sections help develop the self-awareness and social skills needed for today's world.

Citizenship and Competency Skills development are clearly signalled.

CLIL

CLIL section with topics carefully chosen to compliment other areas of the national curriculum.

Real-life tasks to encourage independent study in areas of personal interest.

LITERATURE

Literature Skills section introduces popular literary genres and provides extra skills practice.

Critical thinking activities stimulate class discussion and debate.

Research projects deepen your knowledge and develop independent study skills.

Competency Skills development is clearly signposted.

E-BOOK

- Integrated video and audio
- Interactive activities
- Extra resources

CONTENTS

Starter p. 6   **A** Verbs of routine; present simple; adverbs of frequency   **B** Technology; *there is / are; some / any; a lot, a little, a few; too much / many, too little / few*;   **C** Clothes; past simple: *be* and regular and irregular verbs   **D** Feelings; comparative and superlative adjectives; *(not) as … as*   **E** Jobs; *be going to*; present continuous for future; *will*

		GRAMMAR	VOCABULARY	READING	WRITING
1	**FRIENDSHIP** p. 16	Present simple and continuous; Present perfect; Present perfect with *just*, *already* and *yet*	Adjectives of personality; Vocabulary Extension: Adjective prefixes p. 260	Life online; **Strategy** Identify the writer's views PRELIMINARY IGCSE	Informal emails; **Strategy** Write an informal email PRELIMINARY IGCSE; Writing Expansion p. 250
2	**MIGRATION** p. 24	Present perfect simple and continuous; Defining relative clauses	Geographical features; Vocabulary Extension: Prepositions of movement p. 261	The robin: Myth and reality; **Strategy** Understand the purpose of a text PRELIMINARY IGCSE	Descriptive essays; **Strategy** Write a description of a place; Writing Expansion p. 251

Revise and Round Up pp. 32–33 • **Towards Preliminary – Reading p. 33**

		GRAMMAR	VOCABULARY	READING	WRITING
3	**ENTERTAINMENT** p. 34	*used to* and *would*; Past continuous v past simple	Literary genres; Vocabulary Extension: Literary idioms p. 262	Vampires; **Strategy** Understand chronology and sequence PRELIMINARY IGCSE	Reviews; **Strategy** Write a film or book review; Writing Expansion p. 252
4	**SPORT** p. 42	*can / can't*; *have to / don't have to*; *must* and *have to*; *make* and *let*	Sports and sports equipment; Vocabulary Extension: Compound nouns p. 263	E-sports – The end of sport as we know it?; **Strategy** Transfer information	Essays; **Strategy** Write a 'for and against' essay IGCSE; Writing Expansion p. 253

Revise and Round Up pp. 50–51 • **Towards Preliminary – Reading p. 51**

		GRAMMAR	VOCABULARY	READING	WRITING
5	**CRIME** p. 52	Past perfect; Indefinite pronouns	Crimes and criminals; Vocabulary Extension: Phrasal verbs p. 264	May the force be with us; **Strategy** Take notes IGCSE	Police reports; **Strategy** Write a police report; Writing Expansion p. 254
6	**FREAK WEATHER** p. 60	First conditional; *if / when / unless*; Zero conditional; *will / may / might* for future possibility	The environment; Vocabulary Extension: Weather idioms p. 265	New city dwellers; **Strategy** Cause and effect PRELIMINARY IGCSE	Summaries; **Strategy** Write a summary IGCSE; Writing Expansion p. 255

Revise and Round Up pp. 68–69 • **Towards Preliminary – Reading / Writing p. 69**

		GRAMMAR	VOCABULARY	READING	WRITING
7	**HEALTH OF A NATION** p. 70	Second conditional and *If I were you*; Second conditional v first conditional; *Should / had better / ought to* for advice	Illnesses, injuries and remedies; Vocabulary Extension: Medical collocations p. 266	Health and safety versus common sense?; **Strategy** Insert sentences into a text PRELIMINARY	Proposals; **Strategy** Write a proposal; Writing Expansion p. 256
8	**A POLITICAL WORLD** p. 78	Third conditional; *wish* + past tenses	Politics and society; Vocabulary Extension: Prefixes p. 267	Voting with our feet?; **Strategy** Complete texts PRE FIRST	Biographies; **Strategy** Write a biography; Writing Expansion p. 257

Revise and Round Up pp. 86–87 • **Towards Preliminary – Reading / Writing p. 87**

		GRAMMAR	VOCABULARY	READING	WRITING
9	**PURE GENIUS!** p. 88	The passive: present and past simple; Passive present perfect	Gadgets and creativity; Vocabulary Extension: Collocations with *make* and *do* p. 268	Designing the future; **Strategy** Work on True / False / Doesn't say questions	Formal letters or emails; **Strategy** Write a formal letter / email; Writing Expansion p. 258
10	**IN THE NEWS** p. 96	Reported speech; *say* and *tell*	Media verbs; Vocabulary Extension: Cognates and false friends p. 269	Freedom of the press – but how free is free?; **Strategy** Distinguish between facts and opinions PRELIMINARY IGCSE	Magazine reports; **Strategy** Write a magazine report; Writing Expansion p. 259

Revise and Round Up pp. 104–105 • **Towards Preliminary – Reading / Writing p. 105**

Grammar Reference p. 108 • **Grammar Maps** p. 124 • **Workbook** p. 130 • **Literature Skills** p. 230 • **CLIL** p. 240 • **Wordlist** p. 270

CONTENTS

SPEAKING	CHANGING LANGUAGE / SOUNDS ENGLISH	LISTENING SKILLS	LIFE SKILLS	ACADEMIC SKILLS
Meeting and greeting  **Strategy** Keep the conversation going	**Changing Language:** Greetings 	Conversation about famous friends **Strategy** Focus and eliminate in multiple choice `PRELIMINARY` `IGCSE`	**Life Skills:** Dealing with stress **Citizenship and Competency Skills:** Problem solving	
Having a disagreement  **Strategy** Make an opinion stronger `PRELIMINARY` `IGCSE`	**Sounds English:** Sentence stress: Emphasis	Interview about living in Italy **Strategy** True / False questions	**Academic Skills:** Labelling a map `IELTS`	
Discussing films  **Strategy** Give encouragement	**Changing Language:** Text speak 	Conversation about ghosts **Strategy** Match exercises `IGCSE`	**Life Skills:** Self-regulating **Citizenship and Competency Skills:** Acting autonomously and responsibly	
Explaining rules  **Strategy** Self-correct `PRELIMINARY` `IGCSE`	**Sounds English:** The /r/ sound	Conversation about rugby **Strategy** Identify the main idea `PRELIMINARY` `IGCSE`	**Academic Skills:** Understanding arguments `IELTS`	
Having a discussion  **Strategy** Interrupt politely `PRELIMINARY` `IGCSE`	**Changing Language:** so not  …	Information about crimes **Strategy** Answer *wh-*questions `IGCSE`	**Life Skills:** Judging right from wrong **Citizenship and Competency Skills:** Acting autonomously and responsibly	
Making predictions  **Strategy** Support / Justify an argument `PRELIMINARY` `IGCSE`	**Sounds English:** The sound /θ/	Information about the weather **Strategy** Match pictures to audio information `PRELIMINARY`	**Academic Skills:** Describing a process `IELTS`	
Asking for and giving advice  **Strategy** Show empathy	**Changing Language:** Modal verbs 	Radio interview about healthy eating **Strategy** Complete notes with missing words `PRELIMINARY` `IGCSE`	**Life Skills:** Building your self-esteem **Citizenship and Competency Skills:** Acting autonomously and responsibly	
Apologising and expressing regret  **Strategy** Express regret for your actions `PRELIMINARY` `IGCSE`	**Sounds English:** The /əʊ/ sound	Conversation about personal opinions **Strategy** Identify multiple speakers `IGCSE`	**Academic Skills:** Using the internet for research	
Describing objects  **Strategy** Paraphrasing `PRELIMINARY` `IGCSE`	**Changing Language:** *Literally!* 	Radio interview **Strategy** Select correct information	**Life Skills:** Planning and organising **Citizenship and Competency Skills:** Planning and prioritising	
Gossiping  **Strategy** Change the subject	**Sounds English:** The glottal stop /ʔ/	Conversation about the news **Strategy** Identify relationships between speakers `PRELIMINARY` `IGCSE`	**Academic Skills:** Planning and writing in paragraphs `PRELIMINARY` `IGCSE` `IELTS`	

Speaking Skills – Dialogues p. 276 • Verb Tables p. 280 • Irregular Verbs p. 284 • UK Map p. 285

STARTER A

About us

Grammar: present simple, adverbs of frequency
Vocabulary: verbs of routine

WB pp. 130–131

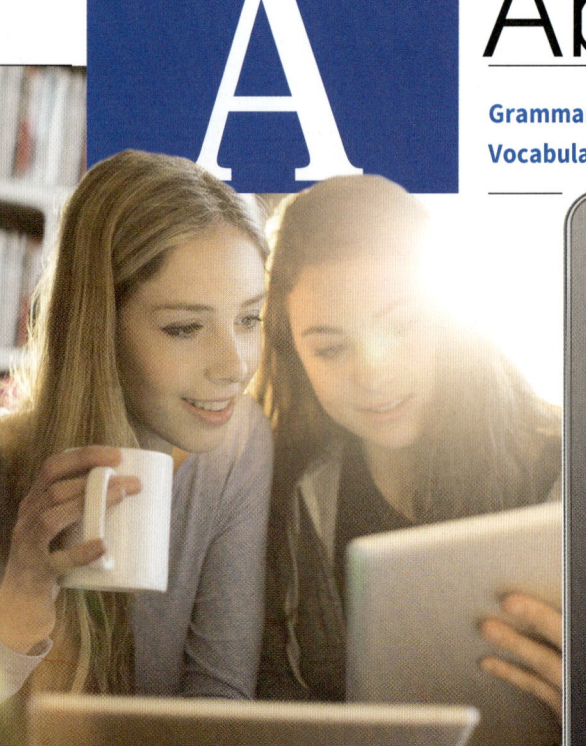

Experience (ex)change!

I'm Emily and this is Sofia. Sofia is from Seville in Spain. She's an exchange student on the Erasmus program and she's here to study English and learn about English life. Sofia is like another member of the family – my bedroom is her bedroom too for the next two weeks.

Sofia thinks life in England is a bit weird! I get up every morning at 7:00 and I always have a shower before breakfast.

In Spain Sofia usually has a shower in the evening after school because it's really hot then. I get dressed in my uniform every day and Sofia thinks that's strange too – Spanish students never wear uniforms – I'm jealous! ☺

After breakfast we walk to school together. In Spain Sofia always takes the bus because it's a long journey and she is often late. The other big difference is mealtimes – in England and Spain we have breakfast and lunch at the same time but in England we have dinner at 6:00 after school. In Spain Sofia has dinner at about 9:00 and sometimes goes out after dinner to meet her friends. She often goes to bed after midnight! I can't wait for my exchange trip to Spain! But my mum is worried!

---

1 PAIRWORK Describe your daily routine to your partner.

2 [1.02] Read and listen to the text. Then answer the questions.

1. Why is Sofia in England?
2. Where does Sofia sleep?
3. When does Emily have a shower?
4. Why does Sofia usually have a shower in the evening in Spain?
5. Why does Emily feel jealous of Sofia?
6. How does Emily travel to school?
7. Why do you think Emily's mum is worried?

VOCABULARY: Verbs of routine

3 Look at the verbs of routine and write when you do these things every day.

1. have breakfast / lunch / dinner
2. get up
3. have a shower
4. get dressed
5. wake up
6. brush your teeth
7. go to school
8. come home
9. go to bed
10. do homework

I wake up at 7 o'clock.
I have breakfast at half past seven.

4 Imagine Emily is on an exchange in Italy. What things would be different for her?

GRAMMAR GUIDE

Present simple

We use the present simple to talk about habits and routines.

Affirmative and negative
I / You / We / They **get** / **don't get up** late.
He / She / It **gets up** / **doesn't get up** late.
Questions
Do I / you / we / they **get up** late?
Does he / she / it **get up** late?
When **do** you **get up**?
What time **does** she **get up**?
Short answers
Yes, I **do**. / No, we **don't**.   Yes, she **does**. / No, he **doesn't**.

➡ GRAMMAR REFERENCE p. 108   WB pp. 130–131

5 Complete the sentences with the correct form of the verbs in brackets.

0   What time ......**do**...... you ....**wake up**.... (wake up) on schooldays?
1   We .... (not / go) to school by bus; we walk.
2   I .... (get dressed) in the bathroom.
3   My parents .... (make) pancakes for breakfast on Sundays.
4   .... you .... (go) to bed late at the weekend?
5   I .... (not / get up) early in the holidays.
6   We .... (play) football on Saturdays.
7   The girls .... (phone) their grandmother every day.
8   What time .... your dad .... (come) home from work?

GRAMMAR GUIDE

Present simple: Spelling rules

- get → get**s**   (+ -s)
- study → stud**ies**   (-y → -ies, with consonants)
- play → play**s**   (+ -s, with vowels)
- bru**sh** → brush**es**
- go → go**es**   } (+ -es)
- ki**ss** → kiss**es**

➡ GRAMMAR REFERENCE p. 108

6 Rewrite the sentences using the third person singular.

0   I get dressed in the bathroom.
    He gets dressed in the bathroom.
1   You study every day after school.
2   We get up at 7 o'clock.
3   I brush my hair before bed.
4   They play football every evening.
5   We go to the cinema on Saturdays.
6   I watch TV after 9 o'clock.
7   They want to visit their mum.
8   You say hello to your teacher every morning.

7 Write the questions for Emily's answers using the prompts.

You   Where / you live?
        0 ....**Where do you live?**........
Emily   I live in Bristol.
You   Who / you / live with?
        1 ....

Emily   I live with my mum, dad and my sister Helen.
You   How old / Helen?
        2 ....
Emily   She's 21 years old.
You   What / Helen do?
        3 ....
Emily   Helen's a student at Bristol University.
You   You / speak Spanish with Sofia?
        4 ....
Emily   No, I don't. We always speak English.
You   Sofia / like English food?
        5 ....
Emily   Honestly? She loves it!

GRAMMAR GUIDE

Adverbs of frequency

100%   0%

always   usually   often   sometimes   hardly ever   never

- Sofia **always** takes the bus.
- Sofia **usually** has a shower in the evening.

Adverbs go before the main verb but after the verb *be*:

- She **often goes** to bed after midnight.
- She **is often** late.

➡ GRAMMAR REFERENCE p. 108   WB p. 131

8 Rewrite the sentences with the adverb in brackets in the correct place.

0   My dad works on Saturdays. (never)
    My dad never works on Saturdays.
1   Keira does her homework on the bus. (always)
2   I play computer games. (hardly ever)
3   Do you wake up at night? (often)
4   You help Mum and Dad in the house. (sometimes)
5   Matt doesn't go to school by bike. (usually)
6   Our English teacher is late. (always)

9 Complete the sentences using your own ideas.

0   I never ....**eat sweets**........!
1   Italian students are always ....
2   Footballers sometimes ....
3   Politicians often ....
4   Teachers are hardly ever ....
5   Parents usually ....

Starter A

STARTER B
My stuff

Grammar: *there is / are; some / any; a lot of, a little, a few; too much / many, too little / few*
Vocabulary: technology

WB pp. 132–133

DECLUTTER YOUR LIFE!

You know the saying 'tidy house, tidy mind'? Well, decluttering is the first step towards a tidy mind. Decluttering means removing all the things that you don't need and creating a clean and tidy space. Here are some simple steps to help you declutter.

1 Keep your memories in your mind

We all collect too many objects. We buy things like souvenirs, medals, certificates, badges to help us remember special places or events in the past – but guess what? You can still remember those special moments without all these objects! You have your memories safe in your mind!

2 Reduce your wardrobe

Have you got too many clothes? What about all those T-shirts from past holidays and events? How often do you wear them? There's too little space in your wardrobe for things you don't wear. Take unwanted clothes to a charity shop – just keep a few favourite items.

3 Go digital

You don't need any CDs or DVDs now! All the music and films you want are on the internet, so download them. And is there any excuse for keeping books? Buy an e-reader and make a little space on your shelves!

10 Think about the things in your room at home. Do you use / wear / need all of them? Write a list.

11 [1.03] Read and listen to the advice in the text. Choose the correct option.
1 You can remember events without *memorabilia / a good memory*.
2 Only keep clothes *you often wear / from a charity shop* in your wardrobe.
3 Download films and music from the internet. *Don't keep / Keep* DVDs and CDs.
4 You only need *digital / print* books in your home.

VOCABULARY: Technology

12 What are these things for?
Match the words below to the definitions.

0 [a] joystick
1 [ ] smartphone
2 [ ] screen
3 [ ] e-reader
4 [ ] mouse
5 [ ] remote control
6 [ ] laptop
7 [ ] speakers
8 [ ] headphones
9 [ ] keyboard

a You use it to move around on screen in a computer game.
b You can hear the audio on your computer with these.
c You use it to text people, make calls and surf the internet.
d You use it to switch on a television and change the channel.
e You use it to read books and other texts.
f You use them to listen to music in private.
g You use it to move things around on your computer.
h It's a small portable computer.
i You use it to type in data on your computer.
j It's the display of your computer.

8 Starter B

B

GRAMMAR GUIDE

there is / there are and some / any

Countable nouns

(+) There **are** some books on the shelf.
(–) There **aren't any** books on the shelf.
(?) **Are** there **any** books on the shelf?

Uncountable nouns

(+) There **is** some space in the wardrobe.
(–) There **isn't any** space on your shelf.
(?) **Is** there **any** space in your wardrobe?

→ GRAMMAR REFERENCE p. 109   WB p. 132

13 Decide which nouns are countable (C) or uncountable (U).

0	U	money	13	....	event
1	....	time	14	....	holiday
2	....	orange	15	....	book
3	....	object	16	....	CD
4	....	souvenir	17	....	DVD
5	....	medal	18	....	e-reader
6	....	badge	19	....	speaker
7	....	memory	20	....	shelf
8	....	T-shirt	21	....	wardrobe
9	....	clothes	22	....	mouse
10	....	music	23	....	smartphone
11	....	film	24	....	joystick
12	....	moment	25	....	keyboard

14 Choose the correct option.

Mum Okay Tanya, there ⁰*is /* (*are*) a lot of things in your wardrobe. Let's take ¹*some / any* to the charity shop.
Tanya OK, but I've got ²*some / any* questions first.
Mum Okay. What?
Tanya Can I keep ³*any / a* T-shirts?
Mum Well, there ⁴*is / are* over 20 in the drawer. Keep ⁵*some / any* that you really love.
Tanya What about my CDs?
Mum There ⁶*is / are* hundreds here! I can't believe you listen to them!
Tanya You're right. I can download them. There ⁷*is / are* ⁸*some / any* space on my laptop.
Mum Good, and these books? There ⁹*isn't / aren't* ¹⁰*some / any* space on your shelves!
Tanya Oh yeah, they can go. I've got them on my e-reader!

GRAMMAR GUIDE

a lot of, a little, a few

Countable nouns

- There **are a lot of** souvenirs. (big quantity)
- There **are a few** souvenirs. (small quantity)

Uncountable nouns

- There **is a lot of** space. (big quantity)
- There **is a little** space. (small quantity)

→ GRAMMAR REFERENCE p. 109   WB p. 132

15 Complete the sentences with *a lot of*, *a little* or *a few*.

0 You've got ....**a lot of**.... bags – can I help you?
1 There's .... cola in the fridge – we've got six bottles!
2 'Have we got any biscuits?' 'Not many, but there are .... in the packet.'
3 I've got .... money to buy Mum a present, just £5.
4 We've got .... time before the train leaves – two hours!

GRAMMAR GUIDE

too much / too many, too little / too few

Countable nouns

- There **are too many** souvenirs. (excess)
- There **are too few** souvenirs. (insufficient)

Uncountable nouns

- There **is too much** space. (excess)
- There **is too little** space. (insufficient)

→ GRAMMAR REFERENCE p. 109   WB p. 133

16 Complete the text with the correct form of *there is / there are*, *some*, *any*, *too much*, *too many*, *too little* or *too few*.

I love watching films and whenever I have ⁰..**some**.. money I always buy a DVD. I really have ¹..................... in my room now – ²..................... any space! I've got hundreds of Hollywood films in my collection and ³..................... animated films, but ⁴..................... old classic black and white films unfortunately – they're very difficult to find. I buy lots of different types but I don't buy ⁵..................... horror films, that's the only film genre I don't like. Too scary!

Starter B   9

STARTER C

School

Grammar: past simple: *be* and regular and irregular verbs
Vocabulary: clothes

WB pp. 134–135

Highcroft School

Then and Now

When did Highcroft first open?
It opened in 1963.

What were the classrooms and the lessons like?
There were around 30 students to a class, and they didn't have any computers in the classrooms. Students sat at individual desks. They didn't do activities in groups, or have class discussions – ever! Teaching methods were very traditional – the teacher read or wrote information on the blackboard for students to copy.

Did students get a lot of homework?
Yes, they did! Students worked very hard. Teachers were strict and corporal punishment was common. Teachers hit the students with a cane (a kind of stick) when they got answers wrong, talked in class or didn't do their homework. Writing out 'lines' (the same sentence a hundred times!) was also a common punishment.

What did students wear?
In the 1960s girls wore skirts, blouses and ties, and white socks. They didn't wear trousers because only boys wore trousers (not jeans or shorts), shirts and ties. Both wore jackets and often there was a school cap (boys) or beret (girls).

17 [1.04] Read and listen to the text and complete the fact file.

HIGHCROFT SCHOOL

Opened in: ....
Class sizes: ....
Teaching methods: ....
Types of punishment: ....
School uniform:
girls ....
boys ....

18 PAIRWORK Answer these questions.

1 How old is your school?
2 Does it have an interesting history?

VOCABULARY: Clothes

19 Which part of the body do you wear the following clothes on?

cap • skirt • trousers • shirt •
jacket • socks • shoes • tie • jumper •
blouse • tights • T-shirt • shorts

Head: *cap* ....
Upper body: ....
Lower body: ....

20 What do you usually wear to school? Write about your clothes.

We don't have a uniform at my school. I wear jeans and a T-shirt and a jumper. I don't wear ...

10 Starter C

GRAMMAR GUIDE

Past simple: *be*

Affirmative	Negative
I **was** strict.	He **wasn't** funny.
You **were** happy.	They **weren't** sad.
Questions	**Short answers**
Was she happy?	Yes, she **was**. / No, she **wasn't**.
Were we happy?	Yes, we **were**. / No, we **weren't**.

➡ GRAMMAR REFERENCE p. 109   WB p. 134

21 Complete the sentences with the correct form of *was* or *were*.

0. My mum ……*was*…… at the same school as me but in the 1980s!
1. Our school uniform at my last school ……………… blue.
2. I ……………… at this school last year. I was at a school in Rome.
3. Your exam results ……………… great, Rita – well done!
4. ……………… you in the scouts when you were young?
5. ……………… Frank in your maths class last term?
6. My friends ……………… at the party, so it was a bit boring.

GRAMMAR GUIDE

Past simple

We use the past simple for completed past actions.

Affirmative and negative
Students **worked** very hard.
They **didn't have** any computers.
Questions
Did students **get** a lot of homework?
Short answers
Yes, they **did**. / No, they **didn't**.

Spelling rules

- open → open**ed**   (+ -ed)
- study → stud**ied**   (+ -ied)
- liv**e** → liv**ed**   (+ -d)
- stop → stop**ped**   (double consonant + -ed)
- do → **did**, make → **made**, have → **had**

➡ GRAMMAR REFERENCE p. 110   WB pp. 134–135

22 Rewrite the sentences in the past simple.

0. I finish school at 4 o'clock.
   I finished school at 4 o'clock.
1. The headteacher talks for hours.
2. The shops open at half past nine.
3. They study every day.
4. You like all my friends.
5. The film starts at 8 o'clock.
6. I try to understand him.
7. They stop serving pizza in the evening.
8. I hug my dog every evening.

23 Find the past simple forms of these irregular verbs in the text.

0. have ……*had*……
1. sit ………………
2. read ………………
3. write ………………
4. wear ………………
5. hit ………………
6. get ………………

24 Complete the dialogue with the correct past simple form of the verbs in brackets.

Anne Where ⁰……*did*…… you ………*go*……… (*go*) to school, Grandad?

Grandad I ¹……………… (*be*) at a school in Yorkshire in the north of England, a boarding school called Granchester Towers.

Anne A boarding school? ²……………… (*be*) you there all the time? ³……………… you ……………… (*sleep*) there too?

Grandad Yes, I ⁴……………… (*study*) there but I also ⁵……………… (*live*) there. I ⁶……………… (*have*) all my meals there and I ⁷……………… (*sleep*) in a dormitory with five other boys.

Anne Weird! ⁸……………… you ……………… (*like*) the school?

Grandad Well, I ⁹……………… (*not / like*) it at first but then I ¹⁰……………… (*make*) some friends and after that I was happy there.

25 PAIRWORK Ask and answer about previous schools you went to and what they were like.

A Where did you go to middle school?
B I went to the Istituto B. Lorenzi.
A Did you like it?

Starter C   11

STARTER D

Friends

Grammar: comparative and superlative adjectives; (not) as … as
Vocabulary: feelings

WB pp. 136–137

TeenLine

Princess Pearl

My problem is with my best friend, Amy. I love Amy – we get on really well and we do a lot of things together – but when other people are there, especially boys, I feel jealous. The thing is, Amy is better than me in every way. She's cleverer than me, she's funnier, she's taller, she's the prettiest girl in our class and she's also the most athletic! She's good at everything and she's not as shy as me – she's more sociable – so people always talk to her and I just … disappear! I know I'm not boring and I'm not stupid, but I'm worried because I'm not as popular as Amy and I'm less confident.
I feel nervous now when I meet new people and I'm embarrassed because I'm not clever like her and I haven't got a lot of friends. I don't want to stop being Amy's friend but I don't want to be invisible! What can I do?

T.L.

Remember Princess Pearl that you have got your own qualities and talents – you aren't less talented than Amy, or the least interesting girl in your class, you're just different! Try to focus on your positive qualities and spend some time with other friends, not just Amy.

26 [1.05] Read and listen to the text. Why is Princess Pearl posting on the TeenLine blog?

27 Circle the correct option.

1. Princess Pearl spends *a lot of / a little* time with Amy.
2. Princess Pearl thinks a lot of people *like / don't like* Amy.
3. Amy is *shy / sociable*.
4. Princess Pearl thinks she *is / isn't* boring and stupid.
5. Princess Pearl is *good / not good* at making new friends.

VOCABULARY: Feelings

28 Match the adjectives to the situations.

0. [g] embarrassed
1. [ ] angry
2. [ ] surprised
3. [ ] jealous
4. [ ] worried
5. [ ] happy
6. [ ] scared
7. [ ] calm

a. You watch a horror film.
b. You get very good grades in your exams.
c. You have an exam tomorrow morning.
d. A classmate gives you a fantastic birthday present.
e. You love a classmate's bag. You want one too.
f. A classmate takes your calculator without asking.
g. You hug your friend, but then realise it isn't your friend.
h. You drink camomile tea before sleeping.

GRAMMAR GUIDE

Comparative and superlative adjectives

regular	comparative	superlative
tall	tall**er** than	the tall**est**
wide	wide**r** than	the wide**st**
big	big**ger** than	the big**gest**
interesting	**more** interesting than	the **most** interesting
happy	happ**ier** than	the happ**iest**
clever	clever**er** / **more** clever	the clever**est** / the **most** clever

irregular	comparative	superlative
good	**better** than	the **best**
bad	**worse** than	the **worst**
far	**further** / **farther** than	the **furthest** / the **farthest**

Look!: *talented* / **less** talented than / **the least** talented

➔ GRAMMAR REFERENCE p. 110   WB pp. 136–137

29 Complete the sentences with the comparative form of the adjective in brackets. Use *less* in two of the sentences.

0 My dog is ……**happier**…… (happy) now we live in the country.
1 This exercise is …………………… (short) than the other one.
2 Your essay is …………………… (good) than my essay.
3 Mum was …………………… (scared) than the children when she saw the film!
4 These jeans are comfortable. They're …………………… (tight) than my other pair.
5 Are you …………………… (sociable) than your brother?
6 Italy is …………………… (hot) than the UK in summer.
7 Today's test was easy! It was …………………… (difficult) than last week's test.

30 Complete the text with the adjectives below. Use the comparative form.

athletic ▪ tall ▪ ~~young~~ ▪ bad ▪ good ▪ strong ▪ fast

My brother Ralph is ⁰ ……**younger**…… than me (he's 12 and I'm 16) but he's already ¹ …………………… than I am. He plays basketball for our school team and he's already ² …………………… than a lot of other players (he scored seven baskets in the last game!). He's ³ …………………… and ⁴ …………………… than the other boys in the team too – the coach says he's a natural athlete. Ralph is definitely ⁵ …………………… than I am, but I'm not jealous. I'm ⁶ …………………… at sport than my brother but I'm good at other things.

31 Complete the dialogue with the words below.

at ▪ the ▪ most (x2) ▪ in ▪ ~~cleverest~~ ▪ intelligent ▪ highest

Nick Who's the ⁰ ……**cleverest**…… student in your class, Mark?
Mark Not me! I think Simon is ¹ …………………… best at maths, but Jane gets the ² …………………… marks ³ …………………… the class in other subjects.
Nick What subjects are you good at?
Mark I like English and I'm probably the ⁴ …………………… creative at writing, but I'm definitely the worst ⁵ …………………… science! What about you?
Nick I'm the ⁶ …………………… athletic but not the most ⁷ …………………… in my class!

GRAMMAR GUIDE

(not) as … as

- He is **as tall as** his brother.   ▪ She's **not as shy as** me.

➔ GRAMMAR REFERENCE p. 111   WB p. 137

32 Rewrite these sentences using *not as … as* and the opposite adjective.

0 My brother is shorter than me.
   My brother isn't as tall as me.
1 Your bike is slower than my bike.
2 A smartphone is smaller than a tablet.
3 Sam's dog is bigger than Jack's dog.
4 Maths is more difficult than geography.
5 Athens is hotter than Venice.
6 Winter nights are longer than summer nights.

STARTER E

Plans

Grammar: *be going to*; present continuous for future; *will*
Vocabulary: jobs

WB pp. 138–139

Project Trust since 1967

WHY VOLUNTEER?

I'm Polly. I applied for a 12-month teaching job with Project Trust after I finished school. I did the training course in August, and I'm leaving for Ghana in Africa in October. I'm really excited about the project because I think that it will challenge me. I'm going to work as a teacher and sports instructor in a primary school. I'm going to teach the children English and help them develop their reading and writing skills. I don't speak their language, Akan, but I'm going to start a language course when I arrive – I'm going to practise every day until I'm fluent! The other volunteer and I are going to live with a family at first; later I think I'll look for an apartment near the school. This job at Project Trust is a fantastic opportunity. Other volunteers say it's tough. I know it's not going to be easy but I'm going to make the most of every minute of my time in Ghana. I hope I'll learn new skills, make new friends, develop confidence and independence and, most of all, learn about a different culture.

Laura, South Africa, Project Trust 2016.

Sarah, Liberia, Project Trust 2008.

33 [1.06] Read and listen to the text. What does Polly want to do next year?

34 Read the text again and decide if the sentences are true (T) or false (F). Correct the false ones.

1. Polly did a course to learn how to teach. T F
2. The teaching job is in India. T F
3. Polly's job is with young children. T F
4. She speaks the local language. T F
5. The accommodation is in a hotel. T F
6. Polly is worried about her year in Ghana. T F

VOCABULARY: Jobs

35 Complete the definitions with the words below.

pilot ▪ police officer ▪ dentist ▪ doctor
sports instructor ▪ vet ▪ office worker ▪ architect
▪ cook ▪ hairdresser ▪ lawyer ▪ teacher

0. A .... *vet* .... looks after sick animals.
1. A .... investigates crimes.
2. A .... looks after people's teeth.
3. An .... designs houses and other buildings.
4. A .... cuts people's hair.
5. A .... teaches people how to do sports.
6. A .... makes food in a restaurant.
7. A .... flies an airplane or a helicopter.
8. An .... uses a computer in an office.
9. A .... helps people with legal problems.
10. A .... teaches children in a school.
11. A .... looks after sick people.

E

GRAMMAR GUIDE

Present continuous v *be going to*

present continuous
I'**m leaving** for Ghana in October. (I've got my ticket.)
be going to
I'**m going to leave** for Ghana in October. (It's my intention, but I still need to buy my ticket.)

We use the present continuous when our plans for the future are certain.

We use *be going to* for future plans which aren't certain yet.

➡ GRAMMAR REFERENCE p. 111 WB pp. 138–139

36 Complete the dialogue with the correct form of the present continuous or *be going to*.

Craig What are you doing tonight, Kevin? Do you want to come to my house?

Kevin I'm sorry Craig, I can't. ⁰ (*I'm going to*) / *I'm going to go to* a football match with my dad. He got the tickets last week.

Craig OK. What about Saturday? ¹*Are you doing / Are you going to do* anything in the morning?

Kevin I'm not sure. Mike says ²*he's calling / he's going to call* me. The basketball team might need a substitute for their match. But ³*I'm not doing / I'm not going to do* anything on Saturday evening. Shall we go out?

Craig Yes, OK. Sally ⁴*is having / is going to have* a party. She invited me yesterday and she says I can bring a friend. Do you want to come?

Kevin Yes, great! Thanks very much. What time ⁵*is the party starting / is the party going to start*?

Craig Eight o'clock. Let's meet at my house. I can call Sally and tell her ⁶*I'm bringing / I'm going to bring* you about 7:45.

Kevin Cool. See you then.

GRAMMAR GUIDE

be going to v *will* for predictions

be going to
Those bags are too heavy. You'**re going to drop** them.
will
I think **I'll be** a good teacher.

We also use *be going to* for future predictions based on present evidence.

We use *will* for future predictions based on our opinion.

➡ GRAMMAR REFERENCE p. 112 WB p. 139

37 Find examples with *be going to* and *will* for different types of predictions in the text.

38 Read the situations, then write a prediction using *be going to* and a verb below.

not / eat ▪ win ▪ sit ▪ not / download ▪ pass

0 Your glasses are on the chair.
   You 're going to sit .... on them.
1 Jake did a lot of revision for his exams.
   He .... all his exams!
2 Rebecca doesn't like brownies.
   She .... any of them.
3 Our team scored five goals!
   They .... the match!
4 These PDF files are too big.
   I .... them.

39 Use the verbs *think, believe, hope, expect, suppose* and *feel* to make predictions about your future life.

I believe I'll be rich in 50 years.

40 Say if the sentences are predictions based on evidence (E) or personal predictions (PP).

0 ...PP... I think I'll be at university when I'm 20.
1 .... The baby's on the table. He's going to fall!
2 .... Kevin hopes his team will win the championship this year.
3 .... My dad believes we'll all drive electric cars in ten years.
4 .... The sun's shining. It's going to be a beautiful day.
5 .... I read your notes. Your project's going to be great!

Starter E 15

1 Friendship

EXAM STRATEGIES
- PRELIMINARY: Reading, Writing and Listening
- IGCSE: Reading, Writing and Listening

SPEAKING SKILLS
- Meeting and greeting

CHANGING LANGUAGE
- Greetings

LIFE SKILLS
- Dealing with stress

Learning goals
Grammar
- Present simple and continuous
- Present perfect
- Present perfect with *just*, *already* and *yet*

Vocabulary
- Adjectives of personality

WB pp. 140–147

LEAD IN

1 PAIRWORK Discuss the descriptions. Which is true for you?

1 A good friend listens to your problems.
2 A good friend agrees with you all the time.
3 A good friend has the same interests as you.

2 [1.07] Read, listen and watch. Which of the descriptions from exercise 1 is mentioned in the text?

HOW TO BE A GOOD FRIEND

Surveys show that good friends are crucial for our happiness and health, but what makes a good friend? Today we're talking about friendship and looking at how you can be a good friend.

Sometimes I just feel sad and I don't really know why. Maybe it's pressure from my parents or stress from schoolwork. My friends are my support system – we talk and chat and I feel happy after. Right now I'm feeling good because it's the start of the new school year, I'm meeting new people and studying new subjects, and we're not studying for exams, but I know when I feel stressed my friends are always there for me. Lily, 15

So, what can you do to be a good friend? Here are some tips:

Listen. A good listener always tries to understand their friend's problem. What are they going through at the moment? How are they feeling? When you're really listening to a person, they feel you care about them.

Ask questions. When your friends aren't feeling happy, try and talk to them. Especially if you're not sure why. Ask them what they need and how you can help. When they're having problems, people don't always want advice. They sometimes just want to talk, or spend time with you.

Show affection. Smiles and hugs are a great way to show friends that you care. Some people are shy and not very talkative but a big hug can make a big difference especially when they're feeling sad!

Maintain contact. Even if you're studying, or busy doing other things, it's important to make time to keep in touch. You can do this through social media, texts and calls. This shows your friends you're thinking about them now, and care for them.

PRACTICE

3 ▶ [1.07] Read, listen and watch the video again. Match the beginnings and ends of the sentences.

1 ☐ Friends make you feel
2 ☐ A good friend
3 ☐ Spend time with your friends
4 ☐ Smiles and hugs can

a when they have problems.
b make your friends feel better.
c happy and well.
d always listens to you.

GRAMMAR GUIDE

Present simple v present continuous

present simple	present continuous
They sometimes just **want** to talk.	Right now I**'m feeling** good.
What **makes** a good friend?	What **are** they **going** through at the moment?
People **don't** always **want** advice.	We**'re not studying** for exams.

State verbs like *want*, *think*, *know*, *like*, *love* don't use the present continuous form.

➔ GRAMMAR REFERENCE p. 113   WB pp. 140–141

4 Look at the time phrases. Write present simple (PS) or present continuous (PC).

0 ..PS.. every day
1 .... at the moment
2 .... usually
3 .... now
4 .... twice a week
5 .... sometimes
6 .... this week
7 .... never

5 Complete the sentences with the present simple or present continuous of the verbs in brackets.

0 I ....**text**.... (text) my best friend every day.
1 Jack always .... (listen) to his brother's problems.
2 'Who .... you .... (talk) to?' 'My friend Frankie. He's online now.'
3 My parents .... often .... (not / use) social media.
4 .... you .... (listen) to me? I need some advice.
5 How often .... you .... (see) your grandparents?

6 Use the prompts to write questions using the present simple or present continuous.

0 How / you / feel / today?
   How are you feeling today?
1 How / you / usually feel / Friday afternoon?
2 When / you / speak to your best friend?
3 What / your best friend / do now?
4 you / sometimes / use / your phone in class?
5 you / text / at the moment?
6 How often / your friends / call you?

7 Complete the text with the present simple or present continuous of the verbs in brackets.

My best friend, Jenny

My best friend is Jenny. Why ⁰......**do I like**...... (like) her? Well, because I ².................... (share) all my problems with her and I ³.................... (know) I can talk to her about any of my worries. To give you an example: at the moment, I ⁴.................... (study) for a really difficult test and Jenny ⁵.................... (help) me every day. I ⁶.................... (talk) to her all the time; my mum often ⁷.................... (shout) at me because I'm always on my phone to Jenny. I ⁸.................... (text) her even now as I ⁹.................... (speak) to you! I ¹⁰.................... (think) Jenny and I are soul mates. Let's hope we can stay best friends forever!

8 Use the phrases to make four true sentences using present simple and present continuous.

verbs	nouns	time expressions
speak to	my friends	every day
call	my teacher	at the moment
ask	music	at weekends
use	problems	
text	my phone	
listen to	my parents	

I speak to my friends every day.
I'm listening to my teacher at the moment.

9 SPEAKING Answer the questions in pairs. Then share your ideas with the class.

- How often do you communicate with your friends?
- When a friend is sad, what do you do?
- Look back at the text on page 16. Can you think of other ways to be a good friend?

Unit 1   17

READING SKILLS

LEAD IN

10 PAIRWORK Discuss the questions. Then share your ideas with the class.

1 Where did you meet most of your friends, online or in real life?
2 Are there any differences between your online friends and your school friends?

PRACTICE

11 [1.08] Read and listen to the text. Choose the best title.

1 What is a good friend?
2 Online friends
3 How teenagers communicate

READING STRATEGY

Identify the writer's views

Clues in the text can help you guess the writer's opinion about the subject. Look closely for these features in the text:

- opinion verbs, e.g., *think, feel, believe*
- the adjectives and adverbs chosen to describe the information
- the use of brackets to comment on points in the text
- the use of exclamation marks to show surprise or shock

PRELIMINARY IGCSE

12 Read the text again and look at the underlined phrases. Match them to the points below. Some phrases belong to more than one point.

1 adjectives and adverbs
2 comments in brackets
3 punctuation

13 Read the text again and decide if the sentences are true (T) or false (F). Correct the false ones.

1 The writer thinks that not many American teenagers have online friends. T F
2 He thinks it's strange that teenagers don't meet their online friends in person. T F
3 He feels many teens lose friends because of online comments. T F
4 He thinks that it is easier to be unkind face-to-face than online. T F
5 He believes teenage boys spend too much time playing games online. T F

GRAMMAR GUIDE

Present perfect

Affirmative	Negative
Social media **has been** around **for** a long time. Most teens **have** never **met** their online friends in person.	You **haven't been** to as many parties as your peers.
Questions	Short answers
Have these boys **ever met** their gaming friends?	Yes, they **have**. No, they **haven't**.

Present perfect v past simple

We use the present perfect to refer to past events that have a link with the present.
We use the past simple to refer to events that are completely in the past.

➡ **GRAMMAR REFERENCE** p. 113   **WB** p. 141

14 Complete the dialogue with the correct form of the verbs in brackets.

A ⁰ ....Have you.... ever ....used.... (you / use) Instagram?
B Yes, I use it all the time. I ¹ .... (send) you an Instagram photo last week from the party.
A Oh yes, of course, so ² .... ever .... (you / hear) of Instagram stories?
B No, I ³ .... What's that?
A Well, it's an app – it combines your photos and videos like a film that you post online.
B Cool, ⁴ .... (you / try) it?
A Yes, I ⁵ .... I ⁶ .... (create) a film this morning of my journey to school and ⁷ .... (post) it online at about 9:30.
B Oh, and ⁸ .... (you / have) any comments or likes?
A No, I ⁹ .... (not / receive) any.
B Maybe your friends ¹⁰ .... (not / look at) the internet today.
A My friends are always online!

15 Critical thinking Discuss the questions in pairs.

1 Do you think your online friendships are different to your real-world friendships?
2 Do you think the differences are important?

18   Unit 1

Social media has been around for a long time and it has certainly changed the way teens communicate every day. Mark Zuckerberg launched Facebook in 2004 and other social media apps, like WhatsApp, Snapchat, Instagram and Twitter quickly followed. Since then, these apps have become one of the main ways that teenagers interact socially, but have they really changed the way young people make friends? A recent survey has shown that more than half of American teenagers have made at least one new friend online in the last year, and a whopping 64% of them used a social networking site. However, in this weird world of online friendships, online friends stay online. Most teens have never met their online friends in person! We all like to have lots of friends, of course, but online friendships can be a negative experience, especially when you feel you haven't been to as many parties as your peers or you haven't made as many friends in the last year. Surveys have shown that over 50% of teens have felt sad when they realise their friends have been to parties, but they didn't invite them. In addition, some teens lie on social media about what is happening in their lives. Around 40% of teenagers have felt pressure to post only content that makes them look good, or that will get a lot of *likes*. More worryingly, 25% of teens have also lost friends because of what happened online (it's easier to post a nasty comment than say it in person!). Both sexes have experienced this, but teenage girls have experienced it more than boys.

Video games now also play an important role in making and maintaining new and old friendships, especially (unsurprisingly!) for teenage boys. Ten or fifteen years ago boys played more sport and socialised through training clubs and sports matches, but nowadays over 57% of boys have made new friends through gaming compared to 13% of girls. Have these boys ever met their gaming friends? No, of course they haven't!

Glossary
whopping : esorbitante   **lie** : mentono

WRITING SKILLS

LEAD IN

16 When do you send an informal email? Tick (✓) the correct options.

1 to make a complaint to a shop
2 to tell a friend some personal news
3 to apply for a university place online
4 to give a friend advice on a personal problem
5 to answer an advert for a job
6 to thank a relative for a gift

PRACTICE

17 Put the parts of the email in the correct order.

a ☐ How are you? How are things with you?
b ☐ Hope to hear from you soon, Write soon, Keep in touch
c ☐ Thanks for your last email, It was great to hear from you, Sorry for not writing sooner
d ☐ All the best, Lots of love, Take care
e ☐ 1 Dear …, Hi …
f ☐ That's all for now, I must go now, Say hi to … for me

WRITING STRATEGY

Write an informal email

Informal emails / letters give personal news, ask for information or give advice.
- They use informal language, contractions and colloquial expressions.
- They ask a lot of questions.
- They show interest and familiarity.

PRELIMINARY | IGCSE

➡ See **WRITING EXPANSION** page 250

Unit 1   19

VOCABULARY

Adjectives of personality

Aquarius – Aquarians are creative, easygoing, generous people. They have brilliant ideas but often they aren't very practical. And they can be very untidy!

Pisces – These people seem practical and reliable but they're also secret dreamers. They've got a sensitive side and can be moody and pessimistic at times.

Aries – These people are confident and sociable leaders with a lot of charisma! However, they can be impatient with others.

Taurus – Taureans are honest, practical and reliable people. They like the good things in life, especially good food! However, they can be impatient and stubborn too.

Gemini – Geminis are intelligent and creative but full of contradictions. One minute they seem easygoing and cheerful, the next minute they're moody and stressed!

Cancer – Cancer people are easygoing home-lovers. They're quiet, kind and rather shy but they're often quite creative. They're very generous with their friends and family.

18 Read the descriptions of the zodiac signs and underline the adjectives of personality. Then answer the questions.

1 Are you or your friends one of the signs described?
2 Do you agree with the personality adjectives for the zodiac signs?
3 Do your friends tend to be the same zodiac sign?

19 Sort the adjectives below into positive and negative.

confident ▪ easygoing ▪ impatient ▪ kind ▪ cheerful ▪ moody ▪ sociable ▪ practical ▪ shy ▪ stubborn ▪ tidy ▪ untidy ▪ generous ▪ reliable ▪ patient

20 Match the adjectives to the definitions.

1 ☐ tidy   5 ☐ reliable
2 ☐ moody   6 ☐ kind
3 ☐ stubborn   7 ☐ easygoing
4 ☐ cheerful

a A person who is always happy and smiling.
b A person who likes order and organisation in his / her home.
c A person who always thinks of others and helps them.
d A person who is flexible and relaxed.
e A person whose emotions change very frequently.
f A person who isn't flexible and thinks they are always right.
g A person you can depend on.

21 [1.09] Listen to the descriptions of three more zodiac signs. Match the signs to the adjectives.

1 ☐ Leo   2 ☐ Virgo   3 ☐ Libra

a creative, kind, shy
b cheerful, sociable, generous
c practical, reliable, tidy

22 [1.09] Listen again and write the negative adjectives for signs 1–3.

23 [1.10] Look at the adjectives for the other signs. Write the opposites of the adjective in brackets. Then listen and check.

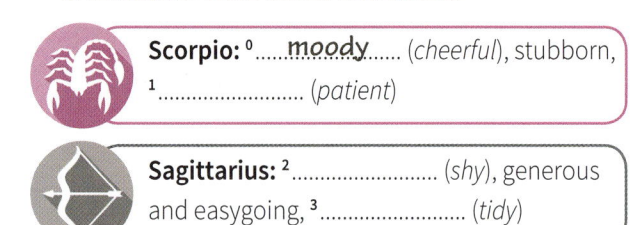

Scorpio: ⁰......moody...... (cheerful), stubborn, ¹........................ (patient)

Sagittarius: ²........................ (shy), generous and easygoing, ³........................ (tidy)

Capricorn: ⁴........................ (impatient), ⁵........................ (sociable), ⁶........................ (easygoing)

24 PAIRWORK Ask your partner about his / her sign and characteristics. Tell him / her what you think about the description.

A What sign are you?
B I'm Virgo. It says I'm practical and reliable.
A Yes, I think you are. You're very practical.

➜ See **VOCABULARY EXTENSION** page 260

20 Unit 1

SPEAKING SKILLS

Meeting and greeting

25 PAIRWORK Discuss these questions.

1 How do you greet your friends when you meet them?
2 How do you greet your teachers?

26 What social expressions are there in your language for the situations below?

1 You meet a friend you haven't seen for a long time.
2 You ask what a friend has done recently.
3 You want to end a conversation with someone you meet in the street.

27 [1.11] Listen and watch the video of Joel and Tom meeting. What are they doing at the moment?

key expressions	
meeting and greeting	ending the conversation
☐ How are you?	☐ I'd better be going.
☐ It's good to see you.	☐ It was great to see you.
☐ How have you been?	☐ Let's catch up soon.
☐ How are things with you?	☐ Have a nice day!
☐ What have you been up to?	☐ Goodbye, take care.

28 [1.11] Listen and watch again and tick (✓) the key expressions you hear.

SPEAKING STRATEGY

Keep the conversation going

When people ask us questions in greetings, it's polite to answer and then turn the question back to them:
A How are you?   B I'm good thanks, *how are things with you?*
A What have you been up to?   B Nothing much. *How about you?*

29 PAIRWORK Act out the following dialogue. Use the key expressions and the strategy box to help you.

- You and your partner meet by chance in a café.
- Greet each other, ask how you are and what you've done recently.
- End the conversation.

CHANGING LANGUAGE

Greetings

30 Sort the phrases out into meeting or ending a conversation or both.

hello · hi · bye · goodbye · ciao · see you later · how do you do · hey

31 Watch the video. Check your ideas from exercise 30.

32 Watch the video again and answer the questions.

1 How many people speak English as a native language?
2 How many people do we estimate speak English as a second or foreign language?
3 What is the most popular way of starting a conversation?
4 What is the most popular way of ending a conversation?

CORPUS

Corpus data can show how frequently we use certain words. Identifying common words and phrases helps ensure that language books contain the most relevant and useful language. Greetings in order of frequency:
1 *Hello* 2 *Hey* 3 *Hi*.
Endings in order of frequency:
1 *Bye* 2 *Goodbye* 3 *See you later*.

Unit 1   21

LISTENING SKILLS

LEAD IN

33 Look at the photos. Which of these pairs of stars do you think are friends in real life?

PRACTICE

34 [1.12] Listen to a journalist talking about famous friends and check your ideas.

LISTENING STRATEGY

Focus and eliminate in multiple choice

In a multiple-choice question, you need to choose one of the three or four options and eliminate the others. The option you choose should closely correspond to the information you hear.
The first time you listen, try to eliminate one statement which you know is wrong. The second time you listen, focus on choosing between the two remaining options.

PRELIMINARY **IGCSE**

35 [1.12] **PAIRWORK** Listen again and cross out the statements that you are certain are wrong. Discuss your answers in pairs.

1. When did Matt and Ben become friends?
   A When Matt was ten years old.
   B When they starred in the film *Good Will Hunting*.
   C Forty-five years ago.
2. What did they have in common when they were young?
   A They both loved acting and filmmaking.
   B They were both shy.
   C They were in love with the same girl.
3. What has Taylor Swift often written about?
   A Her friendship with Selena Gomez.
   B Her romantic relationships.
   C Her musical career.
4. What do Taylor and Selena have in common?
   A They are the same age.
   B They grew up in the same town as children.
   C They had to change their image and music.

36 [1.12] Listen again and choose the correct option.

37 **PAIRWORK** Discuss the following questions. Use the present perfect and the past simple.

1. How long have you know your best friend?
2. Where did you meet?

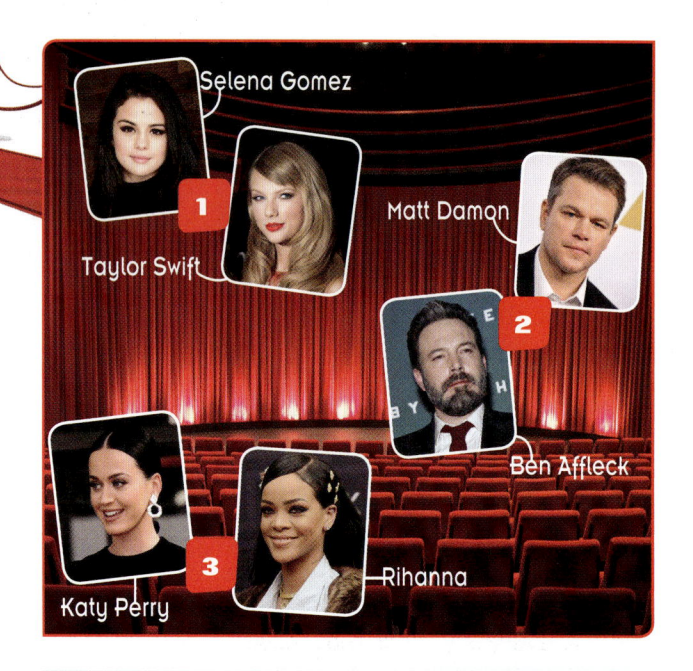

GRAMMAR GUIDE

Present perfect with *just*, *already*, and *yet*

- Selena **has** <u>just</u> **given** an interview on British television.
- She **has** <u>already</u> **written** hundreds of songs.
- Taylor **hasn't written** a song about it <u>yet</u>.

➡ **GRAMMAR REFERENCE** p. 114 **WB** p. 144

38 Use the Grammar guide to complete the rules with *just*, *already* or *yet*.

1. We use the present perfect with not .... in negative sentences to say that something hasn't happened but will happen in the future, and in questions.
2. We use it with .... to say that something happened very recently.
3. We use it with .... to say that a recent action happened sooner than expected.

39 Choose the correct option.

Mum Ryan, have you finished your homework ⁰(*yet*) / *already*?
Ryan Yes, I've ¹*already* / *yet* done all my maths – look.
Mum What about English? Have you done your essay?
Ryan Yes, I have. I've ²*just* / *yet* sent it to my teacher. My PC is still open! Look, he's ³*just* / *yet* replied.
Mum OK, well done. But have you tidied you room ⁴*yet* / *just*? You promised to do it this afternoon.
Ryan Er, no, I haven't tidied it ⁵*yet* / *already*, but I'm going to do it tonight.
Mum Sorry Ryan, I've ⁶*already* / *yet* asked you three times. Tidy your room now.

LIFE SKILLS

Dealing with stress

How stressed are you?

1 In the last week, how often have you felt very tired but couldn't sleep at night?
   A most nights   B 3–5 nights
   C 1–2 nights   D never

2 In the last week, how often have you wanted to eat sweet or salty snacks?
   A every day   B most days
   C on less than two days   D never

3 In the last week, how often have you had headaches?
   A every day   B most days
   C less than five times   D never

4 In the last week, how often have you found it difficult to concentrate at school?
   A every day   B between 2–3 days
   C once or twice   D never

5 In the last week, how often have you felt unsociable and wanted to be alone?
   A every day   B most days
   C once or twice   D never

Answers

Mainly Ds – You don't have much stress in your life, it's manageable.

Mainly Bs and Cs – You have quite a bit of stress in your life. You need to find some strategies to relax before it gets worse.

Mainly As – Your life is very stressful. You need to slow down and find strategies to deal with the stress and improve your health.

LEAD IN

40 Look at the photo. What do you think is happening? How is the girl feeling?

41 PAIRWORK Discuss these questions.
  1 In what situations do people often feel stressed?
  2 What problems can stress cause? Think about health, emotions and relationships.

PRACTICE

42 How stressed are you in your daily life? Take the stress test above.

43 THINKING FURTHER Look at the questions and then discuss with your partner.
  1 What situations do you personally find quite stressful?
  2 How do you deal with them?

LIFE STRATEGY

Tips for dealing with stress

Stress can help us to focus and take action, but when we have too much stress it can affect our health and our feelings. Here are some strategies to de-stress your life.

a Identify the source of your stress.
b Talk to someone about it.
c Socialise more.
d Exercise more.
e Work smarter, not harder.
f Take control of the situation.

44 Read the Life strategy. Match the information 1–6 below to the tips a–f.
  1 ☐ Sharing your problems will help reduce stress.
  2 ☐ Make time for seeing friends at least two evenings a week.
  3 ☐ Prioritise your work – concentrate on the tasks that are the most important.
  4 ☐ Physical activity produces chemicals in the brain that make you feel happy.
  5 ☐ Feeling that you are not in control is often what makes you stressed.
  6 ☐ If you know what is stressing you, you can start dealing with it.

45 Read the Life strategy again. Discuss these questions.
  1 Which strategies do you think are useful / not useful?
  2 Are there any strategies you've already used?
  3 Which strategies do you think you will use in the future?

46 TASK Choose one of the strategies from the Life strategy and try and apply it at least once next week. Report back to the class.
  - say what you did and when
  - explain how you felt afterwards

CITIZENSHIP AND COMPETENCY SKILLS Problem solving ✓

2 Migration

EXAM STRATEGIES
- PRELIMINARY: Reading and Speaking
- IGCSE: Reading and Speaking
- IELTS: Academic

SPEAKING SKILLS
- Having a disagreement

ACADEMIC SKILLS
- Labelling a map

Learning goals
Grammar
- Present perfect simple and continuous
- Defining relative clauses

Vocabulary
- Geographical features

WB pp. 148–157

Glossary
has been shrinking: si è ridotto
coal mines: miniere di carbone
mainland: terraferma
retired: in pensione

LEAD IN

1 Look at the photos and the title of the text. Answer the questions.

1. Would you like to live in this place? Why / Why not?
2. What advantages are there to living in a place like this?
3. What disadvantages are there? Explain your reasons.

2 [1.13] Read, listen and watch. Why are young people moving away from villages?

Ghost villages of rural Britain

When we think of moving populations we think of migrants from war-torn areas such as Syria and Yemen. But population movement is happening much closer to home. In the UK in the last 50 years people in rural areas have been getting older and the number of families living in these communities **has been shrinking**. Why?
5 Because young people are moving to urban areas to look for a brighter future.
In parts of Wales young people have been leaving the rural villages since the 1980s when the **coal mines** stopped production, but when young people leave rural areas, it creates huge problems for the local communities. It means schools, shops and services close and that makes life very difficult for the people left there.
10 In the north of Scotland, for example on the Island of Coll, students like Shona MacLeod make long journeys to school in Oban on the **mainland**. Shona has been travelling to school on Oban since the school in Coll closed. She has caught the ferry every Monday morning and returned Friday evening for the last three years. Her older brother lives in Glasgow now – he's been living there for two years, he has
15 bought a house there and has found a good job. There are no jobs on Coll.
There has been some movement in the opposite direction, a small number of people have been moving from the city to the countryside over the last 50 years. However, these people are generally older. Many of the picturesque English country villages have become 'museum-villages' of expensive homes for **retired** people with no
20 local facilities – no shops, post offices, pubs or schools.

24 Unit 2

PRACTICE

3 ▶ [1.13] Read, listen and watch the video again. Answer the questions.

1. Why are people leaving rural areas for urban areas?
2. Why did people start leaving rural areas in Wales in the 1980s?
3. Why does Shona MacLeod go to school in Oban?
4. How does she get there?
5. What happens to rural villages when a lot of people leave?

GRAMMAR GUIDE

Present perfect continuous

Affirmative	Negative
She **has been travelling**.	They **haven't been leaving**.
Questions	**Short answers**
Has she **been travelling**?	Yes, she **has**. No, she **hasn't**.

➡ **GRAMMAR REFERENCE** p. 115   **WB** pp. 148–149

4 Complete with the present perfect continuous of the verbs in brackets.

0. 'How long <u>have you been working</u> (work) in the city, Dan?'
   'I <u>'ve been travelling</u> (travel) to the city for work for about two months.'
1. 'Has Jane .... (drive) all day?'
   'Yes, she ....'
2. 'How long .... Alfonso .... (stay) with you?'
   'He .... (live) with us since the summer. He's on an exchange programme.'
3. 'How long .... you .... (play) in the school's hockey team?'
   'We .... (play) in it since 2015.'
4. 'Sorry I'm late. .... you .... (wait) for long?'
   'No, I .... Don't worry, I've just arrived.'
5. 'Why .... so many young people .... (leave) rural villages?'
   'Because there are no jobs. They .... (move) to the mainland since 2015.'

5 **PAIRWORK** Make questions to ask your partner, then write his / her answers.

0. How long / you / attend / your present school?
   How long have you been attending your present school?
   Luca has been attending his present school for two years.
1. How long / you / study / English?
2. How long / your family / live / in your present home?
3. How long / you / do / your favourite hobby or sport?
4. How long / your class / use / this English course?

GRAMMAR GUIDE

Present perfect simple v present perfect continuous

*Shona **has been travelling** to school on Oban since the school in Coll closed.*
*She **has caught** the ferry every morning and evening for the last three years.*

The present perfect refers to actions or situations that started in the past and are still happening or have just ended.

- We use the present perfect continuous to emphasise the action, its duration or intensity.
- We use the present perfect simple to emphasise the result or the repetitions of the action.
- We don't use the present perfect continuous with state verbs.

➡ **GRAMMAR REFERENCE** p. 115   **WB** p. 149

6 Write the sentences using the correct form: present perfect simple or present perfect continuous.

0. Jo / write job applications / for hours
   Jo's been writing job applications for hours.
1. Jo / write / 400 job applications
2. People / leave the Island / for ten years
3. Two hundred people / leave the Island / since 2008
4. Andy / take the train / five times this week
5. Andy / take the train / all week

7 **SPEAKING** Answer the questions in pairs.

1. Think of the text on page 24. Does your area have a similar problem?
2. Are there enough things to do in your area?
3. Have people been moving into or out of your area?
   My friend Sabrina has been living in a small town near Rome for two years. There's not much to do there.

READING SKILLS

LEAD IN

8 PAIRWORK Discuss these questions and share your ideas with the class.

1 Which wild animals migrate from your country in the winter?
2 Where do they go?

PRACTICE

9 [1.14] Read and listen to the text and match the summary sentences to the paragraphs.

1 ☐ Immigrant birds
2 ☐ The UK's favourite bird
3 ☐ Friendly or fierce?
4 ☐ Not such a quiet life

READING STRATEGY

Understand the purpose of a text

Analysing a text helps you understand the writer's reason for writing. The purpose of a text can be to entertain, inform or persuade. When you are reading the text, ask yourself these questions:
- form – what type of text is it? e.g., an article, a poem
- source – where is it from? e.g., a newspaper, a novel
- audience – who is it for? e.g., customers, the public

PRELIMINARY | IGCSE

10 Match each text type to its purpose.

☐ medical text book   ☐ an advertising leaflet
☐ a romantic novel   ☐ a newspaper
☐ a travel guide

a entertain   **b** inform   **c** persuade

11 Answer the questions on the European robin from the fact file and the main text.

1 What type of text is the fact file?
   A an advert   B an encyclopaedic description
   C a newspaper article
2 What type of text is the main text?
   A a letter   B an advert   C an article
3 Where has the main text come from?
   A a novel   B a news website
   C a wildlife magazine
4 What is the main purpose of this text?
   A to persuade us to vote for the robin as our favourite bird
   B to tell an entertaining story about robins
   C to inform us about the behaviour of robins

European Robin (Erithacus rubecula)

Length: 13–14 cm
Wing span: 20–22 cm
Weight: 16–22 g
Family: chats and thrushes (*Turdidae*)
Habitat: woods, forest, parks and gardens
Diet: seeds, fruit and insects
Description: a small bird with brown *feathers* and red *breast*. Male and female are identical. It is found across Europe. The robin is highly territorial and can display aggressive *behaviour*.

The robin: Myth and reality

A The robin is a common sight in British gardens and is associated with the winter landscape and Christmas festivities. Postmen in Victorian times wore jackets which were red and they were sometimes called *redbreasts* just like the robins. The tradition of sending Christmas cards started in Victorian times so Christmas was the time when postmen were very busy! Victorians started designing Christmas cards that had robins on them and the robin has been appearing on Christmas cards ever since! People in Britain recently voted for the robin as the nation's favourite bird and there is a campaign to recognise the robin as Britain's national bird. However, recent research has shown that our beloved British robin is not all it seems!

12 Critical thinking Do you think the article gives a positive or negative view of robins? Discuss in pairs, then share ideas with the class.

GRAMMAR GUIDE

Defining relative clauses

- Postmen in Victorian times wore <u>jackets</u> **which** / **that** were red.
- Christmas was <u>the time</u> **when** postmen were very busy.
- Jane is one of the <u>scientists</u> **who** / **that** has been studying robins.
- They live <u>in woods and forests</u> **where** they have little contact with humans.
- There are many <u>robins</u> in the UK **whose** native country isn't Britain.
- They liked <u>the car</u> (**that** / **which**) I bought.

→ GRAMMAR REFERENCE p. 116   WB p. 152

Unit 2

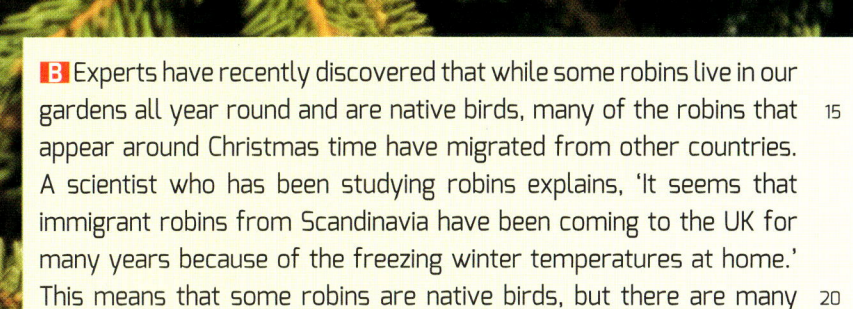

B Experts have recently discovered that while some robins live in our gardens all year round and are native birds, many of the robins that appear around Christmas time have migrated from other countries. A scientist who has been studying robins explains, 'It seems that immigrant robins from Scandinavia have been coming to the UK for many years because of the freezing winter temperatures at home.' This means that some robins are native birds, but there are many robins in the UK whose native country isn't Britain.

C The image of a little bird living sedately in our gardens is certainly not true for Scandinavian robins, whose migration journeys are amazing. First they spend about two weeks eating lots of fruit and insects, which they need to survive their thousand-mile journey. Then they fly non-stop for days, using the moon and the stars to navigate across the mountains, forests and lakes of Scandinavia. They cross the icy North Sea, and finally they arrive at their winter territories returning to the same place each year.

D The popular image of robins as jolly, friendly birds isn't completely true either. Scandinavian robins are not very sociable because they live in woods and forests where they have little contact with humans. What's more, all robins are fiercely aggressive and fight to defend their territory from other robins. The beautiful red of their breasts is a colour of aggression and they use it to frighten and threaten other birds! Luckily they aren't dangerous to humans and wherever they come from they are a welcome sight at any time of the year.

Glossary
wing span : apertura alare **breast :** petto
feathers : piume **behaviour :** comportamento

13 Look at the examples in the Grammar guide and choose the correct option.

1 We use defining relative clauses to give *essential / non-essential* information. Without it the sentence doesn't make sense.
2 We use *who* for *people / things*. We use *which* for *people / things*. We use *whose* for *possessors / people*. We use *that* for *people and things / possessors* instead of *who* and *which*.
3 We *must include / can omit* the relative pronoun when it refers to the object of a sentence.

14 Complete the relative clauses with the correct relative pronoun.

0 Have you seen the book ......**(that)**...... I was reading?
1 Steve Jobs was the person .... started Apple.
2 A smartphone is the only electronic device .... I use.
3 That's the house .... my father was born.
4 Sarah's the girl .... met us on holiday.
5 Sal has a friend .... dad is a teacher at our school.
6 Is this the dress .... was so expensive?

WRITING SKILLS

LEAD IN
15 Which types of information should you include in a descriptive essay?

1 facts and figures
2 feelings, sensations and impressions
3 instructions and explanations
4 points for and against

PRACTICE
16 Read about the structure of a descriptive essay. Complete the sentences with the words below.

details ▪ concluding ▪ summarise ▪ opening ▪ feelings

Firstly, begin with a good ^{1}.................... sentence that talks about the topic. This captures the reader's attention. Then include a main statement which explains why you're writing about your topic. Next include a paragraph with ^{2}.................... which describe the subject and express your thoughts and ^{3}.................... about it. Before you finish, include a final paragraph where you ^{4}.................... your main statement. A memorable ^{5}.................... sentence then finishes off your essay.

WRITING STRATEGY

Write a description of a place

When you are writing a description of a place you know well, explain:
▪ where the place is
▪ what it means to you
▪ the people or memories you associate with it
▪ what you can see, smell, hear and feel in this place
▪ your impressions and feelings

➡ See **WRITING EXPANSION** page 251

VOCABULARY

Geographical features

17 PAIRWORK Discuss these questions.

1 Are there any places you would like to visit outside Italy?
2 Have you read any books or magazines or adverts about them?
3 What is it that attracts you to this place?

18 Read these descriptions of places by two famous writers. Match the photos 1–2 to the paragraphs A–B.

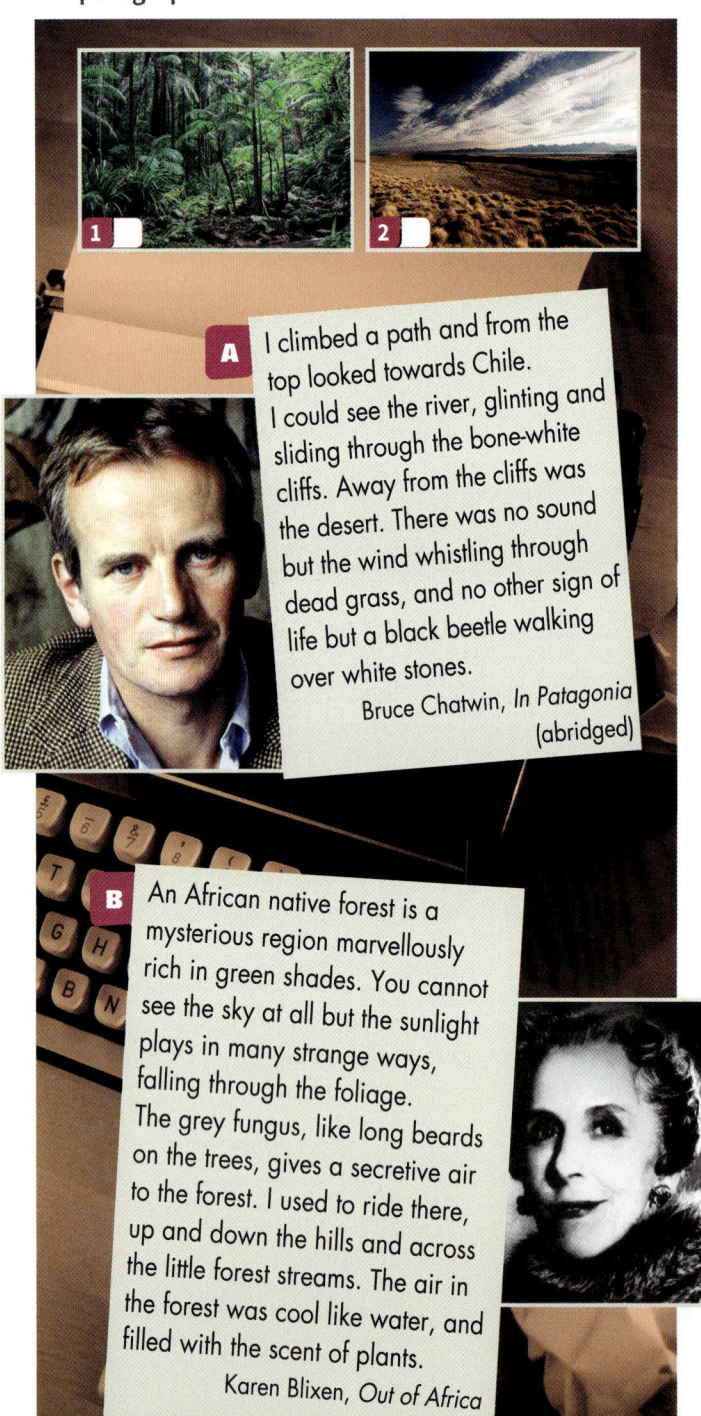

A I climbed a path and from the top looked towards Chile. I could see the river, glinting and sliding through the bone-white cliffs. Away from the cliffs was the desert. There was no sound but the wind whistling through dead grass, and no other sign of life but a black beetle walking over white stones.

Bruce Chatwin, *In Patagonia* (abridged)

B An African native forest is a mysterious region marvellously rich in green shades. You cannot see the sky at all but the sunlight plays in many strange ways, falling through the foliage. The grey fungus, like long beards on the trees, gives a secretive air to the forest. I used to ride there, up and down the hills and across the little forest streams. The air in the forest was cool like water, and filled with the scent of plants.

Karen Blixen, *Out of Africa* (abridged)

19 [1.15] Match the photos to the words. Then listen and check.

a path   e grass   i fungus
b river   f stones   j trees
c cliff   g forest   k hills
d desert   h foliage   l stream

20 [1.16] Match the words to the definitions. Then listen and check.

1 ☐ sea   4 ☐ beach   6 ☐ mountain
2 ☐ valley   5 ☐ field   7 ☐ lake
3 ☐ jungle

a An area of land between two mountains.
b A large amount of water which separates countries and continents.
c An area that has large trees and lots of animals. It is usually hot and sticky. There are many in Africa.
d An area of land that farmers use to grow crops.
e An area of land near the sea. People usually sunbathe here.
f A large amount of water, usually between mountains and hills. There are many in Italy and Switzerland.
g A huge rock, which is very high and very steep. People sometimes go skiing on them.

21 SPEAKING Think of a place you know well and use words from this page to describe it to your partner. Can your partner guess where it is?

SPEAKING SKILLS

Having a disagreement

22 PAIRWORK Why are young people leaving the countryside for the town? Discuss with your partner.

23 [1.17] Listen and watch the video. Why does Grace want to move to London?

key expressions	
express an opinion	
☐ I (don't) think …	☐ In my opinion …
agree	disagree
☐ I know what you mean.	☐ I don't think so.
☐ That's true, but …	☐ I'm sorry I disagree.
☐ You're absolutely right!	☐ You're wrong!
☐ You've got a point.	

24 [1.17] Listen and watch again and tick (✓) the key expressions you hear.

SPEAKING STRATEGY

Make an opinion stronger

We can emphasise an opinion by using an adverb before the verb.

- ☐ I *totally* agree with you.
- ☐ You're *absolutely* wrong!
- ☐ I *really* don't think so.
- ☐ I *completely* agree.
- ☐ You're *definitely* wrong there!
- ☐ I *absolutely* know what you mean.
- ☐ That's *very* true.
- ☐ I *definitely* think …
- ☐ I *completely* disagree.

PRELIMINARY | IGCSE

25 [1.17] Listen and watch again and tick (✓) the expressions from the strategy box you hear.

26 PAIRWORK Choose one of the topics. Express your opinions and react to your partner's. Make some of your opinions stronger.

- It's important for all high school students to study abroad for one year.
- We don't need timetables. It's better for students to study what they want to each day.

SOUNDS ENGLISH

Sentence stress: Emphasis

27 [1.18] Listen to a speaker say the same sentence in three different ways. How does the emphasis change the meaning?

John can't help you with your maths homework.

SOUND STRATEGY

In English sentences the stress pattern is not as regular as in Italian. In English the stress falls on keywords, or words we want to emphasise. This helps you to understand the sense of the sentence better.

- *We* should feed the birds. (no one else, it's our job / duty)
- We *should* feed the birds. (it's the right thing to do)
- We should *feed* the birds. (not frighten them away)

28 [1.19] Listen to three versions of the same sentence. How does changing the emphasis change the meaning? Match 1–3 to a–c, then listen and check.

1 ☐ I love your brother <u>Tom</u>.
2 ☐ I <u>love</u> your brother Tom.
3 ☐ I love your <u>brother</u> Tom.

a He's more than just a friend to me.
b I don't love your sister.
c Not your other brother Sam.

29 GAME Read the sentences. How many ways can you change the emphasis to change the meaning?

1 Where's my dinner?
2 This coffee is awful.
3 I missed you.
4 I'll help the teacher.

Unit 2   29

LISTENING SKILLS

LEAD IN

30 Look at the photos. Which images do you think tourists most associate with Italy?

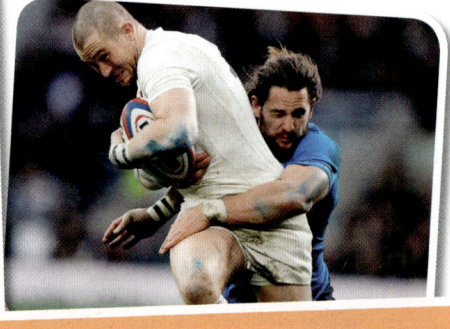

PRACTICE

31 [1.20] Listen to an interview with Megan, a British girl who went to live in Italy. Why did she decide to go there?

1 to look for a boyfriend
2 to look for a job
3 to have a holiday
4 to experience another culture

LISTENING STRATEGY

True / False questions

In some listening exercises you need to decide if sentences are correct (true) or incorrect (false). Remember:
- you will probably hear all the words in the sentences so listen carefully to the context
- True / False statements often state the opposite of what you hear in the recording
- keywords are usually stressed in a dialogue, so listen out for them

32 [1.20] Listen again. Which of the things from the photos on this page does Megan mention?

33 [1.20] Read the sentences, then listen again. Decide if they are true (T) or false (F). Correct the false ones.

1 Megan lives in Italy now. T F
2 She went to Italy to work as a teacher. T F
3 She prefers cities to the mountains. T F
4 She knew a lot about Italian food before she went there. T F
5 She has found it difficult to make friends. T F
6 She speaks Italian very well now. T F

34 [1.20] Listen again. Complete the questions from the interview that correspond to these answers.

1 'How long .... ?'
'I've been living here for three years now.'
2 'Why .... ?'
'I wanted to learn about Italy, the life style and culture …'
3 '.. in Cortina?'
'No, I haven't. When I first came to Italy, I worked in Milan.'
4 '.. Milan?'
'No, I didn't! In winter it was foggy, and in summer it was full of mosquitoes!'
5 'What .... food?'
'I love it! Before I came here I only knew dishes like lasagne and pizza!'
6 '.. don't like?'
'Yes, there is – horse!'

35 **Critical thinking** What do you think English students like or don't like about your town? Make notes on:

- landscape
- weather
- food
- people
- other

36 **PAIRWORK** Take turns to act out an interview with an English student. Use your notes from exercise 35.

Unit 2

ACADEMIC SKILLS

Labelling a map

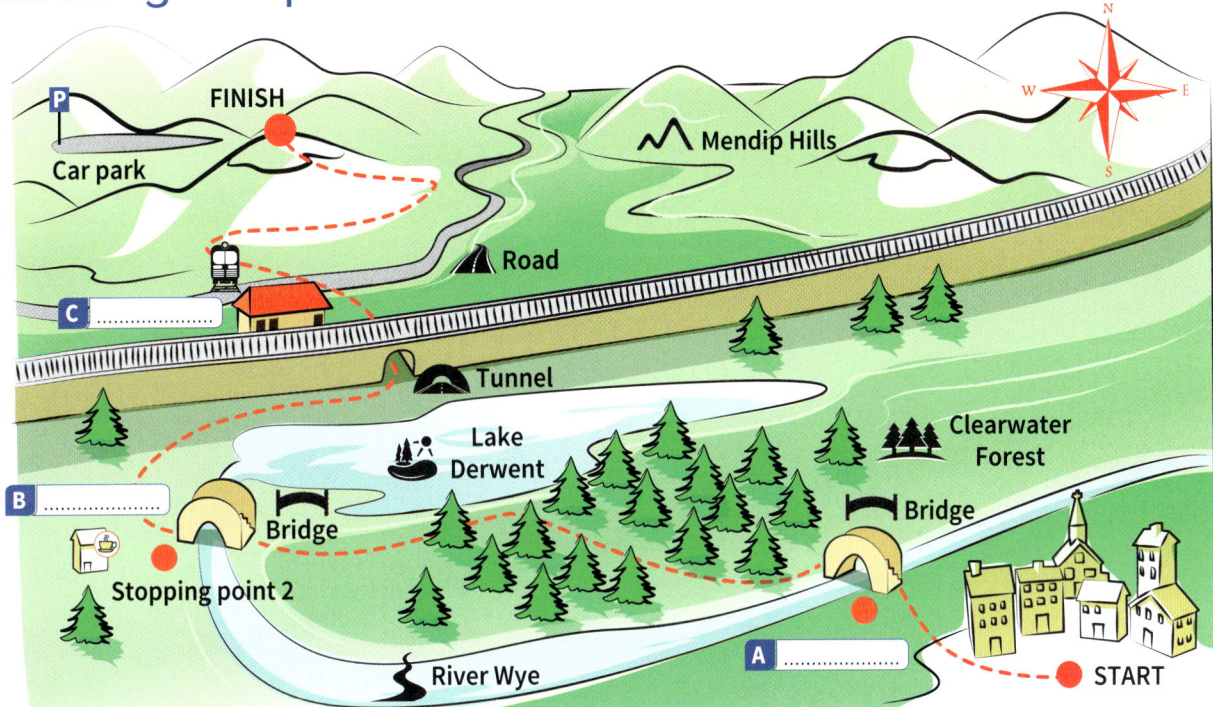

LEAD IN

37 Look at the map. What sort of information does it show?

1 a main road across a region
2 a cross-country running track
3 a walking route through mountains

PRACTICE

38 Match these phrases for locating something on a map to their opposites.

1 ☐ at the top   a to the south
2 ☐ on the left-hand side   b below
3 ☐ to the north   c outside
4 ☐ to the southeast   d at the bottom
5 ☐ above   e on the right-hand side
6 ☐ inside   f to the northwest

39 Complete the sentences with words from exercise 38.

1 Write your name and class .... of the exam paper.
2 Orvieto is .... of Rome.
3 People drive .... in the UK, not the right.
4 Sunset is when the sun drops .... the horizon.
5 London is .... of Cambridge.
6 The cathedral is .... the city walls.

40 Look carefully at these symbols from the map. Match them to the words.

1 ☐   2 ☐   3 ☐   4 ☐
5 ☐   6 ☐   7 ☐   8 ☐

a forest   d hills   g railway line
b lake   e bridge   h tunnel
c river   f road

ACADEMIC STRATEGY

When you label a map, you have to use the information you hear or read to complete blank labels. Look at the map and listen or look for:

- prepositions of place and movement
- the names of the other places on the map that are near the blank labels
- the numbers / letters of the blank labels
- the correct words to fill the gaps

IELTS

41 [1.21] **LISTENING** Listen and complete the labels on the map. Use no more than three words for each answer.

Unit 2   31

REVISE AND ROUND UP

1 **Complete the dialogue with the present simple or present continuous form of the verb in brackets.**

A Hi Leon, how ⁰..**are**.. you ..**feeling**.. (feel) today?
B I ¹.......... (be) good thanks, Ed. I've got some friends in my new class now, so I ².......... (enjoy) school more.
A That's great, Leon! ³.......... you ⁴.......... (take) Spanish this year?
B Yes, I .... (be). I'm in Mrs Pica's class. I really ⁵.......... (like) her. What about you?
A I ⁶.......... (not / do) Spanish. I ⁷.......... (start) French this term instead.
B Cool. ⁸.......... you .... (have) Mr Martin?
A Yes, we ⁹.......... (have). He ¹⁰.......... (give) us our first test this afternoon!

2 **Complete the questions using the present simple or present continuous tense. Then write answers that are true for you.**

0 what / you / do / at the moment?
   What are you doing at the moment?
   I'm studying English.
1 what / you / usually do / after school?
2 how often / you / check / social media / every day?
3 you / look at / a social media site / now?
4 who / sometimes / help / you / with / your school work?
5 they / help / you / with / this exercise / now?
6 you / have / a lot of / online friends?

3 **Complete the sentences using the present perfect form of the verbs in brackets.**

0 Over half of all teenagers ..**have made**.. (make) friends online.
1 Surveys show that over 50% of teens .... (feel) sad because of posts online.
2 25% of teens .... (lose) friends because of things people said online.
3 Which group .... (experience) this more, girls or boys?
4 I .... (not / be) to many parties this term.
5 .... Sam .... (make) a lot of friends since he came to this school?
6 Tanya .... never .... (use) Instagram!
7 .... you .... (text) your friends about the party?

4 **Complete the dialogue with the present perfect or past simple form of the verbs in brackets.**

A ⁰..**Have**.. you ever ..**posted**.. (you / post) things on social media just to get more likes?
B Yes, I have. I do it all the time!
A What sort of content ¹.......... you .... (share)?
B Well, I ².......... (take) some selfies with three kittens that ³.......... (be) really cute. I ⁴.......... (put) them on Instagram because a lot of people love cats so more people will like my photos.
A ⁵.......... you .... (got) a lot of likes, or comments?
B Yeah! Loads of people ⁶.......... (comment) on the photos since I posted them. I ⁷.......... (never / have) so many likes on my profile since I ⁸.......... (create) it!
A Wow. Maybe I need to try kitten power too! My friends ⁹.......... (never / like) any of my photos.
B That's because they're boring. You ¹⁰.......... (post) ten photos of buildings last month.
A I like buildings!
B Yes, but your friends don't!

5 **Choose the correct option.**

Luke I'm going out now, Dad.
Dad Wait a minute, Luke. Have you fixed my laptop ⁰(**yet**) / already?
Luke Yes, I've ¹already / yet done it, Dad. I just needed to reload the software.
Dad Really? What about the problem with the battery? Have you solved that?
Luke Yes, I have. And I've ²already / yet put the battery back in. Now you need to reboot the system. Look – a message has ³just / yet come up on the screen to tell you to reboot.
Dad Oh, yes, you're right. Well done. But have you found those files I lost ⁴yet / just? You promised me to do it this afternoon. I need them for my report.
Luke No, I haven't recovered them ⁵yet / already, but I'm late for the cinema now. Can I do it when I get back?
Dad Come on, Luke, you know I'm useless with computers and I need them now.
Luke Oh, Dad! Okay. Let me have a look.

32 Units 1–2

TOWARDS PRELIMINARY

6 Complete the mini dialogues with the present perfect continuous form of the verbs in brackets.

0 **A** How long <u>have you been working</u> (work) on your history project, Dan?
B I <u>'ve been doing</u> (do) the research online for about two weeks now.

1 **A** Sorry, I'm late. ……………… you ……………… (wait) for long?
B No, I ……………… . Don't worry, I've just arrived too.

2 **A** How long ……………… you ……………… (look after) Karen's dog?
B He ……………… (stay) with us since Easter. Karen's gone to New York for a drama course.

3 **A** ……………… your grandmother ……………… (cook) all day?
B Yes, she ……………… (make) cakes and pies since this morning!

4 **A** How long ……………… you ……………… (study) at Forrester High School, Jess?
B I've been at this school since 2017.

7 Use a relative pronoun to make one sentence from each pair.

0 I'd like to live in a place. There is lots to do there.
I'd like to live in a place where there is lots to do.

1 A crocodile is an animal. It lives in the water.
2 I live in a house. It's near the sea.
3 We ate all the cake. Mum made it for my birthday.
4 That's Connel Castle. A ghost was seen there.
5 This is the film. Its director won the Oscar
6 Can I have that apple? It's green.

8 **TRANSLATION** Translate the sentences into English.

1 Ci sono due pettirossi che vivono nel nostro giardino.
2 Questi uccelli migrano nel Regno Unito?
3 Questo software non sta funzionando bene.
4 Non hanno mai avuto prima problemi di questo tipo.
5 Avete già trovato un posto dove stare?
6 Simon tenta (da tempo) di aiutarci con le nostre richieste per il passaporto.
7 Da quanto tempo leggi questo libro?
8 Credo sia una storia che ha inventato Martine.

Reading

9 Choose the correct option.

My family has been living in Norway for two years now ⁰………… of my dad's job. I like it here but it's very quiet compared to our life in London. We've ¹………… a big house on a beautiful fjord and I've learned to sail and windsurf since we arrived here, which is awesome! The area is very rural and all the students travel long distances to go to school. My brother and I have ²………… taking the ferry four days a week for the last two terms, but next term I ³………… going to get a motorbike and drive us there instead. I have been trying to ⁴………… Norwegian but it's quite a difficult language and I haven't ⁵………… a lot of progress! My older sister lives in Oslo now – she's been living there ⁶………… two years. She went there to look for work and she's ⁷………… her dream job. She's learning how to make animated films for a Norwegian media company. She loves it and she ⁸………… asked me to go and stay with her in the holidays.

0	**A** because	**B** why	**C** when	**D** for
1	**A** had	**B** got	**C** been	**D** get
2	**A** got	**B** being	**C** been	**D** be
3	**A** have	**B** am	**C** was	**D** been
4	**A** learns	**B** learnt	**C** learning	**D** learn
5	**A** had	**B** done	**C** made	**D** studied
6	**A** for	**B** during	**C** since	**D** in
7	**A** find	**B** found	**C** finding	**D** finds
8	**A** was	**B** is	**C** had	**D** has

3 Entertainment

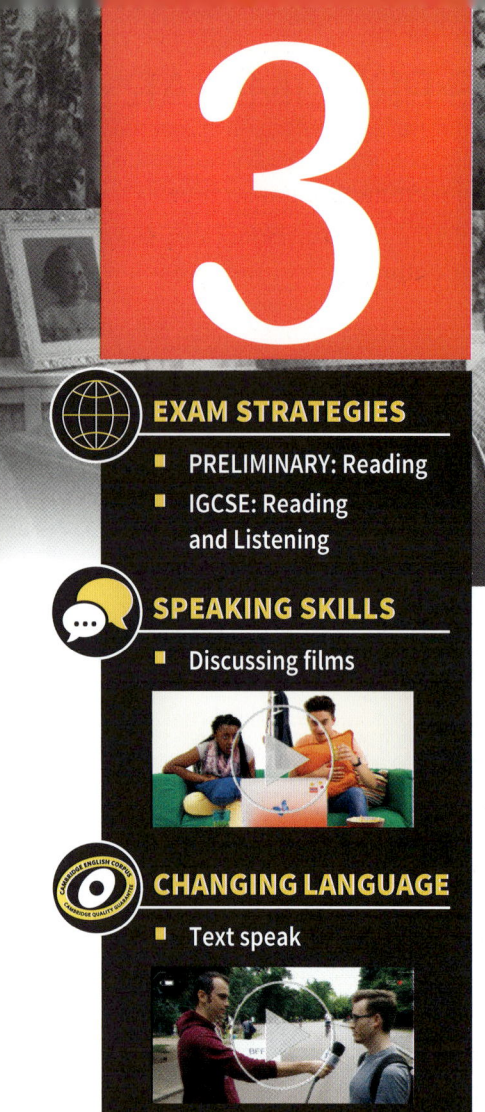

EXAM STRATEGIES
- PRELIMINARY: Reading
- IGCSE: Reading and Listening

SPEAKING SKILLS
- Discussing films

CHANGING LANGUAGE
- Text speak

LIFE SKILLS
- Self-regulating

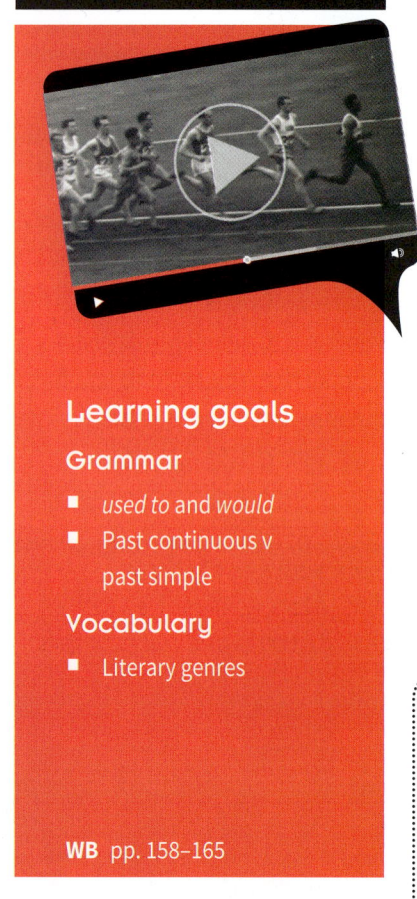

Learning goals
Grammar
- used to and would
- Past continuous v past simple

Vocabulary
- Literary genres

WB pp. 158–165

LEAD IN

1 PAIRWORK Discuss these questions.
1. Do you watch your favourite programmes on TV or on a laptop or a tablet?
2. Do you watch your favourite programmes alone or with your family?
3. Who decides the programmes you watch?

2 [1.22] Read, listen and watch. What type of entertainment is the article about?

Home entertainment: The way we watch

A In the years after World War II watching TV used to be a communal activity. Televisions used to be expensive and not many people had one at home. People would meet in bars and cafés, or go to the home of a lucky friend with a TV, to watch major events like the 1948 Olympic Games in London. These were special occasions, so there would often be food and drink to share and a real party atmosphere!

B In the late 1950s and 1960s televisions became less expensive and more people were able to buy them. However, the technology was still very basic. Televisions were big and they didn't use to switch on immediately. Instead they'd take about half an hour to **heat up** before you could see a picture! Families used to enjoy watching TV in the evenings. They would sit around the TV set in their living room together, but there would be lots of arguments about what to watch as they only used to have one TV!

C As TV became more popular there were more programmes like soap operas and serials. Viewers would wait in anticipation for the next episode and used to discuss it with their friends and colleagues the next day. They didn't want to miss their favourite programmes so video recorders became really popular in the 1970s. Viewers would **preset** their video recorder and then they could choose when to watch. This certainly reduced arguments at home!

D In the last 20 years, the way we watch TV has changed enormously. There are hundreds of channels, **catch-up services** and online streaming. This means we can choose what we watch and when we watch it. But the biggest revolution has been in the technology we use. Tablets, phones and laptops mean we no longer watch with other people. From the communal activity it used to be, watching TV has become an individual activity we enjoy alone.

Glossary
heat up: riscaldarsi
preset: programmare
catch-up services: servizi che permettono di rivedere online programmi già andati in onda

34   Unit 3

PRACTICE

3 ▶ [1.22] Read, listen and watch the video again. Match the headings to the correct paragraphs.

1. ☐ How we watch TV today
2. ☐ Family viewing in the 1950s and 1960s
3. ☐ Television in the 1940s, a communal event
4. ☐ The era of soap operas and video recorders

GRAMMAR GUIDE

used to

Affirmative	Negative
Watching TV **used to be** a communal activity.	They **didn't use to switch on** immediately.
Questions	**Short answers**
Did your grandmother **use to have** a TV?	Yes, she **did**. / No, she **didn't**.

➡ GRAMMAR REFERENCE p. 116   WB p. 158

4 Read the sentences. Tick (✓) the ones that refer to past habits.

0. We had dinner every evening at 6:30. ✓
1. You saw that film last month.
2. They played on the beach all day in the summer holidays.
3. They didn't eat pasta in the UK in the 1940s.
4. The girls didn't understand the question.
5. Did you live near the sea in Ireland?
6. Did James answer the phone earlier?

5 Rewrite the sentences you ticked in exercise 4. Use *used to* or *didn't use to*.

We used to have dinner every evening at 6:30.

GRAMMAR GUIDE

used to and would

Affirmative (habits)	Affirmative (states)
They **would meet** in bars and cafés. They **used to meet** in bars and cafés.	Televisions **used to be** expensive.
Negative	**Questions**
They **didn't use to switch on** immediately.	**Did** people **use to watch** TV during the day?

➡ GRAMMAR REFERENCE p. 116   WB p. 159

6 Look at the examples in the Grammar guide. Complete the sentences with the words below.

didn't use to ▪ used to ▪ would (x2)

1. We use both *would* and *used to* to talk about past habits in the affirmative form.
2. We use ……………… but not ……………… to talk about past states.
3. We don't usually use ……………… to talk about past habits in the negative or interrogative forms. Instead we use ……………… or *Did … use to?*

7 Complete the dialogue with the correct form of *would* or *used to*.

Tanya Did you have a TV when you were a girl, Gran?
Gran No, we didn't. We ⁰ *used to / would* listen to the radio in those days. Nobody had a TV in our street. Televisions ¹……………… be expensive in those days and people ²……………… have much money.
Tanya Really? What ³……………… you ……………… do in the evenings then?
Gran Well, we ⁴……………… go to the cinema – I loved those old black and white films! – and at home we made our own entertainment. We ⁵……………… read, or play cards. We ⁶……………… listen to music on the radio, or my brother ⁷……………… play the piano. He ⁸……………… have strong fingers then, not full of arthritis like now! He ⁹……………… enjoy playing for us!
Tanya Really? ¹⁰……………… you ……………… have a real piano at home?
Gran Yes, we did. There were no electronic keyboards in those days, Tanya!

8 **SPEAKING** Tell about your grandparents' childhood. Use four sentences with *used to* and two sentences with *would* and the prompts below.

- go to school in …
- have a lot of toys and games
- know all their neighbours
- play in …
- share a bedroom
- grow their own food

Unit 3   35

READING SKILLS

LEAD IN

9 PAIRWORK Look at the photos of well-known 'vampires'. Then discuss these questions.

1 Which of the words below do you associate with vampires?
- castle
- teeth
- hairy
- bat
- romantic
- violent
- scientist
- tail
- laboratory
- blood
- full moon
- sad

2 Does the vampire figure scare or fascinate you?

PRACTICE

10 [1.23] Read and listen to the text. How has the image of the vampire changed over time?

11 Read the text again and answer the questions.

1 Which two important people became Bram Stoker's friends in London?
2 What was Stoker doing in Whitby in 1890?
3 What was the usual image of the vampire in the 1950s and 1960s?
4 Which two series about vampires changed their image in the 1990s and 2000s?

READING STRATEGY

Understand chronology and sequence

In longer texts it's important to notice clues like linkers (*first*, *then*, *before*, *after*) and time words (*while*, *when*, *as*) that can help you understand the sequence and chronology of events.

PRELIMINARY | IGCSE

12 Find all the linkers and time words in the text.

13 Read the text again and complete the timeline about vampires in literature.

- **1431** – Vlad the Impaler (Vlad Dracul) is born.
- **1897** – ....
- **..........** – Universal Studios makes *Dracula* the film.
- **1950-1969** – Hammer Horror makes numerous classic horror films about vampires.
- **1997** – ....
- **..........** – Stephenie Meyer publishes the first *Twilight* novel.

VAMPIRES
From Monster To Heartthrob

Bram Stoker was an Irish theatre critic from Dublin. In 1879 he moved to London to work as a theatre manager. While he was working there he met many famous actors, writers and artists. First he met Henry Irving, a celebrated actor and theatre director. Then he got to know Ármin Vámbéry, a Hungarian writer and traveller. These two men became very influential in Stoker's later writing. He was fascinated by Vámbéry's stories of his home in the remote Carpathian Mountains and their strange, dark folklore, and he eventually based his most famous literary character on the dark, charismatic Henry Irving.

In 1890 Stoker went to Whitby in Yorkshire for a holiday. While he was staying there he started studying the history of Romania. He was researching Eastern European legends about vampires, when he discovered the story of an ancient Romanian warrior-prince, Vlad the Impaler. Vlad's family were members of the Order of the Dragon, which was

Glossary
heartthrob : rubacuori **stakes** : pali
Impaler : Impalatore **gory** : macabre

GRAMMAR GUIDE

Past continuous v past simple

past continuous	past simple
While he **was working** there …	he **met** many famous actors.
While he **was staying** there …	he **started** studying the history of Romania.
He **was researching** Eastern European legends about vampires …	when he **discovered** the story of an ancient Romanian warrior-prince.

→ GRAMMAR REFERENCE p. 117   WB p. 162

36   Unit 3

Nosferatu (1922) by F. W. Murnau.

Dracul in Romanian. Vlad was a real historical figure and lived from about 1431 to 1477. He became infamous for his cruelty because he used to execute his enemies by impaling them on **stakes**. He watched them suffer while he was eating his lunch. These **gory** stories and the wild, gothic atmosphere of Whitby inspired Bram Stoker to begin writing a horror story. After working on it for six years, he finally published it in 1897. The title was *Dracula*.

Dracula wasn't very successful during Stoker's life, but it became really famous when Universal Studios made it into a film in 1931. Since then the character of Count Dracula has inspired hundreds of other films and numerous fictional villains. However, during the twentieth century the image of the vampire in popular culture has evolved very noticeably. In the 1950s and 1960s the popular Hammer Horror films were still showing vampires as terrifying monsters, but a few years later writers weren't presenting them as evil, but as romantic, lonely outsiders. In 1997 in the popular TV series *Buffy the Vampire Slayer*, vampires were dangerous, glamorous creatures with supernatural powers. By 2005, in the hugely popular *Twilight Saga* by Stephenie Meyer, they were highly romanticised figures – handsome, troubled and complex heroes. They didn't represent evil, as they were often fighting evil forces. Robert Pattinson, who portrayed the vampire hero on screen, wasn't a monster, but a teen heartthrob. Vampires have certainly come a long way since the days of Vlad the Impaler!

14 Complete the extract from the story of *Dracula* with the past simple or past continuous of the verbs in brackets.

It⁰ ......**was**...... (*be*) a cold, windy night in Whitby.
I¹ .... (*stand*) on the sea wall near the port. I remember
I² .... (*look*) out to sea and ³ .... (*see*)
the moonlight on the water. I⁴ .... (*turn*) to go home,
when I⁵ .... (*notice*) a large ship on the horizon.
It⁶ .... (*move*) towards the shore very fast but there
⁷ .... (*not / be*) any lights on board. The ship
⁸ .... (*seem*) to fly over the water, it ⁹ ....
(*not / touch*) the waves. I¹⁰ .... (*watch*) it for a long time
as it¹¹ .... (*sail*) in to the port, but I¹² ....
(*not / be able to*) see any people on board at all.

15 Critical thinking Discuss the questions in pairs.

1 Do you like horror films? Why / Why not?
2 Why do you think the vampire image is so popular today?
3 Which other figures from folklore have inspired books, plays and films?

WRITING SKILLS

LEAD IN

16 PAIRWORK Discuss these questions.

1 Do you read reviews for any of the following types of entertainment?
- films
- TV programmes
- books
- computer games
- music concerts / gigs

2 Do they influence your choices?
3 Can you think of any other things you can write a review for?

PRACTICE

17 Sort the words and expressions into the correct group: Book, Film and Both.

(Book (Both) Film)

character ▪ plot ▪ special effects ▪
soundtrack ▪ narrator ▪ scene ▪
setting ▪ author ▪ director ▪
chapter ▪ actor ▪ cameraman

WRITING STRATEGY

Write a film or book review

In a review, you briefly explain what the book / film is about and give your opinion of it. A review usually includes:

- background information – for a book: the writer, date of publication, genre; for a film: actors, director, music, date of release, genre
- a brief summary of the main events in the story and characters
- your opinions on the strong and weak points of the book / film and whether you would recommend it

➡ See **WRITING EXPANSION** page 252

Unit 3   37

VOCABULARY

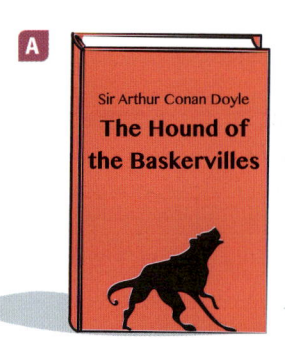

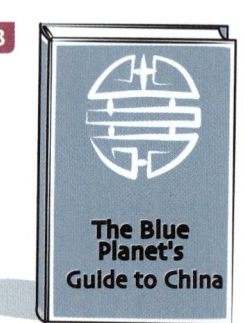

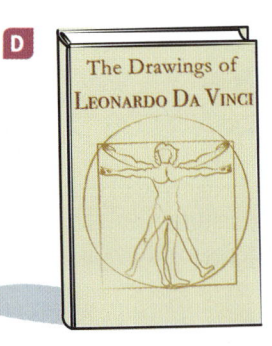

A Sir Arthur Conan Doyle — The Hound of the Baskervilles

B The Blue Planet's Guide to China

C 15 - MINUTE MEALS by JAMIE OLIVER

D The Drawings of Leonardo Da Vinci

E Symbolism in Tibetan Buddhism

F THE LIFE OF ALBERT EINSTEIN — $E = mc^2$

G The American Civil War

H UP YOUR GAME HOW TO IMPROVE YOUR GOLF

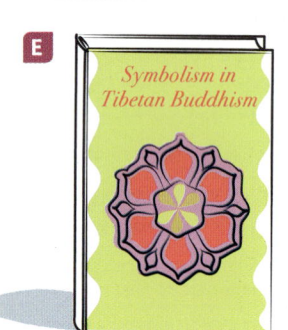

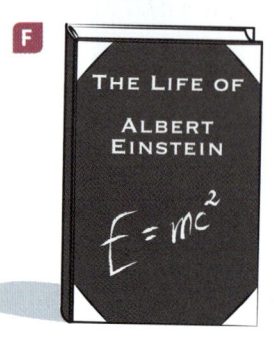

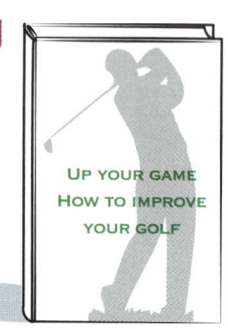

Literary genres

18 PAIRWORK Discuss the questions in pairs.

1. What type of books do you enjoy reading? Why?
2. How do you prefer to read (book, e-reader, smartphone, etc.)?
3. Do you ever buy books? Where do you buy them?

19 Read the titles and decide the genre of books A–H. Then put the books in the correct section of the bookshop 1–12.

12	☐ Children's books
11	☐ Hobbies and Crafts
10	☐ Film and Television
9	☐ Art and Architecture
8	☐ Cookery
7	☐ Religion and Self-help
6	☐ Sport
5	☐ Crime
4	☐ Travel
3	☐ History
2	☐ Biography
1	☐ Fiction A–Z

20 Write examples of books you know for the remaining four sections in the bookshop.

21 Read the descriptions from the back covers of three books.

1. Which genre do you think each belongs to?
2. Underline the information which helped you answer.

1 The 1920s was the Golden Age of silent films in Hollywood, when the first generation of American film stars became international icons. The incredible photographs in this book show us the stars in their glamorous roles on-screen but also in their intimate moments off the film set.

2 Inspector Martin is on the trail of a gang of dangerous criminals who are smuggling diamonds around the world. Will he catch them before they succeed in the biggest robbery of all time – stealing the famous Crown Jewels from the Tower of London?

3 We live in stressful times and more and more people are suffering from anxiety and depression. This helpful guide looks at safe, natural methods like meditation, aromatherapy and yoga to help you relax and reduce stress in your life, to improve your health and well-being.

22 SPEAKING Discuss the questions in pairs.

1. Talk about a book you love and a book you hate.
2. What genre are the two books you chose?
3. What are they about?
4. What do you like / dislike about them?

See **VOCABULARY EXTENSION** page 262

SPEAKING SKILLS

Discussing films

23 PAIRWORK Discuss these questions.
1 Think about the last horror film you saw. Can you describe the story in three sentences?
2 How did you feel while you were watching it?

24 [1.24] Listen and watch the video. What's the name of the film Luke and Anna are talking about? What type of film is it?

key expressions	
questions	answers
setting	
• Where is it set? • Where does the story take place?	• It's set in Transylvania and Germany. • It takes place in a town in Germany.
plot	
• What happens in the story? • What happens next?	• At first … then … after that … in the end …
opinion / reaction	
• Why did you like / not like it? • What did you think of it?	• I thought the characters were brilliant. • I really liked the story.

25 [1.24] Listen and watch again and answer the questions about the film.
1 Where is the film set?
2 In which century does it take place?
3 What happens in the story?
4 Why did Anna like it?

SPEAKING STRATEGY

Give encouragement

When someone is telling us a story, or describing events, we can use these expressions to encourage them to continue and tell us more.
- Go on.
- Then what (happens)?
- What happens after that?
- And … so …?

26 PAIRWORK Think of a film you've seen that you liked a lot. Use the key expressions and the strategy box to talk about it in pairs.

CHANGING LANGUAGE

Text speak

27 Look at the list of text acronyms. Think back to the video in exercise 24. Which acronyms did you hear?
1 LOL
2 YOLO
3 OMG
4 BFF

28 PAIRWORK Use the context of the sentences to discuss the meaning of the acronyms.
1 LOL You're so funny LOL!
2 YOLO Let's go to the party – YOLO!
3 OMG OMG another test!
4 BFF My BFF has just given me a lovely present.

29 Watch the video and check your answers to exercise 28.

30 PAIRWORK Think about your language and discuss in pairs.
1 Which acronyms do young people use a lot in texts?
2 Are there any text acronyms that you now use in speech?

CORPUS

Corpus data can help track the interesting ways our language is changing and adapting. Acronyms are popular in texts but some acronyms are also now seen in informal speech too. Text speak is mostly used by under-30-year-olds.

Unit 3 39

LISTENING SKILLS

LEAD IN

31 Read the statements below and tick (✓) the ones you agree with.

- ☐ Ghosts don't exist.
- ☐ There is a rational, scientific explanation for 'ghosts'.
- ☐ Ghosts are the spirits of dead people and some people can see them.

PRACTICE

32 [1.25] Listen to five people talking about ghosts. Which two people have had personal experience of the supernatural?

33 [1.25] Listen again and answer the questions.

1. Where was Sam when he saw the girl?
2. What happened?
3. Who was she, in his opinion?
4. Where do people usually say they've seen ghosts, according to Kate?
5. What's Adam's possible explanation for ghosts?
6. How does Rebecca describe the human brain?
7. What did Isaac's dog do in their new house?
8. What did his family find out later?

LISTENING STRATEGY

Match exercises

Before you listen:
- read the exercise very carefully. There are usually more options than you need
- underline the keywords in all the options

While you listen:
- you will not probably hear the same words as in the exercise, but synonyms which have a similar meaning
- listen for the keywords
- there may be distractors: these are words and phrases that are not the correct answer but might make you think they are because they are similar in some way
- reread the options. Decide if the information matches the answer or if it is a distractor

IGCSE

34 [1.25] Listen again and match the sentences to the speakers. Use the tips from the strategy box to help you. There is one extra option.

1. ☐ Sam   3. ☐ Adam   5. ☐ Isaac
2. ☐ Kate   4. ☐ Rebecca

a. Animals are more sensitive to the supernatural than people.
b. Ghosts are powerful projections from people's imaginations.
c. I believe ghosts are the spirits of people who died in that place.
d. Ghosts are projections from parallel universes into ours.
e. People get over-imaginative when they're in scary places.
f. There are a lot of things science still can't explain, and ghosts are one of them.

35 Underline the keywords in the summary sentences above which helped you answer exercise 34.

36 **Critical thinking** Discuss the questions in pairs.

1. Which of the five speakers do you strongly agree with? Why?
2. What do you think is the explanation for ghosts and supernatural experiences?

37 **PAIRWORK** Discuss these questions.

1. Are there any ghost stories in your family, or in your area?
2. What do you think is the explanation?
3. Tell your partner the story and give your opinion about it.

LIFE SKILLS

Self-regulating

LEAD IN

38 PAIRWORK Look at the activities below and discuss the questions.

- using social networks
- doing homework
- doing sport / exercise
- revising for exams
- playing computer games
- watching videos

1 Which of these activities do you think you spend too much time on?
2 Which do you not spend enough time on?
3 Do your parents and teachers agree with your ideas?

PRACTICE

39 Read the text. What is self-regulation?

1 the ability to control your temperature
2 skills to help you control your responses to events in your life
3 being able to study for long periods of time

Self-regulation

Self-regulation describes the skills we use to adapt and react to things that happen in our lives. We can't control things that happen in our lives, but we can control how we react to these events. Learning how to effectively regulate your feelings, thoughts and behaviour to adapt to events around you can make your life easier and happier. Good self-regulation skills can help you in many areas: relationships with others, performance at school, physical health and well-being and happiness.
There are three main types of self-regulation skills:
1 Physical – How to calm your body and keep it healthy.
2 Emotional – How to identify and express your feelings.
3 Cognitive – How to identify unhealthy thinking and organise and plan your life.

LIFE STRATEGY

Tips for self-regulation

- Make sure you understand the assignment. Write it in your notebook or homework planner. Ask questions about it.
- Use any extra time you've got at school to do homework. The more work you do at school, the less you have to do at home.
- Plan your time. Be realistic about how much you can do in the time you've got. Remember you may have sports or chores to do at home too. Plan to do an activity you enjoy after your homework. It's motivating!
- Find a quiet place to work. Choose a place with no noise or distractions, but don't study on your bed! Sit at a desk or table. That way you can put your computer on it and it is comfortable to work at.
- Do the hardest tasks first. You've got more energy and focus when you start, so use this on the subjects that are most challenging. Later, when you're more tired, you can do easier things.
- Take a break. Most people's attention spans are short. Take a 15-minute break every hour. (But when you're really concentrating, keep going as long as you can!)

40 Look at the tips in the Life strategy. Decide whether each skill is physical, emotional or cognitive.

41 THINKING FURTHER Discuss the questions in pairs.

1 Read the tips again. Which ones do you think are the most useful? Rank them in order from 1–6.
2 Have you got any other useful tips you can add to the list?

42 TASK Use the internet to find information about one of the topics below. Then write three tips for teenagers on how to deal with the situation.

- how to regulate angry feelings
- how to regulate the time you spend online
- how to eat a healthy diet

CITIZENSHIP AND COMPETENCY SKILLS Acting autonomously and responsibly

4 Sport

EXAM STRATEGIES
- PRELIMINARY: Speaking and Listening
- IGCSE: Writing, Speaking and Listening
- IELTS: Academic

SPEAKING SKILLS
- Explaining rules

ACADEMIC SKILLS
- Understanding arguments

LEAD IN

1 PAIRWORK Discuss the questions and then share your ideas with the class.

1. What sports do students do in your school?
2. Are there different sports for boys and girls?
3. Who do you think plays more sport, boys or girls?

This Girl Can!

This Girl Can is a national campaign by Sport England to encourage more women to do exercise in the UK. Its recent TV advert was very original because it was full of ordinary girls and women, big and small, not slim, fit
5 celebrities. The message was simple: you don't have to be an Olympic champion to do sport, everyone can **have a go**! Before the campaign, Sport England looked at research by universities and other sports organisations. They found that a lot more men participate in sport and exercise than women
10 – 2 million more in fact! Why is this? The most common reasons women gave were:

1. I can't do sport because I'm too **unfit**.
2. I can't do sport because I'm too overweight.
3. I can't do sport because I'm not the **sporty** type.

75% of the women in the survey wanted to start doing sport, but were afraid that others would **judge** them. They believed they had to be fit, in perfect shape and really good at the activity, before they even started!
Sport England believes that all women can do exercise, so don't focus on what you 15
think you can't do. Instead ask the question – what can I do? Do you have to have a perfect body to do sport? Of course not. The This Girl Can advert shows that normal girls can do sport – they don't have to look like Olympic champions. You 20
don't have to be the fastest, or the strongest, or the best on the planet, but you have to do physical activity to be healthy – and sport is fun, it's liberating and it's good 25
for you! These girls can – can you?

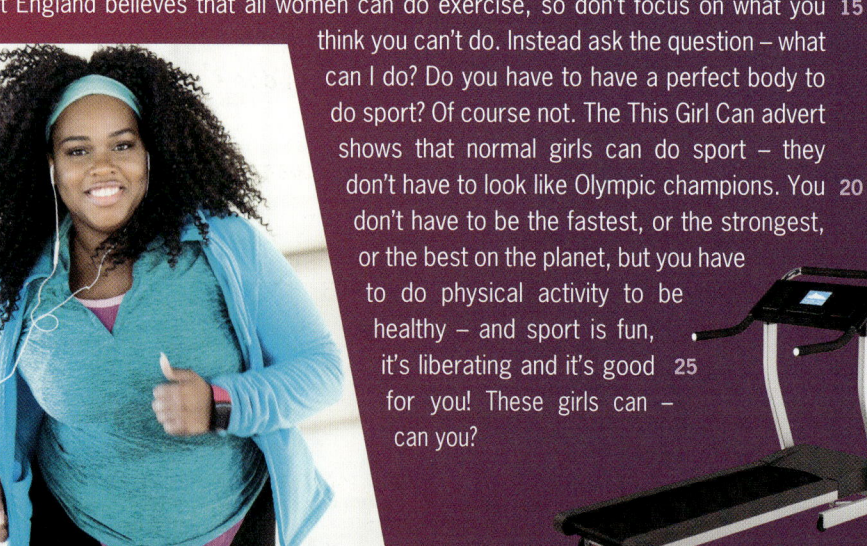

Learning goals

Grammar
- can / can't
- have to / don't have to
- must and have to
- make and let

Vocabulary
- Sports and sports equipment

WB pp. 166–175

Glossary
have a go : fare un tentativo
unfit : fuori forma
sporty : sportiva
judge : giudicare

42   Unit 4

PRACTICE

2 ▶ [1.26] Read, listen and watch. Then choose the correct option.

1 Sport England wants to convince more *men / women* to do exercise.
2 Research shows that in the UK more *men / women* participate in sport.
3 Some women feel other people are *judging / praising* them.
4 The TV advert shows *normal women / women champions* doing sport.

GRAMMAR GUIDE

can / can't for ability, requests, permission and possibility

Affirmative	Negative
She **can** do exercise.	I **can't** do sport.
Questions	**Short answers**
Can you do sport?	Yes, I **can**.
What **can** you do?	No, I **can't**.

➔ GRAMMAR REFERENCE p. 117   WB p. 166

GRAMMAR GUIDE

have to / don't have to

Affirmative	Negative
You **have to do** physical activity.	You **don't have to be** an Olympic champion.
Questions	**Short answers**
Do you **have to have** a perfect body to do sport?	Yes, you **do**.
	No, you **don't**.

Look!: *have to* = obligation; *don't have to* = not necessary

➔ GRAMMAR REFERENCE p. 117   WB pp. 166–167

3 Complete the sentences with *can / can't* or *don't have to*.

0 You *don't have to* be an Olympic champion to do sport.
1 Everyone .... have a go!
2 I .... do sport because I'm too unfit.
3 All women .... do exercise.
4 They .... look like a famous sports champion.
5 You .... be the fastest.

4 What rules are there in your school? Use the prompts and *have to / don't have to* to write sentences that are true for you.

0 We *don't have to* wear special kits for sport.
1 All students .... study two languages in their first year.
2 All students .... do physical education once a week.
3 All students .... do English and maths.
4 We .... meet our form teacher every week.
5 We .... stay indoors during the break.
6 We .... give our phones to the teacher before a test.

5 Complete the text with the correct form of *have to* or *can*.

Exercise keeps you healthy as well as fit. You ⁰ *don't have to* do it every day, but you ¹ .... do it at least three times a week if you ² .... The exercise you do ³ .... be energetic enough to make you out of breath, and you ⁴ .... do it for at least 20 minutes. Exercise makes your heart beat faster and this ⁵ .... lower your cholesterol levels. Exercise ⁶ .... also improve your mood because it releases hormones called *endorphins*, which make you feel positive.
You ⁷ .... buy special equipment to do sport; a good fast walk ⁸ .... also be great exercise.

6 SPEAKING In pairs, find out about the rules in your partner's home. Make questions from these prompts.

- invite your friends / your house / after school
- use the internet / any time you want
- stay out late / at weekends

A Can you invite friends to your house after school?
B Yes, I can. But we have to stay in my room.

Unit 4   43

READING SKILLS

LEAD IN

7 PAIRWORK Discuss the questions and share your ideas with the class.

1. Which video games do you play regularly?
2. Why do you enjoy playing these games in particular?
3. What skills do you need to have in order to play them well?

PRACTICE

8 [1.27] Read and listen to the text on page 45 and answer the questions.

1. What are e-sports?
2. Why are companies like Coca Cola and YouTube now sponsoring gaming teams?
3. Where can you watch e-sports tournaments?
4. Which e-sports event in 2013 attracted more viewers than the baseball World Series?
5. Why are parents worried about teenagers spending a lot of time playing video games?

READING STRATEGY

Transfer information

In this type of exercise, you use information from a written text to complete a chart, table or diagram.
- Look carefully at the chart / table / diagram to understand what type of information to look for.
- Underline the title and headings on the chart / table / diagram and search for related words in the text.
- Don't copy directly from the text. Interpret the information and write it in your own words.

9 Use the headings in the table to help you find the points in favour of e-sports in the text. Then add to the table in your own words.

e-sports: the positives	
sponsors and career possibilities	
community and socialising	
skills and abilities	

GRAMMAR GUIDE

must and *have to*

must	have to
I **must** do more exercise. I feel really unfit.	I **have to** work late on Friday. My boss told me.
I **had to** stay after school to finish my project.	
mustn't	don't / doesn't have to
You **mustn't** use this laptop. It's not yours.	You **don't have to** come. It's not obligatory.

Look!: *must* = personal obligation;
have to = external obligation; *had to* = past obligation;
mustn't = prohibited; *don't have to* = not necessary.

➡ **GRAMMAR REFERENCE** p. 118   **WB** p. 170

10 Complete the competition rules with *have to*, *don't have to* and *mustn't*.

School Athletics Championships

Our school is hosting the School Athletics Championships in June. Students ⁰ *don't have to* participate but we hope to see many of you on the day – athletes and spectators.

Rules
- You ¹............................ be 15 years old or over to participate.
- You ²............................ be in any of the school sports teams or clubs, however you ³............................ be fit and healthy.
- You can participate in up to five events, but you ⁴............................ put your name down for events which are happening at the same time!
- You ⁵............................ buy any equipment. The school can provide everything.
- All participants ⁶............................ complete the form on the school website and send it to Mr Royce. You ⁷............................ print out the form. You can fill it in online and email it if you prefer.
- All forms ⁸............................ be received by May 23rd. Students also ⁹............................ inform their teachers that they'll be absent from lessons on the day of the championships.

11 Critical thinking Discuss the questions in pairs.

1. Do you think e-sports are a good or bad idea?
2. Do you think the writer of the text is for or against e-sports? Which parts of the text helped you decide?

44   Unit 4

E-sports: The end of sport as we know it?

Fifteen years ago video games and professional sport were two very different forms of entertainment. Now, however, they've combined into a new industry: e-sports.

E-sports are competitive tournaments for professional video games players, with big cash prizes. They are now the fastest-growing sports industry in the world, and companies like Microsoft, Coca Cola and YouTube are sponsoring gaming teams for millions of dollars. Talented young gamers around the world can now seriously consider a professional career in e-sports.

Matches take place in big arenas or sports stadiums with up to 50,000 spectators. The teams sit at games consoles on a stage with massive screens behind them. The spectators can watch the state of play on these screens. The atmosphere is electric and fans from the gaming community love meeting up to support their gaming heroes. However, you don't actually have to leave your bedroom to watch your favourite team: you can also watch them live via online streaming and feel like you're really there! In 2013 the world championship of *League of Legends*, a multi-player strategy game, attracted 32 million online viewers, more than double the baseball World Series!

Many parents don't like their teenagers playing video games because they're worried about how much time they spend indoors gaming. They try to persuade them to go out and play traditional sports instead. But is it true that video games **are bad for** you and don't develop any useful skills? We compared professional gamers with top athletes from traditional sports to find out.

Strategy
- Games like *League of Legends* are incredibly complicated and constantly changing. Scientists believe a talent for these types of games can give a better indication of a person's IQ than chess.
- E-sports teams have to spend a huge amount of time and effort working on tactics and strategy. In these games it's the difference between winning and losing.

Fitness
- E-sports players don't have to be as fit as athletes – professional gamers often sit in front of a computer screen for 14 hours a day!
- However, they mustn't turn into **couch potatoes**! A fit body means a fit mind, so top players know they must eat healthily and exercise regularly to improve their reflexes and concentration.

Reflexes
- Professional gamers have **lightning** reflexes and very flexible minds. They have to make more than 300 'actions' per minute during a match and must be 100% focused.
- Research shows that reflexes, hand-to-eye coordination and mental agility are much greater in professional gamers than in the general population.

Glossary
are bad for: fanno male a
couch potatoes: pantofolai
lightning: fulminei, rapidissimi

WRITING SKILLS

LEAD IN

12 Tick (✓) the topics you think are a good choice for a 'for and against' essay.

- ☐ An amazing place I visited
- ☐ My favourite room
- ☐ Is sport educational?
- ☐ Are there boys' and girls' sports?

PRACTICE

13 You can use a simple four-paragraph structure for a 'for and against' essay. Put the paragraphs in the correct order.

a ☐ main body, reasons and examples to support the topic
b ☐ the topic of the essay and a presentation of both sides of the argument
c ☐ conclusion and personal opinion supporting one side of the argument
d ☐ main body, reasons and examples against the topic

14 PAIRWORK Brainstorm a list of topics for 'for and against' essays.

WRITING STRATEGY

Write a 'for and against' essay

This type of essay is normally about a controversial issue. You discuss the reasons for supporting it (for) as well as the opposite point of view (against). This type of essay can be organised into four paragraphs:

- introduction: present the issue objectively
- give reasons in favour and support your ideas with examples
- give reasons against and support your ideas with examples
- conclusion: summarise the issue briefly and give your personal opinion

IGCSE

→ See **WRITING EXPANSION** page 253

Unit 4   45

VOCABULARY

Sports and sports equipment

15 PAIRWORK Discuss these questions.

1 What sports do you like playing?
2 Have you got any special clothes or equipment?

16 [1.28] Which equipment a–l do you need for sports 1–15? Check any words you don't know in a dictionary. Then listen and check.

1 netball
2 hockey
3 basketball
4 football
5 rugby
6 cricket
7 swimming
8 skiing
9 surfing
10 golf
11 cycling
12 badminton
13 tennis
14 boxing
15 baseball

a bat
b stick
c racket
d club
e shuttlecock
f net
g helmet
h ball
i gloves
j wetsuit
k board
l goggles

17 Look at the page from a sports shop's catalogue. Complete the information with the sports equipment from exercise 16.

18 Read the descriptions of three sports from exercise 16. Write the sport. Then check the meanings of the words in bold.

1 .... There are 11 players in each **team**. You play with a ball on a large grass **pitch**. At each end of the pitch there are two nets, the goals. You have to kick the ball into the goal to **score** a point. You can only kick the ball, you mustn't touch it with your hands, but you can use your head.

2 .... This is a sport with seven players in each team. You play on a court with **baskets** at both ends. You have to pass a large ball between team members and then **throw** it into the other team's basket to score points. You can touch the ball with your hands but not your feet. You can run with the ball but you have to **bounce** it while you're running.

3 .... For this sport there can be two players (singles) or four players (doubles). You play it on a **court** with a high net in the middle. You have to use a racket to **hit** a shuttlecock over the net. You score points when your opponent **misses** the shuttlecock and it hits the floor. You can't touch the shuttlecock with your hands.

19 Now write a paragraph for another sport. Use as many words from exercises 16 and 18 as possible. Can the class guess your sport?

SPORT SCENE SUPER SUMMER SALE EVERYTHING MUST GO!

Renton K15 Core
Girls' hockey
1 ....
Colours: 5 available
Sizes: 30/32/34 inch
£18.99   16.99

Dunlok Premier Tour Set Junior
Set of practice golf
2 ....,
in leather golf bag
Colours: black, green, blue
£108   £68

World Cup Z600
Leather rugby
4 ....
Colours: Standard, England, Scotland, Wales, Ireland national team colours
£30   £22

Pitch Perfect III
Easy-to-use baseball
3 ....
Colours: 4 available
£40   £20

46   Unit 4

See **VOCABULARY EXTENSION** page 263

SPEAKING SKILLS

Explaining rules

20 PAIRWORK Do you play board games with your family or friends? When do you usually play? Which board games do you play?

21 [1.29] Listen and watch the video. What is the name of the game the friends are talking about?

key expressions	
asking about rules	explaining rules
☐ What equipment do you need? ☐ How do you do that? ☐ How do you win?	☐ You need a pen and some paper. ☐ You write the name of the famous person on the Post-it™ note. ☐ You have to stick it on another person's forehead. ☐ They mustn't see the name on their Post-it™. ☐ The person has to guess who they are. ☐ The other people can only reply *Yes* or *No*.

22 [1.29] Listen and watch again and tick (✓) the key expressions you hear.

SPEAKING STRATEGY

Self-correct

When you make a mistake while speaking you can use these phrases to show that you are correcting what you have said.

- *Oh no, wait, that's wrong!*
- *No, hang on. That's not right …*
- *Sorry, I've got that wrong.*

PRELIMINARY | IGCSE

23 PAIRWORK Choose a game and explain the rules to your partner. Use the key expressions and the strategy box to correct information if you make a mistake.

This game is called Tiddlywinks. You need a dice and some coloured counters …

SOUNDS ENGLISH

The /r/ sound

24 [1.30] **PAIRWORK** Listen to a British English speaker and a learner of English say these words. Discuss the differences. In which can you hear the sound /r/?

robin   girl

SOUND STRATEGY

In English the sound /r/ is only fully pronounced when it is:
- at the beginning of a word (**r**oad, **wr**ong, **R**ome)
- when it is followed by a vowel (**r**esponsible, i**r**ate)

It is not pronounced when it is:
- after a vowel in the middle of a word (h**ear**t, d**ir**ty, ch**ur**ch)

25 [1.31] Which of these words contain the /r/ sound? Listen and circle them.

1 marked   5 port
2 write   6 around
3 robin   7 rules
4 girl   8 paper

26 [1.32] Listen and repeat the Italian pronunciation of /r/, then the English pronunciation. In which does your tongue move more?

1 Roma   Rome
2 ratto   rat
3 Roberto   Robert
4 regione   region
5 registro   register

27 [1.33] **GAME** Say the tongue-twister. Listen and try and match the speed.

Round and round the ragged rock
The ragged rascal ran.
If you can tell me
How many Rs there are,
I'll call you a clever man.

Unit 4   47

LISTENING SKILLS

LEAD IN

28 Look at the pictures. Which of these sports are *contact sports*? What does the expression mean?

PRACTICE

29 [1.34] Listen to a conversation between a boy and a girl about rugby. Do they both have the same opinion about it?

LISTENING STRATEGY

Identify the main idea

You can often identify the main idea from these features:

- at the beginning of the conversation, speakers often say what they are going to talk about
- word chains: sequences of words which are connected to the same topic and occur throughout the dialogue (rugby match, teammates, players, win)
- at the end of the conversation, speakers often summarise their ideas using phrases such as: *to recap …, to summarise …, so you're saying …*)

PRELIMINARY | IGCSE

30 [1.34] Listen again and write down the following information.

1 a word chain to do with rugby
2 a sentence at the beginning about the girl's point of view
3 a sentence at the end about the boy's point of view

31 Which speaker speaks in favour of banning contact sports in schools and which is against?

32 [1.34] Listen again and say which two points the girl mentions.

1 All rugby matches seem very violent.
2 Head injuries are more frequent than any other injuries in rugby.
3 One player was paralysed after a rugby injury.
4 All other team sports are safer than rugby.

33 [1.34] Now listen again and say which two points the boy mentions.

1 Some of his friends have had injuries from rugby.
2 Being competitive is healthy.
3 His mum doesn't like him playing rugby.
4 Rugby teaches you discipline and strategy.

34 PAIRWORK Are you for or against contact sports in schools? Does your partner agree?

GRAMMAR GUIDE

make and *let*

The school doesn't **make** me play rugby.
She's happy to **let** me play.
Look!: *make* = what someone obliges us to do;
let = what someone gives us permission to do.

→ GRAMMAR REFERENCE p. 118   WB p. 170

35 Complete the sentences with *make* or *let*.

0 Do your parents ……… **let** ……… you stay out after midnight at the weekend?
1 When I was a child my brother ……………… me give him all my sweets.
2 Our parents don't ……………… us watch horror films.
3 Do they ……………… you go to school in jeans on No Uniform Day?
4 The new maths teacher ……………… us do algebra all morning! It was awful.
5 They won't ……………… us in at the cinema if we go too early.
6 Do Ella's parents ……………… her go into the city?

36 Critical thinking Use the information from exercises 32 and 33 to explain what you think about sport in school. Think about:

- health and fitness
- relationships with others
- self-image

ACADEMIC SKILLS

Understanding arguments

The benefits of exercise — why are teenagers not listening?

Teachers and doctors in the USA are worried about the recent rise in cases of obesity and diabetes in American teenagers. They are also alarmed at the drop in the number of teens doing regular exercise. They believe there is a strong link between these two trends.

The US Department of Health and Human Services carried out a national survey into physical activity in American children in 2013. They found that although 77% of primary school children do regular exercise, the figure is only 29% in high school students.

Medical research shows that regular physical activity is good for our bodies and our minds. It helps build healthy bones and muscles in growing teens. It can also reduce the risk of serious illness like diabetes and heart disease in later life. Physical activity also reduces feelings of depression and anxiety and improves concentration. Scientists tell us that students who exercise can concentrate more so they produce better work and are happier. So why are our teenagers not exercising?

Adolescence is a time when our bodies change shape as we become adults. As a result many teenagers feel sensitive about their appearance and abilities. PE classes can be extremely stressful for some teens because they feel uncomfortable about their bodies. Many of them don't enjoy team sports as a result and start avoiding sport and exercise altogether.

But the benefits of physical activity are huge. So why are we making teens participate in team sports they hate? There are so many other enjoyable physical activities they could try! Schools and sports clubs need to start offering non-competitive activities like tai chi or yoga instead, and non-team sports like running or cycling. Most of all we need to convince teenagers that they can all find an activity they enjoy. They can then feel the amazing benefits of exercise. It really doesn't matter what size or shape they are!

LEAD IN

37 Read the title of the text. What do you think it's going to be about?

1. exercise and health
2. exercise and communication
3. e-sports

ACADEMIC STRATEGY

Many academic texts present arguments – the views of the writer or the people he / she is talking about. The writer usually:

- presents and explores points on both sides of the argument
- uses facts like statistics or references to research to support these points
- uses the information to support his / her own ideas about the argument

IELTS

PRACTICE

38 Which three of these points are in the text?

1. Teens who don't exercise all have serious health problems as adults.
2. Schools need to change the types of physical activities they offer teenagers.
3. Regular exercise can improve students' academic performance.
4. Primary school pupils do more exercise than high school pupils in the USA.
5. Many teenagers avoid sports because of bad experiences at school.

39 WRITING Complete the summary with words and expressions from the text. The first letter is given.

Doctors believe there's a [1]l.................. between the [2]r.................. in obesity and diabetes in American teenagers and the [3]d.................. in the number doing regular exercise. Medical research shows that regular [4]p.................. a.................. is good for our bodies and minds and can help improve academic performance, so it's very important that teenagers do more exercise. However, [5]a.................. is a sensitive time for many teenagers and some stop doing exercise because of bad experiences playing [6]t.................. s.................. at school. We need to do more to [7]c.................. teenagers to exercise, for example by offering a wider choice of [8]n..................-c.................. physical activities in schools, not just team sports.

Unit 4

REVISE AND ROUND UP

1 Rewrite the sentences using *used to* or *didn't use to*.

0 I shared a bedroom with my brother.
I used to share a bedroom with my brother.
1 We lived near the sea in Ireland.
2 The students in this school didn't study English.
3 Did you play football in that park when you were a boy?
4 Sam went to the cinema every week.
5 Did people use electricity to cook in the nineteenth century?
6 They drank a lot of tea in Britain in the 1800s.

2 Complete the mini dialogues with *would* or *didn't use to*, or *Did … use to?*

0 A When I was at school we ..**would study**.. (*study*) Latin verbs for hours.
   B That sounds awful! ....**Did**.......... you **use to fall asleep** (*fall asleep*) in Latin?!
1 A Grandma, when you were a girl .... you .... (*have*) a television?
   B No, dear, we didn't. We .... (*listen*) to the radio instead.
2 A I .... (*not / know*) any students in my class but now I've made a few friends.
   B That's great! I .... (*be*) in that class last year and there are some really nice guys in it.
3 A .... (*have*) really long hair when I was young.
   B Me too. I .... (*brush*) 100 times every night before I went to bed.
4 A When a Viking chief died they .... (*burn*) his boat and push it out to sea.
   B Really? .... they .... (*put*) the chief in it too?

3 Complete these sentences with the correct form of the past continuous of the verbs in brackets.

0 We **were having** (*have*) breakfast when we heard the explosion.
1 Fraser .... (*not / work*) in this company last year.
2 Where .... your brother .... (*study*) in Germany?
3 .... you .... (*think*) of me when I texted you?
4 The children .... (*play*) in the garden all day yesterday.
5 .... Picasso .... (*study*) painting when he was in Paris?
6 You .... (*not / go out*) Flora when I met you.
7 Mrs Turner .... (*drive*) down Hope Street when she had the accident.
8 The Romans .... (*fight*) the Visigoths in 416 AD.

4 Find six mistakes in the verb forms in the text.

In the summer of 1816, a young, well-educated woman from England (travelled) with her husband in Switzerland. While they stayed near Geneva the weather turned bad and terrible storms were forcing them to stay inside their villa. A friend of theirs, the poet Lord Byron, was visiting them at the time and he was suggesting that they all write ghost stories to pass the time. While she was planning her story, the young woman was having a dream about a mad scientist who invents an experiment to create a living man. She used her dream as the basis of her story and when they were finishing reading it, her companions agreed that hers was the scariest story, scary enough to become a bestseller! The woman's name was Mary Shelley and the Gothic horror story that she wrote that summer was *Frankenstein*.

5 Complete the school rules with *can, can't, have to* or *don't have to*.

Summer Hill Alternative College
School Rules

▶ Students ⁰ **don't have to** go to all lessons. They ¹........................ choose which ones they want to attend.

▶ Students ²........................ spend 50 % of their week outside. They ³........................ do nature study, or gardening.

▶ Students ⁴........................ do homework at Summer Hill but they ⁵........................ prepare one project every month.

▶ Students ⁶........................ wear their own clothes to school, but they ⁷........................ have obvious tattoos.

▶ Students ⁸........................ use the internet at Summer Hill as we believe wi-fi is bad for their health.

6 Complete the sentences with *must* or *mustn't* or *don't have to*.

0 You ....**must**.... answer all of the questions in the exam paper.
1 Children .... use the lifts unaccompanied.
2 You .... stop drinking so much cola – it's very bad for your teeth!
3 You .... eat the vegetables, if you don't like them.
4 Don't be late. You .... arrive at the station half an hour before we leave.

7 Complete the dialogue with the correct form of *have to* or *must*.

Dad Where have you been, Gemma?
Gemma Sorry, Dad, I ⁰....**had to**.... go out. Hazel wanted to talk to me.
Dad Why didn't you tell us? We ¹................ know where you are when you go out.
Gemma I was in a hurry. I didn't have time.
Mum You ²................ just disappear like that, Gemma. We were worried.
Gemma Mum, it was urgent. I ³................ help my friend.
Dad Why? What happened?
Gemma A girl at school said something unkind about Hazel on Facebook. We ⁴................ find out who it was.
Dad Well, the next time you ⁵................ remember to tell us where you're going.
Mum And text us when you get to Hazel's – it's a long way from here.
Gemma OK, Mum, I will. But you ⁶................ worry about me. I'm 15 now.

8 TRANSLATION Translate the sentences into English.

1 Ero bravo in inglese ma ora lo trovo difficile.
2 Dove andavi a scuola, nonno?
3 Nel diciannovesimo secolo le persone andavano in chiesa più volte a settimana.
4 Dormivo quando è arrivato il tuo messaggio.
5 Mentre parlavamo, un uomo mi ha preso la borsetta dalla sedia.
6 Può dirmi dov'è il laboratorio di scienze?
7 Non dobbiamo (per forza) andare alla partita, possiamo vederla in TV.

TOWARDS PRELIMINARY

Reading

9 Choose the correct option.

A Hi Simona, I haven't seen you for a while. You always ⁰............ coffee here and then we ¹............ have a chat while we ²............ it. Have you found a new café to go to?
B Oh, hi Francine! Actually I ³............ in a clothes shop when I ⁴............ here, but now I've got a job in a restaurant. I only get half an hour for my lunchbreak, so I ⁵............ go somewhere nearer for coffee.
A A new job? That's great. Are you enjoying it?
B Well, yes. There are a lot of rules. For instance, we ⁶............ wear too much make-up and we ⁷............ remember to iron our uniforms. But the money's good, so I want to stay there. I ⁸............ save £500 by September.
A £500! What for?
B I'm going to Morocco with some friends and I ⁹............ pay for the flight ticket. My friend, Hassan, ¹⁰............ there and we're going to stay with his relatives in Fez and Marrakesh.
A Wow! That sounds so cool! Have a great time!

0 A get   B got
   C used to get   D were getting
1 A have   B had   C are   D would
2 A drinking   B were drinking
   C drink   D would
3 A was working   B were working
   C am working   D work
4 A come   B used to come
   C have come   D am coming
5 A can   B have to
   C don't have to D mustn't
6 A mustn't   B don't have to
   C have to   D must
7 A mustn't   B can't   C must   D can
8 A have to   B can
   C had to   D am having to
9 A can   B mustn't
   C don't have to D have to
10 A was living   B would live
   C used to live   D didn't use to live

WB pp. 170–171 Units 3–4   51

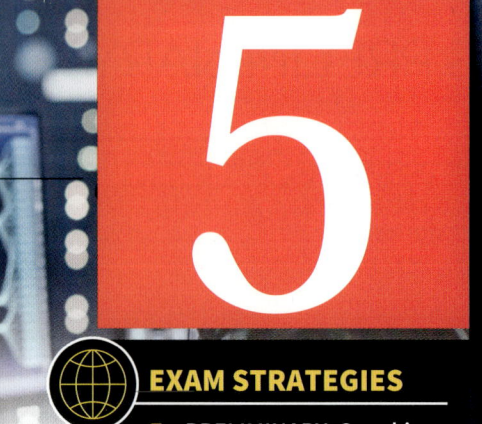

5 Crime

EXAM STRATEGIES
- PRELIMINARY: Speaking
- IGCSE: Reading, Speaking and Listening

SPEAKING SKILLS
- Having a discussion

CHANGING LANGUAGE
- so not …

LIFE SKILLS
- Judging right from wrong

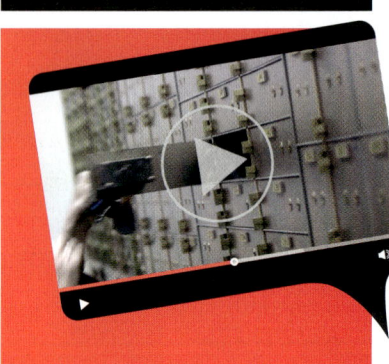

Learning goals
Grammar
- Past perfect
- Indefinite pronouns

Vocabulary
- Crimes and criminals

WB pp. 176–183

LEAD IN

1 PAIRWORK Look at the photos and discuss the questions.

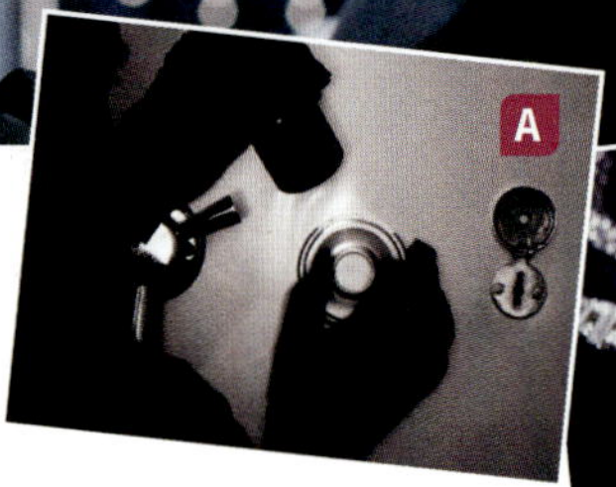

1. What is happening in photo A?
2. What do you think is the value of the jewellery in photo B?
3. Have you heard of any robberies where the thieves stole a lot of jewels or famous paintings?

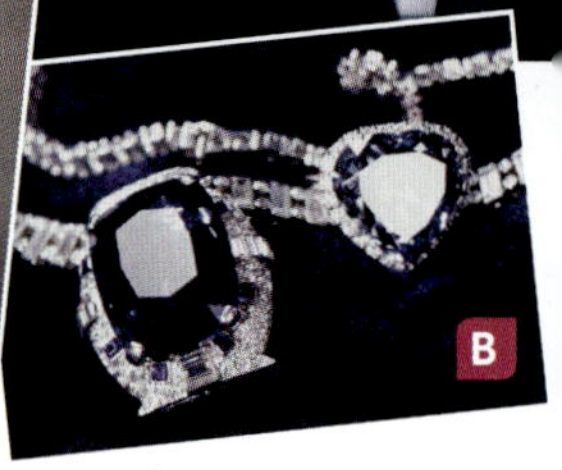

THE HATTON GARDEN HEIST

Hatton Garden is an area of London famous for jewellers and gold specialists. There are also **safety deposit** companies there where people store very expensive items and money. In April 2015 a spectacular news story appeared in the British media. Someone **had broken into** a Hatton Garden Safe Deposit Company during the Easter weekend and stolen everything in the boxes! Security staff hadn't noticed because most of them were on holiday. Amazingly the gang of **thieves** had managed to enter the high-security building by simply **drilling** through a 50-cm-thick wall to get into the **vault**. They had then escaped with around £200 million of diamonds, gold and cash! The newspapers were soon calling it, 'the biggest **heist** in English crime history.'

But then the story became even more bizarre. The police were expecting to find that an international criminal organisation had planned and carried out the **daring** heist. In fact it was a group of **elderly**, local criminals. Two of them were in their seventies and the others were all over 60! They hadn't used sophisticated technology to break into the vault, just an ordinary **electric drill**. One of them had even travelled to the scene of the crime by bus using his pensioner's bus pass and arrived late! The media began to call them 'The Grandads' Gang'!

So why had they decided to carry out this spectacular crime, instead of staying at home and doing crossword puzzles like most grandads? When the police finally arrested them, the gang explained their motives. They had wanted to do something spectacular before they all **retired**, one incredible heist that people would always remember. However, the pensioners didn't know about technology and made a few basic mistakes. For example, they forgot to cancel the search history on their computers! Just before the robbery, they had looked for information online about the best drills to use with concrete, and then they bought a book on Amazon called *Forensics for Dummies*!

Glossary
safety deposit (boxes) : cassette di sicurezza
had broken into : aveva fatto irruzione in
thieves : ladri
drilling : trapanando
vault : caveau
heist : furto di alto livello
daring : audace
elderly : anziani
electric drill : trapano
retired : fossero andati in pensione

PRACTICE

2 ▶ [2.02] **Read, listen and watch. Answer the questions.**

1 What type of crime is the article about?
2 Where did it happen?

3 ▶ [2.02] **Read, listen and watch again. How does the text describe these things?**

1 the building of the Hatton Garden Safe Deposit Company
2 the wall of the vault
3 the people the police thought carried out the heist
4 the people who really carried out the heist
5 the tool the gang used to get into the vault
6 the gang's idea about the crime

GRAMMAR GUIDE

Past perfect and past simple

past perfect	past simple
Staff **hadn't noticed** anything …	because they **were** on holiday.
They **had wanted** to do something spectacular …	before they all **retired**.
They **had looked** for information online …	and then they **bought** a book on Amazon.

We use the past perfect to talk about an event in the past that happened before another event in the past.

➡ **GRAMMAR REFERENCE** p. 118   **WB** pp. 170–171

4 Complete the sentences with the correct past perfect form of the verb in brackets.

0 The thieves ...**had met**... (meet) many times before they robbed the bank.
1 We ……………… (see) the van in the street, before we heard the alarm.
2 The police ……………… (not / arrest) the woman when they first spoke to her.
3 ……………… the thieves ……………… (plan) other attacks before the police arrested them?
4 The people who worked at the bank ……………… (think) it was a safe place before the robbery.
5 My sister ……………… (tell) me all about it before I saw the news report.
6 Why ……………… the thieves ……………… (use) a bus instead of a car?

5 Read the text again and put these events from the story in the correct order.

a ☐ They drilled through the concrete wall of the vault.
b ☐ The police caught the Grandads' Gang.
c ☐ 1 The men looked for information online about the best drill to use with concrete.
d ☐ They bought an ordinary electric drill.
e ☐ One of them travelled to the heist by bus.
f ☐ They escaped with more than £200 million of diamonds, jewellery, gold and cash.
g ☐ The British media reported the story.
h ☐ The police looked at the search history on their computers.

6 Link as many sentences as possible from exercise 5 using *before* or *after* and the past perfect.

The men had looked for information online about the best drill to use before they bought an ordinary drill.

7 Choose the correct option.

Jack Kent ⁰*has spent / was spending / ⒽⒶⒹ ⓈⓅⒺⓃⓉ* all morning at the house. He ¹*took / was taking / had taken* nearly all the contents out, and packed them into his van outside. After that Jack ²*had been / have been / was* so tired, he lay down on the sofa and fell asleep. But Jack ³*didn't live / hasn't lived / hadn't lived* there, and this ⁴*wasn't / hadn't been / haven't been* his house. In fact Jack was a thief! An hour later, the owner of the house ⁵*had arrived / was arriving / arrived*. He saw the van outside his house, found a strange man asleep in his living room and called the police immediately! When the police ⁶*were asking / asked / had asked* Jack why he ⁷*didn't drive / hadn't driven / haven't driven* away, he told them, 'It's hard work stealing the contents of a big house like this. I ⁸*was / have been / had been* exhausted!'

8 SPEAKING What things had you done, or tried, in your life by the time you were: a) six and b) twelve? Think about:

- activities
- school subjects
- friends

Unit 5   53

READING SKILLS

LEAD IN

9 Look at the photos of a Victorian police officer and a modern cyberspecialist and discuss the questions.

1 What types of police are there in your country?
2 What do they do?
3 What are people's attitudes to these different types of police?

PRACTICE

10 [2.03] Read and listen to the text. Match the headings to the paragraphs.

1 ☐ The rise of the detective
2 ☐ The force in our time
3 ☐ The origins of the police force

11 Read the text again and answer the questions.

1 Why did the crime rate go up during the Industrial Revolution?
2 What were two nicknames for the first policemen? Why?
3 What were some of their jobs?
4 When and why did the government establish the CID?
5 How did the public react to the new role of the detective?
6 What are some of the daily jobs for a police officer now?
7 Which two specialist police units does the text mention?
8 What do undercover police officers do in these units?

READING STRATEGY

Take notes

When taking notes, focus on the keywords and concepts.

- Think about what you *need* to know to complete the task, before you start taking notes.
- Identify the relevant information in the text and underline keywords or phrases.
- The keywords and phrases from your notes form the basis of your answer, but use your own words.

IGCSE

12 Underline the key information in each paragraph. Then write notes in your own words.

13 WRITING Write a summary (50 words) about the information in paragraph A of the text. Use your notes from exercise 12.

GRAMMAR GUIDE

Indefinite pronouns

person	thing	place
someone / somebody	something	somewhere
anyone / anybody	anything	anywhere
no one / nobody	nothing	nowhere
everyone / everybody	everything	everywhere

- We use *some* in positive sentences and *any* in negatives and interrogatives.
- We use *every* with all forms.
- We use a singular verb after indefinite pronouns.
- We use a positive verb with *no*.

➡ **GRAMMAR REFERENCE** p. 119 **WB** p. 180

14 Underline all the examples of indefinite pronouns in the text.

15 Complete the sentences with the correct indefinite pronoun.

0 I went to Ellie's house this morning but there was ....*nobody*.... at home.
1 The fridge is empty. We need to buy .... for dinner tonight.
2 I don't want to talk to Adam. I don't have .... to say to him.
3 Miss Houston is a really popular teacher. .... likes and respects her.
4 I can't find my trainers ....
5 Louise is a huge fan of Elvis Presley. She knows .... about him.
6 I've had the flu for the past three weeks. .... is making me better.
7 I think Timbuktu is .... in West Africa.
8 The police searched .... but they didn't find the money.

16 Critical thinking Discuss the questions in pairs.

1 Has the police force in your country changed? How?
2 What kinds of crimes exist today that didn't exist 50 years ago?
3 What qualities do you think good police officers need to have? Why?

MAY THE FORCE BE WITH US ...

A During the Industrial Revolution the population of England's cities increased very rapidly, and consequently the crime rate went up dramatically. In 1829 the Home Secretary, Sir Robert Peel, decided to set up a policing
5 organisation in London. Everybody referred to the first policemen as Peelers, or Bobbies after their founder. It wasn't easy to join the police then, the rules were quite strict. You had to be between 20 and 27 years old. You also had to be at least
10 168 cm tall, physically fit, able to read and write, and of good character. Peelers wore blue coats and top hats. If they heard something suspicious, they used the top hats to stand on, to see over high walls. They also carried a wooden truncheon and a whistle to attract attention. Nobody
15 had guns in those days in the police force. Their main job was to keep order, not to solve crimes, and they were also responsible for lighting streetlamps, calling out the time and checking for house fires.

A typical Peeler

B By the end of the 1800s criminals were committing increasingly complex crimes and so in 1878 the government established the Criminal
20 Investigation Department (CID). The first detectives didn't wear uniforms. They received special training to solve serious crimes such as murder, rape, drug trafficking and fraud. Detective work caught the public's imagination and many of the cases they investigated appeared in the press. The detective became a popular figure in fiction: Conan
25 Doyle created Sherlock Holmes in 1886, and Agatha Christie's Hercule Poirot first appeared in 1920. Even today people find crime fascinating and detective stories are still the most popular TV genre, from *Sherlock* to *NYPD* to *Inspector Montalbano*.

C But the work of fictional detectives is nothing compared to what real
30 police officers have to do today. Detective work today focuses on sophisticated criminal organisations. Cybercrime affects everyone and international terrorist groups don't care about anyone – they strike without warning. The role of today's police officer is to solve crime, catch the perpetrators and prevent future crime. In a typical day a
35 regular police officer responds to emergency calls, helps preserve crime scenes, interviews suspects and witnesses, gathers evidence, prepares reports, and presents evidence in court. Because crime is now so sophisticated, there are many specialist departments within the police force, for example the Anti-terrorist and Cybercrime units. Police
40 officers from specialist units participate in undercover operations in anti-terrorism – this means they join terrorist groups to find out about possible future attacks on our cities and prevent them. These brave officers put their own lives at risk to keep everyone safe.

Glossary
top hats : cilindri, cappelli a cilindro
truncheon : manganello
whistle : fischietto
rape : stupro
suspects : sospettati
witnesses : testimoni
gathers evidence : raccoglie prove
court : tribunale
undercover : sotto copertura

WRITING SKILLS

LEAD IN

17 PAIRWORK Discuss these questions.

1 What crimes have you seen on TV or in films?
2 What happened? Were there any witnesses?
3 What characteristics do you think make a good witness?

PRACTICE

18 Match these common words from police reports to their meanings. Look up any words you don't know in a dictionary.

1 ☐ alibi
2 ☐ suspect
3 ☐ evidence
4 ☐ statement

a the person police think did the crime
b information or objects that give police information about the case
c a formal written account of what happened
d what someone was doing when the crime was committed

WRITING STRATEGY

Write a police report

A police report tells us what a witness saw when a crime happened. It is factual and objective. It records only information about events. It doesn't give subjective descriptions or opinions about them.
A police report contains:
- the date and time of the crime
- information about the suspect
- information about the crime

➡ See **WRITING EXPANSION** page 254

Unit 5 55

VOCABULARY

Crimes and criminals

19 Read the descriptions and match them to the films.

1 ☐ 2 ☐ 3 ☐

a This man is a trickster. He forges cheques and pretends to be other people.
b He steals things from rich people and gives the money to the poor.
c They are a band of pirates. They kidnap the daughter of a famous official and try and steal treasure.

20 Complete the definitions with the words for different types of criminals.

murderer • vandal • terrorist • shoplifter • thief • joyrider • mugger • hacker • kidnapper • burglar • drug dealer • forger • bank robber

1 A ……………… steal cars and drives them dangerously for fun.
2 A ……………… catches a person, hides them and asks for money from the family.
3 A ……………… steals small things from shops.
4 A ……………… buys and sells illegal narcotics like heroin and cocaine.
5 A ……………… attacks people in the street and steals their bags, wallets, etc.
6 A ……………… makes a plan and then kills someone.
7 A ……………… breaks into houses and steals people's possessions and money.
8 A ……………… plants bombs, or takes people hostage, for political reasons.
9 A ……………… deliberately damages private or public property.
10 A ……………… accesses other people's computers and steals information.
11 A ……………… makes copies of documents or artworks, pretends they're real and sells them.
12 A ……………… breaks into banks and steals large amounts of money.
13 A ……………… steals things.

21 Look at these word families about crime. Use a dictionary to help you complete the table.

verb	crime	criminal
burgle	burglary	burglar
kill / murder	killing / murder	1 ………………
rob	2 ………………	3 ………………
mug	mugging	4 ………………
forge	5 ………………	6 ………………
kidnap	7 ………………	8 ………………

22 Complete the sentences with words from the table in exercise 21.

1 Experts have discovered that the famous painting by Raphael is in fact a ……………… .
2 A ……………… has attacked a woman outside Finsbury Park tube station and stolen her bag.
3 The bank ……………… was carried out by a well-organised international gang.
4 The president's son has been ……………… for a ransom of $50 million by a terrorist gang.
5 A 'cat ………………' climbs onto the roofs of houses to break in through the roof.
6 Police say the ……………… is dangerous and might kill again.
7 Detectives believe the butler intended to ……………… his employers of thousands of pounds.

23 SPEAKING Answer the questions in pairs.

1 Put the crimes from the table in exercise 21 in order of seriousness.
2 Which of these punishments do you think is appropriate for each crime? Why?
   - a fine
   - a prison sentence
   - a period of community service
   - other (explain)

See **VOCABULARY EXTENSION** page 264

SPEAKING SKILLS

Having a discussion

24 PAIRWORK Discuss these questions.

1 What do you think the phrase 'Let the punishment fit the crime' means?
2 What is the maximum punishment a criminal can get in your country?
3 What crime is it for?

25 [2.04] Listen and watch the video. Answer the questions.

1 What crime did the man commit?
2 What punishment did he receive?

key expressions	
asking for opinions	asking for clarification
☐ What do you think, (name)?	☐ I'm not sure what you mean.
☐ Have you got a view on this?	☐ What are you trying to say?
☐ What's your take on …?	☐ Sorry? / Pardon?

26 [2.04] Listen and watch again and tick (✓) the key expressions you hear.

SPEAKING STRATEGY

Interrupt politely

When we want to interrupt politely, we can use these expressions.
- Wait a minute. • Sorry, can I stop you there? • Can I stop you for a second?

PRELIMINARY | IGCSE

27 [2.04] Listen and watch again. How many times do you hear the expressions from the strategy box?

28 GROUPWORK Work in groups of three. Choose one of the roles below and use the expressions to discuss the issue.

Student A: You believe prison is the best place for all criminals and it is right that they are punished for their crimes.
Student B: You think prison makes criminals worse. You believe community service and education is the answer.
Student C: You believe some crimes need a prison sentence, but it is important to rehabilitate prisoners afterwards.

CHANGING LANGUAGE

so not …

29 What is Grace referring to when she uses these expressions?

1 so not cool
2 so not vandalism

30 Watch the video and decide if the sentences are true (T) or false (F). Correct the false ones.

1 The construction *so* + adjective is only used by people under 45 years. ☐T ☐F
2 The construction *so* + *not* + adjective / noun was popular in the 1990s. ☐T ☐F
3 The construction *so* + *not* + adjective / noun is more popular now than 30 years ago. ☐T ☐F
4 The construction *so* + *not* + adjective / noun is mainly used by younger people. ☐T ☐F

CORPUS

While intensifiers like:

so, very, really + adjective

are well established in the English language, the construction:

so + *not* + adjective / noun

is relatively new. It is mainly used by young people in informal speech to emphasise the lack of a certain quality:

- *so not hot = very cold*
- *so not good = very bad*

Unit 5   57

LISTENING SKILLS

LEAD IN

31 PAIRWORK Look at the list of different interview situations. Discuss with a partner the type of questions someone would ask you in each case.

1 a job interview with a candidate
2 a first date with a person you really like
3 a police interview with a suspect

PRACTICE

32 [2.05] Listen to four short recordings. Match them to the descriptions.

a ☐ someone reporting a mugging
b ☐ a news bulletin about a robbery
c ☐ a story about a murder
d ☐ a police interview with a suspect

LISTENING STRATEGY

Answer *wh*-questions

When you are asked to answer *wh*-questions in a listening task:
- Read the questions. Circle the question words. What type of information is required?
- Underline the keywords in the questions.
- After the first listening, note down your answers and check they make sense, e.g., *Where = a place*.

IGCSE

33 Match the question words to the types of information they refer to.

1 ☐ where   a   a person
2 ☐ when   b   more than one person, thing
3 ☐ why   or place
4 ☐ how   c   a quantity or measurement
5 ☐ who   or method
6 ☐ what   d   a thing
7 ☐ which   e   a place
                   f   a time
                   g   a reason or cause

34 [2.05] Listen to the four recordings again. Answer the questions. Write no more than three words for each answer.

1 a Where was Mr Atkins last Saturday night?
  b When did he go out?
2 a Who are the police looking for in connection with the robbery in Kensington?
  b What was stolen?
3 a How tall was the mugger?
  b What was he wearing?
4 a Why were the police in the murder case worried?
  b Which of the suspects had an alibi?

35 Write a list of the keywords from the questions in exercise 34 that helped you identify the answers in the recording.

36 [2.05] Listen again. Write down these things.

1 the TV programme the suspect was watching
2 what the woman in the shop robbery looked like
3 the object the mugger was carrying
4 the people who saw Reverend Green in the study

37 Critical thinking Discuss the questions in pairs. Think about how the police interview suspects in films and TV series you've seen.

1 Who is usually present when suspects are interviewed?
2 What is meant by the expression 'nice cop, nasty cop'?
3 How do the police remember what a suspect has told them?

38 PAIRWORK Act out the situation.

There was a burglary last night in Dr Black's house in your town and three valuable paintings were stolen. The police are interviewing a suspect, Dr Black's gardener.

Student A: You are the policeman. Prepare a list of questions to ask the suspect.
Student B: You are the gardener. Prepare an alibi about what you were doing last night.

58   Unit 5

LIFE SKILLS

Judging right from wrong

Right or wrong?

1 You see a classmate stealing DVDs at school. They don't know you're there. What do you do?
- **A** Nothing.
- **B** Tell the thief what you saw and ask them to put the DVDs back.
- **C** Report what you saw to a teacher.
- **D** Write a note and put it in the thief's locker or bag.

2 You see your friend's girlfriend kissing another boy at a party. What do you do?
- **A** Call your friend and tell him.
- **B** Speak to the girl quietly later and ask her why she behaved like that.
- **C** Go over to the girl and say you're going to tell your friend everything.
- **D** Tell everyone at the party what you saw.

3 You find a wallet in the street with £200, an ID card and some bank cards in it. What do you do?
- **A** Keep the money, buy presents for all your friends and throw away the wallet.
- **B** Leave it where it is.
- **C** Take the wallet to the police station.
- **D** Keep the money but take the wallet to the police station.

4 You're having a test at school. A friend has got the answers from a student in another class and tries to pass them to you. What do you do?
- **A** Thank him and copy all the answers he gave you.
- **B** Pretend you can't hear him.
- **C** Say no, it's cheating, and remind him he could get into trouble.
- **D** Tell your teacher.

Glossary
locker : armadietto
cheating : imbrogliare
pretend : fai finta

LEAD IN

39 PAIRWORK Read the situations below. Which ones do you think are the most serious? Discuss and put them in order.
- ☐ stealing someone's mobile phone
- ☐ borrowing your brother / sister's things without asking
- ☐ looking in secret at the messages on someone else's phone
- ☐ cheating in an exam

PRACTICE

40 Read the quiz above and choose the best answers.

41 THINKING FURTHER Read the tips in the Life strategy box and answer the questions.
1. Which of the tips are new for you?
2. Which of them do you already do?
3. Are they all necessary? Which ones are not necessary?
4. Choose a tip for the future and try and follow it.

LIFE STRATEGY

Tips or judging right from wrong

Nobody's perfect, we all make mistakes, but there are different degrees of right and wrong. Here are some tips to help you judge the situation.
- Try and understand people's motives: bad actions are sometimes caused by good intentions.
- Don't judge people until you've heard and considered the whole story.
- Don't just agree with the crowd; crowds can be wrong too.
- Reflect on your own motives before judging someone else's.
- Treat others as you would like them to treat you.

42 TASK Choose one of the situations from the quiz.

Student A: You are the person who did something wrong. Think about your reasons and how you feel now.

Student B: You are the witness to the action. Think about what to say to Student A about his / her actions and how to convince him / her to put it right.

CITIZENSHIP AND COMPETENCY SKILLS Acting autonomously and responsibly ✓

Unit 5   59

6 Freak weather

EXAM STRATEGIES
- PRELIMINARY: Reading, Speaking and Listening
- IGCSE: Reading, Writing and Speaking
- IELTS: Academic

SPEAKING SKILLS
- Making predictions

ACADEMIC SKILLS
- Describing a process

Learning goals
Grammar
- First conditional
- if / when / unless
- Zero conditional
- will / may / might for future possibility

Vocabulary
- The environment

WB pp. 184–193

LEAD IN
1 PAIRWORK Discuss the questions and share your ideas with the class.
1. What is the weather usually like in your area in a) summer and b) winter?
2. Do you know any superstitions or proverbs about the weather?

PRACTICE
2 [2.06] Read, listen and watch. Match the photos to the proverbs and superstitions.
1. ☐ red sky
2. ☐ clear moon
3. ☐ mackerel sky
4. ☐ pine cones

OLD WIVES' TALES

The weather produces many strange phenomena and over the years hundreds of superstitions and proverbs have developed about them. But are any of them true?

'Red sky at night, shepherd's delight. Red sky in the morning, shepherd's warning.'
This superstition is meant to predict the weather for shepherds and their sheep. It does have some basis in fact. If the sky is red, this means there is dust and humidity in the air. If this happens in the evening, calm, dry weather will usually follow. This means shepherds can leave their sheep in the fields. If this doesn't happen in the evening but in the morning, bad weather and rain will arrive soon. Then it's better to move the sheep inside.

'Clear moon, frost soon.'
Will there be frost the next morning if you see a bright moon in a clear winter sky? The proverb says there will be, but is there any scientific evidence for this? Well, scientists say that when the winter moon looks bright and clear, this is because there are no clouds. If there aren't any clouds, the Earth loses heat. The ground cools very quickly, so ice and frost are much more likely.

'Mackerel sky and mares' tails, tall ships lower their sails.'
This superstition refers to the shape of clouds in the sky. A mackerel sky consists of clouds called altocumulus. These give the sky a striped appearance, like the skin of a mackerel. They usually form before heavy rain and storms. Mares' tails are high, thin clouds. They often indicate that strong winds and hurricanes are coming. A tall ship will have to lower its sails if it goes sailing in these dangerous conditions.

'Pine cones predict the weather.'
This one is based on scientific fact. If you look at pine cones during dry weather and then rainy weather, you'll notice a difference. Pine cones contain seeds and the best conditions for a pine tree to disperse its seeds is in clear, dry weather. So if it's warm and dry, pine cones open up, but if it's rainy or very humid, they close.

Glossary
old wives' tales : superstizioni
shepherds : pastori
frost : brina
mackerel sky : cielo a pecorelle
mares' tails : cirri a uncino (lett. code di cavallo)
lower : abbassare
sails : vele
mackerel : sgombro
pine cones : pigne
seeds : semi

60 Unit 6

6

3 ▶ [2.06] Read, listen and watch the video again. Answer the questions.

1. Who benefits when there is red sky?
2. Why does the sky turn red?
3. Which season does the 'clear moon' superstition refer to?
4. What type of animal is a mackerel?
5. What type of weather usually follows a mackerel sky?
6. What type of conditions do pine trees need to disperse their seeds?

GRAMMAR GUIDE

First conditional

condition (*if* + a present tense)	result (*will* + infinitive without *to*)
If this **happens** in the evening,	dry weather **will** usually **follow**.
If this **doesn't happen** in the evening but in the morning,	bad weather and rain **will arrive** soon.
result (*will* + infinitive without *to*)	**condition (*if* + a present tense)**
Will there really **be** frost the next morning,	if you **see** a bright moon in a clear winter sky?

➡ GRAMMAR REFERENCE p. 119 WB p. 184

4 Look at the Grammar guide. Choose the correct option.

1. We use the first conditional to talk about cause and effect in the *future* / *past*.
2. *If* is always followed by a *present* / *future* tense.
3. We use a *future* / *present* tense in the other clause.
4. We *can* / *can't* invert the order of the two clauses in a conditional sentence.

5 Match the clauses to form complete sentences.

0. [e] If you buy Dad's present,
1. [ ] If it snows at the weekend,
2. [ ] Will we have dinner
3. [ ] Climate change will get worse
4. [ ] Will you come and pick me up

a. we'll go skiing.
b. when they arrive?
c. if politicians don't do something soon.
d. if I text you from the station?
e. I'll give you half of the money.

GRAMMAR GUIDE

if / when / unless

condition	result
If this **happens**,	dry weather **will follow**.
When this **happens**,	dry weather **will follow**.
Unless this **happens**,	dry weather **won't follow**.

Look!: *unless* = *if … not*.

➡ GRAMMAR REFERENCE p. 119 WB p. 184–185

6 Complete the sentences with the correct form of the verbs in brackets.

0. If the temperature ....*increases*.... (*increase*), some animals ....*will move*.... (*move*) further north.
1. Unless the students .... (*listen*) to me, they .... (*understand*) what to do.
2. If you .... (*like*) chocolate, you .... (*love*) this dessert.
3. When the weather .... (*get*) warmer, we .... (*go*) to the beach.
4. When I .... (*see*) Gianni, I .... (*explain*) the situation.

GRAMMAR GUIDE

Zero conditional

condition (*if* + a present tense)	result (present simple / imperative)
If it**'s** warm and dry,	pine cones **open up**.
When you **arrive**,	please **send** me a text.

We use the zero conditional to talk about things that are always true.

➡ GRAMMAR REFERENCE p. 120 WB p. 185

7 Choose the correct option.

0. If you visit London, *you go* / (*go*) on the London Eye.
1. When unemployment is rising, people usually *stay* / *are staying* in their present jobs.
2. If you heat water to 100 °C, it *boils* / *might boil*.
3. When I'm concentrating, please *don't talk* / *won't talk* to me.
4. When you *put* / *will put* the money in here, the snacks come out there.

Unit 6 61

READING SKILLS

LEAD IN

8 PAIRWORK Look at the photos of the animals. Discuss these questions.

1 What animal group does each animal belong to: mammal, reptile, amphibian, bird, insect?
2 Where do these animals usually live?
3 What do you know about them?

PRACTICE

9 [2.07] Read and listen to the text. Write down the country and animal each paragraph refers to.

10 Read about the animals and decide if the sentences are true (T) or false (F). Correct the false ones.

1 Leopards usually live in groups. T F
2 They rarely attack humans. T F
3 The bowerbird's natural habitat is in the trees. T F
4 They use colourful objects to scare predators. T F
5 Many British newts now live in ponds in people's gardens. T F
6 Newts are adapting well to polluted urban environments. T F

READING STRATEGY

Cause and effect

We use certain linkers to join two phrases and show the cause-and-effect relationship between events. We put the linker at the start of the phrase it refers to and separate the two phrases by a comma.

- *because* (*of*) and *since* show the cause. This clause can come first or second.
- *so* shows the effect. This clause can only come second.

PRELIMINARY | IGCSE

11 Underline four examples of cause-and-effect linkers in the text. Then explain them.

Linker: *because of*
Cause: *cities are growing very fast and destroying the natural habitats of wild animals*
Effect: *animals are moving into urban environments*

NEW CITY DWELLERS

Cities everywhere are growing fast and in the process they're destroying the natural habitats of many wild animals. Because of this, some animals are moving into urban environments and are
5 managing to adapt successfully to city life.

1 Big cats in Mumbai

Leopards are solitary animals and rarely come into contact with humans. However, reports from Mumbai in India show that the leopard's behaviour
10 may be changing. Recently a film crew filmed leopards as they came into the city at night to hunt. A leopard might attack a man if it's afraid, but humans are not its usual prey, so are these beautiful felines a danger to people in cities? The film shows
15 that in fact these leopards are looking for a different dinner – domestic pigs. Many inhabitants keep pigs in their gardens in Mumbai, and this attracts leopards. It also seems that conditions in the urban environment may give the leopards an
20 advantage as predators. When the leopards approach, the pigs don't hear them because of the constant traffic noise. The leopards will
25 then attack quickly before the pigs even notice they are near.

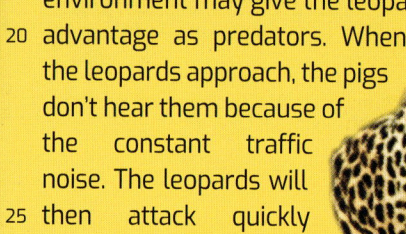

GRAMMAR GUIDE

will / may / might for future possibility

will	may / might
The leopards **will** then **attack** quickly.	Their behaviour **may be** changing.
The eggs **will stick** to the smooth surface.	A leopard **might attack** a man, if it's afraid.

➡ GRAMMAR REFERENCE p. 120   WB p. 188

12 Look at the Grammar guide. Choose the correct option.

1 We use *will* when we feel *certain / uncertain* about something in the future.
2 We use *may* or *might* when we feel *certain / uncertain* about something in the future.

62   Unit 6

2 Nature's interior designers

In its natural forest habitat the Australian bowerbird
builds a nest and decorates it with brightly-coloured
flowers and fruit to attract a mate. However, as
cities expand, these birds are starting to live in urban
environments too, where they're developing a reputation as thieves!
Bowerbirds love colourful objects, which may be the reason that
they steal toys, glass and jewellery. Since there aren't many
flowers, the birds are now using man-made objects for home
decoration, often with bizarre results!

3 Quick-thinking newts

Newts spend most of their lives in **ponds** and rivers. In spring the
female looks for a particular type of aquatic plant to **lay her eggs** on,
since the eggs will stick to the smooth surface of the plant's leaves.
However, in ponds in city gardens where many British newts now
live, these plants are scarce because of water pollution. Recent
research shows that modern female newts might not be as **fussy** as
they used to be, and are adapting quickly to changes in the urban
environment. In polluted water they now look for pieces of plastic
bag, whose smooth surface is an ideal
substitute for the missing leaves. If she
finds one, the female will lay her eggs
on it, then pull more plastic around
them to protect them until they **hatch**
– a truly remarkable adaptation in the
newt's **breeding habits**!

Glossary
newts : tritoni
ponds : stagni
lay her eggs : deporre le uova
fussy : pignole
hatch : si schiudono
breeding habits : abitudini riproduttive

13 Choose the correct option.

0   I'm convinced there (will) / might be more weird weather because of climate change.
1   Etna is still active, so there *may / will* be another eruption soon.
2   I *will / might* call you later if I've got time.
3   When the mixture is ready it *will / might* be yellow and creamy.
4   The situation *will / may* change if enough people protest.
5   I know you *will / may* like Emma when you meet her.
6   My computer isn't working. It *will / might* be a problem with the hard drive, I'm not sure.

14 Critical thinking Look at the pictures of these animals in Italian cities. In pairs, discuss the questions.

1   Have you seen any of these wild animals in towns or cities in your country?
2   What problems might they cause in cities?

Starlings

A peregrine falcon

WRITING SKILLS

LEAD IN

15 PAIRWORK Answer the question.

When do you think a summary is useful?
1   revising for an exam
2   writing a review of a book or a film
3   writing a police report
4   describing a holiday you had
5   describing a friend you know well

PRACTICE

16 Which is the best summary for the first paragraph in the text on pages 62–63?

1   A film crew filmed leopards at night in Mumbai.
2   The behaviour of leopards in India may be changing because they're coming into cities to hunt.
3   Inhabitants of some Indian cities keep domestic animals in their gardens, which attract leopards.

WRITING STRATEGY

Write a summary

Summarising is an important writing skill. A summary is essentially a shortened version of a text, in your own words. It sums up the points in an argument, or presents a large amount of information more concisely. A summary:
- covers the essential points of the original text
- presents the information in short, cohesive sentences
- doesn't contain examples, quotations or any personal opinions

IGCSE

➡ See **WRITING EXPANSION** page 255

Unit 6   63

VOCABULARY

The environment

Want to help the environment? Add your voice to OURS!

We are a group of teenagers from Bristol who are seriously concerned about [1] **climate change** and its effects. We want to make people more aware of just how serious [2] **global warming** is. We want everyone to help us reduce [3] **carbon emissions** from cars by choosing to buy electric and hybrid cars.

The [4] **fossil fuels** we've been using for hundreds of years are now killing our planet. If we don't stop producing vast quantities of carbon dioxide, the Earth will continue to suffer.

The problem is having a huge impact on [5] **weather patterns** around the world.

[6] **Natural disasters** are becoming normal. Terrible [7] **droughts** mean that in some parts of the world vast areas are becoming deserts. In others [8] **floods** and [9] **hurricanes** mean freak winds and water are destroying people's lives. But we can change things. In the 1970s when scientists shocked the world with news of the massive hole in the [10] **ozone layer** over Antarctica, governments from many countries agreed to take action. The result is that now the hole in the ozone layer has stopped growing and is in fact smaller! We can do the same about carbon emissions. Simple changes like more electric cars will help solve the carbon problem. If you care about our planet, subscribe to our newsletter online and add your voice to ours.

www.kidsforclimate.org

17 Look at the text. What type of text do you think it is? Why?

1 an advertisement
2 a blog
3 a twitter feed

18 Match the photos of extreme weather to the words in red in the text.

1 .... 2 .... 3 ....

19 Read the text again and answer the questions.

1 What is the group concerned about?
2 What do they want to do?
3 How do they think we can reduce carbon emissions?
4 What is having an impact on the Earth's weather?
5 What did scientists discover in the 1970s?
6 How did they resolve the problem?

20 Look at the numbered words and expressions in the text. Match them to their definitions.

a ☐ accidents associated with nature that can kill people
b ☐ when it doesn't rain for a long time
c ☐ increasing temperature of our planet
d ☐ when it rains too much for a long time
e ☐ climatic conditions that keep repeating over time
f ☐ severe, destructive winds
g ☐ pollution from petrol, diesel and coal
h ☐ substances we use for power like coal, gas and oil
i ☐ atmospheric gas which protects the Earth from the Sun
j ☐ differences in the weather and temperature of the Earth

21 Now use words from the text to complete these sentences.

1 Earthquakes are a type of .... which often affect Japan.
2 Petrol vehicles are a major cause of .... today.
3 Today it's been sunny and warm, but after tomorrow the .... will change.
4 The tax my dad pays for his car is low, because it's got zero ....
5 Is gas also a type of ...., or is it just coal and oil?
6 The hole in the .... appeared over Antarctica.

22 **Critical thinking** Answer the questions in pairs.

1 Has the weather in your country changed in the last 50 years? How?
2 Are people noticing any other effects of climate change? What?
3 What do you think people can do to help slow climate change? Why?

See **VOCABULARY EXTENSION** page 265

SPEAKING SKILLS

Making predictions

23 PAIRWORK Discuss these questions.

1 Have you ever gone on a school trip? Where?
2 What was the weather like?
3 What clothes and / or equipment did you need?

24 [2.08] Listen and watch the video. What kind of weather was Grace preparing for?

key expressions	
questions	answers
☐ So what do you think the weather will be like?	☐ It might not be sunny.
☐ Will I need to take a coat then?	☐ Yes, you will. A big coat.
☐ Do you think it might snow?	☐ Yes, it might. […] You may get very wet feet.

25 [2.08] Listen and watch again and tick (✓) the key expressions you hear.

SPEAKING STRATEGY

Support / Justify an argument

When we express an opinion, or make a suggestion, we often justify it with reasons. Use these expressions.

☐ What I'm saying is …   ☐ If you think about it, …   ☐ After all …
☐ Actually, …   ☐ In fact …

PRELIMINARY   IGCSE

26 [2.08] Listen and watch again. Tick (✓) the expressions you hear and then write the rest of the sentences.

27 PAIRWORK Choose one of the situations below. Ask your partner about his / her predictions for this event. Ask about:

- weather
- clothes
- equipment
- food

1 Your partner is going to the beach for a picnic with a group of friends on Sunday.
2 Your partner is going to an outdoor music festival in the countryside on Saturday.

SOUNDS ENGLISH

The sound /θ/

28 [2.09] Listen to three speakers saying this sentence. One is a British English speaker. Which one: 1, 2 or 3?

These three things are free.

29 [2.10] Now listen and circle the phrase you hear in each pair.

1 thirsty   first T
2 tree things   three things
3 he's Finnish   he's thin-ish
4 Diesel 2   these'll do
5 that's a lot   VAT's a lot

30 [2.11] **PAIRWORK** Listen and repeat the phrases in exercise 29. Which sounds are difficult to imitate?

SOUND STRATEGY

In English there are two different pronunciations for *th*, the soft sound /θ/ as in *thanks*, and the hard sound /ð/ as in *that*. These sounds are difficult for Italian speakers, as they don't exist in Italian. A common mistake is to say /f/ or /t/ for the soft sound, or /v/ or /d/ for the hard sound.

31 [2.12] Listen and repeat the words.

	/θ/	/f/	/t/
1	thought	fought	taught
2	thin	fin	tin
	/ð/	/v/	/d/
3	weather	ever	wed her
4	there	veer	dare

32 GAME In pairs, say these tongue-twisters as fast as you can.

- He threw three free throws.
- I was thinking of thanking you for the thought.
- Thirty-three thousand people think that this Thursday is their thirtieth birthday.

Unit 6   65

LISTENING SKILLS

LEAD IN

33 PAIRWORK Discuss these questions.

1 How can the weather affect people's mood or well-being?
2 Look at these feelings. What kind of weather do you think they are associated with?
- depression
- happiness
- apathy
- nausea
- headache
- energy levels

PRACTICE

34 [2.13] Listen to four short recordings. Match them to the descriptions.

a ☐ a news programme
b ☐ a radio interview
c ☐ a conversation between a doctor and a patient
d ☐ a conversation between teenage friends

LISTENING STRATEGY

Match pictures to audio information

This sort of task asks you to choose from three possible images where only one accurately represents the information you hear in the recording.
- Read the question and underline the keywords.
- Look at the pictures to understand what type of information to listen for overall.
- Look carefully at the differences between the three pictures to understand the type of detail to listen for.
- Listen carefully and choose the correct picture.

PRELIMINARY

35 [2.13] Listen to the recordings again. For each question choose the correct picture.

1 What type of weather is causing problems in British schools at the moment?

2 Which graph shows the summer weather pattern over the last five years?

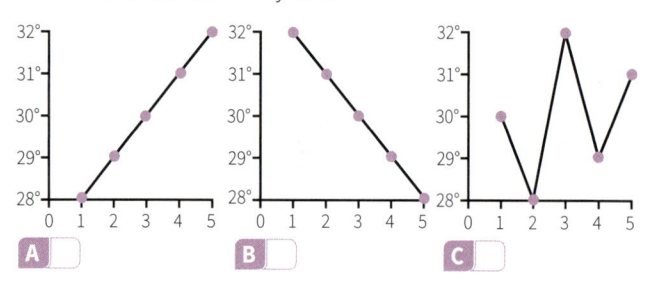

3 What health problems did the heat cause for students?

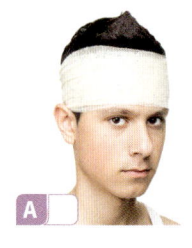

4 What have some schools been giving students to try and keep them cool?

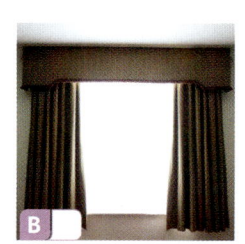

5 What causes Martin's condition, SAD (Seasonal Affective Disorder)?

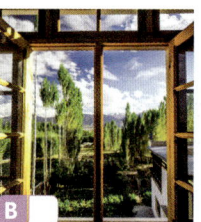

6 What does the doctor recommend for Martin's problem?

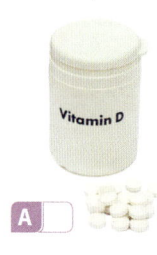

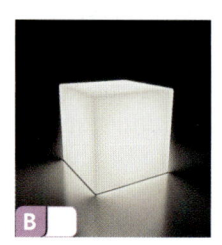

36 Look back at exercise 35 and answer these questions.

1 Which details in the pictures helped you to choose the answer in each question?
2 Explain why the other choices were not correct.

66   Unit 6

ACADEMIC SKILLS

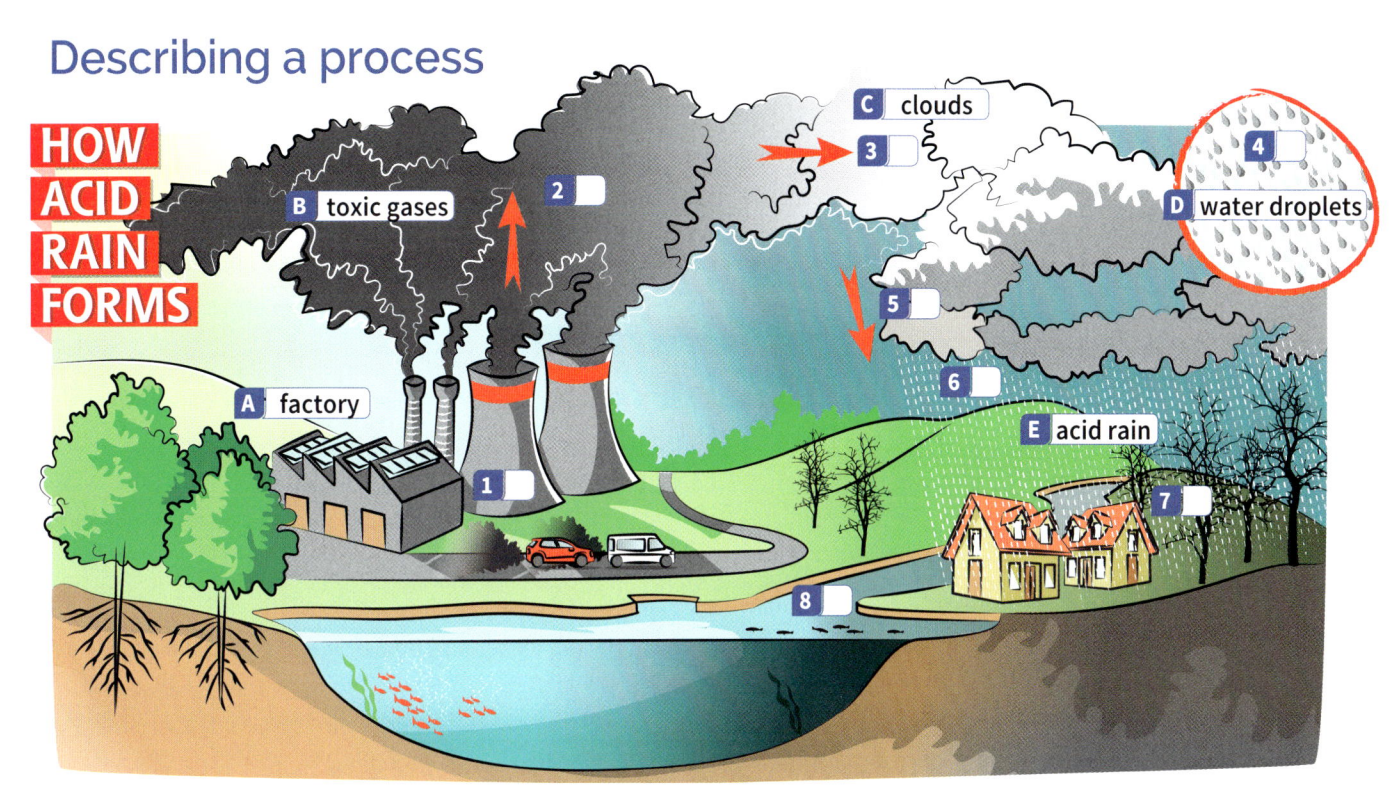

Describing a process

HOW ACID RAIN FORMS

- A factory
- B toxic gases
- C clouds
- D water droplets
- E acid rain

LEAD IN

37 Look at the flow diagram. What sort of process does it show?

1 a natural process 2 a man-made process

PRACTICE

38 Look carefully at the pictures in the diagram. Match the numbers 1–8 to the parts of the process a–h.

- a ☐ water droplets fall as acid rain
- b ☐ gases rise and meet clouds in cooler air
- c ☑ 1 factories, power stations and cars produce toxic gases
- d ☐ clouds fall as temperature rises
- e ☐ plants and animals die
- f ☐ wind carries gases up into atmosphere
- g ☐ acid rain damages plants and pollutes the water supply
- h ☐ gases combine with water droplets in clouds and form acids

ACADEMIC STRATEGY

Before you write the names of the parts of a diagram:
- study the diagram carefully
- look at the position of the parts to label in relation to the rest of the diagram
- predict the words to describe the position of each part

IELTS

39 Look at the pictures and read the summary of a simple process below. Underline the sequencers.

- A kettle
- B teabag
- C cup
- D teapot

How to make a cup of tea

First fill the kettle with water. Next boil the water in the kettle. Then put the teabags in the teapot. After that pour boiling water into the teapot and leave the tea for two minutes. Finally pour some milk into the cup then pour in the tea.

40 WRITING Look at the diagram again and summarise the process of acid rain formation. Use the sentences from exercise 38 and sequencers in your answer.

The illustrations show how acid rain forms. First factories, power stations and cars release toxic gases into the air. Then ...

Unit 6   67

REVISE AND ROUND UP

1 Complete the sentences with the past perfect form of the verbs in brackets.

0   It **had rained** (rain) that morning and it was still cloudy when we left the house.
1   We .... (know) Sally since we were all at primary school together.
2   My friend .... (tell) me all about Barry before I met him.
3   The girls .... (not / understand) the instructions and had failed the test.
4   The king .... (build) a fine castle there, but his enemies destroyed it six years later.
5   There .... (not / be) a prime minister under the age of 40 for over 150 years.
6   Why .... the police .... (discovered) the body before the murder weapon?
7   I .... (not / visit) Paris for 30 years but it was still as beautiful.
8   We all wondered what .... (happen) to the missing student.

2 Complete the dialogue with the past simple or past perfect form of the verbs in brackets, or with short answers.

Policeman Tell me Mr Wilson, ⁰ **had** you ever **met** (meet) this man before last Friday?
Man Yes, I ¹.................. . He ².................. (come) into Bell's Café a few times – that's where I work.
Policeman And ³.................. he .... (speak) to you about any illegal activities when he was there?
Man No, he ⁴.................. . But I ⁵.................. (not / know) him well.
Policeman Before the robbery ⁶.................. you ever .... (have) any suspicions about him?
Man No, I ⁷.................. . I ⁸.................. (think) he just seemed like an ordinary man.
Policeman But ⁹.................. you .... (not / wonder) where he got all his money from?
Man Well, yes, I ¹⁰.................. . But I ¹¹.................. (not / ask) him because my boss ¹².................. (tell) me to be nice to him.

3 Read the paragraph. Choose the correct option.

In December 2010 a woman ⁰ (*walked*) / *was walking* into a police station in Ireland, she ¹ *had* / *had had* no ID, and she couldn't remember her name. Half an hour before that she ² *had woken up* / *woke up* on a beach near Galway. She couldn't remember how she ³ *had got* / *was getting* there. She ⁴ *was* / *had been* wet and cold and she had completely lost her memory. Who was the woman? What ⁵ *had happened* / *happened* to her? Why was she in the water? ⁶ *Had someone attacked* / *Did someone attack* her and stolen her ID and wallet? ⁷ *Had she fallen* / *Did she fall* into the water while she ⁸ *walked* / *was walking* near the sea? Nobody knew. In her bag the police ⁹ *have found* / *found* only a photograph of a child and a phone number. They called the number but no one ¹⁰ *answered* / *was answering*. Who was this mystery woman?

4 Complete the sentences with the correct indefinite pronoun.

0   The detectives searched **everywhere** in the house but they didn't find the gun.
1   Tim can't find his keys .... Have you seen them, Mum?
2   I'm really hungry but there's .... to eat in the fridge.
3   The doorbell rang but when I went to answer it there was .... there.
4   Are you thirsty? Would you like .... to drink?
5   I think I know .... in your French class.
6   Don't worry. I'm sure .... is going to be all right.

5 Write a first conditional sentence for each situation.

0   Phone me tonight. I'll give you my answer.
    If you phone me tonight, I'll give you my answer.
1   Tell Karen the truth. She'll understand.
2   Go to England for the summer. You'll learn to speak English better.
3   Visit your grandma this weekend. She'll be happy.
4   Start going to the gym. You'll soon get fit.
5   Close the window. You won't get cold.
6   Go by bus. The trip won't be expensive.

6 Match the beginnings and ends of the sentences and complete them with the correct forms of the verbs in brackets to form zero conditional sentences.

0. [d] If my sister (*have*) a date with a boy,
1. [ ] If my dad (*be*) late for work,
2. [ ] If you (*heat*) water to 100 degrees,
3. [ ] If I (*listen*) to music,
4. [ ] If our dog (*see*) a cat,
5. [ ] If you (*drink*) a lot of cola,
6. [ ] If you (*mix*) blue and yellow,
7. [ ] If Jon (*not / practise*) the guitar every day,
8. [ ] If students (*not / revise*),

a I (*feel*) calm.
b it (*damage*) your teeth.
c they (*not / pass*) their exams.
d she (*spend*) hours in the bathroom.
e you (*get*) green.
f he (*not / have*) any breakfast.
g he (*not / remember*) the songs.
h it (*boil*).
i he (*start*) barking immediately.

If my sister has a date with a boy, she spends hours in the bathroom.

7 Choose the correct option.

0. When it's brown on the top, the cake (will) / might be ready.
1. We 'll / might pick you up later, around 6 o'clock.
2. This coffee is horrible! It will / might be the milk.
3. If you give me your email address, I'll / may send you the link.
4. Someone's at the door – it might / will be Cal.
5. We need to hurry. It may / will already be too late.

8 TRANSLATION Translate the sentences into English.

1. Sean non vedeva i suoi amici dalle vacanze estive.
2. Da quanto tempo Louise sapeva la verità?
3. Non ci pensavo da molto tempo, ma ora ero preoccupato.
4. Non c'è nulla che qualcuno possa fare.
5. Se il professore di matematica è malato, non ci sarà il compito in classe questo pomeriggio.
6. Se tocchi quest'icona, comincia il gioco.
7. Mi sento molto stanco. Forse sono malato, credo.
8. Ci saranno altre elezioni il 15 gennaio.

TOWARDS PRELIMINARY

Reading

9 Complete the gaps in the text with one word.

ARE YOU SUPERSTITIOUS?

Are you the sort of person ⁰ ...who... believes superstitions are absurd and have ¹ .... to do with modern life? Or are you ² .... believes black cats are lucky and spilling salt is unlucky? If so, you ³ .... not alone: 5.8 million people in the UK admit that they are superstitious.
A new survey shows that over ten million people ⁴ .... not walk under a ladder because they think it will bring them bad luck. A further nine million people believe that ⁵ .... you break a mirror, you will ⁶ .... seven years of bad luck. Almost 1 million people confessed that ⁷ .... have worn "lucky" underwear on special occasions to help their fortunes, while 2.7 million people admitted they believed ⁸ .... the "birthday wish": if you blow out all the candles on your birthday cake in one go, your wish will come true! Many people also thought that having a lucky number ⁹ .... possibly bring them good fortune. And ¹⁰ .... the popular notion that 13 is an unlucky number, it ¹¹ .... actually the second most popular number that most people in the survey ¹² .... chosen.

Writing

10 Write a story in about 100 words.

Your English teacher has asked you to write a story. Your story must begin with this sentence:

Someone had already opened the door.

7 Health of a nation

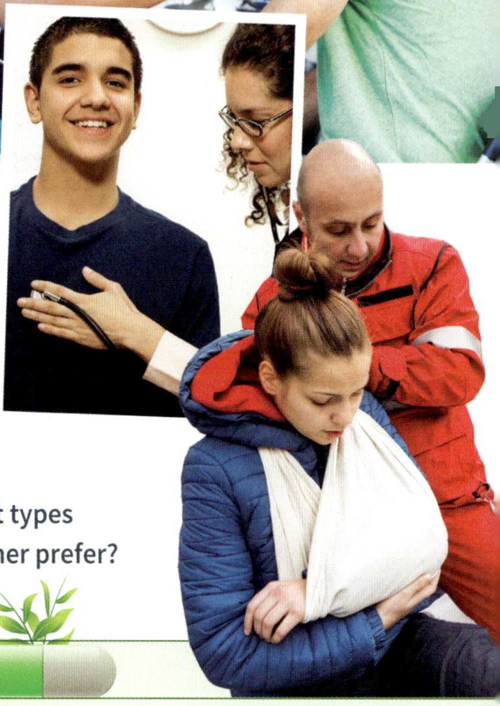

EXAM STRATEGIES
- PRELIMINARY: Reading and Listening
- IGCSE: Listening

SPEAKING SKILLS
- Asking for and giving advice

CHANGING LANGUAGE
- Modal verbs

LIFE SKILLS
- Building self-esteem

Learning goals

Grammar
- Second conditional and *If I were you*
- Second conditional v first conditional
- *should / had better / ought to* for advice

Vocabulary
- Illnesses, injuries and remedies

WB pp. 194–201

LEAD IN

1 **PAIRWORK** Look at the photos. Discuss the questions.
  1 When was the last time you were ill?
  2 What was wrong with you?
  3 What did you do to get better?

2 [2.14] Read, listen and watch. What types of remedies does the writer's grandmother prefer?

PLANT POWER!

Everyone suffers occasionally from a headache, a bad cold or a **skin rash**. Most of us go to the chemist's to buy the usual medicines for these conditions, but some people believe these medicines are a waste of time and that natural remedies are more effective.

Personally, if I had a cold, I'd take a couple of paracetamol. Or, if I my head hurt, I'd take an aspirin. However, my grandmother has other ideas. She has always used natural remedies, common plants from her garden and food from her kitchen, to cure every day illnesses. She believes that if people used natural remedies instead of medicines, they wouldn't suffer from unpleasant **side effects**. And, she says, they would get better just as quickly.

So if you tell my grandmother you're feeling nauseous, she'll make you some ginger and lemon tea. For a sore throat she'll recommend **sucking** a piece of garlic. If you have a rash, she'll make a paste from cold porridge to put on your skin. If you suffer from insomnia, she'll make you a glass of cherry juice to drink at bedtime.

Natural remedies like these are intriguing, but do they really work? If you had a sore throat, would garlic actually help at all? Surprisingly, scientists say that most of these traditional cures have a basis in fact. Garlic contains allicin, a substance that can kill the bacteria that cause throat infections, so it really would help, if you took it for a sore throat. Porridge is made from **oatmeal**, which has anti-inflammatory properties. It's perfect for calming skin irritations like acne or eczema. Cherries are full of melatonin, the same hormone your body produces to regulate sleep. It seems like my grandma knows what she's talking about after all!

Glossary
skin rash : eruzione cutanea
side effects : effetti collaterali
sucking : succhiare
oatmeal : fiocchi d'avena

70 Unit 7

Healthcare

PRACTICE

3 [2.14] Read, listen and watch the video again. Answer the question.

What are the natural remedies for these illnesses?
- nausea
- sore throat
- rash
- insomnia

GRAMMAR GUIDE

Second conditional

condition (*if* + a past tense)	result (*would* + infinitive without *to*)
If I **had** a cold,	I'**d take** a couple of paracetamol.
If people **used** natural remedies […],	they **wouldn't suffer** from side effects.

We use the second conditional to talk about hypothetical present situations.
Look!: to give advice we use *If I were you, I'd …*

➡ **GRAMMAR REFERENCE** p. 120   **WB** p. 194

4 Look at the Grammar guide. Choose the correct option.

1. We use the second conditional to talk about *real / hypothetical* situations.
2. *If* is always followed by a *past / present* tense.
3. We use the *future / conditional* form *would* + past participle in the other clause.

5 Complete the sentences with the correct form of the verbs in brackets.

0. If I ....**lost**.... (*lose*) my phone, I ..**would lose**.. (*lose*) all my music and videos too.
1. If you .... (*have*) a cough, what .... you .... (*take*) for it?
2. If I .... (*receive*) a text like that, I .... (*not / reply*).
3. If I .... (*be*) a better player, I .... (*play*) for the school team.
4. We .... (*be*) really pleased if you .... (*come*) to our party.

6 PAIRWORK Take turns to give advice to your partner in these situations.

0. I can't find my keys. **If I were you …**
1. I feel nauseous and I've got a headache.
2. My back hurts.

GRAMMAR GUIDE

Second conditional v first conditional

First conditional

*If you **tell** my grandmother you're feeling nauseous, she'**ll make** you some tea.*
(real and possible – right now you're nauseous)

Second conditional

*If you **told** my grandmother, she **would make** you some tea.*
(hypothetical or impossible – right now you're fine)

➡ **GRAMMAR REFERENCE** p. 120   **WB** pp. 194–195

7 Match sentences 0–5 to situations a–f.

0. [a] If I win the first prize, I will be perfectly happy.
1. [ ] If I won the first prize, I would be perfectly happy.
2. [ ] If you invite her, she will come.
3. [ ] If you invited her, she would come.
4. [ ] If it snows tomorrow, I'll go skiing.
5. [ ] If it snowed tomorrow, I'd go skiing.

a. I have a good chance of winning.
b. It's January and it might snow tomorrow.
c. You are having a party soon and need more guests.
d. I have some chance of winning, but it's not very probable.
e. You are thinking about maybe having a party.
f. It's January, but it's really mild weather and it's very unlikely that it will snow.

8 Complete the sentences with the correct verb so that it is first or second conditional.

0. Sal is having a baby. If it ....**is**.... (*be*) a boy, she '**ll** .... (*call*) him John.
1. If I .... (*have*) a time machine, I .... (*visit*) the court of Henry VIII.
2. If I .... (*buy*) a sports car, it .... (*be*) a Ferrari.
3. Jack .... (*not / go*) to the football match this afternoon if he .... (*not / finish*) his homework.
4. If it .... (*rain*) tomorrow, we .... (*not / go*) for a picnic.
5. If I .... (*be*) 18, I .... (*learn*) to drive a car.

Unit 7   71

READING SKILLS

LEAD IN

9 PAIRWORK Look at the notices. Discuss the questions.

1. Have you seen any of these notices? Where?
2. Do you think the advice in them is necessary? Why / Why not?
3. Can you think of any similar regulations you've seen in public places?

SWIMMING CAPS MUST BE WORN AT ALL TIMES

This product may contain nuts

No dogs allowed

PRACTICE

10 Scan the text about health and safety regulations. Match the expressions to the paragraphs.

1. ☐ chocolate eggs
2. ☐ swimming pools
3. ☐ planes and technology
4. ☐ petrol stations

READING STRATEGY

Insert sentences into a text

In this type of task you have to insert a number of sentences into the correct places in a gapped text. Read the sentences and look carefully at the text before and after each gap. Look for these things:
- any linking devices (e.g. linkers)
- any useful references (e.g. pronouns)
- any vocabulary which occurs in both the text and one of the sentences (e.g. nouns or adjectives)

Make sure:
- the sentence fits the topic of the paragraph
- the argument / story of the text develops logically if you insert that sentence

PRELIMINARY

11 [2.15] Read the text and put sentences a–f in the correct gaps 1–5. There is one extra sentence. Then listen and check.

a. Actually, there has never been a single instance of a mobile phone blowing up a petrol station.
b. But if they're so dangerous, why are we allowed to take them on board at all?

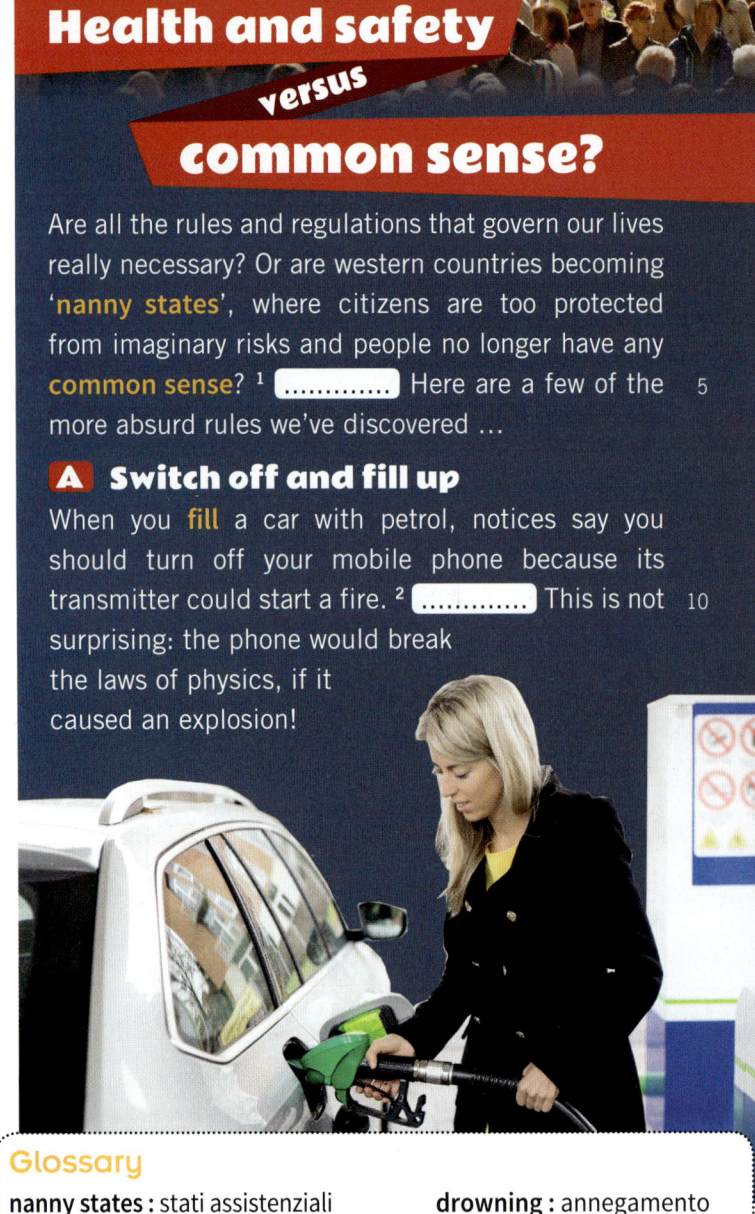

Health and safety versus common sense?

Are all the rules and regulations that govern our lives really necessary? Or are western countries becoming 'nanny states', where citizens are too protected from imaginary risks and people no longer have any common sense? ¹ .... Here are a few of the more absurd rules we've discovered ...

A Switch off and fill up

When you fill a car with petrol, notices say you should turn off your mobile phone because its transmitter could start a fire. ² .... This is not surprising: the phone would break the laws of physics, if it caused an explosion!

Glossary

nanny states : stati assistenziali
common sense : buonsenso
fill : riempite
deep end : parte profonda della piscina
drowning : annegamento
so far : finora
crashes : incidenti, disastri
guns : armi da fuoco

c. That's why we don't need these absurd regulations any more.
d. What type of things are regulators telling us we should and shouldn't do?
e. A small percentage of people have an intolerance to lactose and they may get a stomach ache, if they eat it.
f. In some cases, each child under eight must have an adult with them in the water.

12 Critical thinking Read the following proposals for health and safety regulations. Do you agree with them?

1. Cyclists should all wear reflective jackets.
2. We should close all schools in snowy weather.
3. We should only have fireworks at public events.

72 Unit 7

B In at the deep end?

15 Many municipal swimming pools in Britain have strict rules about young children in the water. ³ .... As a result, many parents can't take all their children together, so fewer kids are going swimming. These rules are supposed to reduce the risk of children drowning, but actually the main cause of drowning is
20 simply the inability to swim. If we want them to learn, sports experts tell us, we'd better take our kids to the swimming pool as often as possible!

C Safety in the air

For more than 20 years air safety regulators
25 have told passengers that they ought to switch off all computers, tablets and phones when the plane is taking off or landing. They say these can interfere with the plane's communications systems. ⁴ ....
30 In fact, statistics show that on every flight at least 20 passengers will forget to switch them off. So far, however, there have been no crashes as a result.

D Dangerous eggs?

In the United States it's illegal to sell a certain type of milk
35 chocolate egg because of regulations about food products which contain lactose, a substance in milk. ⁵ .... So, although in many states in the USA it's illegal to sell types of milk chocolate, it's not illegal to sell guns!

GRAMMAR GUIDE

should / had better / ought to for advice

We use *should*, *had better* and *ought to* to give advice.

We **should** / **ought to** tell our teacher, if Jack is cheating in the text.

Had better is usually used when there are negative consequences if the person doesn't follow the advice.

I've lost my keys. I'd better call my mum. (or she will worry)

➡ GRAMMAR REFERENCE p. 121   WB p. 198

13 Use *should / had better / ought to* and the prompts to give some advice. Use each expression twice.

0 I've got a bad cold. (take / paracetamol)
   You'd better take some paracetamol.
1 My hair is dirty. (wash / tonight)
2 I've got a stomach ache. (drink / ginger tea)
3 I'm worried about my exams. (study more / at weekends)
4 There's nothing to eat in the fridge. (go / supermarket)
5 I've lost my mobile phone. (tell / the police)

WRITING SKILLS

LEAD IN

14 **PAIRWORK** Make a list of changes you would like to see in your school for a healthier lifestyle.

PRACTICE

15 **GROUPWORK** Look at the suggestions below for encouraging teenagers to live a healthier lifestyle. Answer the questions.

1 Which suggestion do you think would be the most successful? Why?
2 Has your school tried any of these suggestions? Did it / they help?

- Include more hours of PE on everyone's school timetable.
- Organise fun exercise classes at lunchtime to get students into the gym.
- Provide only healthy choices on the menu in the school canteen.
- Encourage more students to walk to school.
- Provide different sports after school.

WRITING STRATEGY

Write a proposal

A proposal is a persuasive piece of writing which we use to suggest a solution to a problem. In a proposal you should give details about your idea and support it with background information. A proposal includes:

- the problem and the solution
- the reason why the solution is a good one / why it might work
- persuasive language, e.g. *should*, *had better*, *ought to*
- a request for action
- formal language

➡ See **WRITING EXPANSION** page 256

Unit 7

VOCABULARY

Illnesses, injuries and remedies

16 Write the parts of the body in the correct category: Head, Body, Arms and Legs. Look up any words you don't know in a dictionary.

throat • foot • back • cheek • mouth • toe • finger • shoulder • forehead • neck • thumb • bottom • elbow • chin • eye • hair • chest • knee • teeth • ear • hand • stomach • ankle • hip • nose

17 Look at the photos. Complete the sentences with the words below. Use a dictionary to help you.

cold (n) • pains (n) • blocked (adj) • burn (n) • flu (n) • swollen (adj) • aches (v) • headache (n) • sore (adj) • cut (n) • temperature (n) • cough (n) • hurt (v) • toothache (n) • bruised (adj)

1 He's twisted his ankle. It's ....
2 Her teeth .... She's got ....
3 He's burnt his hand. He's got a bad ....
4 She's got a .... She's got a .... nose and she's got a ....
5 She's cut her finger. She's got a deep ....
6 He's got .... He's got a .... throat and a high ....
7 She's got a ....
8 She's hurt her knee. It's ....
9 His stomach .... He's got .... in his stomach.

18 Read the text. Match the words in bold to the medicines and equipment in the pictures.

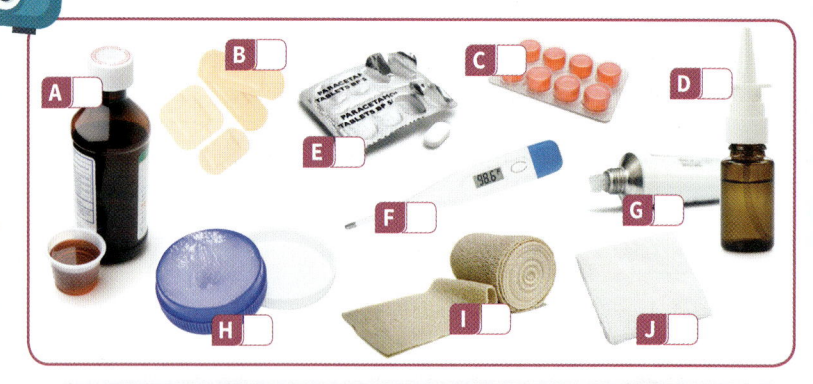

FIRST AID IN THE HOME

Influenza (flu)
If you've got flu, you'll have a fever and aches in your body. The best thing is to go to bed and rest. Use a digital [1]**thermometer** to take your temperature. If it's over 37 °C, you have a fever. You should take two [2]**paracetamol tablets** to lower the fever, and drink a lot of fluids. If you've got a sore throat too, you could try sucking [3]**antiseptic throat lozenges**. If you still have a fever after 48 hours, you should call your doctor.

Colds
The symptoms of a cold are similar to influenza but you don't usually get a fever. If you've got a blocked nose, try using a [4]**nasal spray** every four hours, or put some [5]**menthol ointment** on your chest. For a cough, you should take some [6]**cough syrup** before you go to bed and try to sleep sitting up.

Cuts
Wash the affected area with warm water to clean it, then disinfect it thoroughly. For small cuts and grazes you can put a [7]**plaster** on it. For larger areas, you should put a loose [8]**cotton dressing** on the wound, then a [9]**bandage**.

Burns
You should not put oil or butter on a burn. Instead, hold the affected area under cold, running water for a few minutes. Next you should apply some [10]**antiseptic cream** and cover the area with a loose cotton dressing.

19 SPEAKING Choose one of the problems from exercise 17. Take turns to describe your symptoms to your partner and offer advice.

A I've got a bad headache.
B You should take two paracetamol and go to bed.

74 Unit 7

See **VOCABULARY EXTENSION** page 266

SPEAKING SKILLS

Asking for and giving advice

20 PAIRWORK Discuss the question.

A lot of teenagers are unhappy with their appearance. What sort of things do they worry about?

21 [2.16] Listen and watch the video. Why is Anna feeling bad?

key expressions	
asking for advice	giving advice
☐ What do you think I should do?	☐ You could try …
☐ Should I …?	☐ Yes, you should. / No, you shouldn't.
☐ What would you do?	

22 [2.16] Listen and watch again and tick (✓) the key expressions you hear.

SPEAKING STRATEGY

Show empathy

When someone is upset or down about something, we can use these expressions to show we understand and empathise with them.

- I know how you feel.
- It's awful when that happens.
- It happens to me too.
- I feel exactly the same.
- If you want to talk, give me a call.

23 [2.16] Listen and watch again. How many times do you hear each of the expressions from the strategy box?

24 PAIRWORK Act out the dialogue then swap roles.

Student A: Choose one of the problems below. Explain how you feel to your partner and ask for advice.

Student B: Listen to your partner and express empathy. Then give him / her some advice. Use the key expressions and the strategy box.
1 You feel tired and have problems concentrating at school.
2 You want to get into the athletics team at school but you don't think you're fast enough.

CHANGING LANGUAGE

Modal verbs

25 Which modal verbs do you think British English speakers use most often? *Should, ought to, may* or *might*?

26 Watch the video and complete the sentences with one word.
1 *Should* and ……………… *to* are both used to give advice.
2 ……………… is more frequently used than *ought to*.
3 ……………… is even more popular today than it was 20 years ago.
4 *May* is ……………… popular than ……………… today.

27 PAIRWORK Discuss the statement and decide if you agree or disagree.

Language students should only learn the most frequently used phrases.

CORPUS

Corpus data can reveal whether expressions are becoming more or less popular in spoken English:
- *should* is the most popular modal verb for giving advice
- *might* is the most popular modal verb for expressing probability

Unit 7   75

LISTENING SKILLS

LEAD IN

28 PAIRWORK Look at the covers of some books about food and diet. Discuss with a partner.

1. What types of food do you think they recommend?
2. Why do people usually follow a particular diet?
3. Have you heard of any unusual diets? What foods do they say you should / shouldn't eat?

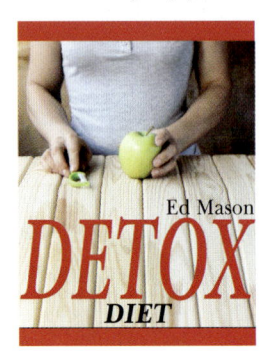

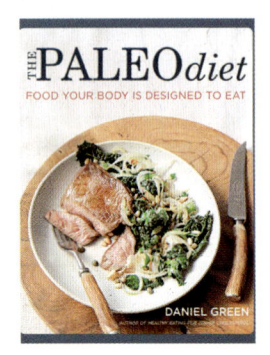

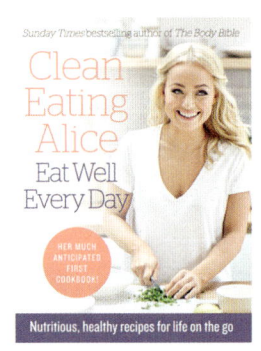

PRACTICE

29 [2.17] Listen to a radio interview about healthy eating. Which of the diets from exercise 28 does the recording mention?

LISTENING STRATEGY

Complete notes with missing words

In this type of task you only have to write down keywords.
- Read the notes. Underline the headings to understand the topic of each section.
- Look at the words before and after the gaps. What type of words are missing?
- Underline the keywords. Listen for these in the recording: the missing words will be near them.
- Listen for the sentences in the notes. Complete them with the missing words.

PRELIMINARY | IGCSE

30 Look at the notes in the fact files. What type of word or clauses are missing in each gap? They could be nouns, verbs or adjectives.

31 [2.17] Listen to the interview again and complete the fact files. Write one or two words in each gap. Then listen and check.

DIET FACT FILES

1

Name
The ¹.................................... diet

Theory behind the diet
Chemicals in the vinegar reduce your appetite, so you ².................................... .

Foods which you should not eat
You can eat ³.................................... .

Advantages
It may help you ⁴.................................... quicker.

Disadvantages
The main problem for most people is the ⁵.................................... of the vinegar.

2

Name
The ⁶.................................... diet

Theory behind the diet
Our bodies ⁷.................................... to eat processed food, so we should only eat the food that paleo man ate.

Foods which you shouldn't eat
You shouldn't eat ⁸...................................., pasta or sugar, and there's no butter or cheese.

Advantages
It's good to avoid ⁹.................................... foods of course.

Disadvantages
Some people find all the raw food gives them ¹⁰.................................... .

32 [2.17] Listen again and answer the questions.

1. How do some people today think food can affect them?
2. Why might the vinegar diet make you eat less?
3. Where does the name *paleo diet* come from?
4. The doctor says most of the food has to be *raw*. What does this mean?
5. Why does she think the paleo diet is boring?

76   Unit 7

LIFE SKILLS

Building your self-esteem

LEAD IN

33 PAIRWORK Look at the photo of the woman. Discuss the questions.

1 How would you describe her?
2 Do you think the image is real?
3 How does it make you feel?

PRACTICE

34 Read the magazine article. Underline four ways people can build their self-esteem.

SELF-ESTEEM

We live in a world of images. We constantly see images in the media of glamorous actors, singers and sports champions, all of them people with amazing bodies, beautiful faces, successful lives and incredible talents. Then we watch adverts on TV with beautiful models in them. We see people we know on social media sites sharing photos of all the exciting moments in their lives, apparently having a great time. At the same time, we have an image of *ourselves* and our own lives in our minds and we often compare this self-image with these media-generated images of others who seem so much better than us. This is good for advertisers – if we want to be like the people in their adverts, we'll buy their products – but it's bad for our *self-esteem*. This is because when we constantly compare ourselves to these exaggerated images of other people it can make us feel unhappy and inadequate. We feel we're not as attractive, successful or popular as they are. Our self-image suffers. A poor self-image leads to low self-esteem, and this can make it hard to be happy in life. So, what should we do to build our self-esteem? Think about how you *judge yourself* and answer these questions:

1 Do you feel proud of your successes, even if they are very small?
2 Do you look for the positive things in yourself, rather than focusing only on the negative things?
3 Do you *aim* for goals that are possible, rather than impossible dreams?
4 Do you actively look for new activities and interests, to discover what your talents are?

If your answer to any of the above questions is no, then try to change it to yes! You can take active steps to build your self-esteem and your life will change if you do!

Glossary
ourselves : noi stessi
self-esteem : autostima
judge yourself : giudichi te stesso
aim : miri, punti

35 Read the article again and answer the questions.

1 Write three examples of places where we constantly see images of others.
2 Are these media-generated images realistic?
3 Why is it good for advertisers if we compare ourselves to these images?
4 How does it make us feel?
5 What is the result of having a low self-image?

LIFE STRATEGY

Tips for building your self-esteem

- Think about yourself in a positive way. Try and avoid negative thoughts.
- It's good that you want to improve, but remember, you don't have to be the best.
- Discover your talents by trying new things.
- Set yourself realistic goals. That way you can be successful.
- Don't be afraid of saying what you think. Join in the conversation because your ideas are valuable too.
- Help others. It will make you feel good and it will be good for your community.
- Be proud of your differences – we don't all have to be the same.

36 THINKING FURTHER Read the questions. Compare your answers with your partner.

1 Which of the tips about improving self-esteem are new for you?
2 Which of them do you already do? Do they help?
3 Choose three you could use to give a friend advice.
4 Choose a tip to follow in the future.

37 TASK Discuss the statement in pairs.

'Make-up really helps improve our image and as a result our self-esteem.'

Student A: You agree with this statement. Think of as many ideas as you can to support it (e.g., hides spots; enhances your natural beauty; increases your confidence very easily and relatively cheaply).

Student B: You disagree with the statement. Think of as many ideas as you can to disagree with it (e.g., self-esteem should come from within; your face to the world should be your natural face; you are supporting a multibillion-dollar industry that exploits people for profit).

CITIZENSHIP AND COMPETENCY SKILLS Acting autonomously and responsibly

8 A political world

EXAM STRATEGIES
- PRELIMINARY: Speaking
- IGCSE: Speaking and Listening
- PRE FIRST: Reading

SPEAKING SKILLS
- Apologising and expressing regret

ACADEMIC SKILLS
- Using the internet for research

LEAD IN

1 PAIRWORK Look at photos 1–4 on this page and discuss the questions.

1. Do you know the year when each of these events happened?
2. What happened in each case?
3. Why do you think it was important?

2 [2.18] Read, listen and watch. Which of the events from the photos are mentioned in the text? When did they take place?

THREE DECISIVE MOMENTS?

The twenty-first century is still very young, but already it's produced many life-changing events, both positive and negative. Which of these events will future generations see as **turning points** in history? We've chosen three. Do you think they were decisive moments?

The terrorist attack on New York's iconic Twin Towers on 11th September 2001 shocked citizens of every nation. Americans watched in horror, unable to believe that extremists from distant lands could attack them in their own country, causing chaos, fear and death. The government reacted by starting the 'War on Terror' and invading Iraq. If the 9/11 attacks hadn't taken place, the Americans would probably never have gone into Iraq. Many believe it was this that radicalised thousands of Muslims and later created ISIS.

On 4th February 2004 two university students at Harvard University launched the first social networking site. Mark Zuckerberg and Eduardo Saverin at first limited **membership** to students at their university, but as the site became more popular, they extended it to other US universities too. Would communication have developed in the same way if the boys hadn't launched their site? We'll never know! But we know that just two years later, in 2006, Facebook had over 12 million users and today it has over 1 billion! It has revolutionised the way we communicate.

On 20th January 2009 millions of people watched the inauguration of Barack Obama, the first African-American US president. Obama's election seemed like a new beginning in the USA's history, an era of tolerance and equality. Unfortunately, he faced many challenges during his presidency and many of his ambitious plans **didn't get approved**. If he'd had fewer difficulties, he would perhaps have achieved more. And if Obama's presidency had been more successful, would Americans have voted for someone so different to him in 2016?

Glossary
turning points : punti di svolta
membership : iscrizione
didn't get approved : non furono approvati

Learning goals
Grammar
- Third conditional
- *wish* + past tenses

Vocabulary
- Politics and society

WB pp. 202–211

78 Unit 8

PRACTICE

3 ▶ [2.18] Read, listen and watch the video again. Answer the questions.

1. How did Americans react to the 9/11 attacks?
2. What do you think the phrase 'War on Terror' means?
3. Who could use the Facebook site when it first started?
4. Why has Facebook been so important?
5. Why did Obama's election seem so important?
6. What kind of president did Americans vote for after Obama, according to the text?

GRAMMAR GUIDE

Third conditional

condition (*if* + a past perfect)	result (*would have* + past participle)
If the 9/11 attacks **hadn't taken** place,	the Americans **wouldn't have gone** into Iraq.
If he **had had** fewer difficulties,	he **would have achieved** more.

We use the third conditional to talk about hypothetical past situations.

➡ See **GRAMMAR REFERENCE** page 121

4 Look at the Grammar guide. Choose the correct option.

1. We use the third conditional to talk about hypothetical situations in the *past / present*.
2. We use it to talk about things that *happened / didn't happen* because the conditions weren't right.
3. We use the *past / present perfect* tense in the *if* clause.
4. We use the *past conditional / past perfect* (*would* + *have* + past participle) in the result clause.

5 Match 1–4 to a–d. Then discuss the statements in pairs. Do you agree or disagree?

0. [b] Zuckerberg wouldn't have invented Facebook
1. [ ] The 2005 London underground attacks wouldn't have happened
2. [ ] Americans wouldn't have voted for Trump
3. [ ] Obama wouldn't have been elected

a. if Britain hadn't joined the USA in invading Iraq.
b. if he hadn't gone to university.
c. if he had been a woman.
d. if he hadn't been a TV star.

6 Complete the sentences with the correct form of the verbs in brackets.

0. If I **had had to** (*have to*) vote in the USA, I **would have voted** (*vote*) Clinton.
1. If you .... (*not / tell*) me, I .... (*not / guess*).
2. We .... (*come*) if you .... (*invite*) us.
3. What .... Harry .... (*say*) if he .... (*found out*) the truth?
4. If our team .... (*score*) one more goal, they .... (*win*) the league.
5. What .... (*happen*) if I .... (*not / notice*) the smoke?

7 Complete the sentences with your own ideas.

0. If I'd gone to bed earlier last night, **I wouldn't have felt tired today**.
1. My parents would have been angry if …
2. If I hadn't eaten all that ice cream …
3. I'd have been better at English if …
4. I would have voted for … if …
5. If I'd had the money, …
6. If you'd told me about it, …

8 **SPEAKING** Choose one of the political events from history below. Tell your partner what you think would have happened in that case. Use the fact files below to help you.

- What would have happened if Henry VIII hadn't married Anne Boleyn in 1533?
- What would have happened if Hitler hadn't invaded Poland in 1939?

HENRY VIII – FACT FILE

- divorced the Spanish queen Katherine of Aragon
- broke from the pope in Rome
- changed the religion of England to become Protestant

WWII – FACT FILE

- Britain declared war on Germany
- Russia took power in Eastern Europe
- millions of people died

READING SKILLS

LEAD IN

9 PAIRWORK Discuss these questions.

1 What are the names of the main political parties in your country?
2 How old do you have to be to vote in elections?
3 Do you know what percentage of people voted in the last election?
4 What was the percentage of voters in the age group from 18–25?

PRACTICE

10 Read the text and answer the questions.

1 Why is the MP Mhairi Black unusual?
2 How have young people in the UK reacted to her election?
3 According to Tamsin, why do young people not connect with UK MPs?
4 Why did Adam not vote in the last election?
5 Why does Laura think the Brexit referendum was unfair?
6 Why does Ishan think that his generation need to get more active in politics?

READING STRATEGY

Complete texts

A monolingual dictionary is an important tool for reading. When you are completing a text, you can use it to:
- check the part of speech of a word to see if it fits the gap
- check the plural of a noun or the past form of a verb
- check synonyms / antonyms to distinguish differences in the meanings of similar words
- look up collocations to see if it fits the gap
- find examples of the use of a word in natural usage

PRE▶ FIRST

11 [2.19] Read the text again and choose the correct option for each gap. Then listen and check.

1 A choose   B chose
  C choice   D chosen
2 A watching   B voting
  C following   D listening to
3 A did   B said
  C made   D told
4 A little   B many
  C few   D some

VOTING WITH OUR FEET?

Mhairi Black was just 20 years old when in 2015 she became the youngest MP (member of parliament) in the UK parliament in 350 years. Her ¹............ of career fascinated people at a time when more and more young
5 people in the UK were feeling completely **disengaged** from politics and weren't even interested in ²............ in elections. Mhairi Black's **commitment** to getting involved and working for change has inspired a new generation of young people and made them realise that
10 they too have a voice and need to use it. When Mhairi ³............ her first **speech** in parliament in 2015, it got 11 million views online.
But why is it that young people, not just in the UK but all over Europe, feel so disillusioned with politics now?
15 We asked four young Brits to explain their views.

Tamsin, 18

The average age of MPs in the UK parliament is 50 and there are very ⁴............ under the age of 30, Mhairi Black is the only one I know. I think that makes it difficult for young people to connect with
20 MPs. There's no one of our age in parliament ⁵............ our problems **at first hand**. I wish we had some younger MPs in parliament!

5 A living   B lived
  C lives   D live
6 A wouldn't know   B would know
  C would have known D wouldn't have known
7 A will affect   B would affect
  C are affecting   D had affected
8 A was able to   B have been able to
  C had been able to D are able to
9 A concerned   B involved
  C occupied   D participated
10 A in   B about
   C out   D with

GRAMMAR GUIDE

wish + past tenses

wish + past simple (for present regret)
I **wish** we **had** some younger MPs in parliament.
I **wish** the voting age **was** 16.

wish + past perfect (for past regret)
I **wish** I'**d been able to** vote in the Brexit referendum.
I **wish** that our candidate **had won**.

➡ **GRAMMAR REFERENCE** p. 121 **WB** p. 206

80 Unit 8

Adam, 19

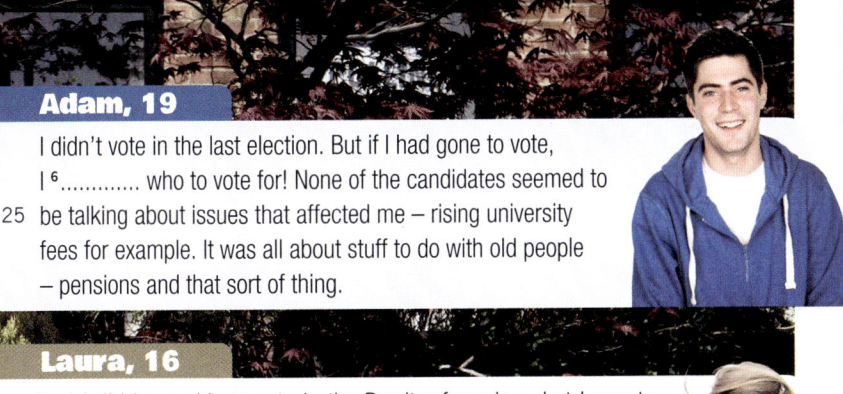

I didn't vote in the last election. But if I had gone to vote, I ⁶............ who to vote for! None of the candidates seemed to be talking about issues that affected me – rising university fees for example. It was all about stuff to do with old people – pensions and that sort of thing.

Laura, 16

I wish I'd been able to vote in the Brexit referendum, but I was too young. I think it was really **unfair** that no one under 18 could vote because actually the future results of leaving the EU ⁷............ me and my generation, not the older people who voted – they'll all be retired by then! If younger people like me ⁸............ vote, the result would have been different. I wish the voting age in the UK was 16.

Ishan, 19

I **campaigned** for the Green Party in the last election. I wish that our candidate had won, but the Tories got the **seat** in my constituency. Anyway, it felt good to get ⁹............, to do something active. It's my generation that in the future will have to deal ¹⁰............ the damage we're doing to the planet and we have to start changing things now.

Glossary

disengaged : disimpegnate
commitment : impegno
speech : discorso
at first hand : in prima persona
unfair : ingiusto
campaigned : fatto campagna elettorale
seat : seggio

12 Rewrite the sentences using *I wish* with the correct past form.

0 If I'd known you were in town, I would have called you.
  I wish I'd known you were in town.
1 If I had remembered to bring my wallet, I would have paid.
2 I would have brought an umbrella if I'd seen the weather forecast.
3 If I was older, I'd campaign for the Green Party.
4 If the voting age was lower, young people would be more interested in politics.
5 Jane would have got the job if she had applied.
6 We wouldn't have been angry if you'd told us the truth.
7 I would have gone to the party if I'd known Joe was there.
8 If you'd listened to me, you wouldn't be in this mess.
9 If politicians were more honest, voters would trust them.
10 I would have bought those trainers if I'd had enough money.

13 `Critical thinking` Discuss the questions in pairs.

1 Are young people in your country engaged in politics? If not, why not?
2 What has discouraged young people from politics in the past?
3 Which of these things do you think would help get them interested and active?
  - younger representatives in parliament
  - a section for young people's issues in every party manifesto
  - lowering the voting age

WRITING SKILLS

LEAD IN

14 Name an example of this type of book.

1 a political biography
2 a historical biography
3 a literary biography
4 an autobiography

1 book about Barack Obama

PRACTICE

15 Tick (✓) the type of information you would expect to find in a biography.

1 arguments for and against political issues
2 events from a person's life
3 jokes and cartoons
4 information about a person's achievements
5 stories about their relationships with family and friends
6 descriptions of fictional characters
7 information about people who influenced the person's ideas

WRITING STRATEGY

Write a biography

A biography is the story of a person's life. The accounts can be long or short. The person can be famous, but they don't have to be. They usually contain:

- some facts about the person's life and their importance
- for a famous person, some analysis or interpretation of the events in that person's life
- chronological events that happened at different stages of the person's life

See **WRITING EXPANSION** page 257

Unit 8   81

VOCABULARY

Politics and society

THE VILLAGE WITH NO CHILDREN

In the UK 70% of the complaints people make about their neighbourhoods concern teenagers – they make a noise, hang out in gangs, drop litter, vandalise buildings and behave without respect for others. One village in Scotland, Firhall, has now decided it's better to just ban teenagers altogether!

The residents have decided to make their village child-free. If you want to buy a home there, you have to be over 45, and agree not to sell your property to a family with kids. If you've got grandchildren, they can't stay with you for more than three weeks.

The Firhall residents say the village is a more peaceful place to live, but their decision has been controversial. Critics say that discrimination based on age is as bad as racism or sexism. If the residents had shown prejudice against a group based on race or gender, it would have been illegal. A healthy society should show tolerance towards everyone, and appreciate the diversity in our society.

But what do teenagers think? Fifteen-year-old Sean says, 'The losers are the residents of the village. Their extremism has turned Firhall into a ghetto for pensioners. I wouldn't live there if you paid me – I'd be bored to death!'

16 What do you think these words mean? Find them in the text and match them to their definitions.

1 ☐ vandalise   5 ☐ extremism
2 ☐ tolerance   6 ☐ ban
3 ☐ prejudice   7 ☐ discrimination
4 ☐ diversity

a acceptance of different beliefs
b disliking someone or something because of their race or religion
c exclude people from a place
d damage public property
e variety and difference
f very strong, exaggerated opinions
g refusing to give some groups the same rights as others

17 Read the text and answer the questions.

1 What do a lot of neighbourhoods in the UK complain about?
2 Where is Firhall and what have its inhabitants decided to do?
3 What are some of the conditions about living in Firhall?
4 Is the ban illegal?
5 What was the reaction of one teenager?
6 What do you think?

18 Look at the example. Complete the table for the other abstract nouns.

abstract noun	root word	suffix
racism	race	-ism
tolerance	1	2 ....
extremism	3	4 ....
diversity	5	6 ....
discrimination	7	8 ....

19 Can you make abstract nouns from the words below? Which group in the table do they belong to? Check your answers in a dictionary.

1 equal ....
2 elect ....
3 fundamental ....
4 accept ....
5 vandal ....

20 Complete the sentences with words from exercises 18 and 19.

1 Terrorist groups sometimes develop out of religious ....
2 The Amazon rain forest has a rich .... of plants and animals.
3 .... in the workplace means that all workers should have the same rights.
4 .... of yourself and your faults can help your self-esteem.
5 Black people in the southern states of the USA faced .... for many years.
6 .... is when some people are prejudiced against others because of the colour of their skin.
7 There have been some acts of .... in our school recently – broken windows and graffiti on classroom walls.

82   Unit 8

See **VOCABULARY EXTENSION** page 267

SPEAKING SKILLS

Apologising and expressing regret

21 PAIRWORK Discuss these questions.

1 Have you ever seen a political demonstration in your area? What was it about? How was it?
2 Do you think the demonstration was effective? Why / Why not?

22 [2.20] Listen and watch the video. Where has Grace been and why is she upset?

key expressions	
making an apology	responding to an apology
☐ I'm so sorry!	☐ Don't worry about it.
☐ I apologise.	☐ Apology accepted.
☐ I'm really sorry.	☐ It doesn't matter.
☐ Please forgive me.	☐ I forgive you.

23 [2.20] Listen and watch again and tick (✓) the key expressions you hear.

SPEAKING STRATEGY

Express regret for your actions

When we have to apologise, we often also express regret for what we've done wrong.
- *I wish I'd remembered about it.*
- *I would have …, if I'd remembered when it was.*
- *I wanted to …, honestly.*
- *I wish I'd been there to …*

PRELIMINARY | IGCSE

24 [2.20] Listen and watch again. How many times do you hear each of the expressions from the strategy box?

25 PAIRWORK Read the situations. In each case decide if you apologise or respond to the apology. Then swap roles.

1 You forgot to buy a present for a friend's birthday from you and two other friends. Apologise and express regret.
2 You borrowed your partner's textbook and lost it. They need it to revise for a test. Apologise and express regret.

SOUNDS ENGLISH

The /əʊ/ sound

26 [2.21] **PAIRWORK** Listen to a British English speaker and a learner of English say these two words. What difference can you hear?

coat   cot

SOUND STRATEGY

The /əʊ/ sound is called a *diphthong*, a vowel formed from two other vowels. Diphthongs are sometimes difficult to pronounce for Italian speakers. Italians often pronounce them as just one vowel, e.g., saying *not* /nɒt/ instead of *note* /nəʊt/.

27 [2.22] Listen and circle the word you hear.

	A /əʊ/	B /ɒ/
1	tote	tot
2	coat	cot
3	goat	got
4	note	not
5	clothes	cloth
6	soak	sock

28 [2.23] Which of these words contain the /əʊ/ sound? Listen and circle them.

1 phone   7 lock
2 close   8 remote
3 stop   9 suppose
4 lonely   10 go
5 cough   11 pot
6 home   12 open

29 GAME Now in pairs say one word to your partner and he / she guesses if it contains the /əʊ/ sound.

Unit 8   83

LISTENING SKILLS

LEAD IN

30 PAIRWORK Look at the picture and answer the questions.

1. Do you recognise this flag? What do the yellow stars represent?
2. Which countries in Europe have you visited?
3. What things were similar to your country and what things were different?

PRACTICE

31 [2.24] Listen to five speakers expressing their personal opinions. Complete the information about them.

name	nationality	lives in (country)
1		
2		
3		
4		
5		

LISTENING STRATEGY

Identify multiple speakers

In this task you will hear five speakers talking about a common topic. For each speaker you have to choose the correct summary of their opinion about it.

- Read the first line of the instructions carefully. This will tell you what the topic is.
- Read the six opinions in the list. (There will be one extra opinion.) Think of ways to paraphrase them.
- As you listen, try to match the ideas and not the words.

IGCSE

32 [2.24] Listen again and match each speaker 1–5 to their opinion a–f. Use each option only once. There is one extra option.

a ☐ The EU offers more career opportunities than my own country.
b ☐ European capital cities are multicultural and international and the inhabitants are European.
c ☐ I feel at home everywhere in Europe because I've got relatives in many countries.
d ☐ I don't feel European because I don't have much contact with Europe or its people.
e ☐ The EU is an artificial concept and it won't survive.
f ☐ Europe is great but people still feel they belong to their own country.

33 Look at the script of the first recording. Underline the parts which helped you choose your answer in exercise 32.

I'm Isabelle. I'm French but I'm living in Brussels in Belgium at the moment. I'm studying here. If someone asks me my nationality, of course I say I'm French, but actually I feel more European. I speak three languages – French, English and German. I've got family in four different European countries – my aunts and uncles have all moved abroad for work. I often travel from one country to another to visit them, so I feel at home everywhere. After I finish university, I'm going to look for a job anywhere in Europe, not just in France.

34 [2.24] Listen again and answer the questions.

1. Which languages does Isabelle speak?
2. Why does she often visit other countries in Europe?
3. Why does Ben feel his country has less contact with mainland Europe?
4. Why does Ben not feel part of Europe?
5. Why is it difficult for Polish young people at the moment in Agata's opinion?
6. What does she want to do after school?
7. Why does Lucia think the EU is a good idea?
8. Where are Elliot's parents from?

35 Critical thinking Discuss these questions as a class.

Many people have strong opinions about the European Union and what it does.

1. What are some of the opinions you've heard about these things?
   - the euro
   - EU laws and regulations
   - freedom of movement across borders
2. What do you think national identity is based on?
3. What things about the place you're from are important to your identity? Why?
4. Is being part of Europe important to you? Why / Why not?

84 Unit 8

Using the internet for research

LEAD IN

36 Look at the list of sources which high school students frequently use for research and answer the questions.

- Wikipedia
- YouTube
- Google Maps
- Google Translate

1 Which of these online tools have you used?
2 Which were the most useful? Why?

37 What are some of the pros and cons of using the internet for research? Sort these points into pros and cons. Add more of your own ideas.

- You can access hundreds of thousands of sources of information.
- You can access information extremely quickly.
- A lot of information comes up that's not really relevant.
- Both primary and secondary sources of information are available.
- You often get distracted by information that's interesting / funny but not relevant.
- Not all of the information is accurate and up-to-date.

ACADEMIC STRATEGY

The internet can be a very effective way of finding the information that you need for projects. However, it's also easy to spend a lot of time searching on the web and still not find what you're looking for. To search effectively you should:

- be sure you know exactly what information you have to find
- use multiple-word searches to get fewer but more relevant results
- put phrases in quotation marks to reduce the number of results, e.g., 'the world's most dangerous animal' will only produce sources which contain all of these words together
- use the minus sign (–) to eliminate unwanted results, e.g., *Hilton – Paris* will produce results for *Hilton Hotels* but not *Paris Hilton* the celebrity
- scan the relevant web pages to decide whether they seem reliable. Check for accuracy, currency, authority, objectivity (ACAO).

ACADEMIC SKILLS

PRACTICE

38 Imagine you had to research the British Prime Minister Winston Churchill and his role in the Second World War. Which search terms would produce the most relevant results?

1 Churchill
2 Churchill Prime Minister
3 Prime Minister Second World War
4 Churchill Second World War

39 WRITING In pairs, you have to write a short biography of 150 words of Winston Churchill. Use the internet for research.

1 Read the question and decide what search terms to use.
2 Refine your search terms to get more relevant results.
3 Write down the top three most relevant web pages that you get from your search.
4 Scan the information on the web pages and decide whether they seem reliable (ACAO).

Winston Churchill was one of the key political figures of WWII. Write a short biography about him and his achievements as British Prime Minister from 1940-1945.

Unit 8

REVISE AND ROUND UP

1 **Match the beginnings and ends of the sentences to make complete second conditional sentences.**

0 [c] If I had a sore throat,
1 [ ] If you got a dog,
2 [ ] If I had more money,
3 [ ] My brother would play on his computer all day
4 [ ] It would be better

a if you all went home now.
b you'd get more exercise walking it.
c would garlic help to cure it?
d I'd go skiing with my friends.
e if my parents let him.

2 **Complete the quiz questions with the correct form of the verbs below. Choose your answers, then write second conditional sentences to explain your choice.**

break down • land • do • ~~react~~ • start

Survival quiz

0 If you met a bear in the forest, how ...**would**... you ...**react**...?
  A turn and run B climb up a tree C stand very still
  Explain your answer: **If I stood still, the bear wouldn't notice me.**

1 If your plane ……………… on a deserted tropical island, how would you find food?
  A fish for fish in the sea
  B make a net to catch birds
  C eat plants and coconuts
  Explain your answer: ………………

2 If your jeep ……………… in the desert, how would you survive?
  A stay in the jeep and wait for help
  B dig under plants to find water
  C try to fix the engine
  Explain your answer: ………………

3 If you lost your way in the mountains in winter, what ……………… you ………………?
  A dig a hole in the snow and sleep in it
  B keep walking downhill
  C make a big sign on the snow with rocks
  Explain your answer: ………………

4 If an earthquake ……………… while you were in bed, where would you go?
  A under the bed B outside C stay in bed
  Explain your answer: ………………

3 **Read the sentences and decide if they are first or second conditional. Then complete them with the correct form of the verb in brackets.**

0 If the weather's good tomorrow, we **'ll go** (go) to the beach. (**first**)
1 If I ……………… (win) the competition, I'll buy a new laptop.
2 If I ……………… (be) you, I'd try again.
3 If you eat less, you ……………… (lose) weight.
4 If her team won the league, Molly ……………… (be) delighted.
5 If you ……………… (show) me how to do it, I could help you.
6 If I ……………… (hear) anything from Jon, I'll let you know.

4 **Correct the mistakes. One sentence is correct.**

0 It's really late. I ~~better~~ go home. **had better**
1 Why is Sarah in her room? She should to be at school.
2 I think we ought tell the police.
3 You shouldn't gave the children so much chocolate.
4 Ought we to go to the cinema now?
5 Should I invite Franca to the party too?
6 You hadn't better drink black coffee, when you feel nauseous.
7 Sally didn't should cycle without a helmet.
8 The boys have better apologise to Mr Brown or he'll go to the police.

5 **Rewrite the sentences using the third conditional.**

0 It rained, so we didn't have a picnic.
  If it hadn't rained, we would have had a picnic.
1 I wasn't hungry, so I didn't have any breakfast.
2 We didn't know his name, so we called him 'the new boy'.
3 Sharon lost her ticket, so she didn't come to the concert.
4 The driver didn't see the red light, so he crashed into the lorry.
5 I couldn't read the Chinese signs, so I got lost in Shanghai.
6 David didn't have any free time, so he couldn't help you.

86 Units 7–8

6 Complete the dialogue with *wish* and the correct form of the verb in brackets.

Anna It was a great end-of-exams party last night.
Sam Yes, it was. I ⁰**wish I'd gone** (I / go) to bed earlier though - I'm really tired!
Fraser So, the exams are finally over. We've finished school forever!
Anna I ¹........................ (we / not / have to) leave. I'm going to miss you guys so much.
Sam Do you really wish you could go back to school for another year? Are you crazy?!
Anna Well, no, but I ²........................ (we / have) more time together this year. More time for parties like last night's!
Fraser Yeah, you're right. I ³........................ (we / not / have to) study all the time.
Sam Yes, me too. I ⁴........................ (there / not / be) so much stress about the exams!
Anna Now everyone is going off to do different things … I ⁵........................ (I / meet) you all earlier.
Sam Don't worry Anna, we'll keep in touch.
Anna I ⁶........................ (we / can) all stay friends forever.
Fraser We will be friends forever – on Facebook!

7 TRANSLATION Translate the sentences into English.

1 Se sapessi l'indirizzo di Claudia, le spedirei una cartolina.
2 Non farebbe così freddo qui dentro, se chiudessi la finestra.
3 Che cosa faresti se vedessi un serpente?
4 Che cosa dovresti fare se qualcuno si rompesse un braccio?
5 Siete sempre stanchi. Dovreste andare a dormire prima.
6 Se mio padre non ci avesse spedito i soldi, saremmo rimasti bloccati a Calcutta.
7 Se avessi ascoltato il professore, non avrei commesso quello stupido errore.
8 Mi avresti sposato, se te lo avessi chiesto?
9 Vorrei non aver mangiato tutti quei dolci.
10 Mia mamma vorrebbe essere andata all'università.

TOWARDS PRELIMINARY

Reading

8 Complete the gaps with sentences from a–f. There are two extra sentences.

A CHANGE FOR THE BETTER

I left university with a degree in Economics. ¹............ Even though the job was interesting and the salary was good, I felt something was missing from my life. After a few years, I gave up my job and went to work as a volunteer on an environmental project by the sea. It was hard work and I had no money but it was the best job I had ever done. ²............ When the winter came, the project ended.
Now, I work for an environmental organisation as an economist. ³............ I'm working for the country's future and making a difference to people's lives. I don't earn as much as before but I feel far more satisfied with life. Do I regret my change of career? ⁴............ If I hadn't spent those years at the bank, I would have been happier.

a I'd never been happier.
b I only wish I had found this job sooner.
c However, I ought to look for a new job.
d I managed to find a good job in a bank in a big city.
e Despite the money, I thought I'd better leave.
f I'm now living in the country and doing a useful job.

Writing

9 Read the email from your English-speaking friend, Ava. Then write your email to Ava using all your notes.

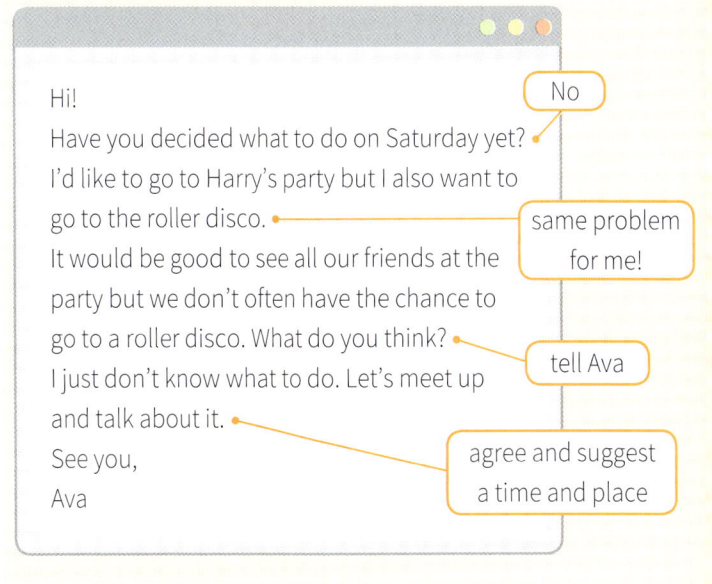

Hi!
Have you decided what to do on Saturday yet? • [No]
I'd like to go to Harry's party but I also want to go to the roller disco. • [same problem for me!]
It would be good to see all our friends at the party but we don't often have the chance to go to a roller disco. What do you think? • [tell Ava]
I just don't know what to do. Let's meet up and talk about it. • [agree and suggest a time and place]
See you,
Ava

9 Pure genius!

EXAM STRATEGIES
- PRELIMINARY: Speaking
- IGCSE: Speaking

SPEAKING SKILLS
- Describing objects

CHANGING LANGUAGE
- Literally!

LIFE SKILLS
- Planning and organising

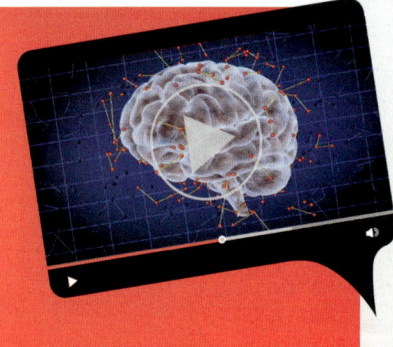

Learning goals

Grammar
- The passive: present and past simple
- Passive present perfect

Vocabulary
- Gadgets and creativity

WB pp. 212–219

LEAD IN

1 Look at the photos and discuss the questions.

1 Who are the three people in the pictures?
2 What special talents did each of them have?
3 What are their most famous works?

2 [2.25] Read, listen and watch. Why are scientists using new technology to investigate the human brain?

WHAT IS CREATIVITY?

Shakespeare's tragic plays, Mozart's sublime symphonies, Einstein's revolutionary theories – how did these creative geniuses create such magnificent and original works? What makes extraordinarily creative people different from the rest of us? Where do their special talents come from? Are their brains made differently from those of ordinary people, or do they perhaps work in different ways?

Recently neuroscientists started to investigate exactly where creativity comes from. Sophisticated new technology was used to monitor the electrical activity of the brain. They found that the brains of very creative people are in fact made differently. It seems that they are able to **access** the **unconscious mind** in ways that most of us can't. How do they do this?

The part of the human brain that's associated with creativity is called the **white matter** and is comprised of around 150,000 kilometres of connections called **neural networks**. Surprisingly, it was discovered that there is actually less white matter than average in very creative brains, not more. Scientists were intrigued by this and started to examine its effects. They found that creative brains weren't organised as tightly as other brains. Impulses therefore travel more slowly along the neural networks and they aren't forced to go in straight lines. They can travel in different directions and link ideas more effectively in the unconscious mind. Flashes of inspiration and new ideas (the Eureka moment) are produced in this way.

The good news is that scientists now believe that if we do certain mental exercises, we can all train our brains to do this and increase our creative potential. Maybe we can't all be William Shakespeare but we can improve our creative writing assignments!

Glossary
access: accedere
unconscious mind: mente inconscia
white matter: sostanza bianca
neural networks: reti neurali

PRACTICE

3 ▶ [2.25] Read, listen and watch again. Answer the questions.

1 What did scientists discover about the brains of creative people when they monitored brain activity?
2 What does the white matter in the brain consist of?
3 What difference does the amount of white matter have on the brain?
4 What is the Eureka moment?
5 How can we all increase our creative potential?

GRAMMAR GUIDE

The passive: Present and past simple

present simple passive	
Affirmative Their brains **are made** differently.	**Negative** They **aren't forced** to travel in straight lines.
Questions **Are** their brains **made** differently?	**Short answers** Yes, they **are**. No, they **aren't**.
past simple passive	
Affirmative It **was discovered** that there was less white matter.	**Negative** Creative brains **weren't organised** as tightly as ordinary brains.
Questions **Were** the results **changed by** the scientists?	**Short answers** Yes, they **were**. No, they **weren't**.

We use the passive to focus on the person or thing affected by the action. To show the person or thing doing the action we use *by*.

➡ **GRAMMAR REFERENCE** p. 122 **WB** pp. 212–213

4 Complete the sentences with the present simple passive of the verbs in brackets.

0 More e-books ....**are sold**.... (*sell*) nowadays.
1 Volkswagen cars .... (*build*) in Germany.
2 Italian .... (*speak*) in many parts of Argentina.
3 Many domestic crimes .... (*not / report*) to the police.
4 Alessi products .... (*design*) in Italy.
5 .... your earrings .... (*make*) of glass?
6 .... these French fries .... (*cook*) in olive oil?

5 PAIRWORK Rewrite the questions from the quiz using the present simple passive. Then answer the questions.

Italian Designers Quiz

0 Which two fashion designers use their initials D&G on their clothes?
   The initials D&G are used by which two famous fashion designers? (Dolce and Gabbana)
1 What does the company Poltrona Frau produce?
2 What animal symbol do they use on Ferrari cars?
3 What do they make in Murano, Veneto?
4 What does the company Fratelli Rossetti make?
5 What does Renzo Piano design?

6 Rewrite the sentences in the past simple passive. Use *by* if necessary.

0 Shakespeare wrote all of these poems and plays.
   All of these poems and plays were written by Shakespeare.
1 They invented electric light in the late 1800s.
2 Christopher Columbus didn't discover America.
3 They didn't find the lost diamonds.
4 Did Alexander Fleming discover penicillin?
5 Picasso painted *Guernica* in 1937.
6 Who designed the Eiffel Tower in Paris?

7 PAIRWORK Use the verbs below in the passive form to write five questions about the works of famous writers, artists and scientists. Ask your partner the questions.

- paint
- design
- discover
- build
- invent
- write

A Who was *The Last Supper* painted by?
B I think it was painted by Leonardo Da Vinci.

READING SKILLS

LEAD IN

8 PAIRWORK Discuss these questions.

1 Which inventions have had the most impact on people's lives in the last 50 years?
2 Which problems do we need solutions for in the next 50 years?

PRACTICE

9 [2.26] Read and listen to the text. Match the headings to the paragraphs.

1 ☐ Transforming polluted water into drinking water
2 ☐ Helping people to find lost items
3 ☐ Smart wound care

READING STRATEGY

Work on True / False / Doesn't say questions

In this type of task you have to decide if the statements correspond to the information in the reading text.

- Read and analyse the statement first. What does it mean? Remember you must match the overall meaning of the statement, not just keywords from it.
- Look for synonyms and antonyms of keywords from the statement in the text.
- Remember the statements are in the same order as the text. The part of the text which corresponds to statement 2 will be after the part about statement 1 and before the part about statement 3. Don't waste time looking for it anywhere else in the text!
- If the information in the text is the opposite of that in the statement, the answer is *false*.
- If the exact information from the statement isn't included in the text, the answer is *doesn't say*.

10 Read the text again and complete the table about the competition winners.

Name	Nationality	Idea
Anushka		sensor to analyse chronic wounds

Designing the future

The Google Science Fair is an online science competition for students between 13 and 18 years old from around the world. The judges look for ideas with the 'Wow!' factor. If you're passionate about science and engineering and can
5 **think outside the box**, your project could win! These are some of the lucky winners this year.

11 Read the text again and decide if the sentences are true (T), false (F) or doesn't say (DS).

1 The judges of the competition prefer surprising and unusual ideas. T F DS
2 Scientists discovered that serious wounds would get better more quickly if they were kept dry. T F DS
3 Anushka's invention helps doctors to evaluate whether a wound is improving without looking at it. T F DS
4 Two Brazilian students invented a system for cleaning dirty water with a handful of seeds. T F DS
5 The seeds decrease the amount of tiny animals in the water so that it becomes drinkable. T F DS
6 Older people can never remember where they put things. T F DS
7 Shriank's invention will help older people to find the medicine they need. T F DS

GRAMMAR GUIDE

The passive: Present perfect

Affirmative	Negative
It **has been shown** that chronic wounds need a wet environment to heal.	Chronic wounds **haven't been exposed** to the air.
Questions	**Short answers**
Has this **been proved** by science?	Yes, it **has**. No, it **hasn't**.

➡ **GRAMMAR REFERENCE** p. 122   **WB** p. 216

A Anushka (13) lives in Portland in the USA and loves chemistry. She wanted to find a solution for treating chronic wounds in hospitals. It has been shown that chronic **wounds** need a wet environment to heal. However, if the cotton **dressings** on wounds are changed too often, the wounds dry and the healing process is interrupted. This means that they can take a very long time to **heal**, which increases the risk of serious infection. Anushka created a unique sensor to help doctors analyse the state of a wound under the bandage without removing it. Thanks to her solution, chronic wounds haven't been exposed to the air unnecessarily and have therefore healed more quickly.

B A revolutionary new system for cleaning polluted water has been developed by Letícia Pereira de Souza, 18, and João Gabriel Stefani Antunes, 15, both from Brazil. In this process the seeds of a common tropical plant, *Moringa oleifera*, were placed in dirty water. The **seeds** make the organic materials in dirty water **stick together**, so they're easier to filter out. They also reduce the quantity of microorganisms, making the water safe to drink. It's a simple and cheap solution to the problem of water pollution in poor communities around the world.

C In Bangalore, India, Shriank (16) noticed that as we get older we often forget where we put things. This is particularly stressful and difficult for older people with conditions like Alzheimer's. Shriank decided to create a portable **device** to track objects in the home. Patients put on the device and use an app on their smartphone to find where their things have been left. Shriank hopes his invention will help improve the quality of life for people with dementia.

Glossary

think outside the box : pensare in modo innovativo
wounds : ferite
dressings : bende
heal : guarire
seeds : semi
stick together : coagulare
device : dispositivo

12 Rewrite the sentences using the present perfect passive form.

0 Someone has stolen my bike. **My bike has been stolen.**
1 Scientists have discovered a new planet.
2 An American millionaire has bought that house.
3 Someone has hacked my email account.
4 No one has seen the boy since last Friday.
5 Politicians haven't told us anything about the referendum.
6 Has anyone heard anything about the exam date?

13 **Critical thinking** What do you think about the inventions in the text? Discuss the questions in pairs.

1 Which is the most useful in your opinion? Why?
2 Which invention surprises you the most?
3 If you could solve one problem in the world, what would it be?

WRITING SKILLS

LEAD IN

14 PAIRWORK In which of these situations would you write a formal letter / email?

1 to say thank you to your grandparents for a present
2 to complain about something
3 to tell your friend about your holiday
4 to apply for a job
5 to present a project for a competition
6 to get in contact with a classmate you haven't seen for a year

PRACTICE

15 PAIRWORK What do you think are some of the different characteristics of informal (I) and formal (F) writing? Tick (✓) I or F.

1 contracted verb forms I F
2 passive verb forms I F
3 first person pronouns I F
4 active verb forms I F
5 slang and colloquial vocabulary I F
6 contractions I F
7 sophisticated vocabulary I F

WRITING STRATEGY

Write a formal letter / email

We use formal letters / emails to make an official request, application or complaint in writing. They contain information relevant to the reason for writing, but not personal information. This type of text includes:
- a reason for writing
- a request for something
- an invitation to the reader to reply
- formal language
- full forms, not contractions

See **WRITING EXPANSION** page 258

Unit 9   91

VOCABULARY

Gadgets and creativity

Made in Italy

Alessi is a world-famous Italian design company that produces high-quality and unusual household objects and kitchen utensils. It was founded in 1921 by Giovanni Alessi in Valle Strona near Lake Orta in the Italian Alps. In the 1950s the company began to specialise in items made of chrome and silver. The idea was to produce carefully designed modern items that looked hand-made but were made with the help of machines.

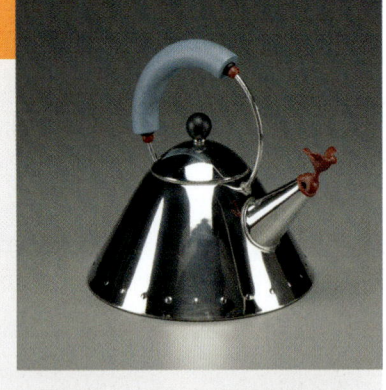

Since the 1970s Alessi has been associated with the concept of 'designer' objects, everyday objects which have been transformed into works of art by unusual and beautiful product designs. During the 1980s and 1990s the company collaborated with famous international designers like Achille Castiglioni, Aldo Rossi, Michael Graves and Philippe Starck to produce a range of iconic homeware products – kettles, coffee makers, lemon juicers, corkscrews. Many of these beautiful Alessi objects have since become design classics.

16 Read the text and underline the names of the gadgets in the photos.

17 What are the gadgets in the photos used for?

18 Read and decide if the sentences are true (T) or false (F). Correct the false ones.

1. Alessi is a company which makes things for the home. T F
2. All of their products are made by hand. T F
3. Designer objects are unusual versions of everyday objects. T F
4. All the designers who have worked with Alessi are Italian. T F
5. Many of Alessi's product designs are considered to be the best ever. T F

19 Now look at the names of some other household objects. What are they used for? Check your answers in a dictionary.

1. tin opener
2. salt and pepper mills
3. cutlery (knives, forks, spoons)
4. teapot
5. cheese grater
6. colander

20 Match the verbs to the nouns they describe.

1. designed by   a films
2. invented by   b statues
3. written by   c clothes
4. directed by   d skyscrapers
5. painted by   e machines
6. sculpted by   f pictures
7. built by   g books

21 Complete the sentences with words from exercise 20.

1. The telephone was .... Antonio Meucci.
2. *The Last Supper* was .... Leonardo da Vinci.
3. *Star Wars* films were .... George Lucas.
4. The statue of David in Florence was .... by Michelangelo Buonarotti.
5. *Macbeth* was .... William Shakespeare.
6. The MAXXI art gallery in Rome was .... Zaha Hadid.

22 How many other famous things were made, invented or designed in Italy? Make a word web for Italian design using the words from exercise 20, the headings below, and your examples.

- clothes
- cars
- perfume
- food
- leather goods

ITALIAN DESIGN — CLOTHES — designed by D&G
ITALIAN DESIGN — CARS — built by Ferrari

23 SPEAKING Choose a different country. How many other famous things can you think of that were made, invented or designed there? Make a list then tell your partner.

See **VOCABULARY EXTENSION** page 268

92 Unit 9

SPEAKING SKILLS

Describing objects

24 [2.27] Listen and watch the video. What do Anna and Luke need to buy?

key expressions	
questions	answers
What is that?	It's a sort of … / It's sort of a …
What's it used for / made of?	It's used for / made of …
How does it work?	It works with / by …
Does it look like a / an …?	Yes, it does. / No, it doesn't.
Are they / Is it big / small?	They're about the same size as a / an …

25 [2.27] Listen and watch again. Which of these things does Luke mention as a present for their friend?

1 a drawing book   2 a graphic tablet   3 an iPad   4 laptop

SPEAKING STRATEGY

Paraphrasing

When you can't remember the correct English word for something, you can explain the concept in a few words instead. This is called *paraphrasing*. Here are some useful expressions to help you do this.

- I don't remember the name …
- It's got a thing like a … that you use to …
- There's a sort of … / It's sort of a …
- It's like / looks like a …

PRELIMINARY | IGCSE

26 [2.27] Listen and watch again. How many times do you hear each of the expressions from the strategy box?

27 PAIRWORK Read the situation. Then act out the dialogue.

Situation: You and your classmates want to buy a present for your favourite teacher who is leaving your school to have a baby.
Student A: Choose one of the things from the list below. Suggest it to your partner and describe it.
- baby monitor
- baby bottle warmer
- baby organiser bag

Student B: You don't know what this thing is. Ask questions to find out what it's like and what it does.

CHANGING LANGUAGE

Literally!

28 Look at the adverbs and choose the words used for emphasis.

1 very   4 so
2 really   5 obviously
3 literally   6 fortunately

29 Watch the video and check your answer to question 28.

30 Watch again and choose the correct option.

1 The adverb *literally has / hasn't* got more than one meaning.
2 The adverb *literally* has become *more / less* popular in recent years.
3 The most common use of *literally is / isn't* for emphasis.
4 *Young / Old* people use the word *literally* most.

CORPUS

Corpus data can track not only how frequently a word is used but also how a word is used. *Literally* can mean 'using the real or original meaning of a word or phrase' but it is more commonly used today for emphasis especially by young people: *This information has left me literally speechless!*

LISTENING SKILLS

LEAD IN

31 PAIRWORK Look at the photos of some objects from the past that are not used now. Answer the questions.

1. When do you think each gadget was used?
2. Which ones were used for the same function?
3. How do you think each one worked?

PRACTICE

32 [2.28] Listen to a radio interview. Which two obsolete gadgets from the photos in exercise 31 are mentioned?

LISTENING STRATEGY

Select correct information

In this type of task you have to choose two correct options from a list of possibilities. Remember to:
- read the question and options carefully before you listen
- underline the keywords in the question to identify the context
- note that the options in the question are not in the same order as the recording
- some of the options may occur in other contexts in the recording – be careful!
- listen for the keywords from the question to locate the correct context
- choose two options from the list

33 [2.28] Listen to the interview again. Which two of the following were steps in the process to use the first gadget?

1. Women went to the hairdresser's.
2. Hairdressers styled their hair and then put the hoods on.
3. Hot air filled the hood.
4. They used curlers to style their hair.
5. They had to keep the hoods on all day.

34 [2.28] Listen again and match each feature of the second gadget to its function. There are two extra functions.

1. ☐ cassette tape
2. ☐ lid
3. ☐ record button
4. ☐ microphone
5. ☐ rewind button

a. it plays back the recording
b. it contains the audio tracks
c. it amplifies the sound
d. it pushes the tape into position
e. it goes back to the beginning of the recording
f. it records audio
g. it starts the recording process

35 [2.28] Listen again and answer the questions.

1. When was the first gadget used?
2. Why did women need this gadget in those days?
3. How long did the gadget take to complete the process?
4. When was the second gadget used?
5. Where could you use it?
6. What was the quality of the audio recordings it produced?

36 Critical thinking Discuss the questions in pairs.

1. What gadgets or utensils from the past can you think of that have become obsolete in our time?
2. Why do people use gadgets?
3. Why do they become obsolete?

LIFE SKILLS

Planning and organising

MY OWN PROJECT

I had always wanted to do something for UNICEF. My friends and I had heard terrible stories of children in poverty in Sudan who desperately needed help. We wanted to support UNICEF's vital project to bring clean drinking water to remote communities
5 there. We decided we would walk along Hadrian's Wall in the north of England to raise money for the charity. We sent a message out on Facebook and 20 other friends decided to join us.

Hadrian's Wall was built by the Romans during the reign of the emperor Hadrian, and marked the northern limit of the
10 Roman Empire. We did some research and found out that it's 117 kilometres long. We calculated that we could walk it in five days, and decided to do it during the summer holidays. We hoped to raise at least £8,000 for UNICEF. Then we began planning the event and deciding who should
15 do what.

We made a **to-do list** and the first priority on it was to **get sponsorship**. We knew we would need to look further than just family and friends, so we set up a blog and spread the word on social media. After that we
20 **approached** a well-known bottled water company and they offered us £4,000 if we could **raise** the other £4,000.

Next, we had to organise the trip, and we had to do it cheaply. We didn't want to **waste** any of the
25 money which could go to UNICEF. So we travelled by bus to the start of our route at the eastern end of the wall, and we stayed in very cheap hostels along the way, which we booked in advance to get the best prices.

We kept posting on our blog during the trip, and got more and more
30 supporters as we went along. When we finally reached the Solway Firth at the western end of the wall, we had raised over £7,000! Altogether we raised £11,000 for UNICEF, which was a fantastic success. Now there is a new water treatment plant in Sudan which wouldn't be there if we hadn't done our sponsored walk.

Glossary

to-do list : elenco di cose da fare
get sponsorship : trovare uno sponsor
approached : abbiamo contattato
raise : raccogliere
waste : sprecare

LEAD IN

37 PAIRWORK Which aspects of your life can planning and organising things in advance help you with?

1 enjoying an experience
2 having the right equipment
3 making new friends

PRACTICE

38 PAIRWORK Read the magazine article and answer the questions.

1 What were the writer's reasons for organising this event?
2 How long did the friends think the walk would take?
3 Which type of charity did they plan to help?
4 How much money did they want to raise?
5 Write two ways they planned to save money on the trip.
6 How much money did they raise in the end?

LIFE STRATEGY

Tips for planning and organising

- Decide what you are going to do and why.
- Write down clear objectives.
- Decide what you'll need to do to achieve your objectives.
- Break the whole job down into smaller tasks.
- Plan a schedule showing the order in which you need to do the tasks.
- Set deadlines for when you need to complete each task.
- Decide who is responsible for each task.
- Decide how much money you need and how you will spend it.
- Decide on an alternative plan if something goes wrong.

39 TASK In pairs, choose one of the events below. Plan your event following the steps in the tips. Explain your plan to another pair.

- preparing a party with food and drink for 20 people
- creating a blog for a group project
- setting up a sponsored swim for a charity

CITIZENSHIP AND COMPETENCY SKILLS Planning and prioritising

Unit 9   95

10 In the news

EXAM STRATEGIES
- PRELIMINARY: Reading, Listening and Academic
- IGCSE: Reading, Listening and Academic
- IELTS: Academic

SPEAKING SKILLS
- Gossiping

ACADEMIC SKILLS
- Planning and writing in paragraphs

Learning goals
Grammar
- Reported speech
- *say* and *tell*

Vocabulary
- Media verbs

Glossary
pretend : fingono
click-baiting : acchiappa-click
pamphlets : opuscoli
rumours : pettegolezzi

WB pp. 220–229

LEAD IN

1 PAIRWORK Look at the photos below and read the headlines. Discuss the questions.

1. Who are the people in the photos? What are they famous for?
2. Why are these headlines unusual?
3. Do you think these two stories are true? Why / Why not?

2 [2.29] Read, listen and watch. What is *fake news*?

WHAT IS FAKE NEWS?

Fake news is something we've been hearing a lot about in the media, but what does it mean? Fake news stories are stories published online that are completely invented, but that writers **pretend** are true. It's also sometimes used to refer to websites that publish very distorted or exaggerated information. These sites often use sensational headlines, so that we are curious about the story and
5 click on a particular web page. This is known as **click-baiting**. Every time we do this, website owners earn money from advertisers – this can often be thousands of pounds. Fake news can be very dangerous because it is not always easy to tell what is fake news and what isn't. In addition, a lot of people in the public eye can use the claim of fake news to say that real news isn't true.
But is fake news a new phenomenon? Historian Graham Brown told us it wasn't new. He explained that
10 his team were doing research into the first printed news **pamphlets**, which appeared in the fifteenth century. He said that actually fake news had been around for centuries. In the past, writers frequently said that the stories they wrote were true, when in fact they were based on **rumours** – and no one ever checked the facts! It wasn't until the first real newspapers were published in the seventeenth century that regulations were gradually introduced and news reporting became more reliable.
15 So why has fake news become such a problem now? Well, this is mainly because fake news stories circulate on the internet, where these regulations don't apply. The good news is that internet regulators have recognised the problem and are starting to design solutions. Facebook promised that it would label suspicious stories in future with an alert that says, 'Disputed by fact-checkers', and browsers like Google Chrome said they were going to add a similar feature to their search engines.

DAILY NEWS

Pope Francis shocks world, endorses Donald Trump as president

David Bowie starred in Spice Oddity in Sussex curry restaurant

PRACTICE

3 ▶ [2.29] Read, listen and watch again. Answer the questions.

1 What is the usual aim of fake news stories online?
2 What is *click-baiting*?
3 When did the first printed news pamphlets appear?
4 Why did news reporting became more reliable after the seventeenth century?
5 Why has fake news become a problem again now?
6 How will Facebook help with the problem?

GRAMMAR GUIDE

Reported speech: Statements

direct speech	reported speech
Present simple 'It **isn't** a new phenomenon.'	**Past simple** He told us it **wasn't** a new phenomenon.
Present continuous 'We**'re doing** research.'	**Past continuous** He explained that his team **were doing** research.
Past simple / Present perfect 'Actually fake news **has been** around for centuries.'	**Past perfect** He said that actually fake news **had been** around for centuries.
will / won't 'We **will label** suspicious stories.'	**would / wouldn't** Facebook promised that it **would label** suspicious stories.
be going to 'We**'re going to add** a similar feature.'	**was / were going to** Google Chrome said they **were going to add** a similar feature.

➡ GRAMMAR REFERENCE p. 122   WB pp. 220–221

4 Transform these sentences into reported speech. Use the verb *said*.

0 Maria: I don't want to go.
   Maria said that she didn't want to go.
1 Rob: My phone isn't working!
2 The boys: We've lost the keys.
3 Megan: I'll be home about 10 o'clock.
4 Mr Heaton: I'm going to give you a maths test.
5 Mum: That was a very stupid thing to do!

5 Rewrite the paragraph as a short dialogue using direct speech.

> Tamsin met her friend Amy at the shopping mall and asked her how she was. Amy said she was fine and that she was shopping with her mum. Tamsin said she had come with her sister, but that now her sister was trying on shoes in another shop. Amy said she was going to look for a new dress for Ben's party on Saturday. Tamsin said Ben hadn't invited her to his party and she was a bit upset. Amy replied that Ben had probably just forgotten, and that she would ask him to call Tamsin to invite her.
>
> Tamsin Hi, Amy, how are you?
> Amy   Hi, Tamsin. I'm fine thanks. I'm …

GRAMMAR GUIDE

Reported speech: *say* and *tell*

He **told us** (that) it wasn't a new phenomenon.
He **said** (that) fake news had been around for centuries.
They **said to me** (that) they wanted to sell the house.

Look!: *say* and *tell* are both used in reported speech.
Tell is followed by a direct object:
- you say something (to someone)
- you tell someone something

➡ GRAMMAR REFERENCE p. 123   WB p. 221

6 Report these sentences using *say* or *tell*.

0 Ben: Mrs Hall, I haven't done my homework.
   Ben told Mrs Hall that he hadn't done his homework.
1 Matt: I'm still not sure what I'm doing on Saturday.
2 Louise: My head hurts and I've got a sore throat, doctor.
3 Teacher: Your results weren't good, Emma.
4 Diane: Dad, I've lost my phone!
5 News reader: The price of petrol is falling fast.
6 Simon: I saw Rob but he didn't see me.

7 SPEAKING Tell you partner three things about you that are true, and three things that are false. Ask him / her to report which things he / she thinks are true or false and why.

Unit 10   97

READING SKILLS

LEAD IN

8 PAIRWORK Discuss these questions.

1. Do you sometimes read a newspaper? Which one?
2. Do you think newspapers should print anything they want?
3. How much evidence do you think they should have before they print a story?
4. Do you believe what you read in the newspapers?

PRACTICE

9 [2.30] Read and listen to the text. What is *freedom of the press*?

READING STRATEGY

Distinguish between facts and opinions

A *fact* is something that you know is true. You can prove it or check to find out if it's true. An *opinion* is something you think, or believe, is true. You can't prove it or check it easily.

The language in a text can help us decide whether a statement is a fact or an opinion.

Facts
The results of the survey have shown …
According to statistics …
Researchers have recently discovered …

Opinions
Advertisers believe that …
In the doctor's view …
Many experts suspect that …

PRELIMINARY | IGCSE

10 Look at three statements from the text. Is any proof given to support them? Are they facts or opinions?

1. 99% of British people say they believe in the freedom of the press.
2. It's true that Britain's newspapers can be provocative and abusive.
3. The government's new legislation will force newspapers to agree to a list of regulations.
4. Britain's position on the Index is not high, but with the passing of this legislation it would be even lower.

11 **Critical thinking** Discuss these questions.

1. What is the writer's opinion about the British press?
2. Are his arguments convincing? Why / Why not?
3. Do you think the press should be more regulated?

FREEDOM OF THE PRESS
– but how free is free?

by Jack Turner

According to a recent survey, when British people were asked, 'Do you believe in the freedom of the press?,' 99% answered, 'Yes.' The concept of *free speech* is absolutely fundamental to our national identity. But now, after more than 300 years of press freedom, we believe the British press is in danger of losing that basic *right*.

It's true that Britain's newspapers can be provocative and abusive. One very obvious case of abuse was the *phone tapping* scandal in 2006-2007, when reporters from a national newspaper listened to the mobile phones of famous people and then published details of private conversations they had heard. The journalists involved were later imprisoned.

GRAMMAR GUIDE

Reported speech: Questions and commands

direct speech	reported speech
questions	
'Do **you believe** in the freedom of the press?'	We asked them if / whether **they believed** in the freedom of the press.
'How **can you** help?'	They asked us how **we could** help.

In reported questions the word order is the same as affirmative statements. We don't use auxiliary verbs. With *yes* or *no* questions we use *if* or *whether*.

direct speech	reported speech
commands	
'**Sign** my petition.'	He told me **to sign** his petition.
'**Don't waste** time!'	He told me **not to waste** time.

In reported commands we use *ask / tell* + direct object + infinitive without *to*.

→ **GRAMMAR REFERENCE** p. 123   **WB** p. 224

Changes in reported speech

- *now* → *then*
- *today, this morning* → *that day, that morning*
- *tomorrow, next week* → *the next day, the next week*
- *yesterday, last week, two days ago* → *the day before, the week before, two days before*
- *here* → *there*   • *in this place* → *in that place*

15 However, the majority of serious newspapers do not behave like this. It's also true that our long tradition of free speech in the United
20 Kingdom has played a vital role in shaping our history, protecting our democracy and keeping our country relatively free from corruption.

We believe this freedom is now under attack. The government's
25 new legislation will force newspapers to agree to a list of regulations about what they can or cannot publish. It says that there will be huge **fines** for those who refuse to conform. The legislation will force newspapers to pay **damages** if they lose a case in court and, incredibly, to pay the legal costs of the losing side even if their
30 reports are proved to be true! This will make newspapers hesitate to publish controversial stories that could lead to legal action, so the public won't get to know about corruption, scandals or abuses of power.

The Press Index **claims** that a country is a true democracy if it has
35 an independent media, and ranks countries according to the freedom of their press. Britain's position on the Press Index is not high, but with the passing of this legislation it would be even lower.

How can you help? If you want to defend your right to read a news website like this one, which refuses to be censored by regulators,
40 sign our online petition against this legislation here.

"I don't think that newspapers should be regulated by the state. Freedom of speech is important in a democracy."
Stacey156

"In my view people's private lives should be protected, whether they're famous or not. The press shouldn't be allowed to publish stories about those things. We need more regulation."
White Pony, Wiltshire

Glossary

free speech : libertà di parola
right : diritto
phone tapping : intercettazioni telefoniche
fines : multe
damages : danni
claims : sostiene

12 Report these questions and commands. Make any other changes necessary.

0 Helen: When are the students arriving?
  Helen asked me when the students were arriving.
1 Waiter: Do you want coffee or tea?
2 Sam: Where did you work in the USA last year?
3 Teacher: Have you all finished the exercise?
4 Mum: Will you go to the supermarket for me this morning?
5 Mum: Give me that knife!
6 Greg: Don't tell my brother about the phone call.
7 Dan: Are we going to the cinema next week?
8 Dad: Do you like it here, kids?

WRITING SKILLS

LEAD IN

13 PAIRWORK Discuss these questions.

1 Have you read magazines like *OK!* and *Hello!*?
2 What sort of articles do they contain?
3 Which people might appear in articles in them?

PRACTICE

14 PAIRWORK What is the difference between a face-to-face interview and a reported interview? Write FI or RI next to the characteristics.

1 .... direct statements, questions
2 .... reported statements, questions
3 .... a lot of first person pronouns
4 .... a lot of third person pronouns

WRITING STRATEGY

Write a magazine report

Magazines often include reports of interviews their writers have done with famous celebrities. They are not usually written in direct speech but report what the person was asked and said. This type of report includes:
- an eye-catching or humorous headline
- reported questions and answers
- chatty, informal language
- information about the interviewees, their career and personal life

➡ See **WRITING EXPANSION** page 259

Unit 10   99

VOCABULARY

Media verbs

15 How do you prefer to get your news? Do the media quiz below to find out.

THE NEWS QUIZ

1 Which of these activities do you prefer doing?
   A chatting online   B listening to music
   C watching TV   D reading

2 Which of these news sources do you use regularly?
   A Twitter   B a news website
   C a TV or radio news D a newspaper
     programme

3 Which of these news sources do you never / rarely use?
   A a newspaper   B a radio news programme
   C news website   D a TV news programme

4 Which of these media do you think publishes or broadcasts the most reliable news?
   A social media   B national news websites
   C TV news programmes D national newspapers

5 Which of these media do you think is the most likely to publish or broadcast fake news?
   A TV news programmes B local news websites
   C national news websites D Twitter

6 How would you pass on information about something you've seen in the news to your friends?
   A post about it on social   B tweet about it
     media
   C send a text about it   D print an article about it

ANSWERS

Mostly As – you are a real digital native and you prefer to get all of your information online.

Mostly Bs – you like a balance of information sources and use all those available to you.

Mostly Cs – you don't like reading much and prefer to get your information through your ears and eyes!

Mostly Ds – you are an old-fashioned sort of person and rely on the printed word for your information.

16 Find five of the verbs below in the quiz. Then match the verbs to the types of media. Some verbs are used more than once.

broadcast ▪ post ▪ print ▪ transmit ▪
show ▪ publish ▪ tweet ▪ circulate

Newspapers
....
....

Radio news
....
....

TV news
....
....

News websites
....
....

Social media
....
....

Types of media

17 Match the definitions to the verbs below.

☐ transmit   ☐ circulate   ☐ broadcast
☐ post   ☐ tweet   ☐ publish

a to send something via a television or radio signal for others to watch / listen to
b to send something via a radio signal for others to listen to
c to send a very short comment on Twitter
d to publish an article online, or a message on a social media site
e to print an article in a newspaper or a magazine
f to send out information to as wide a group of people on social media as possible

18 Complete the sentences with the correct verb from exercise 16.

1 Last night the BBC .... a live talk show about Brexit.
2 Donald Trump likes to .... his opinions to the voters via Twitter.
3 When was *The Times* newspaper first .... ?
4 My friends .... a lot of photos of my birthday party on Instagram.
5 This fake news article was .... to more than 500,000 readers by an American news site.
6 This news programme .... how the refugee crisis is getting worse in Europe.
7 Radio 2 .... a lot of discussion programmes about European politics.

See **VOCABULARY EXTENSION** page 269

SPEAKING SKILLS

Gossiping

19 PAIRWORK Discuss these questions.

1 What is the difference between gossip and just talking about things that happened?
2 What could be some of the negative consequences of gossip?

20 [2.31] Listen and watch the video. What event is Anna talking about? When was it?

key expressions	
☐ You'll never guess what happened!	☐ Apparently …
☐ I shouldn't really tell you this but …	☐ I heard that …
	☐ According to (name) …

21 [2.31] Listen and watch again and tick (✓) the key expressions you hear.

SPEAKING STRATEGY

Change the subject

When we don't want to carry on with a conversation, we can use various strategies to change the subject.
- Ask a question: **By the way,** did you go to Ellie's after, …
- Divert attention: **Speaking of** Tanya, …
- Give a compliment: **I'm really impressed that** …

22 [2.31] Listen and watch again. Complete the sentences in the expressions from the strategy box.

23 PAIRWORK Read the situation. Take turn to act out the dialogue.

Student A: You've just heard that Matteo is going to be captain of the school football team, but everyone thought Luca would become captain. Another student told you that Matteo's uncle paid for the team's new football shirts. Use the key expressions to tell student B this gossip.

Student B: You're a friend of both Matteo and Luca and you don't want to gossip about them. Use the strategy box above to try and change the subject.

SOUNDS ENGLISH

The glottal stop /ʔ/

24 [2.32] **PAIRWORK** Listen to a British English speaker and a learner of English say these two words. Discuss the differences.

mountain   button

SOUND STRATEGY

In informal and fast speech the glottal stop /ʔ/ often replaces the /t/ sound. It is made by closing the back of the throat to stop the air. It often replaces /t/ in these situations:
- before an unstressed /n/ sound, bu**tt**on
- at the end of a statement in an unstressed syllable, I can'**t**
- before a pause, If you find i**t**, call me
- before an unstressed consonant, Le**t** me know

25 [2.33] Listen and circle the pronunciation with the glottal stop /ʔ/ in each pair.

1 A fountain   B fountain
2 A important   B important
3 A certain   B certain
4 A football   B football

26 [2.34] Listen to these statements. Circle any /t/ sound which is replaced with a glottal stop /ʔ/.

1 What can Sam do?
2 Patrick doesn't remember you.
3 Are you certain?
4 Stop it!
5 Tim and Kurt must stop fighting.

27 [2.35] **GAME** Now listen again and repeat the sentences from exercise 26 as fast as you can.

Unit 10   101

LISTENING SKILLS

LEAD IN

28 PAIRWORK Look at the pictures and answer the questions.

1. Where are the people?
2. What do you think they're discussing?
3. What do you think their relationship is? Why?

PRACTICE

29 [2.36] Listen to two conversations. What does the boy have to do?

30 [2.36] Listen again and decide if the sentences are true (T) or false (F). Correct the false ones.

1. Martin has been reading articles on a lot of online news sites. T F
2. There is a list of recommended news sites on a school blog. T F
3. The project had to be ready by last Monday. T F
4. The project should be less than 1,000 words. T F
5. Martin's plan is to look for some information on Google. T F
6. His mum thinks this is a good way to do the project. T F

LISTENING STRATEGY

Identify relationships between speakers

Understanding the relationship between speakers can help you learn more about their opinions and attitudes. Clues in their choice of language and tone of voice give you information about these things. For each speaker listen carefully to:

- the question forms they use (formal or informal questions forms, use of imperatives)
- the type of vocabulary used (everyday vocabulary and slang, or more formal words)
- the use of names / titles (*Mr / Mrs / sir / madam / miss*) are only used in formal relationships
- the tone of voice (people are more polite and controlled in formal relationships)

PRELIMINARY | IGCSE

31 [2.36] Listen again. Choose the correct option.

1. The woman in conversation 1 is Martin's:
   A mother   B sister   C teacher
2. Martin's attitude in conversation 1 is:
   A disinterested and rude
   B respectful but evasive
   C interested and enthusiastic
3. At the end of conversation 1 the woman feels:
   A pleased with Martin
   B a bit irritated with Martin
   C angry with Martin
4. The woman in conversation 2 is Martin's:
   A mother   B sister   C teacher
5. Martin's attitude in conversation 2 is:
   A disinterested and rude
   B respectful but evasive
   C interested and enthusiastic
6. At the end of conversation 2 the woman feels:
   A pleased with Martin
   B a bit irritated with Martin
   C angry with Martin

32 Match the points from the strategy box 1–5 to the examples from the recording a–e.

1. ☐ formal question forms
2. ☐ imperatives
3. ☐ everyday vocabulary or slang
4. ☐ names / titles
5. ☐ informal questions

a. I'll get the info I need.
b. Could you suggest any?
c. I'm sorry, miss.
d. Put that Xbox away!
e. What? What project?

33 Critical thinking Discuss the questions in groups.

1. Which people would you say you have formal relationships with?
2. How is your behaviour different with them than with your friends and family?
3. What are some of the ways people show respect in formal relationships in your language, that are not used in English?

Unit 10

ACADEMIC SKILLS

Planning and writing in paragraphs

LEAD IN

34 Look at the two texts. Answer the questions.

1. Which of these two texts do you find easier to read?
2. Which features does text A have that text B doesn't have?

Text A

These days, more and more people are choosing to go to university. While some people think that the only purpose of a university education is to improve job prospects, others believe that society and the individual benefit in much broader ways.

It is certainly true that one of the main reasons for going to university is to get a better job later. The majority of people want to improve their future career prospects and attending university is one of the best ways to do this. It gives you qualifications and develops important skills and therefore makes you more attractive to employers.

However, there are other benefits too. Firstly, the independence of living away from home, which helps students develop better social skills and become more independent ...

Text B

A lot of young people go to university now so they can get a better job. University can help you get a better job and learn some life skills like being independent and most people want to have these so that's why they go. You can also get more qualifications if you go to university. You need these to find a job.

PRACTICE

35 Match the words and expressions 1–4 from text A to the features of a good paragraph a–d.

1. ☐ firstly
2. ☐ however
3. ☐ therefore
4. ☐ these days

a. a linker of contrast
b. a linker showing a result
c. a sequencer
d. a time expression

ACADEMIC STRATEGY

Writing in paragraphs helps make your text easier to read and understand. Paragraphs can break down a long text into shorter, more memorable chunks and help you to organise the points in an argument, or the events in a narrative, in a logical order. The structure of a well-written paragraph is usually:

- a topic sentence – this comes at the beginning and states what the paragraph will be about
- supporting sentences – explain the ideas in the topic sentence and provide reasons, examples, facts, etc. to support the ideas
- a concluding sentence (optional) – signals the end of the paragraph and paraphrases the topic sentence

PRELIMINARY | IGCSE | IELTS

36 Read the paragraph on the right. Answer the questions.

1. Underline the topic sentence.
2. Find two supporting sentences.
3. What information follows and expands on the supporting sentences?
4. Underline the concluding sentence.
5. What summarising expression introduces it?

Studying Abroad

Studying abroad has two main benefits. Firstly, people who study abroad can get a better job when they return to their home country. This is because their qualifications and experience mean that they tend to get jobs that are higher paid, and they can also gain promotion quickly. Another advantage of studying abroad is the independence students can gain. For example, students have to cope with the challenges of living alone and meeting new people from different cultures. As a consequence, they will become more confident in their life and in their relationships with others. All in all, it is clear that studying abroad is a beneficial experience.

37 WRITING Read the statement below. Make a plan for a paragraph on this topic. Use the strategy box to help you. Then write your paragraph.

Some people think children in secondary school should study international news as part of the curriculum.

Unit 10   103

REVISE AND ROUND UP

1 Match the beginnings and ends of the sentences. Then complete them using the past simple passive form of the verb in brackets and *by*.

0 [i] *I promessi sposi* (*write*)
1 [ ] The dome of Florence Cathedral (*build*)
2 [ ] The *Mona Lisa* (*paint*)
3 [ ] *Madame Butterfly* (*compose*)
4 [ ] The most famous Italian bank (*establish*)
5 [ ] The first radio signal (*send*)
6 [ ] The Sistine Chapel (*paint / decorate*)
7 [ ] The electric battery (*invent*)
8 [ ] The first nuclear reactor (*create*)

a Guglielmo Marconi.
b Enrico Fermi.
c Michelangelo Buonarroti.
d Alessandro Volta.
e Filippo Brunelleschi.
f Giovanni Medici.
g Giacomo Puccini.
h Leonardo da Vinci.
i Alessandro Manzoni.

I promessi sposi **was written by** Alessandro Manzoni.

2 Active or passive? Complete the text with the correct past form of the verbs in brackets.

Amazon ⁰ *was created* (*create*) in the early 1990s by a young American called Jeff Bezos. His idea was that people could buy books directly from an online web site, instead of going to a bookshop. Users ¹ .... (*guide*) round the web site by Amazon's sophisticated but user-friendly search engine. They ² .... (*select*) their books, ³ .... (*order*) them and ⁴ .... (*pay*) for them online. This meant no actual shops ⁵ .... (*need*), so costs ⁶ .... (*keep*) very low. All the books ⁷ .... (*store*) in a central warehouse and posted out to customers as soon as they ⁸ .... (*order*). Amazon's new business model ⁹ .... (*cause*) a revolution in retail and ¹⁰ .... (*copy*) very quickly by many other companies. Online shopping was born!

3 Rewrite these sentences using the passive form.

0 Someone has given me a cheque for £500!
   A cheque for £500 has been given to me!
1 They've built thousands of cars in that factory.
2 We've caused a lot of problems by ignoring the scientists' advice.
3 Doctors have discovered a new drug for Alzheimer's.
4 No one has seen our cat since last Sunday.
5 Our teacher hasn't told us anything about the test.
6 Has anyone heard anything about the wedding?
7 The police have closed this road to traffic.
8 A famous film star has bought that yacht.

4 Complete the text with the correct passive form of the verbs below.

tell ▪ see ▪ choose ▪ train ▪ give ▪ ~~stick~~ ▪ announce ▪ change ▪ discover ▪ know

Her album ⁰ *has been stuck* at No. 1 in the classical charts for five weeks and her face ¹ .... on every chat show on TV recently. Carly Stevens is only 15 years old but already she's an opera super star and ² .... in Europe as the new Maria Callas. Over 1 million copies of her album *Cantata* ³ .... Carly told us, 'When it ⁴ .... that *Cantata* had sold a million copies, I didn't know whether to laugh or cry! I ⁵ .... that it's the fastest-selling album by a new opera singer in 30 years!'
At the age of ten Carly ⁶ .... to sing in the prestigious choir at Wells cathedral. During a performance there she ⁷ .... by the famous opera impresario, Giovanni Bellini. He sent Carly to Italy where she ⁸ .... by the best teachers for a career in classical music. 'My life ⁹ .... forever by meeting Maestro Bellini', she admits, 'But I'm so very lucky to ¹⁰ .... this chance.'

5 Transform these sentences into reported speech. Use the verb *said*.

0 Jennifer: I never eat chocolate.
   Jennifer said that she never ate chocolate.
1 The girls: We're having a party!
2 Mum: I can't believe it!
3 Policeman: I'm going to ask you a few questions.
4 Sally: I've just seen Lisa and Mark.
5 Dad: I've been cooking the Christmas dinner all day!

6 Rewrite these sentences as direct speech.

0 We said that we didn't know London very well.
'We don't know London very well.'
1 Helen said that if we needed help we could text her.
2 John said that he was late because he'd missed the bus.
3 Tess said that she was going to come to visit us in our new flat.
4 My grandparents said they were having a wonderful time in Las Vegas.
5 The children said that they were very hungry.
6 Dad said he would be back by 7 o'clock.
7 Penny said that she had done all of her revision already.
8 The boys said they wouldn't need any dinner because they had had a massive lunch.

7 Report the dialogue using indirect speech.

Mum Simon, where did George go this morning?
Simon I don't know, Mum. Have you tried calling him?
Mum I can't find my phone. Have you seen it?
Simon No, sorry, I haven't. When did you last use it?
Mum It was in the car yesterday, I think. Go and fetch it for me, dear.
Simon Okay. Have you got the car keys?
Mum Yes, they're on the table. Can you see them?
Simon Yes, I've got them. I'll be back in a minute.

Mum asked Simon where George had gone that morning …

8 TRANSLATION Translate the sentences into English.

1 Il ghiaccio si forma quando l'acqua si ghiaccia.
2 Da chi sono progettati i prodotti della Alessi?
3 Questo palazzo fu costruito dal re della dinastia Tudor Enrico VIII.
4 Tutte le stanze sono state completamente ristrutturate.
5 L'orario non è stato ancora approvato dal preside.
6 Rebecca ci disse che partiva il giorno dopo.
7 Il libro diceva che i Romani erano giunti in quest'area nel 400 d.C.
8 Il professore ci disse che non ci sarebbe stato un esame quel quadrimestre.
9 Gli amici di Ed gli hanno chiesto se voleva andare con loro.

TOWARDS PRELIMINARY

Reading

9 Complete the gaps in the dialogue with one word.

Teacher Julia, I ⁰ 've................. been told that you were talking during the maths test.
Julia I'm sorry but I ¹....................... shocked by the test paper. There were things in the test that we haven't ²....................... taught this term. I just said that I ³....................... not think it was fair.
Teacher I see. But Mr Turner the maths teacher ⁴....................... me that you were distracting the other students.
Julia Well, most of them they couldn't ⁵....................... the test either. We've been taught ⁶....................... to do calculus but it wasn't included ⁷....................... the test. We haven't studied trigonometry and it was in the test. I ⁸....................... my classmate, Luke, if he had the same paper as me. It looked ⁹....................... the wrong test!
Teacher Hmm. That sounds very strange. Perhaps the wrong test paper was given ¹⁰....................... . I'll check with the maths department.

Writing

10 Write an article in about 100 words.

You see this notice in an international English-language magazine.

ARTICLES WANTED!

My favourite possession

- What is it? What's it for? How often do you use it?
- Why do you like it? The design? Is it useful? Was it a present from someone special?
- Why can't you live without it?

We will publish the most interesting articles in our magazine.

WORKBOOK and EXTRA MATERIAL

Grammar Reference	page 108
Grammar Maps	page 124
Workbook	page 130
Starter p. 130 • Unit 1 p. 140 • Unit 2 p. 148 • Unit 3 p. 158 • Unit 4 p. 166 • Unit 5 p. 176 • Unit 6 p. 184 • Unit 7 p. 194 • Unit 8 p. 202 • Unit 9 p. 212 • Unit 10 p. 220	
Literature Skills	page 230
CLIL	page 240
Writing Expansion	page 250
Vocabulary Extension	page 260
Wordlist	page 270
Speaking Skills – Dialogues	page 276
Verb Tables	page 280
Irregular Verbs	page 284
UK map	page 285

Grammar Reference

STARTER A

Present simple

affirmative	
I / You	sing.
He / She / It	sing**s**.
We / You / They	sing.

negative		
I / You	don't	
He / She / It	doesn't	sing.
We / You / They	don't	

questions		
Do	I / you	
Does	he / she / it	sing?
Do	we / you / they	

short answers
Yes, I / you / we / they **do**.
Yes, he / she / it **does**.
No, I / you / we / they **don't**.
No, he / she / it **doesn't**.

Form

The affirmative of the present simple is the same for every person (*I*, *you*, *we*, *they*).
The third person singular (*he*, *she*, *it*) is different because we add an -s to the base form without *to*.
For the negative and interrogative form we use the auxiliaries *do* and *does*.
When we use short answers in response to interrogative forms, we use the auxiliaries, *do* and *does*.
With a question word (*what*, *who*, *when*, *where*, *why*, *how often*, *which*) we place the question word in front of the interrogative form:
- *Where do you come from?*

These expressions are not followed by short forms.

Use

We use the present simple:
- to talk about routines and habits:
  I get up at 6:30 on week days.
- for factual information:
  That family are vegetarians. They don't eat meat.
- for permanent truths:
  Water boils at 100 °C.

Present simple: Spelling rules

In most cases, we add -s to the base form without *to*. However, there are some spelling variations:

• Regular + -s:	walk → walk**s**; live → live**s**
• Verbs that end in consonant + -y:	reply → repl**ies**
• Verbs that end in vowel + -y:	play → play**s**; say → say**s**
• Verbs that end in -sh:	push → push**es**
• Verbs that end in -ch:	watch → watch**es**
• Verbs that end in -ss:	pass → pass**es**
• Verbs that end in -o:	go → go**es**; do → do**es**
• Verbs that end in -x:	relax → relax**es**

Adverbs of frequency

We often use the present simple tense with adverbs of frequency such as *always*, *usually*, *often*, *sometimes*, *hardly ever*, and *never*.

Form and use

We use adverbs of frequency to talk about the frequency of an action.
Always means 100% of the time and *never* means 0% of the time. *Never* is used with affirmative sentences even though it has a negative meaning.
The adverbs are usually placed in between the subject and the verb:
- *He always listens to music.*
- *She never eats meat.*

But they are placed **after** the verb *be*:
- *He is often late.*

We use the question *How often* to ask about frequency:
- *How often do you get up early? I always get up early.*

In negative sentences, adverbs of frequency usually precede the main verb but follow the auxiliary:
- *He doesn't always play football.*

But they always follow the verb *be*:
- *He isn't usually late.*

In interrogative forms, adverbs of frequency follow the subject of the sentence:
- *Does Kelly often play football on Saturdays?*

Expressions of frequency

We also talk about frequency using expressions of frequency.

Form

Expressions of frequency are usually placed at the end of the sentence:
- *I go to the gym every day.*
- *I play football once a week.*

These are the most common expressions following the frequency question *How often*:
- *once / twice / three times a week / a month / a year*
- *every day*
- *two times a week*
- *on Saturdays / Tuesdays*
- *in the morning / afternoon / evening*
- *at weekends*

GRAMMAR REFERENCE

STARTER B

there is / there are and some / any

countable	
singular	plural
+ There is **an** egg.	There are **some** eggs.
− There isn't **an** egg.	There aren't **any** eggs.
? Is there **an** egg?	Are there **any** eggs?
uncountable	
+ There is **some** bread.	
− There isn't **any** bread.	
? Is there **any** bread?	

Form and use

There is / are is used with the verb *be* to indicate the location of buildings, people and objects.
In questions and negatives, it does not take an auxiliary form.
Some and *any* are used to talk about unspecified quantities.
A / an is used to talk about a singular item.
Some is used in affirmative sentences and *any* is used in negative and interrogative sentences.
In some requests, *some* can be used in the interrogative form:
- *Can I have some biscuits, please?*

Nouns can be either countable or uncountable – this means they can or cannot be counted.
Countable nouns have a singular and a plural: *a dog, two dogs*.
Singular countable nouns take *a* and plural countable nouns take a specified number or *some*: *a dog, two dogs, some dogs*.
Uncountable nouns cannot be counted and do not have a singular or plural. They do not take *a / an*: *cheese, pasta, bread*.
- *I like cheese but I don't like pasta.*

For quantities of uncountable nouns we use *some* and *any*.
Some is used in plural countable nouns and in singular affirmative uncountable nouns. *Any* is used for plural negative and interrogative countable nouns and for singular negative and interrogative uncountable nouns.
Uncountable nouns take a singular form with a verb:
- *That pasta comes from Italy.*

Some nouns can be countable and uncountable, depending on the context. We can say:
- *I like chocolate.* (uncountable in general as a substance)
- *Please have a few chocolates.* (countable, meaning from a box)

a lot of, a little, a few

Countable nouns
- There **are a lot of** souvenirs. (big quantity)
- There **are a few** souvenirs. (small quantity)

Uncountable nouns
- There **is a lot of** space. (big quantity)
- There **is a little** space. (small quantity)

Form and use

A lot of is used in affirmative sentences. It can be used with countable and uncountable nouns. It means a large quantity.
A little is used with uncountable nouns only. It means there is a small quantity.
A few is used with countable nouns. It means there is a small quantity.

too much / too many, too little / too few

Countable nouns
- There **are too many** souvenirs. (excess)
- There **are too few** souvenirs. (insufficient)

Uncountable nouns
- There **is too much** space. (excess)
- There **is too little** space. (insufficient)

Form and use

Too much / too many means there is an excess of items.
Too many is used with countable nouns and *too much* is used with uncountable nouns.
Too little / too few means there isn't enough of something.
Too few is used with countable nouns and *too little* is used with uncountable nouns.

STARTER C

Past simple: be

affirmative		
I	was	
You	were	
He / She / It	was	late.
We / You / They	were	
negative		
I	was not / wasn't	
You	were not / weren't	late.
He / She / It	was not / wasn't	
We / You / They	were not / weren't	
questions		
Was	I	
Were	you	late?
Was	he / she / it	
Were	we / you / they	
short answers		
Yes, I / he / she / it **was**.		
Yes, you / we / they **were**.		
No, I / he / she / it **wasn't**.		
No, you / we / they **weren't**.		

GRAMMAR REFERENCE

Form and use

The past simple form of the verb *be* is *was* for *I*, *he*, *she* and *it* and *were* for all other subjects.
In interrogative forms, the verb is inverted with the subject:
- *David was 23 yesterday.*
- *Was David 23 yesterday?*

In negative forms, we add *not* to the main verb:
- *He wasn't at school today.*

The past simple is used for actions that have finished and concluded in a past time.

Past simple: Regular and irregular verbs

affirmative		
I / You / He / She / It / We / You / They		**delivered** it. **found** it.
negative		
I / You / He / She / It / We / You / They	did not / didn't	**deliver** it. **find** it.
questions		
Did	I / you / he / she / it / we / you / they	**deliver** it? **find** it?
short answers		
Yes, I / you / he / she / it / we / they **did**. No, I / you / he / she / it / we / they **didn't**.		

Form

The regular past simple is formed by adding *-ed* to the base form of the verb without *to*:
- *play* → *play**ed***; *visit* → *visit**ed***

There are some spelling variations:

• Verbs that end in *-e*:	live → live**d**; arrive → arrive**d**
• Verbs that end in consonant *-y*:	marry → marr**ied**; try → tr**ied**
• Verbs that end in vowel + consonant:	stop → stop**ped**; travel → travel**led**; regret → regret**ted**

The past simple of irregular verbs can be completely different from their base form:
- *have* → *had*; *swim* → *swam*, etc.

The form does not change for all subjects.
The interrogative and negative forms of the past simple are obtained by adding *did* and *did not* to the clause. These forms do not change for all subjects.
Did and *did not* are followed by the base form of the verb without *to*.
Short answers use the auxiliary form: *Yes, I did. / No, I didn't*.
In short answers only the negative can be contracted.
For a list of irregular verbs see page 284.

Use

The past simple is used for:
- completed actions in the past:
  We studied together yesterday.
- a completed period in the past:
  He played football for six months.
- narrative tenses:
  He checked his email, then contacted his boss.

Expressions of past time

We often use time expressions with the past simple to state when something happened. Some common time expressions include the following:
- **last** week / month / year
- **at** ten / twelve o'clock
- **in** 1492 / 2012
- last night
- ten minutes / two hours / six weeks **ago**
- **on** Sunday / Monday (morning, afternoon, evening)
- yesterday
- **last** Christmas / summer

We place the time expressions at the beginning or end of the sentence.
- *My uncle and aunt emigrated to Australia last year.*
- *Last year, my uncle and aunt emigrated to Australia.*
  Look!: we do not use *the* with these time expressions:
  ✗ *He came home from hospital the last week.*

STARTER D

Comparative and superlative adjectives

Form and use

We form the comparative by adding *-er* to one-syllable adjectives and *more* before adjectives that are longer than one syllable.
- *cheap* → *cheaper* (than)
- *quiet* → *quieter* (than)
- *expensive* → *more expensive* (than)

We use the comparative form when we are comparing two things or a group of things. We usually use *than* in the comparative form.
We form the superlative by adding *-est* to one-syllable adjectives and *most* before adjectives that are longer than one syllable.
- *cheap* → (the) *cheapest*
- *quiet* → (the) *quietest*
- *expensive* → (the) *most expensive*

We usually use *the* to form superlatives. We use the superlative when we are contrasting three or more items.
There are important spelling variations. There are also a number of irregular adjectives which change form completely. These are the most common ones.

110 Grammar Reference

GRAMMAR REFERENCE

spelling variations	
• Regular adjectives:	+ -er / -est
• Adjectives ending in -y:	~~y~~ + -ier / -iest
• Adjectives ending in -e:	+ -r / -st
• Adjectives ending in vowel + consonant:	double the final consonant
• Two-syllable (+) adjectives:	add *more* / *most*
• Some two-syllable adjs:	have two forms -er / -est and *more* / *most*

regular adjectives	comparative	superlative
small	small**er** than	the small**est**
happy	happ**ier** than	the happ**iest**
nice	nic**er** than	the nic**est**
big	big**ger** than	the big**gest**
expensive	**more** expensive **than**	the **most** expensive
clever	clever**er** than / **more** clever **than**	the clever**est** / the **most** clever

irregular adjectives	comparative	superlative
good	better than	the best
bad	worse than	the worst
far	further / farther than	the furthest / farthest

LESS THAN AND *THE LEAST*

The comparative and superlative form of *little* is *less* and *the least*. This comparative and superlative form acts in the same way as other comparative and superlative forms.
- *That house is less expensive than the one we saw yesterday. It's the least expensive house in the street.*

(NOT) AS … AS

We use *(not) as … as* to compare equivalent aspects of two things.
- *The apple is as heavy as the banana.*
- *The boy is not as tall his brother.*

In negative sentences we can also use *not so … as* in the same way.

STARTER E

Present continuous v *be going to* for plans

PRESENT CONTINUOUS

affirmative		
I	am / 'm	
You	are / 're	learn**ing**.
He / She / It	is / 's	
We / You / They	are / 're	

negative		
I	am not / 'm not	
You	are not / aren't	learn**ing**.
He / She / It	is not / isn't	
We / You / They	are not / aren't	

questions		
Am	I	
Are	you	learn**ing**?
Is	he / she / it	
Are	we / you / they	

short answers
Yes, I **am**.
Yes, you / we / they **are**.
Yes, he / she / it **is**.
No, I**'m not**.
No, you / we / they **aren't**.
No, he / she / it **isn't**.

Form

The present continuous tense is formed with the verb *be* + *-ing* form. In the interrogative form the verb *be* is put in front of the subject of the sentence. In the negative form the word *not* is added to *be*. There are no other auxiliaries.

In short answers, the negative form can be contracted, but the affirmative cannot:
- ✓ *Yes, you are.*
- ✗ *Yes, you're.*

A question word is placed in front of the inverted verb *be*:
- *What are you doing?*

Use

We use the present continuous:
- to talk about things that are happening at the moment of speaking:
  - *Daniel's not here right now – he's travelling around Europe.*
  - *Mum's not working at the moment – she's sitting on the sofa.*
  - *Why are you packing your suitcase?*
- to talk about temporary situations:
  - *They're showing a great travel programme on TV this week.*
  - *Our internet isn't working this week.*
  - *How's your sister getting on in New York?*
- to talk about things that are changing or developing:
  - *The weather is getting warmer. The Arctic ice cap is shrinking.*
- to describe actions we see in a photo:
  - *In this picture, three girls are swimming in the sea.*

-ing form spelling

The *-ing* form is usually formed by adding *-ing* to the base form of the verb without *to* but there are some spelling variations:

Grammar Reference 111

GRAMMAR REFERENCE

• Regular + -ing:	wait → wait**ing**; stand → stand**ing**
• Verbs ending in -e:	live → liv**ing**; take → tak**ing**
• Verbs ending in -y:	reply → reply**ing**; play → play**ing**; study → study**ing**
• Verbs that have a strong final syllable:	begin → begin**ning**; stop → stop**ping**; travel → travel**ling**
• Verbs ending in -ie:	die → d**ying**; lie → l**ying**

BE GOING TO

affirmative		
I	am / 'm	
You	are / 're	
He / She / It	is / 's	going to leave.
We / You / They	are / 're	

negative		
I	am not	
You	are / aren't	
He / She / It	is not / isn't	going to leave.
We / You / They	are not / aren't	

questions		
Am	I	
Are	you	
Is	he / she / it	going to leave?
Are	we / you / they	

short answers
Yes, I **am**.
Yes, you / we / they **are**.
Yes, he / she / it **is**.
No, I'**m not**.
No, you / we / they **aren't**.
No, he / she / it **isn't**.

Form and use

Be going to is formed with *be + going to +* the base form of the verb without *to*.

We use *be going to* and a main verb to talk about future plans and intentions. These plans are intentional, which means they are there but not definite.
- *I'm going to study hard for my exams. I really want to pass.*
- *Are you going to make a cake for my birthday?*

We can use *be going to* to make predictions when there is strong present or past evidence that something is going to happen. This is also called *evident future*.
- *The temperature is already 20 ºC and it's only 8 am. It's going to be really hot today.*
- *Mum's going to be angry because I haven't tidied my room.*
- *There are clouds in the sky. It's going to rain.*

PRESENT CONTINUOUS V BE GOING TO

We use the present continuous to talk about future events which are already planned.

- *The vet's operating on my dog next week.*
- *'Are we all meeting at Paco's house on Friday?' 'That's right. That's the plan.'*

When we use the present continuous to talk about the future, there is usually a reference to time, either in the sentence or in the context.
- *What are you doing?* (now) *I'm finishing my homework.*
- *Are you doing anything on Friday?* (future) *Yes, I'm meeting Monica.*

We use *be going to* and a main verb to talk about future plans and intentions.
- *They're not going to spend the summer in the mountains this year.*
- *Are you going to make a cake for my birthday?*

We can use *be going to* to make predictions when there is strong present or past evidence that something is going to happen.
- *The temperature is already 20 ºC and it's only 8 am. It's going to be really hot today.*
- *Mum's going to be angry because I haven't tidied my room.*

There is sometimes very little difference in meaning between the present continuous for the future and *be going to*.
'I'm seeing Carlos tonight' is, in theory, a more definite plan than *'I'm going to see Carlos tonight.'* However, here you can use either and British native speakers often use both.

present continuous	be going to
I'**m leaving** for Ghana in October. (I've got my ticket.)	I'**m going to leave** for Ghana in October. (It's my intention, but I still need to buy my ticket.)

We use the present continuous when our plans for the future are certain. We use *be going to* for future plans which aren't certain yet.

be going to v *will* for predictions

be going to	will
Those bags are too heavy. You'**re going to drop** them.	I think I'**ll be** a good teacher.

We also use *be going to* for future predictions based on present evidence. We use *will* for future predictions based on our opinion.

WILL

affirmative		
I / You / He / She / It / We / You / They	will / 'll	go.
negative		
I / You / He / She / It / We / You / They	will not / won't	go.
questions		
Will	I / you / he / she / it / we / you / they	go?

short answers
Yes, I / you / he / she / it / we / they **will**.
No, I / you / he / she / it / we / they **won't**.

GRAMMAR REFERENCE

Form

The future simple is formed with *will* + the base form of the verb without *to*. *Will* is invariable and does not change with all subject forms.
The affirmative is *will* and the negative is formed by adding *not*, *will not* or *won't* as a contracted form.
In questions, *will* is placed before the subject of the sentence. There are no other auxiliary forms.

Use

We use *will* in the following ways:
- to make predictions based on our opinions:
  - *Come and listen to my new CD. You'll love it.*
  - *I don't think you'll like that cake. It's got sultanas in it and you hate them!*
- when we make a spontaneous decision at the time we are speaking:
  - *'I've got to go out to get some eggs.' 'I'll come with you.'*
- when we offer to do something:
  - *Finish your work. I'll cook lunch.*
  - *Don't worry about the tickets. I'll go and pick them up.*
- when we make a promise:
  - *I won't tell anyone. I promise.*
- for certain events that we know will happen:
  - *I'll be 18 next week! It's my birthday on Tuesday.*

BE GOING TO v WILL

The main difference between *will* and *be going to* for predictions is that *be going to* is used with evident future – when there is evidence now that something will happen, while *will* is used for predictions based on our own opinion.
- *Those stairs are wet! You're going to fall down.*
- *She loves him so much. She'll definitely marry him!*

The words *be sure*, *expect*, *probably*, *think* are used with *will*.
- *I'm sure the teacher will understand your explanation.*
- *She doesn't think her parents will mind.*

Words like *definitely* are also used with *will*.
- *John's worked really hard for his exams. He'll definitely pass.*

UNIT 1

Present simple v present continuous

present simple	present continuous
They sometimes just **want** to talk. What **makes** a good friend? People **don't** always **want** advice.	Right now I**'m feeling** good. What **are** they **going** through at the moment? We**'re not studying** for exams.

Use

The present simple is used for habitual actions, while the present continuous is used for actions happening now.
- *He often gets up late. / He is getting up at the moment.*

The present simple is used for permanent actions, while the present continuous is used for temporary actions.
- *Jane lives in Rome. / Jane is living in London at the moment.*

We use different time expressions to identify the different tense forms:

present simple	present continuous
- *always*	- *at the moment*
- *usually*	- *now*
- *often*	- *this evening*
- *sometimes*	- *this weekend*
- *hardly ever*	- *today*
- *never*	- *tonight*
- *every day*	
- *once / twice a week*	
- *on Saturdays*	
- *at the weekend*	

VERBS OF STATE AND VERBS OF PERCEPTION

We don't usually use the present continuous with state verbs. Some examples are *be*, *believe*, *hate*, *know*, *like*, *love*, *understand*, *think*, *want*, *remember*.
- *I believe in God.*
- *I don't understand the question.*

However, there are occasions when we can use the present continuous when we are referring to an action.
- *What do you think of this programme?* (opinion)
- *What are you thinking of?* (action)

We don't usually use the present continuous with verbs of perception like *taste*, *sound*, *smell*, *look*.
- *That coat looks good on you.*
- *The lasagne tastes wonderful.*

Present perfect

affirmative		
I / You	have / 've	
He / She / It	has / 's	left.
We / You / They	have / 've	
negative		
I / You	have not / haven't	
He / She / It	has not / hasn't	left.
We / You / They	have not / haven't	
questions		
Have	I / you	
Has	he / she / it	left?
Have	we / you / they	
short answers		
Yes, he / she / it **has**.		
Yes, I / you / we / they **have**.		
No, he / she / it **hasn't**.		
No, I / you / we / they **haven't**.		

GRAMMAR REFERENCE

Form

The present perfect is formed using *have / has* + the past participle of the main verb.
Regular verbs generally form their past participles by adding *-d*, *-ed* or *-ied*: arriv**ed**, finish**ed**, stud**ied**.
However, many of the verbs we use most frequently are irregular and have irregular participles:

  do → *done*; *lose* → *lost*; *write* → *written*

We form the interrogative by inverting *have / has* with the subject.
- *Have they finished their homework? Yes, they have.*

The short answers are formed using the *have / has* structure.
We form the negative by adding *not* to the *have / has* structure.
- *They haven't seen John for a while.*

Use

We use the present perfect:
- to relate the past with the present:
  Matt's lost his glasses. (He hasn't got them now.)
- to talk about events that took place at an unspecified time in the past:
  Have you ever visited France?

PRESENT PERFECT WITH *EVER* AND *NEVER*

We use the present perfect with the adverbs *ever* and *never*. They go before the main verb. *Ever* is normally used in questions to ask about events. It goes immediately before the past participle.
- *Have you ever seen Rihanna?*
  (This is asking about an event in an unspecified time in someone's life.)

Never is used in affirmative sentences to express a negative sentiment.
- *He has never held a snake.*

Present perfect with *for / since*

We use the present perfect with *for* and *since* to say how long something has been happening.
We use *for* for periods of time (*an hour, two weeks, three months, ten years*, etc.) to talk about duration and *since* with a specific moment in time or to indicate the start of a period (*two o'clock, yesterday morning, Thursday, November, 1995, Christmas*, etc.).
- *Jane has been at the library since two o'clock today.*
- *My mother and my stepfather have been husband and wife for five years.*

Look at the list below. This shows the main expressions used with each form.

for	since
a long time	*yesterday*
a *week / month / year*	*I was born*
three / four days	***last*** *week / month / year*
a few months	*last summer*
five minutes	*2016*
the past year	*Monday 16th June*
the last few *days / weeks / months*	*5:30 pm*
	then

BEEN / GONE

Been and *gone* are the past participles of the verbs *be* and *go*. There are some differences in the meanings of these forms.
- *I've been to the shops. Here's the milk.*
  (This means that the person has visited the shops but is now back at home. The person is now present and shows the milk.)
- *'Where is Joan?' 'She's gone to the shops.'*
  (This means that Joan is not at home because she is still at the shops.)

Present perfect with *just, already* and *yet*

affirmative (+ *just, already*)		
I / You	have / 've	*just /*
He / She / It	has / 's	*already left.*
We / You / They	have / 've	
negative (+ *yet*)		
I / You	have not / haven't	
He / She / It	has not / hasn't	*left yet.*
We / You / They	have not / haven't	
questions (+ *yet*)		
Have	I / you	
Has	he / she / it	*left yet?*
Have	we / you / they	
short answers		
Yes, I / you / we / they **have**. Yes, he / she / it **has**.		
No, I / you / we / they **haven't**. No, he / she / it **hasn't**.		

We can use the adverbs *just, already* and *yet* with the present perfect. They go before the main verb (in between *have / has* and the past participle).
- *Olive has just had a baby girl.* (It happened very recently.)
- *Dani has already posted the news online.* (He has done this faster or before was originally expected.)

Just and *already* normally take the affirmative form. We only use *yet* with present perfect questions and negative statements. It goes at the end of the sentence. If we say *yet*, we are expecting something to happen.
- *Has your sister moved house yet?* (We thought she was moving soon.)
- *I haven't done my homework yet.* (But I will do it soon.)

Present perfect v past simple

Both the present perfect and the past simple are used to express events and actions in the past. The main differences are:
- we use the past simple for events that are finished in a specified time in the past:
  - *He went to school yesterday.*
  - *He moved to Italy in 2015.*
- we use the present perfect to describe events that finished in an unspecified time in the past:

- *He has lost his phone.* (We don't know when, but he hasn't got it now.)
- *What's wrong with Jack? He's broken his ankle.* (We don't know when.)

In these cases, the action is more important than the time.

– we use the present perfect when the effects of the action are still present now:
  - *Oh, look at Phil. He's cut his hair.* (We can see the effects now, even though we don't know when it happened.)
– we use the present perfect when the action began in the past but is still continuing now:
  - *He has lived in London for five years.* (He still lives in London now.)

We can see the difference between the two tenses in a dialogue like this:

Lily Have you ever lived in a different country?
Linda Yes, I have. I lived in Rome.
Lily When did you live there?
Linda I lived there in 2005. It was great.

In this case, the first question is present perfect, because the speaker is asking about an unspecified time in Linda's life. Linda's answer is in the past simple because she lived in Rome some time ago and is now back in the UK. Her time in Rome is finished at a specific time in the past.

Expressions of past time

Expressions of past time help us a lot to identify the difference between the two tenses:

past simple	present perfect
(specified time)	(unspecified time)
• yesterday	• already
• **last** week / month / year	• yet
• at Easter	• just
• on my birthday	• never
• one day / two weeks / three months **ago**	• ever
	• **this** week / month / year
	• for / since
	• today

UNIT 2

Present perfect continuous

affirmative		
I / You	**have** / **'ve**	been travelling.
He / She / It	**has** / **'s**	been travelling.
We / You / They	**have** / **'ve**	
negative		
I / You	**have not** / **haven't**	been travelling.
He / She / It	**has not** / **hasn't**	been travelling.
We / You / They	**have not** / **haven't**	

questions		
Have	I / you	been travelling?
Has	he / she / it	
Have	we / you / they	
short answers		
Yes, I / you / we / they **have**.		
Yes, he / she / it **has**.		
No, I / you / we / they **haven't**.		
No, he / she / it **hasn't**.		

Form

The present perfect continuous is formed with *have / has* + the past participle of the verb *be* + *-ing* form.

Use

We use the present perfect continuous for activities that have recently stopped or have just stopped. There is a connection with the present or now.
- *You're wet. Have you been swimming?* (You're wet now.)
- *Claire is very tired. She hasn't been sleeping well.*
- *I've been talking to Joe about the problem and he agrees with me.*
- *It's been raining all day long!*

We can use *for* and *since* with the present perfect continuous when we ask the question *How long…?* The activity is still happening or have just finished.
- *How long has Alex been playing on his tablet? He's been playing on his tablet for an hour.*

We use the present perfect continuous for actions that are repeated over a period of time.
- *Will is a great pianist. He's been playing since he was six.*
- *Jenny speaks Spanish well. She's been learning it for ten years.*

Present perfect simple v present perfect continuous

The present perfect and the present perfect continuous refer to actions or situations that started in the past and are still happening or have just ended:

– we use the present perfect continuous to emphasise the action, its duration or intensity.
  - *Silvia's hands are covered in paint – she's been painting a mural.*
    (She probably hasn't finished it yet.)
– we use the present perfect simple to emphasise the result or the repetitions of the action.
  - *Silvia has painted the mural – it's full of lots of bright colours.*
    (She's finished painting it.)
– we don't use the present perfect continuous with state verbs.

Grammar Reference 115

GRAMMAR REFERENCE

We use the present perfect continuous with *How long …?* because we are interested in duration.
- *How long have you been learning English? I've been learning English for six years.*

We use the present perfect with *How much*, *How many* and *How many times…?*
- *How much of the book have you read?*
- *How many people have visited the web page this week?*
- *How many times have they been to your house this week?*

Defining relative clauses

Defining relative clauses make clear which person or thing we are talking about. They are essential to understand the meaning of the sentence. Without them, the sentence doesn't make sense.
- *The students **who** cheated in the exam won't get any marks.*
- *The man **who** is over there is my maths teacher.*

RELATIVE PRONOUNS IN DEFINING RELATIVE CLAUSES

who / that	refers to people	The boy **who** / **that** lives next door is my boyfriend.
which / that	refers to things	The car **which** is parked in my drive belongs to my sister.
where	refers to places	That's the house **where** I was born.
whose	refers to possession	Jane is the girl **whose** friend was arrested.
when	refers to time	That's the month **when** I start school.

We can omit the relative pronoun when the person or thing being defined is the object of the sentence. However, it is not wrong if it is inserted.
- *That's the dress (**which** / **that**) I bought for my wedding.*

UNIT 3

used to

affirmative	negative
Watching TV **used to be** a communal activity.	They **didn't use to switch on** immediately.
questions	**short answers**
Did your grandmother **use to have** a TV?	Yes, she **did**. No, she **didn't**.

We use *used to* when we want to express something that happened regularly in the past, but no longer happens.
- *Freddie used to read all the business news online.*
- *Did you use to ride your bike every day?*
- *I didn't use to like ice cream!*

We also use *used to* for something that was true, but isn't true anymore.
- *Evie used to have very long hair when she was a child. Now it's short.*

used to and would

affirmative (habits)	affirmative (states)
They **would meet** in bars and cafés. They **used to meet** in bars and cafés.	Televisions **used to be** expensive.
negative	**questions**
They **didn't use to switch on** immediately.	**Did** people **use to watch** TV during the day?

We use *would* when we want to express something that happened regularly in the past.
- *Whenever Jane was unhappy, she would go to her room and cry.*

Used to can describe actions and states, but *would* can only describe actions.
- ✓ *They used to be crazy about Doctor Who.*
- ✗ *They would be crazy about Doctor Who.*

Past continuous

affirmative		
I	was	working.
You	were	
He / She / It	was	
We / You / They	were	
negative		
I	was not / wasn't	working.
You	were not / weren't	
He / She / It	was not / wasn't	
We / You / They	were not / weren't	
questions		
Was	I	working?
Were	you	
Was	he / she / it	
Were	we / you / they	

short answers

Yes, I / you / we / they **were**.
Yes, he / she / it **was**.
No, I / you / we / they **weren't**.
No, he / she / it **wasn't**.

Form

The past continuous tense is formed with the past simple of the verb *be* + *-ing* form.

Use

We use the past continuous to describe actions in progress at a particular moment in the past.
- *Where were you going yesterday morning?*

We also use it to *set the scene* for a story.

116 Grammar Reference

GRAMMAR REFERENCE

- *It was the first day of spring. The sun was shining, the white clouds were floating in the sky and the flowers were coming out of the ground.*

We also use the past continuous for simultaneous actions in the past.
- *Sue was listening to her MP3 player **while** she was tidying the sitting room.*

Past continuous v past simple

past continuous	past simple
While he **was working** there …	he **met** many famous actors.
While he **was staying** there …	he **started** studying the history of Romania.
He **was researching** Eastern European legends about vampires …	when he **discovered** the story of an ancient Romanian warrior-prince.

We often use the past simple and the past continuous together to describe the relationship between two actions. The past continuous is used to describe a continuous action or to *set the scene* for a shorter completed action.
- *A bee **stung** Jane when she **was sitting** in the garden.*

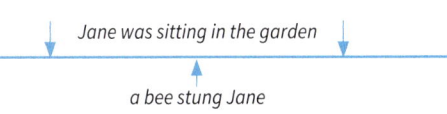

Jane was sitting in the garden

a bee stung Jane

We can use *when*, *while* and *as* to describe situations in which one event interrupts another. *While* and *as* are followed by the past continuous, *when* is followed by the past simple.
- *Mr Neale was sitting in the airport **when** he received the phone call.*
- ***While** the couple were walking, they met Jamie.*

We can use the conjunctions *while* and *as* to join two sentences describing simultaneous actions.
- ***While** we were talking in the garden, a bee was flying from flower to flower.*

UNIT 4

can / can't for ability, requests, permission and possibility

affirmative			
I / You / He / She / It / We / You / They	**can**	play tennis.
negative			
I / You / He / She / It / We / You / They	**can't**	speak English.
questions			
Can	I / you / he / she / it / we / you / they	run fast?
short answers			
Yes, I / you / he / she / it / we / you / they **can**.
No, I / you / he / she / it / we / you / they **can't**.

Form and use

Can is a modal verb. This means:
- it is invariable in all its forms.
- it does not use an auxiliary to form questions or negatives.
- it is followed by the base form of the verb without *to*.

It is used:
- to express ability: *Can you swim? Yes, I can.*
- to express requests: *Can you come to the cinema with me?*
- to express permission: *Can I open the window?*
- to express possibility: *We can go to the shops after school.*

have to / don't have to

affirmative			
I / You	have to		
He / She / It	has to		go.
We / You / They	have to		
negative			
I / You	do not / don't		
He / She / It	does not / doesn't	have to	go.
We / You / They	do not / don't		
questions			
Do	I / you		
Does	he / she / it	have to	go?
Do	we / you / they		
short answers			
Yes, I / you / we / they **do**.
Yes, he / she / it **does**.
No, I / you / we / they **don't**.
No, he / she / it **doesn't**.

Form

Have to is a normal verb and changes with all its forms: *have to* with *I*, *you*, *we*, *they* and *has to* with *he*, *she*, *it*.
For the interrogative and negative we use the auxiliary forms *do* and *does*.
Have to is an irregular verb and the past simple form is *had to*. As with other past simple forms, in the interrogative and negative we use *did / didn't*.
- *I had to go to school yesterday.*
- *I didn't have to do my homework last week.*
- *Did you have to tidy your room on Saturday?*

Use

Have to is used for obligation from an external source, and it is more official and thus stronger than *must*.
- *You have to stop at the red light.* (It's the law.)
- *I have to do my homework.* (My teacher told me.)
- *He had to speak English to his exchange parents because they couldn't understand Italian.*

Have to is also used to ask about obligation.
- *'Do I have to drive on the left in the UK?' 'Yes, you do.'*

Grammar Reference 117

GRAMMAR REFERENCE

Don't / doesn't have to expresses an absence of obligation. It means it is not necessary.
- *You don't have to write out the answer, you can use a computer.*
- *He doesn't have to get up early on Saturday, there's no school.*

must and have to

affirmative		
I / You / He / She / It / We / You / They	**must**	go.
negative		
I / You / He / She / It / We / You / They	**must not / mustn't**	go.
questions			
Do	I / you		
Does	he / she / it	**have to**	go?
Do	we / you / they		
short answers			
Yes, I / you / we / they **do**. Yes, he / she / it **does**. No, I / you / we / they **don't**. No, he / she / it **doesn't**.			

Form
Must is a modal verb and does not change for all its subjects. *Must* is followed by the base form of the verb without *to*.
For negative forms, we do not use auxiliary forms with *must*. The sentence becomes negative by adding *not* to *must*.
- *I must not / mustn't eat peanuts.*

Must is not commonly used in the interrogative form. Instead we use *have to*.
- *'Do you have to go to school tomorrow?' 'No, I don't.'*

Use
Must and *have to* are both used to express obligation or strong recommendation, but there are some differences.
Must is an obligation we put on ourselves (internal / personal obligation).
- *I really must buy my mum a birthday card.*
- *I mustn't get home too late, my parents will worry.*

Must can also be used to give an order.
- *You must finish your homework now.*

Must can also be used as a strong recommendation.
- *You must see that film, it's brilliant.*

Must is also used in formal written notices.
- *You mustn't swim in the sea before 10 am.*

Have to is used for obligation from an external source, and it is more official and thus stronger than *must*.
- *You have to stop at the red light.* (It's the law.)
- *I have to do my homework.* (My teacher told me.)
- *He had to speak English to his exchange parents because they couldn't understand Italian.*

Have to is also used to ask about obligation.
- *'Do I have to drive on the left in the UK?' 'Yes, you do.'*

MUSTN'T AND DON'T / DOESN'T HAVE TO
Mustn't and *don't / doesn't have to* have very different meanings. *Mustn't* expresses prohibition.
- *You mustn't talk during the exam.*
- *You mustn't leave the room before 10 am.*

Don't / doesn't have to expresses an absence of obligation. It means it is not necessary.
- *You don't have to write out the answer, you can use a computer.*
- *He doesn't have to get up early on Saturday, there's no school.*

make and let

My mother **makes** me wash up. My sister **lets** me borrow her clothes.

Form
Make and *let* both have the same construction.
Affirmative: subject + *make* / *let* + direct object + base form of the verb without *to*.
- *The nurse made me take the medicine.*
- *My mum let me go to the party.*

Negative: subject + *doesn't* / *don't* / *didn't* + *make* / *let* + base form of the verb without *to*.
- *My brother doesn't let me use his phone.*
- *My mum doesn't make me wash up.*

Interrogative: *Do* / *Does* / *Did* + subject + *make* / *let* + base form of the verb without *to*.
- *Did your teacher make you re-do the test?*
- *Does your brother let you use his phone?*

Use
Make is used to convey obligation. Someone forces you to do something.
Let is used to convey permission. Someone gives you permission to do something.
They are normal verbs with standard auxiliary forms (*do / does, did*) in the negative and interrogative but always take a direct object, which is usually *me* or the person being.

UNIT 5

Past perfect

affirmative		
I / You / He / She / It / We / You / They	had	done.
negative		
I / You / He / She / It / We / You / They	had not / hadn't	done.
interrogative		
Had	I / you / he / she / it / we / you / they	done.
short answers		
Yes, I / you / he / she / it / we / they **had**. No, I / you / he / she / it / we / they **hadn't**.		

118   Grammar Reference

GRAMMAR REFERENCE

Form

The past perfect is formed using *had* + the past participle of the main verb.
The negative form is formed adding *not* to the auxiliary form *had*.
In the interrogative form *had* is inverted before the subject.
No other auxiliaries are used.

Use

We use the past perfect to talk about two past events when we want to make it clear which event happened first. We use the past perfect for the first event and the past simple for the second event.

- *John **had finished** his homework when someone **knocked** on the door.*
  (John finished his homework. Then someone knocked on the door.)

Indefinite pronouns

person	thing	place
someone / somebody	something	somewhere
anyone / anybody	anything	anywhere
no one / nobody	nothing	nowhere
everyone / everybody	everything	everywhere

Form and use

We use pronouns of *some* to give information about people, things or places.
Some is used in affirmative sentences or when making an offer.

- *There is someone in the library.*
- *Would you like something to drink?*

Any is used in negative and interrogative forms.

- *Is there anyone there?*
- *I don't think anyone is in the garden.*

Every is used with all forms, affirmative, negative and interrogative. It is used with verbs in singular form.

- *Everyone is here.*
- *Is everything ready for the trip?*

Concepts with *no* express negative situations, but are used in affirmative forms.

- *No one was at school today.*

UNIT 6

First conditional

affirmative
If I **have** enough money, I'**ll buy** a new car.
I'**ll buy** a new car if I **have** enough money.
negative
If it **doesn't rain**, we'**ll go** to the beach.
We'**ll go** the beach if it **doesn't rain**.
If it **rains**, we **won't go** to the beach.
We **won't go** to the beach if it **rains**.

questions
If it **rains** tomorrow, **will** you **drive** to the station?
Will you **drive** to the station if it **rains** tomorrow?
short answers
Yes, I **will**. / No, I **won't**.

Form

The first conditional is formed as follows:

conditional clause	result clause
If + present simple,	future simple
result clause	**conditional clause**
future simple	*if* + present simple

The clauses can be inverted, with the *if* clause coming second, but in this case we omit the comma.
The negative form can be in the first or second clause or in both clauses.

- *We won't go to the match if our team isn't playing.*

Use

We use the first conditional to talk about situations which are possible in the present or the future as long as the condition upon which they rely happens. In this way, there is a definite possibility that the event will happen.

- *If I pass my exams, I will go to university.*
- *We will show you how to install that program if you don't know how to do it.*
- *She won't buy the dress if they don't give her a discount.*

IF, *WHEN*, *AS SOON AS*, *UNLESS* WITH THE FIRST CONDITIONAL

conditional clause	result clause
If it **rains,** **When** it **rains,** **As soon as** it **rains,** **Unless** it **stays** dry,	we **will come** home.

Form and use

In the first conditional, *if* can be replaced by other words with a similar meaning such as *when*, *as soon as*, *unless* and *until*. They follow the same form as *if*:

conditional clause	result clause
if / as soon as / unless / when + present simple,	future simple

- *I'**ll lend** you my book **as soon as** I've finished reading it.*
- ***When** it stops raining, we'**ll start** the game again.*

Unless means *if not*.

- *She'll make the cake tonight **if** she **isn't** tired.*
- *She'll make the cake tonight **unless** she's tired.*

Grammar Reference 119

GRAMMAR REFERENCE

Zero conditional

conditional clause	result clause
If there **aren't** any clouds,	the Earth **loses** heat.
If it**'s** warm and dry,	pine cones **open up**.
If you**'ve finished**,	**go** and **have** a coffee.
When you **arrive**,	please **send** me a text.

Form

The zero conditional is formed as follows:

conditional clause	result clause
If + present simple,	present simple
conditional clause	**result clause**
If + present simple,	imperative

Use

We use the zero conditional to talk about things which are generally or always true.
- *If you heat water to 100 °C, it boils.*
- *If you mix yellow and blue, you get green.*

These forms can be inverted: present simple + *if* + present simple
- *Water boils if you heat it to 100 °C.*
- *You get green if you mix yellow and blue.*

We can replace *if* with *when* in zero conditional sentences.
- *When you heat water to 100 °C, it boils.*
- *When you mix yellow and blue, you get green.*

We also use the zero conditional with imperatives and modals to talk about possible future events.
- *If you go to England next week, bring me back some tea.*
- *If you want to pass your driving test, you should get more lessons.*

will / may / might for future possibility

affirmative		
I / You / He / She / It / We / You / They	will / 'll	go.
negative		
I / You / He / She / It / We / You / They	will not / won't	go.
questions		
Will	I / you / he / she / it / we / you / they	go?
short answers		
Yes, I / you / he / she / it / we / they **will**. No, I / you / he / she / it / we / they **won't**.		

will	may / might
The leopards **will** then **attack** quickly.	Their behaviour **may be** changing.
The eggs **will stick** to the smooth surface.	A leopard **might attack** a man, if it's afraid.

Form and use

Will, *may* and *might* are all modal verbs. This means they are invariable in all forms, they are not used with auxiliary verbs and they are followed by verbs in the base form without *to*.
- *Jack will come to the party*
- *They won't listen to you.*
- *Will he help us?*
- *We may see her there.*
- *Her dad might drive her to the party.*
- *They might not come this evening.*

We use the modal verbs *will*, *may* and *might* to express possibility. *Will* is used when we believe something will definitely happen in the future. *May* and *might* are used to say that something is possible.
- *We won't go to the cinema tonight. We have an exam tomorrow.* (We know we aren't going.)
- *We may not / might not go to the cinema tonight. We have an exam tomorrow.* (We aren't sure, we will possibly go.)

UNIT 7

Second conditional

affirmative
If I **had** a cold, I**'d take** a couple of paracetamol.
negative
If people **used** natural remedies, they **wouldn't suffer** from unpleasant side effects.
questions
If you **had** a sore throat, **would** garlic actually **help** at all?
short answers
Yes, it **would**. / No, it **wouldn't**.

Look!: when we give advice we can use the form *If I were you, I'd …* instead of *If I was you, I'd …*

Form

The second conditional is formed as follows:

conditional clause	result clause
If + past simple,	conditional

Use

We use the second conditional to talk about unreal or hypothetical situations.
- *If they had more money, they would buy the computers now.*
- *They would help the poor if they had more money.*

SECOND CONDITIONAL V FIRST CONDITIONAL

first conditional
If it**'s** a girl, we**'ll call** her Poppy. If it**'s** a boy, we**'ll call** him Jack.
second conditional
If I **won** the lottery, I**'d buy** a Ferrari.

120 **Grammar Reference**

GRAMMAR REFERENCE

The first conditional talks of situations that are in the future but probable / likely to happen. The woman is pregnant, she will have a boy or a girl. That is a fact.

The second conditional talks of hypothetical situations. They may never be probable. I may never win the lottery, it's very unlikely.

should / had better / ought to for advice

should
Notices say you **should turn off** your mobile phone. We **should tell** our teacher if Jack is cheating in the text.
had better
Sports experts tell us, we**'d better take** our kids to the swimming pool. I've lost my keys. I**'d better call** my mum.
ought to
Passengers **ought to switch off** all portable electronic devices. It's already midnight, I **ought to be** home by now.

affirmative		
I / You / He / She / It / We / You / They	should	go.
negative		
I / You / He / She / It / We / You / They	should not / shouldn't	go.
questions		
Should	I / you / he / she / it / we / you / they	go?
short answers		
Yes, I / you / he / she / it / we / they **should**. No, I / you / he / she / it / we / they **shouldn't**.		

Form and use

Should is a modal verb. It does not change in all its forms and does not use auxiliary forms. To form the negative we add *not* and to form the interrogative we invert *should* with the main subject.
- *I should see the doctor tomorrow.*
- *'Should Jack come to the party?' 'Yes, he should.'*
- *Jane shouldn't tell her friend about Rob.*

Should is used for advice or a strong recommendation for a future action.
- *You're not well, you should see the doctor.*
- *You should give the lost purse to the police.*

Should is also used for opinions.
- *'What should do the government do about homeless people?' 'They should help them more.'*

Ought to is also a modal verb, but unlike other modal verbs, it takes the base form with *to*.
- *You ought to see a doctor. / You should see a doctor.*

Ought to is used predominantly in affirmative sentences. It can be used in negative and interrogative forms, but it is very formal.
- *You ought to wash your hair tonight.*

Had better is also used to give advice, but is used more when there are negative consequences if the advice is not followed.
- *I've missed the last bus home, I'd better phone my mum or she'll be very worried.*

Had better is used in affirmative and negative sentences, but very rarely in interrogative forms.

UNIT 8

Third conditional

affirmative
If he**'d had** fewer difficulties, he **would** perhaps **have achieved** more.
negative
If the 9/11 attacks **hadn't taken place,** the Americans **would** probably never **have gone** into Iraq.
questions
Would communication **have developed** in the same way if the boys **hadn't launched** their site?
short answers
Yes, it **would**. No, it **wouldn't**.

Form

The third conditional is formed as follows:

conditional clause	result clause
If + past perfect,	*would have* + past participle
result clause	**conditional clause**
would have + past participle	*if* + past perfect

Use

We use the third conditional to talk about things in the past that did or did not happen and what would have happened if we had done something different. We cannot change the consequences of the actions.
- *If he hadn't started working in Bristol, he would never have met his future wife.*
  (But he did work there and now he's married.)
- *I wouldn't have left my job, if the bosses hadn't been so unfair.*
  (But they were unfair and I have now left.)

wish + past tenses

wish + past simple (for present regret)
I wish we **had** some younger MPs in parliament. I wish the voting age **was** 16.
wish + past perfect (for past regret)
I wish I**'d been able to** vote in the Brexit referendum. I wish that our candidate **had won**.

Grammar Reference 121

GRAMMAR REFERENCE

Use

We use *wish* to talk about how we would like a present or past situation to be different.

When we are referring to a present situation, the structure is *wish* + past simple / continuous.

- *There are no cheap restaurants near where I live. I wish there were some cheap restaurants near where I live.* (It's unlikely, but it is possible there may be some in the future.)
- *I wish I could vote, but the voting age is 18 and I'm only 16.* (The voting age may change.)
- *The train is late. I wish we were travelling by car.* (Then we might arrive on time.)

When we are referring to a past situation, we use *wish* + past perfect simple / continuous.

- *Those trousers I bought look awful on me. I wish I hadn't bought those trousers.* (But I did buy them.)
- *We didn't get a good view of the castle because it was raining. I wish it hadn't been raining.* (But it was raining.)

UNIT 9

The passive: Present and past simple

present simple passive	
affirmative	negative
Gadgets **are made** by the company.	Gadgets **aren't made** for Spain.
questions	short answers
Are gadgets **made** for Korea?	Yes, they **are**. No, they **aren't**.
past simple passive	
affirmative	negative
The diseases in the brain **were discovered by** scientists.	A cure for cancer **wasn't discovered by** scientists.
questions	short answers
Was a cure for Alzheimer's **discovered**?	Yes, it **was**. No, it **wasn't**.

Form

The passive is formed by using the verb *be* in the same tense as the normal verb and the past participle of the main verb. When we change sentences into the passive, the object of the active sentence becomes the subject of the passive sentence. The verb tense remains the same.

Present simple: *They **grow** lots of flowers in Holland.* (present simple of *grow*)
→ *Lots of flowers **are grown** in Holland.* (present simple of *be* followed by the past participle of *grow*)

Past simple: *The judge **sentenced** the thief yesterday.* (past simple of *sentence*)
→ *The thief was **sentenced** yesterday.* (past simple of *be* followed by the past participle of *sentence*)

by

When we use the passive, if we say who or what was responsible for the action, we use the preposition *by*.

- *That theatre is owned by a famous actor.*
- *Many people were affected by the Second World War.*

We do not use *by* + agent when it is obvious who performed the action. For example, we would not usually say: *He was arrested by the police.* We would say: *He was arrested.* We would not use *by* + agent in this case, as only the police can arrest people.

The passive: Present perfect

affirmative	negative
The results **have been published**.	The results **haven't been shared** online.
questions	short answers
Has the research **been supported** by the international community?	Yes, it **has**. No, it **hasn't**.

Form

The present perfect passive works in the same way as the other forms. The present perfect of the verb *be* is used with the past participle of the active verb.

Present perfect: *Somebody has stolen my wallet.* (present perfect of *steal*)
→ *My wallet has been stolen.* (present perfect of *be* followed by the past participle of *steal*)

UNIT 10

Reported speech: Statements

When we transfer direct speech to reported, we make some changes to the sentence.

TENSE CHANGES

In general the verb tenses go back one tense, as in the table.

direct speech	reported speech
Present simple He **is** well.	**Past simple** He **was** well.
Present continuous He **is doing** well.	**Past continuous** He **was doing** well.
Past simple He **went** home.	**Past perfect** He **had gone** home.

122   **Grammar Reference**

GRAMMAR REFERENCE

Past continuous	Past perfect continuous
He **was going** home.	He **had been going** home.
Present perfect	Past perfect
He **has done** well.	He **had done** well.
Present perfect continuous	Past perfect continuous
He **has been working** long.	He **had been working** long.
is going to be	was going to be
He **is going to be** home.	He **was going to be** home.
will / won't	would / wouldn't
He **will finish** in time.	He **would finish** in time.

PRONOUNS AND ADJECTIVES

Apart from changing the verb tenses, we also have to remember to change the personal pronouns and possessive adjectives where necessary.

- *'I go skiing every winter,' Jake said.*
  → *Jake said that he went skiing every winter.*
- *'I'm really excited – my story is in the school newspaper,' Edwina said.*
  → *Edwina said (that) she was really excited because her story was in the school newspaper.*

We can omit the word *that* in reported speech.

TIME CHANGES

When we are reporting speech, we often make other changes related to time.

this morning / afternoon / evening / week	→ **that** morning / afternoon / evening / month
today	→ **that** day
tonight	→ **that** night
next week / month / year	→ **that** week / month / year
yesterday	→ **the day before**
last summer / week / month / year	→ **the** summer / week / month / year **before**

- *'I uploaded my post **this morning**,' Fran said.*
  → *Fran said that she had uploaded her post **that morning**.*
- *'Did you go away **last summer**?' Claudia asked.*
  → *Claudia asked me if I had been away **the summer before**.*

SAY AND TELL

When we report what someone has said we use *say* if there is no direct object and *tell* if there is an object.

- She **said** that she wanted to study journalism.
- She **told me** that she wanted to study journalism.

Reported speech: Questions

direct speech	reported speech
Do **you believe** in the freedom of the press?	We asked them if / whether **they believed** in the freedom of the press.
How **can you** help?	They asked us how **we could** help.

To report questions, we make the same tense changes as in reported statements.
When we are reporting *Yes / No* questions (i.e., questions without question words), we use *if* or *whether* before the reported clause and we use statement form rather than question form.

- '**Did you read** that story?' Martin asked.
  → *Martin asked **if / whether I had read** the story.*
- '**Have you read** the papers today?' Kirsten asked.
  → *Kirsten asked **if / whether I had read** the papers that day.*

When we report questions which have question words (*Who, What, How,* etc.), we use the question word in the reported question. The word order is the same as for reported statements.

- '**Where are you going** on holiday?' Melinda asked.
  → *Melinda asked **where I was going** on holiday.*
- '**How much did the printer cost**?' Sam asked.
  → *Sam asked **how much the printer had cost**.*

Reported speech: Commands

direct speech	reported speech
'**Sign** our online petition.'	They told us **to sign** their online petition.
'**Don't waste** time reading fake news!'	He told me **not to waste** time reading fake news.

We use the structure **tell somebody to do something** to report commands.

- *'Turn down the TV,' Lauren said.*
  → *Lauren told me to turn down the TV.*

If the command is negative, then we use the structure **tell somebody not to do something**.

- *'Don't forget to buy some milk,' my mum said.*
  → *My mum told me not to forget to buy some milk.*

Reported speech: Requests

We use the structure **ask somebody to do something** to report requests.

- *'Please, answer the phone,' my dad said.*
  → *My dad asked me to answer the phone.*

If a request is in the negative, then we use the structure **ask somebody not to do something**.

- *'Don't tell my parents,' Emily said.*
  → *Emily asked me not to tell her parents.*

GRAMMAR MAPS

Present simple v present continuous

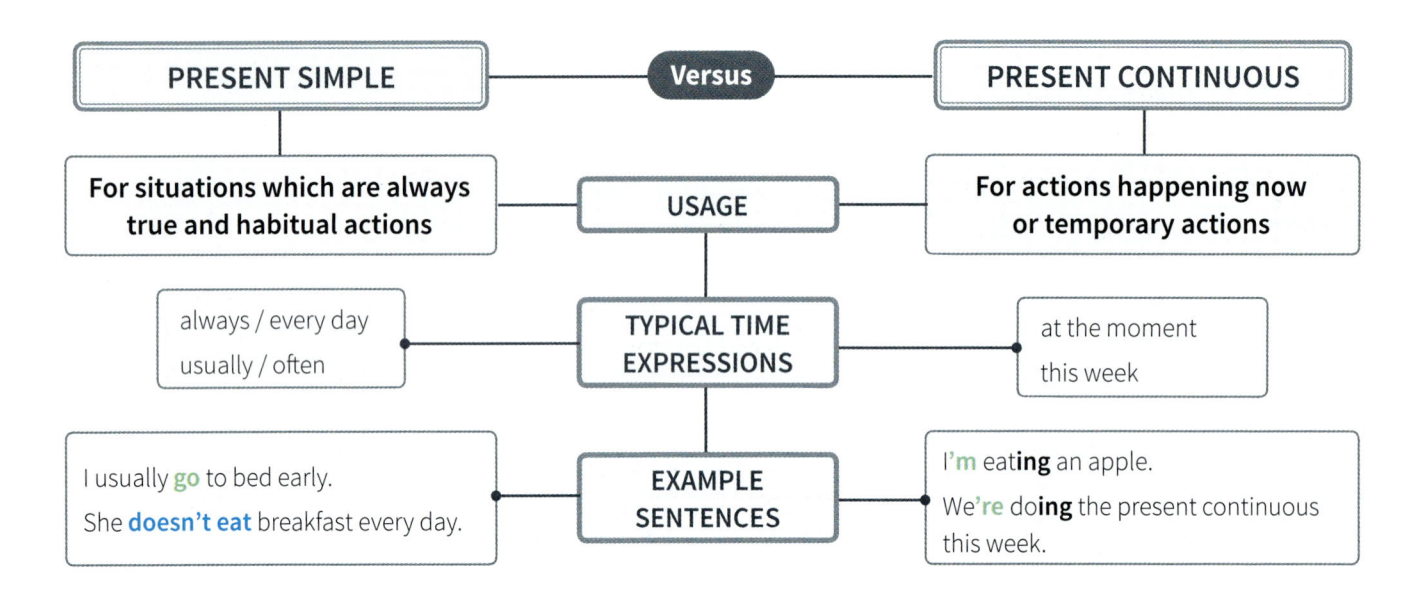

PRESENT SIMPLE	Versus	PRESENT CONTINUOUS
For situations which are always true and habitual actions	USAGE	For actions happening now or temporary actions
always / every day; usually / often	TYPICAL TIME EXPRESSIONS	at the moment; this week
I usually **go** to bed early. She **doesn't eat** breakfast every day.	EXAMPLE SENTENCES	I**'m** eat**ing** an apple. We**'re** do**ing** the present continuous this week.

Past simple v present perfect

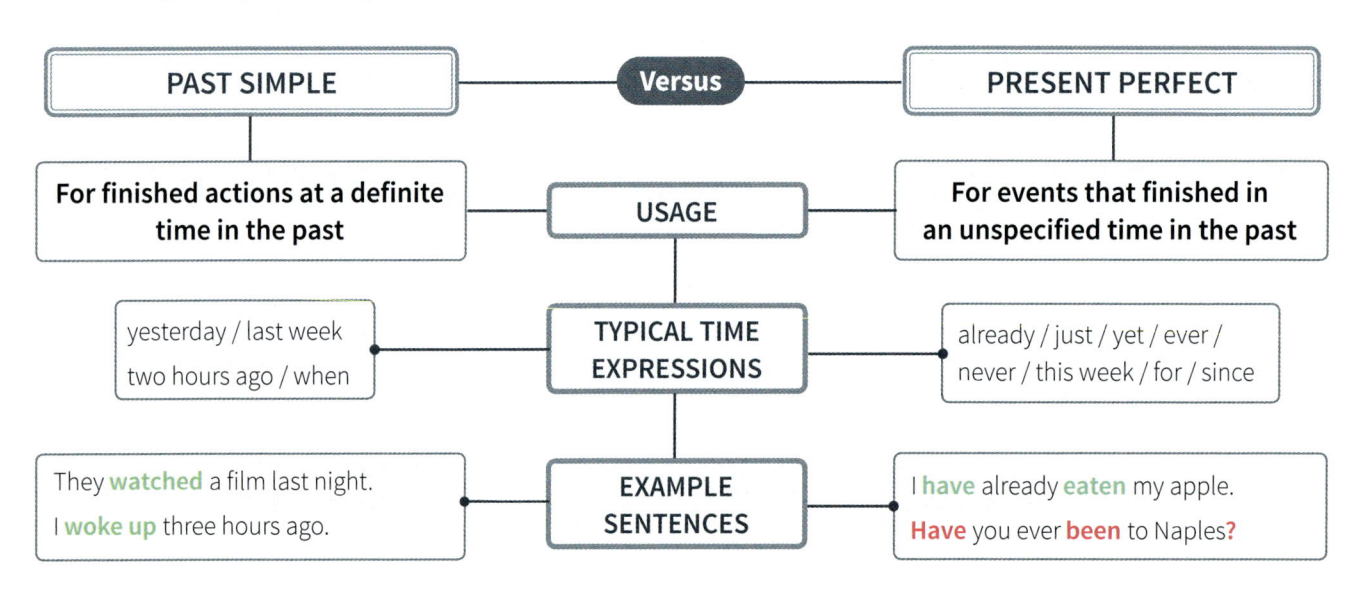

PAST SIMPLE	Versus	PRESENT PERFECT
For finished actions at a definite time in the past	USAGE	For events that finished in an unspecified time in the past
yesterday / last week; two hours ago / when	TYPICAL TIME EXPRESSIONS	already / just / yet / ever / never / this week / for / since
They **watched** a film last night. I **woke up** three hours ago.	EXAMPLE SENTENCES	I **have** already **eaten** my apple. **Have** you ever **been** to Naples?

be going to v present continuous

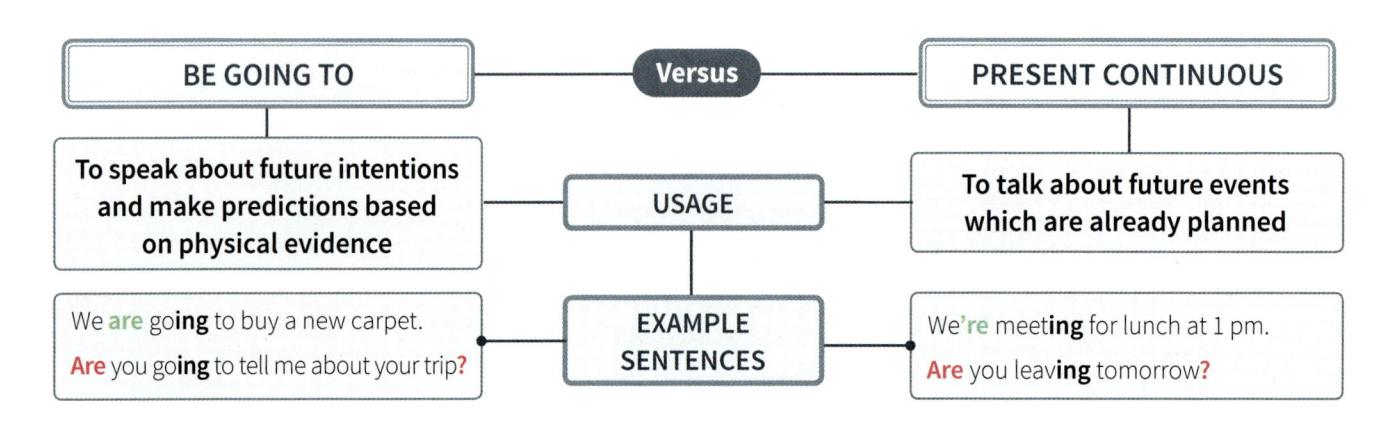

BE GOING TO	Versus	PRESENT CONTINUOUS
To speak about future intentions and make predictions based on physical evidence	USAGE	To talk about future events which are already planned
We **are** go**ing** to buy a new carpet. **Are** you go**ing** to tell me about your trip?	EXAMPLE SENTENCES	We**'re** meet**ing** for lunch at 1 pm. **Are** you leav**ing** tomorrow?

GRAMMAR MAPS

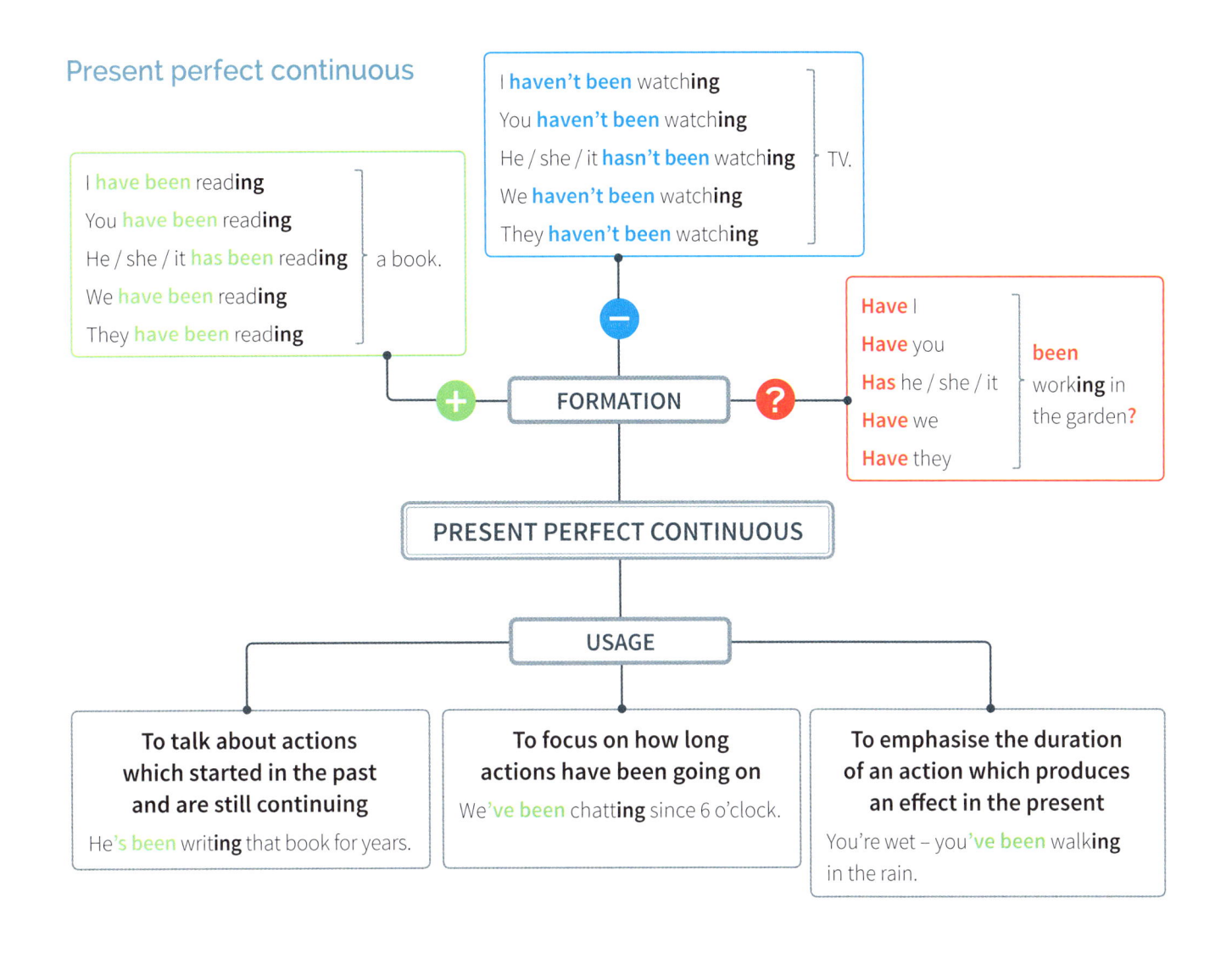

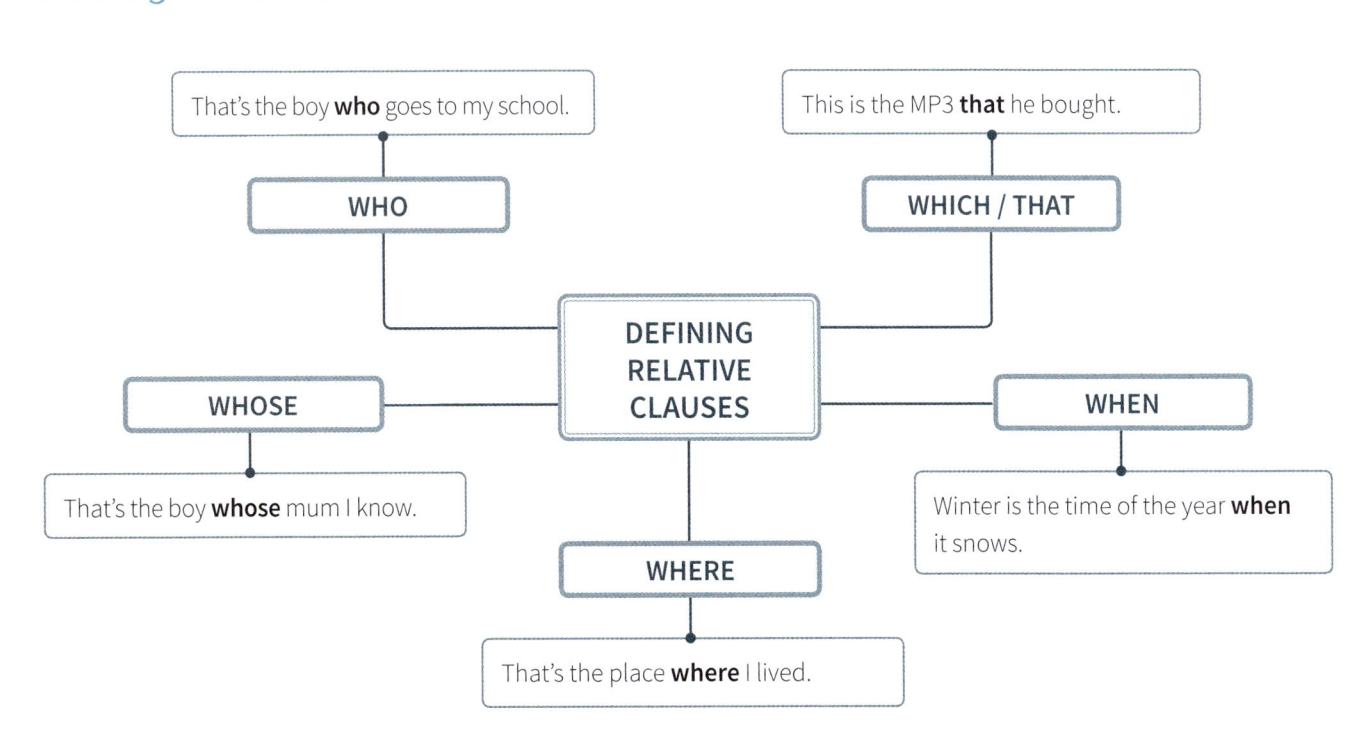

Present perfect continuous

FORMATION

(+)
I **have been** read**ing**
You **have been** read**ing**
He / she / it **has been** read**ing**   a book.
We **have been** read**ing**
They **have been** read**ing**

(−)
I **haven't been** watch**ing**
You **haven't been** watch**ing**
He / she / it **hasn't been** watch**ing**   TV.
We **haven't been** watch**ing**
They **haven't been** watch**ing**

(?)
Have I
Have you
Has he / she / it   **been** work**ing** in the garden**?**
Have we
Have they

PRESENT PERFECT CONTINUOUS

USAGE

- To talk about actions which started in the past and are still continuing
  He**'s been** writ**ing** that book for years.

- To focus on how long actions have been going on
  We**'ve been** chatt**ing** since 6 o'clock.

- To emphasise the duration of an action which produces an effect in the present
  You're wet – you**'ve been** walk**ing** in the rain.

Defining relative clauses

WHO — That's the boy **who** goes to my school.

WHICH / THAT — This is the MP3 **that** he bought.

WHOSE — That's the boy **whose** mum I know.

WHEN — Winter is the time of the year **when** it snows.

WHERE — That's the place **where** I lived.

DEFINING RELATIVE CLAUSES

Grammar Maps 125

GRAMMAR MAPS

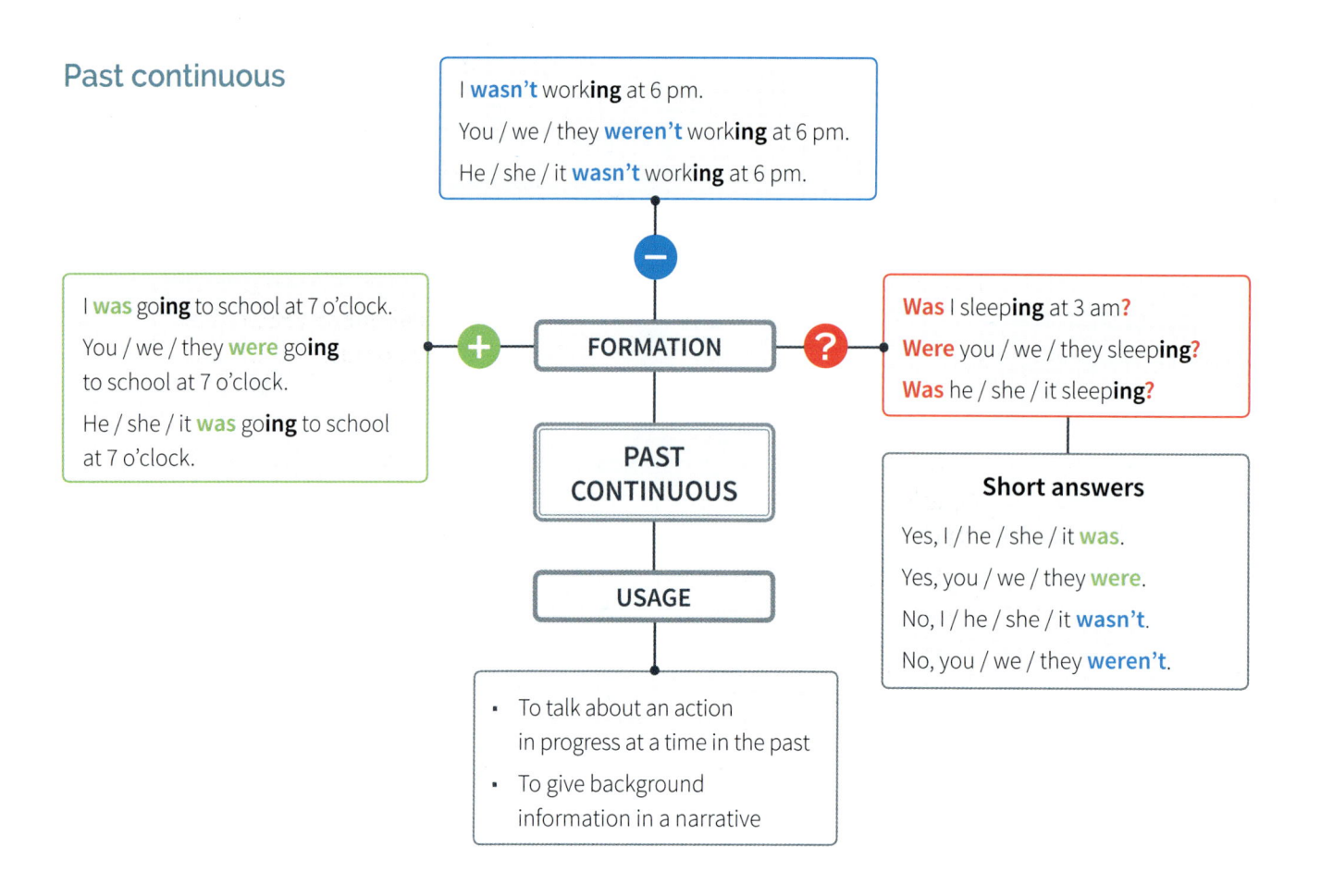

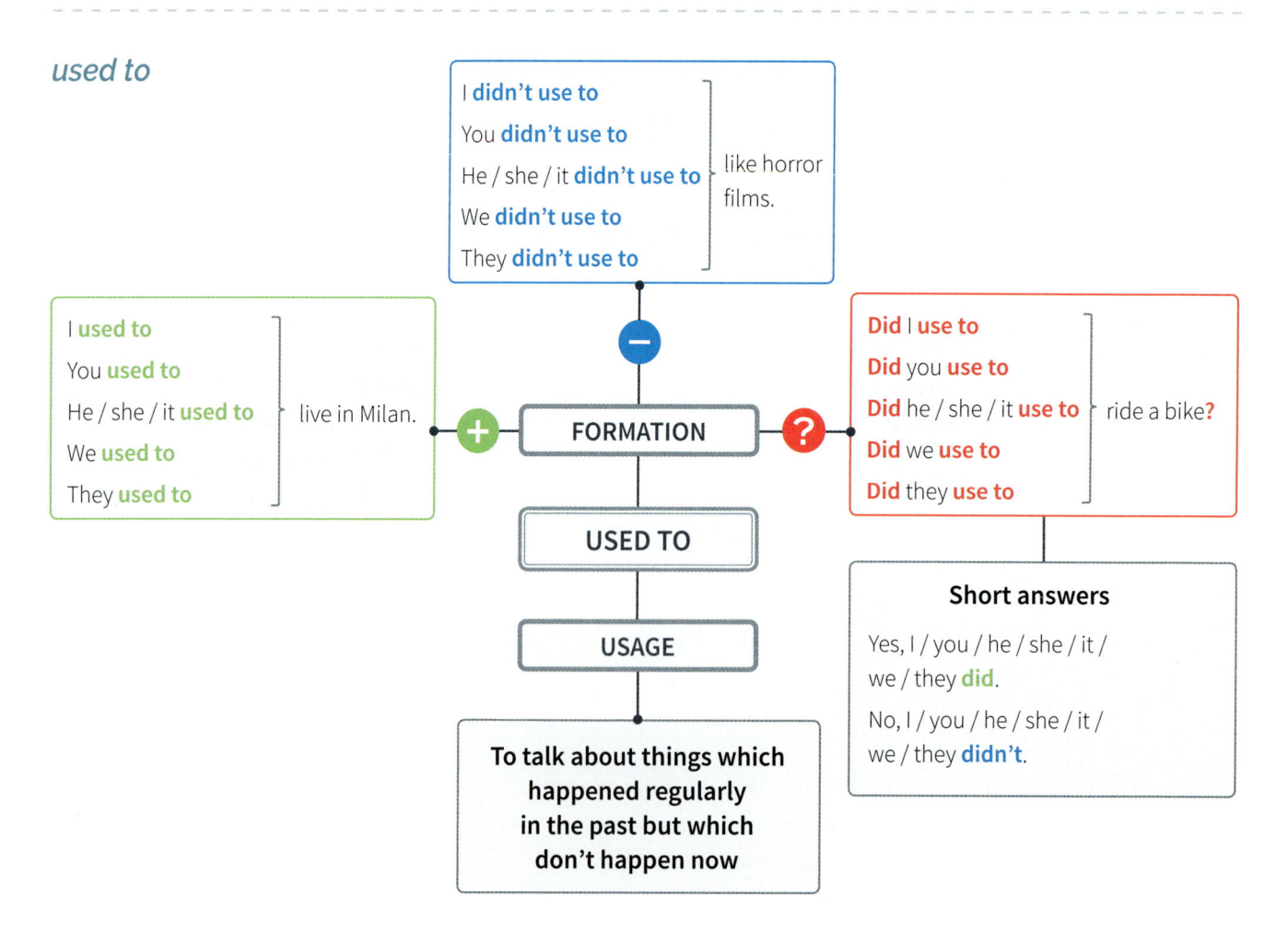

Past continuous

FORMATION

(+)
- I **was** go**ing** to school at 7 o'clock.
- You / we / they **were** go**ing** to school at 7 o'clock.
- He / she / it **was** go**ing** to school at 7 o'clock.

(−)
- I **wasn't** work**ing** at 6 pm.
- You / we / they **weren't** work**ing** at 6 pm.
- He / she / it **wasn't** work**ing** at 6 pm.

(?)
- **Was** I sleep**ing** at 3 am?
- **Were** you / we / they sleep**ing**?
- **Was** he / she / it sleep**ing**?

Short answers
- Yes, I / he / she / it **was**.
- Yes, you / we / they **were**.
- No, I / he / she / it **wasn't**.
- No, you / we / they **weren't**.

PAST CONTINUOUS

USAGE
- To talk about an action in progress at a time in the past
- To give background information in a narrative

---

used to

FORMATION

(+)
- I **used to**
- You **used to**
- He / she / it **used to**
- We **used to**
- They **used to**

live in Milan.

(−)
- I **didn't use to**
- You **didn't use to**
- He / she / it **didn't use to**
- We **didn't use to**
- They **didn't use to**

like horror films.

(?)
- **Did** I **use to**
- **Did** you **use to**
- **Did** he / she / it **use to**
- **Did** we **use to**
- **Did** they **use to**

ride a bike?

Short answers
- Yes, I / you / he / she / it / we / they **did**.
- No, I / you / he / she / it / we / they **didn't**.

USED TO

USAGE

To talk about things which happened regularly in the past but which don't happen now

126 Grammar Maps

GRAMMAR MAPS

Second conditional

```
FORMATION ── SECOND CONDITIONAL ── USAGE
                                     │
                                     To talk about a hypothetical
                                     present or future situation
```

Condition:
if + past simple,

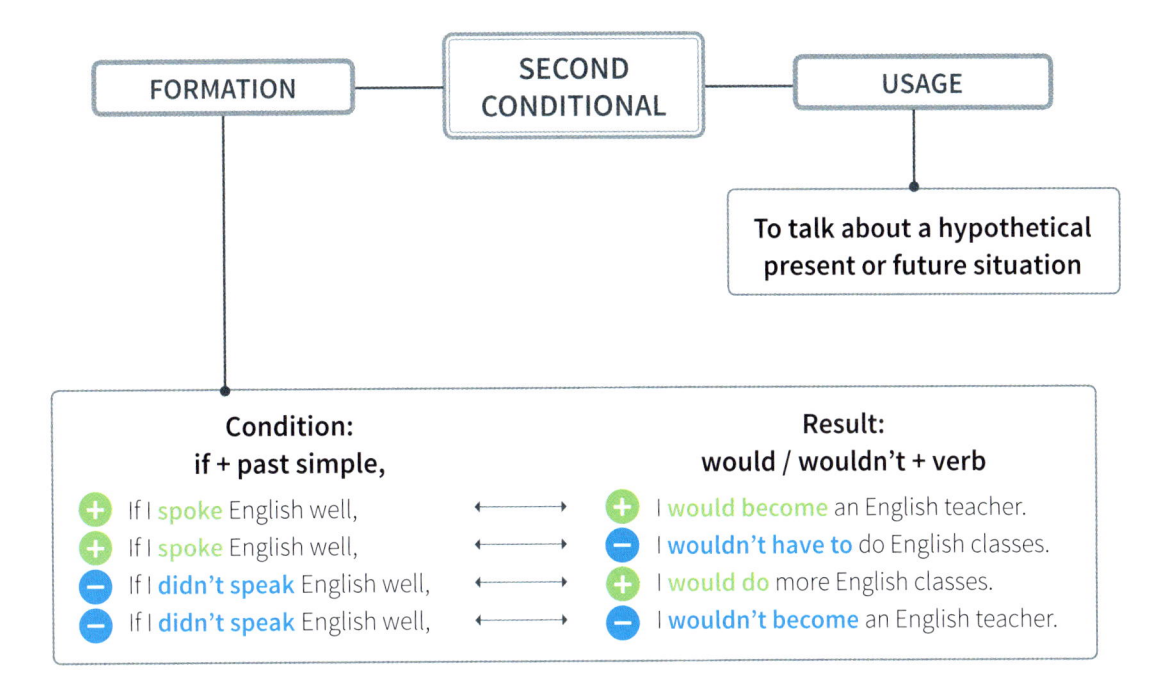

Result:
would / wouldn't + verb

- (+) If I **spoke** English well, ⟷ (+) I **would become** an English teacher.
- (+) If I **spoke** English well, ⟷ (−) I **wouldn't have to** do English classes.
- (−) If I **didn't speak** English well, ⟷ (+) I **would do** more English classes.
- (−) If I **didn't speak** English well, ⟷ (−) I **wouldn't become** an English teacher.

Third conditional

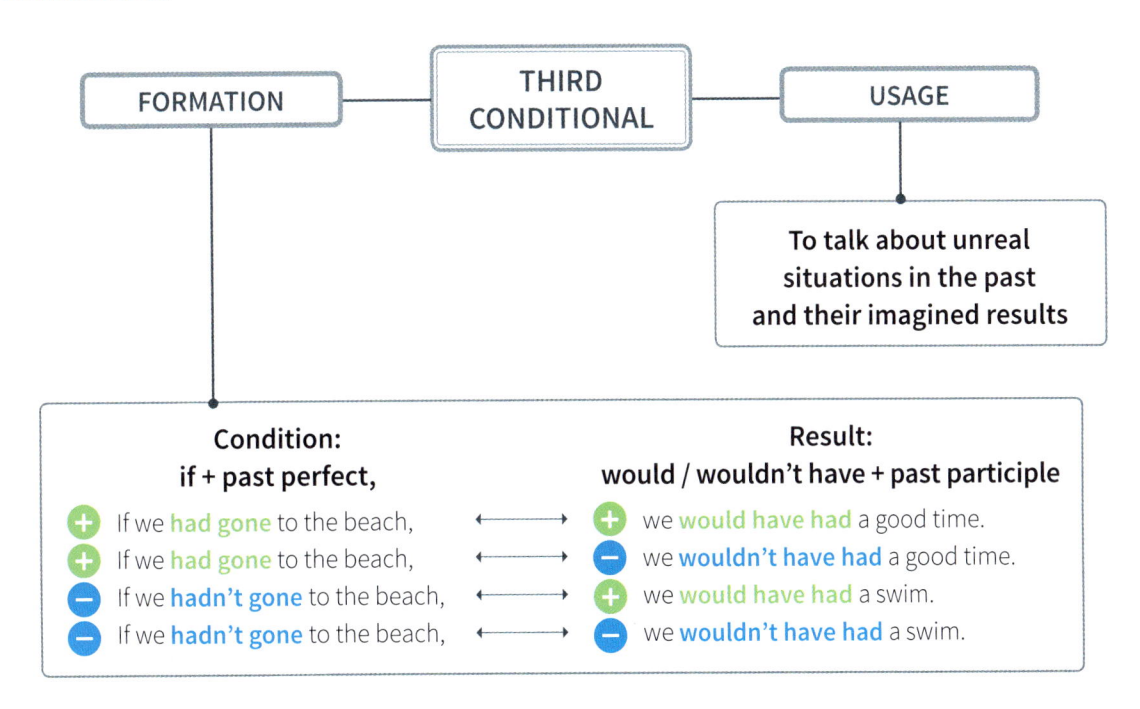

```
FORMATION ── THIRD CONDITIONAL ── USAGE
                                    │
                                    To talk about unreal
                                    situations in the past
                                    and their imagined results
```

Condition:
if + past perfect,

Result:
would / wouldn't have + past participle

- (+) If we **had gone** to the beach, ⟷ (+) we **would have had** a good time.
- (+) If we **had gone** to the beach, ⟷ (−) we **wouldn't have had** a good time.
- (−) If we **hadn't gone** to the beach, ⟷ (+) we **would have had** a swim.
- (−) If we **hadn't gone** to the beach, ⟷ (−) we **wouldn't have had** a swim.

Grammar Maps   127

GRAMMAR MAPS

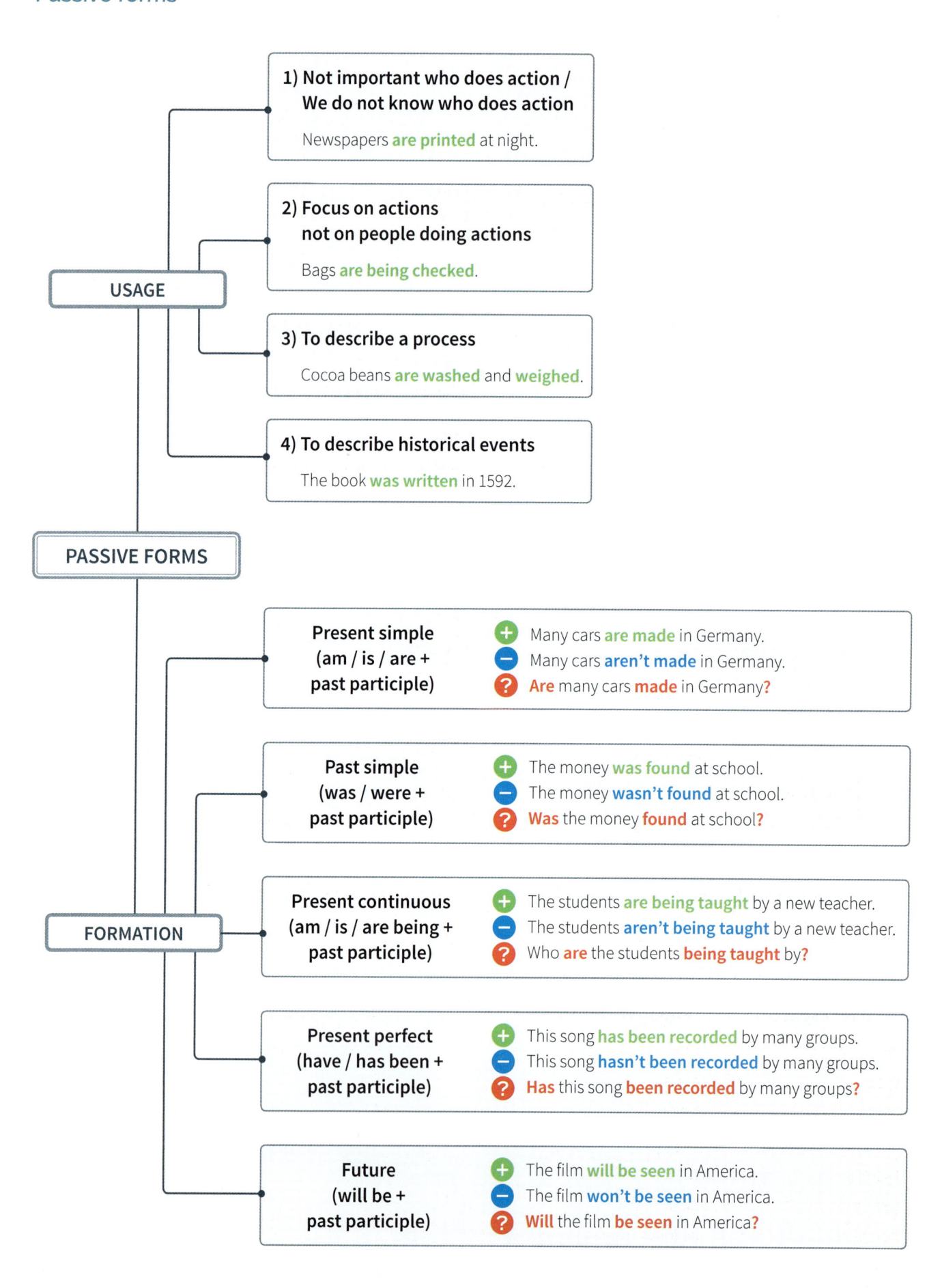

Passive forms

USAGE

1) Not important who does action / We do not know who does action
   Newspapers **are printed** at night.

2) Focus on actions not on people doing actions
   Bags **are being checked**.

3) To describe a process
   Cocoa beans **are washed** and **weighed**.

4) To describe historical events
   The book **was written** in 1592.

PASSIVE FORMS

FORMATION

Present simple
(am / is / are + past participle)
- ➕ Many cars **are made** in Germany.
- ➖ Many cars **aren't made** in Germany.
- ❓ **Are** many cars **made** in Germany?

Past simple
(was / were + past participle)
- ➕ The money **was found** at school.
- ➖ The money **wasn't found** at school.
- ❓ **Was** the money **found** at school?

Present continuous
(am / is / are being + past participle)
- ➕ The students **are being taught** by a new teacher.
- ➖ The students **aren't being taught** by a new teacher.
- ❓ Who **are** the students **being taught** by?

Present perfect
(have / has been + past participle)
- ➕ This song **has been recorded** by many groups.
- ➖ This song **hasn't been recorded** by many groups.
- ❓ **Has** this song **been recorded** by many groups?

Future
(will be + past participle)
- ➕ The film **will be seen** in America.
- ➖ The film **won't be seen** in America.
- ❓ **Will** the film **be seen** in America?

128   Grammar Maps

GRAMMAR MAPS

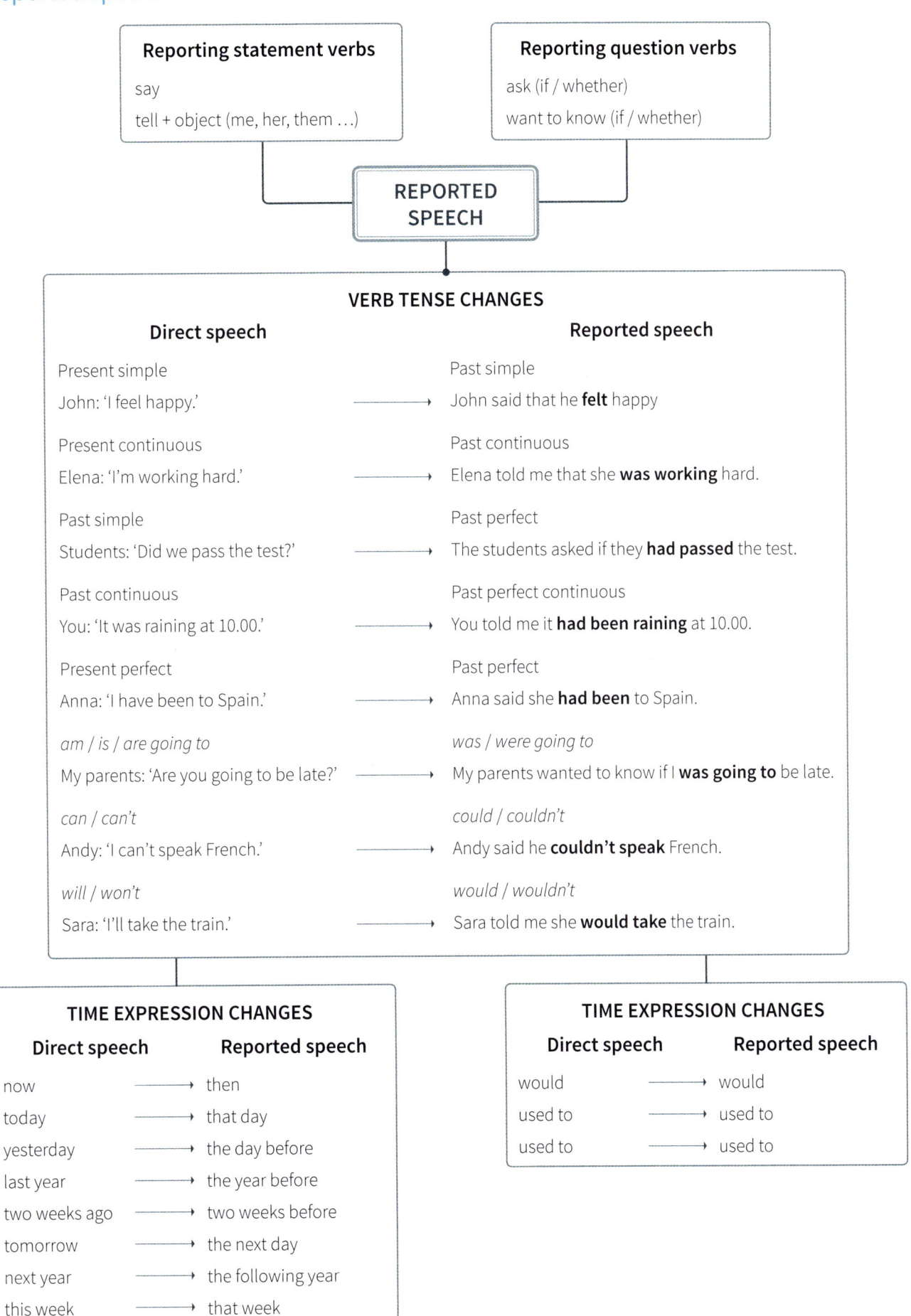

Reported speech

Reporting statement verbs
say
tell + object (me, her, them …)

Reporting question verbs
ask (if / whether)
want to know (if / whether)

→ **REPORTED SPEECH**

VERB TENSE CHANGES

Direct speech	Reported speech
Present simple John: 'I feel happy.'	Past simple John said that he **felt** happy
Present continuous Elena: 'I'm working hard.'	Past continuous Elena told me that she **was working** hard.
Past simple Students: 'Did we pass the test?'	Past perfect The students asked if they **had passed** the test.
Past continuous You: 'It was raining at 10.00.'	Past perfect continuous You told me it **had been raining** at 10.00.
Present perfect Anna: 'I have been to Spain.'	Past perfect Anna said she **had been** to Spain.
am / is / are going to My parents: 'Are you going to be late?'	*was / were going to* My parents wanted to know if I **was going to** be late.
can / can't Andy: 'I can't speak French.'	*could / couldn't* Andy said he **couldn't speak** French.
will / won't Sara: 'I'll take the train.'	*would / wouldn't* Sara told me she **would take** the train.

TIME EXPRESSION CHANGES

Direct speech	Reported speech
now	then
today	that day
yesterday	the day before
last year	the year before
two weeks ago	two weeks before
tomorrow	the next day
next year	the following year
this week	that week

TIME EXPRESSION CHANGES

Direct speech	Reported speech
would	would
used to	used to
used to	used to

Grammar Maps 129

STARTER A About us

VOCABULARY: Verbs of routine

1 Complete this sport star's blog with the words below.

> have breakfast ▪ go to bed ▪ come home ▪
> ~~wake up~~ ▪ brush my teeth ▪ get up ▪ get dressed

My name's Jay Fox and I'm a professional volleyball player. I know that some of you want to know how I spend my day. Well, I ⁰ **wake up** at 8 am. I stay in bed for about 10 minutes and then I ¹.......................... .
I ².......................... because I don't like to ³.......................... in my pyjamas! I have a wash and ⁴.......................... .
I'm out of the house at 9.
I basically train all day, with just a light lunch with my teammates.
Then around 5 pm I ⁵.......................... .
I relax, watch TV and then I ⁶.......................... at around 10 or 11. It's a good life, I know.

GRAMMAR: Present simple

2 Complete the sentences with the correct form of *be*.

0   We ......**are**...... twin brothers.
1   They .... my friends.
2   I .... at home.
3   She .... 16.
4   He ....very happy today.
5   Ivan .... from Russia.
6   My uncles .... Spanish.

3 Change into negative sentences.

0   We're sisters.
    We aren't sisters.
1   I'm Spanish.
2   French is a difficult language.
3   They're late for the film.
4   This is the right street.
5   Nicky is at school today.
6   My maths lessons are easy.

4 Complete the dialogue with the correct form of *be*.

A   This ⁰..........**is**.......... my family. Here we ¹.......................... in Tenerife, Spain, with my cousin. As you can see, it ².......................... really beautiful. My parents ³.......................... on the right. That ⁴.......................... my sister and I ⁵.......................... next to her. We ⁶.......................... a really happy family …
B   ⁷.......................... that your cousin there?
A   No, it ⁸.......................... . She ⁹.......................... just a friend on holiday with us.
B   ¹⁰.......................... you still friends?
A   Yes, we ¹¹.......................... still in touch.
B   So where ¹².......................... your cousin?
A   She ¹³.......................... the one with the camera. She ¹⁴.......................... really nice.

5 Correct the mistakes. Two sentences are correct.

0   I no have a ticket for a train.
    I haven't got a ticket for the train.
1   She not has got dark hair.
2   We hasn't got a nice car.
3   My brother's got a bike.
4   They hasn't got the right books with them.
5   I hasn't a good French teacher.
6   My sisters have got blue eyes.

6 Match the correct questions to the answers.

0   [c] Have you got many films on DVD?
1   [ ] Have you got any brothers or sisters?
2   [ ] Have they got any good beaches here?
3   [ ] Have I got time to go on the internet?
4   [ ] Have we got food for this evening?
5   [ ] Has your brother got a girlfriend?
6   [ ] Has your mum got dark hair?

a   No, you haven't – we're late.
b   Just a brother. His name's Marcus.
c   No, just one or two of my favourites.
d   No, blonde.
e   Not really, just a piece of cheese.
f   There's a nice one five minutes from here.
g   Yes, he has. She's really nice.

A

7 Complete the dialogue with the correct form of *have got*.

Liz Hi Ben, ⁰ *have you got* time for a walk?
Ben Yes, sure.
Liz So, is everything OK?
Ben Yes, fine. Look, I ¹........................... my photos from the holiday on my phone.
Liz Great! Is that your brother? He ²........................... really nice eyes!
Ben That's true! ³........................... any brothers or sisters?
Liz Yes, I ⁴........................... a brother – he ⁵........................... dark hair like me. And I ⁶........................... a sister, too.
Ben Tell me about your sister …
Liz Well, she ⁷........................... dark hair, too.
Ben ⁸........................... a photo of her?
Liz Yes, I think so. Ah, here you are …

8 Choose the correct option.

0 I (*play*) / *plays* tennis at the weekend.
1 My brother *read* / *reads* a lot.
2 Her sisters *live* / *lives* in the city centre.
3 We *meet* / *meets* here every Tuesday.
4 Estella *loves* / *love* Coldplay.
5 Guy and Anna *use* / *uses* Facebook all the time.

9 Complete the text with the correct form of the verbs in brackets.

Paolo ⁰ *is* (be) in Edinburgh for six months to study English. His host family ¹........................... (be) nice and they ²........................... (have) a son, Luke. He ³........................... (be) 16 like Paolo. Paolo really ⁴........................... (like) his English course. Lessons ⁵........................... (start) at 9:00 and he ⁶........................... (study) all morning. In the afternoon he ⁷........................... (go) into the city centre and he ⁸........................... (have) a sandwich in a café or he just ⁹........................... (walk) around with friends. In the evening he ¹⁰........................... (watch) TV with the family – it's good for his English.

10 Change into negative sentences.

0 Holly sings in a band.
  Holly *doesn't sing in a band.*
1 My cousin wears expensive clothes.
2 She studies a lot in the evening.
3 My parents speak Spanish.
4 We play sports at school on Friday afternoons.
5 My brother likes spaghetti on toast.

11 Write questions using the prompts.

0 Where / your sister / live?
  Where *does your sister live?*
1 you / like the theatre?
2 Michael / play the guitar?
3 How / you go to school?
4 What / Samir / study at university?
5 your parents / speak French?
6 Why / Tim like / that music?

12 Complete the blog with the correct form of the verbs in brackets.

My best friend is Freddie. He ⁰ *doesn't live* (not / live) near me, he actually ¹........................... (live) over 200 km away, but we ²........................... (speak) regularly on Instant Chat. What ³........................... (he / look like)? Well, he's quite tall with blonde hair. He ⁴........................... (look) like his older brother, Ben. Freddie ⁵........................... (study) at his local school but, to be honest, he ⁶........................... (not / study) very much – he ⁷........................... (prefer) sports, especially football. What team ⁸........................... (he / support)? Chelsea, of course.

GRAMMAR: Adverbs of frequency

13 Put the words in the correct order.

0 never / use / smartphone / lessons / in / I / my
  I *never use my smartphone in lessons.*
1 always / they / leave / at 8:30 am / do / home / ?
2 never / she / at weekends / in / 's
3 you / late / always / are / ?
4 grandparents / his / visits / he / sometimes
5 me / doesn't / often / call / she
6 at home / they / usually / aren't

14 Complete the sentences with an adverb of frequency so that they are true for you.

0 I meet my friends at the weekend
  I *often meet my friends at the weekend.*
1 I listen to music on the radio.
2 My parents go out at the weekend.
3 I get angry with my friends.
4 I go to bed before 10 pm.
5 I have breakfast on school days.
6 I do my homework in the afternoon.

Starter A 131

STARTER B: My stuff

VOCABULARY: Technology

15 Match the items to their definitions.

0 [h] e-reader
1 [ ] smartphone
2 [ ] screen
3 [ ] program
4 [ ] remote control
5 [ ] laptop
6 [ ] speakers
7 [ ] headphones
8 [ ] programme
9 [ ] keyboard

a You use this to change the TV channels.
b You use these to listen to music by yourself on the train or bus.
c This is software you use on the computer.
d You use this when you need to work in different places.
e You use this to type in letters and words on the computer.
f This is where you see what you are writing on the computer.
g You use this for practically everything: calls, music, emails, etc.
h You use this to read ebooks.
i This is something you watch on the TV.
j You use these to listen to music in your room with friends.

16 Complete the sentences with words from exercise 15 and from the Student's Book.

0 I never use the keyboard. I prefer the ......mouse...... .
1 The sound on these .... is terrible. I want to change them.
2 My mum needs to work on the train to the office, so she has a ....
3 I don't like this .... The quality of the graphics is really bad.
4 I take my .... with me on holiday – I love reading a book on the beach.
5 This programme is terrible! Where's the .... ?
6 I can't use a .... for this game. I need a joystick.

GRAMMAR: *there is / there are* and *some / any*

17 Complete the sentences with the correct form of *there is / there are*.

0 ......There's...... a T-shirt on the bed.
1 .... new students in my class.
2 .... good headphones with this new smartphone.
3 .... eggs in the fridge, if you want.
4 .... no space in the car, sorry.
5 .... some nice T-shirts in this shop.
6 .... a letter for you.
7 .... any chocolate in this cake?
8 .... any good programmes on TV tonight.
9 .... any tests next week?
10 .... any programs on this PC?
11 .... a coffee bar near here?
12 .... any interesting people at the party?

18 Complete the text with *some* or *any*.

My room isn't very tidy. I've always got ⁰......some...... jeans or T-shirts on the floor or on my bed. I haven't got ¹.................. computers or video games in my room, but I've got a small TV, a DVD player and ².................. DVDs on my bedside table. I haven't got ³.................. posters, but I've got ⁴.................. postcards of my favourite places. My wardrobe is really full and there isn't ⁵.................. space for my things – that's why I leave them on the floor. I've always got ⁶.................. biscuits for when I'm hungry in the evening. There aren't ⁷.................. books on my table – I keep them under the bed! I've got ⁸.................. lovely photos of my family, too.

GRAMMAR: *a lot of, a little, a few*

19 Correct the mistakes. Two sentences are correct.

0 We've only got a ~~few~~ money for the shopping.
   a little money
1 I've got a few souvenirs from my holiday in Kenya.
2 Have you got a few time for me?
3 Can you help with a little homework exercises?
4 There are only a little people at the party.
5 I've got a lot of clothes in my wardrobe.

GRAMMAR: *too much / too many, too little / too few*

20 Choose the correct option.

0 We've got (too much) / *too many* homework.
1 I don't want *too much / too many* people at my party.
2 I've got *too much / too many* problems at the moment.
3 You're putting *too much / too many* salt in the pasta.
4 My brother and I have got *too much / too many* clothes.
5 My sister has got *too much / too many* DVDs in her room.
6 You've got *too much / too many* money with you.
7 There's *too much / too many* food in the fridge.
8 I cannot make up my mind, there are *too much / too many* options.

21 Choose the correct option.

0 There are *too little* / (too few) schools in this area.
1 I've got *too little / too few* money for the weekend.
2 There are *too little / too few* glasses for the party.
3 We have *too little / too few* information.
4 We've got *too little / too few* food in the fridge.
5 She's got *too little / too few* friends.
6 We've got *too little / too few* time.
7 The hall was empty, *too little / too few* people attended the conference.
8 There's *too little / too few* water in the jug.

22 Complete the dialogue with *too much / too many* or *too little / too few*.

Amy Hello Lucy, how are things?
Lucy Oh, hi Amy. I'm OK, thanks, but I've got ⁰ *too much* schoolwork at the moment.
Amy And ¹............... time, I imagine!
Lucy Yes. It's my English and geography teachers really. They give us ²............... tests!
Amy Well, we've got the opposite problem – our parents say we've got ³............... homework – just 20 minutes a day, and that the teachers give us ⁴............... tests – only one per semester!
Lucy And my parents aren't happy because there are ⁵............... teachers in the school – only one for every forty students.
Amy I think our parents give us ⁶............... problems …
Lucy You're right about that!

23 Choose the option which is *not* possible.

0 There's *a little* / (a few) / *some* cheese in the fridge.
1 I've got *too many / too few / too much* friends.
2 We need *some / any / a little* sugar.
3 There are *too little / too few / too many* cinemas in this city.
4 She's got *some / any / a few* Spanish books.
5 We've got *some / any / a little* orange juice.
6 We've got *some / a little / too many* time for a break.
7 There are *a lot of / a little / too many* people on the train.

24 Complete these sentences so that they are true for you.

0 I haven't got much ...*time to study*... .
1 I've got too many ....
2 I've got too little ....
3 I've got some ....
4 I haven't got any .... in my bedroom.
5 In my family we've got too few ....
6 I've got too much .... at the moment.
7 My friends have got a lot of ....

25 Complete the forum chats with *some, any, too much, too many, too little* or *too few*. You can use the same expression more than once.

Andy, Sheffield

I think young people have ⁰ *too many* electronic devices these days – smartphones, tablets, e-readers, etc., and because of these they have ¹............... time to talk to each other. When I see ²............... young people sitting together I notice they don't have ³............... conversations – they just sit there looking at their screens!

Eleanora, Bristol

That's not true. I think we have ⁴............... devices – young people need a lot of devices these days. We often don't have ⁵............... free time at school, so when we go out with ⁶............... friends we use our smartphones to chat to other people at the same time – what's the problem? Teachers and parents put ⁷............... stress on young people. They give us ⁸............... things to do and then say we never chat to each other …

STARTER C School

VOCABULARY: Clothes

26 Write these people's descriptions.

1 Suzanne's got *a black skirt, a white blouse, …*
....
....

2 Tom's got ....
....
....

GRAMMAR: Past simple: *be*

27 Choose the correct option.

I ⁰(*was*)/ *were* a student at your school when I ¹*was* / *were* young. The teachers ²*was* / *were* different in those days – they ³*was* / *were* very strict with us, not like now. Of course there ⁴*was* / *were* also the school uniform. It ⁵*was* / *were* horrible in those days – red with grey stripes … ugh!
Some of the teachers ⁶*was* / *were* really nice and they ⁷*was* / *were* actually quite kind. But there ⁸*was* / *were* one teacher I really liked. His name ⁹*was* / *were* Mr Howard and he ¹⁰*was* / *were* a great teacher.

28 Complete the sentences with the past simple of *be*.

0 Britain ....*wasn't*.... (not) a Republic in 1930.
1 Enzo Ferrari, the creator of Ferrari cars, ... from Modena.
2 Turin .... the first capital of Italy in the 1860s.
3 The members of the pop group Abba .... (not) Danish.
4 France and Italy .... founder members of the European Coal and Steel Community.
5 Berlin .... (not) the capital of West Germany in the 1970s.
6 John Lennon .... (not) American.

29 Complete the questions with *was* or *were* and then match them to the answers.

0 [b] Why ......*were*........ you late this morning?
1 [ ] Who .... those people at the party?
2 [ ] What .... the name of your first school?
3 [ ] .... you a good student at primary school?
4 [ ] How .... the film?

a They were my brother's friends.
b Because there was a problem with the bus.
c Very exciting.
d Tiffin Girls School.
e Not really.

GRAMMAR: Past simple

30 Complete the text with the past simple of the verbs below.

> speak · finish · try · ~~open~~ ·
> start · invite · listen · go

A new school ⁰......*opened*...... in our town.
I ¹........................ to see the opening ceremony.
It ²........................ at 9:00 am. I ³........................ to see some of my friends, but there were too many people. The new headteacher ⁴........................ for 20 minutes about the new school, but I think nobody ⁵........................ to him. Luckily, the ceremony ⁶........................ after that and the headteacher ⁷........................ everybody to a really nice buffet in the new school playground.

31 Put the verbs in the past simple and then match them to the final part of the sentence.

0 [d] She (*have*) ......*had*......
1 [ ] We (*meet*) ....
2 [ ] I (*know*) ....
3 [ ] They (*run*) ....
4 [ ] I (*see*) ....
5 [ ] He (*sing*) ....

a in a local rock band.
b the answer.
c for the train but missed it.
d a problem with her new PC.
e a really good film last night.
f Carla on holiday in Spain.

32 Make the sentences negative.

0 I walked two miles yesterday.
   I didn't walk two miles yesterday.
1 I did my school project at the weekend.
2 I saw Andy at the party.
3 Schools had computers 30 years ago.
4 She spoke to her friends at the station.
5 The students went on a trip to London.
6 We met our friends in the park.
7 I wore my favourite shirt at the party.
8 She stood next to him for the photo.

33 Complete the questions.

0 'I had a great pizza last night.'
   'What pizza ......**did you have**...... ?'
1 'I read a good book on Saturday.'
   'What .... ?'
2 'My parents got angry with me last night.'
   'Why .... ?'
3 'I arrived late for school this morning.'
   'What time .... ?'
4 'Maggie told me about the party on Saturday.'
   'What .... ?'
5 'I made a cake.'
   'What cake .... ?'

34 Write possible questions for the answers using the past simple.

0 **Where did you go for your holidays?**
   To Minorca, in Spain.
1 Yes, I loved it.
2 We travelled around and went to the beach every day.
3 We stayed in a big hotel near Son Bou.
4 Yes, we met lots of other Italians.
5 Yes, we ate really well.
6 On Saturday.

35 Correct the mistakes. Two sentences are correct.

0 She ~~call~~ me at midnight last night. **called**
1 I not received your text.
2 What time did you arrive yesterday?
3 How went you to the match on Sunday?
4 I eated a really good hamburger last night.
5 Why you call me this morning?
6 I spoke to Helen about the trip.

36 Tim Smith is a journalist. Complete the interview with the past simple of the verbs below.

~~be~~ (x2) • not / be • enjoy • learn • teach • not / have • send • study (x2) • wear

Tim Beth, congratulations on your 100th birthday!
Beth Thank you, my dear.
Tim School ⁰......**was**...... very different in your days, I imagine.
Beth Oh, yes. We ¹................ computers or mobile phones or anything, just a pen and paper!
Tim ²................ you .... a uniform?
Beth Yes, definitely. And the teachers ³................ us home when our uniform ⁴................ clean.
Tim ⁵................ you .... the same subjects as children today?
Beth I honestly don't know what students study today! We ⁶................ a lot of English, literature and maths. I ⁷................ English a lot, especially the compositions.
Tim Who ⁸................ your favourite teacher?
Beth Mrs Farrow. She ⁹................ really well and I still remember her lessons. I ¹⁰................ a lot from her.

37 Complete the story with the past simple of the verbs below.

jog • put • go • ~~happen~~ • turn • not / see • call • start • not / answer • be (x2) • hear • run

Something really funny ⁰......**happened**...... to me yesterday. I ¹................ for a run with my best friend, Mandy, in the morning as usual. We ²................ our headphones on and we ³................ along the river for a few miles. I run really fast so she ⁴................ about 20 or 30 metres behind me as usual, but when I ⁵................ round to speak to her I ⁶................ her. I ⁷................ her name three times, but she ⁸................ me. I ⁹................ to panic a bit. Then I ¹⁰................ a voice in the distance so I ¹¹................ towards it. And there ¹²................ my friend, in one metre of water, looking very unhappy.

STARTER D Friends

VOCABULARY: Feelings

38 Choose among the words below to answer the questions.

> embarrassed · angry · surprised ·
> jealous · worried · ~~happy~~ ·
> scared · nervous · calm

0 How do you feel when it's your birthday?
  I feel happy.
1 How do you feel when you see your friend with a new smartphone?
2 How do you feel when you watch a horror film?
3 How do you feel when you are on holiday?
4 How do you feel when you win first prize in a competition?
5 How do you feel before a big test at school?
6 How do you feel when you get a nice present?

GRAMMAR: Comparative and superlative adjectives

39 Correct the mistakes. Two sentences are correct.

0 It's ~~hoter~~ today than yesterday. **hotter**
1 Your bike's more safe than mine.
2 My aunt's younger than my uncle.
3 This film's less exciting than the first one.
4 My brother's clever than me.
5 Am I late than usual?
6 Is this homework more difficulter than last week's?

40 Complete the text.

I really admire my volleyball teammate, Anita. She's a bit older ⁰ **than** me – six months, to be precise.
At 1 m 90 she's ¹ .... than all the other players. She's also really athletic and she's ² .... than all the rest of us – she can run 100 m in 12 seconds. She's got lots of friends and she's generally ³ .... than me because she enjoys meeting and talking to people.
So she's ⁴ .... than me in practically everything, but there's one thing that she is
⁵ .... than me at: schoolwork. She always wants to copy my homework!

41 Complete the questions with the correct superlative and then choose the correct option.

0 Which is the **driest** (dry) place on Earth?
  A the Great Victoria Desert in Australia
  B the Sahara   **C** the Atacama Desert in Chile
1 What is .... (large) island in the world?
  A Iceland   B Greenland
  C South Island (New Zealand)
2 Who is .... (old) of these three star actors?
  A Brad Pitt   B Angelina Jolie   C Kate Winslet
3 Who is .... (young) of these music stars?
  A Adele   B Taylor Swift   C Lady Gaga
4 Who is .... (rich) of these sports stars?
  A Maria Sharapova   B Lewis Hamilton
  C Roger Federer
5 Which is the world's .... (busy) airport?
  A Amsterdam   B Beijing International
  C Atlanta International (US)
6 How tall is the world's .... (tall) living man?
  A 2 m 51   B 2 m 39   C 2 m 28

42 Complete the sentences with the superlatives of the adjectives below.

> hot · short · ~~difficult~~ · good · young · long · bad

0 This is **the most difficult** exercise of all.
1 At 13 years old, she's .... member of our family.
2 Today is .... day of the year – it's 38°C.
3 That was our .... result of the season – 0–5 at home!
4 June 21st is .... day of the year.
5 She's .... student in our class – she always gets 9 or 10 in tests.
6 December 21st is .... day of the year, just about eight hours of sunlight in England.

D

43 Complete the superlatives and then write answers that are true about your city.

0 Where is ...**the biggest**... (big) shopping centre?
1 What's .... (good) cinema?
2 Which is .... (tall) building?
3 Which is .... (crowded) place?
4 What's .... (bad) pizzeria?
5 Which is .... (popular) meeting place for young people?
6 What's .... (trendy) fashion outlet?

44 Correct the mistakes.

0 This is the ~~less expensive~~ ice-cream shop in town.
   ...**the least expensive**...
1 She's the more athletic in my family.
2 I'm the worst in French in my family.
3 They're best students in my class.
4 This is the most long film in the series.
5 My friend is the taller in the class.
6 I want least complicated model.

GRAMMAR: (not) as … as

45 Rewrite the sentences so that they mean the same. Use (not) as … as.

0 I'm 1 m 60 and my friend Anita is 1 m 60, too.
   Anita is ...**as tall as me**... .
1 Mike's really friendly, but François isn't at all.
   François isn't ....
2 The new Samsung mobile costs 700 euros and the new Apple mobile costs 700 euros, too.
   The new Samsung is ....
3 I'm a bit shy, but my best friend Alper is really shy.
   I'm not ....
4 These headphones are cheap, but the others are cheaper.
   These headphones aren't ....
5 *Avatar* is a long film, but *The Wolf of Wall Street* is longer.
   Avatar ....
6 This pizza is very good. That pizza is very good, too.
   This pizza is ....

46 Put the words in the correct order.

0 I'm / tall / my / as / brother / as
   I'm as tall as my brother.
1 cold / not / it's / as / yesterday / as
2 as / good / not / at physics / she's / me / as
3 entertaining / game / this / the / of / season / is / the / most
4 this / the / least / exciting / series / in / is / the / film
5 Germany / Italy / hot / as / as / isn't
6 I'm / tired / as / you / as

47 Choose the correct option.

I really love my family – they're the [0] (*best*) / *better* in the world. My mum is [1] *the cleverest* / *cleverer* in the family. My sister Debbie is also [2] *more good* / *better* at academic subjects [3] *that* / *than* me. My dad's [4] *taller* / *more tall* than me and my sister, but we're [5] *more thin* / *thinner* – ha ha. My sister's [6] *tall as me* / *as tall as me* – we're both 1 m 65.
I think that my dad's [7] *the craziest* / *the more crazy* in our family – he does [8] *strangest* / *the strangest* things, often at [9] *the less* / *the least* convenient moments. He's got [10] *more dark* / *darker* hair than all the rest of us and [11] *the more loud* / *the loudest* voice. Luckily, our mum's not [12] *loud like him* / *as loud as him*.

48 Compare the two sentences using as many comparative forms as possible.

0 Pete weighs 85 kg; Steff weighs 65 kg.
   Pete is heavier than Steff.
   Steff is lighter than Pete.
   Steff isn't as heavy as Pete.
1 The Nile is about 6,853 km long; the Mississippi is about 3,700 km long.
2 Pete is a bit nervous; Jim is very, very nervous.
3 A Ferrari can go 349 km/h; a Lotus can go 240 km/h.
4 Claire's funny; Sue's incredibly funny.
5 James is 1 m 90 tall; Scott is 1 m 80.

Starter D   137

STARTER E Plans

VOCABULARY: Jobs

49 Match the jobs to the words.

0	d	pilot	a	food
1	☐	police officer	b	gym
2	☐	sports instructor	c	criminal
3	☐	vet	d	airport
4	☐	office worker	e	design
5	☐	lawyer	f	shampoo
6	☐	architect	g	meeting
7	☐	cook	h	pets
8	☐	hairdresser	i	judge

GRAMMAR: Present continuous v *be going to*

50 Write what the person is going to do.

> ~~travel around Europe~~ • reply to the message • buy a train ticket • eat something • see a film • do his homework • do some sport

0 Sammie has got her luggage ready and a European Rail Pass in her pocket.
   Sammie's going to travel around Europe.
1 Jamir is in his room with some schoolbooks.
2 Amy and Sue are outside the cinema.
3 Ann is in the kitchen and she's hungry.
4 Jill is in the queue for tickets at the station.
5 I'm outside the sports centre with my sports bag.
6 There's a new text from me on your smartphone.

51 Write the questions.

0 going / after school / to / what / are / you / do / ?
   What are you going to do after school?
1 last / our / this / is / be / going / to / lesson / ?
   ....
2 how / home / you / to / going / are / get / ?
   ....
3 call / they / to / us / later / are / going / ?
   ....
4 going / Jen / is / to / visit / next year / the USA / ?
   ....
5 when / finish / you / going / to / are / the course / ?
   ....
6 this evening / what / going / watch / we / to / are / ?
   ....

52 Read the programme and complete the sentences with the present continuous.

Activity Weekend Programme

TIME	SATURDAY	SUNDAY
9–10	arrival	visit a farm
10–12	swimming	the 5-mile run
12–1	lunch	lunch with local students
1–3	basketball	meet local athletes
3–5	training	departure at 5:00

0 We**'re arriving** at 9 am.
1 We .... a local farm at 9 am on Sunday.
2 We .... basketball at 1 pm on Saturday.
3 We .... lunch with local students on Sunday.
4 We .... swimming just before lunch on Saturday.
5 We .... some local athletes at 1 on Sunday.
6 We .... a 5-mile run after the farm visit.
7 We .... after the basketball.
8 We .... at 5 pm on Sunday.

53 Write sentences in the present continuous.

0 We / not / meet / the others this evening.
   We're not meeting the others this evening.
1 I / not / go on holiday / this summer.
   ....
2 She / not / have a party / this year.
   ....
3 Liz / not / visit / her friends / this weekend.
   ....
4 When / you / start / your new Twitter account?
   ....
5 What / we / take / to the party?
   ....
6 How / your friends / travel / to London?
   ....

138 Starter E

E

54 Complete the sentences with *be going to* or the present continuous.

0   My hands are dirty. I '*m going to wash* (wash) them.
1   I .... (have) a pizza with Jenny this evening. Do you want to come?
2   I'm cold. I .... (close) the window.
3   I can't remember the time of the film. I .... (check) on the website.
4   I'm thirsty. I .... (have) a drink.
5   We .... (leave) at 7:00 am.

GRAMMAR: *be going to* v *will* for predictions

55 Make predictions. Use *will* or *won't*.

0   People / watch TV in 2050.
    People won't watch TV in 2050.
1   Cars / use petrol in 2050.
2   People / work in offices in 2050.
3   I'm sure cars / have a driver in 2050.
4   I think people / work long hours in 2050.
5   People / read paper books in 2050.

56 Write the questions, then give answers that are true for you.

0   Where / you / be / five years from now?
    Where will you be five years from now?
    I'll be at university. I want to study medicine.
1   How old / you / be in 2035?
2   people / still use / tablets in 2040?
3   your school / still be open / in 2050?
4   What jobs / disappear / in the next ten years?
5   Where / your best friend / be five years from now?

57 Write predictions using *be going to* and a verb below.

   pass · ~~fall~~ · have · miss · snow · come

0   Get off the table, you '*re going to fall* !
1   It's 7:30! You .... the train.
2   It's –5°C outside. It .... in a minute!
3   They're a really popular band. A lot of people .... to the concert.
4   You're cycling too fast. You .... an accident!
5   She's studying a lot for that exam. She .... this time.

58 Complete the sentences with *be going to* or *will*.

0   She hopes she '*ll* pass the test.
1   I think I .... be a doctor when I'm older.
2   That car's driving so fast. It .... crash!
3   The baby's on the table. He .... fall!
4   Kevin hopes his team .... win tonight.
5   My dad believes that everybody .... drive electric cars ten years from now.
6   The sun's shining. It .... be a beautiful day.
7   I'm sure they .... call you later.

59 Complete the interview with the correct form of *going to* or *will*.

A   Our interview today is with a young woman with a great plan. First of all, what's your name?
B   My name's Lia and I'm really excited because from next month I ⁰ '*m going to spend* (spend) three months in Argentina.
A   What ¹........................ (you / do)?
B   I ²........................ (study) history.
A   OK. Do you think Latin American history ³........................ (be) difficult?
B   Maybe, but I think I ⁴........................ (learn) a lot. I really hope the other students ⁵........................ (help) me with my Spanish.
A   What ⁶........................ (you / do) after that?
B   I ⁷........................ (come back) here.

60 Complete the dialogue with a correct form of the future. In some cases two options are correct.

A   Hey, Rob! Guess what … I ⁰ '*m going* (go) to Sweden on Tuesday. I ¹........................ (do) an Erasmus course there.
B   Wow, that sounds great! How long ²........................ (you / stay)?
A   About six months.
B   Wow! I think you ³........................ (have) a great time.
A   I hope so. ⁴........................ (you / come) and visit me?
B   Thanks, but I don't think I ⁵........................ (have) time with all the exams. Anyway, where ⁶........................ (you / study)?
A   At Uppsala University. I ⁷........................ (take) a course in international law.
B   That ⁸........................ (be) interesting!

Starter E   139

1 Friendship

GRAMMAR PRACTICE

Present continuous

Complete the rules.
We use the present continuous to talk about .... happening now.
We form the present continuous with subject + present of *be* + ... form of the verb.

➡ See **GRAMMAR REFERENCE** page 111

1 **Complete the text with the present continuous of the verbs in brackets.**

Today is a typical Saturday. Everybody's at home so it's difficult to study. I ⁰ *'m doing* (do) my maths homework. My brothers ¹ .... (eat) breakfast downstairs and they ² .... (make) a lot noise as usual. My dad ³ .... (work) on the car in the garage. My mum ⁴ .... (speak) to her best friend – the conversation always goes on for hours. Now my brothers ⁵ .... (fight) about something and my mum ⁶ .... (get) very angry with them because she can't hear her friend. Is your family as noisy as this?

2 **Write the negative and interrogative forms of these sentences.**

0 I'm studying today.
   I'm not studying today. / Am I studying today?
1 They're coming to see us.
2 His friends are chatting online.
3 She's texting her friends about the party.
4 We're arriving on the 9 o'clock train.
5 His brothers are travelling to Germany.
6 They're waiting for an answer.

3 **Write the questions in the present continuous.**

0 Why / you / leave / ? **Why are you leaving?**
1 What / your sister / do / ?
2 Where / your parents / stay / ?
3 How / you / feel / today / ?
4 What / Michael / study / ?
5 Why / she / laugh / ?

4 **Answer these questions so that they are true for you.**

0 How are you feeling today? **I'm feeling quite well.**
1 What are your parents doing right now?
2 What are your friends doing at the moment?
3 What's happening in your country in this period?
4 What are you doing in the evenings these days?
5 What events are going on in your town / city?
6 How are you travelling to school in this period?

Present simple v present continuous

Complete the rules.
We use the .... to talk about facts, habitual actions and routines.
We use the .... to talk about temporary actions happening now.
We use the .... with time phrases like *at the moment*, *now*, *today*, *this week*, *these days*, *currently*.
We use the .... with adverbs of frequency like *always*, *sometimes*, *often*, *never*, etc.

➡ See **GRAMMAR REFERENCE** page 113

5 **Put the time phrases below in the correct group.**

usually ▪ at the moment ▪ often ▪ every Saturday ▪
now ▪ today ▪ always ▪ three times a week ▪
occasionally ▪ this morning ▪ in these days

1 with present simple: **usually**, ...
2 with present continuous

6 **Choose the correct option.**

0 (*I see*) / *I'm seeing* my best friends every day.
1 *I'm usually going* / *I usually go* to the shopping centre on Saturday afternoon.
2 *I have* / *I'm having* a lot of arguments with Sally in this period.
3 *I use* / *I'm using* Facebook every evening.
4 My boyfriend *is giving me* / *gives me* a lot of problems at the moment.
5 My best friend *is living* / *lives* in China for a few months to study the language.
6 Look! Jeannie *is speaking* / *speaks* to those boys from the other school.

140 Unit 1

GRAMMAR PRACTICE

7 🔊 **Complete the sentences.**

0 My brother usually **comes** (come) to dinner on Sunday, but today he **'s visiting** (visit) his girlfriend.
1 I .... (take) the coach to school this week, but I normally .... (go) by train.
2 She usually .... (play) well, but today she .... (play) really badly.
3 My mum always .... (read) a lot – she .... (read) something by Dickens at the moment.
4 We .... (study) literature in our English lessons this week, but we normally .... (do) a lot of grammar.
5 She .... (use) Twitter today – strange! She usually .... (message) via Facebook.
6 We .... (train) twice a week in the regular season, but this month we .... (train) every day because of the final next week.

8 🔊 **Complete the questions.**

0 'What **are you doing** (you / do)?' 'My homework.'
1 'Where .... (you / go)?' 'To the shops.'
2 'What .... (your mother / do)?' 'She's a nurse.'
3 'How .... (the course / go)?' 'Oh, great. It's really interesting.'
4 'How often .... (you / see / Pete)?' 'Once or twice a week.'
5 'What time .... (the lessons / start)?' 'At 9 during the week and at 9:30 on Saturdays.'
6 'Why .... (you / call) Jacob?' 'Because he's late!'

9 🔊 **Correct the mistakes. Three sentences are correct.**

0 ~~Do you speaking to me?~~ **Are you speaking to me?**
1 I'm meeting my friends every Saturday.
2 I'm often visiting my grandparents at the weekend.
3 How often are you tweeting during the school day?
4 Why do you always call me at 10 in the evening?
5 My brothers never tell me anything.
6 I'm really enjoying this film – it's so exciting.
7 Are you knowing any of these people?
8 My Irish friend's often contacting me on Facebook.

Present perfect

Complete the rule using *ever*, *never*, *for* and *since*.

We use the present perfect with .... and .... to talk about something which began in the past and is still happening now.
We use .... when we want to express the duration of the situation. We use .... when we want to indicate when the action began.
We use .... in questions and .... in statements to signify *at any time until now*.

➡ See **GRAMMAR REFERENCE** page 113

10 🔊 **Complete the sentences.**

0 **Have you spoken to Paul** (you / speak to Paul) since your argument?
1 .... (you / ever / be) out with Jo?
2 She .... (have) the same pencil case since primary school.
3 .... (she / ever / work) in a shop?
4 I .... (never / hear) that name before.
5 We .... (know) them for ages.

11 🔊 **Complete the sentences with *for* or *since*.**

0 Rob and Matt have been friends **for** about ten years.
1 I haven't spoken to Pete .... a few days.
2 I've had this bike .... my last birthday.
3 He's been my teacher .... I started school.
4 I haven't played any sport .... months.
5 Your English has improved a lot .... last year.

12 🔊 **Complete the sentences with the present perfect of the verbs below.**

speak • receive • see • be • win • know • ~~make~~

0 I **'ve made** lots of new friends since I moved here.
1 She .... here for the last three days.
2 .... your team ever .... the championship?
3 We .... just once since Christmas.
4 I .... never .... an indie film.
5 Jim .... Chen for about ten years.
6 I .... never .... a birthday card or present from them.

Unit 1   141

READING SKILLS

13 Read the blog post once quickly and complete the sentence.

The post is specifically about:
1 friendships that have gone wrong
2 the statistics around bullying and what we can do
3 the risks and dangers of young people going online
4 how to stop bullying

14 [2.01] Read and listen to the post and decide if the sentences are true (T) or false (F). Correct the false ones.

1 Bullying is not a serious problem nowadays. T F
2 Schools are aware of the problem and want to stop it. T F
3 More than 5 million people have experienced bullying of some form. T F
4 More than 1 million people have experienced extreme bullying every day in the last couple of years. T F
5 It's easy for young people to avoid cyberbullying. T F
6 The majority of victims don't know their bullies. T F
7 Cyberbullying is possible because it is easy to do it online. T F
8 Less than half of teens have taken part in cyberbullying. T F
9 The Diana Awards have helped to stop bullying. T F
10 Only parents and schools can change the behaviour of young people. T F

15 Read the post again and match the headings to the paragraphs. There is one extra title.

1 ☐ The importance of social media in communication
2 ☐ We all take part
3 ☐ It's our responsibility
4 ☐ A lot of young people have experienced bullying
5 ☐ The negative effects of bullying
6 ☐ Why people bully

16 Underline the words, expressions or punctuation in the text that show the writer's opinion.

Cyberbullying: The shocking facts

When you hear about cyberbullying, many people think it is old news. It no longer happens in schools and schools have resolved bullying issues. Many schools have adopted 'zero tolerance' against bullying and say they have controlled the problem in their schools. These are all good objectives, but the reality is very different.

A

The Anti-Bullying campaigners have worked tirelessly with schools and teenagers to tackle bullying in schools. Its figures showed that in the last couple of years an estimated 5.4 million young people have experienced
5 cyberbullying and 1.3 million unfortunate teenagers have experienced extreme cyberbullying on a daily basis!

B

'Why don't they just turn off their phones?', you may ask, but, as we know, social media is very important for teens and that's not so easy. An estimated 96% of teens from
10 11–19 years old use social media as their main form of communication. 'I need my phone to talk to my friends, but when I turn on my phone, I don't just see friendly chats, but extreme abuse, threats and maybe even humiliating images.' It's a vicious circle and it's often an
15 easy one to fall into as a lot of cyberbullying begins with friendships that have gone wrong.

17 Choose the correct summary of the writer's opinion about the topic.

1 Cyberbullying was serious a few years ago, but schools have stopped it now.
2 Cyberbullying is a serious problem and it is up to parents and schools to stop it.
3 A lot of cyberbullying still exists, we are all responsible for it and we can stop it together.

VOCABULARY

ADJECTIVES OF PERSONALITY

19 Complete the sentences with the words below.

easygoing ▪ cheerful ▪ sociable ▪ practical ▪ ~~shy~~
intelligent ▪ quiet ▪ untidy ▪ generous

0   Bill gets very embarrassed when new people speak to him. He's really ......**shy**...... .
1   Sue's bedroom is terrible – books, food, CDs and clothes everywhere! She's incredibly ....
2   Lily never gets angry or stressed. She's really ....
3   I don't see my aunt very much, but she always gives me great presents at Christmas. Everybody thinks she's really ....
4   Tim's really good at school. He gets top marks in every test – he's very ....
5   My parents have a lot of friends and enjoy meeting new people. They're really ....
6   My uncle likes fixing things and he's very good with cars. He's a very .... person.
7   I really envy Joe – he's always smiling and happy. How can he be so .... all the time?
8   My sister is really .... She doesn't talk much.

20 Match the opposites.

0   *g*   untidy   a   outgoing
1   ☐   quiet   b   nervy
2   ☐   shy   c   miserable
3   ☐   easygoing   d   talkative
4   ☐   generous   e   unpractical
5   ☐   cheerful   f   mean
6   ☐   practical   g   tidy

21 Complete the sentences with words a–g in exercise 20.

0   My cousin looks really ......**miserable**...... . I think she got a bad mark in the test.
1   He's really .... – he drinks too much coffee!
2   Your house is really .... – not like mine!
3   Sally loves meeting people – she's very ....
4   Tim's very ...., and he tells great stories.
5   Frank's so .... – he never buys me presents.
6   Jim's so ....: lots of ideas, all of them impossible!

C

The effects of cyberbullying are very serious. For many young people it becomes a source of constant anxiety. In the UK around 20% of young people have felt worried
20   about going to school because of cyberbullying.

D

So, what can we do? Well, we can refuse to take part in this. 81% of young people admit that bullying is easier online and a shocking 53% of teens admit to sharing posts that encourage bullying.

E

25   Schools and parents have a duty to educate their children, but young people also know the difference between right and wrong. We know it is wrong to target someone online, make fun of them and isolate them. We can stop this terrible behaviour. The inspirational
30   Anti-Bullying campaigners have set up the Diana Awards Anti-Bullying Ambassadors, which trains young people in schools to identify bullying and support victims of bullying. We are all responsible for what happens to our classmates, so let's work together to put
35   an end to this serious misery that is damaging so many adolescents.

18 Find the words and phrases in the text that mean the same as these.

1   sorted out (intro)   ....
2   try and stop (para A)   ....
3   very serious (para A)   ....
4   every day (para A)   ....
5   an approximate (para B)   ....
6   make me feel embarrassed (para B)   ....
7   not agree (para D)   ....
8   hurting, harming (para E)   ....

Unit 1   143

GRAMMAR PRACTICE

Present perfect v past simple

Choose the correct option.
- We use the *past simple / present perfect* with time phrases like *five years ago, yesterday, last week*, etc. to refer to finished events in the past.
- We use the *past simple / present perfect* to talk about something that happened in the past but is connected to the present.
- *Been* and *gone* are both the past participle of *go*. We use *been / gone* when the person went to a place and then left it. We use *been / gone* when the person went to a place and is still there.

→ See **GRAMMAR REFERENCE** page 114

22 Put the time phrases in the correct group.

> last year • since then • in 1998 •
> on January 17th • lately •
> when I was five • this week •
> a week ago • this year • on Friday morning •
> for two weeks • today

1 present perfect: ....
2 past simple: last year, …..................................
3 both: ....

23 Choose the correct option.

0 She *had / 's had* a difficult time this week.
1 I *didn't speak / haven't spoken* to them today.
2 My friend's *been / gone* to Madrid for a few days – she's really enjoying it.
3 I haven't *gone / been* to the US, but I'd love to go.
4 I *went / have gone* clubbing on Saturday night.
5 I *wrote / have written* three essays so far this term.
6 She *didn't train / hasn't trained* much recently.

24 Complete the text with the present perfect or past simple of the verbs in brackets.

I ⁰ **have known** (know) my best friend Benji for five years now. We ¹.......................... (meet) in 2012 when he ².......................... (arrive) from India with his parents. I ³.......................... (not / go) to his house lately, but I ⁴.......................... (see) his brother a few months ago. I ⁵.......................... (never / visit) India, but Benji ⁶.......................... (receive) an invitation from his cousin this week, so maybe we can go together.

Present perfect with *just*, *already* and *yet*

Complete the rules.
- To say that something happened very recently we use the present perfect with ....
- To say that a recent action happened before we expected we use it with ....
- To say that something we expected did not happen but can happen in the future we use the present perfect negative with ....
- We also use .... with questions to check if something we expected has happened.

→ See **GRAMMAR REFERENCE** page 114

25 Complete the dialogue with *just*, *already* or *yet*.

A Where are you going, Dele?
B I'm going out with a friend.
A Have you ⁰ **already** finished those maths exercises?
B I haven't finished them all ¹.......................... but Jan's ².......................... called and she wants to meet up.
A Well, I've ³.......................... finished most of my homework, so I'm going to the gym.
B Have you done that English composition ⁴.......................... ? It's really difficult …
A Which composition?
B The one about Shakespeare, of course. I've ⁵.......................... written three paragraphs, but I haven't finished it ⁶.......................... .
Hey, where are you going?
A Home – to write my composition …

26 Write sentences about what Janan's done and hasn't done this week. Use *just*, *already* and *yet*.

She hasn't studied for her geography test yet.

This week's 'To do' list
- study for geography test ✗
- text Mary about trip ✓
- call Patricia (before she leaves Paris) ✗
- clean up bedroom ✓ (five minutes ago!)
- go shopping with Sally and Eva ✗
- Helen's birthday – buy present! ✗
- visit grandparents ✓

SPEAKING SKILLS

MEETING AND GREETING

27 Put the expressions in the correct group.

> Let's catch up soon ▪ Hi, how are you? ▪
> It was great to see you ▪ Have a nice day! ▪
> It's good to see you ▪ How have you been? ▪
> Keep in touch ▪ How are things with you? ▪
> What have you been up to? ▪ Nice to see you!

1 greeting people
2 finding out how people are
3 ending the conversation

28 Complete the dialogue with the words below.

> too ▪ big ▪ moment ▪ let's ▪ great ▪ studying ▪
> up to ▪ you ▪ meet ▪ hear ▪ hope

Tom Hello, Rick. Good to see you.
Rick Hi, Tom. Good to see you, ¹.......................... .
What have you been ².......................... ?
Tom Oh, just the usual. Playing football,
³.........................., you know. And what about
⁴.......................... ?
Rick Well, studying like you, but I'm not playing
volleyball at the ⁵.......................... because I've got
a problem with my leg.
Tom Oh, I'm sorry to ⁶.......................... that.
I ⁷.......................... it's nothing serious.
Rick It's OK, it's not a ⁸.......................... problem.
Oh, there's my bus. Well, it was ⁹..........................
to see you, Tom.
Tom You too, Rick. Let's ¹⁰.......................... up soon. Bye!
Rick Yes, ¹¹.......................... . Have a great weekend! Bye!

29 Write a dialogue using the suggestions.

A Greet your friend and ask him / her how he / she is.
B Greet A and reply to his / her question. Ask how A is.
A Reply. Ask about B's news.
B Reply. Ask A the same question.
A Reply with your news.
B Indicate you need to finish the conversation.
A Suggest that you meet soon.
B Agree and suggest a day and something to do.
A Say you're busy and suggest a different day.
B Reply and say goodbye.
A Say goodbye.

LISTENING SKILLS

30 [2.02] Listen to the podcast and write the names of the two pairs of actors who are good friends in real life.

31 [2.02] Listen again and tick (✓) the words you hear.

☐ romance ☐ like brothers ☐ friendship
☐ close ☐ a couple ☐ family
☐ film set ☐ got married ☐ real life

32 [2.02] Listen again and choose the correct option.

1 During the filming of *An Officer and a Gentleman* Richard Gere and Debra Winger:
A liked each other a lot.
B didn't like each other at all.
C had a big romance in real life.
2 Shirley Esteban is:
A a celebrity gossip journalist.
B a famous actress.
C an ex-actress.
3 Christian and Winona met:
A at a celebrity party.
B on the set of a film.
C on a TV programme.
4 Christian Bale:
A married Winona Ryder.
B married Winona's personal assistant.
C married Winona's best friend.
5 Winona thinks Christian is:
A generous and reliable.
B self-confident and cheerful.
C generous and practical.
6 Brad Pitt and George Clooney became friends after:
A *Ocean's 11*.
B a celebrity party.
C *Ocean's 12*.
7 According to Shirley:
A Brad Pitt is easygoing and sociable.
B Brad Pitt and George Clooney have similar personalities.
C George Clooney is easygoing.
8 Shirley says that:
A Brad and George are making a new comedy film.
B they're probably making a new adventure film.
C she wants to find out what they're doing.

Unit 1   145

TOWARDS PRELIMINARY

> **EXAM STRATEGY**
>
> **Reading – Multiple choice**
>
> Look at the short text carefully and think about what it is and where you might see it. Don't worry about words you don't know, try to get the general meaning from the context. Read through the three options A, B, C carefully and choose the one that has the same meaning as the short text.

33 Read the signs and the three options below each. Choose the correct option A, B or C and explain why the other options are wrong.

0

Big autumn sale next week – up to 50% off many articles

   A <u>50% of articles</u> will be on sale next week.
   B <u>All articles</u> will cost 50% less next week.
   C Some articles will cost half price next week.

The sign means that next week many articles will be on sale at half price.
A says that half the articles will be on sale; the sign says half price, not half the articles.
B says all the articles will be half price next week; the sign says 'many articles', not all of them.
C says that some articles will be half price. This is the correct answer.

1

The parents' evening will take place at the school on Friday 15th December at 8 pm. All subject teachers will be present.

   A Students need to come to school on Friday 15th December in the evening.
   B Parents can come to the school and meet teachers on Friday 15th December.
   C Classes for parents start on Friday 15th December.

2

Please stand on the right of the escalator during busy periods and let people pass on the left

   A You can stand where you want on the escalator.
   B Do not stand on the left of the escalator when there are a lot of people.
   C You need to let people pass on the right.

3

Please order and pay for food at the bar. We will deliver the food to your table

   A You can order food from the table.
   B You can eat your food at the bar.
   C You need to pay for the food before eating.

4

Special summer offer 20% off this item (batteries excluded) Offer ends August 30th

   A You can only have this offer before the end of August.
   B You get the item and the batteries as part of the offer.
   C The price is 20% cheaper on August 31st.

5

This film is suitable for people over 15 years of age

   A People younger than 15 can watch this film.
   B The film is only for adults.
   C A 16-year-old can watch this film.

6

Dogs must be kept on their lead at all times in the park

A You can let dogs go where they want in the park.
B Dogs can only enter the park at certain times.
C You always need to keep your dog under control in the park.

7

NO vacancies

A The hotel is open only for business people.
B The hotel is full.
C The hotel is closed during the holidays.

8

BUY ONE GET ONE FREE!

A You pay less for the second article you buy.
B The second article you buy is half price.
C You don't pay for the second article you buy.

9

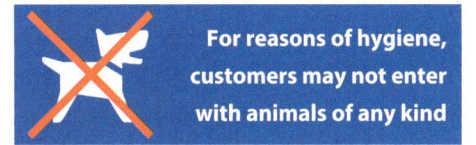

For reasons of hygiene, customers may not enter with animals of any kind

A You can enter only with a dog.
B You can enter with small animals.
C No animals can enter the shop.

10

Caution WET FLOOR

A You can enter but you need to be careful.
B You cannot enter this building.
C The floor has some damage.

TOWARDS PRELIMINARY

EXAM STRATEGY

Reading – Gap fill

When you are thinking of words to complete the gaps, remember that you can only use one word in each gap and that contractions count as two words: *isn't = is not*; *she's = she is / has*.
The words you need to use are mostly grammar words, so think about words such as:

- pronouns: *he*, *it*, *we*; *me*, *him*; *they*; *mine*, *ours*
- verb auxiliaries: *do*, *does*, *did*, *has*, *have*, *will*
- articles: *a*, *an*, *the*
- relative pronouns: *who*, *that*, *which*
- negatives: *no*, *not*, *never*
- adverbs: *just*, *always*, *yet*
- linkers: *and*, *but*, *however*, *instead*
- prepositions: *on*, *in*, *at*

Read the text once to understand the general meaning. Then for each gap, read the complete sentence and pay particular attention to the words before and after the gap. When you have written a word in the gap, read the sentence again to check it fits.

34 Complete the gaps with one word.

ONE FRIEND OR LOTS OF FRIENDS?

My brother, Ed, and I ⁰ **have** got different personalities but we get on well together. I'm quiet and quite shy ¹ .... he's very sociable and talks non-stop. I have ² .... a few close friends. I prefer this because I feel I know my friends well. Obviously, I'm friendly with ³ .... people, too but I don't find it easy to meet new people and make friends. Ed's exactly the opposite, he loves meeting people and talking to them. He often invites his friends to ⁴ .... house and I find that a bit difficult sometimes ⁵ .... they make a lot of noise. Ed says I'm impatient and that I should be more easygoing. Actually, he's probably right. I'd like to be as friendly and confident ⁶ .... he is.

Unit 1 147

2 Migration

GRAMMAR PRACTICE

Present perfect continuous

Complete the rules.
We form the present perfect continuous with *have / has* + *been* + the .... form of the verb.

→ See **GRAMMAR REFERENCE** page 115

1 Complete the sentences with the present perfect continuous of the verbs in brackets.

0   We **'ve been reading** (read) the same book since the start of school.
1   I .... (live) here for the last six months.
2   She .... (study) Spanish since she was five.
3   My brothers .... (play) in the same team since February.
4   I'm tired – I .... (work) all day.
5   They .... (write) compositions since the first year.
6   Zak .... (get) bad marks in tests recently.

2 Write six sentences about what Janen has been doing.

2005	drove a car for the first time
2007	went out with Gary for the first time
2009	played her first tennis match
2012	went to live in Essex
2013	worked as a doctor for the first time
2014	did yoga for the first time
2015	sang in an R&B group for the first time

Janen's been driving since 2005.

3 Rewrite the sentences in the negative present perfect continuous.

0   We started playing chess two weeks ago.
    We **haven't been playing** (play) for long.
1   Amy moved here from Wales last month.
    Amy .... (live) here for long.
2   We began studying *Hamlet* last lesson.
    We .... (study) it for long.
3   They learnt English last year.
    They .... (speak) it for long.
4   My brother had his first driving lesson this morning.
    He .... (drive) for long.
5   Liz got her first bike for her birthday on Monday.
    She .... (cycle) for long.
6   She started reading *Romeo and Juliet* yesterday.
    She .... (read) it for long.

4 Complete the questions with the present perfect continuous of the verbs in brackets.

0   Look at the state of Tim's shoes!
    Has he been walking (he / walk) in the park?
1   You look really hot!
    .... (you / run)?
2   This is a lot of food!
    .... (Mum / cook) all day?
3   I can't find my tablet!
    .... (you / use) it?
4   You look tired!
    .... (you / go) to bed late?
5   Jim and Tom are improving fast!
    .... (they / practise) a lot?
6   His answers are exactly the same as mine!
    .... (he / copy)?

5 Complete the dialogue with the present perfect continuous of the verbs below.

| ~~do~~ • help • train • study • not / go out • run • give • read |

A   So, what ⁰ ......**have**...... you ......**been doing**...... since the last time I saw you?
B   Well, I ¹ .... for the half marathon next month.
A   Oh great! ² .... you .... a lot?

148   Unit 2

GRAMMAR PRACTICE

B Yes, 10 km every morning – it's great. What about you? ³..................... you .... a lot for your exams?

A Yes, a lot. I ⁴..................... books and articles every evening and I ⁵..................... much in the evening, so my friends aren't very happy with me.

B ⁶..................... your brother .... you with your studies?

A Yes, he's been great. He ⁷..................... me a lot of help and support. I have to go now. Good luck with the marathon!

B And you with the exams!

Present perfect simple v present perfect continuous

Choose the correct option.

- We use the present perfect and the present perfect continuous for actions that started in the past and are still in progress or have just ended.
- We use the present perfect continuous when we want to refer to the *duration / result* of an action.
- We use the present perfect simple when we want to refer to the *duration / result* of an action.

See GRAMMAR REFERENCE page 115

6 Complete the sentences with the present perfect simple or continuous of the verbs in brackets.

0 We **'ve been working** (work) all day. I'm tired.
1 We .... (run) 10 km already – let's stop.
2 They .... (study) for over two hours.
3 They .... (study) every book by Charles Dickens.
4 I .... (wait) for you for hours.
5 My sister .... (talk) on the phone since 5 o'clock.
6 I .... (do) all my homework exercises. Let's go out.
7 I .... (finish) 50 pages of that new ebook.
8 I .... (love) chocolate biscuits since I was a child.
9 My brother .... (drive) since he passed his test.

7 Complete the dialogue with the present perfect simple or continuous of the verbs in brackets.

A Guess what? I ⁰ **'ve started** (start) a new karate course.

B Really? How long ¹..................... (you / do) that?

A About six months. I ²..................... (obtain) my yellow and orange belts.

B Great! What kinds of things ³..................... (you / practise) in karate?

A Oh, movements, defence … that kind of thing.

B ⁴..................... (you / have) any competitions?

A Yes, I ⁵..................... (be) in three and we ⁶..................... (win) two of them!

A Well done. So you ⁷..................... (you / not / study) much with all this karate …

B No, not really … I ⁸..................... (get) some really bad marks recently.

A ⁹..................... (you / explain) the reason to your teachers?

B You're having a laugh, right?

8 Complete the blog with the present perfect simple or continuous of the verbs in brackets.

Hello everyone
Sorry I ⁰ **haven't written** (not / write) for a few weeks. I ¹..................... (be) really busy with my new job in London. That's right – I ²..................... (work) in Café Bianco for the last three weeks. ³..................... (make) over 1,000 coffees in the last week and I ⁴..................... (talk) to people from all over the world. Thanks to my new job I ⁵..................... (move) to a bigger flat and in the last two weeks I ⁶..................... (have) over 20 visitors! I ⁷..................... (put) some photos of my new flat here on my blog. See you soon.

9 Write answers that are true for you.

0 How long have you been living in your current home?
I've been living here since 2012.
1 How many times have you been abroad in your life?
2 What have you been studying recently?
3 What sports have you done in the last 3 months?
4 How many books have you read since Christmas?
5 What has been happening in the world in the last few weeks?
6 How long have you been using instant messaging apps?

Unit 2 149

READING SKILLS

10 [2.03] Read and listen to the article and choose the best heading for it.

1. Living in the desert
2. Populations on the move
3. Tourism in Egypt
4. Discrimination against minority groups

11 Read the text again and match the titles to the paragraphs. There is one extra title.

1. ☐ Not wanted here
2. ☐ A true desert people
3. ☐ Moved on by tourism
4. ☐ Nearly a 1,000 years on the move
5. ☐ Returning to their origins
6. ☐ In search of an education

12 Read the text again and decide if the sentences are true (T) or false (F). Correct the false ones.

1. The article is about two different populations. T F
2. The Bedouin live in small towns and villages. T F
3. The Bedouin all live in the same continent. T F
4. The development of tourism in Egypt has been positive for the Bedouin. T F
5. The Roma people have Indian origins. T F
6. The Romani's first destinations were towns and cities. T F
7. The main purpose of the text is to stop discrimination against Roma and Bedouin people. T F
8. The main purpose of the text is to inform people about two different cultures. T F

13 Now write short answers to these questions.

1. What does *Bedouin* mean in Arabic?
2. Which animals do the Bedouin keep?
3. Where do the Bedouin get water from?
4. Why did the Romani move to city areas?
5. What do some people accuse the Romani of doing?
6. Why do Romani people continue to move from one place to another?
7. What two things have made it difficult to integrate Romani children in some cases?

In this article we look at nomadic populations and in particular the Bedouin and Roma peoples.

A

Bedouin means 'someone who lives in the desert' in Arabic. The Bedouin have been living in the desert or remote mountain areas for over a thousand years. You can find the Bedouin in the Arabian peninsula and North Africa. They traditionally keep animals such as camels and **goats** and move regularly, looking for streams to provide them with freshwater.

B

In Egypt the Bedouin also lived by the coast, but the arrival of tourism in the Red Sea in resorts such as Sharm el Sheikh made it impossible for them to continue living there. So for the past few years they have been living inland in desert areas. Some Bedouin have been working in the new tourist resorts, which meant giving up their traditional nomadic lifestyle, and many find it difficult to adapt to the new conditions.

C

In Europe we find the Roma or Romani people. Like the Bedouin, they are a traditionally nomadic population. The Romani are actually a Hindi people from Northern

14 Find the opposite of these expressions in the text.

1. near towns and cities (para A) ....
2. infrequently (para A) ....
3. starting (para B) ....
4. living in one place (para B) ....
5. noisy (para C) ....
6. remain in a place (para D) ....
7. approximate (para D) ....
8. isolate (para E) ....

150 Unit 2

India and those who live in Europe are part of a migration process that has been continuing for over 900 years. The Romani first moved to quiet country areas, including forests and woods, in East European countries like Romania and Bulgaria. However, they found it difficult to survive there, so they had no choice but to move to urban areas to find work and food for their families.

D

Many people do not understand the Roma culture, which is often based on distant Hindi traditions. As a result, the Romani have often **suffered** discrimination and persecution. This means that they migrate to other countries in search of better jobs and living conditions. It is difficult to know the exact Romani population in the world because they often prefer not to register when they move to a new place.

E

Several governments have been trying to integrate the Romani into local culture. They have introduced programmes that give Romani children the chance to attend local schools, but integration is not easy and changing habits and traditions that date back hundreds of years is a difficult process.

GLOSSARY

| goats | ➤ capre |
| suffered | ➤ subito |

15 Find the words or phrases in the text that mean the same as these.

1 small rivers (para A)
2 away from the sea / coast (para B)
3 places with lots of leisure facilities and hotels (para B)
4 to change habits / customs (para B)
5 movement of large numbers of people (para C)
6 places containing lots of buildings and offices (para C)
7 looking for (para D)
8 go to a place, like a school, on a regular basis (para E)

VOCABULARY

GEOGRAPHICAL FEATURES

16 Complete the sentences with the words below.

lake · forest · coast · hills · stream · mountains · path · desert

0 We often go swimming in the ......lake........ near my aunt's house.
1 There's usually little or no water in a ....
2 There are lots of really old trees in this ....
3 My grandparents' holiday house is on the Atlantic ....
4 People often go skiing in the ....
5 .... are similar to mountains but smaller.
6 We get our water from a .... that runs near the house.
7 We followed the .... along the river.

17 Choose the correct option.

California is on the west [0] (coast) / desert of the United States. There are beautiful golden [1] beaches / lakes and some spectacular [2] cliffs / rivers that look onto the ocean. There are many [3] rivers / coasts in California but the most important is the Sacramento, which provides water to 19 Californian counties. It starts high up in the Klamath [4] beaches / mountains and divides into hundreds of small [5] streams / cliffs on its way to San Francisco Bay.
Just north and south of San Francisco are three very large national [6] hills / forests called Redwood, Sierra and Angeles, where you can find trees that are thousands of years old and over a 100 metres high. The whole region is not very flat. Many towns and cities are built on [7] deserts / hills, meaning there is a lot of going up and down. One of the most famous of these cities is Beverly [8] Hills / Cliffs, where most people actually live on flat land.
Last but not least, California also has three very large [9] mountains / deserts, the Mojave, Colorado and Great Basin. The first two are extremely hot and dry, receiving only 50 millimetres of rain every year. The Great Basin is a strange [10] forest / desert because it actually snows there in the winter.

18 Write a 100-word description of your local area using at least five of these words: *coast*, *lake*, *mountain*, *forest*, *wood*, *river*, *cliffs*, *stream*, *hill*.

Unit 2   151

GRAMMAR PRACTICE

Defining relative clauses

Complete the rules with *where, who, that, subject, possessor* **and** *which*.

- We use a defining relative clause to identify .... or what we are talking about.
- We use *who* to refer to people, ... to refer to things and .... for places.
- We use .... as an alternative to *who* or *which*, especially when speaking.
- We use *whose* to indicate the .... of something.
- No relative pronoun is necessary when the verb already has a ....; for example: *Is this the shop (that) you mentioned?*

➡ See **GRAMMAR REFERENCE** page 116

19 Choose the correct option.

0 Have you seen the film (that) / who everybody is talking about?
1 She's the person *that / where* I told you about.
2 This is the teacher *whose / which* book we use in class.
3 The internet is something *which / who* has changed our lives.
4 German is a language *who / that* is difficult to speak really well.
5 I have a friend *whose / which* mother works in that school.
6 This is the town *where / which* I was born.

20 Choose the option which is *not* possible. The symbol '–' means 'no relative pronoun'.

0 This is the hotel *which* / (who) / *that* we stayed in for our last summer holidays.
1 I'd like a new phone *that / whose / which* takes really good photos and video.
2 Bill is the person *which / – / that* you need to speak to.
3 There are many populations *that / where / which* migrate annually.
4 The Aborigines are the people *who / that / whose* originally lived in Australia.
5 This is the test *who / which / that* worries me.
6 This is the girl *that / whose / which* parents I met.

21 Delete the relative pronouns you can omit.

0 The film ~~that~~ I saw was really good.
1 I have a friend that always knows all the answers.
2 This is the new smartphone that I bought.
3 This is the band whose song is No. 1 in the charts.
4 She's the girl who won the quiz show on TV.
5 That's the song which everybody is talking about.
6 I like to visit places whose name I can pronounce.

22 Match the start of each sentence with its end and write sentences with relative pronouns.

0 [f] A nurse is someone …
1 [ ] A pilot is a person …
2 [ ] A modem is a device …
3 [ ] A desert is a place …
4 [ ] A teacher is a person …
5 [ ] A Eurozone country is a nation …

a job is to help students.
b flies planes as a job.
c sends and receives data.
d currency is the euro.
e there's little or no water.
f looks after sick patients.

A nurse is someone who / that looks after sick patients.

23 Complete the text with relative pronouns.

Steve Jobs is the person ⁰ *who / that* created the touchscreen smartphone. He was also the person ¹........................ creative spirit helped the personal computer to become reality in the form of the Apple Macintosh. This was a rudimentary device ²........................ was first built in his friend Steve Wozniak's garage using parts ³........................ Steve Jobs bought from a local electrical shop. Jobs grew up in California. He wasn't a very good student and he never finished his college studies. In 1977 he went to India ⁴........................ he studied Zen Buddhism. It was this experience ⁵........................ encouraged him to return to the US and start a computer company, Apple. He also joined a group of young inventors at Rank Xerox: one of their innovative projects included the first ever mouse. This is the device ⁶........................ changed computers because it made them accessible to people ⁷........................ weren't very technical and didn't like computer code.

152 Unit 2

SPEAKING SKILLS

HAVING A DISAGREEMENT

24 Complete the dialogues with the words below.

know • wrong • opinion • stand • believe
agree • totally • so • afraid • sorry • don't

1 **A** I think online shopping is a waste of time.
   B I .... completely.
2 **A** This party is a shocker, let's go home.
   B I .... agree with you, let's go.
3 **A** I'm sure my last maths test was terrible.
   B I don't .... that. You always do really well.
4 **A** The food's really bad here.
   B I .... what you mean, but at least it's cheap!
5 **A** This town's so boring.
   B I think you're .... there.
6 **A** This homework's impossible.
   B I really don't think ....
7 **A** We decided to go home early.
   B I .... think that was a good decision.
8 **A** I love this music.
   B Really? I'm sorry, but I can't .... it.
9 **A** I go to sleep in her lessons …
   B In my .... they're really useful.
10 **A** Their latest song is fantastic.
   B I'm .... I don't agree.
11 **A** You've got my bag.
   B I'm ...., but this is my bag.

25 Complete the dialogue with the expressions below.

In my opinion it's a bit boring. •
No, I think you're wrong there. • In my opinion •
I'm afraid I don't agree. • I agree • I know

A So, what do you think of the new *Star Wars* film?
B ¹.........................
A Really? I thought it was really exciting!
B ².......................... – It's slow and too long, over three hours.
A ³.......................... – It was only two hours long.
B In any case the acting was terrible.
A ⁴.......................... – it was pretty bad! But these are action films after all …
B ⁵.........................., but that's no excuse for bad acting.
A You're right. ⁶.......................... they need to finish the series right here.

LISTENING SKILLS

26 [2.04] Listen to the interview. Why did Afrar leave her country?

1 to continue her studies
2 to escape a dangerous situation
3 to know a different culture
4 to find a job

27 [2.04] Revise the Listening strategy on page 30 of your Student's Book. Then listen again and decide if the sentences are true (T) or false (F). Correct the false ones.

1 Afrar is a teenager.   T F
2 Afrar is from West Africa.   T F
3 Afrar felt excited when she left her home town.   T F
4 Afrar has been in the UK for two years.   T F
5 She stayed in a centre for immigrants when she arrived.   T F
6 She's studying in Winchester.   T F
7 She likes her school.   T F
8 She's had a difficult experience with the family since she was adopted. T F
9 A large part of Sudan is desert.   T F
10 She enjoyed going to the Lake District.   T F

28 [2.04] Listen again and answer the questions.

1 How old is Afrar?
2 Where was the migrant camp located in the UK?
3 Who told Afrar to leave her country?
4 What was the journey from Sudan like?
5 What was good about it in the end?
6 What has Afrar learnt about from her adopted family?
7 How much of Sudan is desert?
8 What conditions are there in the desert area?
9 What can you find in the Lake District?
10 What's the weather like in the Lake District?

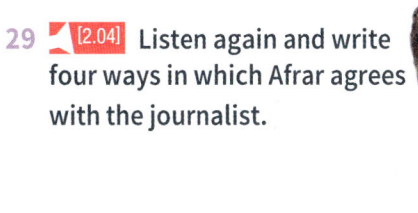

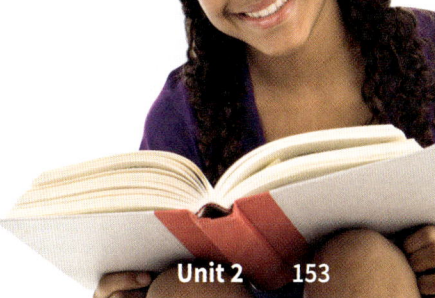

29 [2.04] Listen again and write four ways in which Afrar agrees with the journalist.

Unit 2 153

ACADEMIC SKILLS

LABELLING A MAP

30 Complete the following expressions with *on*, *in*, *at* or – (no preposition).

0 ...on... the left / the right
1 .... the top / bottom
2 .... the left-hand side / right-hand side
3 .... the middle / centre
4 .... the north / south / east / west
5 .... above / below
6 .... front of
7 .... opposite / behind

Which of the expressions above can also be used with *to*?

31 Read Lucy's email and label the six missing elements on the map she sent.

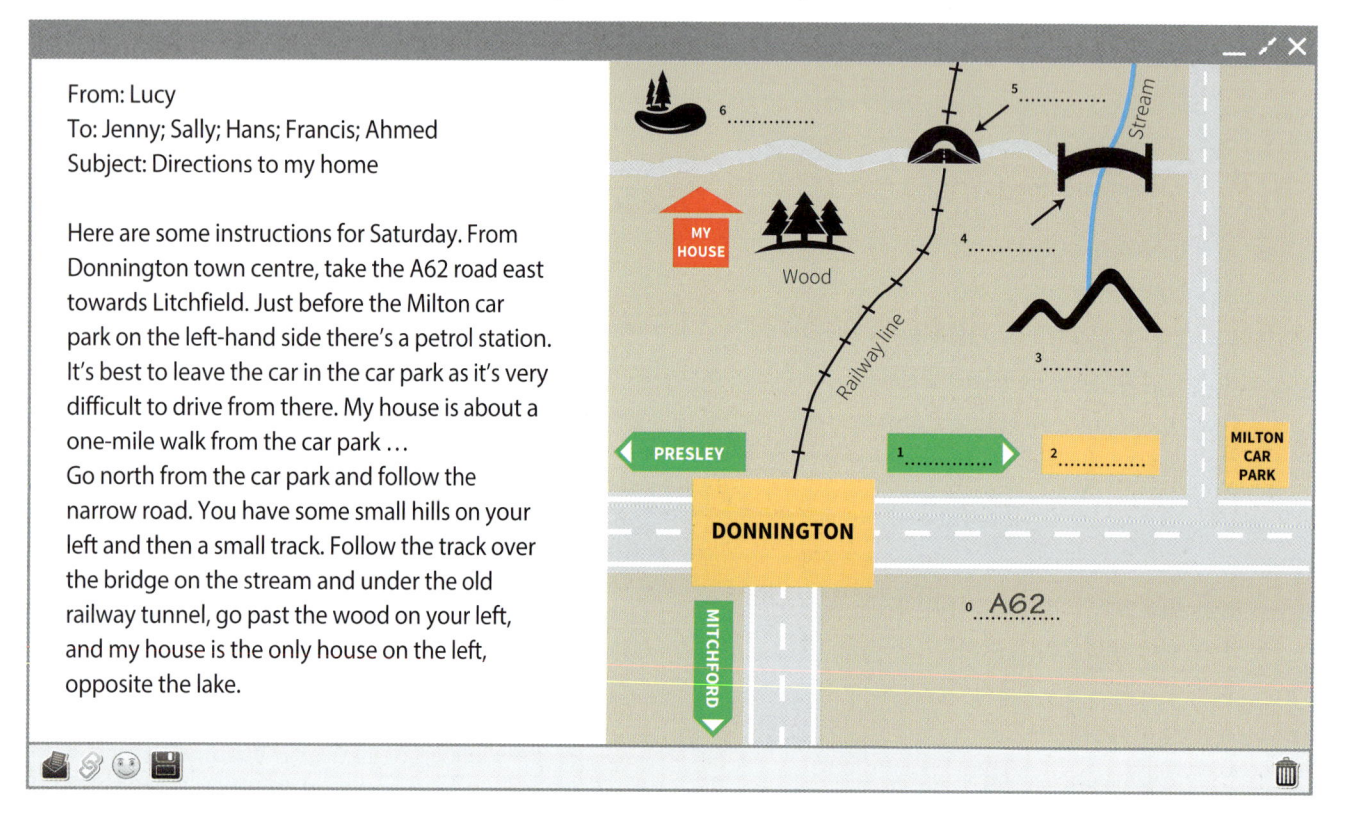

From: Lucy
To: Jenny; Sally; Hans; Francis; Ahmed
Subject: Directions to my home

Here are some instructions for Saturday. From Donnington town centre, take the A62 road east towards Litchfield. Just before the Milton car park on the left-hand side there's a petrol station. It's best to leave the car in the car park as it's very difficult to drive from there. My house is about a one-mile walk from the car park …
Go north from the car park and follow the narrow road. You have some small hills on your left and then a small track. Follow the track over the bridge on the stream and under the old railway tunnel, go past the wood on your left, and my house is the only house on the left, opposite the lake.

32 [2.05] Listen to the headteacher's welcome speech and label the six buildings on the map with the words below.

assembly room ▪ bike racks ▪ drinks area ▪ canteen ▪ administration office ▪ gym

MALDEN SCHOOL PLAN

154   Unit 2

TOWARDS PRELIMINARY

EXAM STRATEGY

Listening – Multiple choice (pictures)

Depending on the question, you will need to listen either for gist, specific information or opinions. Before you listen, read the question and focus on the differences and similarities between the three pictures. When you listen, remember that you will probably hear all the things in the pictures mentioned, so it's important to listen to exactly what the speakers say and mean. Make sure the picture you have chosen answers the question.

33 [2.06] **Listen and choose the correct picture.**

0 Where have they been?

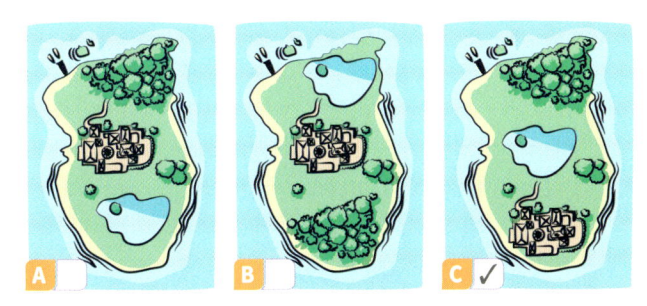

The audio says the forest is in the north, the lake in the middle and the town in the south. So A and B are wrong and C is the correct answer.

1 Where is the photocopier?

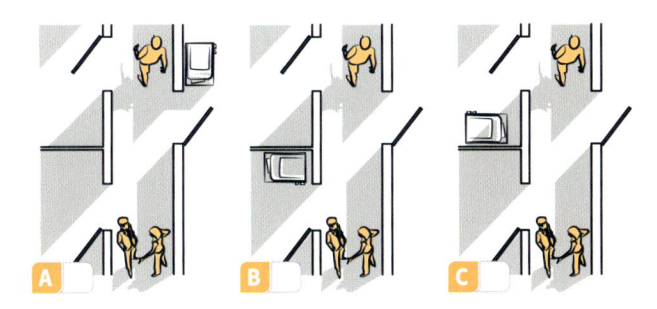

2 Where is the exercise book?

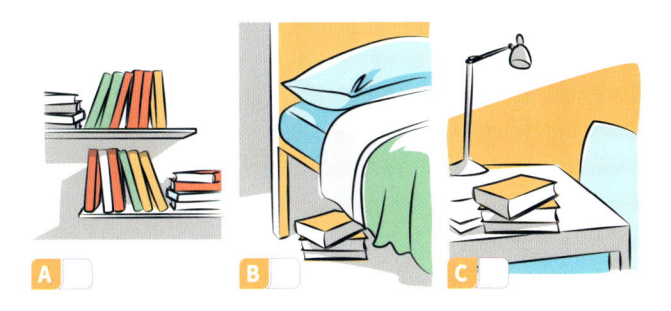

3 Where's the library?

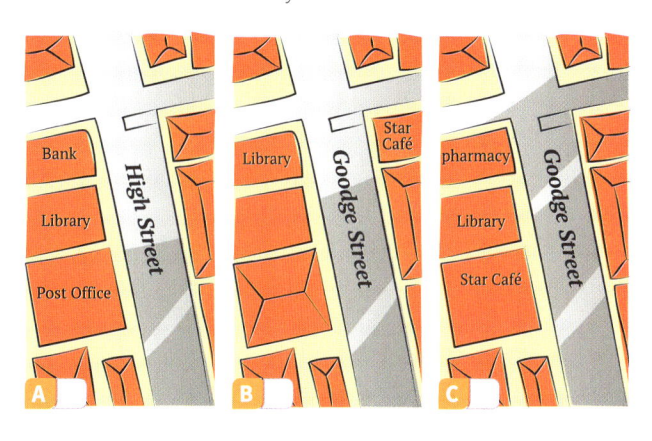

4 What's your country like?

5 Where's the football shirt?

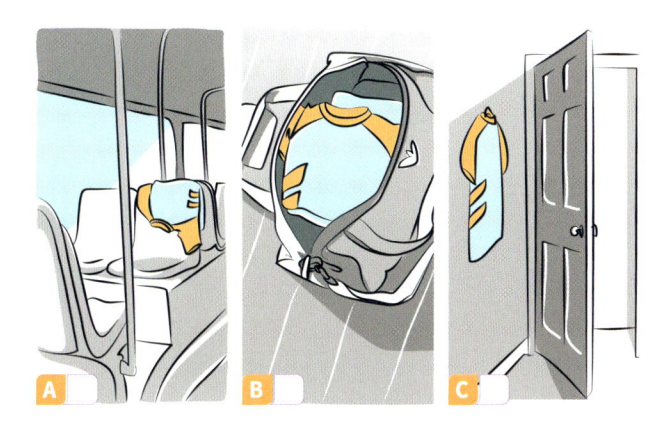

6 Which house did the man stay in?

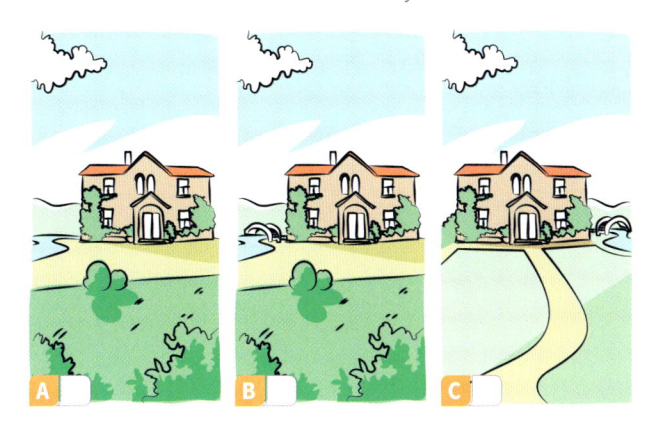

Unit 2 155

REVISE AND ROUND UP

1 Complete the sentences with the correct form of the verbs below.

~~meet~~ • come • do • listen • go • happen • chat

0 We ......**meet**...... in the shopping mall on Saturday afternoons.
1 What .... in their classroom? It's really noisy in there today!
2 What type of music .... you normally .... to?
3 She .... to the gym every Monday.
4 'What .... you .... ?' 'Nothing!'
5 Oh no, my parents .... back.
6 My brother always .... to friends on social media when he's finished his homework.

2 Choose the correct option.

0 Don't disturb me – I *('m talking)* / *talk* on the phone.
1 My parents *like* / *are liking* opera.
2 *I'm thinking* / *think* it's a good idea.
3 Where *are you coming from* / *do you come from*?
4 Where *is Ed going* / *does Ed go* with that funny hat?
5 My dad *drives* / *is driving* 30,000 km every year.
6 *I'm usually getting up* / *usually get up* at 7 during the week.
7 I *always have* / *am always having* a party for my birthday.
8 I *really like* / *am really liking* my new school.

3 Complete the sentences with the present perfect simple.

0 She ...**hasn't answered**... (not / answer) my email.
1 They .... (finish) their homework.
2 I .... (see) that film twice.
3 How many pages .... (you / read) of that book?
4 My aunt .... (visit) Israel many times.
5 Jo, where .... (you / put) my shirt?
6 We .... (not / be) to the mountains for a long time.
7 I .... (never / speak) French in my life.
8 How long .... (they / know) you?
9 I .... (see) that film twice – let's watch something else.

4 Rewrite the sentences with the present perfect and *for* or *since*.

0 I met my friend Ritchie three months ago.
Ritchie and I have been friends for three months.
1 I'm in class 3B. I started it three months ago.
2 Lara's got a new bike. She got it for her birthday.
3 The last time I saw Jo was a week ago at the party.
4 My brother has a girlfriend. They met two years ago.
5 I know Gayle. I met her in April.
6 I live in Manchester. I was born here and I've never wanted to move away.

5 Choose the correct option.

0 I *had* / *('ve had)* this jacket since I was 12.
1 I've *never met* / *never met* a famous person.
2 We *arrived* / *have arrived* two days ago.
3 *Have you ever been* / *Did you ever go* to the US?
4 We *started* / *'ve started* the lesson at 4 pm.
5 I *knew* / *have known* her since primary school.
6 We *saw* / *'ve seen* Lucy last week.

6 Complete the sentences with the present perfect simple and *just*, *yet* or *already*.

0 They ...**haven't arrived yet**... (not / arrive) – let's wait five more minutes.
1 We .... (arrive) – literally two minutes ago.
2 I .... (not / finish) so I can't come out.
3 She .... (do) two exercises – she's just got one more to do.
4 I .... (hear) the news – no school tomorrow!
5 .... (you / call) your mum and dad .... ?
6 They .... (not / speak) to their parents about the party ....

7 Put the words in the correct order.

0 years / been / 've / I / here / ten / living / for
I've been living here for ten years.
1 Christmas / last / doing / been / since / have / what / you / ?
2 shop / local / she / working / been / 's / a / in
3 long / how / Twitter / using / you / been / have / ?
4 studying / you / have / your / for / been / test / ?
5 playing / Easter / team / how / since / been / has / your / ?

156 Units 1–2

8 Choose the correct option.

Hi Bryony,
I ⁰do / **'m doing** my maths homework, but it's really boring so I ¹'ve decided / 've been deciding to write you a few lines. First, I want to tell you about someone ²which / that I really like. He's the boy ³where / who works in the supermarket – you know him, he's the guy ⁴who / whose sister's got purple hair. Anyway, I ⁵saw / 've seen him there a few weeks ago, but I ⁶haven't spoken / haven't been speaking to him yet. He looks really friendly and I have a friend ⁷who / whose knows him, so I hope he can introduce us. Anyway, I ⁸'m getting / get good results in my tests in this period and my parents ⁹are / are being happy about that. There was one test ¹⁰which / who was really difficult and I ¹¹didn't have / haven't had the results yet, but I hope they're OK.
I ¹²play / 'm playing volleyball every week and the training is very hard. Last week we ¹³'ve been playing / played against a team ¹⁴whose / which best player is in the national team – not bad, huh? Anyway, we ¹⁵do / 're doing quite well and we ¹⁶'ve been winning / 've won five matches out of six so far …

9 Complete the sentences so that they are true for you.

0 A friend is someone who … **calls you when you are having a bad day.**
1 A good teacher is a person who …
2 I have a cousin / relative that …
3 I love holidays where …
4 A good parent is a person who …
5 I know somebody whose brother …
6 I like films in which …

10 TRANSLATION Translate the sentences into English.

0 Vado a trovare i miei nonni ogni mese.
   I visit my grandparents every month.
1 Ho visto tre film questo mese.
2 Sto studiando per il test.
3 Ho già fatto tre esercizi ma non ho ancora finito.
4 Sono andata al cinema sabato scorso.
5 Conosco una persona che lavora in quella banca.
6 (Io) Sono in Germania da tre mesi.
7 Qual è lo studente il cui padre è un famoso pilota?
8 Sono due ore che ti aspetto!

CONCEPT CHECK

Read the sentences and answer the questions.

1 *Our team's playing really well today.*

(Answer Yes / No / Your own words)
0 Is the action happening now? **Yes**
1 Can you see it?
2 Do you know the final result?
3 Is this past, present or future?

2 *My sister lives in Birmingham city centre.*

(Answer Yes / No / Not sure / Your own words)
0 Is my sister normally in Birmingham? **Yes**
1 Is she in Birmingham at this moment?
2 Is this a permanent or a temporary situation?
3 Is this past, present or future?

3 *I've been in France for two years.*

(Answer Yes / No / Your own words)
0 When did I arrive in France? **Two years ago**
1 Am I in France at the moment?
2 Is this past, present or future?

4 *I've just finished that science-fiction book.*

(Answer Yes / No / Your own words)
0 Am I reading the book now? **No**
1 Do I have other pages to read?
2 Did I finish the book in the distant or in the recent past?
3 Is this past, present or future?

5 *I've been studying Roman history for the last three weeks.*

(Answer Yes / No / Not sure / Your own words)
0 Am I studying Roman history in this period? **Yes**
1 And in the future?
2 When did I start studying it?
3 Is this form past, present or future?

6 *Liz, this is the man who helped me.*

(Answer Yes / No / Not sure / Your own words)
0 Does Liz know the man? **Not sure**
1 Does Liz know that somebody helped me?
2 Are this man and the man who helped me the same person?
3 Can you omit the word *who* in this sentence?

➡ See **GRAMMAR REFERENCE**
pages 113, 114, 115, 116

Units 1–2 157

3 Entertainment

GRAMMAR PRACTICE

used to

Choose the correct option.
We use *used to* when we want to talk about *a single action / a habit* in the past. We can also use *used to* to talk about *past / present* states or situations: for example: *I used to be in the Scouts*.
Used to is followed by the *infinitive / infinitive without to*.

➤ See **GRAMMAR REFERENCE** page 116

1 Rewrite the sentences using *used to*.

0 My father drove a lorry in his first job.
My father used to drive a lorry in his first job.
1 We played tennis a lot when I was young.
2 My mum always told us a story before bedtime.
3 My friends went to Spain on holiday every year when they were young.
4 She visited her aunt in York every weekend when she was at university.
5 My school was the best in the area until two years ago.
6 I thought disco music was rubbish when I was twelve.

2 Complete the first part of the sentence with the negative form of *used to* and match it to the second part.

0 [c] People not / have
1 [ ] People not / send
2 [ ] London buses not / be
3 [ ] People not / play
4 [ ] Northern Ireland not / be
5 [ ] UK monarchs not / live
6 [ ] People / not click

a part of the United Kingdom.
b on icons in 1980s computers.
c smartphones in 2006.
d football in the street in 1830.
e in Buckingham Palace.
f red.
g emails in 1995.

People didn't use to have smartphones in 2006.

3 Complete the dialogue with *used to* and the verbs below.

call ▪ communicate ▪ write ▪ have ▪ be ▪
not / make ▪ meet ▪ wait ▪ feel

A Excuse me, Madam, have you got a moment?
B Yes, why?
A We're interviewing people about how they ⁰ **used to communicate** before the internet.
B I see. Well, we ¹ ………………………… each other a lot – the phone was the quickest way to speak to someone. But it ² ………………………… really expensive!
A Did you write a lot of letters in the past?
B Yes, I ³ ………………………… letters all the time. But you ⁴ ………………………… for days or weeks for an answer!
A How frustrating!
B No, not really. We ⁵ ………………………… more time for things in general, there was no hurry.
A What other things have changed in your opinion?
B Me and my friends ⁶ ………………………… every day after school and so we ⁷ ………………………… our things public like people do now with social media. In a way, our conversations ⁸ ………………………… much more private and personal than they do now.

4 Complete the sentences with the correct form of *used to* and the verbs in brackets.

0 I **didn't use to understand** (understand) anything in French, but now I can catch everything.
1 She ………………………… (like) him, but now they're not friends.
2 ………………………… (you / study) English at primary school?
3 I ………………………… (eat) lots of vegetables, but now I hate them.
4 They ………………………… (use) social networking sites, but now they're on them all the time.
5 Where ………………………… (you / live) before you moved?
6 Tim ………………………… (send) me messages, but now he sends them to me every five seconds!

158 Unit 3

GRAMMAR PRACTICE

used to and would

Choose the correct option.

We use *would* to talk about past *habits / states* but not past *habits / states*. We don't normally use *would* in the *affirmative / negative* and interrogative forms.

➡ See **GRAMMAR REFERENCE** page 116

5 🔊 Put the words in the correct order.

0 often / visit / grandmother / Dublin / in / my / would / I
I would often visit my grandmother in Dublin.
1 our / to / the cinema / Saturdays / on / take / us / parents / would
2 sister / things / would / always / my / take / my
3 river / go / in / would / swimming / the / I / summer / the / during
4 every / them / up / she / at 7 / wake / would / morning
5 nice / give / us / they / presents / Christmas / for / would
6 visit / and / come round / friends / would / my / evening / every / me

6 🔊 Complete the text with *would* and the verbs below.

bring · play · have · visit · lie · spend · eat · watch · talk · travel · explore · ~~go~~

We had fantastic holidays when I was very young. We always went to Wales and we ⁰ **would go** to the seaside in Pembroke and ¹........................ wonderful days playing near the beach. Unfortunately it sometimes rained and on those days we ²........................ museums like Big Pit, located in old Welsh mines. We actually liked these museums because we ³........................ down over 100 m into the ground, at great speed and in the same cage that transported the miners. Then we ⁴........................ the long dark mine tunnels for several hours. After that, we ⁵........................ tea back in the hotel at 5 pm, but we didn't drink tea – we ⁶........................ lots of cakes and biscuits. On sunny evenings we ⁷........................ in the park with the other children and my parents ⁸........................ on the grass and relax. Sometimes we ⁹........................ a film on TV in the hotel lounge. My parents ¹⁰........................ with their friends in the hotel bar and they ¹¹........................ us some crisps and lemonade into the lounge.

7 🔊 Correct the mistakes. Two sentences are correct.

0 ~~Would you~~ be good at French? **Did you use to be**
1 I didn't use to like their music.
2 David Beckham would play for Manchester United in the 1990s.
3 My aunt would to make us wonderful homemade orange juice in the summer.
4 Did you use to wearing a uniform at primary school?
5 My parents used to live next door to each other when they were children.
6 Our uncle use to help us with our maths homework exercises, but he hasn't got time now.

8 🔊 Look at these people and write sentences about the differences. Use *would* and *used to*.

Sally used to play basketball. / Sally didn't use to watch TV.

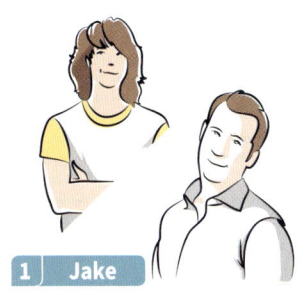

0 Sally
1 Jake
2 Ben
3 Joe
4 Gina
5 Selina
6 Carol

Unit 3 159

READING SKILLS

HOLLYWOOD AND

9 Before you read match the words to their definitions.

1. ☐ cinemagoer
2. ☐ filmmaker
3. ☐ landscape
4. ☐ setting
5. ☐ fans
6. ☐ the establishment

a The place where the action in a book or film takes place.
b A person who creates movies.
c A large area of countryside.
d A person who goes to the cinema to watch films.
e Important or powerful people who control an organisation.
f People who support something, e.g., a football team or a type of music.

10 [2.07] Read and listen to the article and answer the question.

What is the main focus of the article?
1 the importance of Hollywood
2 the problems of Hollywood directors
3 the birth and progress of indie cinema
4 the decline of indie cinema

11 Read the text again and decide if the sentences are true (T) or false (F). Correct the false ones.

1 At the beginning of the 1900s there were a lot of opportunities for small filmmakers. T F
2 Filmmaking on the East Coast was expensive for small companies. T F
3 Indie cinema arrived in Hollywood before the big studios. T F
4 The Hollywood area was popular because it was cheaper than New York. T F
5 TV was bad for independent cinema. T F
6 Indipendent films were popular in Europe before the Second World War. T F
7 People started to become tired of Hollywood movies in the 1970s. T F
8 The big Hollywood studios tried to compete with indie filmmakers. T F

A

Have you seen an indie movie recently? *Indie* is short for *independent* and it refers to films from small studios and relatively unknown film directors. In the past these directors used to need one of the major Hollywood
5 studios to finance their films, but now they can find film companies which are happy to experiment with new material.

B

Ironically, it was independent filmmakers who first started making movies in Hollywood on the West coast
10 of the USA. There were two main reasons for this. First of all, they wanted to move away from the East Coast where big film studios controlled the use of film technology. This meant making movies was expensive. Secondly, the landscape in California was perfect
15 for film setting. Unfortunately the big studios soon followed them.

C

At the same time, things were developing in Europe. In Britain a group set up The London Film Society in 1924. During the 1930s film societies were established all over
20 the continent and people would watch independent foreign language films in small **arthouse theatres**. But the Second World War changed everything. After the war indie films became less popular, reflecting the changing habits of cinemagoers, the growing popularity
25 of TV and the powerful monopoly of the big Hollywood studios such as MGM and 20th Century Fox.

GLOSSARY
arthouse theatres ➤ cinema d'essai

12 Match the headings to the paragraphs. There is one extra title.

1 ☐ Go West
2 ☐ Indie or not indie
3 ☐ An alternative
4 ☐ A revival
5 ☐ Famous indie movies
6 ☐ Changing society

INDIE CINEMA

D

In the 1950s and 1960s Hollywood produced some films that became classics, such as *To Kill a Mocking Bird* and *East of Eden*, but by the 1970s its productions were predictable and boring. So people turned their attention to filmmakers who were exploring alternative topics and who were using innovative filmmaking techniques. More and more people became interested in this new cinema. Cinema fans organised independent film festivals to promote this innovative filmmaking, for example the Sundance Film festival, which started in 1978.

E

The major film companies noticed the increasing interest in indie cinema and so they created their own independent divisions to compete. However, the true indie fans never accepted films from what they regarded as part of the Hollywood establishment.

13 Write the words that show the order of the events.

In the past, …

14 Reorder the events according to the text.

a ☐ Big Hollywood studios became successful.
b ☐ TVs became popular.
c ☐ Independent film festivals started.
d ☐ Small filmmakers moved away from East coast.
e ☐ Large studios moved to Hollywood.
f ☐ Filmmaking started in Hollywood.
g ☐ Second World War started.

VOCABULARY

LITERARY GENRES

15 Match the word clouds to the book category they describe. There is one extra category.

children's books • biography • history • travel • art and architecture • crime • sport • cookery • hobbies and crafts

0 children's books

magic world, toys, dreams, enchanted, fairy tale

1 ....

Berlin Wall, revolution, territory, Cold War, conflict

2 ....

victim, detective, murderer, suspense, mystery

3 ....

creative, innovative design, painting, new technique, beautiful shapes, GLASS FRONT

4 ....

precision, practice, dedication, skills, free time, creativity

5 ....

dedication, 10 consecutive victories, training routine, fame and success, controversial decision

6 ....

crowded beaches, exotic, authentic restaurants, attractive, tourist trap

7 ....

professional success, incredible life, dynamic personality, family difficulties, personal struggle

Unit 3   161

GRAMMAR PRACTICE

Past continuous v past simple

Complete the rules with *in progress*, *interrupts* and *background*.

We use the past continuous for the .... to a story and to indicate that an action was .... at a certain point in time. We use the past simple to indicate an action that .... another past action.

➡ See **GRAMMAR REFERENCE** page 117

16 Complete the sentences with the past continuous of the verbs below.

> not / expect • listen • rain • ~~speak~~ • live • tidy • wait

0 I ....was speaking.... to the head teacher yesterday afternoon.
1 We .... our room when our parents got back.
2 My brother .... in France this time last year.
3 I .... to my favourite music when you called.
4 They .... for you outside the cinema, not the school.
5 It .... when I left the party yesterday evening.
6 I .... a call from you – what a nice surprise!

17 Put the words in the correct order.

0 hoping / meet / you / to / were / we
   ....We were hoping to meet you.....
1 looking / was / of / you / I / a photo / for
   ....
2 happening / was / what / in / street / the / ?
   ....
3 morning / this / why / you / were / crying / ?
   ....
4 mum / calling / now / was / your / just / you
   ....
5 just / text / was / reading / I / your
   ....
6 talking / what / he / about / was / ?
   ....

18 Complete the sentences with the past continuous.

0 How ....were you feeling.... (you / feel) this morning?
1 We .... (think) of inviting Alisdair to the party.
2 What film .... (show) last night?
3 Who .... (your brother / text) just now?
4 Where .... (you / go) on your bike yesterday evening?
5 How .... (they / plan) to travel to the game?
6 Sorry, can you repeat that? I .... (not / concentrate).

19 Complete the sentences with the past simple or continuous.

0 I ....was dreaming.... (dream) of my holidays when the alarm clock ....started.... (start) ringing.
1 When you .... (phone) me I .... (fix) my bike.
2 Where .... (you / go) when I .... (see) you yesterday?
3 How .... (your grandmother / do) when you .... (visit) her last weekend?
4 I .... (lose) my wallet while I .... (walk) down to the shops.
5 We .... (discuss) that when you .... (arrive).
6 Where .... (they / stand) when the accident .... (happen)?

20 Complete the story with the past simple or continuous.

When I ⁰ ....woke up.... (wake up) I ¹ .... (look) outside the window. And guess what? It ² .... (snow) – at last! Children ³ .... (make) snowmen on the road in front of the house and cars ⁴ .... (try) to pass around them. I ⁵ .... (go) downstairs and I ⁶ .... (see) that my mother ⁷ .... (prepare) a big breakfast. I ⁸ .... (sit) down and ⁹ .... (start) to eat. I ¹⁰ .... (be) really happy to be home after so long.

162 Unit 3

SPEAKING SKILLS

DISCUSSING FILMS

21 Use the words below to complete the expressions we use to encourage someone to tell a story.

next • then • end • on • so
think • after • more • know

1 .... what happens?
2 Go ....
3 What happens ....?
4 What happens .... that?
5 Tell me ....
6 And ....?
7 I want to .... more.
8 How does the story .... ?
9 What did you .... of it?

22 Write A's part of the dialogue using B's answers.

A ¹..
B I haven't been to the cinema much recently, but I saw *Welcome* on DVD last weekend. It's really good.
A ²..
B It's a realistic story, really.
A ³..
B It's about Bilal, a 17-year-old Kurdish boy from Iraq who wants to join his girlfriend who's in Britain.
A ⁴..
B In Calais.
A ⁵..
B Bilal meets Simon, who used to be a swimming coach, but is in a difficult period in his life.
A ⁶..
B Well, at first Simon's not very kind, but then he teaches Bilal to swim and they become friends. But then a neighbour notices that Bilal is living in Simon's flat and reports him to the police.
A ⁷..
B Well, Bilal decides to swim across the Channel to meet his girlfriend.
A ⁸..
B I think it's a great film – no special effects but good actors.
A ⁹..
B Probably because it's a simple story, but also because it's about real friendship.
A ¹⁰..
B I can't tell you that, but here's the DVD – watch it!

LISTENING SKILLS

23 Complete the sentences with the words below.

get into • film script • proposal •
youth culture • charts • chance

1 The film company accepted their .... immediately.
2 Their new song has been number one in the .... for about three weeks now.
3 Adults usually have a negative opinion of ....
4 She sent her .... to the producer, who liked it but made a lot of changes.
5 A lot of young filmmakers don't get a .... to show their films to big film companies.
6 It takes people a long time to .... the world of cinema.

24 [2.08] Listen to the interview and answer the questions.

1 What do the two filmmakers have in common?
2 Are they successful?

25 [2.08] Listen again and write who did these things, Samir Khan (SK) or Jennifer Keeble (JK).

1 .... made a film set in Eastern Europe.
2 .... is an ex-cameraman.
3 .... wrote film scripts when he / she was young.
4 .... made a film about social change.
5 .... thought it was difficult to become a film director.
6 .... got the idea for a film while he / she was travelling.
7 .... had ideas for films while he / she was watching movies.
8 .... wasn't enjoying working on a big Hollywood film.
9 .... thinks that originality is very important in indie cinema.

26 [2.08] Listen again and answer the questions.

1 What was the name of Samir's film about youth culture?
2 What was the name of his film company?
3 Which country inspired Jennifer's film *New World Blues*?
4 Where is *New World Blues* in the indie charts?
5 What is the name of her film company?

Unit 3   163

TOWARDS PRELIMINARY

> **EXAM STRATEGY**
>
> **Reading – Multiple matching**
>
> This task requires careful reading and attention to detail. Start by reading the profiles and underlining the key information. As you read the texts, look back and check the profiles. Remember the text and profile must match exactly. There are more texts than people, so three of the texts won't be used but they contain distractors.

27 Read the descriptions of the films and the profiles of the cinemagoers. Then answer the questions.

0 **a** Which film will probably interest Michael?
1 ☐ Which film will probably interest Areefa?
2 ☐ Which film will Jay probably like most?

Michael loves sport, drama and films about nature. He loves the theatre and opera in particular. He has children and enjoys contemporary films about family life and its complications.

Areefa is into anything that has lots of action in it, from contact sports and adventure films to science-fiction and even horror films. She gets really bored by human-interest films and documentaries.

Jay spends all her time on the internet and often streams cartoons and adventure movies for kids. She sometimes takes part in internet-based sci-fi competitions.

The Trouble with the Truth
This is an intriguing film about people, relationships and some of the difficulties that they can cause. It starts when Robert (*John Shea*) meets his daughter Jenny (*Danielle Harris*) who announces that she is getting engaged. Robert isn't happy about this and criticises her choice of future husband. He then has to look at his own relationships and realises they are far from perfect.

a

What Made Pokemon Go
Sci-fi has always looked to the future, but the current popularity of virtual reality has its origins in computer games like *Pokemon*, which exploded into our homes in the 1990s. In *What Made Pokemon Go*, director Adam Campbell looks at the history of this popular game as well as providing lots of information on its founder, John Hanke, on his journey to being rich and famous.

b

Arrival
Arrival is the new sci-fi drama by the director of *Sicario*, Denis Villeneuve. It is an amazing film that mixes incredible action scenes with moments of deeper reflection. When aliens arrive on Earth, there is usually death and destruction, but this film takes an alternative look at intelligent life from other planets.

c

Amy
Amy is an independent production by Film 4 and follows singer Amy Winehouse's life from difficult teenager to internationally famous pop star. This is an honest and emotional movie with personal clips that show her feelings about fame. The film has extensive interviews with all the important people in her life.

d

28 Write the keywords from the film descriptions that helped you answer the questions in exercise 27.

a *people, relationships, getting engaged*

164 Unit 3

TOWARDS PRELIMINARY

29 Decide which book would be suitable for the following people.

1 SAMANTHA loves reading about people's lives and what they have achieved, especially famous people in society and politics. She's keen on finding out what famous people are really like in private.

2 MARCUS wants to go on a one-month train trip round Europe with his friends before starting university. He'd like to see as many places as possible, as cheaply as possible.

3 SUSAN is a big fan of NBA basketball and watches it when she can. She knows all about the leading players and keeps an eye on the results of her favourite teams every weekend.

4 HUGO has always had an interest in detective films and stories. He loves to read about police investigations into complex and mysterious cases around the world.

5 BARBARA has always enjoyed doing jobs around the home, but now she's interested in attempting to make more complicated things like furniture. She wants to improve her basic skills and make some really nice things for her home.

Books

A HOUSECRAFT This is the perfect companion for people who love DIY – do-it-yourself! Become an expert in making things from cushions to bookcases. Clear, simple instructions including tips on how to get started and expert advice on how to attempt more complicated items.

B TOP STORIES FOR TEENS In this collection of classic and modern short stories there's something for everyone. None of the stories is more than twenty pages long so it's a book you can pick up when you feel like having a quiet read. There's adventure, comedy, mystery, crime and romance. An ideal book to take with you on holiday.

C CELEBRITY HOMES This beautiful book takes you on a trip round the world to discover the amazing homes of the famous – from a top floor apartment in one of London's skyscrapers to a beach villa in California and a mountain chalet in Canada. See for yourself the incredible luxury and comfort of celebrity homes and how the stars live.

D AN AMAZING LIFE Follow the fascinating events in Barack Obama's life, from his birth in Hawaii to when he was a candidate for the presidential primaries to his incredible election as the President of the United States. Follow every single event in his eight momentous years, complete with personal anecdotes from the people that really knew him.

E WHO DID IT? In this second collection of unresolved crimes, we look at why the police cannot find the solution to an apparently obvious case. We also examine a series of robberies in which a total of £100 million disappeared over five years. Nobody has any idea who the criminal was or where the money is.

F ALL-SPORTS ALMANAC Do you know everything about your favourite team? Test your knowledge with this new collection of the results and action of the last 10 years of your favourite sport. Everything from interviews with star players to match-by-match summaries, all in one volume.

G €20 A DAY! Do you want to see the world on a budget? This guide is all you need to escape the tourist traps and really experience life in different countries. In the first book in the series, we'll show you how to eat well and cheaply in Italy, France, Spain and other Mediterranean countries and give you money-saving tips on travel.

H PLAY BASKETBALL IN ONE WEEK This book is aimed at complete beginners who know nothing about the sport! We start with the basics using step-by-step guides. Ideal for sporty people who learn quickly. In seven days you'll be ready to join your local team!

4 Sport

GRAMMAR PRACTICE

can / can't for ability, requests, permission and possibility

Complete the rules with the words below.

infinitive ▪ permission ▪ future ▪ past ▪ ability ▪
past participle ▪ without ▪ questions ▪ same

- We use *can* to talk about .... ,
  .... and possibility.
- *Can* is a modal verb, which means that:
  - it uses the .... form for all subjects;
  - after *can* we use the .... of the main verb .... to;
  - it has no infinitive, -ing or .... form;
  - it doesn't need an auxiliary to make .... or negatives;
- We use *could* and *was / were able to* to talk about the .... We use *will be able to* to talk about the ....

→ See **GRAMMAR REFERENCE** page 117

1 🔊 **Sort the sentences into the correct group: Ability (A), Permission (P) and Possibility (PO).**

0 ..PO..   I can't come tomorrow.
1 ....   I asked him but he couldn't help me.
2 ....   You can call me after lunch.
3 ....   I can't receive calls up in the mountains.
4 ....   Can he swim?
5 ....   I can't see anything – it's too dark.
6 ....   We can't use our dictionaries in the test.
7 ....   I can pick you up at your house.

2 🔊 **Match the two parts of the sentences and complete them with *can* or *can't*.**

0 [e]   I ...can't... hear
1 [ ]   .... you remember
2 [ ]   I .... sing
3 [ ]   Who .... tell
4 [ ]   Sorry, I .... talk
5 [ ]   He .... speak German,

a her name?
b me the answer?
c opera – too difficult!
d just French.
e anything.
f to you right now.

3 🔊 **Write questions with *can* and the verbs in brackets.**

0 My brother wants to take us to the party. (*he / drive*)
   Can he drive?
1 He's really busy at the moment! (*I / help*)
2 My sister's going to live in China. (*speak / Chinese*)
3 Martha would like to become a chef. (*she / cook*)
4 You can't use credit cards here. (*we / pay in cash*)
5 My friend plays the trumpet. (*he / read music*)
6 Something's happening outside. (*what / you / see*)

4 🔊 **Put the words in the correct order.**

0 can / ski / they / well / ? **Can they ski well?**
1 can't / tomorrow / why / you / come / ?
2 dialect / understand / she / the / can't / local
3 your / address / you / remember / can / friend's / ?
4 the / can / send / pictures / you / tomorrow / I
5 couldn't / at / Milan / in / 9 / be / we
6 find / anywhere / can't / bag / school / my / I

5 🔊 **Complete the sentences with the correct form of *can* or *could* and the verbs below.**

~~sleep~~ ▪ chat ▪ feel ▪ open ▪ run ▪
watch ▪ come ▪ decide ▪ be

0 It's really hot and I ..**can't sleep**.. very well at night.
1 My friends and I .... all day with Skype.
2 I .... the document you sent me.
3 Good news – I .... to your party after all!
4 He .... 100 m in 11 seconds ten years ago.
5 With streaming you .... videos straight away.
6 It was so cold I .... my feet.
7 I .... where to go for my holidays.
8 Wait there. We .... with you in 20 minutes.

have to / don't have to

Complete the rules.

We use *have to* to express .... We use *don't / doesn't have to* to indicate there is no ...., so the action is optional or not necessary. *Have to* is not a modal verb, so it can be used in all ....

→ See **GRAMMAR REFERENCE** page 117

166   Unit 4

GRAMMAR PRACTICE

6 🔊 Choose the correct option.

0 You *have to* / *don't have to* wear a uniform in this school – it's compulsory.
1 You *have to* / *don't have to* come – you decide.
2 I want to go, but I *have to* / *don't have to* check with my parents first.
3 You *have to* / *don't have to* buy eggs. We have lots.
4 I *have to* / *don't have to* talk to you – it's important.
5 I can't stop – I *have to* / *don't have to* catch my train.
6 You *have to* / *don't have to* pay to enter today. It's free.

7 🔊 Complete the sentences with the correct form of *have to*.

0 It was closed, so we ......*had to*...... wait outside.
1 I've put some cash in your wallet so you .... use your card when you're away.
2 .... (you) to pay to get into the stadium last night?
3 My friends and I .... walk home because someone gave us a lift.
4 We never .... prepare for history tests – they're so easy.
5 .... (she) repeat the exam last year?
6 You .... answer that question – maybe it's a bit personal.

8 🔊 Complete the text about schools in Britain with *have to* / *don't have to* and the verbs below.

wear • go • decide • pass • keep • stay • do

Going to school in the UK

In UK schools you sometimes ⁰......*have to go*...... to assembly in the morning. At assemblies the headteacher makes important announcements. In most schools you ¹........................... a school uniform, usually a blazer and grey trousers or a grey skirt for girls. Luckily you ²........................... your blazer on when it's hot in summer, just a blue or white shirt is normally OK in this case. When students do something wrong, they sometimes ³........................... a detention. This is not good because they ⁴........................... at school for an hour or more after normal school time. At 4, students ⁵........................... which ten or more subjects they want to do as GCSEs (the final exams at the end of their secondary school). They ⁶........................... their exams if they want to continue their studies at college.

must and *have to* (1)

Choose the correct option.

- *Must* is used for *permission* / *obligation* / *possibility*. *Must* *is* / *isn't* a modal verb, so it *changes* / *doesn't change* according to the subject.
- The negative form means something is *prohibited* / *not necessary* to do.
- The *affirmative* / *interrogative* form of *must* is rare. In this case we normally use *have to*.
- Like *can*, *must* has no *infinitive* / *present*, past or future forms. In these cases we also normally use *have to*.

➡ See **GRAMMAR REFERENCE** page 118

9 🔊 Complete the sentences with *must* or *mustn't*.

0 They ......*mustn't*...... be late this time – make sure they know that.
1 You .... go into the teachers' room. They get really angry when we do.
2 You .... study harder this time.
3 You .... tell anyone what I said.
4 I .... remember to take my science books to class – I forgot them last time.
5 You .... leave anything on the train.
6 All visitors .... go to reception.

10 🔊 Match the two parts of the sentences and complete them with *must* or *mustn't*.

0 [b] You ......*must*...... tell
1 [ ] You .... listen
2 [ ] She .... do
3 [ ] They .... arrive
4 [ ] He .... get
5 [ ] Jill .... take

a better care of her things.
b me the truth.
c to them. They're only joking.
d angry all the time.
e at the station on time.
f that again. It was dangerous.

11 🔊 Complete the sentences with *must* or *mustn't* and an appropriate verb.

0 All gym users ......*must wear*...... clean shoes in the gym.
1 You .... personal items in a safe place.
2 You .... any food in school.
3 You .... loudly in the library.
4 Students .... other people with loud music.

Unit 4   167

READING SKILLS

12 Read the title. What do you think the article is about?

13 [2.09] Read and listen to the article and check your answer.

14 Read the text again and complete the timeline of events.

- 1968 ....
- 1970s ....
- 1988 ....
- 1994 ....
- 1997 ....
- 1999-2005 ....
- 2010 ....
- 2011 ....
- 2012 ....
- 2013 ....

15 Complete the table.

athlete/s	type of drug used	how it helps an athlete
1	....	....
2	....	....
3	....	....
4	....	....
5	....	....

16 Read the text again and answer the questions.

1. What did Ben Johnson win in Seoul?
2. How much slower was Ben Johnson when he returned after his suspension for drugs?
3. How long did Lance Armstrong stay away from competition because of cancer?
4. Why did Armstrong take the drugs?
5. Which sport had particular problems in 1994?
6. According to Nadzeya, who was giving her drugs?
7. What first action did the IOC take to fight drugs in sport?
8. Why were the first drugs tests on athletes not very useful?
9. What does the writer think about the current situation involving drugs and sports people?

WHEN SPORT GETS DIRTY

A I remember Ben Johnson beating the 100 m world record and winning the gold medal at the 1988 Olympics in Seoul. I can't forget seeing the same athlete a few years later, returning after a 2-year ban for doping. Ben Johnson used
5 anabolic steroids to improve his body strength. When he returned to running 2 years later, without the help of steroids, he was nearly a second slower.

B Johnson wasn't the first or the last high-profile case, of course, of doping in sport. Cyclist Lance Armstrong got ill
10 with cancer in 1997, but in 1999 he returned to cycling and, incredibly, won the Tour de France seven times in a row. Armstrong eventually admitted on a popular American talk show in 2013 that he used illegal drugs, including a hormone that made him go much faster. He knew he couldn't take
15 this hormone because it was against the sport regulations, but he took it anyway because he wanted to win.

17 Read the text again and decide if the sentences are true (T), false (F) or doesn't say (DS). Correct the false ones.

1. Ben Johnson returned to athletics immediately after testing positive in 1988.   T F DS
2. Anabolic steroids can kill people.   T F DS
3. Armstrong was completely cured from cancer in 1999.   T F DS
4. Alberto Contador lost all his titles because of drugs.   T F DS
5. Some sports are completely without drugs, according to the writer.   T F DS
6. Nadzeya said she didn't take any drugs.   T F DS
7. Drugs testing means that doping in sport no longer happens.   T F DS

168   Unit 4

C Armstrong was not alone, of course. Alberto Contador, the Spanish cyclist, has won several major cycle races but lost his 2010 Tour de France and 2011 Giro d'Italia titles a year later when he tested positive for a powerful bronchodilator drug which athletes use in order to lose fat very quickly.

D No sport can say it is totally clean. In 1994, 11 athletes in China's women's swimming team tested positive for a male hormone just before the 1994 Asian Games. This hormone is responsible for increased muscular and skeletal growth.

E More recently, Belarusian **shot-putter** Nadzeya Ostapchuck won gold at the 2012 London Olympics but then tested positive for drugs. Nadzeya claimed that her coach made her take drugs by secretly putting into her food an anabolic steroid used to promote muscular growth.

F The International Olympic Committee first made athletes take drug tests in 1968, but these tests could not identify all types of drugs, so doping in sport continued. Over the years drugs testing in sport has become more sophisticated but recent news stories show that doping in sport still happens today.

GLOSSARY
shot-putter ➤ pesista

18 Find the words or phrases in the text that mean the same as these.

1. suspension (para A) ....
2. almost (para A) ....
3. sick (para B) ....
4. came back (para B) ....
5. competitions (para C) ....
6. strong (para C) ....
7. masculine (para D) ....
8. development (para D) ....
9. trainer (para E) ....
10. improve (para E) ....
11. top (para F) ....
12. highly developed (para F) ....

VOCABULARY

SPORTS AND SPORTS EQUIPMENT

19 Complete the sentences with the words below.

clubs ▪ boots ▪ shuttlecocks ▪ wetsuit ▪ hoop ▪ board ▪ helmet

0. The exercise with the ......*hoop*...... in gymnastics looks really difficult.
1. I need some new golf .... – these ones are really old.
2. We can't play badminton. We've lost all the ....
3. Junior skiers have to wear a .... in Italy.
4. You need a good .... for scuba diving. It's cold down there!
5. Windsurfers pay a lot for their .... because it's the most important piece of equipment.
6. Mountaineering means difficult terrain and sometimes bad weather, so you need great ....

20 Write the name of the sport described.

0. ......*baseball*...... This is a sport played with a bat and it consists of one person hitting the ball as far as possible and then running from base to base to score points for the team.
1. .... This is a game that people play on grass or on ice. You use a stick to move a ball or a puck on ice and try to score goals for your team.
2. .... You need a helmet and a good bike for this sport. You can practise it on the street or cross-country.
3. .... This sport is an important part of the Olympic Games. It consists of many different disciplines from running on the track to complex disciplines like the decathlon and heptathlon.
4. .... For this sport you need a ball, two teams of five players and two hoops. The players cannot touch the ball with their feet.
5. .... In this sport there are different categories for the athletes according to their weight: athletes have to be of similar weight to be able to compete against each other. Matches take place on a square ring between two competitors who wear special gloves and cannot kick each other.

Unit 4   169

GRAMMAR PRACTICE

must and have to (2)

Complete the rules with the words below.

internal · negative · external · prohibited · necessary · past

Must and *have to* are both used to express obligation.
Must is common for an .... obligation: the speaker feels he / she has a duty.
Have to is common for an .... obligation: the duty comes from someone else or from the situation itself.
Must is also used for rules.
We use the verb *have to* and not *must* for obligation in the ....
Mustn't means something is ...., but *don't have to* means something is not ....; so in the .... form *must* and *have to* are completely different in meaning.

➡ See **GRAMMAR REFERENCE** page 118

21 🎙 **Complete the interview with the correct form of *must* or *have to*. In some cases two options are correct.**

A What's the secret to becoming a world triathlon champion?
B I think you ⁰ **must be / have to be** (be) really dedicated – you ¹.................... (stop) at the first difficulty you meet!
A What lifestyle changes ².................... (you / make) when you started?
B Well, I ³.................... (learn) to get up at 6 every morning, but in this period we don't have any competitions, so I only ⁴.................... (start) at 8 o'clock, which means I can sleep until later!
A Are you on a special diet?
B Yes, I ⁵.................... (be) very careful about that. I ⁶.................... (drink) coffee or fizzy drinks.
A And what's the best part of being an athlete?
B Probably that when I was at school I ⁷.................... (do) all my homework because I was away at competitions!

make and let

Choose the correct option.

We use *make* / *let* to talk about what somebody or something obliges us to do.
We use *make* / *let* to say that a person or situation gives the possibility to do something.
Make and *let* are followed by *a subject* / *an object* and the *infinitive* / *infinitive without to*.

➡ See **GRAMMAR REFERENCE** page 118

22 🎙 **Choose the correct option.**

0 Our teachers (let) / make us eat in class.
1 My parents don't *let* / *make* me go out during the week.
2 My mother *lets* / *makes* me clean my room – I hate it!
3 My phone broke and Tim *let* / *made* me use his.
4 My English teacher *lets* / *makes* us use a dictionary in tests, but I prefer to use my own words.
5 The inspector *let* / *made* me get off the bus because I didn't have a ticket.
6 Does the cinema *let* / *make* you bring your own food in?

23 🎙 **Put the words in the correct order.**

0 early / get / she / me / made / up
   She made me get up early.
1 teacher / the / make / do / me / the test / didn't
2 tablet / let / use / Jim / me / his
3 coach / home / go / us / our / let / early
4 sing / you / they / did / make / ?
5 win / let / didn't / easily / we / them
6 up / parents / you / stay / let / your / do / late / ?

24 🎙 **Complete the sentences with the correct form of *make* or *let*.**

0 You can't ....**make**.... me go – it's my decision!
1 Our parents .... us watch TV until late – we always have to switch off at 9 pm.
2 Can you .... me know before the weekend?
3 She .... me use her bike all weekend – that was really kind of her.
4 .... your primary school teacher .... you learn poems by heart?
5 .... your English teacher .... you speak Italian in class?

170 Unit 4

SPEAKING SKILLS

EXPLAINING RULES

25 Put the words in the correct order.

1 fun / is / watch / it / to / ?
2 play / how / you / do / ?
3 players / the / other / what / do / do / ?
4 win / do / you / how / ?
5 need / equipment / you / what / do / ?
6 points / you / do / score / how / ?
7 main / objective / the / what's / ?
8 long / how / typical / is / match / a / ?
9 got / wrong / sorry / I've / that

26 Match the sentences of exercise 25 to these responses.

a ☐ Yes, it's really exciting.
b ☐ A bat and a ball.
c ☐ By winning 3 sets.
d ☐ To hit the ball as far as possible and score as many points before it comes back.
e ☐ No problem.
f ☐ About 90 minutes.
g ☐ One person hits the ball and the other tries to stop it.
h ☐ They try to help their teammates.
i ☐ By getting the ball to go through the hoop.

27 TRANSLATION Write these dialogues in English.

Dialogue 1
A Chiedi a B se sa giocare a cricket.
B Rispondi di sì.
A Chiedi come si gioca.
B Spiega che è un po' complicato.
A Di' che non importa.

Dialogue 2
A Chiedi a B se gioca a squash.
B Rispondi di sì.
A Chiedi come si vince una partita di squash.
B Spiega che devi fare 20 punti per vincere un set. Di' che hai sbagliato – devi fare 21 punti.
A Chiedi a B quanti set bisogna vincere.
B Rispondi che bisogna vincerne tre.
A Chiedi che attrezzatura serve.
B Rispondi che servono solo una racchetta e una pallina.
A Chiedi se è divertente da guardare.
B Rispondi non tanto, e che è bello giocare a squash ma non guardarlo.

LISTENING SKILLS

28 [2.10] **Listen and answer the question.**

Which of these groups has Frank *not* worked with?
1 people with disabilities
2 young people
3 mothers with babies
4 school children
5 Paralympians

29 [2.10] **Listen again and decide if the sentences are true (T) or false (F). Correct the false ones.**

1 Frank was born in the Netherlands. T F
2 He joined the army as a teenager. T F
3 He helped people with disabilities in the army. T F
4 He qualified as a swimming instructor before he arrived in Paris. T F
5 Frank thinks there is some psychology in coaching swimming. T F
6 He thinks preparation for swimming is similar to that in football. T F
7 Frank enjoys his work with Paralympians. T F

30 [2.10] **Listen again and answer the questions.**

1 Where does Frank work?
2 What did he do before becoming a swimming instructor?
3 Who went with Frank to Amsterdam?
4 What are the two elements of a good swimming lesson?
5 What does an instructor have to tell people?
6 Why does he enjoy the work with schools?
7 What do Paralympian swimmers want to make people see?

31 [2.10] **Listen again and choose the correct option.**

1 What is Frank's main idea about coaching?
   A It needs to be a balance between difficulty and fun.
   B It needs to be hard and difficult.
   C It needs to be light and fun.
2 What is Frank's general opinion of swimming?
   A You need to use your natural talent.
   B You must swim at least eight hours a day.
   C You need to swim regularly.
3 How does Frank describe Paralympians?
   A Competitive and great to work with.
   B Really difficult to work with.
   C Rich and difficult to work with.

Unit 4 171

ACADEMIC SKILLS

UNDERSTANDING ARGUMENTS

WOMEN'S FOOTBALL – WHERE NOW?

Talk to most people about women's football and they will probably mention the film *Bend It like Beckham*. The football scenes in the film did a lot to make people accept women's football, especially in popular culture. But where does the women's game stand now, nearly 20 years after the film, and what difficulties does it still have?

It's important to understand that women's football did not start with *Bend It like Beckham*. In the early 1900s the sport became very popular, with around 150 women's teams in England. Matches attracted more people than most men's games – sometimes more than 50,000 – and they had to create larger areas for the spectators at both men's and women's matches. But then in 1921 the English Football Association decided that football was 'unsuitable for females', officially because of the high level of physical contact, but probably also for political and financial reasons. Amazingly, the FA only let women play regular matches from 1971, two years after the foundation of the Women's Football Association.

Since then women's football has grown rapidly in popularity. According to UEFA, there were 1,208 million registered female players for the 2014–2015 season and 750,000 players are under the age of 18. The number of players has doubled in the last few years and continues to go up. In fact there are now 51 countries with a women's national league.

Despite this popularity, there is practically no women's football on ordinary television, and TV football is still synonymous with the men's game. More importantly, there is very little money in the women's game. At the elite level of women's football in England, the Women's Super League, the top players earn around £1,000 per month. That is equivalent to what the top men make every 30 minutes … Can you imagine Cristiano Ronaldo playing for so little money? So, in the end, we need to ask the question, do we really want to take this sport seriously? And are we still happy with enormous gender inequality in sport in the twenty-first century?

---

32 Read the text quickly and answer the question.

What is the main purpose of the article?
1 To promote women's football.
2 To denounce discrimination against women.
3 To discuss past and present problems faced by women's football.
4 To talk about the differences between men's and women's football.

33 Read the text and answer the questions.

0 Why was *Bend It like Beckham* good for women's football? **Because it made more people accept it.**
1 How do we know that women's football was popular in the past?
2 Who stopped women from playing in official matches?
3 Did women wait for the FA's permission to play before forming their own football association?
4 According to the writer, what were the real reasons why the FA stopped women's football?
5 For how long were women officially not able to play football?
6 How much money do the best male players earn in one hour?

34 Choose the points the writer makes.

0 Some women's football matches were more popular than men's in the past. ✓
1 Women's football was the victim of discrimination in the past.
2 The popularity of women's football is growing fast.
3 Most women players are middle-aged.
4 TV coverage of women's football is generally good.
5 Women players are well paid.
6 Women players earn far less than their male counterparts.
7 Top male players receive far too much money.

35 Find the opposites of these words in the text.

0 convincing — **unconvincing**
1 refuse — ....
2 suitable — ....
3 slowly — ....
4 halved — ....
5 decrease — ....
6 bottom level — ....
7 very small — ....
8 equality — ....

TOWARDS PRELIMINARY

> **EXAM STRATEGY**
>
> **Listening – Multiple choice**
>
> Before listening to the interview, read the questions and the answers carefully. The questions will give you an idea about what you are going to hear. Remember that the questions always follow the order of the dialogue. The first time you listen, choose an answer, then check it in the second listening.

36 🔊 [2.11] **Listen and answer the first question.**

0 How did Jeena become a top volleyball player?
  A She spent a lot of time training.
  B She trained hard and was fortunate.
  C She is a very competitive person.

The correct answer is B because she says she worked hard and was lucky.
A is wrong because she says it wasn't only hard work.
C is wrong. The sport is competitive. She doesn't speak about herself.

37 🔊 [2.12] **Now listen to the interview and choose the correct option.**

1 Jeena went to play in Italy because:
  A she wanted to live in Milan.
  B an Italian team asked her to play.
  C she went there to look for a team.

2 What do volleyball players spend most of their time doing, according to Jenna?
  A Preparing for matches.
  B Playing matches.
  C Travelling to competitions.

3 According to Jeena, the worst aspect of being a professional player is:
  A training.
  B playing matches.
  C travelling.

4 What does Jeena say about the coaches?
  A They let the team have fun if they win.
  B They don't let them eat snacks.
  C They have invented a lot of rules.

5 Which food does Jeena not mention as part of the prematch meal?
  A Steak.
  B Fruit.
  C Pasta.

6 How long is the discussion with the coach about tactics?
  A An hour.
  B 30 minutes.
  C 45 minutes.

7 How long is the prematch warm-up?
  A 30 minutes.
  B 40 minutes.
  C 45 minutes.

8 What's the last thing they do before a match?
  A Have a big meal.
  B Talk about the match plan.
  C Prepare physically for the match.

9 What's a 'smash'?
  A A type of shot.
  B A bonus point in the match.
  C A way of jumping.

10 Last year Jeena's team won:
  A a championship.
  B promotion and a cup.
  C promotion.

11 What has been the highlight of Jeena's career so far?
  A Learning to do smashes.
  B Moving up to the next category.
  C Playing with top class players.

12 Jeena's team now plays in:
  A the second division.
  B the first division.
  C the third division.

Unit 4   173

REVISE AND ROUND UP

1 **Choose the correct option. In some cases both are correct.**

0 My mum (used to) / (would) wait for us outside school.
1 We would / used to climb the trees near the river.
2 Max would / used to play for the Juventus youth team.
3 My parents would / used to call me every day.
4 She would / used to be my teacher.
5 Mobile phones would / used to be big and heavy.
6 My dad would / used to have a sports car.
7 A famous writer used to / would live there.
8 We used to / would cycle along the coast.

2 **Complete the sentences with the past simple or continuous of the verbs in brackets.**

0 I **was walking** (walk) to the shops when you **called** (call) me.
1 What .... (you / think) when you .... (say) that to him?
2 Greg .... (phone) while you .... (have) a shower.
3 I .... (not / expect) a call from you, so it .... (be) a nice surprise to hear your voice.
4 Who .... (you / talk) to just now?
5 Why .... (you / stop) in front of that house?
6 They .... (hope) to catch the last bus but they .... (arrive) too late.

3 **Complete the dialogue with used to, the past simple or the past continuous of the verbs below.**

> be (x2) ▪ walk ▪ wear ▪ have ▪ go ▪
> stop ▪ not / recognize ▪ leave ▪ ~~meet~~ ▪ tell

Sue Hey, guess who I⁰ **met** last night?
Tim No idea. Who?
Sue I¹ .... home after the party when someone² .... me in the street.
Tim Who³ .... it?
Sue Fiona! I⁴ .... her at first. She⁵ .... blonde hair and she⁶ .... army trousers.
Tim Strange. She⁷ .... really elegant … And⁸ .... she .... you anything interesting?
Sue No, she⁹ .... to a dinner party, so she¹⁰ .... in a hurry.

4 **Look at the table and complete the sentences with can or can't and the correct verb.**

	Frances	Dave	Mike
play squash	✓	X	✓
speak Japanese	X	X	✓
play the piano	X	✓	X
cook	✓	✓	✓
ski	X	X	X
run 10 km	X	✓	✓
sing	✓	X	X

0 Frances **can't run** 10 km, but Dave and Mike can.
1 Frances and Mike ...., but Dave can't.
2 None of them ....
3 All three ....
4 Only Mike ....
5 Frances and Mike ...., but Dave can.
6 Mike and Dave ...., but Frances can.

5 **Look at the signs and complete the sentences with the correct form of have to or can and a verb.**

0 You **can't use** mobiles in here.
1 You .... and let ducks pass here.
2 You ...., eat or drink in here.
3 You .... the building before tweeting.
4 You .... wear clothes after this point.
5 You .... plastic and cans here.
6 You .... back.
7 You .... this sign – it's sharp.

174   Units 3–4

CONCEPT CHECK

6 **Choose the correct option.**

0 You *don't have to* / *mustn't* arrive late for the meeting.
1 You *don't have to* / *mustn't* walk on the grass.
2 We *don't have to* / *mustn't* change train – it's direct.
3 You *don't have to* / *mustn't* tell anyone – it's a secret.
4 They *don't have to* / *mustn't* use their phones in class.
5 You *don't have to* / *mustn't* bring your book – it's here.

7 **Complete the dialogue with the correct form of *must*, *have to* or *can* and the verbs below.**

> copy • do • ~~study~~ • send •
> use • keep • pass • be

Jim So how's the graphics course going?
Amy Not bad, but we ⁰ *have to study* a lot. It's really tiring.
Jim How's that?
Amy Well, we have lessons in the morning and then we ¹ .... our project work in the afternoon.
Jim ² .... (you) an exam at the end?
Amy No, luckily it's all based on the coursework. But we ³ .... anybody else's work. They ⁴ .... original designs.
Jim OK. Are you learning anything useful?
Amy Yes, I ⁵ .... all kinds of graphic design programmes now.
Jim Great – ⁶ .... (you) me one or two examples?
Amy No, unfortunately I ⁷ .... We ⁸ .... all our work on pen drives and the wi-fi's a bit slow around here.
Jim No worries … see you soon!

8 **Complete the sentences with the correct form of *make* or *let*.**

0 She *didn't let* me use her dictionary.
1 He told me to shut up and .... me explain what happened.
2 The teacher .... me copy my homework because I wrote it all in pencil.
3 The security guards .... us wait for hours outside in the rain.
4 My parents .... me apologise to my brother.
5 .... (your parents) you go to the party last night?

Read the sentences and answer the questions.

1 *I used to cycle to school.*

(Answer Yes / No)

0 Am I cycling to school these days? **No**
1 Did I cycle to school in the past?
2 Did I cycle to school regularly in the past?

2 *I was cleaning my room when he texted me.*

(Answer with your own words)

0 Does the sentence refer to the past, present or future? **Past**
1 Did I start cleaning the room first or did he text me first?
2 Was the cleaning finished when I received his text?
3 Which is the longer action, the cleaning or receiving the text?

3 *You can't take this train with that ticket.*

(Answer Yes / No)

0 Do I have a ticket? **Yes**
1 Is it the right ticket for this train?
2 Is it possible for me to take this train?
3 Does the sentence refer to the past, present or future?

4 *You must study harder.*

(Answer Yes / No)

0 Do I study? **Yes**
1 Do I need to study more?
2 Is the other person happy with my results?
3 Is the person giving me the choice to not study more?
4 Does the sentence refer to the past, present or future?

5 *She doesn't have to drive to work.*

(Answer Yes / No)

0 Can she drive to work? **Yes**
1 Is it necessary for her to use the car for work?
2 Can she take an alternative means, e.g., a bus?

→ See **GRAMMAR REFERENCE**
pages 116, 117, 118

Units 3–4

5 Crime

GRAMMAR PRACTICE

Past perfect and past simple

Complete the rules.
We use the past perfect to indicate that an action happened .... another one in the past.
We form the past perfect with the past of .... followed by the past .... of the main verb.
  I had lunch before I met Joe.

➡ See **GRAMMAR REFERENCE** page 118

1 Complete the sentences with the past perfect.

0 I **'d never been** (never / be) there before.
1 We .... (already / stay) in that hotel.
2 She .... (always / tell) me the opposite.
3 The President .... (promise) not to build a wall.
4 That kind of thing .... (never / happen) around here.
5 They .... (always / book) their holiday on another website.
6 I .... (often / hear) these rumours.

2 Put the words in the correct order.

0 before / there / been / you / had / ever / ?
   Had you ever been there before?
1 called / before / two / we / days / had / them
2 email / received / she / by / had / answer / the
3 good / a / then / been / he / until / hadn't / student
4 accident / seen / they / hadn't / the
5 brother / your / mentioned / ever / had / it / ?

3 Choose the correct option.

0 When Dan (arrived) / had arrived the film *already started* / (had already started).
1 Patricia *felt* / *had felt* sick last night because she *ate* / *had eaten* too many crisps.
2 I *was never* / *had never been* there before.
3 George *didn't pass* / *hadn't passed* the exam, though he *studied* / *had studied* hard.
4 All the plants died because it *didn't rain* / *hadn't rained* all summer.

4 Look at the pictures. Complete Jay's blog about the changes to her room using the verbs below.

> fix ▪ move ▪ tidy up ▪ buy ▪ hang up ▪
> transform ▪ leave ▪ replace

I couldn't believe it when I got back from my holiday. My parents had completely ⁰ **transformed** my bedroom. First of all, they ¹........................ my bed to the middle of the room and they ²........................ my horrible old desk with a nice new one. Then they ³........................ my lamp and ⁴........................ all the CDs I ⁵........................ on the floor. They ⁶........................ some nice curtains and, best of all, they ⁷........................ me a new TV – wow!

5 Rewrite the two sentences using the past perfect and *after* or *when*.

0 The robbers left. Somebody called the police.
   Somebody **called the police after the robbers had left**.
1 The cat ran away and the children were sad for ages.
   After ....
2 Tim heard the good news. He felt much better.
   Tim felt ....
3 Alice tried on 20 T-shirts. She finally bought one.
   After ....
4 The team won the match. They celebrated with a pizza.
   They ....
5 Jess cleared away her books. They had dinner.
   When ....

GRAMMAR PRACTICE

6 Complete the dialogue with the past perfect of the verbs below.

have ▪ cancel ▪ plan ▪ tell ▪ not / win ▪ call ▪ finish ▪ not / see ▪ ask ▪ play ▪ not / go

A How was your weekend?
B Not bad, but it didn't go exactly as I ⁰'d planned.
A Oh. Why not?
B Well, do you remember the party at Carrie's house?
A Sure. She ¹.............................. everybody about it at school a few days before.
B Right. Well, when I got there, there was no one there – she ².............................. it!
A Just like that, at the last minute?
B Apparently she ³.............................. a big argument with her boyfriend earlier in the afternoon … so no party. Anyway, what about you? Did you do anything special?
A Yes, after I ⁴.............................. my homework I went to see the football match.
B Really? I'm sure you enjoyed that!
A Absolutely. I ⁵.............................. to the stadium since last season and the atmosphere was electric.
B You were lucky, we ⁶.............................. at home for at least ten games before Saturday. But how did they play?
A Not bad, but remember, I ⁷.............................. them for nearly a year, so I don't know how they ⁸.............................. in the last few matches.
B Terribly, believe me! Oh, by the way, I saw you with Suzy in the evening.
A Oh yes, she ⁹.............................. me in the afternoon and ¹⁰.............................. to go shopping after the match.

7 Finish the sentences using the past perfect.

0 By the time the film finished we had cried several times.
1 I was a bit surprised that they ....
2 When I called her she ....
3 Before the school party they ....
4 The day before I left for my holiday we ....
5 When I got home I realised that ....

8 Complete the sentences with the past simple or past perfect of the verbs in brackets.

0 I had already left (already / leave) when they got (get) to the station.
1 When I .... (arrive) they .... (go) home so I .... (not / see) them.
2 When I .... (open) the door the burglars .... (run off) immediately.
3 Luckily the rain .... (stop) by the time we .... (leave).
4 .... (they / hear) the news before you .... (arrive)?
5 My mobile .... (switch off) because I .... (not / charge) the battery.
6 I .... (not / know) you .... (change) team recently.
7 They .... (watch) a horror movie after the kids .... (go) to bed.
8 She .... (know) a lot of people at the party because she .... (be) there many times before.
9 We .... (be) afraid because we .... (not / fly) before.
10 He .... (love) that big old house. After all, he .... (live) there for the past 30 years.

9 Choose the correct option.

I had the shock of my life the other day.
I got home and I saw that the light in the hall ⁰(was) / had been on. I clearly remembered that I ¹turned / had turned it off before going out.
I ²entered / had entered the house a bit nervously. Inside, I saw my visitors ³didn't take / hadn't taken anything important and my stereo, tablet and TV ⁴were / had been still there. And then I ⁵saw / had seen some empty glasses on the kitchen table.
The thieves ⁶enjoyed / had enjoyed a drink before they left! I ⁷walked / had walked into the living room and ⁸turned / had turned the light on. What did I see?
The smiling faces of my closest friends. They ⁹organised / had organised a surprise party for my birthday.
After my initial shock I ¹⁰laughed / had laughed about it and we ¹¹partied / had partied until 2 am.

Unit 5 177

READING SKILLS

10 [2.13] Read and listen to the article and choose the best headings for paragraphs A and B.

1 .... Underage criminals
2 .... Death of murderer
3 .... Innocent man found guilty of murder
4 .... Unclear intention
5 .... Terrorists freed
6 .... In the wrong place at the wrong time

11 Read the text again and decide if the sentences are true (T), false (F) or doesn't say (DS). Correct the false ones.

1 Bentley was 16 at the time of the crime. T F DS
2 Bentley had brought his own gun. T F DS
3 Bentley did not kill a policeman. T F DS
4 Police thought that Bentley had encouraged his friend to kill the policeman. T F DS
5 Craig was also found guilty of murder. T F DS
6 The Birmingham bomb exploded late at night. T F DS
7 Police knew about the bomb before it exploded. T F DS
8 The Birmingham Six knew who had left the bomb. T F DS

12 Read the text again and answer the following questions.

1 What were Bentley and Craig trying to do?
2 What kind of weapons did Bentley and Craig have?
3 Who called the police?
4 What did the policeman ask Craig?
5 What are the two interpretations of the phrase 'let him have it'?
6 What was the man cause of conflict in Ireland during the troubles?
7 When did the Birmingham bombing happen?
8 Where were the six Irish men travelling to?
9 What was the evidence that linked the six Irish men to the bomb scene?
10 How long did the Birmingham Six spend in prison?

ROUGH JUSTICE

Films and novels often tell stories of innocent people who wrongly go to prison, sometimes these stories are pure fiction, but there are many stories about **miscarriage of justice** that are tragically true.
5 Today we look at two famous historic cases.

A

The first is the case of Derek Bentley. Bentley was 19 at the time of his crime in 1952. He and a 16-year-old friend, Christopher Craig, tried to burgle a factory in London. Bentley had a knife which Craig had given him earlier,
10 Craig had a gun. A young girl saw the boys going into the factory and called the police. When the police arrived the boys tried to escape. One policeman grabbed Bentley and shouted at Craig to give him the gun. Then Bentley said 'let him have it', and Craig shot the policeman dead. Craig
15 was too young to be held responsible for murder, but Bentley was an adult. Bentley's defence **lawyers** argued that when Bentley said 'let him have it' he had intended – let the policeman have the gun. But the **prosecutors** insisted that Bentley had actually meant – kill him.
20 Bentley **was** declared guilty of encouraging murder and **sentenced** to death in 1953. Bentley's family continued to protest his innocence even after Bentley had died and eventually in 1993 he received a royal pardon.

B

The second is the case of the Birmingham Six. 1968–1998
25 was a period of violence and conflict in Northern Ireland between the Irish Catholics who, believed that Northern Ireland had been wrongfully occupied by the British, and

GLOSSARY

rough justice	▶ cattiva giustizia
miscarriage of justice	▶ errore giudiziario
lawyers	▶ avvocati
prosecutors	▶ pubblico ministero
was … sentenced	▶ fu condannato
conviction	▶ condanna
freed	▶ liberati
evidence	▶ prova
compensation	▶ risarcimento

13 Read the text again and fill in the gap with one word. Sometimes more than one answer is possible.

1 hold someone .... for a crime
2 declare someone .... of a crime
3 sentence someone to .... for a crime
4 protest against your ....
5 convict someone of ....
6 claim to be ....

178   Unit 5

The Birmingham Six after their release, 1991.

Irish Protestants, who strongly supported British rule. The conflict spread to Britain and in 1974 in a busy pub in
30 the centre of Birmingham a bomb exploded and killed 21 people and injured 182. The police had received a phone call about the bomb before it exploded but they didn't have enough time to locate it.
Police arrested six Irish men who had left Birmingham
35 that evening and were on their way to Belfast to attend the funeral of a friend. The only thing that connected them to the bomb was the fact that they were Irish and lived in Birmingham.
The six men were convicted of murder and given life
40 sentences. They always claimed they were innocent and continued to protest against their **conviction**. In 1991 after the men had spent over 16 years in prison they were finally **freed**. The courts finally admitted that there was not sufficient **evidence** to prove that the men were
45 connected to the bombing. They each received **compensation** payments of close to a million pounds.

14 Now complete the notes for the crimes.

Crime 1
Date of crime: 1..
Place of crime: 2..
Victim(s) 3..
Person / people found responsible: 4............................
Person / people really responsible: 5............................
Sentence: 6..
Eventual result: 7..

Crime 2
Date of crime: 1..
Place of crime: 2..
Victim(s) 3..
Person / people found responsible: 4............................
Person / people really responsible: 5............................
Sentence: 6..
Eventual result: 7..

VOCABULARY

CRIMES AND CRIMINALS

15 Read the texts and write the name of the criminal.

0 This person captures famous or rich people and asks for money. **kidnapper**
1 This person sells dangerous substances to people to make money.
2 These people break and destroy things like property.
3 These people take other people's cars and drive them usually really fast before they abandon them.
4 These people believe they are fighting for a cause – they often use violence and shock tactics to promote their cause.
5 These people target places where lots of money is stored. They often spend years planning a job and looking at ways to get into buildings.

16 Complete the texts with words from the same word family as these verbs.

to murder
The police are looking for convicted 0 **murderer** Keith Joseph after he escaped from prison last night. He was responsible for the infamous shopping centre 1.......................... in July.

to forge
The police are concerned about the number of high quality 2.......................... of high value euro notes in shops and restaurants. They believe the 3.......................... have a lot of experience in this field.

to burgle
The police are looking for two audacious 4.......................... who managed to take over £500 from the police station officers' changing room. The police think that the 5.......................... took place last night.

to terrorise
The police are looking for a group of 6.......................... who planted a bomb in the city centre. Experts on 7.......................... say this may be a new group.

to mug
There was another 8.......................... in Kingston town centre involving an 80-year-old pensioner. Two 9.......................... took her bag with all her pension money.

Unit 5   179

GRAMMAR PRACTICE

Indefinite pronouns

Complete the rules with the words below.
singular • non-specific • any •
affirmative • some • every

We use indefinite pronouns (*someone*, *anything*, *somewhere*, *nothing*, etc.) to talk about a .... person, thing, place, etc.
We use pronouns with .... in affirmative sentences and pronouns with .... in interrogatives and negatives.
.... can be used in affirmative, negative and interrogative sentences.
We use a .... verb with *no*.
We follow indefinite pronouns with a .... verb.

➡ See **GRAMMAR REFERENCE** page 119

17 Choose the correct option.

0   I'd like to know (something) / anybody / anyone about this new phone.
1   *Nobody / Anybody / Everybody* likes Jenny – she's really popular at school.
2   I can't understand *nothing / anything / something* when I watch English TV programmes.
3   I'd like to go *somewhere / something / someone* new.
4   *Nobody / Everybody / Nothing* can spell my name correctly – it makes me really angry!
5   I've put my book *anywhere / nowhere / somewhere* here – I just can't remember where.
6   Is there *anyone / anything / anywhere* you need from the shops?
7   I met *anybody / somebody / nobody* you know at the party – you went to the same primary school.
8   Did you hear *anything / somewhere / everything* about the test?

18 Complete the sentences with the correct indefinite pronouns.

0   She didn't say **anything** about the present I bought her – I was really disappointed.
1   I asked for some help with the shopping but .... came down – that's typical!
2   Wait – there's .... I'd like to tell you.
3   I'm sorry, but there's .... I can do to help.
4   .... told me you were looking for me.

5   Ah, here you are! I've been looking for you .... !
6   There are police officers .... – I think there's been a robbery at the bank or something.
7   I've prepared .... special for dinner tonight – chicken curry!
8   I'm sure I've seen your jeans .... in your room.
9   Has .... seen Bob recently?
10 I'm going to the shop – we've got .... to eat!
11 Have you got .... to say about this?
12 He called many times, but .... answered.

19 Rewrite the sentences replacing the underlined words with an indefinite pronoun. Change the verb form if necessary.

0   I saw <u>an object</u> on the floor.
    I saw something on the floor.
1   Put the light on – I can't see <u>a thing</u>.
2   Do <u>you all</u> know where the party is?
3   Did you get <u>all the things</u> we need from the supermarket?
4   I didn't see <u>one person</u> I knew at the club.
5   <u>A thief</u> stole my car.
6   I've looked <u>in all the places I can think of</u> for my mobile, and I still can't find it.

20 Complete the dialogue with indefinite pronouns.

Jan   I can hear 0 **someone** outside.
Steve Let me have a look. No, there's 1 .... there.
Jan   I'm sure I heard 2 .... talking just outside the window.
Steve Well, it's dark, but I can't see 3 .... outside.
Jan   Listen … I can hear voices … and now 4 ....'s opening the front door.
Steve What shall we do?
Jan   Well, we can't just sit here and do 5 .... ! Let's go and see.
Steve After you …
Jan   Thanks. There. I've locked the front door so they can't go 6 .... now.
Steve Maybe it's Jean who's forgotten 7 .... and come back to get it.
Jan   No, she always remembers to take 8 .... when she goes out.
Steve So who can it be …?

180   Unit 5

SPEAKING SKILLS

HAVING A DISCUSSION

21 Put the words in the correct order.

1 think / what / you / do / ?
2 sure / I'm / not / mean / what / you
3 you / this / view / have / got / a / on / ?
4 say / trying / what / are / you / to / ?
5 take / on / what's / this / your / ?
6 second / you / for / I / can / a / interrupt / ?
7 there / stop / you / can / I / ?
8 why / that / did / he / do / ?

22 Complete the dialogue with expressions from exercise 21.

Anna Bea, have you heard about the boy who ran away from home when the police came to his house?
Bea ¹..................
Anna Because his mother had called them and …
Bea ²........................., Anna – his mother had contacted the police about her own son?
Anna Yes, that's right. But only because someone was bullying him at school and she was worried.
Bea ³.................................... – the son wasn't actually in trouble?
Anna No.
Bea So why did he run away?
Anna Because he was frightened of the bullies, he didn't want them to think he called the police …
Bea Well, I think the mother made a big mistake – she didn't help her son at all and …
Anna ⁴............................... – why did she make a mistake? She was trying to help.
Bea ⁵.., Carla?
Carla Personally, Bea, I think the boy caused all this.
Bea ⁶.. ? That he was responsible for all this?
Carla I mean, he didn't have to run away …
Bea ⁷............................... . I can't believe what you're saying. That's completely wrong. The bullies clearly caused all this.
Carla Sorry?
Bea I said, the bullies were behind all this – it's obvious.
Anna Anyway, the police spoke to the school and the bullying stopped.
Bea And what about the boy?
Anna Oh, he came home that evening – when he started to feel hungry!

LISTENING SKILLS

23 🎵 [2.14] Listen to the interview. What's the person's name and what does he do?

24 🎵 [2.14] Listen again and decide if the sentences are true (T) or false (F). Correct the false ones.

1 Jake is a criminal hacker. T F
2 Jake learned about computers at university. T F
3 Companies pay Jake to hack into their systems. T F
4 He worked for a bank at the beginning. T F
5 He sells people's personal information. T F
6 You can't go to prison for hacking. T F
7 He wants people to protect their data. T F
8 He thinks hacking is not a serious crime. T F

25 🎵 [2.14] Listen again and answer the questions.

1 Why do companies pay Jake to hack into their systems?
2 Which places developed at Jake's university when the internet had started?
3 What job did Jake want to find when he left university?
4 What was Jake's first job?
5 Why did Jake go freelance?
6 What do hackers try and steal?
7 What does he think about security systems today?
8 What is Jake's advice to people?

26 Choose the best summary of Jake's activity.

1 He is a young professional who works for the police. He helps big businesses like banks to find and arrest people who have hacked into their systems and stolen data.
2 He is a young IT expert. He tests the security systems of big businesses by trying to hack into them. He does this to see if their systems are vulnerable and help them to prevent real hackers from getting the company data.
3 He is a young professional who used to work for a bank. He worked out how to hack into their system because they often asked him for help with their security systems. He is freelance now and enjoys the challenge of hacking into systems and stealing data.

Unit 5   181

TOWARDS PRELIMINARY

> **EXAM STRATEGY**
>
> **Reading – Gapped text**
>
> This exercise tests reading for gist and understanding text structure. Read the title and the text quickly to understand what it is about, then look at sentences a–h. Remember that there are three extra sentences that you will not need to use. Read both before and after each gap, then choose a sentence. Reread with the new sentence in position to check it sounds right. Look out for:
> - sentences on the same subject as the paragraph
> - linkers such as: *However, Actually, On the contrary*
> - reference words, such as: *this / that, it / she / they* that could refer to a person or thing that has been previously mentioned.

27 Complete the gaps in the text with sentences a–h. There are three extra sentences that you won't need to use.

a I love wearing my uniform because it makes me feel important.
b They also work with the local community, visiting schools, businesses and local people.
c The police obviously arrest criminals but they do so much more.
d Here I am now, just finishing the first part of my training to be a police officer.
e You have to be ready for anything and everything.
f I'm just coming to the end of the 12-week course.
g I started my 2-year police training straight afterwards.
h I wasn't very keen but she persuaded me to go too.

A CAREER FIGHTING CRIME

My name is Leonie Sanders and I am at police training college. This is a sentence I never thought I would say. I had never even thought about joining the police until about a year ago. [1]............ It was the best decision I ever made! This is definitely the right job for me!

How did it happen? In my last year, my school invited ex-students with a variety of different jobs to give some talks. My friend, Lara, was interested in going to the talk by a police officer. [2]............ I liked what I heard. Until that day, I had always imagined that all police officers did was arrest bank robbers and other criminals. I was so wrong!

A police officer's job is to stop crime and that can mean stopping criminals after they have committed a crime but it also means stopping people from getting involved in crime in the first place. They spend a lot of their time on crime prevention, which is very important. [3]............ Their job is to make sure everyone feels safe living and working in their local area.

I left that talk knowing what I wanted to be. The fact that every day is different for a police officer attracted me to the job. Obviously, there is a certain amount of routine work but you never know what is going to happen next. [4]............ As soon as I got home, I started finding out about police training courses.

I enjoyed the basic qualification course because I learnt all about the law and the legal system, which were subjects I had never studied before. [5]............ I'm really looking forward to the next part as I'll be learning the job in real life situations with trained police officers. If everything goes well, I'll be a police officer in 2 years' time!

EXAM STRATEGY

Writing – An email

Before you write your reply:
- read your friend's email and the notes very carefully
- focus on each note and decide what you want to say

When you are writing your reply, remember to:
- start by thanking your friend for the message and making a friendly comment
- write in an informal style
- write answers to all the notes
- finish your email with a friendly reply.

28 Read the email then match the sentences 1–4 to the notes.

To: ....
From: Artem

Hi Kacper,

Would you like to meet up in the summer holidays? — ᵃ Yes!

I've got a new tent and I'd like to go camping. Are you interested? — ᵇ Definitely.

I'm free next week. Are you? — ᶜ Which day?

Have you got any ideas for good places to go camping? — ᵈ suggest

Let me know as soon as you can!

Artem

1 [a] I'd love to!
2 [ ] Why don't we go to the lake?
3 [ ] Not Saturday or Sunday.
4 [ ] Cool! You know I love camping.

TOWARDS PRELIMINARY

29 Now add some extra information to the short answers above. Write the letter on the box.

[3] I'm free any other day during the week.
[ ] I haven't seen you for a long time.
[ ] It isn't far and there's a campsite.
[ ] I'd like to see your new tent.

30 Write your personal answers to Artem's questions. Remember to answer and then add some extra information.

31 Read the email and complete the writing plan.

To: ....
From: Alyssa

Hi Ewa,

You said you wanted to join my theatre group – well now they're looking for actors. Are you interested? — ² Yes!

We're doing a play about a murder mystery. Is that OK? — ³ Great!.

Can you come to the practice with me tomorrow? — ⁴ What time?

Let's meet up before! Where could we meet? — ⁵ suggest

Let me know as soon as you can!

Alyssa

Writing plan
1 Greeting
2 ....
3 ....
4 ....
5 ....
6 Ending

32 Write your reply to Alyssa in about 100 words.

33 When you've written your answer, reread the notes in the Strategy box and check your email includes all of the points. Also check your spelling and grammar is correct.

Unit 5   183

6 Freak weather

GRAMMAR PRACTICE

First conditional

Complete the rules with *present, order, future, will*.
We use the first conditional to talk about consequences that are probable in the .... *If* is followed by subject + verb in a .... tense, and we use the future with .... in the other clause. We can change the .... of the two clauses in a conditional sentence.

➡ See **GRAMMAR REFERENCE** page 119

1 Write the sentences using the first conditional.

0 I / text / you / if / there / be / any / changes
   I'll text you if there are any changes.
1 you / go / to the party / if / I / come / too?
2 If / it / not / rain / we / go for a picnic / next weekend
3 If / it / be / late / we / not / stop / at the supermarket
4 If / you / pass / in front of the cinema / you / get / me / a ticket / for the film?
5 If / they / confirm / the strike / we / not / be able to leave / on time
6 If we / lose / another match like that / I / change sport

2 Complete the sentences with the first conditional.

0 If I ......**don't hear**...... (not / hear) from you, I '......**ll meet**...... (meet) you outside the station at 6:30.
1 If you .... (get) lost, I .... (come) and pick you up.
2 If the weather .... (be) good tomorrow, we .... (go) for a walk.
3 I .... (cook) dinner for you if you .... (buy) everything at the shops.
4 If the train .... (not / arrive) in five minutes, we .... (take) the coach.
5 If you .... (revise) for the test, you .... (do) much better.
6 If the sky .... (be) clear tonight, then it .... (be) really icy tomorrow morning.

3 Complete the blog with the correct form of the first conditional.

HOW TO SURVIVE A SHARK ATTACK

If you ⁰......**go**...... (go) swimming in Australia's Great Barrier Reef, you ¹............................ (probably / meet) a shark sooner or later. If this ²............................ (happen), you ³............................ (need) to stay very calm, because if you ⁴............................ (start) swimming, you ⁵............................ (attract) the shark's attention and interest! The best thing is not to move. If the shark ⁶............................ (swim) directly towards you, ⁷............................ (have to) decide what to do. One option is to defend yourself. For example, if you ⁸............................ (hit) the shark on the nose as it attacks you, it ⁹............................ (swim) away – if you ¹⁰............................ (be) lucky! Alternatively, you can pretend to be dead: if you just ¹¹............................ (stay) there in the water, the shark ¹²............................ (go) and look for something more interesting – that's the theory. I haven't tried these methods, but if I ¹³............................ (do), I ¹⁴............................ (let) you know if they ¹⁵............................ (work)! And if you ¹⁶............................ (not / hear) from me, then at least you ¹⁷............................ (know) that these suggestions are pretty useless. And, of course, if you ¹⁸............................ (have) any better suggestions I'll be happy to post them.

if / when / unless

Complete the rules with *negative, sure, positive*.
We can use *when* or *unless* in the conditional part of the sentence.
We use *when* for situations where we are .... something will happen.
Unless means the same as *if not*. We use a .... verb with *unless* because the meaning is already ....

➡ See **GRAMMAR REFERENCE** page 119

GRAMMAR PRACTICE

4 Complete the sentences with *when*, *if* or *unless*.

0 You won't pass ......**unless**...... you study harder.
1 I'll call you .... I'm ready.
2 .... I know the dates, I'll email you to confirm all the details.
3 You won't resolve the problem .... you speak to them directly.
4 Will this food go bad .... we don't keep it in the fridge?
5 It won't work .... you switch it on!
6 I won't give you the money .... you give me the sweets.
7 .... you have any problems, just call me.
8 We'll celebrate .... the exam results come out.

5 Put the words in the correct order.

0 happened / won't / me / unless / you / tell / I / leave / what
   I won't leave unless you tell me what happened.
1 badly / play / match / win / I / unless / 'll / the / I
2 home / party / go / we / finishes / 'll / when / the
3 there's / if / we / stop / hello / say / 'll / time / to

Zero conditional

Choose the correct option.

We use the zero conditional to talk about consequences that are *always true* / *probable*. *If* is followed by a subject + *present* / *future* tense. We use a *future* / *present* tense or the *past* / *imperative* in the other clause.

➡ See **GRAMMAR REFERENCE** page 120

6 Match the beginnings and ends of the sentences.

0 [c] Babies cry
1 [ ] Sports fans feel sad
2 [ ] I only do sport
3 [ ] I don't like fizzy drinks
4 [ ] He doesn't eat meat
5 [ ] She's usually late
6 [ ] He doesn't like it
7 [ ] Tom calls me
8 [ ] Exams are hard
9 [ ] People like you

a if their team plays badly.
b if they're very cold.
c if they're hungry.
d if the weather's nice.
e if he's got a problem.
f if there's a good alternative.
g if I use his mobile.
h if she misses the train.
i if you're kind to them.
j if you don't study for them.

7 Complete the dialogue with the zero or first conditional.

Ali This is KAT Radio, and this is Ali with the *Young People's Problems Phone-In* – hello everybody. This is *your* space: if you ⁰..........**call**.......... (*call*) us, I ¹.......................... (*promise*) to help. Our first caller is Jo. Hi, Jo! How can we help?

Jo Well, I'm having some problems with my mum. I have a new boyfriend and she ².......................... (*always / become*) angry if I ³.......................... (*spend*) time with him.

Ali I see. Well, if you ⁴.......................... (*explain*) that this person is important to you, I'm sure she ⁵.......................... (*understand*).

Jo But if I ⁶.......................... (*speak*) to her about it, she ⁷.......................... (*start*) to shout.

Ali Are you doing OK at school?

Jo I ⁸.......................... (*usually / get*) good marks if I ⁹.......................... (*study*), but recently I've failed some tests …

Ali Mmm, maybe this is the problem. If you ¹⁰.......................... (*take care*) of your schoolwork, then I'm sure your mum ¹¹.......................... (*feel*) more relaxed. Parents ¹².......................... (*worry*) if their children ¹³.......................... (*start*) to do badly at school.

8 Complete the text about study tips with the first or zero conditional.

Try to break up your study into periods of 30 minutes. If you ⁰..........**try**.......... (*try*) to do everything in one session, you ¹.......................... (*probably / get*) really tired and you ².......................... (*not / be able to*) concentrate.
Set specific times for your activities. If you ³.......................... (*plan*) your studies, you ⁴.......................... (*not / get*) into a panic before your next big exam.
Try to study at the same time each day. People's brains ⁵.......................... (*work*) better if they ⁶.......................... (*have*) a regular routine.
Also make sure your friends know that if they ⁷.......................... (*call*) you at these times, they ⁸.......................... (*not / receive*) an answer because you're busy studying. Good students know that if you study at the same time each day, this ⁹.......................... (*gradually / become*) a normal part of your life.

Unit 6 185

READING SKILLS

9 Match the terms to the definitions.

1. ☐ renewable energy
2. ☐ wind turbines
3. ☐ solar panels
4. ☐ recycled paper
5. ☐ environmentally friendly
6. ☐ hydroelectric power
7. ☐ greenhouse gases
8. ☐ hybrid cars

a Power coming from wind, sun or water.
b That does not damage the environment.
c Rectangular units on buildings that generate energy from sun.
d Substances that keep heat in the atmosphere.
e Paper that someone has used before.
f Vehicles that run on electricity and petrol.
g Energy from water.
h Large structures that turn and create energy.

10 Read the web page quickly and answer the question.

What is the main topic of discussion?
1 dangers connected with the environment
2 causes of environmental pollution
3 young people's attitudes to the environment
4 protecting the environment

11 [2.15] Read the text again and put sentences a–d in the correct gaps 1–4. Then listen and check.

a They're so taken by city life, they forget there's a world around them.
b But by then it's too late to do anything about it.
c I sometimes wonder if people like that can really be friends of mine.
d I suppose I'm just an ordinary person in that respect.

12 Read the text again and answer the questions.

Which writer …
1 only considers the environment at certain moments?
2 has friends who don't care much about the future?
3 seems most worried about climate change?
4 thinks people only pay attention to the environment when something happens to them?
5 says that climate change causes mass movements of people?
6 is actively trying to make a difference?
7 tries to change his / her friends' attitudes?
8 thinks global warming is a very immediate danger?
9 thinks there is no alternative to using the car?

We asked you for your views on global warming and lots of you answered. Here's a selection of your answers:

Kyle, Sheffield, UK

I'm really shocked by the opinions of some of my friends. Many of them just don't care about the environment. They simply say, 'I'm a very busy person so I need my car'. These comments make me really angry, because
5 this way people don't consider the effect of their actions on the future. ¹............. Well, I am worried about the future. And since we can all do something about it, I'm doing my part. I have renewable energy at home and I ride to work on an electric bike.

Katrina, New York, US

10 If I see stories on the news about floods and drought, they shock me and I start to think about the environment, but only for a few minutes. These stories are often about distant places so I just forget about it straight away. I must admit that I'm not
15 particularly environmentally friendly. ²............. Since fuel is cheap here in the States, a lot of people have really big cars, including me, and public transport's useless. Anyway, world leaders ignore the Paris Climate Agreement, so why should I change my lifestyle?

13 Read the text again and decide if the sentences are true (T), false (F) or doesn't say (DS).

1 Kyle agrees with his friends on the environment. T F DS
2 Kyle thinks it's important to think about the future. T F DS
3 Kyle tells his friends they are wrong about the environment. T F DS
4 Kyle uses public transport to get to work to protect the environment. T F DS
5 Certain stories make Katrina briefly consider climate change. T F DS
6 Katrina thinks governments give a good example to people. T F DS
7 Frida goes to the country with her cousins. T F DS
8 She thinks her cousins are a bit ridiculous. T F DS
9 Jordan tries to protect the environment. T F DS
10 Flood water damaged his house. T F DS
11 He thinks people do not know enough about the environment. T F DS

186 Unit 6

Frida, Granada, Spain

20 I have many cousins who have never been camping, they don't recycle and hate the idea of spending a day in the country. ³............. They actually believe that the solution to climate change is to adopt another planet! They also complain about migration towards
25 Europe and don't understand that it's often the result of climate change we cause in other countries. Since this is the only planet we've got for the moment, I tell them to look after it!

Jordan, Christchurch, New Zealand

The whole issue of global warming is really scary for me.
30 Because of it, young people from my generation have a really uncertain future. I mean, will we still have a planet that we can live on in one hundred years? Unless we do something fast, I really believe that climate change will destroy large areas of the Earth, and in the near
35 future as well. Most people only start talking about climate change when a terrible flood damages their house. Then they discover that the flood was the result of years of global warming – and this shocks them. ⁴.............

14 Find words and phrases in the text that mean the same as these.

1. be interested in (Kyle) ....
2. think about (Kyle) ....
3. make my contribution (Kyle) ....
4. cycle (Kyle) ....
5. hit (Katrina) ....
6. far (Katrina) ....
7. confess (Katrina) ....
8. petrol / gas (Katrina) ....
9. strongly dislike (Frida) ....
10. protest (Frida) ....
11. problem (Jordan) ....
12. frightening (Jordan) ....
13. devastate (Jordan) ....
14. very bad (Jordan) ....
15. find out (Jordan) ....

15 Underline the examples of cause and effect in the text.

VOCABULARY

THE ENVIRONMENT

16 Complete the texts with the words below.

drought ▪ carbon footprint ▪ flood ▪ climate change ▪
natural disasters ▪ ozone layer ▪ global warming ▪
carbon emissions ▪ hurricane ▪ fossil fuels

0 ....Climate change.... is a problem for all of us, not just governments and scientists. Every generation passes this problem on to the next and nobody really does anything about it.

1 We still use too many .... in the twenty-first century, especially for industry and domestic use, when there are greener alternatives.

2 You can see the effects of .... all around you – just look at your own summers and winters. The temperatures are different now and it rarely snows in the mountains before Christmas here.

3 This was the first .... we have ever had in this area. It started off with heavy rain but then the wind came and it was really strong; trees came down and houses lost their roofs.

4 Many people thought that diesel cars were clean and that they had lower .... than petrol engines, but in the end it seems that they produce even more. So there is no choice – we need a good alternative to the private car to save our cities.

5 The .... started two years ago and in this region the people have had no rain at all. This is a disaster for agriculture as the farmers are not able to grow anything. It's quickly becoming a desert here.

6 .... are everyday news now. They include droughts, floods, earthquakes and we feel helpless. I don't think these things happened so regularly in the past, but maybe I'm wrong.

7 The .... was a complete surprise. It came after three days of heavy rain. The river was full but something like this has never happened. I had two metres of water in my house.

8 We need to protect the .... After all, it protects us from the sun. Scientists have told us that CFC chemicals from aerosol sprays damage it, but we continue to use them every day.

9 The .... is the total amount of greenhouse gases produced by human activity, usually expressed in quantities of carbon dioxide (CO_2).

Unit 6   187

GRAMMAR PRACTICE

will / may / might for future possibility

Complete the rules with *possible, subjects, sure, modal, past.*

We use *will* when we feel .... about something in the future.

We use *may* or *might* to indicate that something is .... in the future.

Will, *may* and *might* are all .... verbs so they don't change with different .... and they have no .... form.

→ See **GRAMMAR REFERENCE** page 120

17 🔊 **Complete the sentences with *will* or *won't*.**

0 I promise I ......**won't**...... tell anyone.
1 Your mobile .... get a signal in the mountains.
2 I'm sure she .... win. She's the best.
3 Your parents .... be happy with your school report – you've got bad marks in every subject!
4 Don't worry, I .... help with the maths exercises.
5 Sorry, I .... be at the party tomorrow because my parents .... let me go.
6 Amy .... like that dress you bought her for her birthday. You know she never wears dresses.
7 I .... make sure that they call you.
8 The history test .... be easy – you know the teacher always asks really difficult questions.

18 🔊 **Rewrite the sentences using *might* or *may*.**

0 There's a small possibility of rain later.
It ....**might rain later**.................... .
1 There's a good possibility we will buy that new house.
We ....
2 That film has a small chance of winning an Oscar.
It ....
3 There's good possibility that we will go to Spain on holiday this summer.
We ....
4 There's a good chance of snow later on.
It ....
5 There's a good chance he will not play in the final.
He ....
6 There's a very small chance that we will win today.
We ....

19 🔊 **Put the words in the correct order.**

0 OK / 'm / I / everything / will / be / sure
I'm sure everything will be OK.
1 arrive / not / might / Dave / on / time
2 late / may / I / hour / an / half / be
3 afternoon / it / this / about / will / you / I / text
4 might / problem / dates / be / there / a / those / with
5 any / week / have / I / money / pocket / this / not / might
6 they / want / check / you / with / to / may / first
7 brother / definitely / that / like / will / my / T-shirt

20 🔊 **Complete the dialogue with *may, might, will* or *won't*.**

Jim Hi, I heard there ⁰......**may**...... be another test next week, but the teacher's not sure.
Pat That's right. We ¹.................... definitely have the test, but she hasn't decided if it's next week or the one after.
Jim I just hope it ².................... be really difficult like last time.
Pat It ³.................... be, you just never know with her.
Jim Mmm, she ⁴.................... even forget about it – it's happened before.
Pat No, she ⁵.................... remember, don't worry. In any case, you ⁶.................... fail this time, OK? Just study a bit and you ⁷.................... pass it, no problems.

21 🔊 **Complete the prediction with the correct form of *will, might* or *may* and the verbs below.**

agree • ~~rise~~ • be • take • find • do • become

0 Temperatures ....**will rise**.......... in the next 50 years. (*definite*)
1 People .... regular trips to space in the next century. (*impossible*)
2 There .... more floods in Bangladesh. (*definite*)
3 Space explorers .... life on Mars. (*small possibility*)
4 Governments .... anything about climate change in the next 10 years. (*impossible*)
5 Winters .... warmer and warmer. (*good chance*)
6 Political leaders .... on effective measures to stop climate change. (*impossible*)

188 Unit 6

SPEAKING SKILLS

MAKING PREDICTIONS

22 Complete the dialogue with the expressions below.

> do you suggest • will I need to book •
> what I'm saying is • actually • won't be able to get •
> you might • it might not be • after all •
> won't come • if you think about it •
> might make you pay • you enjoy • will be like

A Hi. What are you doing?

B I'm looking at the theatre websites in London. I want to see something at the theatre with my aunt.

A Cool! I went to see *Cats* there last year. What are you going to see?

B I don't know – what ¹...................... ?

A Maybe a musical? That's what we did.

B That's not a bad idea, but ²...................... ?

A Yes, definitely – sometimes you need to book six months before the show.

B Oh no! So I ³...................... a ticket.

A No, that's not necessarily true.
⁴......................, if you're lucky.
⁵...................... that you really need to organise that before you go.

B ⁶......................, I'd quite like to see the *Queen* musical.

A That's a good idea, because it started a few years ago and ⁷...................... fully booked now. In fact you might be able to find special last minute tickets that people send back when they can't go.

B That'd be great!

A If you can't find those, you can go to one of those small ticket sellers. ⁸......................, the centre of London is full of them! But be careful, they ⁹...................... a lot unless they have those special offers.

B What do you think the *Queen* musical ¹⁰......................?

A I heard it's really good, I hope ¹¹...................... it.

B I hope so, too. ¹²......................, a musical is probably the best choice. My aunt doesn't normally go to the theatre and she probably ¹³...................... to London with me if I suggest a play by Shakespeare or something boring like that.

LISTENING SKILLS

23 Match the words to the definitions.

1 ☐ industry   4 ☐ data
2 ☐ invention   5 ☐ cycle
3 ☐ smog   6 ☐ Ice Age

a Factories and forms of production.
b Numbers describing something.
c Unhealthy air full of pollution.
d Something you create, not existing.
e An extremely cold pre-historical period.
f A repeated series of connected events.

24 [2.16] Listen to the interview and answer the questions.

1 Who is the person in the interview?
   A a university teacher
   B a political leader
   C a businessman

2 What is his general opinion on climate change?
   A It's a serious problem.
   B It's a serious problem but some people say it is bigger than it really is.
   C It's not a problem at all.

25 [2.16] Listen again and decide if the sentences are true (T), false (F) or doesn't say (DS).

1 Professor Haider thinks that climate change does not exist. T F DS
2 He agrees that cars are polluting our cities. T F DS
3 He says that electric cars are responsible for polluting cities. T F DS
4 He thinks that pollution in towns is worse now than in the past. T F DS
5 He thinks global warming is a very old phenomenon. T F DS
6 He says that there were fewer hurricanes and floods 50 years ago. T F DS
7 He thinks real temperatures are different from those in official statistics. T F DS
8 He thinks we will go back to the Ice Age in the future. T F DS
9 He does not agree with limits on carbon emissions. T F DS

26 [2.16] Tick (✓) the things that Professor Haider says are *not* the result of climate change.

1 floods   4 heavy / torrential rain
2 droughts   5 ozone disappearing
3 hurricanes   6 melting ice caps

Unit 6   189

ACADEMIC SKILLS

DESCRIBING A PROCESS

The greenhouse effect is both a natural and man-made process. First, when the Sun shines, its rays reach the Earth's atmosphere. This blocks some of the Sun's rays but lets others pass, and these then warm the Earth's surface.
5 After that, natural radiation from the warming process rises from the Earth into the atmosphere. Most of the radiation escapes through the atmosphere into space, but some of it does not and comes back down to Earth. This is the actual *greenhouse effect*, since the Earth's atmosphere is like a glass
10 roof and this return of heat to the Earth's surface makes sure that it stays nice and warm.
When people burn fossil fuels, for example in factories or simply when using cars, these produce carbon emissions. Since these gases (and other man-made gases) rise,
15 they collect in the Earth's atmosphere together with natural greenhouse gases. When it reaches the atmosphere, the radiation from the Earth finds more resistance. If the radiation cannot escape, it goes back to Earth and heats it up, but much more than in the natural process.
20 This means that temperatures on Earth go up – in fact, nearly 1 °C in the last 100 years. Since the temperature changes in some parts of the world are greater than in others, this causes very different levels of air pressure. These pressure differences may cause extreme weather
25 events, like hurricanes and drought. And, finally, people notice climate change and the damage it creates.

27 Match the following English and Italian terms.

0	i	sun rays	a	calore
1	☐	fossil fuels	b	riscaldare
2	☐	atmosphere	c	radiazione
3	☐	to warm	d	gas serra
4	☐	heat (noun)	e	combustibili fossili
5	☐	greenhouse gases	f	pressione atmosferica
6	☐	radiation	g	atmosfera
7	☐	air pressure	h	effetto serra
8	☐	greenhouse effect	i	raggi solari

28 Read the description of the greenhouse effect and then complete the flowchart.

29 Underline the sequencers in the text.

First, …

30 Write the expressions about cause and effect in the text.

When the Sun shines, its rays reach the Earth's atmosphere.

START

0 The sun ……shines……… .

1 Some rays ……………………… and others don't.

2 The Earth ……………… and radiation ……………………… .

3 Some radiation escapes, but ……………………… .

4 The result is that ……………………… .

5 Burning fossil fuels ……………………… .

6 All the greenhouse gases ……………………… .

7 Because the gases block a lot of it, more ……………………… .

8 As a result, temperatures ……………… and climate ……………… .

9 Higher temperatures and pressure differences result in ……………………… .

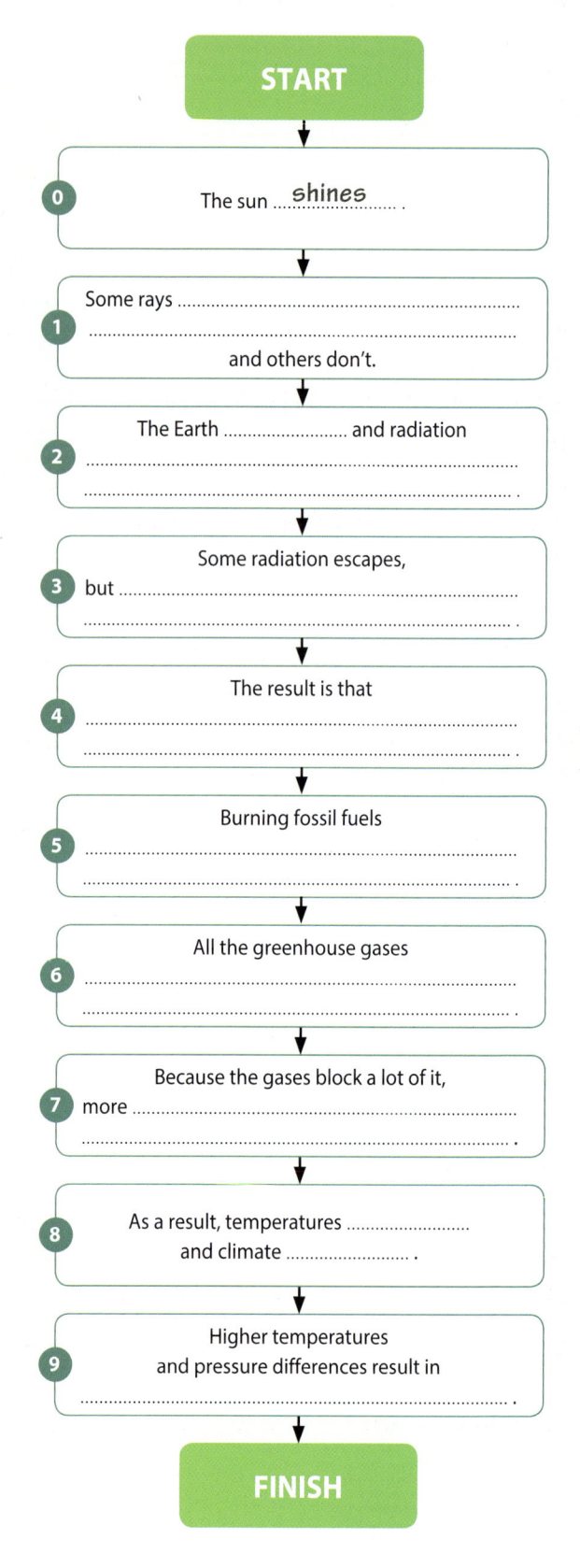

FINISH

31 Create a flowchart of the stages of a process you know well. Include 6–8 stages, from start to finish. Then write a full description of it (60–80 words). Choose one of these topics:

- How to download something from the internet
- How to cook your favourite dish
- A science experiment
- How to play a computer game

1 First of all, …
2 Then …

190   Unit 6

EXAM STRATEGY

Listening – Sentence completion

When you need to listen for precise information, make sure you know what details you need before you listen. You usually have to complete notes with one or two words, a number, a name / spelling or a date. Look out for symbols and abbreviations in the notes such as £, $, km, %, as they give useful clues. You will hear just one person speaking who may repeat some of the missing details.

32 Complete the information about the person below.
Name: ⁰ Viola Willis
Address: ¹ ....
Age: ² ....

Look at the text below and highlight the information you need to complete the task.

My name's Viola Willis. I'm 16 and I've got two brothers and a sister and I'm a student at Gray's College in Winchester. I live in the town centre and my address is 25 Northcote Road. My hobbies include cinema and kickboxing.

33 [2.17] Listen and complete the person's profile.

First and last name: ⁰ Pete
Nationality: ¹ ....
Address: ² ...., Camden Town
Postcode: ³ ....
Age: ⁴ ....
Profession: ⁵ ....
Hobbies: ⁶ ....
⁷ ....
Accommodation: ⁸ ....

34 [2.18] Listen to a tour guide welcoming some visitors to a hotel and complete the notes.

Breakfast: in the Square Mile Room on the ⁰ top floor from ¹ .... to 9:45 am.
Packed ² .... **for trips:** collect until 11 am.
Dinner: hotel restaurant famous for its ³ ....
⁴ ....: from 7 to 10 pm every evening.
Free drinks: ⁵ .... only.
Hotel facilities: ⁶ .... – opening times from 8 am to ⁷ .... pm.
Please remember it is closed for ⁸ .... over lunchtime. ⁹ .... are provided.
Enjoy a cup of ¹⁰ .... at no extra cost after your swim at the hotel's terrace café.

TOWARDS PRELIMINARY

35 [2.19] Listen to the same tour guide explaining a day trip and complete the notes.

Boat trip to Camden
Depart from hotel at: ⁰ 11:15 .
Boat leaves from: Little Venice in ¹ .... London.
Boat departs at: ² ....
Boat stops at: the ³ ....; ideal for families with ⁴ ....
Remember to bring ⁵ .... with you.
Time in Camden market: ⁶ .... hours.
What to do: visit market, buy ⁷ .... and bags there, eat ⁸ ....
Boat departs at: ⁹ ....
Cost: ¹⁰ ....

36 [2.20] Listen to a weather centre guide and complete the notes.

Name of centre: ⁰ North-West Weather Centre.
Number of floors: ¹ ....
Ground floor: ² .... Forecast Room
  Hours of operation: ³ .... per day.
  Activity: prepare internet and ⁴ .... forecasts.
  Number of staff: ⁵ .... maximum.
  Internet forecast: available from ⁶ .... pm.
  Every day, data collection until ⁷ .... am.
First floor: ⁸ .... Monitoring Centre.
  Hours of operation: from ⁹ .... am to ¹⁰ .... pm.
  Number of staff: ¹¹ .... maximum.
  Activities: checking air ¹² ....,
  ¹³ .... changes, monitoring events.
Second floor: ¹⁴ .... Centre.
  Number of staff: ¹⁵ .... people.
  Activities: updating and maintaining ¹⁶ ...., interacting with users on ¹⁷ .... and Twitter, recording video ¹⁸ .... for other ¹⁹ ....

Unit 6   191

REVISE AND ROUND UP

1 🔊 **Complete the sentences with the past simple or past perfect of the verbs in brackets.**

0 Mandy ......**threw**...... (throw) away the flowers her boyfriend ..**had bought**.. (buy) her the day before.
1 When I .... (go) to the beach in August I .... (be) shocked because I .... (never / see) so many people.
2 Dan .... (open) the window that I .... (just / close).
3 Some kids .... (destroy) the snowman we .... (build) earlier that morning.
4 After the sun .... (go) down it .... (be) much cooler.
5 Luckily I .... (already / save) the file before the computer .... (crash).
6 I .... (feel) tired that morning because I .... (not / sleep) well the night before.
7 When they .... (arrive) we .... (already / start) cooking dinner.
8 She .... (tell) us about the film she .... (see).
9 The group .... (sing) a song that I .... (never / hear) before.
10 The film .... (start) just as we .... (sit) down.

2 🔊 **Complete the text with the correct form of the verbs in brackets.**

I ⁰......**arrived**...... (arrive) home maybe just a couple of minutes after the thieves ¹.................. (go). In any case, they ².................. (have) enough time to do plenty of damage to my flat and ³.................. (leave) it in a terrible condition. The first thing that I ⁴.................. (notice) was that they ⁵.................. (take) my favourite picture from the wall. Why? It ⁶.................. (have) no value at all. In the bedroom, they ⁷.................. (open) all the drawers in my bedside table, but luckily they ⁸.................. (not / find) my passport, which ⁹.................. (be) on top of the wardrobe. I ¹⁰.................. (feel) really upset when I ¹¹.................. (see) that they ¹².................. (break) my favourite photo of me and my family on holiday in Spain and I ¹³.................. (start) to cry. After I ¹⁴.................. (tidy) everything up, I ¹⁵.................. (need) to be with someone so I ¹⁶.................. (call) a friend I ¹⁷.................. (not / see) for ages and we ¹⁸.................. (go) for a pizza.

3 🔊 **Complete the sentences with an indefinite pronoun.**

0 I can't see ......**anything**...... – put a light on.
1 There's .... we can do now – only wait.
2 I've looked .... but I can't find my keys.
3 I'd like to go .... warm this summer.
4 Can .... help me with this exercise?
5 The film didn't win .... at the Oscars.
6 Is there .... home?
7 Come here – there's .... you have to see!
8 Does .... remember the name of that town in France we stayed in?
9 I need .... to sleep in the town centre.
10 I asked all my friends, but .... knew the answer, so I had to find it on the internet.

4 🔊 **Complete the sentences with the correct form of the verbs in brackets.**

0 If you ......**heat**...... (heat) water, normally it ......**boils**...... (boil) at 100 °C.
1 If you .... (not / study) for that test, you .... (not / pass) it.
2 If you .... (take) your coat, you .... (not / feel) cold later.
3 If Pete .... (get) the job, he .... (move) to London.
4 If you .... (not / like) this model, I .... (bring) you another one.
5 If I .... (stay) on the beach too long, I .... (go) really red.
6 If temperatures .... (rise), they .... (cause) extreme events.

5 🔊 **Choose the correct option.**

0 I think we (*may*) / *can* be in trouble here.
1 I won't call you *if* / *unless* there are problems.
2 If I *see* / *'ll see* them, I'll tell them.
3 It *might* / *will* rain, so take your umbrella just in case.
4 *If* / *Unless* you see something unusual, you must tell us.
5 It *may* / *will* be a difficult match – you never know with our team.
6 Unless you *are* / *'ll be* more careful, you'll have an accident.
7 I'll call you *if* / *when* I get there.
8 *When* / *Unless* I hear some news, I'll text you.
9 She *will* / *won't* come to the party unless you call her.
10 I *will* / *may* be late tonight, but I'll text you to confirm.

192 Units 5–6

6 🔊 **Complete the dialogue with** *might, might not, unless, if, when, will, won't.*

Joe Hello, Dave. You look worried – what's up?
Dave I have to repeat the history exam on Friday and I'm sure I ⁰......*will*...... fail it again.
Joe Oh, come on, you never know. It ¹.......................... be so difficult this time.
Dave Well, ².......................... I pass it, I'll have to repeat the school year!
Joe Oh, don't worry, ³.......................... you study a bit you ⁴.......................... be fine.
Dave What do you think the teacher ⁵.......................... put in the test?
Joe It's difficult to say. It definitely ⁶.......................... be about the Roman period because we didn't do that properly, but it ⁷.......................... be on the Anglo-Saxons as we covered that a lot.

7 🔊 **Correct the mistakes. Two sentences are correct.**

0 I've been looking for those slippers ~~somewhere~~.
   everywhere
1 When you'll arrive, you'll find the keys under the mat.
2 She may to call you later on.
3 Unless we don't leave now, we'll be late.
4 When I got home, my friends already left.
5 If we'll have heavy rain, there's always a risk of a flood.
6 I didn't know nobody in my new school.
7 Don't throw it away, you might need it one day.

8 🔊 **TRANSLATION** **Translate the sentences into English.**

0 Non conosco nessuno qui.
   I don't know anybody here.
1 Quando sono arrivato in aeroporto mi sono ricordato che avevo lasciato il passaporto a casa.
2 Ho cercato il libro dappertutto ma non l'ho trovato.
3 A meno che non ci sia qualcos'altro che mi vuoi dire, vado a casa.
4 Ho sentito qualcosa su in camera tua.
5 Quando li hai visti, avevano già finito di fare la spesa?
6 Se fai tanto sport, rimani in forma.
7 Se sento qualcosa riguardo al test di martedì ti chiamo.
8 Quando arrivi chiamiamo Adele.
9 Mike potrebbe arrivare in ritardo – vuoi aspettarlo?
10 Non avevo mai sentito questa canzone.

CONCEPT CHECK

Read the sentences and answer the questions.

1 *When I got to the station, my train had already left.*

(Answer Yes / No)

1 Was my train still at the station when I arrived? **No**
2 Did the train leave the station before I arrived?
3 Did it leave after I arrived?
4 Was I able to take it?

2 *If it rains tomorrow, I won't go to the match.*

(Answer Yes / No / Your own words)

1 Am I planning to go to the match? **Yes**
2 Am I sure about the weather?
3 Will I definitely go to the match?
4 What does it depend on?

3 *I won't call him unless he says sorry to me.*

(Answer Yes / No / Your own words)

1 Am I angry with this person? **Yes**
2 Will I definitely call him?
3 When will I call him?

4 *I want to go somewhere warm for our holiday.*

(Answer Yes / No)

1 Do I want to go on holiday? **Yes**
2 If so, do I know exactly where?
3 Have I already decided the destination?
4 Am I happy to go to a cold place?

5 *I know you'll really enjoy the film.*

(Answer Yes / No)

1 Do you want to go and see a film? **Yes**
2 Have I seen the film?
3 Am I sure that you will like it?

6 *It might rain tomorrow.*

(Answer Yes / No / Your own words)

1 Will it definitely rain tomorrow? **No**
2 Is there a possibility of rain tomorrow?

➡ See **GRAMMAR REFERENCE**
pages 118, 119, 120

Units 5–6 193

7 Health of a nation

GRAMMAR PRACTICE

Second conditional

Complete the rules.
We use the second conditional to talk about
.... situations.
If is followed by subject + verb in a .... tense.
We use .... + infinitive without *to*
in the other clause.
When we give advice we often use the form
If I .... *you, I'd …*

➡ See **GRAMMAR REFERENCE** page 120

1 🔊 **Put the words in the correct order.**

0 had / tennis / at / if / time / be / I'd / better / I / more
   If I had more time, I'd be better at tennis.
1 if / it / so / wasn't / we'd / out / go / cold
2 would / be / left / OK / if / we / early / it / ?
3 told / wouldn't / surprised / I / if / she / be / that / you
4 better / would / we / be / called / first / if / them / it
5 worry / if / I / you / wouldn't / it / about / were / I
6 exam / university / to / be / able / go / to / she'd / passed / she / that / if
7 happened / that / like / me / if / complain / I'd / something / to
8 gave / clearer / instructions / if / us / we'd / you / to / do / what / know
9 trouble / if / this / would / lost / key / be / in / we / we
10 lived / speak / abroad / they'd / language / another / they / if

2 🔊 **Write the sentences in the second conditional.**

0 if / you / study / more / you / get / better marks
   If you studied more, you'd get better marks.
1 if I / be him / I / talk to my parents about it
2 if you / have less homework / how often / you / go out / ?
3 if we / have a cinema in this town / I / see more films
4 if petrol / cost a lot / people / use public transport more
5 if they / not speak so much in class / they / understand a lot more
6 if I / know the answer to that / I / tell you
7 if we / win the lottery / we / travel round the world
8 your parents / listen / if / you / try to explain / ?

3 🔊 **Choose the correct option.**

0 I *'d come* / *came* to the match with you if I *didn't* / *wouldn't* have a maths lesson.
1 I *wouldn't* / *didn't* do that if I *would be* / *were* you.
2 What *did* / *would* you say if you *would meet* / *met* a very famous person?
3 He *wouldn't* / *didn't* say it if he *wouldn't* / *didn't* mean it.
4 What *did* / *would* you do if you *saw* / *'d see* a UFO?
5 They *come* / *'d come* and see you more often if you *didn't* / *wouldn't* live so far.
6 If I *knew* / *didn't know* this town so well I*'d have* / *had* trouble getting around.
7 If I *weren't* / *were* you I *went* / *'d go* home.

4 🔊 **Rewrite the sentences in the second conditional.**

0 I haven't got much free time, so I don't go out much.
   If I had more free time, I'd go out more.
1 I don't swim very often; the swimming pool is very far.
2 They don't do any jobs around the house, so their parents don't give them much pocket money.
3 She doesn't check her homework, so she makes a lot of spelling mistakes.
4 We always do the same things in geography class, so we get really bored.
5 I get up late and I often miss the school bus.
6 My friends don't do their homework, so they always get bad test marks.
7 She hasn't got his number, so she can't call him.
8 Bill never writes things down; he often forgets them.
9 Ben knows a lot about IT, so he can fix his own computer.
10 Pat isn't feeling well. She isn't going to the party.

Second conditional v first conditional

Choose the correct option.
We use the second conditional when we think the situation in the *if*-clause is *likely* / *unlikely* to happen.
We use the first conditional when we think the situation in the *if*-clause is *likely* / *unlikely* to happen.
We often use conditionals to give advice.

➡ See **GRAMMAR REFERENCE** page 120

194   Unit 7

GRAMMAR PRACTICE

5 Read the sentences and write likely (L) or unlikely (U).

0 ...L... You'll get there early if you leave now.
1 .... If I won a million pounds, I'd buy a nice house.
2 .... If I have the time, I'll finish that job.
3 .... We'd win more matches if we trained more often.
4 .... I'll get in touch with you if there's any news.
5 .... If I knew more people, I'd like this city much more.
6 .... She'll help you if you ask her.
7 .... If Sam felt ill, he wouldn't tell anyone.
8 .... If you miss the train, I'll come and pick you up.

6 Choose the correct option.

0 If it *is* / *was* cold tomorrow, I'll cancel the trip.
1 If I *have* / *had* time, I'd come round.
2 If that's OK with everybody, I *'ll* / *'d* call and book.
3 What *will* / *would* you say if you see them?
4 Where *would* / *will* you like to go if we went away at the weekend?
5 She *wouldn't* / *won't* be very happy if you didn't tell her about it.
6 Ahmed *will* / *would* call you if he arrives early.
7 What *will* / *would* you think if he said that to you?
8 Where will you study if you *pass* / *passed* your exams?

7 Match the beginnings and ends of the sentences.

0 [b] If I were you,
1 [ ] If she's got time,
2 [ ] If you get some tomatoes,
3 [ ] You'll get us in trouble
4 [ ] If your parents find out,
5 [ ] I'd travel the world
6 [ ] I'd prefer it
7 [ ] You'll hear this track
8 [ ] She'll be upset
9 [ ] If it wasn't so cold,
10 [ ] If you tried harder,

a she'll send you a text.
b I'd go home right now.
c if you go to their concert.
d if you're not careful.
e I'll make some pizza.
f if we lived in the country.
g if I had the money.
h if we arrive late.
i they'll be angry.
j you'd get better results.
k I'd wear my new T-shirt.

8 Correct the mistakes. Two sentences are correct.

0 If I ~~have~~ no homework, I'd go out much more. **had**
1 If you got in touch, they'll be really pleased.
2 If it doesn't stop raining, we'll go home.
3 If we spoke German, we can make more friends here.
4 What will they think if I didn't pass the test?
5 What would you do if you were in my situation?
6 Will you call me if you'd be late?
7 I wouldn't recognise Palek if I see him now.

9 Complete the sentences with the correct form of the verbs below.

be • rain • rent • get • have •
let • ~~not / eat~~ • talk • happen

0 I **wouldn't eat** that if I were you.
1 If you .... a film, we'll watch it together.
2 If Harry was tall and slim, he .... still .... unhappy with his looks.
3 You .... more visits if you had more pictures on your Facebook page.
4 If I already .... my driving licence, I wouldn't have to catch the bus to school.
5 If I were you, I .... to the teacher about it.
6 If it .... a bit more often, the grass would be a lot greener around here.
7 They .... you know if the party was off.
8 If that .... to me, I'd be very unhappy.

10 Complete the dialogue with the first or second conditional of these verbs.

~~be~~ • not / be able • post • do •
not / want • have to • put • limit • comment

Sue I'm setting up my Facebook page. Any advice?
Phil Well, if I ⁰ **were** you, I ¹ .... lots of pictures and information on it.
Sue OK. And what ² .... you .... to get more visits and likes?
Phil I ³ .... a piece of news or a story everyone's talking about. And then I ⁴ .... on that particular post.
Sue OK, that's a good idea. If I ⁵ .... strangers to see my page, what ⁶ .... I .... do?
Phil It's easy. If you ⁷ .... access to your page, people you don't know ⁸ .... to see your information.

Unit 7 195

READING SKILLS

11 Match the terms to the definitions.

1 ☐ infection   4 ☐ ward
2 ☐ treatment   5 ☐ antibiotics
3 ☐ care   6 ☐ injection

a The act of looking after someone when they're ill.
b What the hospital provides to make a patient better.
c A room in a hospital for a certain type of patient.
d An illness caused by bacteria.
e A drug that doctors prescribe to kill bacteria.
f A method for administering a drug to a patient.

12 [2.21] Read the text and put sentences a–e in the correct gaps 1–5. Then listen and check.

a how has this dramatic change happened?
b and many countries copied it.
c so it's simply not enough.
d the result is that many hospitals simply can't manage in certain periods.
e but this isn't without its problems.

13 Match the headings to the paragraphs. One heading is extra.

1 ☐ More cash please!
2 ☐ Our health expectations
3 ☐ Hospitals at breaking point
4 ☐ Is there a doctor around here?
5 ☐ How to become a doctor in the UK
6 ☐ A fairer system for all

14 Read the text again and answer the question.

What is the main point of the article?
1 The health system is very effective.
2 The health system used to be very good, but now it has several problems.
3 There are no good doctors and nurses in British hospitals.
4 Doctors from abroad do not speak good English.

15 Read the text again and decide if the sentences are true (T), false (F) or doesn't say (DS). Correct the false ones.

1 The NHS started in the 1930s. T F DS
2 Other countries created similar services to the NHS. T F DS
3 Before the NHS, people had to pay for treatment. T F DS
4 An official report gave a negative opinion of the NHS. T F DS

SAVE OUR HEALTH SERVICE!

A If you felt ill, you would go to a hospital and you would expect someone to see you and explain the problem and you would also probably expect them to make you feel better. These are basic things that modern Europeans expect now but how long can our governments continue to provide free healthcare?

B The British National Health Service was one of the best systems in the world when it started in 1948 [1]............. It was the first time nobody had to pay a doctor or a hospital to use their services. But now, according to the Organisation for Economic Co-operation and Development, the NHS is starting to suffer.

C So, [2]............ Well, one of the problems is that staff numbers per patient are low – lower than in countries such as Turkey and Poland. The NHS needs an estimated 75,000 more staff to maintain its high standards but finding and keeping good doctors and nurses is not easy. As a consequence many doctors and nurses have to work very long hours and are very stressed. Many doctors and nurses in UK hospitals come from other countries, [3]............ For example there can be language obstacles and cultural differences. In addition after the UK's decision to leave Europe, it may become much more complicated to employ EU doctors in the future.

5 The NHS has fewer staff than in 1948. T F DS
6 There are more doctors in Poland than in the UK. T F DS
7 NHS doctors and nurses are under pressure because of their low numbers. T F DS
8 The NHS uses foreign doctors because British doctors are not very good at their job. T F DS
9 Winter is the worst time for the health system. T F DS
10 Older people use the NHS more than younger people. T F DS
11 The government is spending more than ever before on the NHS. T F DS
12 Hospital costs are going up. T F DS

16 Read the text again and answer the questions.

1 How many more doctors and nurses does the NHS need?
2 Why is it difficult to have more qualified staff in UK hospitals?

25 Another problem is the growing number of people who
need to use hospitals and the health service in general
due to an aging population – people are living longer
and older people need more health treatment. Recently,
nearly 6 million people received treatment at Accident
30 and Emergency wards in just three months – a record.
And ⁴............ The situation is critical in winter when elderly
people need injections for influenza and
the number of people with infections that need treatment
with antibiotics increases.

35 What should the government do about this? Well, nearly
everybody agrees they need to invest more in the service.
They already spend £150 billion on it, but operations
and treatment are becoming more expensive, ⁵.............

D

E

3 Why are doctors and nurses feeling more stressed?
4 What problems do foreign staff have to face in the UK?
5 What might happen after Britain leaves the EU?
6 What's an additional pressure on hospitals?
7 What happens in some hospitals during very busy periods?
8 What do people think the government needs to do?

17 Find the words or phrases in the text that mean the same as these.

1 in the opinion of (para B) ....
2 workers (para C) ....
3 levels (para C) ....
4 give a job to (para C) ....
5 increasing (para D) ....
6 very difficult (para D) ....
7 spend money (para E) ....

VOCABULARY

ILLNESSES, INJURIES AND REMEDIES

18 Write the name of the health problem.

0 **toothache** You go to the dentist because of this. It makes it difficult to eat and think!
1 .... You often get one of these in the winter and they can make it difficult for you or the rest of the family to sleep at night. They are also a problem if you're at the cinema.
2 .... It is very common to have one of these, usually in winter, but sometimes in the other seasons, too. The symptoms are a cough, a headache and generally not feeling too well, but nothing as bad as the flu.
3 .... You get one of these if you are under stress, or very worried about something, or if you have a cold or flu. It can make it difficult to concentrate and some people take an aspirin to minimise it.
4 .... You normally have this when you eat food that's bad for you or if you've got flu or something similar. It's difficult to eat because you don't feel hungry.
5 .... This is when you feel really hot, for example if you've got flu or just a bad cold. You normally check it with a thermometer and anything above 37.5 °C is a problem.

19 Circle the odd word out in each group.

0	*swollen*	knee	ankle	eye	(teeth)
1	*feel*	ill	sick	twist	well
2	*break a*	leg	wrist	finger	liver
3	*bruised*	elbow	knee	teeth	toe
4	*sore*	throat	knee	neck	stomach
5	*hurt your*	back	neck	shoulder	cough
6	*blocked*	eye	nose	ear	chest
7	*put a ... on*	plaster	dressing	syrup	cream
8	*burn your*	finger	lip	teeth	mouth
9	*twist your*	knee	ankle	chest	back

20 Match the problems to the treatments.

0 [d] small cut — a antibiotics
1 [ ] antiseptic — b bandage
2 [ ] headache — c paracetamol
3 [ ] bacterial infection — d plaster
4 [ ] sore throat — e spray
5 [ ] big cut — f cream
6 [ ] blocked nose — g lozenges

Unit 7   197

GRAMMAR PRACTICE

should / had better / ought to for advice

Complete the rules.
We use *should*, *had better* and *ought to* to give ....
We don't usually use *had better* or *ought to* in .... sentences.
Should, *had better* and *ought to* use the same form for all ....
The negative forms are .... and ....
Ought to isn't often used in the negative.
These verbs are always followed by the ....

➡ See **GRAMMAR REFERENCE** page 121

21 📶 Match the problems to the advice.

0. [c] I've got a really bad headache.
1. [ ] Tim's really worried about the test.
2. [ ] I haven't got any nice clothes for Emily's party.
3. [ ] We haven't got any food for this evening.
4. [ ] I'm so tired.
5. [ ] Helen can't understand the French book she's reading.
6. [ ] Christian wants to do an exchange programme abroad.
7. [ ] We're really late for the lesson.
8. [ ] My friends and I don't know where to go this summer.
9. [ ] There are no trains after 10 pm.
10. [ ] My brother is getting lots of nasty comments on Twitter.

a You should have a look at Greece.
b He shouldn't be. He's studied very hard for it.
c You'd better take some aspirin.
d She should use a dictionary.
e We'd better hurry up then.
f He should cancel his account.
g You'd better go to the shops.
h We should get a takeaway.
i He ought to consider Norway.
j You'd better take a taxi then.
k You'd better not stay up late again tonight.

22 📶 Put the words in the correct order.

0 to / Gus / them / like / talk / shouldn't / that
   Gus shouldn't talk to them like that.
1 better / few / minutes / home / go / we'd / in / a
2 read / more / ought / you / to / books
3 outside / Suzy / better / bike / her / leave / had
4 people / told / tell / what / secret / shouldn't / she / you / you / in / other
5 right / tell / you'd / now / them / better
6 bedroom / ought / we / up / tidy / our / to
7 our / should / call / parents / we / them / OK / everything / is / to / tell
8 ask / should / I / the US / for / to / go / a / visa / to / ?
9 not / late / better / be / you'd / time / this
10 much / you / food / shouldn't / so / junk / eat

23 📶 Complete the dialogue with the verbs below and the verbs in brackets.

try • ~~do~~ • give up • speak • find • give • play • get

Mark Hello Pat, are you OK?
Pat Hi Mark. Yeah, not bad, but I don't know which sport I ⁰ **should do** (should) next year.
Mark Well, I think you ¹ .... (shouldn't) tennis – you're so good at it.
Pat Thanks, but I'm a bit tired of it, to be honest.
Mark You ² .... (should) to your coach – she won't be happy about that.
Pat I know! Perhaps I ³ .... (ought to) a new sport before I do that.
Mark Well, what about squash? You ⁴ .... (ought to) it at least.
Pat Well, maybe I ⁵ .... ('d better) the squash club a call.
Mark Yes, I think you ⁶ .... (should) once or twice, just to see if you like it.
Pat You're right. I ⁷ .... ('d better) in touch with Simon – he's already a member there.

24 📶 Write advice for these situations using *should*, *ought to* and *had better*.

0 I don't know where to have my birthday party.
   You ought to see if Papa Joe's is available.
1 I can't decide which T-shirt to wear.
2 My brother's not sure which language to study.
3 My parents never go out in the evening.
4 My best friend spends too much time on Facebook.
5 I do really badly in my history tests.
6 My sister and I are always late for school.
7 I can never remember words when I study a language.
8 I always do my homework late in the evening, and I'm tired in the morning.

198 Unit 7

SPEAKING SKILLS

ASKING FOR AND GIVING ADVICE

25 Put the words in the correct order.

1. ankle / left / my / hurts / really
2. think / what / should / do / do / you / I / ?
3. call / talk / if / want / you / to / a / me / give
4. me / to / happens / it / too
5. pain / you / are / a / of / lot / in / ?
6. go / better / you'd / see / and / doctor / your
7. painkillers / maybe / try / some / I / should
8. first / better / I'd / doctor / my / with / check

26 Complete the dialogue with expressions from exercise 25.

A Hey, you haven't been to training all week – what's going on?
B ¹.. .
A When do you feel the pain?
B Every time I jump, especially when I hit the ground.
A I know. ².. .
B Really?
A Yes. Just the same. ³.. ?
B Quite a lot, yes.
A So on a scale from 1 to 10?
B 9 or 10. ⁴.. .
A What if you make it worse?
B You're right. So what ⁵.. ?
A I think ⁶.. .
B Yes, maybe you're right. I ⁷...................................... .
A OK, and ⁸.. .

27 Write a dialogue using the suggestions.

A A chiede a B come sta.
B B risponde che sta bene ma che gli / le fa male la spalla.
A A chiede quando succede.
B B risponde che succede quando si alza la mattina.
A A chiede se gli / le fa molto male.
B B risponde di sì, gli / le fa molto male.
A A consiglia a B di andare dal medico.
B B risponde che non ha tempo in questo periodo.
A A dice che gli / le conviene prendere degli antidolorifici se non riesce ad andare dal medico.
B B ringrazia A del consiglio.
A A risponde e dice che B può chiamare se vuole parlarne.

LISTENING SKILLS

28 Match the verbs to the expressions.

1. ☐ work   a signs of illness
2. ☐ see   b a problem
3. ☐ finish   c with patients
4. ☐ solve   d a patient
5. ☐ look for   e long hours
6. ☐ communicate   f a course

29 [2.22] Listen to the interview and answer the questions.

1. What job does the man do?
2. Does he generally like his job?

30 [2.22] Listen again and complete the sentences.

1. Dr Numan works in .... London.
2. He sees around .... patients every hour.
3. Junior doctors usually work .... hours per week.
4. He sometimes finishes at .... or .... in the morning.
5. The most difficult cases are those with ....
6. He says that doctors are like ....
7. Doctors need good .... skills.
8. If he wasn't a doctor, he'd like to be a ....

31 [2.22] Listen again and choose the correct option.

1. What happened to some of his fellow students at university?
   A They changed course.
   B They stopped studying.
2. What does he say about being a modern doctor?
   A It's really exciting.
   B It's a lot of work but always interesting.
3. What does he say about working long hours?
   A He doesn't usually notice them.
   B They make him really tired.
4. What does he say about people who prefer to work regular hours?
   A They should be pilots.
   B They should work in an office.
5. What is the difference between child and adult patients?
   A The adults complain more.
   B The children remain positive.

Unit 7   199

TOWARDS PRELIMINARY

> **EXAM STRATEGY**
>
> **Reading – Four-option multiple choice**
>
> The first and the last questions test gist understanding of the text. The first question is usually about the purpose of the text and the last question is often about the text as a whole. The other three questions focus on details and are in the same order as the text. Read the text once through for general understanding before you start answering the questions. Always refer carefully to the text when choosing your answers.

I am writing about a recent visit to Holby hospital. My mother went to Accident and Emergency after a fall in the kitchen. The nurse in reception said there was a waiting time of several hours.
First of all, I was shocked to see at least 50 people in the waiting room, some with nasty injuries, too. I asked one person and he told me he'd been there for over three hours and hadn't seen a doctor yet. There were also four or five patients parked on trolleys in the corridor, but nobody moved them in the three hours I was there.
My mother was feeling really uncomfortable when we finally saw a doctor. She examined her and said we ought to come back the next day. I asked the reason for this and I was shocked to hear that both X-ray machines were broken!
I have been using this hospital for many years and this is the worst experience I've ever had. I took my mother to a private clinic the same afternoon and we resolved her problem immediately. I'm lucky I have the money, but a lot of people can't afford private healthcare.
I know that the health service has financial problems and I accept you often have to wait hours for treatment, but the poor organisation in this hospital is a danger to patients.
I hope the hospital managers are reading this letter and take some action to improve the situation at Holby.

32 Read Will's letter and choose the correct option.

  0 Will went to hospital because:
   A he wasn't feeling well.
   B he had a car accident.
   C his mother had had a domestic accident.
   D his mother wasn't feeling well.

  1 What is Will trying to do in the text?
   A Advise patients to go to Holby hospital.
   B Complain about the hospital.
   C Suggest improvements to the service.
   D Explain how the accident happened.

  2 His first problem was:
   A the other injured patients.
   B the unfriendly receptionist.
   C the long waiting times.
   D the patients in shock.

  3 When he spoke to other patients, he realised that:
   A other people had also been waiting a long time.
   B there were no nurses in the hospital.
   C his mother was in a worse condition than them.
   D his mother's condition wasn't very urgent.

  4 Will thinks that:
   A the hospital managers are not good at their jobs.
   B money is the real problem.
   C it's not acceptable to have broken equipment.
   D the hospital puts patients at risk.

  5 What would Will write in a letter to the local newspaper?
   A I wanted to say what wonderful service Holby hospital offers all its patients.
   B Something needs to be done about the poor level of care at Holby hospital.
   C If I were ill, I wouldn't go to Holby hospital to be treated.
   D I would particularly like to thank the nurse who treated my mother yesterday.

33 Read Alice's blog and choose the correct option.

I started to feel bad just after Christmas. I had this terrible pain on the right side of my tummy and I was very sick. My parents called the doctor and she came round straight away to visit me. She checked my temperature and put some pressure on different points of my tummy, but it didn't hurt very much. She told my parents that I had flu, so I wasn't too worried after that. I went back to school a few days later, but I still didn't feel completely right. I found it difficult to do sports and I had a lot of pain when I jumped for the ball in volleyball.
The week after I felt too ill to go to school and my parents took me to the doctor again. I was now quite thin because I didn't have much appetite because of my tummy pains. The doctor said I had a urinary infection, gave me antibiotics and ordered some blood tests.
The next day I felt terrible so my dad took me to hospital. They did a scan and found the doctor was wrong and that I had appendicitis. So they rushed me into the operating room. I obviously don't remember anything about it, but I know that it was a very difficult operation. After that I spent two weeks in hospital. It wasn't too bad there because all my friends came to visit me and some clowns came round in the evening and made us laugh, but in the end I was really glad to get home, still alive.

Alice

0 Alice's doctor:
  A visited her immediately.
  B visited her after a few days.
  C didn't come and visit her.
  D visited her but didn't do a physical exam.
1 What is the writer trying to do in the text?
  A Explain about her illness.
  B Describe how terrible she felt.
  C Suggest what to do if you feel ill.
  D Thank the doctors and nurses.
2 On the second visit, the doctor:
  A sent her to hospital.
  B gave the wrong diagnosis.
  C told her not to eat much.
  D said there was nothing wrong.
3 Alice says she:
  A will never forget her operation.
  B had to wait a few days for the operation.
  C felt nervous before the operation.
  D knew that the operation was complicated.
4 Alice's stay in hospital was:
  A long and uncomfortable.
  B long but sometimes enjoyable.
  C not very long but very boring.
  D short and not very enjoyable.
5 What would Alice write to a friend who lives a long way from her?
  A I had appendicitis but I was only in hospital for a few days and didn't miss much school.
  B I had a terrible Christmas! I was in hospital all the time but I got lots of presents from my friends.
  C I've had an operation but I've got to go back into hospital because the doctor made a mistake.
  D Sorry I haven't been in touch recently but I've been ill. It's a long story. I'll tell you about it later.

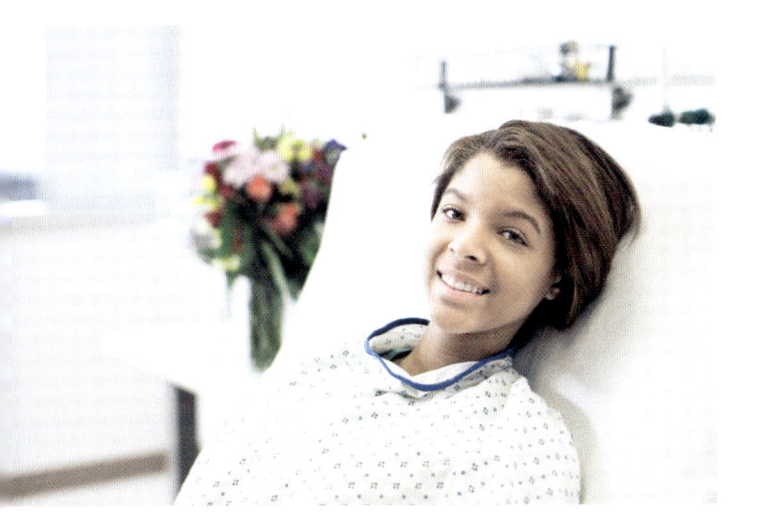

TOWARDS PRELIMINARY

EXAM STRATEGY

Speaking – Interview

When the examiner asks you questions, try to give complete answers. It's important not to answer with one word or a very short phrase. Try to give complete answers to the questions by adding some information.

34 Complete the questions.

0 ……**What**……'s your name?
1 Where ……………………… you live?
2 How long ……………………… you lived there?
3 What do you ……………………… in your free time?
4 Do you ……………………… English at school?
5 Do you ……………………… studying English?

35 Now match the questions in exercise 34 to these answers.

a [5] Yes, quite lot. But it's quite hard to learn new words.
b [ ] I go out with my friends and I do tae kwon do.
c [ ] My name's Denise.
d [ ] Yes, we've got three hours a week, plus one hour of conversation class.
e [ ] I live near the main square.
f [ ] We moved there about ten years ago.

36 Put the words in the correct order.

0 got / brothers / I've / two / younger
  I've got two younger brothers.
1 like / really / I'd / Russian / try / to /
2 Shakespeare / *Henry V* / doing / we're / by
3 Greek / June / islands / in / went / the / to / we
4 lively / it's / evenings / in / quite / the
5 all / boring / think / I / they're
6 try / I / sport / like / a / would / to / team

37 Give answers that are true for you. Try to make them as complete as possible.

1 Where do you live?
2 Tell us about the type of music you like.
3 Tell us about your journey to school.
4 What's your favourite time of year?
5 What sort of clothes do you like wearing?
6 Where do you like to go shopping?
7 Tell us about a holiday you enjoyed.
8 What job would you like to do in the future?

Unit 7 201

8 A political world

GRAMMAR PRACTICE

Third conditional

Choose the correct option.
We use the third conditional to refer to the *past / present*.
We use it to speculate about the probable consequences of something that *happened / didn't happen*.
We use the *past / present* perfect in the *if*-clause and *would have / would had* + past participle in the main clause.
You *can't / can* invert the order of the *if*-clause and the main clause.

➡ See **GRAMMAR REFERENCE** page 121

1 🔊 **Match the beginnings and ends of the sentences.**

0 [c] If you had said it in a different way,
1 [ ] If someone had called an ambulance,
2 [ ] If Tony had left home earlier,
3 [ ] If I had taken that special offer,
4 [ ] If we'd played better in the first half,
5 [ ] If they had been a bit cheaper,
6 [ ] If the group had played in a smaller venue,

a we would have won the match easily.
b they would have saved more people.
c he wouldn't have reacted so badly.
d he wouldn't have missed his plane.
e Sue would've bought those shoes.
f I would have saved quite a lot.
g the music would have sounded much better.

2 🔊 **Put the words in the correct order.**

0 if / have / known / I / had / you / helped / I / would
   if I had known, I would have helped you.
1 problems / she / had / if / called / have / had / she / would
2 wouldn't / lost / checked / map / on / if / they / had / the / it / got / have / they
3 if / you / argument / wouldn't / anything / happened / that / have / said / hadn't
4 been / done / you / would / have / you / had / if / situation / same / the / in / my
5 called / if / him / out / have / you / had / come / Mike / tonight / would
6 to / if / Jennifer / late / wouldn't / been / have / sent / text / a / confirm / we / had / the time / us

3 🔊 **Complete the sentences with the third conditional of the verbs in brackets.**

0 She **wouldn't have had** (not / have) that accident if she **had respected** (respect) the speed limit.
1 If Samir .... (not / study) French, he .... (not / take) that job in Paris.
2 What .... (your parents / say) if you .... (choose) another school?
3 You .... (not / believe) me if I .... (tell) you.
4 If the shop .... (close) five minutes earlier, we .... (not / manage) to get the food for this evening.
5 Where .... (your friends / stay) if they .... (visit) London?
6 If Kelly .... (check) her stuff more carefully, she .... (not / lose) her trainers.
7 If my parents .... (find out), they .... (get) really angry.
8 If Gina .... (consider) things more carefully, she probably .... (not / make) that decision.

4 🔊 **Rewrite the sentences using the third conditional.**

0 I arrived late and I missed my train.
   If I hadn't arrived late, I wouldn't have missed my train.
1 She didn't call me, so I didn't know about the party.
2 They didn't see the speed limit, so they went too fast.
3 She didn't receive my present, so she didn't call to say 'thank you'.
4 It wasn't very cold, so I didn't take my jacket.
5 I heard someone call my name. I stopped and turned around.
6 52% of the people voted for Brexit in the EU referendum. Britain left the EU.
7 The government increased public spending. The economy improved.
8 The government made some popular decisions. People re-elected it.
9 Robert Kennedy was the favourite to become President of the US. An assassin killed him.
10 The government cut workers' pay. The workers went on strike.

GRAMMAR PRACTICE

5 🔊 **Complete the sentences with the third conditional and the verbs below.**

not miss / take ▪ know / help ▪ not do / be ▪
go / stop ▪ not know / ask ▪ let / cancel ▪
tell / bring ▪ have / won ▪ think / not do ▪
book / save ▪ do / not get

0 If she ......**had known**...... about the problem, she ......**would have**...... helped.

1 I did OK in the race. If I .... another couple of weeks of preparation, I .... it.

2 We .... outside if the rain ....

3 They .... that if you .... nice to them.

4 I .... how to answer that if they .... me the same question.

5 If you .... me you were thirsty, I .... something to drink.

6 Marcus .... you know if the match ....

7 If he .... about the consequences, he .... that.

8 If we .... a bit earlier, we .... lots of money on the flight.

9 If you .... all the exercises like I told you, you .... such a bad mark.

10 My parents .... the flight if they .... a taxi as I suggested.

6 🔊 **Read about these historical events and write sentences with the third conditional.**

0 Germany invaded Poland in 1939. Britain declared war on Germany soon after.
   If Germany hadn't invaded Poland, Britain wouldn't have declared war on Germany soon after.

1 Gandhi campaigned for independence in India. British colonial rule ended in 1947.

2 The Berlin Wall divided the city in 1961. People were not free to go from East to West Berlin.

3 A killer assassinated J. F. Kennedy in Dallas. Lyndon Johnson became the new president.

4 The US lost 64,000 soldiers in the war and 1.3 million Vietnamese soldiers died. There were violent protests in the US against the Vietnam War.

5 The French carried out nuclear tests in the South Pacific in the 1960s and 1970s. Serious contamination reached large areas of Polynesia.

6 Israel fought the Six Day War against Egypt in 1967. It occupied the West Bank and Gaza territories.

7 The Soviet Union invaded Afghanistan. The US boycotted the 1980 Moscow Olympic Games.

8 The Soviet Union broke up in 1991. Fifteen states gained their independence.

9 The Yugoslavian Republic broke up in 1991. A war followed and 140,000 people died.

10 Protestant Unionist and Catholic Republican groups in Northern Ireland signed the Good Friday Agreement in 1998. Paramilitary operations on both sides stopped within a year.

7 🔊 **Complete the sentences with the verbs below.**

study ▪ eat ▪ teach ▪ not / have ▪
give ▪ not / lose ▪ do ▪ buy ▪
look ▪ not / miss ▪ get ▪ not / feel ▪
land ▪ not / be ▪ not / have ▪
get better ▪ make ▪ go

0 If the boy ......**had looked**...... before crossing the road, he ......**wouldn't have had**...... the accident.

1 If the students .... a bit harder for the test, they .... much better marks.

2 If the weather .... so bad, we .... outside on the terrace yesterday.

3 If my teachers .... me to speak the language, I .... so many problems when I actually went to the country.

4 If the shop assistant .... me just a little discount, I .... that T-shirt.

5 If the flight .... on time, we .... the connection in Hong Kong.

6 If the government .... more for young people, it .... their votes.

7 The economy .... if they .... the right decisions.

8 You .... so tired last night if you .... to bed a bit earlier the night before.

Unit 8   203

READING SKILLS

8 Write the expressions below close to their definitions.

charity ▪ campaign ▪ rights ▪ majority ▪ right-wing ▪ advocate ▪ political thinking ▪ aid worker

1 .... This refers to people who have very conservative political opinions.
2 .... You do this when you organise political action to change a situation.
3 .... A person who helps on humanitarian projects in difficult areas.
4 .... Somebody's general opinion in politics.
5 .... A not-for-profit, non-political organisation that tries to help people in difficulty.
6 .... Someone who argues for (or against) something.
7 .... You have these guaranteed in law when something is morally or legally yours – for example, freedom.
8 .... In an election, at least 50% of the votes plus 1.

9 Read the article and answer the question.

What is the main focus of the article?
1 the migrant crisis
2 the rise of a talented young politician
3 being a woman in Westminster

10 [2.23] Read the text again and put sentences a–d in the correct gaps 1–3. Then listen and check. One sentence is extra.

a and started her new career in parliament in Westminster.
b She would always cycle from the boat to Parliament.
c She was very politically active during her period there.
d and her parents never agreed with her career choice.

11 Read the text again and answer the questions.

1 Which party did she belong to?
2 What subject did she study?
3 What effect did her work for Oxfam have on her?
4 Which political issues was she active in?
5 Where did she live?
6 Why did people like her in Yorkshire?
7 What kind of personality did she have?

A LIFE LESS ORDINARY

A

Joanne Cox, a Labour politician, was born into a working-class family in Yorkshire in 1974. She went to university in Cambridge and studied political sciences. [1]............. After graduating, she worked for several years as an assistant to various politicians and then joined the international charity Oxfam, working in Brussels and then in the UK. While she was at Oxfam, she worked on humanitarian projects in Afghanistan and Darfur, which changed her political thinking. She later said that if she hadn't entered politics, she would have become an aid worker in one of these countries.

B

Her first opportunity to become a politician was in May 2015, when she was the Labour candidate for Parliament for her hometown of Batley. She won the local election for her party [2]............. Once in Parliament, she campaigned for the British government to find a solution to the civil war in Syria and criticised it for not doing enough to help the civilian population there. She published a report about islamophobia (fear of Islam) in the UK and was very anti-racist, she was also a strong supporter of women's rights. She was pro-European and often spoke about the need to be more open to migrants entering Britain.

12 Read the text again and decide if the sentences are true (T) or false (F). Correct the false ones.

1 Joanne Cox was British. T F
2 She went to university in her hometown. T F
3 She worked for Oxfam in just one country. T F
4 She became an aid worker after working for Oxfam. T F
5 She wasn't happy with the British government's approach to the Syrian crisis. T F
6 She wrote a report on the dangers of Islamism. T F
7 She tried to stop migration to Britain. T F
8 She wanted Britain to leave the EU. T F
9 She lived in a big house on the river. T F
10 She was well known in Parliament for her dynamism. T F
11 A man killed her with a gun. T F

C

When she became an MP (Member of Parliament),
Jo moved to a distinctive houseboat on the River Thames,
25　where she lived with her husband and two children.
³............ She spent time in London and in her Yorkshire
constituency where people described her as 'one of us'.
Her friendly, fun-loving nature and enthusiasm for life,
and particularly for politics, made her a very popular figure
30　in Westminster.

D

On June 16th 2016 a man approached her. Jo was always
very welcoming and stopped to talk but the man had a gun
and he shot her three times. Jo died at the scene. Everybody
was shocked by this horrific event and people had difficulty
35　understanding the motive. Politicians from all parties spoke
out about the need for tolerance and understanding –
qualities that Jo Cox always demonstrated. Jo Cox wanted
to change society for the better and for people to live
together in peace so in her memory every year people
40　in the UK organise community events on the anniversary
of her death called 'the Great Get Together'. The events are
to encourage people who live in the same area or street
to socialise and meet each other and make their
communities better, more friendly places.

GLOSSARY

constituency ➤ collegio elettorale

13 Choose the expression that means the same.

1　working class (para A)
　A　proletarian　　　B　high society
2　graduating (para A)
　A　getting grades　　B　finishing your studies
3　joined (para A)
　A　entered an organisation
　B　united an organisation
4　humanitarian (para A)
　A　for the benefit of people　B　economic
5　supporter (para B)
　A　member　　　B　defender
6　distinctive (para C)
　A　very large　　B　easy to notice
7　tolerance (para D)
　A　acceptance　　B　support

VOCABULARY

POLITICS AND SOCIETY

14 Complete the gaps with the words below.

~~racism~~ ▪ tolerance ▪ segregated ▪
extremism ▪ diversity ▪ ban ▪ discrimination ▪
integration ▪ prejudice

0　During apartheid in South Africa, black and white people could not study together or even sit in the same part of a bus. These were obvious manifestations of ......**racism**...... .

1　........................... occurs when people do not have the same opportunities because of race, colour, religious belief or gender – for example, when a company pays men more than women for the same work.

2　........................... is the act of accepting that people and culture are different and considering this difference as a positive thing.

3　The term .... refers to the presence in a community of people who are not all the same in terms of age, race, culture, ability, etc.

4　........................... refers to the situation when people have very strong views that are different from the majority of people and it often describes people who are on the far left or far right of politics.

5　When we talk about .... we mean that we create a negative opinion of somebody because they belong to a group we don't accept or don't like in some way. This can be based, for example, on ethnic origin, skin colour, nationality, gender, disability or other.

6　A .... is a prohibition on something – for example, smoking in many public places.

7　........................... is when individuals from one culture manage to live and work successfully in another.

8　A society is .... when different races or ethnic groups live in separate areas of a city, don't have equal rights and rarely interact with each other.

15 Put the abstract forms of the words below into the correct group. Some have more than one form.

~~resist~~ ▪ popular ▪ commune ▪ fascist ▪ persevere ▪
equal ▪ diverse ▪ federal ▪ allow ▪ terror ▪ active ▪
tolerate ▪ capital ▪ assist ▪ important ▪ sex

-ance:　**resistance,** ....
-ism:　..
-ity:　..

Unit 8　205

GRAMMAR PRACTICE

wish + past tenses

Choose the correct option.

We use *wish* with the *present simple / past simple* to express regret about a present situation.
We use *wish* with the *present perfect / past perfect* to express regret about a past situation.

➜ See **GRAMMAR REFERENCE** page 121

16 Complete the sentences with the correct form of the verbs in brackets.

0 I wish I ....**had**.......... (*have*) a room of my own instead of sharing it with my sister.
1 I wish our teachers .... (*give*) us a bit less homework.
2 I wish I ....(*be*) the president, so I could really change things around here.
3 I wish you .... (*live*) a bit closer – we can never meet up apart from Skype.
4 I wish I .... (*know*) the answer to this last question.
5 I wish the weather .... (*not / be*) so cold – I didn't bring any warm clothes.
6 I wish my brother .... (*not / talk*) so loudly on the phone all the time.
7 Who wishes school exams .... (*not / exist*)?
8 I wish you .... (*not / take*) my things all the time without asking me.

17 Match the beginnings and ends of the sentence.

0 [d] I wish we were
1 [ ] They wish they had
2 [ ] She wishes she could
3 [ ] I wish they didn't make
4 [ ] Do you wish you knew
5 [ ] He wishes we texted
6 [ ] I wish politicians told
7 [ ] Do you wish you lived

a relax a bit more.
b lots of languages?
c fun of me all the time.
d on holiday.
e more free time.
f him a bit more often.
g in another country?
h the truth.

18 Complete the sentences with the correct form of the verbs in brackets.

0 I wish you ..**hadn't told**.. (*not / tell*) me the end of the film.
1 Do you wish you .... (*choose*) another subject?
2 Amanda wishes she .... (*not / buy*) that dress – it's not the colour she really wanted.
3 Tom wishes he .... (*have*) stop the penalty, but the player hit it too hard.
4 I wish Europe .... (*do*) more to help in previous international crises.
5 Frank wishes he .... (*not / say*) that to Betty – she got really angry …
6 Does your brother wish he .... (*go*) to live in Wales instead of Scotland?
7 Do you ever wish you .... (*be born*) in another period?
8 I really wish I .... (*study*) harder.
9 Kay wishes she .... (*not / eat*) such a hot curry last night.
10 I wish I .... (*remember*) your birthday.

19 Rewrite the sentences with *wish*.

0 I haven't got much free time. I would like to have more.
I ....**wish I had more free time**................ .
1 My friend Liz would like to be taller.
Liz ....
2 Judith regrets choosing chemistry at university.
She ....
3 I live in a small town, but I'd prefer to live in a big city.
I ....
4 My brother has to do Latin translations every evening, but he hates them.
He ....
5 My neighbours made a lot of noise last night. I couldn't get off to sleep.
I ....
6 She works in an office, but she really wants to be a TV presenter.
She ....
7 Jeff's sorry he didn't speak to his grandparents more often.
Jeff ....
8 My best friend Sophie sends me Snapchat messages during lessons and I don't like that.
I ....

206 Unit 8

SPEAKING SKILLS

APOLOGISING AND EXPRESSING REGRET

20 Complete the expressions with the words below.

forgive ▪ worry ▪ sorry ▪ accepted ▪ apologise ▪ matter ▪ known ▪ wanted ▪ wish

1 I'm so ……………… .
2 Don't ……………… about it.
3 I ……………… for all the trouble I caused.
4 Apology ……………… .
5 It doesn't ……………… .
6 Please ……………… me.
7 I wish I'd ……………… about it.
8 I ……………… to call, honestly.
9 I ……………… I'd been there for you.

21 Put the dialogue in order.

a ☐ Hey, you don't look so happy. What's up?
b ☐ Oh no, I completely forgot …
c ☐ Well, just this once …
d ☐ It's OK, it doesn't matter.
e ☐ No, that's really bad. Please forgive me.
f ☐ It was my birthday yesterday.

22 Write the dialogue.

A call / did / Beth / you / remember / to / ?
B I / something / knew / was / there / I / do / had / to / !
A it / it's / do / OK, / I'll
B I / I / call / to / and / forgot / then / wanted / just
A not / don't / problem / worry / it, / it's / about / a / big
B I / terrible / memory / really / my / apologise / for
A accepted / apology

23 Write a dialogue using the suggestions.

A Chiede a B se ha finito di usare il libro di matematica che gli / le ha prestato la scorsa settimana.
B Risponde di sì.
A Chiede se può restituirgli / le il libro domani perché gli / le serve per un compito.
B Risponde che c'è un piccolo problema.
A Chiede qual è.
B Dice che voleva chiamare A e spiegare di avere lasciato il libro sull'autobus. Dice che è veramente dispiaciuto / a.
A Dice che avrebbe voluto che B glielo avesse detto prima.
B Si scusa e promette di comprarne un'altra copia.
A Dice che non importa e che lo prenderà in prestito dalla biblioteca.

LISTENING SKILLS

24 Complete the sentences with the words below.

celebrations ▪ barrier ▪ land ▪ border ▪ cross

1 When Leicester City won the Premier League there were mass ……………… in the streets.
2 It will take us hours to ……………… London by car.
3 We have a small piece of ……………… near our house – we use it to grow vegetables.
4 There are a lot of armed guards on the ……………… between the two countries.
5 There is a large ……………… at the checkpoint between the two countries and they check your ID.

25 🔴 [2.24] Listen and answer the question.

How many different walls do you hear about?

26 🔴 [2.24] Listen again and decide if the sentences are true (T) or false (F). Correct the false ones.

1 The Berlin Wall divided Berlin for more than 30 years. T F
2 Over 100 people died trying to cross from East Berlin to the West. T F
3 After Berlin, other big walls started to come down. T F
4 The West Bank wall causes big difficulties for some. T F
5 The French government paid for the Calais wall. T F
6 The wall in Calais is 4 km long. T F
7 The walls in Cyprus separate two different ethnic groups. T F
8 Alphaville is an area of high criminality. T F

27 🔴 [2.24] Listen again and answer the questions.

1 How did Berliners celebrate the fall of their wall?
2 What was the Israeli government's justification for building the West Bank wall?
3 Why did the British government build a wall in France?
4 What is the purpose of the walls in Belfast?

ACADEMIC SKILLS

USING THE INTERNET FOR RESEARCH

28 Match the search suggestions to the examples and definitions below.

0. [a] Use unique or very specific terms where possible.
1. [ ] Use only keywords and no punctuation.
2. [ ] Avoid long and complicated questions.
3. [ ] Try different search engines.
4. [ ] The use of the article *the* can make a difference.
5. [ ] Use the base word.
6. [ ] Word order makes a difference.
7. [ ] Remember GIGO: Garbage In, Garbage Out (garbage = rubbish in American English).
8. [ ] Use a colon (:) and a domain name if you want to find results only on a specific site.

a. For example, if you want to go to the Cotswolds and spend July staying and doing lessons at your teacher's home, searching *English courses uk* gives 96,000,000 results, while *english homestay july cotswolds* gets 178,000.

b. If you enter a badly-worded or wrong search enquiry, you'll get a bad set of results back.

c. It may change your search results. For example, type *who* and you will get pages on the World Health Organization first. Type *the who* and you'll find out about a British rock band.

d. So, for example, a good search enquiry would be: *cheap accommodation London*.

e. Google is not the world's only search engine, so others, like Yahoo, may give better results.

f. Typing in *What are the exact requirements to do an exchange course with another student in the UK in the summer period?* will include a lot of irrelevant pages.

g. For example, *wind turbine energy* will give different results to *energy wind turbine*.

h. If you want some gossip about Beyoncé but know the best information is on guardian.com, enter *gossip beyoncé:guardian.com*.

i. For example, use *talk* rather than *talks* or *talking*, unless you are specifically searching for those terms.

29 Write the search terms for these questions.

0. My two-year old puppy has got big red eyes and is not running around and playing all the time. What's the matter with it? **puppy red eyes tired**
1. Who was the leader of China before the Communist Party took over in 1949?
2. I have a strong pain in my left shoulder when I do my tennis serve. What's causing it?
3. I remember that Mars bars looked and tasted completely different some years ago. They also looked much bigger. Is this true?
4. I heard there is a completely deserted town not far from San Francisco. What's it called?
5. I remember that a woman US politician was the victim of a shooting like Jo Cox, but survived the attack. What was her name?
6. I know there are a lot of Italian people working in the UK but I'm not sure exactly how many. What's the exact number?

30 Use the strategy described above to find information for a school project on European and world politics.

0. What was the name of the British policy towards Hitler in the years before World War II?
   ....*appeasement*..............................
1. How many countries are members of the EU?
   ....
2. Which two sides fought the Spanish Civil War from 1936?
   ....
3. Why was General Franco's government unpopular in Catalonia?
   ....
   ....
   ....
4. When did apartheid officially start in South Africa?
   ....
5. What was the name of the anti-apartheid activist who was freed in South Africa in 1990?
   ....
6. Where and when did the Easter Rising take place?
   ....
7. What did the Schengen Treaty guarantee for European citizens?
   ....
   ....
   ....

TOWARDS PRELIMINARY

EXAM STRATEGY

Speaking – Collaborative task

When you are doing a collaborative task, make sure you and your partner discuss all the options in the pictures and reach a conclusion at the end of the task. You need to make and respond to suggestions, discuss alternatives and agree or disagree in an appropriate way.

31 Read the conversation for the speaking text and decide which student does the task more successfully and why.

Examiner Your friend is going to spend six months in Britain. Discuss the things she will need during her stay and decide which she should take with her.

A OK. I think she'll need a dictionary. It'd be difficult without that. But, just a minute, she could use an app on her phone so she doesn't need to take a dictionary after all!

B No, you're right. I also think she'd better take an umbrella.

A Good idea! It rains a lot in Britain. She also needs a school bag: she'll go to lessons there and she'll have a lot of books.

B I agree.

A What about a camera? I think she can use her mobile phone, don't you? I don't think a camera's very important.

B Yes. She can take photos with her phone.

A OK then, so we've decided she should take her bag and the umbrella.

B Yes, OK.

32 Read the task and look at the pictures, then complete Student B's part of the dialogue. Remember to expand your answers and ask Student A's opinion.

Examiner A friend of yours has just moved to a new town and wants to make new friends. Look at the pictures and discuss the different things your friend can do to meet new people, then decide which is best.

A Right. I think Pete should get a dog. People with dogs often talk to each other!

B ....
....

A Yes, that's a good point but not everyone likes clubs. A youth club with some activities might be OK. What do you think?

B ....
....,
you know, organising a show and things like that …

A In my opinion you need special skills for that. Not everyone is good at acting! Do you agree that the youth club is the best option?

B ....
....

Let's go for that.

EXAM STRATEGY

Speaking – Discussion

When the examiner reads out a question, you should answer it together. Develop interaction with your partner by listening to what he / she says and commenting on it. Continue the discussion by exchanging opinions, giving examples and contributing new ideas.

33 Write your answers to the questions.

1 What's the best way to meet new friends in your town?
....

2 Do you think real life friends are more important than online friends?
....

3 Do you prefer to have a few close friends or lots of friends?
....

4 Do you prefer to talk to your friends or family about important things?
....

Unit 8   209

REVISE AND ROUND UP

1 **Correct the mistakes. Two sentences are correct.**

0 Would you go and live in a place if you ~~don't~~ know anybody there? **didn't**
1 If that is what really happened, you better apologise.
2 If you'll see a message, it'll be from me.
3 If I had a driving licence, I'd be able to go and see my friends every weekend.
4 If you would have told me, I'd have helped you.
5 If my cousins lived a bit closer, we'd meet more regularly.
6 If that'd been me, I'd said something to them.
7 If I don't know you better, I'd say you were lying.
8 Do you visit me if I go to the States next year to study?
9 If we have more time, we could visit the funfair.
10 If they had left earlier, they would catch the train.

2 **Rewrite the sentences so that they mean the same using the verbs in brackets.**

0 I think it's a good idea for you to speak to your teachers about your progress. (*should*)
   You **should talk to your teachers about your progress**.
1 I don't want you to arrive late this time. (*'d better*)
   You ....
2 I think it's important that Alice studies medicine at university. (*ought to*)
   Alice ....
3 They mustn't forget their English dictionary tomorrow. (*'d better*)
   They ....
4 It'd be a good idea for your mum to stop smoking. (*should*)
   Your mum ....
5 I think it's time for us to go now. (*ought to*)
   We ....
6 I think it's a good idea if you don't mention this for a few days. (*'d better not*)
   You ....
7 I think it's a bad idea for us to meet them this evening. (*should not*)
   We ....
8 I think it would be a good idea for him to let them know that he's bought the food for this evening. (*ought to*)
   He ....

3 **Choose the correct option.**

0 If Judith (*had*) / *have* seen us, she'd have said hello.
1 If I *have* / *had* more time in class tests, I wouldn't make so many mistakes.
2 I wish you *'d* / *'ve* told me earlier.
3 If you play like that tomorrow, you *'ll* / *'d* win, I'm sure.
4 You *ought to* / *ought* speak to your parents more often.
5 You *would* / *had* better explain to them straight away.
6 They *shouldn't to* / *shouldn't* copy during the exam.
7 If somebody *have* / *had* helped me with the homework, I *would have* / *had* got a better mark.
8 She wishes she *didn't decide* / *hadn't decided* not to go university.

4 **Rewrite the sentences using the words provided.**

0 I chose history as my main subject. I don't enjoy it.
   I wish **I hadn't chosen history as my main subject**.
1 I took lots of photos of my holiday, but not enough.
   I wish ....
2 I didn't send my aunt a birthday card because I didn't have time.
   If I ....
3 Lily left her boyfriend. She regrets it now.
   She wishes ....
4 We didn't want to eat a pizza so we didn't go to Joe's Place.
   If we ....
5 We had a little bit of time to talk, but then I had to run off and catch my train.
   I wish ....
6 Fiona wants to buy clothes, but she's spent all her money.
   She wishes ....
7 She didn't see the 'Stop' sign and she crashed into the other car.
   If she ....
8 They left the concert before the end and they regret it because they missed the best songs.
   They wish ....
9 My dad left school at 16 and now he's really sorry he did that.
   My dad wishes ....

210 Units 7–8

5 Complete the interview with the verbs below.

be (x2) • have (x2) • complain • ask • make • spend • be able • do (x2) • say • want

A Marty – you're a regular user of social media. What experiences have you had?

B Good and bad. I wish there ⁰ **was** more protection in general. And I wish people ¹............................ so many silly or unfriendly comments. A friend wrote something unkind about me and now she wishes ²............................ that – too late!

A So you haven't enjoyed your experiences …

B Oh no, I love the interaction with friends. In fact I just wish I ³............................ more time to follow everything. And if I ⁴............................ a faster connection, I ⁵............................ to download everything at once. And then my friends ⁶............................ that I don't reply to their comments and videos.

A You should ⁷............................ your parents to get fibre optic broadband …

B If I ⁸............................ that, they ⁹............................ 'And what about your schoolwork? You shouldn't ¹⁰............................ all your time on the internet.'

A Do you interact with your parents on social media?

B They're not on social media. But even if they ¹¹............................, I ¹²............................ to do that.

6 TRANSLATION Translate the sentences into English.

0 Ti conviene partire presto per il concerto – ci sarà un sacco di gente.
   You'd better leave early for the concert – there'll be lots of people.
1 Se avessi tempo finirei questo libro subito.
2 Dovresti controllare il telefono – non riesco a mandarti SMS.
3 Dovrebbero fare più esercizio fisico – sono sempre davanti alla TV.
4 Se l'avessero saputo, me lo avrebbero detto in quel momento.
5 Vorrei non aver comprato queste scarpe.
6 Farai meglio a non dirlo a nessuno.
7 Vorrei poter stare a casa oggi.
8 È meglio se prenoti l'albergo online.
9 Che cosa avresti detto se fossi stato al mio posto?

CONCEPT CHECK

Read the sentences and answer the questions.

1 *If you call them, they'll tell you the start time.*

(Answer Yes / No / Your own words)
0 Do we already know the start time? **No**
1 Do we need to call to know the start time?
2 Am I absolutely sure you will call them?

2 *If he made them a decent offer, they'd probably accept.*

(Answer Yes / No / Your own words)
0 Do I think he will definitely make them an offer? **No**
1 Is it probable that he will make them an offer?
2 Would they accept if the offer was OK?
3 What is the condition for them to accept the offer?

3 *You should be more careful of what you download.*

(Answer Yes / No)
0 Do I think you're careful with downloads? **No**
1 Am I prohibiting you from downloading files?
2 Am I giving you advice?

4 *If the weather had been a bit better yesterday, we'd have stayed out until late.*

(Answer Yes / No)
0 Was the weather good yesterday? **No**
1 Did we stay out until late?
2 Did we want to stay out until late?

5 *I wish the people upstairs didn't make so much noise in the evenings.*

(Answer Yes / No)
0 Do I live in a flat? **Yes**
1 Do people live in a flat above me?
2 Do they make a lot of noise?
3 Do they disturb me?

6 *Aly wishes he hadn't been rude to his neighbour.*

(Answer Yes / No)
0 Was Aly rude to the neighbour? **Yes**
1 Is he sorry for what he did?
2 Is it too late to change the situation?
3 Does he regret the situation?

→ See **GRAMMAR REFERENCE** pages 119, 120, 121

9 Pure genius!

GRAMMAR PRACTICE

The passive: Present and past simple

Choose the correct option.

- We use the passive form when the person or thing that does the action is obvious or not important, or we don't know the person or thing that does the action.
When we want to specify who or what does the action we use *by* / *from*.
- To make the present simple passive we use the *present* / *past* simple of *be* + the past participle of the main verb.
- To make the past simple passive we use the *present* / *past* simple of *be* + the past participle of the main verb.

See **GRAMMAR REFERENCE** page 122

1 Write sentences in the present simple passive.

0 the windows / clean / every week
   The windows are cleaned every week.
1 passengers / request / to remain in their seats
2 cash / not accept / in some shops in the US
3 internet orders / send out / every morning
4 all calls / monitor / to improve customer service
5 here cars / wash / by hand, not by a machine
6 students / request / to wear their school uniform at all times
7 mobile phones / not allow / in the exam room
8 guests' rooms / clean / between 10 and 11 every day

2 Complete the sentences with the verbs below.

use • not / check • ~~find~~ • play
pay • accept • record • make

0 If your wallet ...**is found**..., we will get in touch.
1 The game *petanque* .... a lot in France.
2 Euros .... in some big stores in London.
3 Top sports stars .... a lot of money.
4 This device .... to memorise the shape of someone's face.
5 Glass .... from sand.
6 Videocalls .... by some government agencies.
7 Passports .... always .... when you go from one EU country to another.

3 Rewrite the sentences using the present simple passive.

0 People send a lot of messages on instant messaging apps.
   A lot of messages are sent on instant messaging apps.
1 People spend billions on Christmas presents in the UK.
2 Cars injure 10,000 UK pedestrians every year.
3 People produce around 300 million tonnes of rubbish every year in the UK.
4 Nearly 1 billion people speak English worldwide.
5 They sell those T-shirts at the market.
6 Our teachers tell us to do our homework on time.

4 Write sentences in the past simple passive.

0 our local post office / rob / last week
   Our local post office was robbed last week.
1 I / tell / you wanted to see me
2 when / that tweet / send / ?
3 this picture / take / by a newspaper reporter
4 we / show / a film about healthy eating at school
5 where / your parents / teach Spanish / ?
6 my friend / give / a nice present by the class when she moved to a new school

5 Complete the sentences with the past simple passive of the verbs in brackets.

0 She ...**was paid**... (*pay*) £10 for getting 10,000 views on her web channel last month.
1 I .... (*meet*) by my host family at the airport.
2 My team .... (*beat*) by the favourites in the final.
3 We .... (*amaze*) by people's kindness in Peru.
4 This picture .... (*sign*) by the artist herself.
5 My brother .... (*tell*) by his teachers to study harder.
6 The Italian lira .... (*replace*) by the euro in 2002.

GRAMMAR PRACTICE

6 Choose the correct option.

0 The telephone *is* / *was* invented by Alexander Bell.
1 Penicillin *is* / *was* used to kill all kinds of bacteria.
2 Around 500 emails *are* / *were* sent by the average office worker every month.
3 The new club *is* / *was* opened by a famous actor in May.
4 Pop concerts *are* / *were* often held at San Siro.
5 Why *aren't* / *weren't* we told about the change in plans? We arrived late because of that.
6 Some cheese *is* / *was* made from goat's milk – it's really tasty.

7 Put the words in the correct order.

0 smartphone / your / where / made / was / ?
Where was your smartphone made?
1 given / you / were / when / that / book / ?
2 letter / who / this / was / by / written / ?
3 bike / damaged / was / how / your / ?
4 school / decided / was / in / meeting / the / what / ?
5 president / made / she / when / was / ?
6 why / film / banned / was / this / ?

8 Complete the sentences with the past simple or present simple passive of the verbs below.

~~stop~~ ▪ steal ▪ direct ▪ knock down ▪ find ▪ hold ▪ make ▪ sing ▪ produce ▪ show ▪ conduct

0 One of my friends **was stopped** by the police last night.
1 My sister .... managing director of her company last month.
2 70% of the world's electronic devices .... in China.
3 This film .... by Ben Affleck.
4 £1m of jewellery .... in that robbery last week.
5 A lot of American TV series .... on British TV.
6 My passport and wallet .... in a waste basket near the station.
7 The experiment .... at the CERN laboratory last April.
8 The hit song *Yesterday* .... by The Beatles in the 1960s.
9 The Berlin Wall .... in 1989, nearly 30 years after it first went up.
10 The 2012 Olympics .... in Beijing, China.

9 Match the beginnings and ends of the sentences and put the verbs below in the correct form.

shipwreck ▪ make (x2) ▪ disqualify ▪ invent ▪ ~~produce~~ ▪ give

0 [a] Coffee
1 [ ] *Robinson Crusoe* is about a man who
2 [ ] Fiat cars
3 [ ] One of the leading roles in *Supernatural*
4 [ ] Many medicines
5 [ ] The first computer with icons
6 [ ] Maria Sharapova

a in many parts of South America.
b from tennis for one year for taking banned drugs.
c from tropical plants.
d by Apple Macintosh.
e to Jensen Ackles.
f on a desert island.
g in Italy and 15 different countries.

Coffee is produced in many parts of South America.

10 Complete the text with the correct passive form of the verbs below.

throw away ▪ ~~invent~~ ▪ keep ▪ damage ▪ use ▪ heat ▪ kill

Pasteurisation ⁰ **was invented** by French scientist Louis Pasteur in 1864. He found that a lot of wine ¹.................. by bacteria and on many occasions it ².................. because it tasted bad. He discovered that if wine ³.................. to quite a high temperature, the bacteria ⁴.................. off and the wine remained drinkable for much longer. Later the same technique ⁵.................. by Pasteur with milk and new filtering techniques mean that that nowadays milk ⁶.................. often .... for weeks without going bad.

11 Correct the mistakes. Two sentences are correct.

0 I ~~wasn't informing~~ about the risks. **wasn't informed**
1 This invention were made in 2010.
2 My phone was stolen last week.
3 All students were telling to bring their gym shoes.
4 Students are not allowing to use dictionaries in the exam.
5 Most people's salaries are paying at the end of every month.
6 I'm often asking that question by my teachers.
7 It was surprising to hear the good news.
8 All the food is freshly cooked from our chef.

Unit 9   213

READING SKILLS

12 Match the words to the definitions.

1. ☐ indestructible
2. ☐ target
3. ☐ object
4. ☐ amusing
5. ☐ curved
6. ☐ bullseye
7. ☐ double-decker
8. ☐ cast iron
9. ☐ carriage
10. ☐ symbol
11. ☐ pillar

a Something you want to achieve.
b Something that makes you laugh because it's funny.
c A general word to refer to a thing.
d Something that represents something else.
e The place where people sit when a horse is transporting them.
f A shape or line that is not straight but rounded.
g A strong and resistant metal.
h Something that cannot be broken or destroyed.
i Something in the shape of a column.
j The exact centre of something.
k Something with two floors or layers.

13 [2.25] Read and listen to the article. Then answer the question.

Which of the following items are *not* discussed by the three people: letterboxes, phone boxes, red buses, train stations, transport company logos?

14 Read the text again and decide if the sentences are true (T), false (F) or doesn't say (DS).

1. The article is focused on objects that we don't pay much attention to each day. ☐T ☐F ☐DS
2. The Underground symbol was created by two people. ☐T ☐F ☐DS
3. The font and format on the logo have been changed several times since its introduction. ☐T ☐F ☐DS
4. Some designers have copied the Underground symbol. ☐T ☐F ☐DS
5. British post boxes have a different colour to most of their European counterparts. ☐T ☐F ☐DS
6. The post boxes were specifically designed to be impossible to damage. ☐T ☐F ☐DS
7. The most popular model of London bus is the Routemaster. ☐T ☐F ☐DS
8. Fraser thinks that the new models are less practical because they have doors. ☐T ☐F ☐DS

CAPITAL DESIGN

This week we asked several London professionals to research iconic designs in the capital among those things we see and use all the time but don't even notice after a while. And here's what they
5 *came up with.*

SUSAN, ARCHITECT, EARLS COURT
I love the London Underground symbol. The concept was actually created over 100 years ago by commercial manager Frank Pick and then designed by a graphic artist, Edward Johnston.
10 They worked on the idea of a target or *bullseye* and it was eventually called the *roundel*. The use of sans-serif capital letters in the text was decided a few years after the original design. The logo was used in all
15 stations from the 1930s on and is instantly recognised by travellers. Many variations, some of them strange and amusing, have been created by other designers over
20 the years.

MAURICE, GRAPHIC DESIGNER, FINCHLEY
For me it has to be the post box. Think about it: they've been used since 1852, just after the first postage stamps were introduced and had created an obvious need for them! Their beauty

15 Read the text again and answer the questions.

1. What was Edward Johnson's profession?
2. What was the specific name that the designers gave to the London Underground symbol?
3. What have designers done with the Underground logo in the past?
4. Why were post boxes created?
5. What are British post boxes made of?
6. How many parts are they made up of?
7. What are the two main differences between British and many European letterboxes?
8. What was the purpose of the rear platform on buses?
9. What is the main difference between the old and the more recent versions of the famous red bus?
10. Where can you still travel on the old-style bus?
11. Why do you think they kept the buses on these lines?

CLASSICS

25 is their simple but elegant design. They're made of a cast-iron body with a separate top section. They are different from their European
30 counterparts because they are not fixed on the wall, but they're pillars in the street and are painted bright red unlike in most other European countries, which use yellow. They look solid, almost indestructible, and if a design hasn't been
35 changed in nearly 200 years, then it's obviously good.

FRASER, ARTIST, HAMMERSMITH

I think London's best design feature is the iconic red bus. They were introduced in 1911, when horse-drawn carriages were finally stopped. The model everyone knows is the double-decker
40 Routemaster, which had an open platform at the back and let people jump on and off when they wanted, even between stops. It had a great design, nice curved lines, together with its distinctive pantone 485 red colour. Later models, with doors,
45 were much less elegant and in some cases less practical. Luckily, some of the old buses have been preserved and you can still take one, for example on Route 15 from Trafalgar Square to the
50 Tower of London.

16 Find the words or phrases in the text that mean the same as these.

1 representative (Intro) ....
2 pay attention to (Intro) ....
3 suggested (Intro) ....
4 idea (Susan) ....
5 in the end (Susan) ....
6 immediately (Susan) ....
7 strong (Maurice) ....
8 almost (Maurice) ....
9 aspect (Fraser) ....
10 highly representative (Fraser) ....
11 pulled (Fraser) ....
12 characteristic (Fraser) ....
13 stylish (Fraser) ....

VOCABULARY

GADGETS AND CREATIVITY

17 Identify the objects using the words below.

tin opener • corkscrew • colander • cheese grater • kettle

0 It's used for opening food containers that are made of metal and quite difficult to open at times.
tin opener
1 A type of electric jug that is used to boil water.
2 Unless you've got one of those special pots, you'll need one of these to drain your pasta or rice.
3 You really need one of these, especially if you like a lot of parmesan cheese on your pasta.
4 This is usually made of metal and is used to remove the stopper from a wine bottle for example.

18 Look at the pictures and say what the objects are used for.

0 a teapot: *This is used for pouring tea.*
1 salt and pepper mills: ....
2 cutlery: ....

19 Complete the questions.

0 Who ......**was**...... the ballpoint pen ......**invented**...... by? (László and György Bíró)
1 Who .... the book *Emma* .... by? (Jane Austen)
2 Who .... Guggenheim Bilbao Museum .... by? (Frank Gehry)
3 Who .... *Guernica* .... by? (Picasso)
4 Who .... *The Lord of the Rings* films .... by? (Peter Jackson)
5 Who .... *The Kiss* statue .... by? (Auguste Rodin)
6 Who .... the hit songs *Mamma Mia* and *Waterloo* .... by? (Abba)

Unit 9 215

GRAMMAR PRACTICE

The passive: Present perfect

Complete the rule.
To make the present perfect passive we use the
.... of *be* + the past participle of the main verb.

➡ See **GRAMMAR REFERENCE** page 122

20 🔊 Put the words in the correct order.

0 recently / your / has / updated / been / antivirus / ?
Has your antivirus been updated recently?
1 book / ordered / been / has / your / you / for
2 yet / given / I / money / my / pocket / haven't / been
3 touched / this / hasn't / been / food
4 textbook / why / our / changed / has / been / ?
5 new / released / their / single / been / has / just
6 moved / has / burger / the / restaurant / been
7 passport / stamped / has / been / my / times / twenty
8 often / song / covered / this / been / has / too

21 🔊 Complete the sentences with the verbs in brackets.

0 This operation **'s been performed** (*perform*) only a few times up to now.
1 I .... (*tell*) you want to join a band!
2 My sister .... (*promote*) at work.
3 Tomorrow's match .... (*cancel*).
4 This film .... (*not / advertise*) very well.
5 .... these exercises .... (*check*)?
6 Ryan Gosling's new film .... (*nominate*) for an Oscar.
7 A new app .... (*introduce*) that does your homework for you.
8 Our bedroom .... (*not / tidy up*) for at least a month.

22 🔊 Rewrite the sentences in the present perfect passive.

0 They've finally cleaned their room.
Their room has finally been cleaned.
1 She's warned him about the danger.
2 The police have caught the robber.
3 We have delivered your parcel.
4 We have accepted your application for a place on the course.
5 The organisers have confirmed the date and time of the match.

6 Our teacher hasn't given us our test back yet.
7 They've recently released a new kind of tablet.
8 Someone has given her a great present.

23 🔊 Choose the correct option.

0 We (*haven't been*) / *weren't* informed of the changes yet. I think they should tell us.
1 This palace *hasn't been* / *wasn't* built in the eighteenth century but in the seventeenth.
2 My favourite teacher *has been* / *was* moved to another school last year.
3 *Have you been* / *Were you* vaccinated against malaria for your trip next month?
4 Sorry we're a bit a late – we*'ve been* / *were* held up at customs at the airport.
5 That film you wanted to see *has just been* / *was just* released. Let's go and see it.
6 Driverless cars *have first been* / *were first* tested by Google in 2015.
7 We *haven't been* / *weren't* contacted last night.
8 Oh no! My phone *has been* / *was* stolen!

24 🔊 Complete the text with the past simple passive or the present perfect passive.

The TV has come a long way since it ⁰**was invented** (*invent*) by German student Paul Gottlieb Nipkow in 1884. Since then over a billion TVs ¹.......................... (*produce*) and the way people watch TV ².......................... completely .... (*transform*) over this time. It's amazing if you think that it was only in the 1970s that more colour televisions ³.......................... (*sell*) than black and white sets. In the UK there were only four channels right up to the 1990s, but since then many thousands of specialty channels ⁴.......................... (*set up*) for all kinds of tastes and interests.
In the early 2000s the traditional TVs with big cathode ray tubes ⁵.......................... (*replace*) by elegant flatscreen TVs, which ⁶.......................... (*make*) in just a few giant factories in China.
In George Orwell's book *1984*, the flatscreen TV ⁷.......................... (*use*) by Big Brother to watch what people were doing in their own homes. This nightmare scenario ⁸.......................... (*make*) a reality now by new smart TV apps that record what people like doing and their habits.
In the last few years, 3-D TVs ⁹.......................... (*introduce*) as the move towards complete virtual reality continues.

SPEAKING SKILLS

DESCRIBING OBJECTS

25 Complete the sentences with the words below.

what ▪ work ▪ used ▪ looks ▪ made ▪ called ▪
thing ▪ remember ▪ small ▪ sort ▪ size

1 There's a .... of handle at the top.
2 ....'s that?
3 How does it .... ?
4 It .... like a calculator but it's not.
5 What's it .... for?
6 What's it .... again?
7 It's got a .... like a USB stick that you use to load it.
8 It's about the same .... as a wallet.
9 I don't .... the name.
10 What's it .... of?
11 Is it big or .... ?

26 Complete the dialogues with expressions from exercise 25 (adapt them if necessary).

Dialogue 1

A ¹..................................... on your tablet?
B It's a brand new app called Prisma. I downloaded it yesterday.
A ²..................................... ?
B Making your own paintings!
A ³..................................... ?
B You just take one of your photos and enter it into the app. Your photo becomes a painting.
A Awesome. ⁴..................................... ?
B Prisma. It only costs a couple of pounds.

Dialogue 2

A OK, let's play a guessing game. I think of a gadget and you try to guess what it is – OK?
B OK. ¹..................................... ?
A Quite small.
B ²..................................... ?
A Metal and some plastic.
B ³..................................... ?
A For finding your way around.
B OK, I've got it. It's a satnav for the car.
A No, ⁴..................................... a 50 pence coin, so it's smaller than a satnav.
B Can you help me a bit?
A Well, ⁵..................................... like a pointer to guide you.
B A pointer? OK, I've got it – it's a compass.
A Yeah, that's right. You took your time …

LISTENING SKILLS

27 Match the English to the Italian terms.

1 ☐ charge   a tubo di scappamento
2 ☐ exhaust pipe   b convertire
3 ☐ carbon dioxide c immagazzinare, tenere
4 ☐ convert   d fotosintesi
5 ☐ store   e lattina
6 ☐ photosynthesis f caricare
7 ☐ tin can   g lampade LED
8 ☐ LED lamps   h raccogliere
9 ☐ collect   i anidride carbonica

28 [2.26] Listen to the interview and answer the questions.

1 How many people are interviewed on the programme?
2 What do they have in common?

29 [2.26] Listen again and choose the correct option.

1 Which two pieces of information are true for Sasha?
  A Her idea is not complicated.
  B Her invention charges a phone in a few hours.
  C The device stores energy for 24 hours.
  D The device can be charged up to 1000 times.
  E Her device has been tested in mobile phones.
2 Which two pieces of information are true for Parvez?
  A He invented a new component to reduce fuel consumption by cars.
  B His device creates oxygen.
  C He is already selling his invention on the market.
  D He has been given an award for his invention.
  E He has sold the concept to a car maker.

30 [2.26] Listen again and answer the questions.

1 What is a frustrating situation according to Sasha?
2 How long does it take to charge tablets and laptops?
3 How long does Sasha's device take to do this?
4 How long does it take to charge her device?
5 Apart from quick charging, what's the other main advantage of Sasha's invention?
6 What happened when the device was used inside a mobile phone?
7 Why did Parvez decide to make his device?
8 What is it similar to in the way it works?
9 What does it look like?
10 Why has Parvez not accepted car makers' offers?

Unit 9   217

TOWARDS PRELIMINARY

> **EXAM STRATEGY**
>
> **Listening – Multiple choice (gist)**
>
> When you are listening to the short dialogues, concentrate on general ideas, opinions and attitudes, not on facts or specific information. Read the questions carefully before you listen so that you know what information you need to listen for. The first time you listen eliminate one of the options; on the second listening, choose between the remaining two.

31 Match the verbs to their meanings.

0 [c] suggest   4 [ ] disagree
1 [ ] advise   5 [ ] complain
2 [ ] persuade 6 [ ] feel
3 [ ] agree   7 [ ] decide

a express dissatisfaction
b choose after thinking
c express an idea for a plan
d have the same opinion
e convince
f have the opposite opinion
g experience an emotion
h say what is best to do

32 [2.27] Read and listen to the example, then choose the best option.

0 You hear two friends talking about a television programme. What did the boy like best about it?
   A the action scenes
   B the story
   (C) the last part

Example

Boy Did you watch *Black Planet*?
Girl Of course! I wouldn't miss it. It's my favourite programme. I didn't think this episode was as good as some of the others, though. There wasn't much action in it.
Boy Not until the end. I really wasn't expecting that ending. It was a total surprise. I thought it was brilliant!
Girl You're right there. The ending was really good.
Boy The rest of it was a bit slow and nothing much happened. I can't wait to see the next episode. What's going to happen now?

The correct answer is C.

33 Read the audioscript in exercise 32 and do the following tasks.

1 Underline the part in the audioscript that contains the correct answer.
2 Look at the other two options and explain why they are incorrect.

34 [2.28] Listen to the dialogues and choose the correct option.

0 You hear two friends talking about a birthday. What does the girl suggest?
   (A) a day out
   B a picnic
   C a party

1 You hear two friends talking about shopping. How does the boy feel?
   A angry
   B cheerful
   C bored

2 You hear two friends talking about food. What do they agree about?
   A Running makes you hungry.
   B Fruit is a healthy snack.
   C Breakfast is an important meal.

3 You hear two friends talking about sport. What is the girl doing?
   A complaining
   B offering
   C warning

4 You hear two friends talking about homework. What does the girl advise the boy to do?
   A Do all the work by himself.
   B Change partner.
   C Speak to the teacher.

5 You hear two friends talking about a concert. What do they disagree about?
   A The band's music.
   B Watching concerts online.
   C Going to live concerts.

TOWARDS PRELIMINARY

EXAM STRATEGY

Writing – An article or a story

In the second part of the writing test, you can choose to write either an article or a story.

Article
- Read the question carefully and focus on the questions.
- Think about your answers to the questions and use them as the basis of your email.
- Remember to include a short introduction at the beginning and finish with a brief conclusion.

Story
- Either the title or the first line is given and you must write the story.
- Plan your story before you start writing.
- Think about the sequence of events and use linkers to connect them.
- Write your story using past tenses.

36 Choose either the article or the story. Write your answer in 100 words.

1 Article

ARTICLES WANTED!

A GREAT DAY OUT

What makes a good day out?
Is it the people,
the place
or exciting activities?

Why is it important
to go out with friends or family?

Tell us what you think!

2 Story
Write a story that begins with the sentence:
I took the parcel into the house and opened it.

35 The paragraphs below come from an article and a short story. Divide the paragraphs into the two groups and then put them in order.

1 an article: *My Lucky Day*
  1 [E] 2 [ ] 3 [ ] 4 [ ]

2 a short story that begins: *I went downstairs and opened the door.*
  1 [ ] 2 [ ] 3 [ ] 4 [ ]

A My day got even better in the evening because I beat my brother at our favourite video game and we had my favourite food for dinner.

B Funny joke! But at least they weren't burglars! I finally went back to bed and had a good sleep.

C Later on a friend helped me with my maths homework because I'd bought her the sweets in the morning.

D I looked around but there was nobody. I felt a bit nervous because there had been some robberies in the area. I went back inside and went back to bed.

E My day started really well because on the way to school I found a 5 euro note in the street. I went to the shop and bought a bag of sweets to share with my classmates.

F Then I heard some voices. They sounded familiar. I looked out the window and saw three of my friends laughing and running away.

G On the way home, I couldn't believe it when I saw my favourite basketball player in a shop. He signed his autograph for me!

H And then there was another knock on the door. That's when I started to feel scared. Who could it be? I wasn't sure if I should go to bed or call the police.

Unit 9   219

10 In the news

GRAMMAR PRACTICE

Reported speech: Statements

Complete the rules with the words below.
somebody else ▪ past ▪ person ▪ reporting ▪ that

- We use reported speech when we tell somebody what .... has said.
- In reported speech there is always a .... verb (*say*, *tell*, *explain*, etc.) and sometimes there is the .... the speaker was talking to.
- When the reporting verb is in the ...., we often change the tense of the verb of the original direct speech. Other words may also need to change, such as: *Gina said, 'This is my book.'* becomes *Gina said that .... was her book.*

→ See **GRAMMAR REFERENCE** page 122

1 Transform the sentences into direct speech.

0 Yousef told me he was leaving at 5 am.
   I'm leaving at 5 am.
1 Hannah told us she didn't feel very well.
2 Marcus promised he would call us later.
3 Laetitia promised she would send us all the photos she had taken at the party the day before.
4 I told him I couldn't remember his name.
5 He explained that he was going to book the trip.
6 Our parents said that we had to get back before 11.

2 Transform the sentences into reported speech. Use the reporting verb *said*.

0 Teacher: I'm really pleased with your homework.
   The teacher said she was really pleased with my homework.
1 Jill: I'm not going to call Tim if he doesn't call me.
2 Andy: I can't make it for 3 o'clock.
3 Fiona: I don't want anything for my birthday.
4 Gus and Helen: We haven't invited anyone to our party yet.
5 Dele: My phone isn't working, so I can't text anybody.
6 Rosie: I've seen the TV series before.
7 Nigel: I must finish my project this evening.
8 Vincent: I can do the shopping this afternoon.

3 Put the words in the correct order.

0 late / me / told / she / was / she
   She told me she was late.
1 Garth / me / told / wasn't / he / sure / today / come / would / he / school / to
2 teacher / Friday / us / would / have / test / a / we / on / told / the
3 say / what / time / leaving / she / was / Gina / didn't
4 couldn't / the man / repair / shop / tablet / my / he / explained / the / in / that
5 friends / me / liked / they / told / my / shirt / new / my
6 promised / day / she / she / visit / would / us / one
7 know / the / told / I / teacher / I / didn't / question / his / answer / the / to
8 tired / he / said / stop / to / few / a / needed / for / minutes / and / was / he

4 Transform these quotes into reported speech.

0 Marcus Tullius Cicero (philosopher): If you have a garden and a library, you have everything you need.
   Cicero said that if you had a garden and a library you had everything you needed.
1 Forrest Gump (film character): Life is like a box of chocolates. You never know what you're going to get.
2 Mae West (US actress): You only live once, but if you do it right, once is enough.
3 Elbert Hubbard (writer): A friend is someone who knows all about you and still loves you.
4 Friedrich Nietzsche (philosopher): We hear only those questions for which we are in a position to find answers.
5 Oscar Wilde (writer): The proper aim is to try and reconstruct society on such a basis that poverty will be impossible.
6 Marilyn Monroe (actress): I believe that everything happens for a reason.
7 Ayn Rand (writer): You can avoid reality, but you cannot avoid the consequences of avoiding reality.
8 Madeleine Albright (ex-US Secretary of State): It took me quite a long time to develop a voice, and now that I have it, I am not going to be silent.
9 Mahatma Gandhi (leader of Indian independence movement): The future depends on what we do in the present.

GRAMMAR PRACTICE

5 **Write the dialogue between Li and her mother.**

> The argument started when Li told her mother she was just going out for a bit. Her mother told her she couldn't because she had to finish her homework. Li said she'd been at home all afternoon and wanted to go out for a few hours. Li's mum told her she wasn't doing very well in maths and had to spend more time on it.
> She explained that school was really important for Li's future. Li agreed, but said that she was also young and needed to live her life a little. She promised her mum she would do a couple of hours' study when she got back. Li's mum told her that wasn't good enough and that she was going to speak to her father. Li said she wasn't worried about that because her father at least understood her problems a little. Li's mum said she was tired of arguing and that they would speak later.
>
> **Li** *Mum, I'm just going out for bit.*

6 **Report the dialogue between the two friends.**

Irina I didn't enjoy the meal.
Ross I found it quite good.
Irina What? The food was horrible and badly cooked. I'm going to write a review about it.
Ross I don't know what you're talking about. My pizza was really tasty.
Irina Well, I think the service was slow and the waiter was quite rude to me on a couple of occasions as well.
Ross Really, I didn't notice that.
Irina I'm not surprised. You were too busy eating pizza and drinking cola!
Ross That's not true!
Irina Mmm … Anyway, I must go home. I've just had a text from Mum and she wants me to go back home straight away.
Ross OK, I'll call you later. I'm sorry about the meal.
Irina It's all right, but I will decide where we go next time, OK?
Ross That's fine, but you'll have to pay …
Irina But I paid this time.

Irina said that she hadn't enjoyed the meal.

Reported speech: *say* and *tell*

Choose the correct option.
If you want to include who the speaker spoke to, you can use **tell** with to / without to or **say to**.
If you do not want to include who the speaker spoke to, you can use **say** (but not **tell**). You *have to / can* omit *that*.

➡ See **GRAMMAR REFERENCE** page 123

7 **Complete the sentences with the correct form of *say* or *tell*.**

0 We ......**told**...... him the pizza was this evening.
1 They didn't .... what train they were taking.
2 Janice .... she would call us later.
3 I .... you the test would be difficult.
4 I think they .... 3 pm outside the school gates.
5 My teacher .... me my story was really good.
6 I .... to you we'd be late and I was right.
7 Nobody .... me we needed to bring our ID card.
8 Pat .... she hoped she could make it in time.
9 They forgot to .... me the dates of their holiday.
10 Harry .... to everyone that the party was off.

8 **Transform the sentences into reported speech.**

0 She said, 'I can do this for you.'
   She said she could do that for me.
1 She said, 'I can't come to the party next weekend.'
2 Frank said, 'I didn't understand the lesson yesterday.'
3 Pat said, 'We have to be careful in the next match.'
4 The teacher said to me, 'You're not studying enough to pass the exam next June.'
5 Kyle said, 'I think this film is better than the one we saw last month.'
6 'You'll have to train hard for the next two years,' my coach told me.

Unit 10   221

READING SKILLS

9 Match the expressions to the definitions.

1. ☐ assumption
2. ☐ nitrate
3. ☐ court
4. ☐ to expose
5. ☐ prize
6. ☐ to hire
7. ☐ to pollute
8. ☐ to praise

a This is when you employ somebody for a fixed period of time.
b This is when you speak positively of someone's performance.
c This is a chemical compound often found naturally in foods but dangerous in high quantities.
d This is when you put dangerous substances into the air or the land.
e This is when you automatically think that you know something is true even if you do not know it for sure.
f This is a group of people who have to make a decision on whether somebody is guilty of a crime or not.
g This is what you win when you come first or do well in a competition.
h This is when you make something public.

10 [2.29] Read and listen to the article and answer the question.

What is the main focus of the article?
1 industrial pollution
2 living in rural USA
3 a small newspaper taking on big companies
4 a strange decision by the Pulitzer Prize jury

11 Read the first two paragraphs and decide if the sentences are true (T), false (F) or doesn't say (DS). Correct the false ones.

1 *The Storm Lake Times* is based in New York. T F DS
2 *The Storm Lake Times* has untidy offices. T F DS
3 *The Storm Lake Times* is in the same newspaper group as the *New York Times*. T F DS
4 The newspaper normally reports only local events. T F DS
5 The newspaper always sells more than 3,000 copies. T F DS
6 The newspaper was voted the best US newspaper of the year in 2017. T F DS
7 The newspaper exposed pollution by local farming companies. T F DS

David takes on Goliath – pt 2

A The offices of the *The Storm Lake Times* in Iowa are not very tidy. There are piles of old newspapers and magazines everywhere – on the floor, on desks, even on chairs. This is very different from the fashionable and tidy designer offices of *The New York Times*. Iowa is a quiet and, some people might say, quite boring part of rural America. Not much happens here and even the newspaper's owner admitted that they put stories about babies, dogs, fires or car accidents on every front page because nothing really exciting or drastic really happens.

B *The Storm Lake Times* employs ten people. It is published twice a week and, in a good week, sells over 3,000 copies. So that's quite normal, but what is extraordinary is that the newspaper was awarded the prestigious Pulitzer Prize in Editorial Writing in 2017. The reason: a brave campaign against pollution of local water by big agricultural companies in Iowa. The newspaper investigated and found that nitrates used by agriculture were going directly into the water supply. Newspaper owner Art Cullen explained in one of his editorials that anyone with eyes and a nose knew that Iowa had the dirtiest water in America.

12 Read the last three paragraphs and answer the questions.

1 Why was the campaign about water pollution difficult for the newspaper?
2 What was Art Cullen's reaction to losing friends and sponsors because of the campaign?
3 What was the decision of the court about water pollution by agricultural companies?
4 Who paid for the legal defence of the agricultural companies?
5 What was Cullen's reaction to the court's decision?
6 What three things did the jury appreciate about his work?

222   Unit 10

C In a predominantly farming area, this was a risky story to expose. Indeed, the newspaper lost some of its regular advertisers and there were rumors that the newspaper might close.
30 Cullen also lost a few of his friends, but his reply was that it was a newspaper's job to challenge people's assumptions and that that was what every good newspaper should do.

D These problems didn't damage their circulation
35 numbers and in the end the local water company took legal action against the agricultural industry for polluting the water. A court recognised there was a nitrate contamination problem, but did not find the
40 agricultural companies directly responsible and said that they couldn't prove it. The companies had hired expensive lawyers to defend their position, but it was never clear where the money for this had come from.

E
45 Cullen was disappointed by the outcome, but felt the campaign had been worthwhile because it had brought the problem to everybody's attention. Cullen's writing certainly caught the eye of the Pulitzer jury, who praised
50 the paper for their 'tenacious reporting, impressive expertise and engaging writing that successfully challenged powerful corporate agricultural interests in Iowa'. This story is an inspiring example of how good journalism can
55 change the world.

13 Read the sentences from the text. Decide if they are fact (F) or opinion (O) in the context of the article.
1 Iowa itself is a quiet and, to be honest, quite boring part of rural America. F O
2 *The Storm Lake Times* employs ten people, is published twice a week and, in a good one, sells over 3,000 copies. F O
3 [They] found that nitrates used by agriculture were finishing up in the water supply. F O
4 The companies had hired expensive lawyers to defend their position. F O
5 The story is an inspiring example. F O

VOCABULARY

MEDIA VERBS

14 Look at these media words from the text. Write the Italian translation. Which words are false friends?
0 magazine ....
1 prove ....
2 circulation ....
3 journalism ....
4 rumours ....
5 campaign ....
6 publish ....

15 Circle the odd word out in each group.
0 print   publish   circulate   (tweet)   } newspapers
1 broadcast   show   publish   transmit   } TV news
2 circulate   publish   print   broadcast   } a newspaper story
3 tweet   post   print   circulate   } on social media
4 post   publish   print   show   } on news websites
5 publish   forward   post   transmit   } a tweet
6 broadcast   transmit   circulate   post   } on a radio news programme

16 Complete with the correct form of the verbs from exercise 15.
0 I ....*tweeted*.... all my followers about the election result.
1 The story .... on all national news channels.
2 Newspapers .... the day before they come out.
3 Orwell's last book .... in 1949.
4 You can .... comments whenever you like.
5 Some famous newspapers .... abroad.

Unit 10   223

GRAMMAR PRACTICE

Reported speech: Questions and commands

Choose the correct option.
- When we report a question we *are / aren't* asking the question. So a reported question has the same word order as a *statement / question*.
- To introduce a reported *Yes* or *No* question we use *that / if* or *whether / how*. To introduce a reported *wh*-question we use *that / the wh-word*.
- In reported commands we use the *infinitive / past simple* of the main verb.

➡ See GRAMMAR REFERENCE page 123

17 Put the words in the correct order.

0 me / asked / if / free / was / I / that evening / she
   She asked me if I was free that evening.
1 I / park / whether / wanted / my brother / he / come / the / to / to / asked / me / with
2 text / she'd / my / asked / I / got / her / if
3 Skin / if / me / asked / he / heard / song / latest / I'd / by / the
4 us / asked / Mum / housework / help / we'd / the / with / if
5 asked / together / them / they / we / if / work / on / wanted / project / the / to
6 hadn't / called / brother's / him / asked / my / why / girlfriend / week / he / before / the / her
7 before / evening / dad / why / asked / late / I'd / so / the / my / got back
8 them / after / week / wanted / they / go / me / if / I / to / and / visit / the / asked

18 Transform the sentences into direct speech.

0 Sally asked Janice what time she had arrived.
   What time did you arrive, Janice?
1 She asked her boyfriend what he thought of the film the day before.
2 My parents asked me how my test had gone.
3 She asked her dad if he would take her to the station the next day.
4 My uncle asked me why I was in such a hurry.
5 Tom asked Jenny where she was going on holiday the following summer.
6 Jan asked why I'd been so silent the evening before.
7 Harry asked Andy if he could borrow his car for the following three days.

19 Transform the sentences into reported speech.

0 Chris asked Kelly, 'Do you want to play tennis tomorrow?'
   Chris asked Kelly if she wanted to play tennis the day after.
1 Meira asked Jamie, 'Are you coming to the cinema?'
2 Pat asked Maurice, 'Are you engaged?'
3 Fiona asked me, 'Did your trip go well?'
4 Sam asked Tim, 'Have you ever been to Canada?'
5 Jo asked Ed, 'Will you come to visit me next week?'
6 Anne asked me, 'How long have you been a member of the tennis club?'
7 Sue asked Tim, 'Why are you talking to me like this?'
8 Wendy asked her mum, 'Can I take the car tonight?'

20 Transform the sentences into reported speech.

0 Tess told Flo, 'Be careful with my bike this evening.'
   Tess told Flo to be careful with her bike that evening.
1 I told my cousin, 'Don't forget to give me my CD back tomorrow.'
2 Dave told his parents, 'Give me time to think!'
3 We told them, 'Don't be late this evening!'
4 My brother told me, 'Don't listen to my phone calls.'
5 She told him, 'Call me next week.'
6 Jen told Tom, 'Do something useful for once.'

21 Read the text and then write the dialogue.

I met my old friend Camilla in town yesterday. She asked me how I was and I told her that everything was OK and that I'd finished school the week before. She said that was good and then told me she was going through a very difficult period. I asked why that was and she told me she'd broken up with her boyfriend the month before. I said I was really sorry to hear that. She thanked me and explained that she didn't have so many friends and asked if she could go out with me and my group some time. I said that would be fine and then told her that I was meeting up with Susie and the others the following evening. I asked her if she wanted to come and she said that she would be happy to come. I told her to leave me her number so that I could text her the details of where we were meeting. She said that she was really looking forward to meeting everybody again and told me she hadn't been out for weeks. I said goodbye and that I'd see her the next day.

Camilla Hello! How are you?

SPEAKING SKILLS

GOSSIPING

22 Complete the sentences with the words below.

shouldn't ▪ apparently ▪ heard ▪ according to ▪ by the way ▪ guess ▪ speaking of ▪ impressed

1 I've just ……………… that Emily's out of the team for tomorrow.
2 ………………, they're not talking to each other.
3 I'm really ……………… that you know so much about coaching and tactics.
4 I ……………… really tell you this, but they had a big argument about tactics.
5 ……………… the coach, she hasn't been playing too well recently.
6 ………………, did anybody tell you when and where we were meeting for the match?
7 ……………… coaches, what do you think of the new coach at Team Albatross?
8 You'll never ……………… what I just found out!

23 Complete the dialogue with the sentences from exercise 22.

A Hello Alice. Are you looking forward to the match?
B Yes, I am. But ¹……………… !
A What? Am I playing in defence for once?
B No, nothing like that … ²……………… .
A You're joking. She always plays well and we'll lose without her. Why isn't she playing?
B Well, it's top secret and ³……………… .
A But what have tactics got to do with Emily? The coach decides all that anyway.
B I know that, but that's the situation. ⁴……………… because they had an argument over it.
A Oh that's great, we'll have a really nice trip to the match … in total silence.
B If I were you, I'd travel with someone else.
A But what's the real reason for this? It can't just be about tactics.
B No, not completely. ⁵……………… .
A Well, that's rubbish. She's been our best player in the last three matches. Look at the way she led the attack in our last match.
B ⁶……………… .
A Well, I want to be a coach one day, so I need to know a little bit about them. ⁷……………… ?
B I think she's doing really well. It'll be a tough match!

LISTENING SKILLS

24 Complete the sentences with the words below.

news item ▪ news agency ▪ publish ▪ platform ▪ front page

1 A ……………… is a specific medium that you use to publish and promote your material.
2 Journalists need to ……………… several articles a week to make a living.
3 That story was ……………… news and people were talking about it for months.
4 A ……………… is any story that deals with a particular topic or argument in the news.
5 A ……………… has a large number of independent journalists and provides stories for newspapers and TV news programmes.

25 [2.30] Listen to Matt and Evie and answer the questions.

1 What course is Matt doing?
2 What's his ambition?

26 [2.30] Listen again and decide if the sentences are true (T) or false (F). Correct the false ones.

1 Matt thinks the journalism course gives good preparation for his career. T F
2 He has to write three news articles every day. T F
3 The articles are not checked by his tutors. T F
4 His tutor is satisfied with his progress. T F
5 Evie knows someone else who's still on the course. T F
6 Angie is currently looking for a job. T F
7 Matt thinks it's difficult to find online journalist work. T F
8 Big newspapers prefer to use their own journalists for stories rather than news agencies. T F
9 Journalists working for agencies are paid for every story they write. T F

27 [2.30] Listen again and answer the questions.

1 What was the tutor's comment on Matt's progress?
2 What kind of work has Angie been doing?
3 What does Matt think about the work Angie does?
4 What does Matt say about blogs in journalism?
5 What was his article for the local paper about?
6 How could you describe the relationship between Matt and Evie, and why?

Unit 10   225

ACADEMIC SKILLS

PLANNING AND WRITING IN PARAGRAPHS

28 Look at the content list for an essay on British newspapers and put the paragraphs into logical order.

a ☐ History of British newspapers
b ☐ 1 Introduction
c ☐ Conclusion
d ☐ Challenges for the future

29 Read the sentences from the opening paragraph and put them in order.

a ☐ Tabloids. These are the most popular newspapers.
b ☐ The other is broadsheet newspapers. As the name suggests, these are larger in size and contain fewer pictures than tabloids.
c ☐ They are small in size, generally have large print characters and often include stories about celebrities and scandals.
d ☐ So the UK newspaper-reading community is usually divided into two very distinct groups.
e ☐ 1 When people think about British newspapers, the first thing that they do is to divide them into two categories.
f ☐ They also have more detailed articles and are more serious than the tabloids.

30 Now find the sentence(s) from exercise 29 which:

0 contains the topic sentence for the paragraph. ......e......
1 are supporting sentences for the topic sentence. .... and ....
2 expand on the supporting sentences by giving more information. .... and ....
3 concludes the paragraph by reaffirming the topic sentence. ....

31 Look at the second paragraph and complete it with the linking words below.

> however • in the end • ~~firstly~~ •
> these days • therefore • then

Newspapers have a very long history in Britain and several periods were critical to their development. ⁰ ...**Firstly**..., in the early nineteenth century all the big newspapers set up their offices on a single street in central London, called Fleet Street. This remained the focus of British journalism for nearly 50 years.

¹..................., this changed in the 1980s, when the owner of *The Times* and *The Sun* newspapers moved to the east of London. ²................... many journalists and support operations had to move out of Fleet Street, and when other newspapers followed, the traditional home of British newspapers went into decline. ³................... technology changed even more rapidly and it became easier to print newspapers from remote locations and even abroad. ⁴................... the newspaper industry is very flexible and mobile compared to the past but ⁵................... the history of British newspapers will always be linked to its very first home, Fleet Street.

32 Identify the sentences of the third paragraph on challenges for the future.

0 Topic sentence: ....*e*....
1 Support sentence 1: ....
2 Expansion of support sentence 1: .... and ....
3 Support sentence 2: ....
4 Expansion of support sentence 2: .... and ....

a Firstly, new technology is the biggest danger to the survival of printed newspapers.
b The other main issue, however, is the fact that people simply buy fewer newspapers than they used to.
c One reason for this is that people's lives are busier and most find it impossible to read up to 30 pages of articles in a normal day.
d For example, some newspapers are free, and people don't want to pay for similar content.
e The future of Britain's newspaper is unclear in this rapidly changing digital world.
f Nowadays people can assess online newspapers so they don't need to buy one.
g As a result, sales have fallen by 10% in just two years and will probably continue to fall.

33 Now write an appropriate concluding sentence to the third paragraph.

34 Write the conclusion to the essay. Look at the points below, decide on the best order for them and write your concluding paragraph.

- newspapers need to change to survive
- many changes over the last 30 years
- very competitive world
- need to innovate / make people want to read newspapers rather than online materials

EXAM STRATEGY

Speaking – Describing a photo

When you describe a photograph, start with a sentence saying what the photo shows and then describe the picture in more detail:
- say what the people are doing
- talk about the place where they are
- make some guesses based on what you can see, for example the time of day / year, situation.

If you don't know the name of an object, describe it or explain what it is used for. Use expressions and prepositions of place to describe where the people and objects are.

35 Complete the description of the picture with the prepositions below.

behind ▪ on the right ▪ in the middle ▪ in the background ▪ on the left ▪ above ▪ <u>in the foreground</u>

This is a scene in London, I think. ⁰ **In the foreground**, ¹ .... of the picture, there is a man on his bike. He's wearing gloves and a helmet, and he's got a backpack; maybe he's going to work. ² .... of the picture there's another cyclist; ³ .... the cyclist there's a red bus and ⁴ .... the bus there's a big building made of glass and metal. ⁵ .... there are some people who look like they're chatting to each other. ⁶ .... the red bus I can see street lights.

TOWARDS PRELIMINARY

36 Look at the picture and then complete the first part of the description. Then write the second part. Use some of the words below to help you.

sunny ▪ on holiday ▪ blue sky ▪ palm trees ▪ in the background ▪ beach hut ▪ white sand ▪ sandy beach ▪ shorts ▪ acquamarine ▪ beach mattress

In this ⁰ ....**picture**...... we can see a family at the ¹ .... ² .... are a man and a woman, the mother and father I ³ ...., and their two ⁴ ....
I think they're on ⁵ .... because everyone ⁶ .... very relaxed. In the ⁷ .... I can see palms and a straw ⁸ ...., so I think it's a place for tourists.
The family are …

Unit 10 227

REVISE AND ROUND UP

1 **Complete the sentences with a passive form.**

0 There's been really heavy rain recently and a lot of damage *has been done* (do) to houses.
1 Facebook .... (set up) by Mark Zuckerberg in 2004.
2 *Bedroom in Arles* .... (paint) by Van Gogh in 1888.
3 Good news! Our entry to the school engineering project .... (accept).
4 Pesto .... (make) with basil, parmesan, pecorino cheese and pine nuts.
5 The 2008 Olympics .... (hold) in Beijing.
6 We are getting reports that several people .... (hurt) in a car accident on the city's ring road.
7 We .... (shock) by the state of the room we had booked on the internet and left immediately.
8 All Year 3 students .... already .... (tell) about the changes in the programme for next year.

2 **Transform the sentences using the passive.**

0 Someone found my lost passport yesterday.
 My lost passport was found yesterday.
1 This book tells the story very well.
2 The police caught the bank robbers last night.
3 You can wear this cardigan in spring and summer.
4 Who took this picture?
5 How often do your teachers check the class register?
6 Has anyone ever taught you to swim?
7 You should keep your dog on its lead inside the park.
8 They make coffee from roasted coffee beans.
9 Nobody told me about the accident.
10 Has someone checked the weight of this suitcase?

3 **Transform the sentences into reported speech.**

0 They said, 'We're waiting for you outside.'
 They said they were waiting for me outside.
1 Mark said, 'I'll help you with this exercise.'
2 Jeff said, 'I bought a new tablet yesterday.'
3 Sylvia asked me, 'Do you come here often?'
4 I asked my dad, 'Will you take me to the match?'
5 Paul said, 'I didn't play football last week.'
6 My sister said, 'I lost my schoolbag three days ago.'

4 **Report the conversation between the two friends.**

Helen	How did the test go?
Jay	Can we talk about something else?
Helen	Sorry, I just wanted to show some interest.
Jay	I'm sorry I reacted like that. It went pretty badly.
Helen	Why do you think that?
Jay	The questions were really hard. I'm sure I'll fail.
Helen	Just forget about it. I'm going for an ice cream, do you want to come?
Jay	That's a great idea. I'll just wait here a moment.
Helen	So what ice cream do you want?
Jay	A chocolate and mint one, please. It's very kind of you.
Helen	So, are you feeling better now?
Jay	Yes, thanks. I was really nervous before the test and I just panicked when I saw some of the questions.
Helen	I know, the same thing happens to me sometimes. But don't worry, you'll be fine for the next test.
Jay	At least it can't be any worse than this one!

Helen asked Jay how the test had gone.

5 **Correct the mistakes. Two sentences are correct.**

0 The changing rooms have been ~~moving~~ to the front of the sports centre. **moved**
1 This video on this new smartphone is improved compared to the old model.
2 *Winter Landscape* was painting by Rembrandt.
3 Our classroom has just been painted; it looks really white and fresh.
4 She asked them if they want to go to the match.
5 They said me they were late.
6 I told him be careful.
7 The new shopping centre was opened in June.
8 This song is covered so many times in the past – it's not original at all.
9 Applications for the job are considering on the basis of the candidate's CV and experience.
10 My parents told me go home at once.

Unit 10

6 Complete the text with the correct form of the verbs below.

~~post~~ • limit • improve • post • verify • have • not / expect • launch • send • close • call • introduce • interview

Twitter is an online news and social networking service where messages **⁰ are posted** by users. Twitter **¹** .... online in March 2006 by Jack Dorsey and some friends. Messages on Twitter **²** .... *tweets* and in 2016 more than 1 billion tweets **³** .... every day. Tweets **⁴** .... to 140 characters to allow such a high number of tweets, and people can only post tweets after their account **⁵** .... to stop abuses of the system. When he **⁶** ...., the inventor told reporters that he **⁷** .... the idea during a brainstorming session for a podcasting company. He also said that he **⁸** .... the idea to become so incredibly successful when it **⁹** .... first .... to the public. The first Twitter message consisting of 'just setting up my twttr' **¹⁰** .... by Dorsey on March 21, 2006.
Since the beginning, many user accounts **¹¹** .... because the owners didn't respect the rules. Dorsey recently promised reporters that he **¹²** .... security across the Twitter platform.

7 TRANSLATION Translate the sentences into English.

0 Questo formaggio è prodotto in Francia?
   Is this cheese produced in France?
1 Ti avevo detto di non fare tardi.
2 Sono state cotte abbastanza queste patate?
3 Questo dispositivo viene usato per salvare i dati importanti sul tuo computer.
4 Questi compiti non sono stati ancora corretti dall'insegnante.
5 Quando è stata costruita questa scuola?
6 Non siamo ancora stati informati sul nuovo programma per il terzo anno.
7 Sono stati fatti tanti cambiamenti nella tua città negli ultimi anni?
8 Ti ho detto che questa non era la strada giusta.
9 Marie ha promesso che sarebbe venuta più tardi.

CONCEPT CHECK

Read the sentences and answer the questions.

1 *All your school marks are loaded onto the school portal after every test.*

(Answer Yes / No)

0 Do students have to load their marks onto the portal? **No**
1 Does someone else load the marks onto the portal?
2 Do I know who will put my marks on the school portal?
3 Is it important for me to know this information?

2 *Were you given a copy of the new timetable?*

(Answer Yes / No / Your own words)

0 Does the sentence refer to the past or present? **Past**
1 Is the person asking about who gave you the timetable?
2 Is it important who gave you the new timetable?
3 What does the person really want to know?

3 *I told you the match would be easy.*

(Answer Yes / No / Your own words)

0 Was the match easy? **Yes**
1 Did I tell you this before the match started?
2 What did I say to you exactly?

4 *They asked me if I was free the following afternoon.*

(Answer Yes / No / Your own words)

0 Are they asking me this now? **No**
1 Am I reporting a conversation I had in the past?
2 What question did they ask me exactly?

5 *She told me she was going to do a six-month Erasmus exchange the following term.*

(Answer Yes / No / Your own words)

0 Am I speaking directly to the person who is going on the Erasmus course? **No**
1 Am I reporting a conversation I have already had with the person going on the Erasmus course?
2 What did that person say to me exactly?

→ See **GRAMMAR REFERENCE**
pages 122, 123

Units 10   229

LITERATURE SKILLS 1

The action / adventure novel

LEAD IN

1 **PAIRWORK** Talk together about what makes a good friend. Give examples of things that people do which prove they are real friends.

Moby Dick (1851)
by Herman Melville

Moby Dick is a magnificent white whale and it has been Captain Ahab's lifelong ambition to kill it. Ishmael, the narrator in the novel, and Queequeg, a native of an island in the South Pacific where cannibalism is practised, are sailors on Captain Ahab's boat, the Pequod. *In this excerpt, Ishmael and Queequeg, who only met a few days before, are staying at an inn on the coast of Massachusetts as they wait to set sail on the* Pequod.

from CHAPTER 10

Returning to the Inn[1] from the Chapel, I found Queequeg there quite alone. He was sitting on a bench[2] before the fire. He went to the table, took up a large book, placed it on his lap[3] and began
5 counting the pages with deliberate regularity; at every fiftieth page he stopped a moment, looked around him and gave a whistle[4] of astonishment. He was amazed at how many pages there were in the book.
10 With much interest I sat watching him. Although he was a savage and his face was covered in tattoos there was something special about him. You cannot hide[5] the soul[6]. Through all his tattoos, I thought I saw a simple honest heart and his head
15 was an excellent one. Queequeg was the cannibal version of George Washington.
Here was a man some twenty thousand miles from home, living among people as strange to him as though he were on the planet Jupiter and yet he
20 was totally relaxed, content with his own company. As I sat there in that lonely room I suddenly realized that I was in the presence of a brave, noble man. He was a savage but in many ways he was better than many of the Christians I knew. I'll try a
25 pagan friend, I thought.
I pulled my chair over to his and we started looking at the book together. I tried to explain some of the words to him but he was more interested in the pictures. Gradually he began to relax in my
30 company and as a sign of friendship he pulled out his pipe which we passed from one to the other, exchanging puffs[7]. And when our smoke was over, he pressed his forehead against mine, clasped[8] me around the waist[9], and said that from now on we
35 were married, which meant, in his country's language, that we were best friends.

(abridged excerpt)

1. **inn** : locanda
2. **bench** : panca
3. **lap** : grembo
4. **whistle** : fischio
5. **hide** : nascondere
6. **soul** : anima
7. **puffs** : boccate
8. **clasped** : abbraccio
9. **waist** : vita

PRACTICE

2 🔊 [3.02] Read and listen to the extract. Decide if the sentences refer to Ishmael (I), Queequeg (Q), or both (B).

1 He can't read.   I Q B
2 He observes his companion attentively.   I Q B
3 He takes out a pipe to smoke.   I Q B
4 He reads the book.   I Q B

3 Read the extract again and answer the questions.

1 Why did Queequeg give 'a whistle of astonishment'?
2 What did Ishmael deduce from the fact that Queequeg's face was covered in tattoos?
3 What could Ishmael see through the tattoos?
4 Was Queequeg homesick?
5 Why do you think Queequeg wanted Ishmael to smoke a pipe with him?

4 🔊 [3.03] Listen to a summary of the story of Moby Dick. Does Ahab capture Moby Dick?

5 🔊 [3.03] Listen again and order the events.

☐ a The sailors extracted oil from two dead whales.
☐ b Another ship rescued Ishmael.
☐ c Ahab gave a speech.
☐ d The sailors saw Moby Dick for the first time.
☐ e The *Pequod* set sail.
☐ f Moby Dick destroyed the *Pequod*.
☐ g Queequeg fell ill.
☐ h The sailors killed two whales.

6 Choose one of the following tasks.

1 Find an example of a friendship between people who are or were very different either in real life or in a book or film. Write down briefly how and why they became friends.
2 In pairs write a dialogue in which one of you is Captain Ahab and the other is an animal-rights activist who believes that it's wrong to hunt and kill whales.

RESEARCH SKILLS

7 **Critical thinking** Read the questions and note down your ideas. Then share in groups.

1 Do our friends tend to come from our own background and social class?
2 Is it harder to build up a friendship with people from very different backgrounds?
3 Do friendships become stronger if they involve facing difficulties or dangers together?

8 **RESEARCH** Find out when each adventure story was written or made and put them in chronological order.

☐ a *Jurassic Park* by M. Crichton
☐ b *Treasure Island* by R. L. Stevenson
☐ c *Gulliver's Travels* by J. Swift
☐ d *Indiana Jones and the Temple of Doom* by S. Spielberg
☐ e *Star Wars: A New Hope* by G. Lucas
☐ f *Captain America: Civil War* by A. and J. Russo

9 **RESEARCH** Choose one of the stories above and find out the main events in the story.

10 Make a timeline listing the events in the story and use your timeline to describe the story to the class.

COMPETENCY SKILLS

- Acting autonomously and responsibly (exs 1, 7)
- Acquiring and interpreting information (exs 8, 9)
- Problem solving (ex 10)

Literature Skills 1   231

LITERATURE SKILLS 2

The gothic novel

LEAD IN

1 **PAIRWORK** With a partner make a list of the things that people are afraid of. Are you afraid of these things? Compare your lists with the rest of the class.

Dracula (1897)
by Bram Stoker

Jonathan Harker, a young English lawyer, is a guest in Count Dracula's castle in Transylvania. At first the Count was very polite but now Jonathan has the impression that there is something very strange about the castle and its owner. In this extract he is in his bed.

from CHAPTER 3

I was not alone. I could see along the floor, in the brilliant moonlight, my own footsteps marked where I had disturbed the long accumulation of dust. In the moonlight opposite me were three young women, ladies by their dress and manner. I thought at the time that I was dreaming when I saw them, for, though the moonlight was behind them, they threw no shadow on the floor. They came close to me, and looked at me for some time, and then whispered[1] together. Two were dark, and had high aquiline noses, like the Count, and great dark, penetrating eyes that seemed to be almost red when contrasted with the yellow moon. The other was fair, as fair as can be, curly golden hair and eyes like sapphires[2]. They whispered together, and then they all three laughed—such a light, musical laugh, but as hard as though the sound never could have come through the softness of human lips. The fair girl shook her head and the other two encouraged her. One said:—

'Go on! You are first, and we shall follow; yours is the right to begin.' The other added:—

'He is young and strong; there are kisses for us all.' I lay quiet, in anticipation. The fair girl advanced and I could feel the movement of her breath upon me. Sweet it was in one sense, honey-sweet. I was afraid to open my eyes, but looked out and saw perfectly under the lashes[3]. Her lips went below my mouth and chin and seemed about to kiss my throat. I could feel the soft touch of the lips on the super-sensitive skin of my throat, and hard sharp teeth, just touching and pausing there. I closed my eyes and waited—waited with beating heart.

But at that instant, another sensation swept through me as quick as lightning. I was conscious of the presence of the Count.

'How dare you touch him, any of you? This man belongs to me! Keep away from him, or you'll have to deal with me.'

(abridged excerpt)

1. **whispered** : sussurrarono
2. **sapphires** : zaffiri
3. **lashes** : ciglia

PRACTICE

2 [3.04] Read and listen to the extract. How does the author describe the women?

3 Read the text again and decide if the sentences are true (T) or false (F). Correct the false ones.

		T	F
1	Jonathan's room was clean.	T	F
2	Jonathan could hear what the women were saying.	T	F
3	Only one of the women walked over to Jonathan.	T	F
4	Jonathan's eyes were closed.	T	F
5	The woman touched Jonathan's throat with her lips and her teeth.	T	F
6	The Count was angry with the women.	T	F

4 This report is about the popular series *The Vampire Diaries*. Before you listen, in pairs discuss the questions.

1. What do you know about the series? Did you like it?
2. Do you know the actors in the picture?

5 [3.05] Listen to the report and answer these questions.

1. What has become popular recently?
2. Who is the main character in the series?
3. Does the town of Mystic Falls really exist?
4. Who does Elena fall in love with?
5. Who does Damon fall in love with?
6. What age group is most interested in vampires according to the speaker?

6 Choose one of the following tasks.

1. Write a short account of a situation where you or somebody you know was afraid. Describe what happened.
2. In pairs, write the dialogue between Jonathan Harker and Count Dracula the morning after the incident in the extract.

RESEARCH SKILLS

7 **Critical thinking** Read the questions and discuss in pairs.

1. Do you think that horror stories appeal more to certain types of people (e.g., young or old, male or female)?
2. Do you think that it is acceptable for small children to watch horror films? Why / Why not?

8 **PAIRWORK** Look at the list of classic horror books / films. Which do you think is the most frightening and why?

- *Frankenstein* (1818)
- *The Turn of the Screw* (1898)
- *The Shining* (1977)
- *Psycho* (1960)
- *Alien* (1979)
- *The Blair Witch Project* (1999)

9 **RESEARCH** Choose a book, film or TV series that involves the supernatural. Write a review explaining:

1. Who the main characters are.
2. What the main events are.
3. Whether you found the characters and events convincing. Give reasons.

COMPETENCY SKILLS

- Planning and prioritising (ex 1)
- Acting autonomously and responsibly (ex 7)
- Identifying links and relations (ex 7)
- Communicating (exs 7, 8)
- Acquiring and interpreting information (ex 9)

Literature Skills 2   233

LITERATURE SKILLS 3

The short story

LEAD IN

1 Do you prefer reading short stories or novels? Can you tell the class about any short stories you have read and enjoyed?

The Murders in the Rue Morgue (1841)

by Edgar Allan Poe

Edgar Allan Poe is widely regarded as the inventor of the short story in English and The Murders in the Rue Morgue *is one of the finest examples of the genre.*
Here is a newspaper report about what happened in Rue Morgue, in Paris, in the early hours of the morning.

EXTRAORDINARY MURDERS.—This morning, at about three o'clock, the inhabitants of the Quartier St. Roch were woken from sleep by a succession of terrific screams, coming, apparently, from the fourth storey[1] of a house in the Rue Morgue, home to Madame L'Espanaye, and her daughter Mademoiselle Camille L'Espanaye. After some delay[2], eight or ten of the neighbors accompanied by two *gendarmes* broke the gate with a crowbar[3], and entered. By this time the screams had stopped; but, as everyone ran up the stairs, two or more, angry voices were heard which seemed to come from the upper part of the house. When they reached the fourth storey everything remained perfectly quiet.

The apartment was in the wildest disorder—the furniture broken and thrown about in all directions. On a chair lay a razor, covered in blood. On the hearth[4] were two or three long and thick pieces of grey, bloodied human hair. Upon the floor were an earring, three large silver spoons, and two bags, containing nearly four thousand francs in gold. The drawers of a *bureau*, which stood in one corner, were open, and had been, apparently, rifled[5], although many articles still remained in them. A small metal box was discovered under the bed. It was open, with the key still in the door. It contained a few old letters, and other papers of little consequence.

Madame L'Espanaye was nowhere to be seen but there was an unusual quantity of soot[6] in the fireplace[7] so a search was made of the chimney, and (horrible to relate!) the dead body of the daughter was found in it.

Then, after investigating the rest of the house, the police made their way to a small yard[8] at the back of the building where they found the dead body of the old lady.

(abridged excerpt)

1. **storey** : piano
2. **delay** : ritardo
3. **crowbar** : piede di porco
4. **hearth** : focolare
5. **rifled** : frugati
6. **soot** : fuliggine
7. **fireplace** : caminetto
8. **yard** : cortile

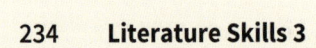

PRACTICE

2 [3.06] Read and listen to the extract. Underline where the writer describes what is out of place in the room.

'the drawers of a bureau […] were open'.

3 Read the text again and answer the questions.

1 What woke people in the middle of the night in the Quartier St. Roch?
2 Why couldn't the *gendarme*s get into the house immediately?
3 Did it seem that anything was stolen from the apartment?
4 Why did they look in the chimney?
5 Where did the police find Madame L'Espanaye's body?

4 Look at the picture. What do you think is happening? Share your ideas with the class.

5 [3.07] Listen to a sailor explaining the murders. Do you believe the story? Why / Why not?

6 [3.07] Listen again and put these events in the correct order.

- [ ] a The orangutan murdered Madame L'Espanaye.
- [ ] b The sailor captured an orangutan.
- [ ] c The orangutan escaped and ran into the street.
- [ ] d The orangutan was shaving.
- [ ] e The orangutan murdered Madame L'Espanaye's daughter.
- [ ] f The sailor tried to take the razor from the orangutan.

7 Choose one of the following tasks.

1 Invent an alternative ending to the story starting from the moment when the sailor saw the orangutan in the woman's house.
2 Imagine that the police have decided to kill the orangutan. Write a letter to the police explaining why you think the orangutan should or should not be killed.

RESEARCH SKILLS

8 **Critical thinking** Discuss the questions in groups.

1 Do you think that animals are more violent than humans?
2 Should animals have the same rights as humans?
3 Are experiments on animals always justified?
4 Do you think stories about crimes encourage people to commit similar crimes?

9 **PAIRWORK** Look at the list of famous short stories. Can you guess what each one is about?

- *The Happy Prince* (1888)
- *The Gift of the Magi* (1905)
- *To Build a Fire* (1908)
- *The Dead* (1914)
- *The Snows of Kilimanjaro* (1936)
- *The Secret Life of Walter Mitty* (1939)

10 RESEARCH Read a short story (in English or Italian) and design a mind map to reflect the story, main characters and main themes.

11 Do some research to find a critical review of the story / collection of stories you chose. Do you agree with the review?

COMPETENCY SKILLS

- Acting autonomously and responsibly (ex 8)
- Communicating (ex 9)
- Learning to learn (ex 10)
- Acquiring and interpreting information (ex 11)

Literature Skills 3   235

LITERATURE SKILLS 4

The historical novel

LEAD IN

1 How much do you know about the city of Florence? Make a list of famous Florentine buildings, works of art and people.

Romola (1863)
by George Eliot (Mary Ann Evans)

Romola is a young woman who lives through some of the most turbulent years in Florence's history. The novel traces her life story in a period when the governing Medici family were exiled from the city by invading French forces. This excerpt explains how Florence had become one of the most powerful cities in Italy.

from CHAPTER 8

It is easy for northern people to rise early on Midsummer morning, to notice the fresh grass and the dark green of the oak[1] in the wood, and to look over the gate at the cut field, without remembering
5 that it is the Nativity of Saint John the Baptist. Not so to the Florentine—still less to the Florentine of the fifteenth century: to him on that particular morning the brightness of the eastern sun on the Arno had something special in it; the ringing of the bells was
10 articulate, and declared it to be the great summer festival of Florence, the day of San Giovanni. San Giovanni had been the patron saint of Florence for at least eight hundred years—ever since the Lombard Queen Theodolinda had ordered her
15 subjects to honour him. Florence had become a powerful state but whereas in the past that power was based on military strength, now it was based on gold florins. For military strength could be bought by gold florins, and on the gold florins there
20 had always been the image of San Giovanni.

Much good had come to Florence despite some quarrelling[2] and bloodshed[3], between Guelf and Ghibelline, between orthodox sons of the Church and heretics, some floods[4], famine[5], and pestilence; but still much wealth and glory. 25
Florence had conquered powerful walled cities especially the hated Pisa, whose marble[6] buildings were too high and beautiful and whose ships were honoured on Greek and Italian coasts. The name of Florence had been growing prouder and prouder in 30
all the courts of Europe, even in Africa itself, thanks to its pure gold coins, finest dyes[7] and textures[8], illustrious scholars, sophisticated diplomacy and flourishing[9] banks. It was a name so omnipresent that a Pope had called the Florentines 35
'the fifth element'. And this high destiny was reached thanks to San Giovanni, whose image was on the fair gold florins.

(*abridged excerpt*)

---

1. **oak**: quercia
2. **quarrelling**: litigi, dispute
3. **bloodshed**: spargimento di sangue
4. **floods**: alluvioni
5. **famine**: carestia
6. **marble**: marmo
7. **dyes**: tinture
8. **textures**: tessuti
9. **flourishing**: fiorenti

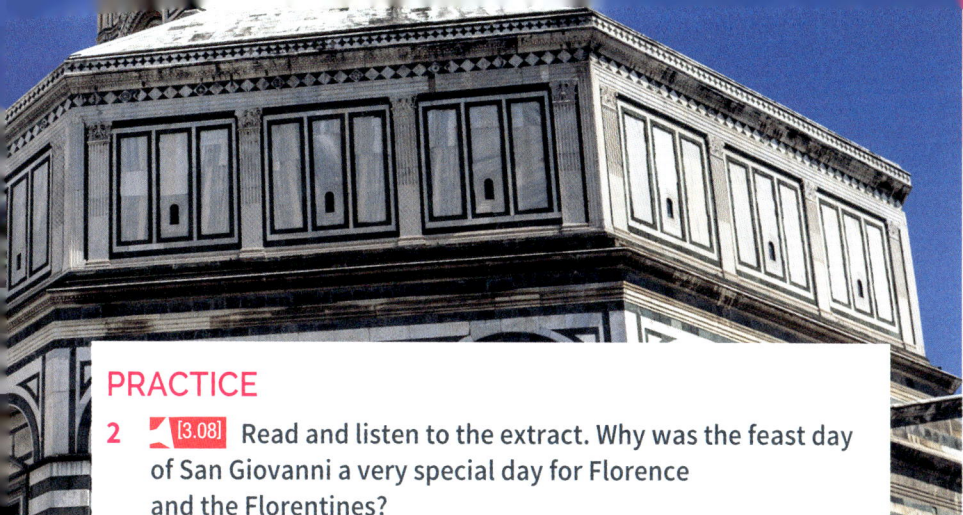

PRACTICE

2 [3.08] Read and listen to the extract. Why was the feast day of San Giovanni a very special day for Florence and the Florentines?

3 Read the extract again and answer the questions.

1. Who decided that San Giovanni would be the patron saint of Florence?
2. What was the power of Florence based on in the past?
3. What is its power based on now?
4. The Pope called the Florentines 'the fifth element' to underline their importance. What are the other four elements?

4 [3.09] Listen to this description of Bloomsday in Dublin and say whether you think it is more of a social or a cultural event.

5 [3.09] Listen again and answer the questions.

1. Who is honoured on Bloomsday?
2. Who is Leopold Bloom?
3. Why did Joyce choose June 16th as the day when all the events in *Ulysses* take place?
4. What do some people wear on Bloomsday?
5. Why do Joycean fans go to pubs on Bloomsday?
6. Has Joyce always been honoured in Dublin?

6 Choose one of the following tasks.

1. Choose one of the dates and write an email to an English friend explaining why it is a national holiday and explain what happens in your town.
   - 1st May
   - 25th April
   - 2nd June
2. In pairs, think of a historical period that you think you would like to experience. Explain to your partner what you think you would like about living in that period.

RESEARCH SKILLS

7 **Critical thinking** Discuss the quotations in groups. Do you agree or disagree?

1. 'Power corrupts and absolute power corrupts absolutely. Great men are almost always bad men.' *Lord Acton*
2. 'Those who cannot remember the past are condemned to repeat it.' *George Santayana*

8 Chose one of the questions and write a paragraph explaining your answer.

1. Is corruption inevitable in politics?
2. Can studying history help us build a more peaceful and prosperous world?

9 **PAIRWORK** Here is a list of historical books and films. Do you know when or where they are set?

- *A Tale of Two Cities* (1859)
- *The Name of the Rose* (1980)
- *Gone with the Wind* (1939)
- *Braveheart* (1995)
- *Gladiator* (2000)
- *300* (2007)

10 **RESEARCH** Choose one of the books / films and answer the questions.

1. Where and when is it set?
2. Are the main characters based on real people or are they fictional?

COMPETENCY SKILLS

- Planning and prioritising (ex 1)
- Collaboration and participating (ex 7)
- Acting autonomously and responsibly (ex 8)

Literature Skills 4   237

LITERATURE SKILLS 5

The utopian / dystopian novel

LEAD IN

1 **PAIRWORK** Discuss these questions.

1 Have you ever taken part in a political demonstration?
2 Do you ever discuss politics with friends and family? Do you usually agree or disagree?

The Iron Heel (1908)
by Jack London

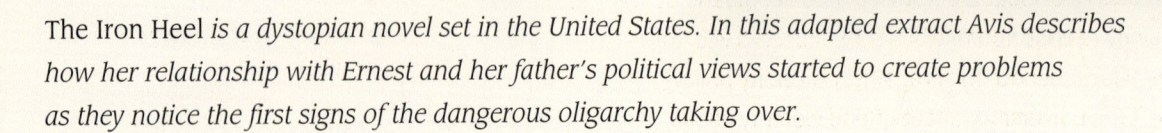

The Iron Heel is a dystopian novel set in the United States. In this adapted extract Avis describes how her relationship with Ernest and her father's political views started to create problems as they notice the first signs of the dangerous oligarchy taking over.

It was about this time that the warnings[1] of coming events began. Ernest had already questioned father's policy of having socialists and labor leaders at his house, and of openly attending socialist meetings; and father had only laughed at him. As for myself, I was learning much from the working-class leaders and thinkers. I was delighted with their unselfishness[2] and high idealism. I was learning fast, but not fast enough to realize then the danger of our position.

There were warnings. I noticed my friends' disapproval[3] of my intended marriage with Ernest. Ernest warned me, 'you have given love to an enemy of your class,' he said. 'Think not that you will escape being penalized.'

But it was before this that father returned one afternoon. Ernest was with me, and father was angry. 'I was invited for lunch with Wilcox, the president of the university,' father announced. 'I was sent for. I was reprimanded[4]. I!'

'I know what you were reprimanded for,' Ernest said. 'For your private life. I warned you before about it.'

'Yes, you did,' father meditated. 'But I couldn't believe it.'

Ernest went on, 'It is nothing to what will come, if you continue to have these socialists and radicals at your house, myself included.'

'Just what old Wilcox said. He said it was not university policy. It wasn't a pleasant task for him. I could see he didn't like it. He said that the university needed money; and that it must come from wealthy personages who could not be offended. Also, he said that there was talk about my daughter being seen in public with so notorious a character as you, and that it was not in keeping with university tone and dignity.'

Ernest considered this for a moment, and then said: 'Somebody has put pressure on President Wilcox.' Ernest said. 'The swift[5] changes in our industrial system are causing equally swift changes in our religious, political, and social structures. A terrible revolution is taking place in the structure of society. There is a shadow of something menacing[6] that is falling across the land. The shadow of an oligarchy and you are in a perilous position.'

(abridged excerpt)

1. **warnings**: avvertimenti
2. **unselfishness**: altruismo
3. **disapproval**: disapprovazione
4. **reprimanded**: redarguito
5. **swift**: rapidi
6. **menacing**: minaccioso

utopian: Describes a society where everything is perfect and life is wonderful.

dystopian: Describes a society where life is a nightmare and where people suffer.

PRACTICE

2 🔊 [3.10] Read and listen to the extract. Which characters share socialist views?

1. Avis
2. Ernest
3. Avis' father
4. Avis' friends
5. Mr Wilcox

3 Read the text again and answer the questions.

1. How did Avis' father react at first to Ernest's warnings about mixing with socialists?
2. What impresses Avis about the working-class people she is meeting?
3. Why don't Avis' friends approve of her relationship with Ernest?
4. What does Avis' father do that is against university policy?
5. Why doesn't the university want to offend wealthy people?
6. How does Ernest feel about the changes that are taking place in society? Support your answer with examples from the text.

4 🔊 [3.11] Listen to the start of a lecture about another famous dystopian novel and complete the lecture notes.

Author	George [1].............................
Title of book	[2]........................ written in [3]........................
Setting	[4]........................
Main character	[5]........................, works for [6]........................

5 🔊 [3.11] Listen again and explain in your own words what the following are.

1. Big Brother
2. Ministry of Truth
3. the Thought Police

6 Choose one of the following tasks.

1. Find out which political party won the most votes in your local area and make a list of their main policies.
2. Choose a route that you often walk. Count the number of video surveillance cameras you see on this route. Map the route, map the cameras.

RESEARCH SKILLS

7 **Critical thinking** Discuss the question in groups.

1. Who has real power in our society – wealthy citizens, politicians, journalists, celebrities?
2. Governments are assessing privacy rules of social media providers. They say they are doing this to combat terrorism. Is it ever justifiable for the government to have access to your social media posts and emails?

8 **PAIRWORK** Try to guess from titles below if each work is utopian or dystopian. Give a reason for your choices.

- *Island* (1962)
- *A Clockwork Orange* (1962)
- *Always Coming Home* (1985)
- *The Handmaid's Tale* (1985)
- *The Plot against America* (2004)
- *The Hunger Games* (2008)
- *Divergent* (2011)

9 **RESEARCH** Freedom of the press is important in guaranteeing democracy. Find out your country's ranking in freedom of press surveys.

COMPETENCY SKILLS

- Acquiring and interpreting information (exs 6, 8)
- Acting autonomously and responsibly (exs 6, 7, 9)
- Identifying links and relations (ex 7)
- Collaborating and participating (ex 7)

Literature Skills 5 239

CLIL A Science

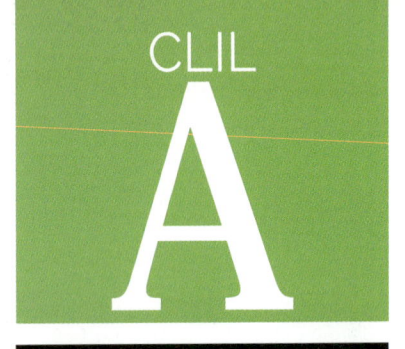

Biodiversity

In this Module, you will see why diversity in biological systems is important for the general well-being and survival of not only individual species but also our entire planet.

1 **LEAD IN** Discuss in pairs. What is biodiversity? Can you give any examples?

2 Read the definitions of three levels of biodiversity and match the images A–C to the types of diversity 1–3.

> **1 Genetic diversity** Different variants within a species, but individuals in that species can *breed*, e.g., different ethnic groups.
>
> **2 Species diversity** Different species, but all living in the same place, and individuals cannot breed, e.g., a sheep and a cow.
>
> **3 Ecosystem diversity** Lots of different organisms (plants and animals) that live in a large area and interact with each other and with their habitat (e.g., water, soil, weather).

A   B   C

3 [3.12] Why is *genetic diversity* important? Read the Introduction about peppered moths. Then, work in pairs to choose the best explanation A or B. Then listen and check.

INTRODUCTION
The example of peppered moths helps us understand how *genetic diversity* within a species increases that species' chances of survival when there are changes in its habitat. In the mid-1800s entomologists noticed that, in the area around industrialised cities like Manchester, the population of *dark-bodied* peppered moths greatly outnumbered the white-bodied peppered moths. This was surprising because before the Industrial Revolution black peppered moths were rare, but by the end of the 1800s more than 90% of the peppered moths around Manchester were dark-bodied.

EXPLANATION A
Pollution from *coal-burning* darkened the trees and surfaces in industrial areas, so the white moths were easily seen and eaten by predators. By contrast, the black peppered moths were more likely to live and breed.

EXPLANATION B
The pollution from coal-burning darkened the trees and surfaces in industrial areas. The same pollution darkened the white-bodied moths. In this way, they could hide from birds.

CONCLUSION
Now that pollution is under control and the air is cleaner, the white-bodied variety of peppered moths is able to survive and their numbers have increased. Not surprisingly, in today's cleaner environment, the population of the dark-bodied variety is decreasing.

CLIL A

4 VISUAL LITERACY Use the diagram to complete the text below about the importance of *species diversity*.

Food Web

- Quaternary consumers
- Tertiary consumers
- Secondary consumers
- 'Carnivores and omnivores'
- Primary consumers 'Herbivores'
- Capable of producing their own food

The diagram illustrates a food web that is typical of ecosystems in many areas in Europe. At the top of this food web, are [1].................... and at the bottom there are different species of [2]...................., which produce their own food through photosynthesis. Plants are food for primary consumers such as insects like [3].................... and herbivores like [4].................... and mice. Secondary consumers feed on primary consumers. In this food web, the secondary consumers are mammals such as [5]...................., amphibians like [6]...................., and both small birds and big birds such as [7].................... . Here there is only one tertiary consumer, the snake, that feeds on frogs and small [8].................... . Since hawks also feed on snakes, they are considered quaternary [9].................... .

5 REAL-LIFE TASK How does species diversity help keep ecosystems stable? Work in groups of four to investigate the following questions.

1. Imagine that a virus totally eliminated the rabbits in the ecosystem in exercise 4.
   - What would happen to the food supply of foxes? And the population of foxes?
   - Would many hungry foxes change the mouse population?
   - What impact would introducing other species of small mammals that the fox could eat have?
   - How would increasing species diversity ensure the survival of the entire ecosystem?
   - Present your ideas to the class.
2. There are many ecosystems on the planet: ecosystem diversity. However, many consider our planet one big ecosystem. One example is how plastic trash from one part of the planet can affect life in another part of our ecosystem. Investigate this and find another example that demonstrates 'We are all one ecosystem'.

Glossary
breed : riprodursi
coal-burning : combustione del carbone
dark-bodied : di colore scuro

CITIZENSHIP AND COMPETENCY SKILLS Identifying links and relations

CLIL B
The Industrial Revolution
History

In this Module, we look at the Industrial Revolution: why it started in England and how it affected the English people.

1 LEAD IN When did the Industrial Revolution start and why was it considered a revolution? Read the following text to find out.

The Agricultural and Industrial Revolution of the eighteenth and nineteenth century changed, in only 100 years, the way people had worked for over 900 years. This is why it is called a *revolution*. The Industrial Revolution started in England around 1750. At the time, other regions in the world such as China and India had the same technological capabilities as England. So, why did the Industrial Revolution take off in England and not elsewhere? Many factors contributed.

2 PAIRWORK Look at the three factors below. Why do you think they were important for the Industrial Revolution?

During the Industrial Revolution, people invented machines. Machines were more efficient than manual labour.

1 Property rights
English laws protected inventors and made it illegal to steal **intellectual property**.

2 Inexpensive coal
Coal was an important fuel and provided energy for running machines. Initially, since coal in England was found near the surface, it was cheap and easy to **mine**.

3 Small population size
Since the population size in England was small, the speed of production was always limited by how many manual workers were available.

3 VISUAL LITERACY Read the text below. Which image (A or B) best summarises the information?

Before the Industrial Revolution, the transformation of cotton, from cotton plant to cotton fabric, was a very labour-intensive manual process. Cotton had to be imported from India because textile production in England was too slow and could not keep up with the demands. Since India had a population of around 24 million compared to England's 6 million, the Indian cotton industry was much more efficient. The English **textile** industry could not compete with the Indian cotton industry simply because there were fewer people in England to work in the cotton industry.

Glossary
fabric : stoffa
fuel : combustibile
intellectual property : proprietà intellettuale
mine : estrarre
steam : vapore
textile : tessile

CLIL B

4 [3.13] **VISUAL LITERACY** Why was the Industrial Revolution so successful? Read and listen to the text. Then, in pairs, decide which graph correctly represents the information.

Textile production in England was slow, so people invented machines that were faster. Early machines first used water for power and this tripled production. Water-operated machines were soon substituted by much more efficient steam-operated machines. To generate steam, coal was used to heat water. England had abundant supplies of coal and much of it was near the surface so it was very cheap to mine. As more and more industries began using steam-operated machines, more coal was needed, making it necessary to mine deeper. Eventually, machines were invented to facilitate this. At first, coal was transported by water, via rivers and canals. But with the invention of the light weight steam engine in 1769 it became possible to transport coal, and also other goods, much faster, cheaper and farther. That is why, once the Industrial Revolution started in England, the production and transportation of coal ensured its continued growth. This can be seen in the amount of coal usage before and after the Industrial Revolution. In 1700 England used under 3 million tons of coal but by 1830 it was using 30 million tons. In fact, by 1900, 200 million tons of coal was being mined to meet the fuel needs of England.

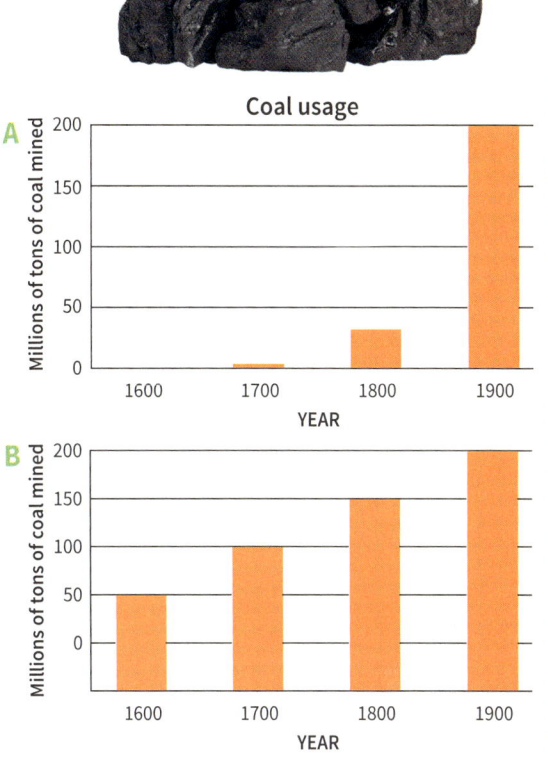

5 **Critical thinking** Look at the photos of some of the negative effects of the Industrial Revolution. Which do you think was the worst? Why?

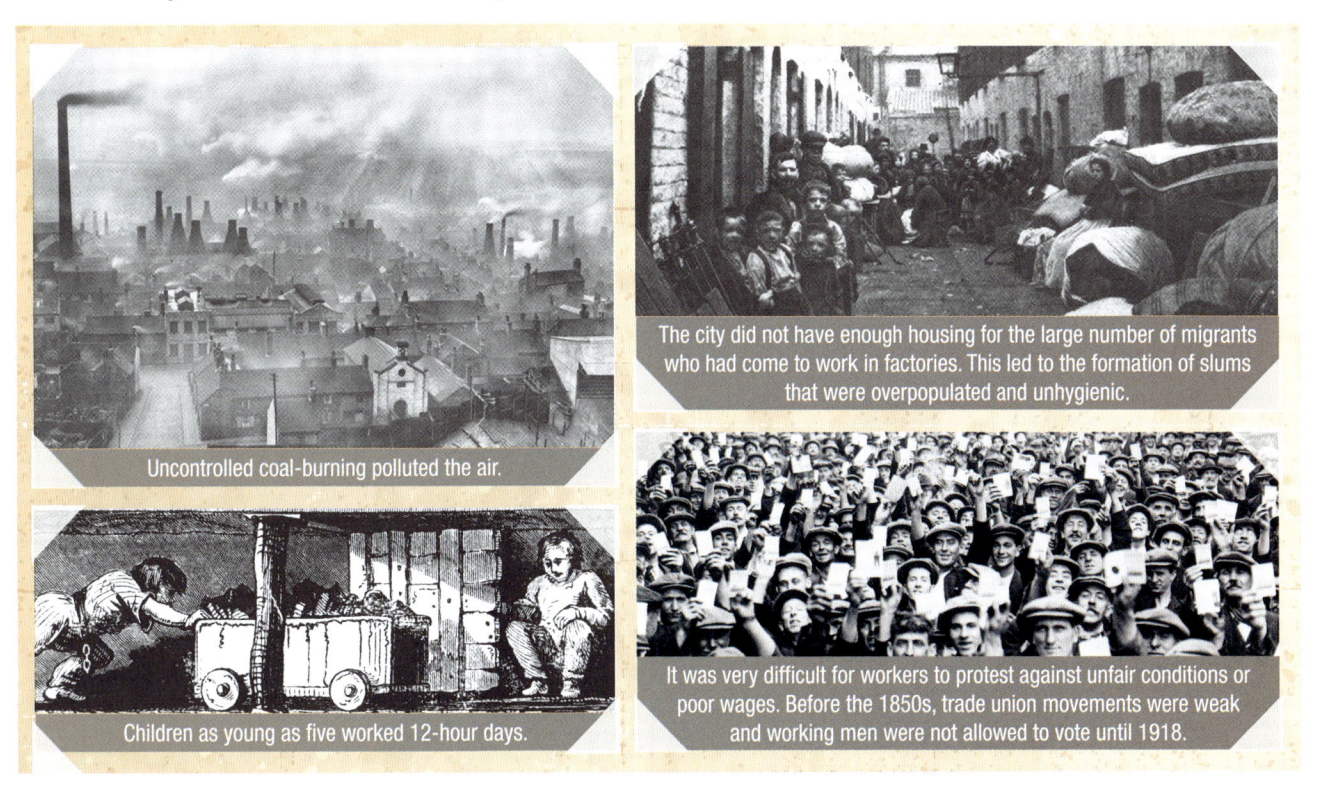

Uncontrolled coal-burning polluted the air.

The city did not have enough housing for the large number of migrants who had come to work in factories. This led to the formation of slums that were overpopulated and unhygienic.

Children as young as five worked 12-hour days.

It was very difficult for workers to protest against unfair conditions or poor wages. Before the 1850s, trade union movements were weak and working men were not allowed to vote until 1918.

6 **REAL-LIFE TASK** Work in groups of five to make a poster about the Industrial Revolution.

1 Decide which issues you will focus on in your poster.
2 Research it using reliable sources, cite these, and summarise your findings.
3 Find images and create graphs that help reinforce your message.

CITIZENSHIP AND COMPETENCY SKILLS Communicating

CLIL C
Geography
Migration

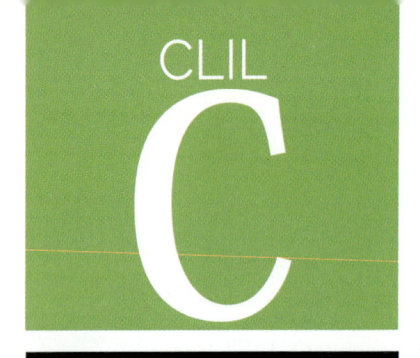

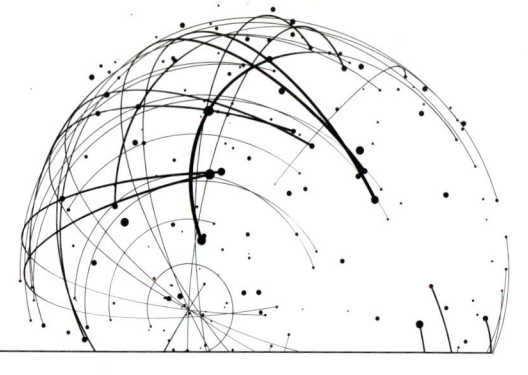

In this Module, we explore the distribution of populations and look at the problems caused by the rise of urbanisation.

1 [3.14] **LEAD IN** Where do most people in the world live? Read and listen to the following report to find out.

More and more people are moving from rural areas into urban areas. Geographers classify *rural areas* as those with a population density of less than 400 people/km² and urban areas are classified into three categories, depending on the number of people who are living in a **settlement**. For example, a *city* has at least 50,000 inhabitants while a *metropolis* has at least 500,000 people. When many metropolises form a continuous urban **spread**, they become an enormous *megalopolis* or a *megacity*. Some megacities have more than 10 million people!

2 **PAIRWORK** Use the information from exercise 1 to complete the definitions.

1 **Rural area:** .... than .... /km²
2 **City:** a settlement of .... 50,000 people.
3 **Metropolis:** a large urbanised area with at least .... inhabitants.
4 **Megalopolis / megacities:** A .... urban .... formed by many ....

3 Look at the diagrams of population distribution and use the information to correct the sentences.

1 In 1955, most of the megacities were in the Southern Hemisphere.
2 In 1955, there was one megacity in North America and one in South America.
3 The pie chart shows that, in 1955, only a little more than a quarter of the total world population lived in rural areas.
4 According to the pie chart, in 2015, a little less than half of the total world population lived in urban areas.

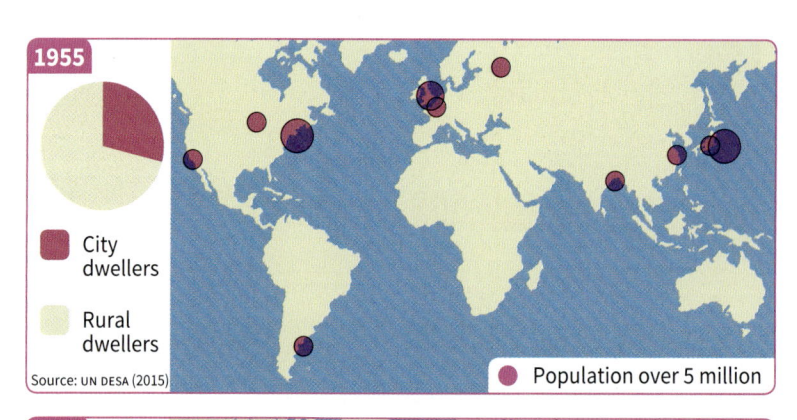

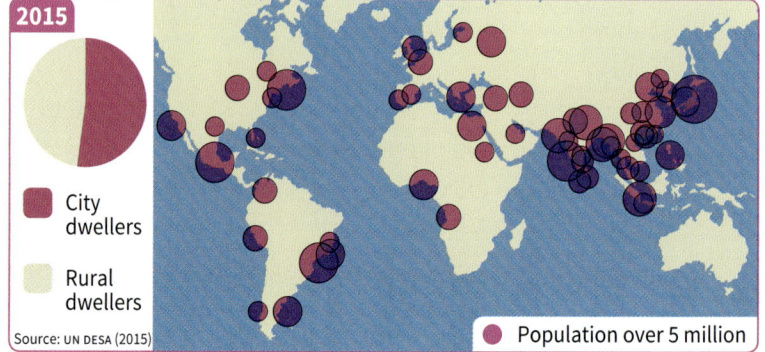

1955
- City dwellers
- Rural dwellers

Source: UN DESA (2015)

● Population over 5 million

2015
- City dwellers
- Rural dwellers

Source: UN DESA (2015)

● Population over 5 million

CLIL C

4 Why is urbanisation today more problematic? Read the text below to find out.

In older times, cities formed for pragmatic reasons: living close together gave settlements safety and socioeconomic benefits. However, the size of such settlements depended on the amount of food local farmlands could produce (Fig. **1**☐). With the Industrial Revolution, efficient machines replaced manual workers. This pushed people into cities to look for jobs. Even though living conditions for the newcomers were often difficult and harsh, most found jobs because the rapidly growing Industrial Revolution needed many workers (Fig. **2**☐). The movement from rural areas is continuing today. However, developing countries are facing what experts call *premature urbanisation*, where the number of jobs that cities can offer is far less than the number of migrants to the cities. This results in the creation of **slum areas** outside megacities (Fig. **3**☐). In addition, many of these people cannot return to their farms because new processes in agriculture such as overfarming and the use of pesticides have rendered these lands infertile (Fig. **4**☐). Slum areas are growing, which means that the number of destitute people without homes, or jobs or clean water or hope is now a serious problem in our globalised society.

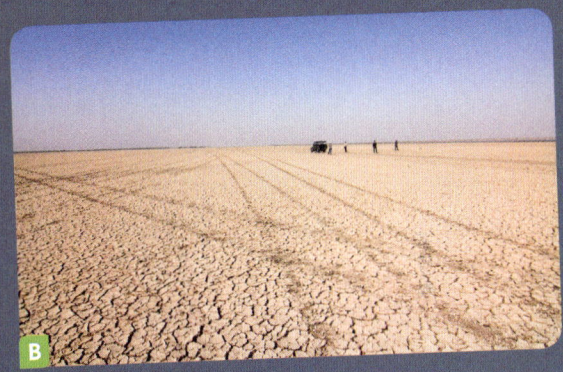

A

B

C

D

5 Now match the images A–D to the correct gaps 1–4 in the text.

6 **REAL-LIFE TASK** Work in groups of four. Choose one of the topics below and do some research on it. Then produce a short summary to present to the class.

1 The United Nations Millennium Declaration aimed to 'significantly improve the quality of life for 100 million slum dwellers by 2020'.
   - How many megacities are there in the world? Are these surrounded by slums? Approximately how many people live in these slums?
   - Research a slum around a megacity. What kind of social and health problems do people living there have?

2 Consider Italian history. What was the process of urbanisation? Look at the nineteenth century. Were there differences between urbanisation then and now?

Glossary
settlement : insediamento
slum areas : baraccopoli
spread : estensione

CITIZENSHIP AND COMPETENCY SKILLS Identifying links and relations ✓

CLIL D

Art

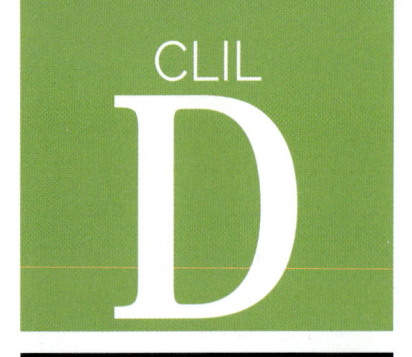

Conservation

In this Module, we explore how our cultural heritage is being threatened by processes in industry.

1 LEAD IN Work in pairs to answer the questions.

1. Look at the images. When you think of art, which of these three genres do you think of?
2. Do you have a preferred genre?
3. Do you have a favourite piece of art? If so, what is it?
4. Describe your favourite piece to your partner.

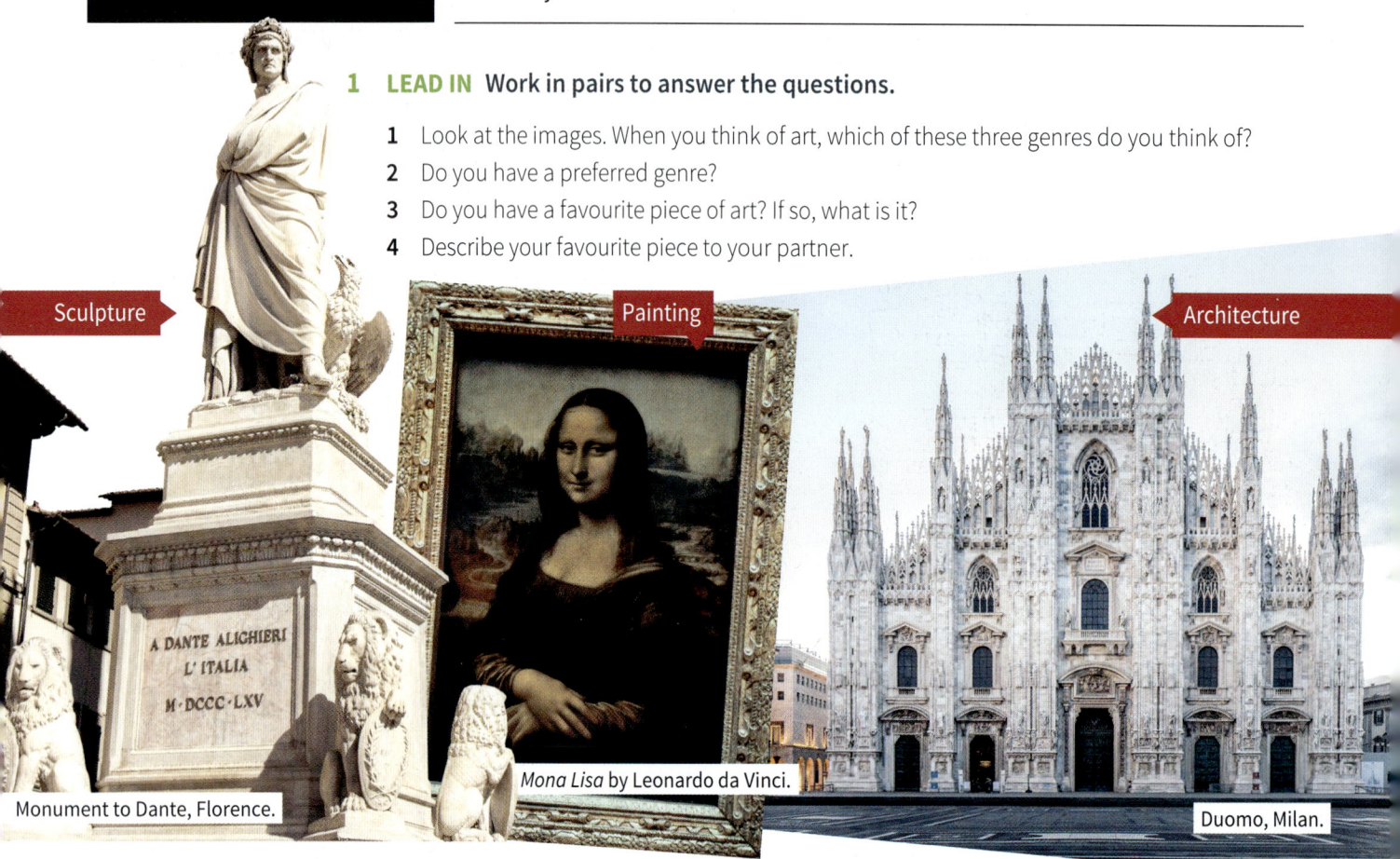

Sculpture

Painting

Architecture

Monument to Dante, Florence.

Mona Lisa by Leonardo da Vinci.

Duomo, Milan.

2 PAIRWORK Look at these images of a bronze statue before and after restoration and answer the questions.
Then share your thoughts with the class.

1. What are the main differences between the images?
2. What do you think caused the deterioration to the statue?

Glossary
cultural heritage : beni culturali
shells : gusci
threatened : minacciati
vinegar : aceto

BEFORE

AFTER

Martin Luther, Wittenberg.

246 CLIL D

CLIL D

3 **[3.15]** Listen and complete the three texts. Some letters of the missing words are given.

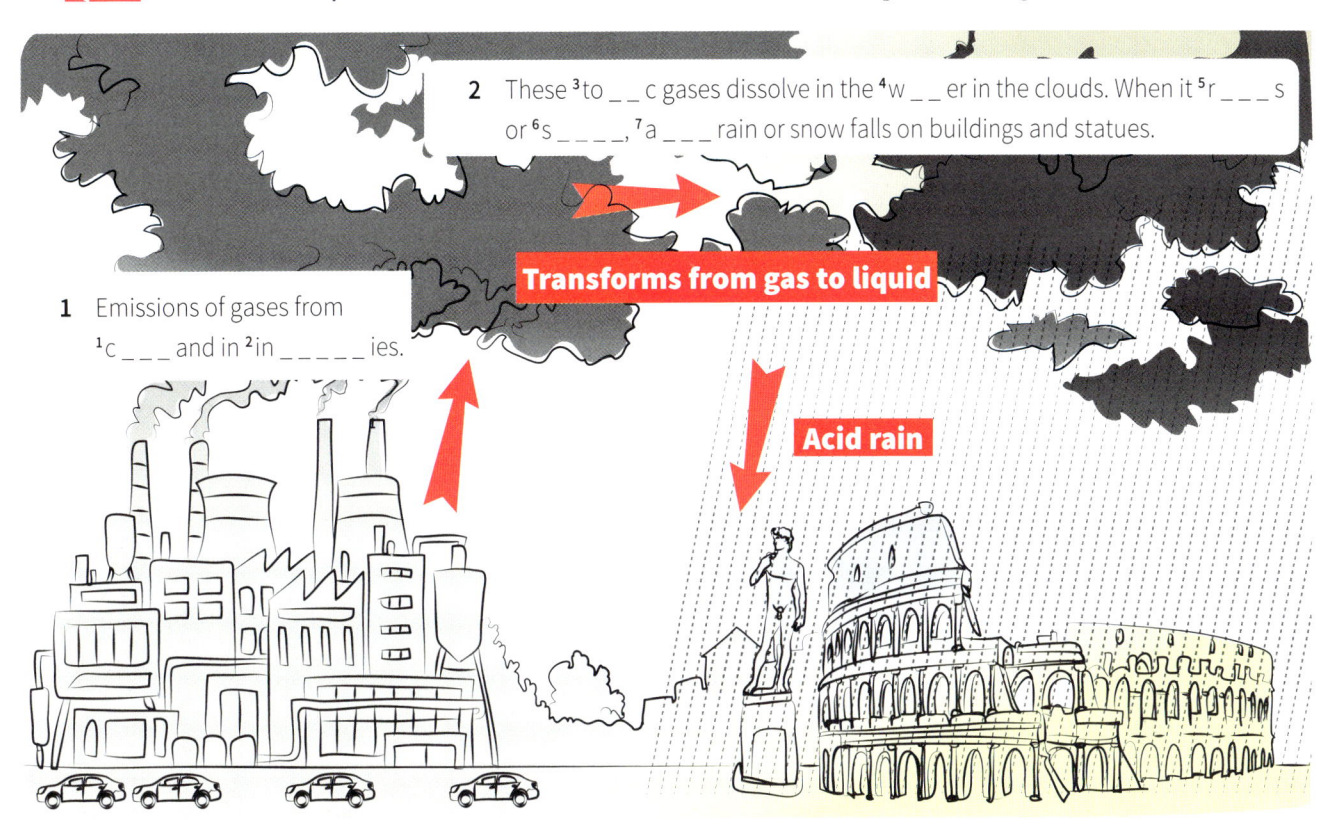

Transforms from gas to liquid

Acid rain

1 Emissions of gases from ¹c _ _ _ and in ²in _ _ _ _ _ ies.

2 These ³to _ _ c gases dissolve in the ⁴w _ _ er in the clouds. When it ⁵r _ _ _ s or ⁶s _ _ _ _, ⁷a _ _ _ rain or snow falls on buildings and statues.

3 ⁸M _ _ _ le is calcium carbonate, the same substance as egg **shells**. The sulphuric acid and nitric acid in acid rain dissolves the marble, like **vinegar** dissolves the shell of an ⁹e _ _. In time, the details are ¹⁰l _ _ t and ¹¹s _ _ _ ces become eroded and dark. Likewise, acid rain also ¹²e _ _ des metals which become rough and also lose their ¹³d _ _ _ ls.

Gargoyle, Notre Dame Cathedral, Paris.

Porta Nigra, Trier.

Mark the Evangelist, Vienna.

Archduke Charles of Austria, Vienna.

4 **REAL-LIFE TASK** Work in groups of four to identify a building or a sculpture that represents your local cultural heritage. Do some research on it. Use the questions to help you.

1 When were these pieces made, by whom and with what materials?
2 Find out if and how local agencies are protecting this local cultural heritage.
3 Prepare a 'report' to present to your class to help others understand why it matters that we pay attention to our local cultural heritage.

CITIZENSHIP AND COMPETENCY SKILLS Acquiring and interpreting information

CLIL E — Urbanisation and pollution

Maths

In this Module, we look at trends in urbanisation and pollution and consider how this affects health.

1. **LEAD IN** In pairs, think of two health-related problems that might be associated with life in big cities.

2. **PAIRWORK** Use the information in the text and Figures 1, 2 and 3 to complete Figures A, B and C.

The Urbanisation Trend

Some sources estimate that in 2030 there are going to be 8.1 billion people in the world and 5 billion will be living in urban areas (**Figure 1**). This is consistent with other reports that estimate that by 2050 67% of the 10 billion people in the world will be living in cities (**Figure A**). Increasing urbanisation has been a trend all over the world. **Figure 2** shows that, although only 30% of the world population in 1950 lived in urban areas, by 2014 55% of all the people in the world were **urban dwellers**. This data is presented in **Figure B**. How does Italy compare? **Figure 3** presents data regarding the distribution of people in rural and urban areas throughout Italy in 1950 and 2014, plus the **forecast** for 2050. These data are illustrated in **Figure C**.

Figure 1 — estimated % distribution of inhabitants (2030): urban 62%, rural 38%.

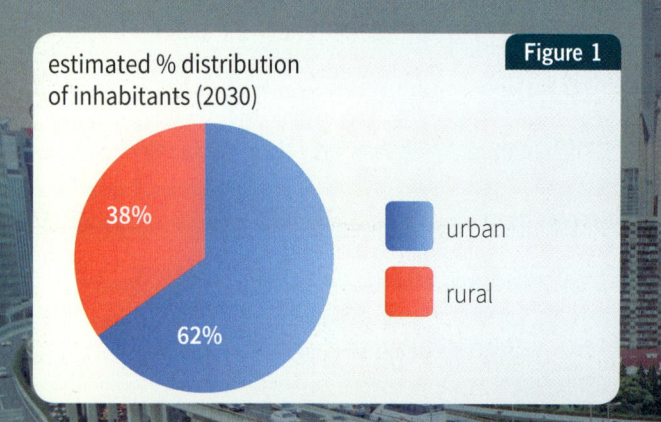

Figure A — estimated % distribution of inhabitants (2050): urban ☐, rural ☐.

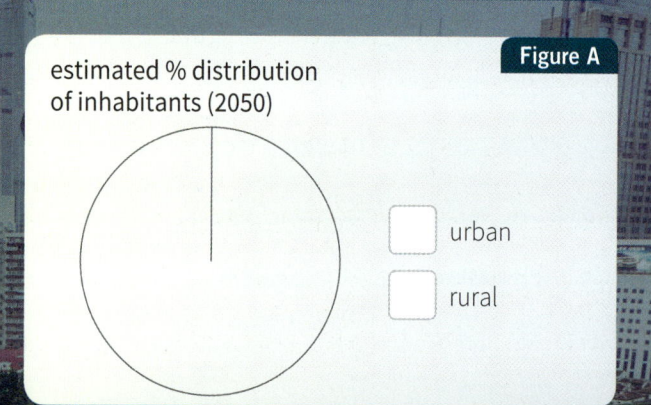

Figure 2 — World population distribution (1950, 2014, 2050): urban/rural.

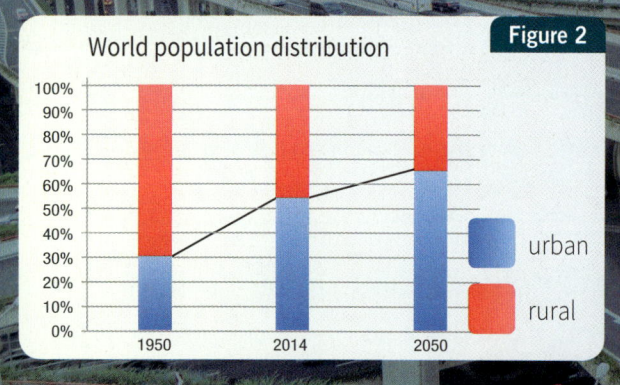

Figure B — World population distribution (actual and projected)

	% Rural	% Urban
1950		
2014	45%	
2050		65%

Figure 3 — Italy population distribution (actual and projected)

	% Rural	% Urban
1950	45%	55%
2014	30%	70%
2050	22%	78%

Figure C — Italy population distribution (1950, 2014, 2050): urban ☐, rural ☐.

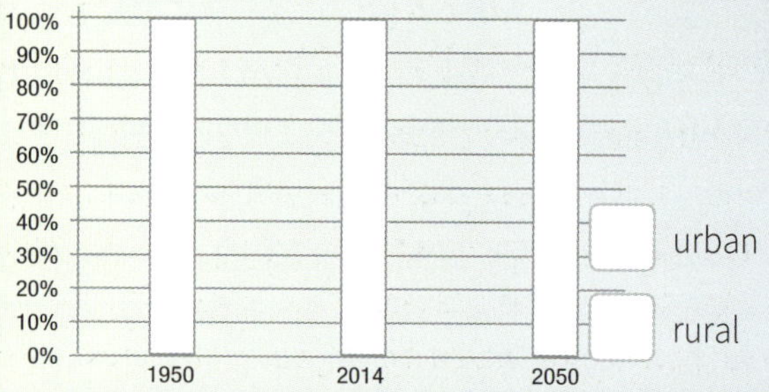

CLIL E

3 🎧 [3.16] **Listen to the text on air pollution and answer the questions.**

1. Why is air pollution more dangerous than malaria and HIV/AIDS?
2. Which gases cause air pollution and where do they come from?
3. What do gases mix with in the air to form microscopic particulate matter (PM)?
4. How can these particulate matters affect our health?

4 PAIRWORK How does urbanisation affect our health? Use the information from the map and graphs below to choose the correct option.

THE AIR WE BREATH

Polluting gases such as nitrogen oxides (NO_x) and sulphur dioxide (SO_2) are emitted from vehicles and factories every day: the famous smog that covers industrialised cities. When we **¹** *eat / breathe* these microscopic particles, they enter our lungs and can pass into the bloodstream, causing respiratory and cardiovascular problems.

Air-control stations have been installed throughout Europe to monitor **²** *water quality / air quality*. The map below shows the average concentration of PM measured at these stations in **³** *2014 / 2016*: each dot represents a control station. In Italy, the highest PM values were recorded in **⁴** *small agricultural towns / large industrial cities*. Stations in Spain and France registered **⁵** *the lowest / the highest* PM values while countries in **⁶** *Northern Europe / Eastern Europe* recorded higher PM values. The European Environmental Agency (EEA) reported that, of the 491,000 deaths in Europe that were related to air pollution, **⁷** *17% / 83%* were reported in Italy. Italy was, in fact, the country with the highest number of air-pollution-related deaths. Of the 84,400 cases reported, **⁸** *26% / 70%* were related to particulate matter exposure, **⁹** *26% / 70%* caused by exposure to NO_2 and **¹⁰** *4% / 26%* caused by exposure to other pollutants.

Concentration of particulate matter (PM) measured at air-quality control stations across Europe in 2014

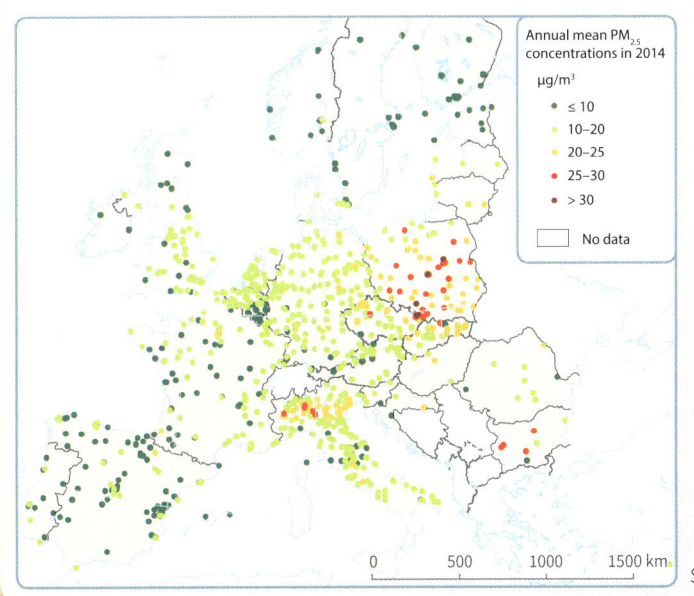

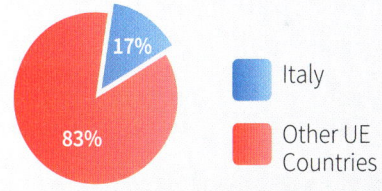

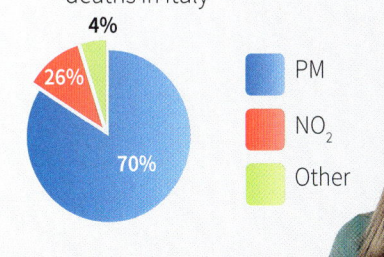

Source: EEA – European Environment Agency.

5 REAL-LIFE TASK Work in groups of four. Choose one of the topics below and do some research into it. Then present your findings to the class.

1. Investigate how geographical terrain affects air quality in Italy. Industries are often built where land is flat so transportation is easy. How do nearby mountains worsen the air pollution in industrial cities?
2. Exercise enthusiasts say jogging is an excellent way to keep fit. But how healthy would it be to jog when there is pollution?

Glossary
forecast : previsione
urban dwellers : persone che vivevano in città

CITIZENSHIP AND COMPETENCY SKILLS Identifying links and relations

1 WRITING EXPANSION

An informal email

Hi Tamsin!
How are things with you? Thanks for your last email. Sorry for not writing sooner, I've been very busy recently.
I've got some interesting news for you, I've made a new friend online and she lives in Bristol! How weird is that? I started chatting to her a few weeks ago and we immediately clicked. Now we've become great friends. Her name's Rebecca and she's very friendly and easygoing – I really like her. In fact, you both live in the same street! Her family lives at number 34 and their name's Brown. Do you know her? I haven't met her in person yet but we're planning to meet up in the school holidays. Maybe you could come too?
Anyway, that's all for now. Write soon and tell me your news.
Lots of love,

Claudia

1 Read the email. Choose the main reason Claudia is writing to Tamsin.

1 She wants to meet up with Tamsin.
2 She feels bad because she hasn't written to her for a long time.
3 She wants to tell her about her new online friend.

2 Answer these questions.

1 How did Claudia meet Rebecca?
2 How long have they been friends?
3 What is Rebecca like?
4 Where does she live?
5 What's her surname?
6 What is Claudia planning to do in the holidays?

3 Find phrases in Claudia's email to match to the sections of an informal email.

1 a greeting
2 a question asking how the person is
3 opening comments
4 closing comments
5 a suggestion for future contact
6 a phrase to say goodbye

4 Adjectives and adverbs make sentences more interesting. Add adverbs or adjectives below to the sentences. Use each word once.

really ▪ quickly ▪ adorable ▪ surprisingly ▪
disappointing ▪ fascinating ▪ finally

1 My parents gave me an ………………………… tiny kitten for my birthday.
2 I'm ………………………… happy. My brother is getting married!

3 After three days of calling him, I've ………………………… managed to talk to Graham.
4 Rob and I met in an online game and ………………………… became friends.
5 I've just read a ………………………… story about friendship.
6 I've just had some ………………………… news. I'm feeling a bit down.
7 I'm a terrible driver but I took my driving test yesterday and ………………………… I passed it!

5 TASK Write an informal email to a friend (100–150 words). Choose one of the following topics.

▪ Give advice on how to be a good friend to someone who is feeling sad (look back at the text on page 16 to get some ideas).
▪ Tell your friend about a new person you've met recently and why you like / don't like him / her.
▪ Reply to a friend's email with suggestions about how and where to make new friends.

Steps to writing

1 Choose your reason for writing.
2 Follow the sections in exercise 3 to organise your writing (make sure you include clear paragraphs: introduction, middle and end).
3 Include appropriate phrases in each section.
4 Use colloquial language and contractions.
5 Add adjectives and adverbs to make your writing interesting.

Writing Expansion

WRITING EXPANSION

A description of a place

A place I love

My grandmother lives in Derbyshire in a lovely old house above the town of Matlock. My family have been going there every summer
5 since I was three years old. My first happy memories of playing outside, surrounded by nature, are of that place near Matlock.
When we were children, my sister
10 and I always stayed with my grandmother for a month in the summer holidays. We loved going there because we were usually outside from morning till night, playing on the open **moor** in the sunshine, or in the **shady** woods near my grandmother's house. We played hide-and-seek for hours and I
15 remember the sweet smell of summer flowers as I lay in the long grass, waiting for my sister to find me. The ground was soft under me and the sun was warm on my face. Bees **buzzed** lazily in the still air. Sometimes my sister and I found **blackberries** on the moor and ate them. They were juicy and
20 sweet and the juice painted our fingers purple. There was a small stream nearby where we washed our hands and drank the cold, clear water, or **paddled our** white **feet** in it.
In my memory it seems the weather was always sunny on those long summer days – it never rained, it was never cold and we
25 were free and innocent, like birds. When I feel sad or worried now I think of that place I love, and it always makes me feel calm and happy.

Glossary
moor : brughiera
shady : ombroso
buzzed : ronzavano
blackberries : more
paddled our … feet : ci bagnavamo i piedi

1 Read the description of a place. Why does the writer love it?

2 Answer the questions with adjectives from the text.
1 What type of house does the writer's grandmother live in?
2 What sort of memories does the writer have about it?
3 What places did he and his sister play in?
4 Where did the writer hide from his sister?
5 How were the blackberries they sometimes found and ate?
6 What was the water in the stream like?
7 How is the weather in his memories of the place?

3 Find parts of the text to match the sections of a descriptive essay.
1 A good opening sentence stating why you've chosen that place.
2 Details of the location, special features, atmosphere, etc.
3 Your thoughts / feelings about it.
4 A memorable concluding sentence that summarises your reasons for choosing it.

4 Feelings related to the senses add a lot of interest to a descriptive essay. Complete the sentences with the words below. Then say which sense each word refers to.

loud ▪ wet ▪ bitter ▪ shady ▪ soft ▪ sweet

> **Senses:** sight, sound, smell, taste, touch

1 My feet were cold and ……………… from the snow by the time I arrived home.
2 The garden was full of the ……………… perfume of roses.
3 The rock music was so ……………… that we couldn't talk at all.
4 It was green and ……………… under the trees in the vast forest.
5 The sand under my feet was warm and ……………… .
6 The coffee he brought us was black, ……………… and hot.

5 TASK Write a descriptive essay (100–150 words). Choose one of the following topics.
▪ a place I loved when I was a child
▪ a place I visited that moved me
▪ a place I visited that scared me

Steps to writing
1 Choose your topic.
2 Brainstorm adjectives to describe the place and your feelings about it.
3 In paragraph 1 introduce the place, say where it was and why you chose it.
4 In paragraph 2 provide a detailed description with plenty of adjectives.
5 Finish your essay with a memorable concluding sentence.

3 A review

This production at the National Theatre is an adaptation of Michael Morpurgo's novel *War Horse*. It tells a story of love and war through the eyes of a horse. In the play the horses are
5 represented on stage by amazing, life-sized **puppets**. The story is about a horse called Joey and his relationship with Albert, the teenage boy who trains him. It is set against the events of WW1 in England and France.

10 The story begins in 1914 on a farm in England. Albert trains Joey to work on their farm, but the family are poor and Albert's father sells Joey to the army, who need horses for the war. The action then moves to wartime France. There
15 we see all the horrors of war through Joey's eyes and he has a couple of lucky **escapes** from **death**. For me, the **highlight** of the play was the incredible realism of the life-sized puppets. Their movements are so realistic that they are
20 completely convincing. It's an unusual idea to talk about love and war from the point of view of an animal but it works. I would definitely recommend this production: the story is **touching** and makes you think, and the puppets are superb.

Glossary
puppets : pupazzi
escapes : fughe
death : morte
highlight : punto forte
touching : commovente

1 Look at the photo and answer the questions.
  1 What do you notice about the horse?
  2 What type of entertainment do you think the review is going to be about?
     A a film   C a cartoon
     B a play   D a book

252 Writing Expansion

WRITING EXPANSION

2 Now read the review and answer the questions.
  1 Where did the performance take place?
  2 Where does the original story of the play come from?
  3 What's the main theme?
  4 Who is the main character?
  5 What happens to the main character?
  6 How does the writer feel about the production? Why?

3 Underline the phrases / sentences in the review about these things.
  - setting
  - characters
  - plot / main events
  - special effects / characteristics
  - personal recommendation

4 Look at these phrases for describing a story. Find them in the text and complete the sentences with the missing information.
  1 It tells a story of …
  2 The story is about …
  3 It is set …
  4 The story begins in …
  5 The action then moves to …

5 Think about a play, film or book you've seen or read. Use the prompts below to make notes about it.
  - setting and characters
  - plot and events
  - good / bad points
  - personal opinion

6 TASK Write a review (140–190 words) about the work you chose. Use the Steps to writing box, your notes from exercise 5 and the phrases from exercise 4 to help you.

Steps to writing
1 Choose a film / play / book, etc. you know well.
2 Makes notes about setting, characters, plot and reasons why you liked it.
3 In paragraph 1 give the title and background, describe the setting and characters.
4 In paragraph 2 use appropriate phrases to summarise the main events.
5 In paragraph 3 explain why you liked it and give a personal recommendation.
6 Check your spelling and grammar.

WRITING EXPANSION

A 'for and against' essay

Must we ban contact sports for children?

We all want children to enjoy physical activities. Playing team sports is an important part of learning to work together, and it's a great way to stay fit and healthy. However, many parents are worried about the dangers of contact sports like rugby and football, specifically the risk of serious **head injuries**. But how real are the risks from contact sports?

If we're going to ban risky activities for children, we need to look at the wider picture. Although we've all heard about the possible risks from contact sports, research shows that the greatest risks of serious head injuries are actually from skiing, snowboarding and horse riding. Do we need to ban all sports to eliminate risk from our children's lives?

In fact, is eliminating risk from children's lives the best solution? In team sports, children learn to **assess** risk and how to deal with it, an important ability in their later professional lives. Are we creating a generation of adults who are afraid of taking risks – no more astronauts, artists or entrepreneurs?

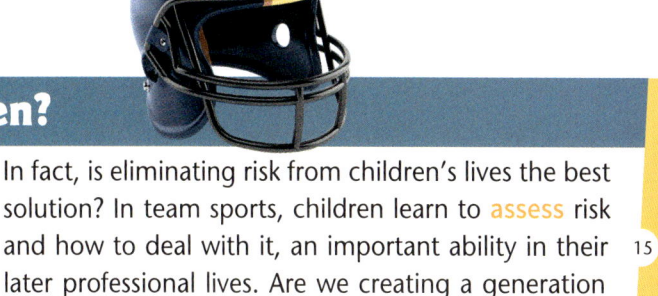

Although there are lots of alarmist stories about head injuries from contact sports, serious injuries are very rare. There is simply not enough **evidence** to support the argument that the dangers of contact sports **outweigh** the benefits.

Glossary
head injuries : traumi cranici
assess : valutare
evidence : prove
outweigh : sono maggiori di

1 Read the essay. Does the writer agree or disagree with the argument in the title?

2 Answer these questions.
1 Why are parents worried about contact sports in schools?
2 Which other sports have a high risk of head injuries?
3 What do some people think is the solution to avoid this risk?
4 What is a possible negative consequence of eliminating risk from children's lives?
5 How does the writer describe the stories about head injuries from contact sports?

3 Underline the phrases / sentences in the paragraphs which tell us these things.

Para 1: the two sides of the argument
Para 2: reasons for the argument
Para 3: reasons against the argument
Para 4: the writer's opinion about the argument

WRITING STRATEGY

Linkers for contrast

Look at these sentences:
- *Playing team sports is a great way to stay fit and healthy. **However**, many parents are worried about the dangers of contact sports like rugby and football, …*
- ***Although** we've all heard about the possible risks from contact sports, research shows that the greatest risks of head injuries are actually from skiing …*

4 TASK Write a 'for and against' essay (140–190 words) on one of these topics. Use linkers to contrast points for and against the argument.

- team sports help to develop the team spirit in life too
- schools must include e-sports on their PE curriculum
- some sports are only for boys and some are only for girls

Steps to writing
1 Choose your topic.
2 Brainstorm ideas for and against the argument.
3 In paragraph 1 introduce the topic and both sides of the argument.
4 In paragraphs 2 and 3 provide reasons and examples for both sides.
5 In the last paragraph write a conclusion and state your opinion.
6 Remember to use linkers to contrast your ideas.
7 Use formal language and avoid direct speech.
8 Remember to check your spelling and grammar.

5 WRITING EXPANSION

A police report

Willow Bank Police Station, Middleton

Date: Wednesday January 16th
Time: h 14:15
Witness: Miss Julie Fellows
Address: 27 Forest Road, Middleton

It was January the 15th. I was watching TV at home. At 9:30 pm I went into the kitchen to make a cup of tea. I know it was 9:30 pm because the news had just finished on TV. I opened the back door to call my cat. While I was waiting, I noticed something unusual. There was snow on the ground and someone had made **footprints** in my garden. The footprints went towards my neighbour's garden. It was dark, so I couldn't see anyone at first. Then I saw a man. He came out of the trees and went towards my neighbour's garage.

He was quite short and he was wearing a dark **hoodie**. I don't know how old he was because his face was hidden. He tried to open the garage door but it was **locked**. Then he went around the back of the garage and I couldn't see him.
I went into the living room to phone my neighbour. While I was looking for her number, I heard a car **engine**. Then I saw my neighbour's blue car go past my house. The car was going very fast and I noticed that the side window on the right was broken. After that I phoned the police and told them what I had seen.

Glossary
footprints: orme
hoodie: felpa con cappuccio
locked: chiusa a chiave
engine: motore

CLASSIFIED

1 Look at the pictures and answer the questions.
   1 What type of crime do you think the report is about?
   2 What time of year did it happen?

2 Read the report and put the pictures in exercise 1 in the correct order.

3 Complete column 1 of the table with information from the text. Is Julie a good witness?

	1 Julie's report	2 My report
Date of crime		
Time		
Place		
Name of witness		
Relationship to victim		
Description of crime		

4 Choose one of the situations below. Imagine you were a witness to this crime. Complete column 2 of the table in exercise 3 with your ideas.

1 You were in the shopping mall. You saw a woman. She was stealing a dog from outside a shop.
2 You were on a train. You saw a gang of teenagers. They were painting graffiti on the wall of a church.
3 You were in the bank. You saw two men in masks come in. You heard them tell the bank clerk to give them all the money.

5 TASK Write a report (140–190 words) about the crime you chose in exercise 4. Use the Steps to writing box and the information from the table to help you.

Steps to writing
1 Makes notes about when and where the crime happened.
2 Say what time it happened and why you remember.
3 Describe the events using appropriate past tenses.
4 Describe the suspect.
5 Use short sentences and factual language.
6 Leave out unnecessary adjectives and adverbs.
7 Use indefinite pronouns (*someone*, *something*, etc.).
8 Check your spelling and grammar.

WRITING EXPANSION

A summary

> **WRITING TIP**
>
> A **topic sentence** is the key sentence in a paragraph of text. It tells us the main message of the paragraph and contains important keywords. In summarising a passage it's useful to identify the topic sentence first.

1 Look back at the text on pages 62–63. Read three possible topic sentences for paragraph 1. Which is correct?

> 1 Leopards are solitary animals and rarely come into contact with humans.
>
> 2 However, reports from Mumbai in India show that the leopard's behaviour may be changing.
>
> 3 The film shows that in fact these leopards are looking for a different dinner.

2 **PAIRWORK** Discuss with a partner. Why are the other two sentences not good topic sentences?

3 Now underline the topic sentences in paragraphs 2 and 3.

4 Which of these are keywords and expressions in paragraph 1 of the text? Tick (✓) the keywords and cross out the rest.

1 leopards
2 solitary
3 cities
4 rarely
5 felines
6 India
7 hunting
8 Mumbai
9 attack
10 pigs
11 constant
12 noise

5 Now circle the keywords in paragraphs 2 and 3.

6 Read a summary in 58 words of the introduction and paragraph 1 of the text. Tick (✓) the types of information that it <u>doesn't</u> contain.

1 names   4 impressions
2 facts   5 times
3 places   6 descriptions

> Cities are growing and are destroying the habitats of many wild animals. Because of this, some animals are moving into cities and are adapting to life there. In India a film crew filmed leopards hunting in the city at night. The film shows leopards going into the city to attack pigs, which the inhabitants keep in their gardens.

7 **TASK** Now use the topic sentences from exercise 3 and the keywords from exercise 5 to produce a summary of the other two paragraphs in the text. Use the Writing tip and the Steps to writing boxes to help you. Write about 100 words.

> **Steps to writing**
>
> 1 Identify the topic sentence(s) in the text.
> 2 Underline the key information and make a list of bullet points.
> 3 Circle the keywords.
> 4 Rewrite the bullet points in short, clear sentences.
> 5 Use your own words.
> 6 Don't include additional details, descriptions or impressions.
> 7 Avoid repetition.

Writing Expansion 255

7 WRITING EXPANSION

A proposal

How to make us healthier – a proposal

A Introduction
The aim of this proposal is to present a plan to make our community healthier. **Furthermore**, our objective is to encourage young people in particular to become more physically active and socialise more often.

B Background
We believe that the general population is not active enough and this is causing health problems, even in teenagers. Treating these problems puts huge pressure on local health services. If people did more exercise, the number of people with these problems would decrease and the health service could treat more serious **illnesses**.

C The proposal
We suggest that schools should get together with the council to coordinate regular sporting events. These could include fun runs and cycle races, perhaps once a month. In addition, improved sports facilities could include cycle paths, running tracks and exercise machines in parks, and free fun exercise classes in schools.

D Concluding remarks
In conclusion, we believe young people in our area are not sufficiently active and this is affecting their health. Our proposal is to improve this situation by creating better facilities and more occasions to get active. **Admittedly**, it will not be cheap to implement these suggestions. However, we believe that if we do this, eventually these solutions will create real **savings** in the health service.

Glossary
furthermore : inoltre   admittedly : certamente
illnesses : malattie   savings : risparmi

---

1 Read the proposal. Which of the suggestions from the Writing strategy on page 73 does it mention?

2 Read the proposal again and decide if the sentences are true (T) or false (F). Correct the false ones.

1. The writers believe lack of exercise causes major health problems for a lot of teenagers. T F
2. Their suggestions include indoor and outdoor facilities. T F
3. They think these suggestions won't cost a lot of money. T F

3 Match the phrases from the proposal to their functions.

1. ☐ In conclusion
2. ☐ We suggest that …
3. ☐ In addition
4. ☐ We believe that …
5. ☐ The aim of this proposal is …

a introducing the reason for the proposal
b explaining the background to the problem
c presenting the solution
d giving additional details
e summarising the proposal and its benefits

4 TASK Read the situation and write a proposal with your suggestions (140–190 words). Use the Steps to writing box and the phrases from exercise 3 to help you.

Your town has won a large amount of lottery money to make it a healthier place to live. The local council is holding a competition to decide the best way to use the money.

Steps to writing

1. Introduce the topic and state the reason for the proposal.
2. Use appropriate phrases to add background information.
3. Present the solution and add details about it.
4. Summarise the proposal and mention some of its benefits.
5. Use formal, factual language.
6. Use appropriate language to make recommendations.
7. Check the sentences are logically connected.
8. Check your spelling and grammar.

WRITING EXPANSION

A biography

1 Read the biography. Where did Nelson Mandela spend most of his life?

NELSON MANDELA: FATHER OF A NATION

Nelson Mandela was called the 'Father of a Nation' because, after many years campaigning for racial equality in South Africa, he eventually became the first black president. By the time he became president in 1994, he had convinced the government to end the
5 racist system called *apartheid*, which discriminated against black people. But Mandela wasn't only the father of a nation. He was also the father of six children of his own and had 18 grandchildren!

Nelson had four children with his first wife, Evelyn, before they divorced in 1958. He then had two children with his second wife,
10 Winnie, before they divorced in 1996, six years after his release from prison. He didn't have any children with his third wife. He
15 dedicated his life to politics and spent 27 years in prison because of his anti-apartheid
20 beliefs. However, he always felt that if he hadn't been in prison for most of his life, he would have been able to enjoy his family more.
25 When he retired in 2004, he was finally able to spend more time being a father. Before he died in 2013 he said, 'To be the father of a nation is a great honour, but to be
30 the father of a family is a greater joy'.

2 Write the dates for these events in Nelson Mandela's life and put them in chronological order.

a ☐ .... He became the first black president.
b ☐ .... He died.
c ☐ .... He went to prison.
d ☐ .... He divorced Evelyn.
e ☐ .... He divorced Winnie.
f ☐ .... He left prison.

3 Biographies often focus on particular areas of the person's life. Which two aspects of Mandela's life does the text focus on?

1 childhood   3 career and achievements
2 family   4 travels

4 Only one of these sentences about Mandela is true. Decide which one then correct the others.

1 He changed the system of government in South Africa after he became president. ☐ T ☐ F
2 He married three times. ☐ T ☐ F
3 He had four children. ☐ T ☐ F
4 He always spent a lot of time with his family. ☐ T ☐ F
5 He felt his political success was more satisfying than being a father. ☐ T ☐ F

5 Choose the best time markers below to complete these sentences.

after ▪ before ▪ by the time ▪ then ▪
eventually ▪ later ▪ when

1 Ed and Sue got married. They had been together for 2 years.
   When / By the time / Before Ed and Sue got married, they had been together for 2 years.
2 Jake had been married to Lily. He divorced her and married Ronnie.
3 Harry joined Greenpeace. He had been interested in green politics for years.
4 Jo campaigned for a long time. She became an MP.
5 Callum and Olivia adopted Greg. He was a baby.
6 First the family lived in Vienna. They moved to Prague.

6 TASK Write a biography (140–190 words) of a person you like. Use the Steps to writing box and exercise 5 to help you. Focus on some of these areas.

▪ childhood   ▪ career   ▪ travels
▪ family life ▪ achievements

Steps to writing

1 Choose a person you are interested in.
2 Find out the basic facts of the person's life.
3 Think about what else you'd like to know about the person and research these aspects.
4 Decide how to present the events, chronologically or by theme.
5 Choose one area of their life or one theme and focus on that.
6 Use time markers to present the events clearly and in an interesting order.
7 Check your grammar and spelling.

Writing Expansion 257

9 WRITING EXPANSION

A formal letter or email

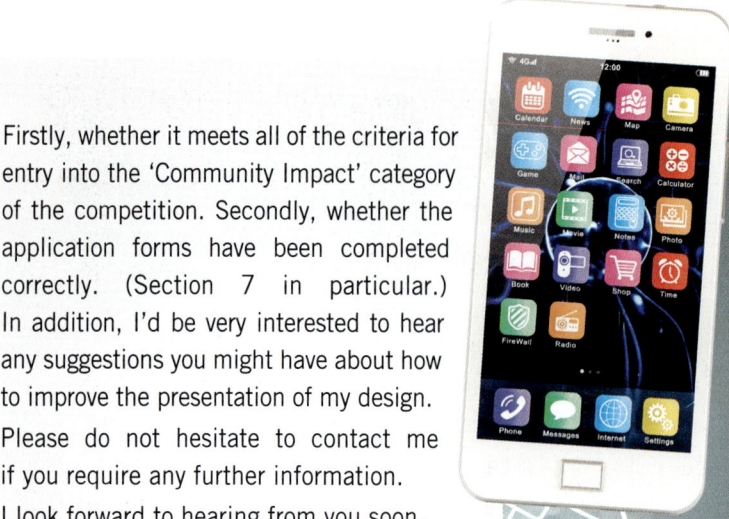

Dear Mrs Morley,

I am writing to the British Design Association to present my design for the Young Inventor of the Year competition in the 14–16 years category.

5 My project is a smartphone app for young people which has been designed to help *maximise* the use of the available sports facilities in their areas. The aim of the app is to increase the use of communal sports facilities by young people.

10 It does this by creating groups *at short notice* who can use the spaces together, as they become available, to do sports and socialise.

I would be *grateful* if you could read the attached description of the project and give me
15 your *feedback* on the following points.

Firstly, whether it meets all of the criteria for entry into the 'Community Impact' category of the competition. Secondly, whether the application forms have been completed
20 correctly. (Section 7 in particular.) In addition, I'd be very interested to hear any suggestions you might have about how to improve the presentation of my design.

Please do not hesitate to contact me
25 if you require any further information.

I look forward to hearing from you soon.

Yours sincerely,

Michael Appleton

Glossary
maximise : ottimizzare
at short notice : con breve preavviso
grateful : grato
feedback : riscontro

---

1 Read the letter. What is the writer's reason for writing it?

2 Read and decide if the sentences are true (T) or false (F). Correct the false ones.

1 Michael is between 14 and 16 years old. T F
2 His project is an app for sport centres. T F
3 The aim of the app is to make teenagers do exercise. T F
4 Michael would like to hear Mrs Morley's opinions on the app. T F
5 He had some difficulty completing the application forms. T F
6 He hopes she'll reply soon. T F

3 Find the phrases in Michael's letter which correspond to the features of a formal letter / email listed below.

1 greeting
2 the reason for writing
3 a request
4 encourage someone to reply
5 end the email

4 Find formal expressions in Michael's letter which correspond to these informal expressions.

1 Hi!
2 Call me if you want to
3 Love,
4 Can you …?
5 My project's for …
6 Write back soon!

5 TASK Read the situation and do the task.

Situation: Your region has organised a songwriting competition for high-school students. The songs have to be about the town where you live. A famous popstar is going to perform the winning song on national television. You've written a song that you think has a good chance of winning.

Task: Write a formal letter asking to submit your song in the competition. Explain what it's about and ask for feedback from the organisers (140–190 words). Use the Steps to writing box and expressions you found in exercise 4.

Steps to writing

1 Include a formal greeting with the person's title (*Mr, Mrs, Dr*, etc.).
2 Give your reason for writing.
3 Make a request.
4 Encourage the reader to reply quickly.
5 Include a formal ending (*Yours sincerely, Kind regards*).
6 Use formal language and full verb forms.
7 Check your spelling and grammar.

WRITING EXPANSION

A magazine report

BEAUTY, and the BEST!

The Emma Watson interview

Emma Watson is the kind of girl you'd want as your best friend – intelligent, attractive, talented and an all-round really nice gal! In celebration of her new movie *Beauty and the Beast*, we sat down with Disney's newest star to
5 talk films and feminism.

Firstly, I asked Emma whether she had kept anything from the film set as a souvenir. She told me that the costume designer had designed a ring for Belle which Emma thought was really beautiful. She asked if she could keep
10 it after the film and now she wears it all the time.

The film has a happy-ever-after ending, when Belle and the Beast get married. I asked Emma what she imagined happened to her character after that. She said she thought Belle opened a school and a public library in the
15 castle, which she ran for the local people!

When she's not acting, Emma campaigns for women's rights, so I asked what she thought was the biggest problem for young women today. She pointed out that although girls are told they don't need feminism anymore,
20 they're still treated differently to men in the workplace so there's still a lot to do to achieve 100% equality.

Glossary
nice gal : tipa piacevole
happy-ever-after : tutti vissero felici e contenti
anymore : non più

---

1 Read the interview. Why has Emma Watson been interviewed?

2 Answer the questions.
  1 Which film company made Emma's latest film?
  2 What did Emma keep as a souvenir of the film?
  3 What did Emma imagine happens to her character after the film ends?
  4 What work is Emma involved in apart from acting?
  5 Does she think that feminism is still relevant in today's society? Why / Why not?

3 The interviewer asks Emma three questions. Underline the reported questions in the text. Rewrite them in direct speech.

4 Underline two facts about Emma in the text (blue) and an opinion (red).

5 TASK Read the situation and do the task.

Situation: You've been asked to write an imaginary report of an interview with a famous celebrity for your school blog. Think of someone you would like to interview from the world of entertainment, film or sport. Research some information about them online. What do you think people would like to know about them?

Task: Write the report of your interview (140–190 words). Think of three or four key questions you want to ask the celebrity and how to report them. Then write their 'answers' to your questions, based on your research. Use the Steps to writing box to help you with the interview and the Writing strategy on page 99 to invent a good headline.

Steps to writing
1 Invent an eye-catching headline.
2 Include some background information about the celebrity (career successes, family, etc.).
3 Express your opinion about them.
4 Give a reason for interviewing them.
5 Report the questions you asked them using reported speech.
6 Give their answers using reported speech.
7 Use informal language.
8 Check your spelling and grammar.

1 VOCABULARY EXTENSION

Adjective prefixes

> **WORD STRATEGY**
>
> **Prefixes**
>
> You can give an adjective the opposite meaning by adding a prefix like *un-*, *im-* and *in-*. These prefixes usually make adjectives with negative connotations.
>
> | prefix | example | |
> |--------|---------|---|
> | un- | tidy | → untidy |
> | | kind | → unkind |
> | | reliable | → unreliable |
> | im- | patient | → impatient |
> | | practical | → impractical |
> | in- | sensitive | → insensitive |
> | | sincere | → insincere |

1 Study the table in the Word strategy box. Then use a dictionary to find the opposites of the adjectives below. Then write them in the correct group in the diagram.

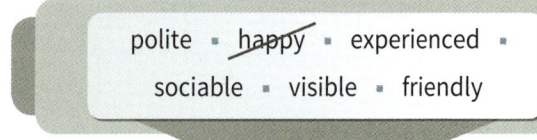

polite · ~~happy~~ · experienced · sociable · visible · friendly

un-
unhappy
....
....
....

im-
....
....
....

in-
....
....
....

2 Complete the sentences with the opposites of the adjectives in exercise 1.

0 I don't think Sharon is right for the job. She's too young and **inexperienced**.
1 It's wrong to speak to the teacher like that. It's ....
2 My sister's boyfriend has left her and now she's very ....
3 Frank hasn't got many friends – he's shy and rather ....
4 I don't like Frank. He's moody and ....
5 You fixed that vase really well. The break is almost ....

3 PAIRWORK Discuss the following.

1 Describe your personality.
2 Use three positive and three negative adjectives from this page and from the Vocabulary lesson on page 20.
3 Does your partner agree?

I'm easygoing, kind and cheerful, but I can be stubborn, moody and unreliable.

260 Vocabulary Extension

VOCABULARY EXTENSION

Prepositions of movement

WORD STRATEGY

Prepositions of movement
- Prepositions of movement describe the direction of an action.
- They come after the verb in the sentence.
- They are usually followed by a noun.

1 Write the prepositions below under the pictures.

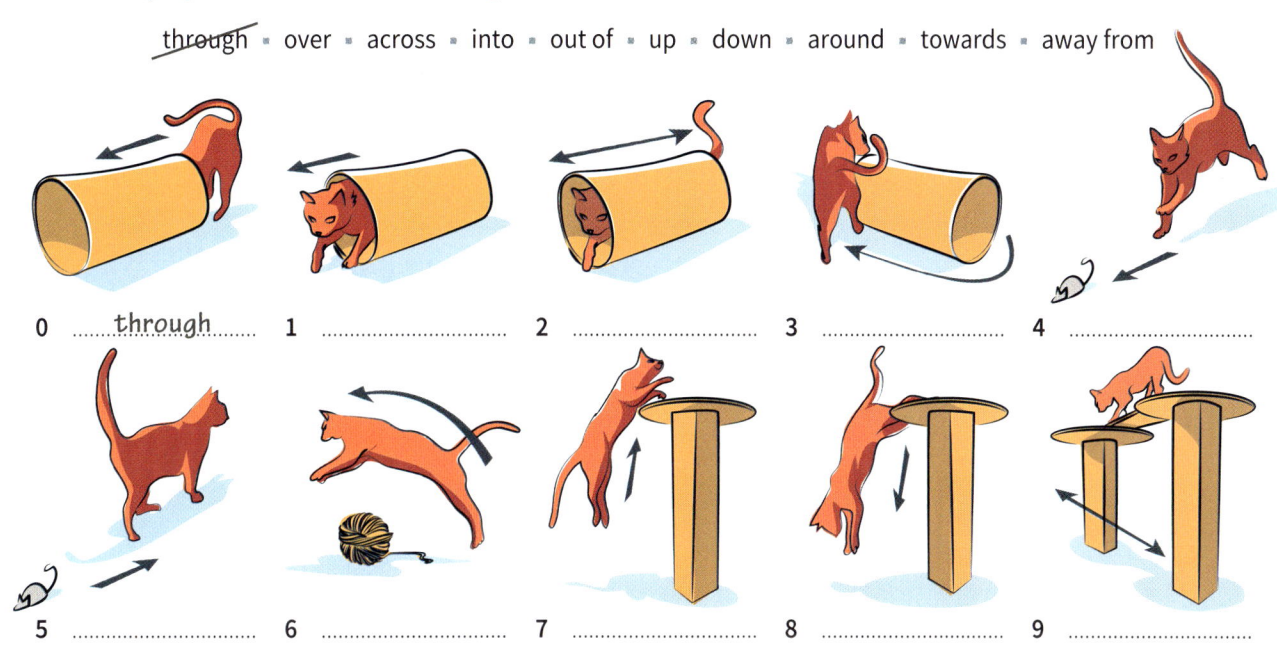

through • over • across • into • out of • up • down • around • towards • away from

0 ...through...   1 ....   2 ....   3 ....   4 ....

5 ....   6 ....   7 ....   8 ....   9 ....

2 Match the beginnings and ends of the sentences.

1	c	The tiger walked slowly through …
2		Tower Bridge is a bridge over …
3		We drove around …
4		The fire is coming towards …
5		My brother fell into …
6		It took us five hours to climb up …

a	the city for hours.
b	the river and got wet.
c	the long grass.
d	the mountain.
e	the River Thames in London.
f	the houses. Call the fire brigade!

3 PAIRWORK Act out the situation.

Student A: Draw a route from your house to the school. Describe it to Student B.

Student B: Draw the route your partner describes.

Compare maps: are they the same?

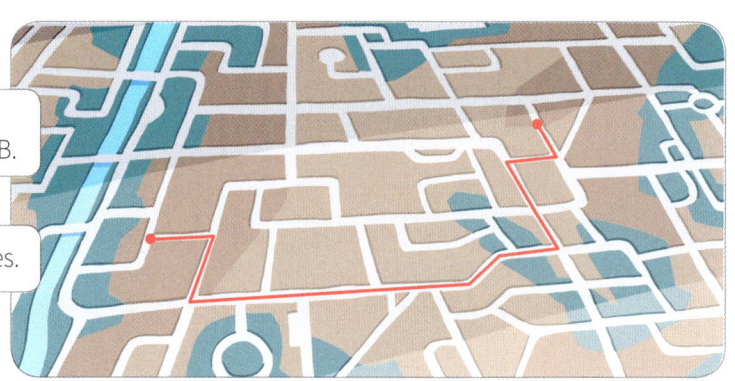

Vocabulary Extension 261

3 VOCABULARY EXTENSION

Literary idioms

1 Read some of the most common idioms about books in English. Match them to their meanings. Check your answers in a monolingual dictionary.

1. [d] be an open book
2. [ ] turn over a new leaf
3. [ ] be on the same page as someone
4. [ ] be in someone's good books
5. [ ] read someone like a book
6. [ ] to bring someone to book
7. [ ] do things by the book
8. [ ] cook the books

a. have the same view or opinion
b. do things correctly, follow all the rules
c. falsify or hide financial information
d. be very honest and open
e. get rid of a bad habit, change your behaviour
f. another person likes you and approves of you
g. intuitively understand a person
h. punish a person when they've done wrong

2 Complete the sentences with idioms from exercise 1.

0. I've been very honest with you. I've been ...*an open book*... .
1. I'm really unfit, I never do any exercise, but I've decided that next month I'm going to .... and start running.
2. Dan and I get on very well. We think the same and we're always .... about every topic.
3. When you sit your driving test you need to do things ....
4. Deacon Brodie was a famous thief. The Scottish police eventually ....
5. I helped my mum a lot last weekend, so now I'm ....!

3 Many of the most common idioms in English come from plays by William Shakespeare. Can you guess what these ones mean?

1. He wears his heart on his sleeve.
2. She's a real night owl.
3. There's no point in going. It's a wild goose chase.
4. I know you don't want to tell him, but you have to be cruel to be kind.

4 PAIRWORK Answer these questions.

1. What idioms are there in your language?
2. Think of three and say them to your partner.
3. Does your partner know what they mean?
4. Try to find out where the idioms come from.

WORD STRATEGY

Idioms

Idioms are expressions that have a figurative meaning which is different from their literal meaning.
For example, *break a leg* is a common English idiom. This isn't an instruction to fall, but an idiom that means *good luck!*

262 Vocabulary Extension

VOCABULARY EXTENSION

Compound nouns

1 Look at the compound nouns. Which are made from two nouns (N+N) and which from an adjective and a noun (A+N)?

0	...N+N...	cricket ball
1	....	football
2	....	swimming pool
3	....	goalkeeper
4	....	wetsuit
5	....	boxing gloves
6	....	tennis shoes
7	....	snowboard

2 Complete the sentences with words from exercise 1.

0 My sister plays water polo at our local ....swimming pool.... .

1 Jack's the best .... in our class because he's got the biggest hands!

2 Surfers in the UK always have to wear a .... The water's freezing!

3 It's impossible to pick objects up when you're wearing ....

> ### WORD STRATEGY
> **Compound nouns**
> - They are often made from two nouns, or an adjective and a noun.
> - The first word modifies or describes the second word, e.g., *toothpaste*, *blackboard*.
> - Some compound nouns are two words, but over time some have become one word.

3 Many words for sports equipment and facilities are compounds. Complete column 2 of the table with words you know. Then use the words below to make compounds to complete column 3.

court (x2) • course • ~~pitch~~ (x2) • ring

1 Sport	2 Sports equipment	3 Sports facility
football	football boots	football pitch
golf		
boxing		
tennis		
cricket		
basketball		

4 GAME Work in groups of four. How many compound nouns can you make from these words? You have one minute! Check your answers in a dictionary. The group with the most words wins!

- police
- post
- black
- sun
- bus
- hot

5 VOCABULARY EXTENSION

Phrasal verbs

1 Replace the words in bold with the phrasal verbs below in the correct form.

> blow up · lock up · break into · ~~run off~~ ·
> hold up · turn in · pay back

0 The mugger **escaped** with the man's laptop bag.
   ran off
1 Bank robbers **took money from** a bank using machine guns.
2 Some burglars **entered** a pop star's home **by force** and stole paintings and jewellery.
3 The terrorists wanted to **make** the London Eye **explode**, but their plan was discovered.
4 A mother **reported** her son to police for shoplifting.
5 The judge said he was a danger to society and **sent** the man **to prison** for life.
6 The judge ordered the thief to **return** the money he has stolen.

2 Put the words in the correct order. There are two possibilities in three of the sentences.

0 the English parliament / Guy Fawkes / blow / tried to / in 1605 / up
   Guy Fawkes tried to blow up the English parliament in 1605.
1 the detectives / the drug dealers / up / locked / last week
2 decided to / the thief's family / turn / her / in
3 into / the shop / the boy / break / said / he didn't
4 promised / to pay / the / my sister / money / back
5 three homes / in / blew / Manchester / up / a gas explosion / yesterday
6 ran / into / the crowd / a tall man / off / the robbery / after

WORD STRATEGY

Phrasal verbs

These are idiomatic phrases formed from a verb and a preposition or adverb, e.g., *hold up*. Remember:
- when the object is a personal pronoun, it comes between the verb and the preposition / adverb:
  *They held **it** up.*
- when the object is a noun, it can come between the verb and the preposition / adverb, or at the end of the phrase:
  *They held **the bank** up.* / *They held up **the bank**.*

3 Look at the word web for phrasal verbs with the verb *hold*. Make examples with *hold* + these prepositions. Check your answers in a dictionary, then add the correct ones to the web.

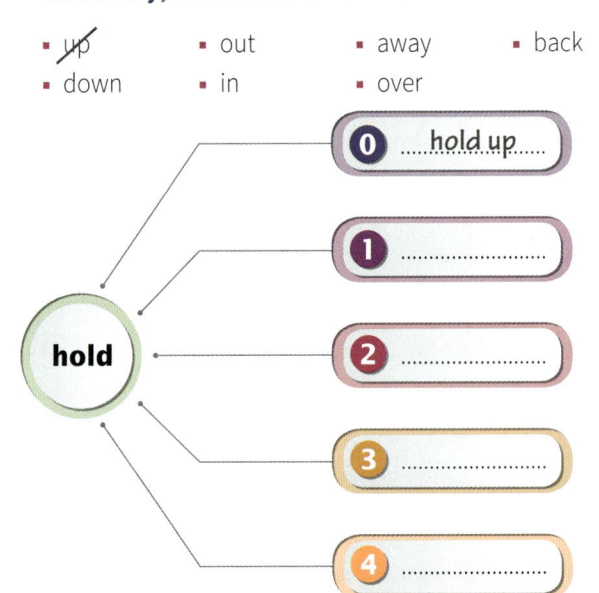

- ~~up~~
- out
- away
- back
- down
- in
- over

0 hold up
1 ....
2 ....
3 ....
4 ....

4 **GAME** How many phrasal verbs can you make from these common verbs in one minute? Choose one each. Use a dictionary to check your partner's answers.

- take
- put
- go
- give

264 Vocabulary Extension

VOCABULARY EXTENSION

Weather idioms

1 Read the idioms. Can you match them to their meanings?

0 [e] We had a lot of problems with this project last year, but I think we've *weathered the storm* now.
1 [ ] Take this medicine and you'll be *as right as rain*.
2 [ ] Someone stole Harry's bike. He had to go to school by bus for a month, but he met his new girlfriend on the bus – *every cloud has a silver lining*!
3 [ ] I'm not very good with girls. What questions can I ask to *break the ice*?
4 [ ] The surprise party has to be a secret. Don't let Katie *get wind of it*!
5 [ ] I'm worried the thieves who burgled my flat will come back, but the police say *lightning never strikes twice in the same place*.

a in every bad situation you can find something good
b to hear about something
c to get completely well again
d to make someone relax and start talking
e to get over difficult problems
f the same problem doesn't occur twice in the same place / situation

2 Write the idioms from exercise 1 next to the weather conditions they refer to.

weather	idiom
rainy	0 *to be as right as rain*
windy	1
stormy (thunder and lightning)	2
cloudy	3
frosty / icy	4

3 Rewrite these sentences using idioms from exercise 1 to replace the underlined expressions.

0 I was ill all last week but now I'm <u>feeling completely well again</u>.
   I was ill all last week but now I'm as right as rain.
1 Frank told some jokes at the dinner which really <u>helped to make everyone relax and talk</u>.
2 My boyfriend and I had a lot of arguments at first but we get on really well now, we've <u>got over our difficulties</u>.
3 Don't let everyone <u>hear about</u> the sale, or there will be nothing left when we get there!
4 I lost my keys but I found my ID card while I was looking for them. <u>Something positive always comes out of a bad situation!</u>

4 Look at the expressions and answer the questions.

1 Which of these are idioms in English? Use a dictionary to check your answers.
2 Correct the idioms that are wrong.
3 What do they mean?

1 come rain or shine ✓
   in good times and in bad times
2 to be always chasing rainbows
3 as cold as fog
4 to have a face like thunder
5 to be a fair weather friend
6 good winds blow good fortune

5 PAIRWORK What idioms about the weather are there in your country? Try to think of one for each type of weather below. Does your partner know what it means?

- sunshine
- wind
- snow
- rain
- clouds

A I know one, 'cadere dalle nuvole'.
B What does that mean?
A It means …

Vocabulary Extension   265

7 Medical collocations

VOCABULARY EXTENSION

WORD STRATEGY

Collocations

A collocation is usually two words (but can be more) that usually go together. For example, in English, we usually say *heavy rain*. It's correct grammatically to say *strong rain* or *big rain*, but both of these sound very strange to a British English speaker, because the collocation with *rain* is *heavy*. There are many collocations in English about illnesses and medicine.

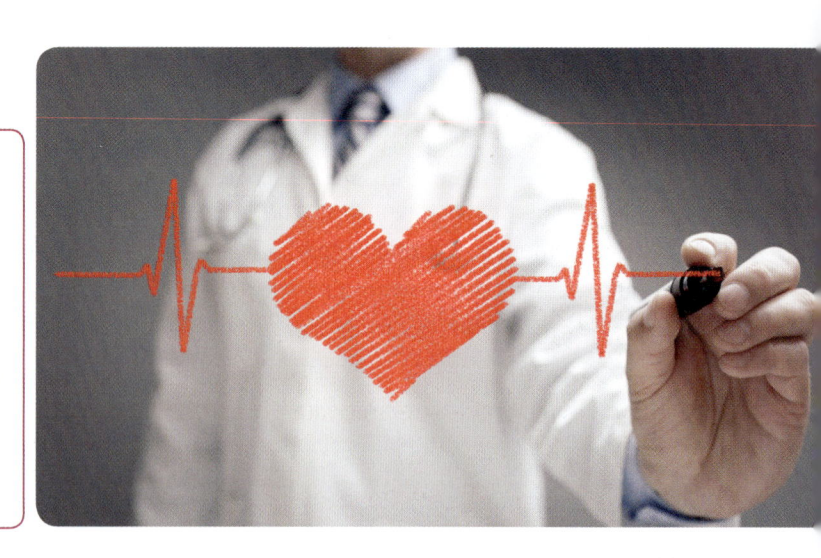

1 Look at the diagram. Complete the collocations with the words below. Use a dictionary to check any words that you don't know.

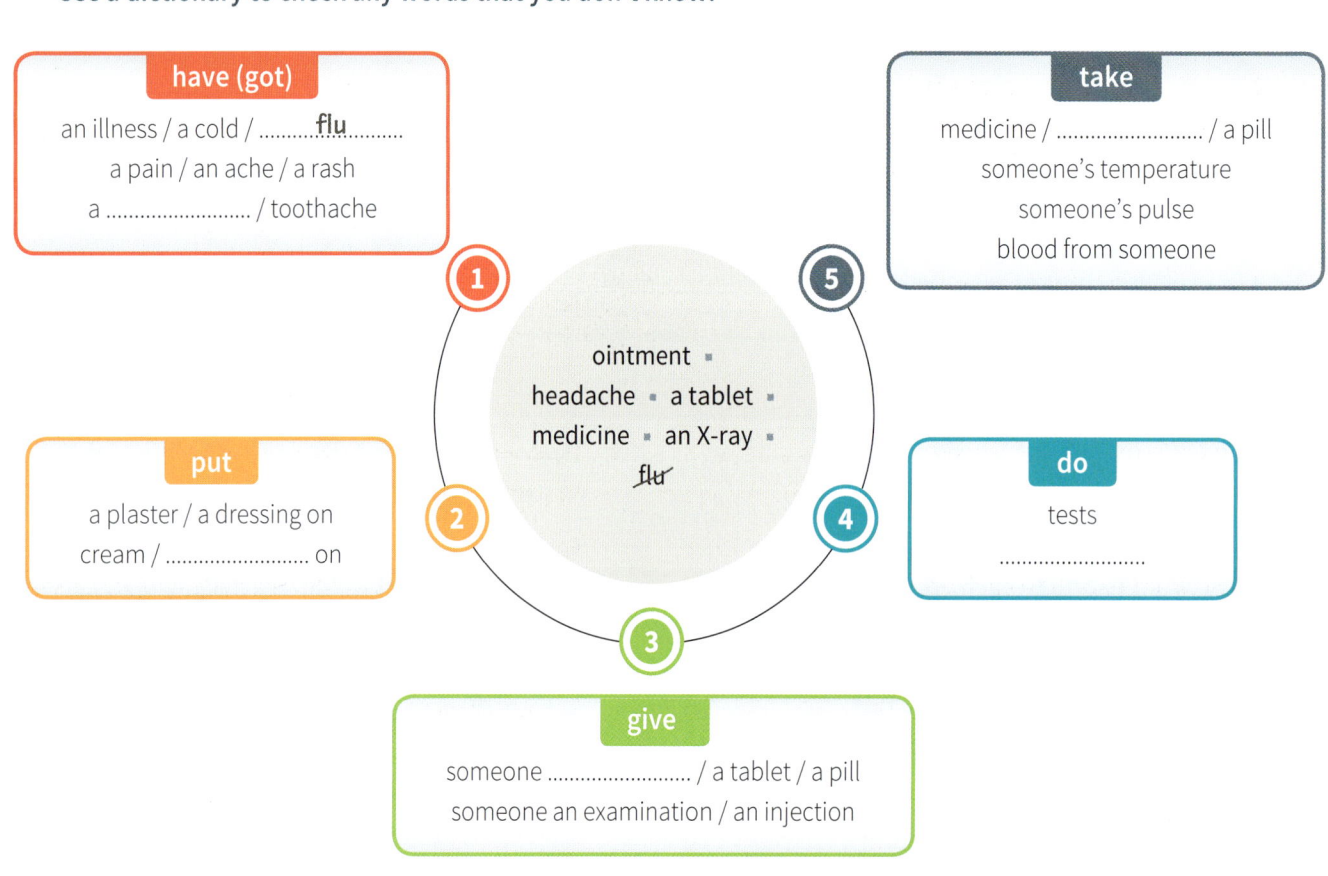

have (got)
an illness / a cold / ......**flu**......
a pain / an ache / a rash
a .... / toothache

take
medicine / .... / a pill
someone's temperature
someone's pulse
blood from someone

ointment
headache • a tablet
medicine • an X-ray
~~flu~~

put
a plaster / a dressing on
cream / .... on

do
tests
....

give
someone .... / a tablet / a pill
someone an examination / an injection

2 What other collocations do you know? Circle the odd word out in each group.

0   have a bath   (have hunger)
    have a snack   have an idea
1   take a break   take a train
    take a meal   take a message
2   put on a dress   put on a show
    put on an appointment put on some music
3   do well   do your homework
    do sport   do a mistake

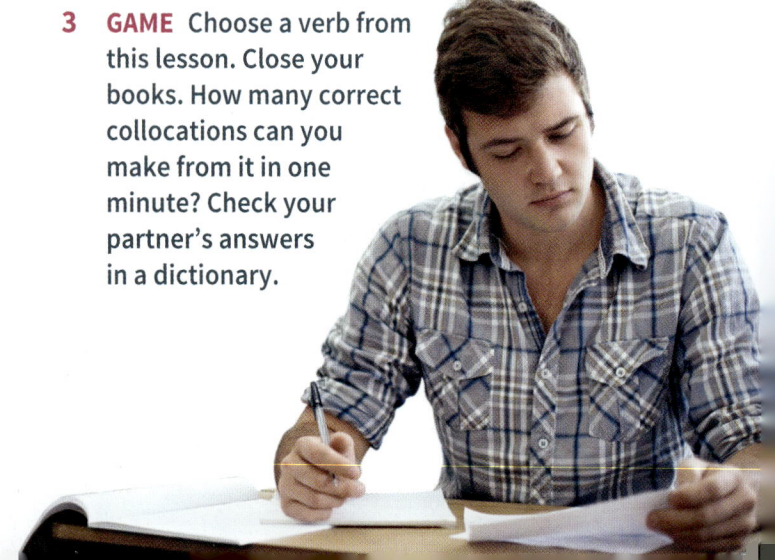

3 **GAME** Choose a verb from this lesson. Close your books. How many correct collocations can you make from it in one minute? Check your partner's answers in a dictionary.

266   Vocabulary Extension

VOCABULARY EXTENSION

Prefixes

WORD STRATEGY

Prefixes

There are a number of prefixes in English which come from Latin. We add them to words to change their meaning. The most common are *anti-*, *auto-*, *multi-*, *non-*, *pro-*, and *super-*. A good dictionary will tell you which words with prefixes we write with a hyphen (-).

1 Look at the table. Match five of the example words to these definitions.

0 ...*autobiography*... : a book about your own life
1 .... : in favour of education
2 .... : an event that didn't happen or was very disappointing
3 .... : a very special road
4 .... : opposed to the government
5 .... : having a lot of different cultural influences

prefix	meaning	example
anti-	against / opposed to	anti-government, anti-apartheid
auto-	self	autobiography, autograph
multi-	many	multicultural, multitasking
non-	not	non-payment, non-event
pro-	for / in favour of	pro-democracy, pro-education
super-	very special / powerful	superhero, superhighway

2 Now write definitions for the other six example words.

3 Use a word below and a prefix to make a new word to add to each group. Check your answers in a dictionary.

drug
mobile · life
believer · war
climax

4 Use words from the table and exercise 3 to complete the sentences.

0 Scientists are working to develop a ......*superdrug*...... to cure many types of cancer.
1 Who is your favourite .... in the film *Fantastic Four*?
2 My mother isn't religious at all. She's a ....
3 I'm reading a really interesting book at the moment, the .... of Barack Obama.
4 Today there were .... protests in London by people who oppose the conflict in Afghanistan.
5 The first commercial .... was built by Ford in 1908 in the USA.
6 The music festival was very disappointing, a real ....

5 **GAME** Choose a prefix from this lesson. Look up five words with this prefix in a dictionary. Read their definitions to your partner. Can he / she guess the words?

Vocabulary Extension 267

9 VOCABULARY EXTENSION

Collocations with *make* and *do*

1 Write the expressions below in the correct group.

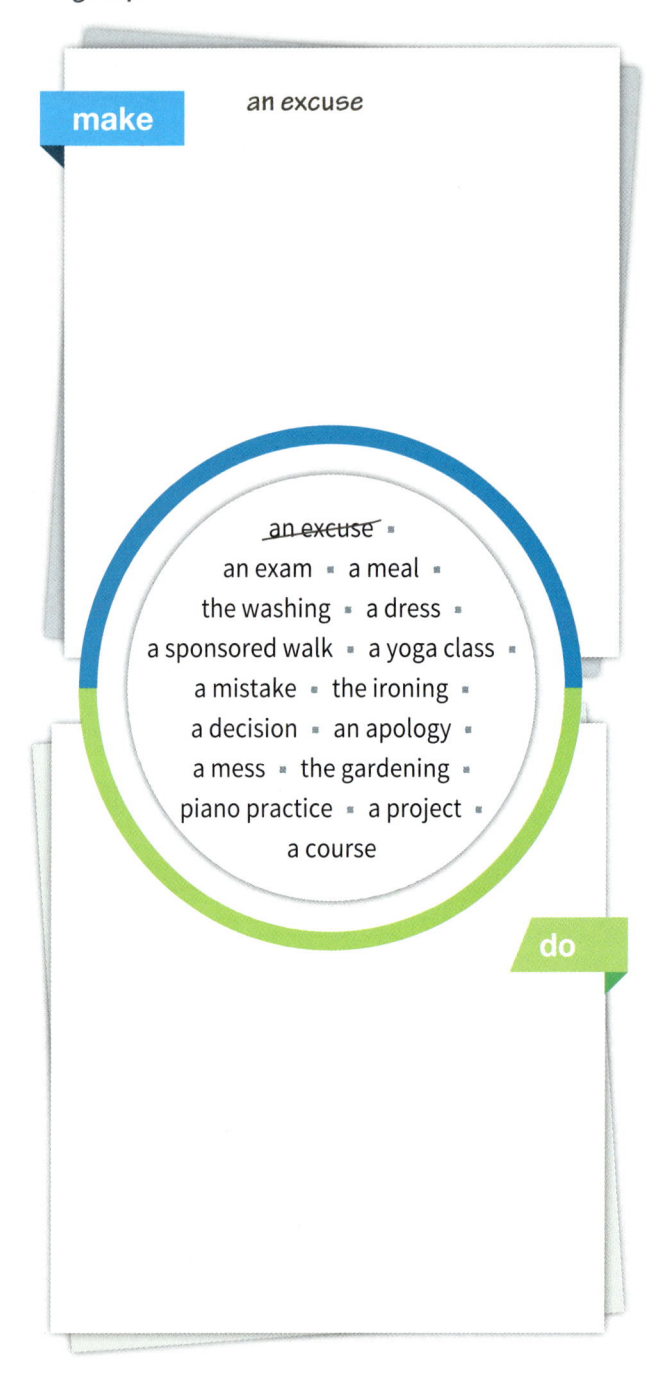

make
- an excuse

an excuse • an exam • a meal • the washing • a dress • a sponsored walk • a yoga class • a mistake • the ironing • a decision • an apology • a mess • the gardening • piano practice • a project • a course

do

WORD STRATEGY

make and do

These two verbs are frequently confused by students because their equivalents are used differently in other languages. As a general rule we use *make* for creative or mental activities and *do* for every day and practical actions / jobs. (However there are quite a lot of exceptions to this rule!)
- *make a plan*
- *do your homework*
- *make music*
- *do the shopping*

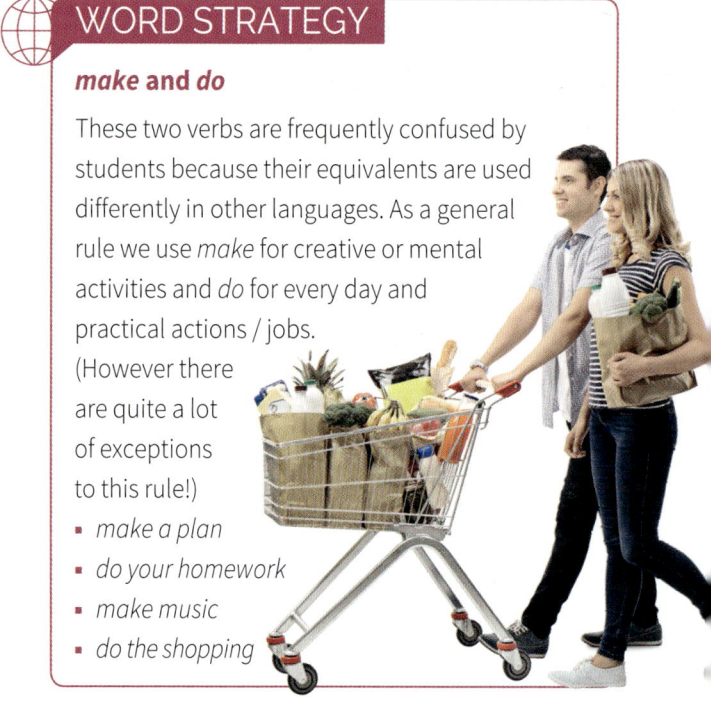

3 Complete the sentences with the correct form of *make* or *do*.

0 Your exercise is excellent, you haven't ......**made**...... any mistakes!
1 My brother is .... research in genetics at Cambridge University.
2 My prom dress was .... by Aunt Shirley. It was really lovely.
3 Can I use your phone to .... a phone call, please?
4 On Saturdays I usually help my mum to .... the shopping.
5 I love lazy Sundays because I like .... nothing!
6 Don't worry too much about the exams, you can only .... your best.
7 My friend .... me a big favour and let me use his bike for the race.
8 Sam, you are so naughty! Look at the mess you've .... !

2 Which group do these expressions go in? Use a dictionary to check your answers.

0 a decision ......**make**......
1 a phone call ....
2 nothing ....
3 your best ....
4 a donation ....
5 progress ....
6 someone a favour ....
7 research ....

4 GAME Work in pairs. Choose a verb each, either *make* or *do*. Close your books. How many correct collocations can you make from it in one minute? Check your partner's answers in a dictionary.

VOCABULARY EXTENSION

Cognates and false friends

1 Which of these English words are cognates (C) in Italian and which are false friends (F)? Write C or F.

0 ...F... magazine
1 .... prove
2 .... circulate
3 .... journalist
4 .... camera
5 .... rumours
6 .... campaign
7 .... library
8 .... publish
9 .... sensational

2 Write the meanings in Italian of the five false friends from exercise 1. The first one has been found for you.

1 rivista

WORD STRATEGY

Cognates and false friends

Cognates are words in two different languages which come from a common root in another language. They look similar and have the same meaning.
In English and Italian, cognates come from Latin, e.g., *letter = lettera* and *lettera = letter*.
False friends are words that look similar but have different meanings. They often have a common root but over time have evolved in the two languages to mean different things, e.g., *educated = istruito / colto* but *educato = polite / well-mannered*.

3 Match these translations to the five false friends in exercise 1. Then write the Italian word they are usually confused with and its meaning in English.

English false friend	Italian translation	Italian word	English translation
1 magazine	rivista	magazzino	warehouse
	macchina fotografica		
	dimostrare		
	pettegolezzi		
	biblioteca		

4 Here is a list of false friends that are often confused in English and Italian. Choose the correct option. Use a dictionary to check your answers.

0 *actually*
  A attualmente
  B correntemente
  C (in realtà)

1 *arrange*
  A disporre
  B maneggiare
  C arrangiare

2 *comprehensive*
  A completo
  B comprensivo
  C simpatico

3 *pretend*
  A fare finta
  B pretendere
  C ingannare

4 *sensible*
  A sensitivo
  B sensibile
  C ragionevole

5 *sympathetic*
  A empatico
  B simpatico
  C comprensivo

5 GAME Follow the steps and play the game.

1 Write 12 English false friends on squares of paper.
2 Write 12 squares with their true translations.
3 Write 12 squares with the translations they're confused with.
4 Use the cards to play a game of Vocabulary Snap.
5 Only shout 'Snap!' when the English word and its Italian meaning are a true match!

WORDLIST

A

above (prep) /əˈbʌv/ al di sopra di
access (v) /ˈæk.ses/ accedere a
ache (n) /eɪk/ dolore
acid rain (n) /ˌæsɪd ˈreɪn/ pioggia acida
across (prep) /əˈkrɒs/ attraverso (da un lato all'altro)
actor (n) /ˈæk.tər/ attore
admittedly (adv) /ədˈmɪt.ɪd.li/ certamente, in effetti
adorable (adj) /əˈdɔː.rə.bl/ adorabile
after (adv) /ˈɑːf.tə/ in seguito
aim (v) /eɪm/ mirare, puntare
angry (adj) /ˈæŋ.gri/ arrabbiato
ankle (n) /ˈæŋ.kl/ caviglia
anti- (pref) /ˈæn.ti/ anti-
antiseptic cream (adj) /ˌæn.tiˈsep.tɪk kriːm/ pomata antisettica
antiseptic lozenge (adj) /ˌæn.tiˈsep.tɪk/ pastiglia ad azione antisettica
anymore (adv) /ˌen.iˈmɔːr/ non più
apathy (n) /ˈæp.ə.θi/ apatia
apology (n) /əˈpɒl.ə.dʒi/ scusa
approach (v) /əˈprəʊtʃ/ contattare
approve (v) /əˈpruːv/ approvare
architect (n) /ˈɑː.kɪ.tekt/ architetto
architecture (n) /ˈɑː.kɪ.tek.tʃər/ architettura
around (prep) /əˈraʊnd/ intorno a
art (n) /ɑːt/ arte
assess (v) /əˈses/ valutare
at first hand (phr) /ət ˈfɜːst hænd/ in prima persona
at short notice (phr) /ət ʃɔːt ˈnəʊ.tɪs/ con breve preavviso
at the bottom (phr) /ət ðə ˈbɒt.əm/ in fondo
at the top (phr) /ət ðə tɒp/ in cima
author (n) /ˈɔː.θər/ autore
auto- (pref) /ˈɔː.təʊ/ auto-
away from (prep) /əˈweɪ frɒm/ via da

B

back (n) /bæk/ schiena
badminton (n) /ˈbæd.mɪn.tən/ badminton, volano
ball (n) /bɔːl/ palla, pallone
ban (v) /bæn/ proibire
bandage (n) /ˈbæn.dɪdʒ/ benda, fasciatura
bank robber (n) /bæŋk ˈrɒb.ər/ rapinatore di banche
baseball (n) /ˈbeɪs.bɔːl/ baseball
basket (n) /ˈbɑː.skɪt/ canestro
basketball (n) /ˈbɑː.skɪt.bɔːl/ pallacanestro
bat (n) /bæt/ mazza
beach (n) /biːtʃ/ spiaggia
be bad for (phr v) /biː bæd fɔːr/ far male a
before (adv) /bɪˈfɔːr/ prima
behaviour (n) /bɪˈheɪ.vjər/ comportamento
below (prep) /bɪˈləʊ/ al di sotto di
bench (n) /bentʃ/ panchina
biography (n) /baɪˈɒg.rə.fi/ biografia
bitter (adj) /ˈbɪt.ər/ amaro
blackberry (n) /ˈblæk.bər.i/ mora
blocked (adj) /blɒkt/ bloccato
blood (n) /blʌd/ sangue
bloodshed (n) /ˈblʌd.ʃed/ spargimento di sangue
blouse (n) /blaʊz/ camicetta
blow up (phr v) /ˈbləʊ.ʌp/ far esplodere
board (n) /bɔːd/ tavola da surf
bottom (n) /ˈbɒt.əm/ sedere
bounce (v) /baʊns/ rimbalzare
boxing (n) /ˈbɒk.sɪŋ/ pugilato
boxing gloves (n) /ˈbɒk.sɪŋ glʌvz/ guantoni da boxe
break into (phr v) /breɪk ˈɪn.tuː/ fare irruzione in
breast (n) /brest/ petto
breed (v) /briːd/ riprodursi
breeding habit (n) /ˈbriː.dɪŋ ˈhæb.ɪt/ abitudine riproduttiva
bridge (n) /brɪdʒ/ ponte
broadcast (v) /ˈbrɔːd.kɑːst/ trasmettere
bruised (adj) /bruːzd/ graffiato, contuso
brush your teeth (phr v) /brʌʃ jɔːr tiːθ/ lavarsi i denti
build (v) /bɪld/ costruire
burglar (n) /ˈbɜː.glər/ scassinatore
burglary (n) /ˈbɜː.glər.i/ furto con scasso
burgle (v) /ˈbɜː.glər/ svaligiare
burn (v) /bɜːn/ scottatura
buzz (v) /bʌz/ ronzare
by the time (adv phr) /baɪ ðiː taɪm/ quando
bye (excl) /baɪ/ ciao, arrivederci

C

calm (adj) /kɑːm/ calmo
camera (n) /ˈkæm.rə/ fotocamera, telecamera
cameraman (n) /ˈkæm.rə.mæn/ cameraman
campaign (n) /kæmˈpeɪn/ campagna
campaign (v) /kæmˈpeɪn/ fare una campagna
cap (n) /kæp/ berretto
carbon emission (n) /ˈkɑː.bən ɪˈmɪʃ.ən/ emissione di diossido di carbonio
catch-up service (n) /kætʃ ʌp ˈsɜː.vɪs/ servizi che permettono di rivedere online
chapter (n) /ˈtʃæp.tər/ capitolo
character (n) /ˈkær.ɪk.tər/ personaggio
cheat (v) /tʃiːt/ imbrogliare
cheek (n) /tʃiːk/ guancia
cheerful (adj) /ˈtʃɪə.fəl/ allegro
cheese grater (n) /tʃiːz ˈgreɪ.tər/ grattugia
chest (n) /tʃest/ petto, torace
chin (n) /tʃɪn/ mento
ciao (excl) /tʃaʊ/ ciao
circulate (v) /ˈsɜː.kjʊ.leɪt/ far circolare
claim (v) /kleɪm/ sostenere
clasp (v) /klɑːsp/ abbracciare forte
click-baiting (n) /klɪk beɪtɪŋ/ acchiappaclick
cliff (n) /klɪf/ scogliera, dirupo
climate change (n) /ˈklaɪ.mɪt ˌtʃeɪndʒ/ cambiamento climatico
cloud (n) /klaʊd/ nuvola, nube
cloudy (adj) /ˈklaʊ.di/ nuvoloso
club (n) /klʌb/ mazza
coal-burning (n) /kəʊl ˈbɜː.nɪŋ/ combustione del carbone
coal mine (n) /ˈkəʊl.maɪn/ miniera di carbone
colander (n) /ˈkɒl.ən.dər/ colino, scolapasta
cold (n) /kəʊld/ raffreddore
come home (phr v) /kʌm həʊm/ tornare a casa
commitment (n) /kəˈmɪt.mənt/ impegno

WORDLIST

common sense (n) /ˌkɒm.ənˈsents/ buonsenso
confident (adj) /ˈkɒn.fɪ.dənt/ sicuro di sé
cook (n) /kʊk/ cuoco
cookery (n) /ˈkʊk.ər.i/ cucina
cotton dressing (n) /ˈkɒt.ən ˈdres.ɪŋ/ benda di cotone
couch potato (n) /kaʊtʃ pəˈteɪ.təʊ/ pantofolaio
cough (n) /kɒf/ tosse
cough syrup (n) /kɒf ˈsɪr.əp/ sciroppo per la tosse
course (n) /kɔːs/ corso
court (n) /kɔːt/ campo; tribunale
crafts (n) /krɑːfts/ artigianato
crash (n) /kræʃ/ incidente, disastro
creative (adj) /kriˈeɪ.tɪv/ creativo
cricket (n) /ˈkrɪk.ɪt/ cricket
cricket ball (n) /ˈkrɪk.ɪt bɔːl/ palla da cricket
crime (n) /kraɪm/ (romanzo) poliziesco
crowbar (n) /ˈkrəʊ.bɑːʳ/ piede di porco
cultural heritage (n) /ˈkʌl.tʃər.əl ˈher.ɪ.tɪdʒ/ beni culturali
cut (n) /kʌt/ taglio
cutlery (n) /ˈkʌt.lə.ri/ posate
cycling (n) /ˈsaɪ.klɪŋ/ ciclismo

D

damages (n) /ˈdæmɪdʒɪz/ danni
daring (adj) /ˈdeə.rɪŋ/ audace
dark-bodied (adj) /dɑːk ˈbɒd.id/ di colore scuro
death (n) /deθ/ morte
decision (n) /dɪˈsɪʒ.ən/ decisione
deep end (n) /diːp end/ parte profonda della piscina
delay (n) /dɪˈleɪ/ ritardo
dentist (n) /ˈden.tɪst/ dentista
depression (n) /dɪˈpreʃ.ən/ depressione
desert (n) /ˈdez.ət/ deserto
design (v) /dɪˈzaɪn/ progettare
device (n) /dɪˈvaɪs/ dispositivo
direct (v) /daɪˈrekt/ dirigere
director (n) /daɪˈrek.təʳ/ regista
disappointing (adj) /ˌdɪs.əˈpɔɪn.tɪŋ/ deludente
disapproval (n) /ˌdɪs.əˈpruː.vəl/ disapprovazione
discrimination (n) /dɪˌskrɪm.ɪˈneɪ.ʃən/ discriminazione
disengaged (adj) /ˌdɪs.ɪnˈgeɪdʒd/ disimpegnato
diversity (n) /daɪˈvɜː.sɪ.ti/ diversità
do homework (phr v) /də ˈhəʊm.wɜːk/ fare i compiti
doctor (n) /ˈdɒk.təʳ/ dottore, medico
down (prep) /daʊn/ giù da
dress (n) /dres/ vestito, abbigliamento
drill (v) /drɪl/ trapanare
drought (n) /draʊt/ siccità
drowning (n) /ˈdraʊn.ɪŋ/ annegamento
drug dealer (n) /drʌg ˈdiː.ləʳ/ spacciatore di droga
dye (n) /daɪ/ tintura, tinta

E

ear (n) /ɪəʳ/ orecchio
early (adv) /ˈɜː.li/ presto, in anticipo
easygoing (adj) /ˌiː.ziˈgəʊ.ɪŋ/ calmo, accomodante
elbow (n) /ˈel.bəʊ/ gomito
elderly (adj) /ˈel.dəl.i/ anziano
electric drill (n) /ɪˈlek.trɪk drɪl/ trapano elettrico
embarrassed (adj) /ɪmˈbær.əst/ imbarazzato
energy levels (n) /ˈen.ə.dʒi ˈlev.əlz/ livelli di energia
engine (n) /ˈen.dʒɪn/ motore
e-reader (n) /ˈiː.riː.dəʳ/ lettore e-book
escape (n) /ɪˈskeɪp/ fuga
evidence (n) /ˈev.ɪ.dəns/ prove
exam (n) /ɪgˈzæm/ esame
examination (n) /ɪgˌzæm.ɪˈneɪ.ʃən/ esame, visita
excuse (n) /ɪkˈskjuːz/ scusa, pretesto
extremism (n) /ɪkˈstriː.mɪ.zəm/ estremismo
eye (n) /aɪ/ occhio

F

fabric (n) /ˈfæb.rɪk/ stoffa
factory (n) /ˈfæk.tər.i/ fabbrica
famine (n) /ˈfæm.ɪn/ carestia
fascinating (adj) /ˈfæs.ɪ.neɪ.tɪŋ/ affascinante
feather (n) /ˈfeð.əʳ/ piuma
feedback (n) /ˈfiːd.bæk/ riscontro
fiction (n) /ˈfɪk.ʃən/ narrativa
field (n) /fiːld/ campo
fill (v) /fɪl/ riempire
film (n) /fɪlm/ film
finally (adv) /ˈfaɪ.nə.li/ alla fine
fine (n) /faɪn/ multa
finger (n) /ˈfɪŋ.gəʳ/ dito della mano
fireplace (n) /ˈfaɪə.pleɪs/ caminetto
fit / unfit (adj) /fɪt/ /ʌnˈfɪt/ in forma / fuori forma
flood (n) /flʌd/ inondazione, alluvione
flourishing (adj) /ˈflʌr.ɪ.ʃɪŋ/ fiorente
flu (n) /fluː/ influenza
foliage (n) /ˈfəʊ.li.ɪdʒ/ fogliame
foot (n) /fʊt/ piede
football (n) /ˈfʊt.bɔːl/ calcio; pallone
footprint (n) /ˈfʊt.prɪnt/ orma
forecast (n) /ˈfɔː.kɑːst/ previsione
forehead (n) /ˈfɒr.ɪd/ fronte
forest (n) /ˈfɒr.ɪst/ foresta
forge (v) /fɔːdʒ/ falsificare
forger (n) /ˈfɔː.dʒəʳ/ falsario
forgery (n) /ˈfɔː.dʒər.i/ falsificazione
fossil fuel (n) /ˈfɒs.əl fjʊəl/ combustibile fossile
free speech (n) /friː spiːtʃ/ libertà di parola
frost (n) /frɒst/ brina
frosty / icy (adj) /ˈfrɒs.ti/ /ˈaɪ.si/ ghiacciato / gelato
fuel (n) /fjʊəl/ combustibile
fungus (n) /ˈfʌŋ.gəs/ fungo, muffa
furthermore (adj) /ˌfɜː.ðəˈmɔːʳ/ inoltre
fussy (adj) /ˈfʌs.i/ pignolo

G

gal (n) /gæl/ tipa
gardening (n) /ˈgɑː.dən.ɪŋ/ giardino
gather evidence (phr v) /ˈgæð.əʳ ˈev.ɪ.dəns/ raccogliere prove
generous (adj) /ˈdʒen.ər.əs/ generoso
get dressed (phr v) /get drest/ vestirsi
get sponsorship (phr v) /get ˈspɒnt.sə.ʃɪp/ trovare uno sponsor
get up (phr v) /ˈget.ʌp/ alzarsi
global warming (n) /ˌgləʊ.bəlˈwɔːr.mɪŋ/ riscaldamento globale
gloves (n) /glʌvz/ guanti

WORDLIST

goalkeeper (n) /ˈɡəʊlˌkiː.pər/ portiere
goggles (n) /ˈɡɒɡ.l̩z/ occhialini
golf (n) /ɡɒlf/ golf
goodbye (excl) /ɡʊdˈbaɪ/ arrivederci
gory (adj) /ˈɡɔː.ri/ violento, cruento
go to bed (phr v) /ɡəʊ tuː bed/ andare a letto
go to school (phr v) /ɡəʊ tuː skuːl/ andare a scuola
grass (n) /ɡrɑːs/ erba
grateful (adj) /ˈɡreɪt.fəl/ grato
gun (n) /ɡʌn/ arma da fuoco

H

hacker (n) /ˈhæk.ər/ pirata informatico
hair (n) /heər/ capelli
hairdresser (n) /ˈheəˌdres.ər/ parrucchiere
hand (n) /hænd/ mano
happiness (n) /ˈhæp.i.nəs/ felicità
happy (adj) /ˈhæp.i/ felice
happy-ever-after (adj) /ˈhæp.i ˈev.ər ˈɑːf.tər/ (tutti vissero) felici e contenti
hatch (v) /hætʃ/ schiudersi
have a go (phr v) /hæv ə ɡəʊ/ fare un tentativo
have a shower (phr v) /hæv ə ʃaʊər/ fare la doccia
have breakfast (phr v) /hæv ˈbrek.fəst/ fare colazione
have dinner (phr v) /hæv ˈdɪn.ər/ cenare
have lunch (phr v) /hæv lʌntʃ/ pranzare
head injury (n) /hed ˈɪn.dʒər.i/ trauma cranico
headache (n) /ˈhed.eɪk/ mal di testa
headphones (n) /ˈhed.fəʊnz/ cuffie
heal (v) /hiːl/ guarire
hearth (n) /hɑːθ/ focolare
heartthrob (n) /ˈhɑːt.θrɒb/ rubacuori
heat up (phr v) /hiːt ʌp/ scaldare
heist (n) /haɪst/ furto di alto livello
hello (excl) /helˈəʊ/ salve
helmet (n) /ˈhel.mət/ casco
hey (excl) /heɪ/ ehi

hi (excl) /haɪ/ ciao
hide (v) /haɪd/ nascondere
highlight (n) /ˈhaɪ.laɪt/ punto forte
hill (n) /hɪl/ collina
hip (n) /hɪp/ anca
history (n) /ˈhɪs.tər.i/ storia
hit (v) /hɪt/ colpire
hobbies (n) /ˈhɒbiz/ hobby
hockey (n) /ˈhɒk.i/ hockey
hold up (phr v) /ˈhəʊld.ʌp/ rapinare
honest (adj) /ˈɒn.ɪst/ onesto
hoodie (n) /ˈhʊd.i/ felpa con cappuccio
how do you do (phr) /ˌhaʊ.dʒəˈduː/ piacere
hurricane (n) /ˈhʌr.ɪ.kən/ uragano
hurt (v) /hɜːt/ far male

I

illness (n) /ˈɪl.nəs/ malattia
impaler (n) /ɪmˈpeɪ.lər/ impalatore
impatient (adj) /ɪmˈpeɪ.ʃənt/ impaziente
impractical (adj) /ɪmˈpræk.tɪ.kəl/ poco pratico
injection (n) /ɪnˈdʒek.ʃən/ iniezione
inn (n) /ɪn/ locanda
insensitive (adj) /ɪnˈsen.sɪ.tɪv/ insensibile
inside (prep) /ɪnˈsaɪd/ dentro
insincere (adj) /ˌɪn.sɪnˈsɪər/ falso
intellectual property (n) /ˌɪn.təlˈek.tju.əl ˈprɒp.ə.ti/ proprietà intelletuale
into (prep) /ˈɪn.tuː/ dentro
invent (v) /ɪnˈvent/ inventare
ironing (n) /ˈaɪə.nɪŋ/ stiratura

J

jacket (n) /ˈdʒæk.ɪt/ giacca
jealous (adj) /ˈdʒel.əs/ geloso
journalist (n) /ˈdʒɜː.nə.lɪst/ giornalista
joyrider (n) /ˈdʒɔɪˌraɪ.dər/ ladro di macchine
joystick (n) /ˈdʒɔɪ.stɪk/ joystick
judge (v) /dʒʌdʒ/ giudicare
judge yourself (v) /dʒʌdʒ jɔːˈself/ giudicare se stessi
jumper (n) /ˈdʒʌm.pər/ maglione
jungle (n) /ˈdʒʌŋ.ɡl̩/ giungla

K

keyboard (n) /ˈkiː.bɔːd/ tastiera
kidnap (v) /ˈkɪd.næp/ rapire
kidnapper (n) /ˈkɪd.næpər/ rapitore
kidnapping (n) /ˈkɪd.næp.ɪŋ/ rapimento, sequestro
kill / murder (v) /kɪl/ /ˈmɜː.dər/ uccidere / assassinare
killing / murder (n) /ˈkɪl.ɪŋ/ /ˈmɜː.dər/ omicidio / assassinio
kind (adj) /kaɪnd/ gentile
knee (n) /niː/ ginocchio

L

lake (n) /leɪk/ lago
lap (n) /læp/ grembo
laptop (n) /ˈlæp.tɒp/ laptop, portatile
lash (n) /læʃ/ colpo di frusta
later (adv) /ˈleɪ.tər/ più tardi
lawyer (n) /ˈlɔɪ.ər/ avvocato
lay eggs (phr v) /leɪ eɡz/ deporre le uova
library (n) /ˈlaɪ.brər.i/ biblioteca
lie (v) /laɪ/ mentire
lightning (adj) /ˈlaɪt.nɪŋ/ fulmineo, rapidissimo
literally (adv) /ˈlɪt.ər.əl.i/ letteralmente
lock up (phr v) /ˈlɒk.ʌp/ mettere in galera
locked (adv) /lɒkt/ chiuso a chiave
locker (n) /ˈlɒk.ər/ armadietto
loud (adj) /laʊd/ rumoroso
lower (v) /ˈləʊ.ər/ abbassare

M

mackerel (n) /ˈmæk.rəl/ sgombro
mackerel sky (n) /ˈmæk.rəl skaɪ/ cielo a pecorelle
magazine (n) /ˌmæɡ.əˈziːn/ rivista
mainland (n) /ˈmeɪn.lənd/ terraferma
marble (n) /ˈmɑː.bl̩/ marmo
mares' tails (n) /ˈmeəz.teɪlz/ cirri a uncino
maximise (v) /ˈmæk.sɪ.maɪz/ ottimizzare
meal (n) /mɪəl/ pasto
membership (n) /ˈmem.bə.ʃɪp/ iscrizione

WORDLIST

menacing (adj) /ˈmen.ɪ.sɪŋ/ minaccioso
menthol ointment (n) /ˈmen.θəl ˈɔɪnt·mənt/ balsamo al mentolo
mess (n) /mes/ caos, disordine
mine (v) /maɪn/ estrarre
miss (v) /mɪs/ mancare
mistake (n) /mɪˈsteɪk/ errore
moody (adj) /ˈmuː.di/ di umore mutevole
moor (n) /mɔː/ brughiera
mountain (n) /ˈmaʊn.tɪn/ montagna
mouse (n) /maʊs/ mouse
mouth (n) /maʊθ/ bocca
mug (v) /mʌg/ aggredire per rapinare
mugger (n) /ˈmʌg.ər/ rapinatore
mugging (n) /ˈmʌg.ɪŋ/ aggressione a scopo di rapina
multi- (pref) /ˈmʌl.ti/ multi-
murderer (n) /ˈmɜː.dər.ər/ assassino

N

nanny state (n) /ˈnæn.i steɪt/ stato balia
narrator (n) /nəˈreɪ.tər/ narratore
nasal spray (n) /ˈneɪ.zəl spreɪ/ spray nasale
natural disaster (n) /ˈnætʃ.ər.əl dɪˈzɑː.stər/ disastro naturale
nausea (n) /ˈnɔː.zi.ə/ nausea
neck (n) /nek/ collo
net (n) /net/ rete
netball (n) /ˈnet.bɔːl/ netball
neural network (n) /ˈnjʊə.rəl ˈnet.wɜːk/ rete neurale
newt (n) /njuːt/ tritone
non- (pref) /nɒn/ non-
nose (n) /nəʊz/ naso

O

oak (n) /əʊk/ quercia
oatmeal (n) /ˈəʊt.miːl/ fiocchi d'avena
obviously (adv) /ˈɒb.vi.əs.li/ ovviamente
office worker (n) /ˈɒf.ɪs ˈwɜː.kər/ impiegato

on the left-hand side (phr) /ɒn ðə left hænd saɪd/ sul lato sinistro
on the right-hand side (phr) /ɒn ðə raɪt hænd saɪd/ sul lato destro
ourselves (n) /ˌaʊəˈselvz/ noi stessi
out of (prep) /aʊt əv/ fuori da
outside (prep) /ˌaʊtˈsaɪd/ fuori da
outweigh (v) /ˌaʊtˈweɪ/ avere maggior peso di
over (prep) /ˈəʊ.vər/ sopra, al di sopra di
ozone layer (n) /ˈəʊzəʊn ˌleɪər/ strato di ozono

P

paddle your feet (phr v) /ˈpæd.l̩ jɔːr fiːt/ bagnarsi i piedi
pain (n) /peɪn/ dolore
paint (v) /peɪnt/ dipingere
pamphlet (n) /ˈpæm.flət/ opuscolo
paracetemol tablet (n) /ˌpær·əˈsiː·tə·mɒl ˈtæb.lət/ compressa di paracetamolo
path (n) /pɑːθ/ sentiero
patient (adj) /ˈpeɪ.ʃənt/ paziente
pay back (phr v) /ˈpeɪ.bæk/ restituire
phone tapping (n) /ˈfəʊnˌtæp.ɪŋ/ intercettazioni telefoniche
pill (n) /pɪl/ pillola, pastiglia
pilot (n) /ˈpaɪ.lət/ pilota
pine cone (n) /ˈpaɪnˌkəʊn/ pigna
pitch (n) /pɪtʃ/ campo
plaster (n) /ˈplɑː.stər/ cerotto
plot (n) /plɒt/ trama
police officer (n) /pəˈliːsˌɒf.ɪ.sər/ agente di polizia
pond (n) /pɒnd/ stagno
post (v) /pəʊst/ postare (sul web), imbucare (lettera)
practical (adj) /ˈpræk.tɪ.kəl/ pratico
prejudice (n) /ˈpredʒ.ʊ.dɪs/ pregiudizio
preset (v) /ˌpriːˈset/ programmare
pretend (v) /prɪˈtend/ fingere
print (v) /prɪnt/ stampare
pro- (pref) /prəʊ/ pro-
project (n) /ˈprɒdʒ.ekt/ progetto

prove (v) /pruːv/ dimostrare
publish (v) /ˈpʌb.lɪʃ/ pubblicare
puff (n) /pʌf/ boccata d'aria
pulse (n) /pʌls/ battito, polso
puppet (n) /ˈpʌp.ɪt/ pupazzo

Q

quarrelling (n) /ˈkwɒr.əlɪŋ/ litigi, dispute
quickly (adv) /ˈkwɪk.li/ velocemente

R

racism (n) /ˈreɪ.sɪ.zəm/ razzismo
racket (n) /ˈræk.ɪt/ racchetta
railway line (n) /ˈreɪl.weɪ laɪn/ linea ferroviaria
rainy (adj) /ˈreɪ.ni/ piovoso
raise (v) /reɪz/ raccogliere
rape (n) /reɪp/ stupro
rash (n) /ræʃ/ eruzione cutanea
realise (v) /ˈrɪə.laɪz/ accorgersi
really (adv) /ˈrɪə.li/ veramente
reliable (adj) /rɪˈlaɪə.bl̩/ affidabile
religion (n) /rɪˈlɪdʒ.ən/ religione
remote control (n) /rɪˌməʊt.kənˈtrəʊl/ telecomando
reprimand (v) /ˈrep.rɪ.mɑːnd/ rimproverare
retired (adj) /rɪˈtaɪəd/ in pensione
rifle (v) /ˈraɪ.fl̩/ frugare
right (n) /raɪt/ diritto
river (n) /ˈrɪv.ər/ fiume
road (n) /rəʊd/ strada
rob (v) /rɒb/ rapinare / derubare
robber (n) /ˈrɒb.ər/ rapinatore, ladro
robbery (n) /ˈrɒb.ər.i/ rapina
rugby (n) /ˈrʌg.bi/ rugby
rumour (n) /ˈruː.mər/ pettegolezzo
run off (phr v) /ˈrʌn.ɒf/ scappare, fuggire

S

safety deposit box (phr) /ˈseɪf.ti dɪˈpɒz.ɪt bɒks/ cassetta di sicurezza
sail (n) /seɪl/ vela
salt and pepper mill (phr) /sɒlt ænd ˈpep.ər mɪl/ saliera e pepiera
sapphire (n) /ˈsæf.aɪər/ zaffiro

WORDLIST

savings (n) /ˈseɪvɪŋz/ risparmi
scared (adj) /skeəd/ spaventato
scene (n) /siːn/ scena
score (v) /skɔːr/ segnare
screen (n) /skriːn/ schermo
sculpt (v) /skʌlpt/ scolpire
sea (n) /siː/ mare
seat (n) /siːt/ seggio
see you later (phr) /siː juː ˈleɪ.tər/ a dopo
seed (n) /siːd/ seme
self-esteem (n) /ˌself.ɪˈstiːm/ autostima
self-help (n) /ˌselfˈhelp/ (libro per la) crescita personale
sensational (adj) /senˈseɪ.ʃən.əl/ sensazionale
setting (n) /ˈset.ɪŋ/ ambientazione
settlement (n) /ˈset.l̩.mənt/ insediamento
shady (adj) /ˈʃeɪ.di/ ombroso
shell (n) /ʃel/ guscio
shepherd (n) /ˈʃep.əd/ pastore
shirt (n) /ʃɜːt/ camicia
shoes (n) /ʃuːz/ scarpe
shoplifter (n) /ˈʃɒpˌlɪftər/ taccheggiatore
shorts (n) /ʃɔːts/ shorts, pantaloncini
shoulder (n) /ˈʃəʊl.dər/ spalla
show (v) /ʃəʊ/ mostrare
shrink (v) /ʃrɪŋk/ restringersi
shuttlecock (n) /ˈʃʌt.l̩.kɒk/ volano
shy (adj) /ʃaɪ/ timido
side effect (n) /ˈsaɪdɪfekt/ effetto collaterale
skiing (n) /ˈskiː.ɪŋ/ sci
skin rash (n) /skɪn ræʃ/ eruzione cutanea
skirt (n) /skɜːt/ gonna
slum area (n) /slʌm ˈeə.ri.ə/ baraccopoli
smartphone (n) /ˈsmɑːt.fəʊn/ smartphone
snowboard (n) /ˈsnəʊ.bɔːd/ snowboard
so (adv) /səʊ/ così
so far (phr) /səʊ fɑːr/ finora
sociable (adj) /ˈsəʊ.ʃə.bl̩/ socievole
socks (n) /sɒks/ calzini
soft (adj) /sɒft/ morbido
soot (n) /sʊt/ fuliggine
sore (adj) /sɔːr/ che fa male
soul (n) /səʊl/ anima

soundtrack (n) /ˈsaʊnd.træk/ colonna sonora
speakers (n) /ˈspiː.kəz/ altoparlanti
special effects (n) /ˌspeʃəl ɪˈfekts/ effetti speciali
speech (n) /spiːtʃ/ discorso
sponsored walk (n) /ˈspɒnt.səd wɔːk/ camminata sponsorizzata
sport (n) /spɔːt/ sport
sports instructor (n) /spɔːts ɪnˈstrʌk.tər/ istruttore sportivo
sporty (adj) /ˈspɔː.ti/ sportivo
spread (n) /spred/ distesa
stake (n) /steɪk/ palo
steam (n) /stiːm/ vapore
stick (n) /stɪk/ bastone
stick together (v) /stɪk təˈgeð.ər/ rimanere attaccati
stomach (n) /ˈstʌm.ək/ stomaco, pancia
stone (n) /stəʊn/ pietra
storey (n) /ˈstɔː.ri/ piano
stormy (adj) /ˈstɔː.mi/ tempestoso
stream (n) /striːm/ ruscello
stubborn (adj) /ˈstʌb.ən/ ostinato
suck (v) /sʌk/ succhiare
super- (pref) /ˈsuː.pər/ super-
surfing (n) /ˈsɜː.fɪŋ/ surf
surprised (adj) /səˈpraɪzd/ sorpreso
surprisingly (adv) /səˈpraɪ.zɪŋ.li/ sorprendentemente
suspect (n) /səˈspekt/ sospettato
sweet (adj) /swiːt/ dolce
swift (adj) /swɪft/ rapido
swimming (n) /ˈswɪm.ɪŋ/ nuoto
swimming pool (n) /ˈswɪm.ɪŋˌpuːl/ piscina
swollen (adj) /ˈswəʊ.lən/ gonfio

T

T-shirt (n) /ˈtiː.ʃɜːt/ maglietta
teacher (n) /ˈtiː.tʃər/ insegnante
team (n) /tiːm/ squadra
teapot (n) /ˈtiː.pɒt/ teiera
television (n) /ˈtel.ɪ.vɪʒ.ən/ televisione
temperature (n) /ˈtem.prə.tʃər/ febbre
tennis (n) /ˈten.ɪs/ tennis

tennis shoes (n) /ˈten.ɪs ʃuːz/ scarpe da tennis
terrorist (n) /ˈter.ə.rɪst/ terrorista
test (n) /test/ analisi
textile (n) /ˈtek.staɪl/ tessile
texture (n) /ˈteks.tʃər/ tessuto,
then (adv) /ðen/ poi
thermometer (n) /θəˈmɒm.ɪ.tər/ termometro
thief (n) /θiːf/ ladro
threaten (v) /ˈθret.ən/ minacciare
throat (n) /θrəʊt/ gola
through (prep) /θruː/ attraverso (passando dentro)
throw (v) /θrəʊ/ tirare
thumb (n) /θʌm/ pollice
tidy (adj) /ˈtaɪ.di/ ordinato
tie (n) /taɪ/ cravatta
tights (n) /taɪts/ calze, collant
tin opener (n) /ˈtɪn ˌəʊpənə/ apriscatole
to-do list (phr) /tuː də lɪst/ elenco di cose da fare
toe (n) /təʊ/ dito del piede
tolerance (n) /ˈtɒl.ər.əns/ tolleranza
tooth (n) /tuːθ/ dente
toothache (n) /ˈtuːθ.eɪk/ mal di denti
top hat (n) /tɒp hæt/ tuba, cilindro
to the north (phr) /tuː ðə nɔːθ/ a nord
to the south (phr) /tuː ðə saʊθ/ a sud
touching (adj) /ˈtʌtʃ.ɪŋ/ commovente
towards (prep) /təˈwɔːdz/ verso
toxic gas (n) /ˈtɒk.sɪk gæs/ gas tossico
transmit (v) /trænzˈmɪt/ trasmettere
travel (n) /ˈtræv.əl/ libro di viaggi
tree (n) /triː/ albero
trousers (n) /ˈtraʊ.zəz/ pantaloni
truncheon (n) /ˈtrʌn.tʃən/ manganello
tunnel (n) /ˈtʌn.əl/ tunnel, galleria
turn in (phr v) /tɜːn ɪn/ consegnare (alla polizia)
turning point (n) /ˈtɜː.nɪŋ.pɔɪnt/ punto di svolta
tweet (v) /twiːt/ twittare

274 Wordlist

WORDLIST

U
unconscious mind (n) /ʌnˈkɒn.ʃəs maɪnd/ mente inconscia
undercover (adj) /ˌʌn.dəˈkʌv.ər/ sotto copertura
unfair (adj) /ʌnˈfeər/ ingiusto
unkind (adj) /ʌnˈkaɪnd/ scortese
unreliable (adj) /ˌʌn.rɪˈlaɪə.bl̩/ inaffidabile
unselfishness (n) /ʌnˈsel.fɪʃnɪs/ altruismo
untidy (adj) /ʌnˈtaɪ.di/ disordinato
up (prep) /ʌp/ su per
urban dweller (n) /ˈɜː.bən ˈdwel.ər/ persona che vive in città

V
valley (n) /ˈvæl.i/ valle
vandal (n) /ˈvæn.dəl/ vandalo
vandalise (v) /ˈvæn.dəl.aɪz/ danneggiare
vault (n) /vɒlt/ caveau, camera blindata
very (adv) /ˈver.i/ molto
vet (n) /vet/ veterinario
vinegar (n) /ˈvɪn.ɪ.gər/ aceto

W
waist (n) /weɪst/ vita
wake up (phr v) /weɪk ʌp/ svegliarsi
warning (n) /ˈwɔː.nɪŋ/ avvertimento
washing (n) /ˈwɒʃ.ɪŋ/ bucato
waste (v) /weɪst/ sprecare
water droplet (n) /ˈwɔː.tər ˈdrɒp.lət/ gocciola d'acqua
weather pattern (n) /ˈweð.ər ˈpæt.ən/ pattern meteorologico
wet (adj) /wet/ bagnato, umido
wetsuit (n) /ˈwet.suːt/ muta subacquea
when (adv) /wen/ quando
whisper (v) /ˈwɪs.pər/ sussurrare
whistle (n) /ˈwɪs.l̩/ fischietto; fischio
white matter (n) /waɪt ˈmæt.ər/ sostanza bianca
whopping (adj) /ˈwɒp.ɪŋ/ esorbitante
windy (adj) /ˈwɪn.di/ ventoso
wing span (n) /wɪŋ spæn/ apertura alare
witness (n) /ˈwɪt.nəs/ testimone
worried (adj) /ˈwʌr.id/ preoccupato
wound (n) /wuːnd/ ferita
write (v) /raɪt/ scrivere

X
X-ray (n) /ˈeks.reɪ/ radiografia

Y
yard n /jɑːd/ cortile
yoga n /ˈjəʊ.gə/ yoga

SPEAKING SKILLS – Dialogues

Unit 1, page 21, exercises 27 and 28

Tom Hi, Joel!
Joel Tom, hello. I haven't seen you for ages! Since school right?
Tom Yes, that's right. You're looking good! How are you?
Joel I'm good thanks, how are things with you?
Tom Oh, you know – the usual.
Joel So, what have you been up to?
Tom Well, I'm working with my dad now. In the garage. How about you?
Joel Oh, I'm at college, so I'm still studying, playing football, you know.
Tom Oh, cool! What are you studying? A science course, right?
Joel Yes, that's right. How's work?
Tom Yeah, it's all good. My dad's happy I'm working with him.
Joel Cool so …
Tom Yeah …
Joel Right … erm …
Tom Well, I … erm
Joel Yes, I'd better be going. It was great to see you, Tom.
Tom Yes, you too Joel. See you soon.
Joel Yes, have a good one! Bye.
Tom Goodbye, take care.

Unit 2, page 29, exercises 23, 24 and 25

Grace Joel, listen I've been thinking …
Joel Oh yes?
Grace Yes, I've been thinking about it a lot … and I've decided to move to London.
Joel Are you serious? Why? London is dirty and polluted!
Grace Well, I know what you mean but London's a really exciting place. There are more opportunities in London.
Joel That's true but in my opinion it's dangerous, not exciting.
Grace I really don't think so, I've been to London lots of times. I think it's a safe place, just as safe as here.
Joel You're definitely wrong there! Have you been reading the news?
Grace Look, London is a big place, there are more people so more stuff happens.
Joel You're absolutely right! Bad stuff! And what about … pollution? No forests, no lakes, no hills – just ugly grey buildings.
Grace I'm sorry but I completely disagree – there are lots of parks in London and green spaces. It's a very green city, certainly not all grey buildings.
Joel OK, you've got a point, but I still think London is a really bad idea.
Grace Well, I don't think so. You can't change my mind by disagreeing with me.
Joel How can I change your mind? Please please don't go, Grace! Say you'll stay! Please, please!

Unit 3, page 39, exercises 24 and 25

Luke What's the best horror film you've seen, Anna?
Anna You mean the scariest? It's actually a classic one from the 1920s.
Luke The 1920s! OMG! Did they even make films in the 1920s? What's it called?
Anna It's called *Nosferatu*. It's in black and white and there's no soundtrack – it's a silent film.
Luke Go on. What's it about?
Anna It's about a vampire. It's basically the Dracula story.
Luke Where's it set?
Anna First it's set in Transylvania, and then in Germany in the early nineteenth century.
Luke What happens in the story?
Anna Well, like Dracula, Nosferatu is a vampire. He lives in a remote castle, he only goes out at night and he drinks blood.
Luke And … so …?
Anna Well, people in the town start to die and they don't know why.
Luke Then what?
Anna Well, then people realise that there's a vampire in the town. It's Nosferatu. They make a plan to try and catch him and destroy him.
Luke What happens after that? Does their plan work?
Anna So many questions! LOL! I can't tell you! You need to watch the film yourself.
Luke Uff! So, why did you like it?
Anna Nosferatu is really creepy and sinister. He looks grotesque, a real monster. You see his shadow on the walls before you see him, with pointed teeth and hands … I felt terrified when he was on the screen.
Luke It sounds great – I want to see it!
Anna OK. Let's see if we can download it …

Unit 4, page 47, exercises 21 and 22

Grace Anna, I must tell you about this new game I've been playing with Matt. It's so funny!
Anna What game?
Grace It's called *Who am I?*
Anna *Who am I?* What's that?
Grace The basic idea is that you write down the name of a famous person on a piece of paper …
Anna Can it be any famous person?
Grace Yes, that's right. But you must choose a person a lot of people know.

SPEAKING SKILLS – Dialogues

Anna OK, so what equipment do you need?
Grace Well, you need a pen and some paper.
Anna OK.
Grace Oh no, wait, that's wrong! You need Post-It™ notes, not paper. That's important.
Anna Post-It™ notes? Why?
Grace Well, you write the name of the famous person on the Post-It™ note. Then you have to stick it on another person's forehead! But they mustn't see the name on their Post-It™. All their friends can read it, but not them!
Anna What's the point of that?
Grace Well, the person with the Post-It™ on their head has to guess who they are!
Anna How do they do that?
Grace Their friends ask them questions …
Anna What?
Grace Sorry, I've got that wrong … the person with the Post-It™ has to ask their friends questions, like, 'Am I male or female?' or 'Do I live in the USA?'
Anna Oh, I see. And then their friends tell them where the famous person lives?
Grace Yes. No, hang on. That's not right … The other people can only reply *Yes* or *No*.
Anna So, how do you win?
Grace You just keep going until the person guesses who they are. Then it's another person's turn. It's for fun!
Anna It doesn't sound much fun.
Grace Believe me. It's hilarious. I was Donald Trump!
Anna Really? Actually you look a bit like him. I think it's the hair …

Unit 5, page 57, exercises 25, 26 and 27

Grace Have you seen this?
Joel No, what is it?
Grace It's a post about a guy who was fined £5,000 for spraying graffiti on trains. It's absolutely ridiculous …
Joel Wait a minute, what happened exactly?
Grace This guy sprayed a picture with his tag on a railway carriage …
Luke Sorry, can I stop you there? His *tag*? I'm not sure what you mean …
Grace A tag is a sort of symbol a graffiti artist uses on all his stuff. It's like his signature.
Luke Right. OK, go on.
Grace So, he sprayed graffiti on a carriage at the railway station. The railway company reported it to the police. They said it was vandalism and that he had damaged their property. So not cool!
Joel Well, they have got a point.

Grace Seriously? He just sprayed some designs on a dirty old railway carriage! No one was using it!
Joel Well, you don't know that for sure, but you can't let people damage private property.
Luke What are you trying to say, Joel?
Joel I agree with the company. I think it is vandalism.
Grace Oh, please! Graffiti is so not vandalism, it's art! Think about Banksy.
Joel Sorry? Who?
Grace Banksy, the famous British graffiti artist. When Banksy paints graffiti on a building now, it's worth thousands of pounds. He isn't given a stupid fine …
Joel Can I stop you for a second? Is spraying graffiti on public property a crime in England?
Grace Yes, it is.
Joel And what's the punishment for it?
Grace You get a fine, or sometimes you have to do community service.
Joel Well, that seems right to me. When people break the law, they have to face the consequences.
Grace You sound like my dad! What's your take on this, Luke?
Luke I'm with you. I don't think spraying graffiti is a crime at all. It's art!
Joel You too? Give me a break!

Unit 6, page 65, exercises 24, 25 and 26

Joel Hi. What are you doing?
Grace I'm making a list of things to take on my school trip next week.
Joel A school trip? Cool. Where are you going?
Grace Venice! I can't wait! It'll be amazing. But I still need to buy some new clothes for it – a bikini, some new sunglasses …
Joel A bikini? It's February! It won't be hot in Venice now.
Grace Why do you say that? It's in Italy!
Joel What I'm saying is it isn't always hot in Italy – it's not on the equator!
Grace Oh. So what do you think the weather will be like? It will be sunny, right?
Joel Actually, it might not be sunny. It's often cold and foggy in Venice in winter.
Grace Foggy! So I won't need sunglasses?
Joel Er, not really … unless you want to fall into a canal.
Grace Will I need to take a coat then?
Joel Yes, you will. A big coat – it will be about 5 or 6 degrees Celsius …
Grace Oh!
Joel And probably an umbrella. It may rain while you're there.
Grace You're kidding! It never rains in Italy! It's a Mediterranean country.

SPEAKING SKILLS – Dialogues

Joel What? Are you nuts? Mediterranean?
Grace Why? What d'you mean?
Joel If you think about it, Venice isn't on the Mediterranean, it's on the Adriatic coast.
Grace Is it?
Joel Yes. You might need wellie boots too.
Grace What? Do you think it might snow?
Joel Yes, it might. But Venice is often flooded in winter. In fact you may get wet feet.
Grace OMG. It sounds like a week in Wales.
Joel Oh, come on! After all it is an amazing city. You'll have a great time!

Unit 7, page 75, exercises 21, 22 and 23

Grace You look fed up.
Anna I feel bad. My skin's a mess. I've got these horrible spots! I hate being a teenager!
Grace I know how you feel, Anna. It's awful when that happens.
Anna What do you think I should do?
Luke You could try eating more fruit. My mum says that helps.
Grace It happens to me too and I feel exactly the same. If I were you, I'd try porridge.
Anna Porridge? Should I have porridge for breakfast?
Grace No, you shouldn't. I mean you should put it on your face.
Anna What? That's ridiculous!
Grace No, it isn't. Porridge is a natural remedy for skin irritations. It works – you ought to try it.
Anna Oh, please!
Luke Wait a minute Anna, Grace might have a point. A lot of natural remedies do work.
Grace Actually, my sister and I washed our faces in milk once. They say it gives you beautiful skin!
Anna And did it give you beautiful skin? Apparently not.
Grace Hey, that's really mean!
Anna So, what would you do, Luke?
Luke I'd get some cream from the doctor, not try remedies from medieval times!
Grace Well, that's just your opinion. Listen Anna, if you want to talk, give me a call. I know it can be depressing when your skin's bad.
Anna Thanks, Grace, you're a star.

Unit 8, page 83, exercises 22, 23 and 24

Grace Joel! There you are! Where have you been? I had to go to the demonstration without you!
Joel I'm so sorry! I forgot all about it! I was playing *World of Weapons*! I completely lost track of time.
Grace Seriously? You were playing video games? You promised you'd come with me. You said you felt really strongly about university fees. You said …
Joel OK, OK. I apologise. I wish I'd remembered about it. I wanted to come, honestly. I would have come, if I'd remembered when it was.
Grace Hmm. OK, apology accepted. It doesn't matter.
Joel So, how did it go? Did you walk all the way?
Grace Yes, I did, but I needed help with my banner. I made it extra large but I thought you'd be there to carry it with me.
Joel Look Grace, I'm really sorry. I wish I'd been there to give you a hand. Oh, please forgive me, Grace.
Grace Get up, stupid. I forgive you. Don't worry about it.
Joel Can I see the banner?
Grace Yes, sure. Uff! It's really big.
Joel That's great. It's … er … really …
Grace What? What is it?
Joel Nothing. It doesn't matter.
Grace Come on, tell me. What's wrong with it?
Joel Well, that's not how you spell *opportunities*.
Grace What? Are you sure?
Joel Of course, I'm sure! It's o-double p-o-r-t-u-n-i-t-i-e-s.
Grace I don't believe it. I went on a demonstration about education with a banner full of spelling mistakes! I'm so embarrassed.
Joel Well, think positive. It's another reason for the government to help students to go to university – we can't spell when we leave school!
Grace Shut up!

Unit 9, page 93, exercises 24, 25 and 26

Anna Luke? What are we going to get Ed for his birthday?
Luke I'm not sure yet – have you got any ideas?
Anna Well, he's really into drawing. So, what about something for that?
Luke You mean like a graphic tablet?
Anna A graphic tablet. What is that?
Luke It's an electronic drawing book.
Anna What's it used for?
Luke It's used for digital drawings. Hang on … see?
Anna Really? How does it work?
Luke I think it works with – what's it called again? Oh yes – touchscreen technology.
Anna Does it look like an iPad?
Luke Yes, it does a bit. But it's a bit bigger than an iPad. And it's got a thing like a pen that you use to draw directly onto the screen. I don't remember the name …
Anna You mean a stylus?
Luke Exactly. You draw lines on the screen with the stylus. And you can colour the drawing with it too.

SPEAKING SKILLS – Dialogues

Anna How do you do that?

Luke Well, there's sort of a menu on the screen – it's like a little box of paints …

Anna A colour palette?

Luke Exactly! That's the word! It's got a virtual colour palette.

Anna Right. Are graphic tablets big?

Luke It depends. Most of them are about the same size as a laptop, others are a bit bigger.

Anna Are they expensive?

Luke The cheapest ones are about eighty pounds.

Anna Eighty pounds! I literally have no money, Luke. How can we afford that?

Luke We could ask Sally and Ian to buy it with us. If they help, it will only cost twenty pounds each.

Anna But I only earn money from walking our dog. I'll literally have to walk him from here to the North Pole to get twenty pounds!

Luke Oh, come on Anna, Ed's our best friend. And it's his eighteenth birthday.

Anna All right.

Unit 10, page 101, exercises 20, 21 and 22

Grace Hi, Anna, you look excited. What's up?

Anna I've just been talking to Katie about the party last Saturday night. You'll never guess what happened!

Grace Oh, what happened?

Anna Well, I shouldn't really tell you this but …

remember? We left at about half past eleven and when we got our coats Danny was talking to Roberta.

Grace Was he? I didn't really notice … By the way, did you go to Ellie's after, or did you go home?

Anna I went home. Anyway, Danny and Roberta were talking on the stairs for ages. They looked very … friendly. Apparently Jake, Roberta's boyfriend, was pretty angry about it …

Grace Seriously?

Anna Yes, he was furious actually, and I heard that Jake told his sister Tanya and she had a big argument with Roberta about it!

Grace Right. Speaking of Tanya, she's in my English class this year.

Anna Yeah, OK, whatever. So, according to Katie, Tanya told Roberta that she was behaving really badly towards Jake because she'd spent all night talking to Danny. Roberta said that it was none of her business and …

Grace Hey, I'm really impressed that you can remember the conversation so well. You've got an amazing memory. What's your secret?

Anna Oh, thanks. Well, I don't really know. I memorise a lot of song lyrics; maybe that helps.

Grace Do you? Do you know the lyrics to *Bohemian Rhapsody* by Queen? I love that song!

Anna Yes, I do! I love it too. But listen, Roberta was really angry then and she said that …

VERB TABLES

Present simple

affirmative	negative		questions	short answers	
full	full	contracted		affirmative	negative
I read	I do not read	I don't read	Do I read?	Yes, I do.	No, I don't.
you read	you do not read	you don't read	Do you read?	Yes, you do.	No, you don't.
she/he/it reads	she/he/it does not read	she/he/it doesn't read	Does she/he/it read?	Yes, she/he/it does.	No, she/he/it doesn't.
we read	we do not read	we don't read	Do we read?	Yes, we do.	No, we don't.
you read	you do not read	you don't read	Do you read?	Yes, you do.	No, you don't.
they read	they do not read	they don't read	Do they read?	Yes, they do.	No, they don't.

Past simple: be

affirmative	negative		questions	short answers	
full	full	contracted		affirmative	negative
I was	I was not	I wasn't	Was I?	Yes, I was.	No, I wasn't.
you were	you were not	you weren't	Were you?	Yes, you were.	No, you weren't.
she/he/it was	she/he/it was not	she/he/it wasn't	Was she/he/it?	Yes, she/he/it was.	No, she/he/it wasn't.
we were	we were not	we weren't	Were we?	Yes, we were.	No, we weren't.
you were	you were not	you weren't	Were you?	Yes, you were.	No, you weren't.
they were	they were not	they weren't	Were they?	Yes, they were.	No, they weren't.

Past simple

affirmative	negative		questions	short answers	
full	full	contracted		affirmative	negative
I played	I did not play	I didn't play	Did I play?	Yes, I did.	No, I didn't.
you played	you did not play	you didn't play	Did you play?	Yes, you did.	No, you didn't.
she/he/it played	she/he/it not play	she/he/it didn't play	Did she/he/it play?	Yes, she/he/it did.	No, she/he/it didn't.
we played	we did not play	we didn't play	Did we play?	Yes, we did.	No, we didn't.
you played	you did not play	you didn't play	Did you play?	Yes, you did.	No, you didn't.
they played	they did not play	they didn't play	Did they play?	Yes, they did.	No, they didn't.

Present continuous

affirmative		negative		questions	short answers	
full	contracted	full	contracted		affirmative	negative
I am talking	I'm talking	I am not talking	I'm not talking	Am I talking?	Yes, I am.	No, I'm not.
you are talking	you're talking	you are not talking	you aren't talking	Are you talking?	Yes, you are.	No, you're not.
she/he/it is talking	she/he/it's talking	she/he/it is not talking	she/he/it isn't talking	Is she/he/it talking?	Yes, she/he/it is.	No, she/he/it isn't.
we are talking	we're talking	we are not talking	we aren't talking	Are we talking?	Yes, we are.	No, we aren't.
you are talking	you're talking	you are not talking	you aren't talking	Are you talking?	Yes, you are.	No, you aren't.
they are talking	they're talking	they are not talking	they aren't talking	Are they talking?	Yes, they are.	No, they aren't.

VERB TABLES

be going to

affirmative		negative		questions	short answers	
full	contracted	full	contracted		affirmative	negative
I am going to eat	I'm going to eat	I am not going to eat	I'm not going to eat	Am I going to eat?	Yes, I am.	No, I'm not.
you are going to eat	you're going to eat	you are not going to eat	you aren't going to eat	Are you going to eat?	Yes, you are.	No, you aren't.
she/he/it is going to eat	she/he/it's going to eat	she/he/it is not going to eat	she/he/it isn't going to eat	Is she/he/it going to eat?	Yes, she/he/it is.	No, she/he/it isn't.
we are going to eat	we're going to eat	we are not going to eat	we aren't going to eat	Are we going to eat?	Yes, we are.	No, we aren't.
you are going to eat	you're going to eat	you are not going to eat	you aren't going to eat	Are you going to eat?	Yes, you are.	No, you aren't.
they are going to eat	they're going to eat	they are not going to eat	they aren't going to eat	Are they going to eat?	Yes, they are.	No, they aren't.

will

affirmative		negative		questions	short answers	
full	contracted	full	contracted		affirmative	negative
I will	I'll	I will not	I won't	Will I?	Yes, I will.	No, I won't.
you will	you'll	you will not	you won't	Will you?	Yes, you will.	No, you won't.
she/he/it will	she/he/it'll	she/he/it will not	she/he/it won't	Will she/he/it?	Yes she/he/it will.	No, she/he/it won't.
we will	we'll	we will not	we won't	Will we?	Yes, we will.	No, we won't.
you will	you'll	you will not	you won't	Will you?	Yes, you will.	No, you won't.
they will	they'll	they will not	they won't	Will they?	Yes, they will.	No, they won't.

Present perfect

affirmative		negative	
full	contracted	full	contracted
I have seen	I've seen	I have not seen	I haven't seen
you have seen	you've seen	you have not seen	you haven't seen
she/he/it has seen	she/he/it's seen	she/he/it has not seen	she/he/it hasn't seen
we have seen	we've seen	we have not seen	we haven't seen
you have seen	you've seen	you have not seen	you haven't seen
they have seen	they've seen	they have not seen	they haven't seen

questions	short answers	
	affirmative	negative
Have I seen?	Yes, I have.	No, I haven't.
Have you seen?	Yes, you have.	No, you haven't.
Has she/he/it seen?	Yes, she/he/it has.	No, she/he/it hasn't.
Have we seen?	Yes, we have.	No, we haven't.
Have you seen?	Yes, you have.	No, you haven't.
Have they seen?	Yes, they have.	No, they haven't.

Verb Tables

VERB TABLES

Present perfect continuous

affirmative		negative	
full	contracted	full	contracted
I have been waiting	I've been waiting	I have not been waiting	I haven't been waiting
you have been waiting	you've been waiting	you have not been waiting	you haven't been waiting
she/he/it have been waiting	she/he/it's been waiting	she/he/it has not been waiting	she/he/it hasn't been waiting
we have been waiting	we've been waiting	we have not been waiting	we haven't been waiting
you have been waiting	you've been waiting	you have not been waiting	you haven't been waiting
they have been waiting	they've been waiting	they have not been waiting	they haven't been waiting

questions	short answers	
	affirmative	negative
Have I been waiting?	Yes, I have.	No, I haven't.
Have you been waiting?	Yes, you have.	No, you haven't.
Has she/he/it been waiting?	Yes, she/he/it has.	No, she/he/it hasn't.
Have we been waiting?	Yes, we have.	No, we haven't.
Have you been waiting?	Yes, you have.	No, you haven't.
Have they been waiting?	Yes, they have.	No, they haven't.

Past continuous

affirmative	negative	
full	full	contracted
I was waiting	I was not waiting	I wasn't waiting
you were waiting	you were not waiting	you weren't waiting
she/he/it was waiting	she/he/it was not waiting	she/he/it wasn't waiting
we were waiting	we were not eating	we weren't waiting
you were waiting	you were not waiting	you weren't waiting
they were waiting	they were not waiting	they weren't waiting

questions	short answers	
	affirmative	negative
Was I waiting?	Yes, I was.	No, I wasn't.
Were you waiting?	Yes, you were.	No, you weren't.
Was she/he/it waiting?	Yes, she/he/it was.	No, she/he/it wasn't.
Were we waiting?	Yes, we were.	No, we weren't.
Were you waiting?	Yes, you were.	No, you weren't.
Were they waiting?	Yes, they were.	No, they weren't.

VERB TABLES

Past perfect

affirmative		negative	
full	contracted	full	contracted
I had seen	I'd seen	I had not seen	I hadn't seen
you had seen	you'd seen	you had not seen	you hadn't seen
she/he/it had seen	she/he/it'd seen	she/he/it had not seen	she/he/it hadn't seen
we had seen	we'd seen	we had not seen	we hadn't seen
you had seen	you'd seen	you had not seen	you hadn't seen
they had seen	they'd seen	they had not seen	they hadn't seen

questions	short answers	
	affirmative	negative
Had I seen?	Yes, I had.	No, I hadn't.
Had you seen?	Yes, you had.	No, you hadn't.
Had she/he/it seen?	Yes, she/he/it had.	No, she/he/it hadn't.
Had we seen?	Yes, we had.	No, we hadn't.
Had you seen?	Yes, you had.	No, you hadn't.
Had they seen?	Yes, they had.	No, they hadn't.

Passive tenses

affirmative	negative	questions	short answers	
present simple				
it is made	it isn't made	Is it made?	Yes, it is.	No, it isn't.
they are made	they aren't made	Are they made?	Yes, they are.	No, they aren't.
past simple				
it was made	it wasn't made	Was it made?	Yes, it was.	No, it wasn't.
they were made	they weren't made	Were they made?	Yes, they were.	No, they weren't.
present perfect				
it has been made	it hasn't been made	Has it been made?	Yes, it has.	No, it hasn't.
they have been made	they haven't been made	Have they been made?	Yes, they have	No, they haven't.

IRREGULAR VERBS

base form	past simple	past participle
be	was / were	been
beat	beat	beaten
become	became	become
begin	began	begun
bend	bent	bent
bet	bet	bet
bite	bit	bitten
bleed	bled	bled
blow	blew	blown
break	broke	broken
bring	brought	brought
build	built	built
burn	burned / burnt	burned / burnt
burst	burst	burst
buy	bought	bought
catch	caught	caught
choose	chose	chosen
come	came	come
cost	cost	cost
cut	cut	cut
deal	dealt	dealt
dig	dug	dug
do	did	done
draw	drew	drawn
dream	dreamed / dreamt	dreamed / dreamt
drink	drank	drunk
drive	drove	driven
eat	ate	eaten
fall	fell	fallen
feed	fed	fed
feel	felt	felt
fight	fought	fought
find	found	found
fly	flew	flown
forbid	forbade	forbidden
forget	forgot	forgotten
forgive	forgave	forgiven
freeze	froze	frozen
get	got	got
give	gave	given
go	went	gone
grow	grew	grown
hang	hung	hung
have	had	had
hear	heard	heard
hide	hid	hidden
hit	hit	hit
hold	held	held
hurt	hurt	hurt
keep	kept	kept
know	knew	known
lay	laid	laid
lead	led	led
learn	learned / learnt	learned / learnt
leave	left	left
lend	lent	lent
let	let	let
lie	lay	lain

base form	past simple	past participle
lie	lied	lied
light	lit	lit
lose	lost	lost
make	made	made
mean	meant	meant
meet	met	met
pay	paid	paid
put	put	put
read /riːd/	read /red/	read /red/
ride	rode	ridden
ring	rang	rung
rise	rose	risen
run	ran	run
say	said	said
see	saw	seen
seek	sought	sought
sell	sold	sold
send	sent	sent
set	set	set
sew	sewed	sewn / sewed
shake	shook	shaken
shine	shone	shone
shoot	shot	shot
show	showed	shown
shrink	shrank	shrunk
shut	shut	shut
sing	sang	sung
sink	sank	sunk
sit	sat	sat
sleep	slept	slept
smell	smelled / smelt	smelled / smelt
speak	spoke	spoken
spell	spelled / spelt	spelled / spelt
spend	spent	spent
split	split	split
spread	spread	spread
spring	sprang	sprung
stand	stood	stood
steal	stole	stolen
stick	stuck	stuck
sting	stung	stung
stink	stank	stunk
strike	struck	struck
swear	swore	sworn
sweep	swept	swept
swim	swam	swum
swing	swung	swung
take	took	taken
teach	taught	taught
tear	tore	torn
tell	told	told
think	thought	thought
throw	threw	thrown
understand	understood	understood
wake	woke	woken
wear	wore	worn
win	won	won
write	wrote	written

284 **Irregular Verbs**

UNITED KINGDOM
Total Area : 244 820 sq. km
(94 525 sq. miles)
POPULATION
over 5 000 000
over 500 000
over 100 000
over 50 000
over 10 000
under 10 000
LAND HEIGHT
1000m/3280ft
500m/1640ft
200m/656ft
Sea Level
N
0
100 km
0
100 miles
SHETLAND ISLANDS
Mainland
Lerwick
Fair I.
ORKNEY ISLANDS
Kirkwall
Mainland
Thurso
John o'Groats
Wick
OUTER HEBRIDES
Stornoway
Isle of Lewis
St Kilda
The Minch
Ullapool
North Uist
South Uist
Little Minch
Isle of Skye
Rhum
Sea of the Hebrides
INNER HEBRIDES
Isle of Mull
Jura
Islay
Firth of Lorn
Oban
Fort William
Ben Nevis 1343m
NORTH WEST HIGHLANDS
Dornoch Firth
Moray Firth
Elgin
Inverness
Loch Ness
Spey
GRAMPIAN MOUNTAINS
Peterhead
Aberdeen
Dee
Tay
Dundee
Firth of Tay
SCOTLAND
Perth
Loch Lomond
Stirling
Forth
Dunfermline
Firth of Forth
Falkirk
Greenock
Glasgow
Airdrie
Edinburgh
Firth of Clyde
Hamilton
Motherwell
Kilmarnock
Isle of Arran
Ayr
Berwick-upon-Tweed
Tweed
SOUTHERN UPLANDS
Hawick
CHEVIOT HILLS
Dumfries
Stranraer
North Channel
ATLANTIC OCEAN
NORTH SEA
Lough Foyle
Londonderry
Coleraine
Lower Bann
ANTRIM MOUNTAINS
Ballymena
NORTHERN IRELAND
ULSTER
Lough Neagh
Foyle
Newtownabbey
Bangor
Belfast
Omagh
Lower Lough Erne
Enniskillen
Lisburn
Armagh
Upper Bann
Newry
Upper Lough Erne
REPUBLIC OF IRELAND
Solway Firth
Carlisle
Eden
Penrith
CUMBRIAN MOUNTAINS
Isle of Man
Douglas
Barrow-in-Furness
Lancaster
Tyne
Newcastle upon Tyne
Sunderland
Durham
Tees
Middlesbrough
Stockton-on-Tees
Darlington
PENNINES
Ribble
Scarborough
Ouse
York
IRISH SEA
Blackpool
Bradford
Leeds
Kingston upon Hull
Humber
Preston
Blackburn
Huddersfield
Grimsby
Scunthorpe
Bolton
Manchester
Doncaster
Liverpool
Birkenhead
Mersey
Warrington
Sheffield
Lincoln
Trent
Anglesey
Holyhead
Bangor
Chester
Caernarfon
ENGLAND
The Wash
Cromer
Wrexham
Dee
Derby
Nottingham
King's Lynn
Norwich
Great Yarmouth
Severn
Stoke-on-Trent
Shrewsbury
Walsall
Leicester
Great Ouse
THE FENS
Wolverhampton
Peterborough
Cardigan Bay
Aberystwyth
Birmingham
Coventry
St George's Channel
CAMBRIAN MTS
WALES
Wye
Worcester
Northampton
Cambridge
Ipswich
Stratford-upon-Avon
Milton Keynes
Stansted Airport
Hereford
COTSWOLD HILLS
Luton
Luton Airport
Colchester
Fishguard
Carmarthen
Usk
Merthyr Tydfil
Gloucester
Watford
Southend-on-Sea
Swansea
Port Talbot
Pontypridd
Oxford
Heathrow Airport
Thames
Newport
Cardiff
LONDON
Ramsgate
Canterbury
Bristol
Bath
Swindon
Reading
CELTIC SEA
Bristol Channel
MENDIP HILLS
SALISBURY PLAIN
Gatwick Airport
Ashford
Dover
Barnstaple
Bridgwater
Taunton
Salisbury
Crawley
Folkestone
Channel Tunnel
Winchester
Southampton
Yeovil
Bournemouth
Portsmouth
Brighton
Hastings
Tamar
Exe
Poole
Isle of Wight
DARTMOOR
Exeter
Lyme Bay
Weymouth
Torquay
St Austell
Plymouth
Penzance
Truro
Isles of Scilly
English Channel
FRANCE

THANKS AND ACKNOWLEDGEMENTS

The authors and publishers acknowledge the following sources of copyright material and are grateful for the permissions granted. While every effort has been made, it has not always been possible to identify the sources of all the material used, or to trace all copyright holders. If any omissions are brought to our notice, we will be happy to include the appropriate acknowledgements on reprinting and in the next update to the digital edition, as applicable.

Key: T = Top, TL = Top Left, TR = Top Right, CL = Centre Left, CR = Centre Right, C = Centre, B = Below, BL = Below Left, BR = Below Right, L = Left, R = Right, Ex = Exercise, B/G = Background, U = Unit.

Text

Cover photo on p. 76 taken from *The Paleo Diet by Daniel Green*, photography by Peter Cassidy, published by Kyle Books. Reproduced with kind permissions; Cover photo on p. 76 reprinted by permission of HarperCollins Publishers Ltd. Copyright © 2016 Alice Liveing. Reproduced with kind permissions; Text on p. 85 adapted from "How to do internet research". Copyright © Paul Shoebottom 1996-2017. Reproduced with kind permissions; Maps on p. 244 adapted from "UNDESA, (2005)". Copyright © United Nation Department of Economic and Social Affairs; Text on p. 259 adapted from "We Interviewed Emma Watson While She Played with Kittens and It Was Absolutely Adorable" by Lindsay Farber, Mike Rose, Christian Zamora, © BuzzFeed, Inc.

Photo

All photos are sourced from GettyImages.

p. 6 (L) & p. 6 (R): Hoxton/Tom Merton; p. 6 (icons): Wonderfulpixel/iStock/Getty Images Plus; p. 6 (B/G): TCmake_photo/iStock/Getty Images Plus; p. 6 (tablet): Youzitx/DigitalVision Vectors; p. 6 (breakfast): etorres69/iStock/Getty Images Plus; p. 8 (header): Lonely Planet; p. 8 (CL): David Cleveland/Cultura; p. 8 (DVDs): kiev4/iStock/Getty Images Plus; p. 8 (DVDs): bibikoff/E+; p. 8 (CR): onurdongel/iStock/Getty Images Plus; p. 8 (TL): by_nicholas/iStock/Getty Images Plus; p. 8 (C): ChristinLola/iStock/Getty Images Plus; p. 9 (T): urfinguss/iStock/Getty Images Plus; p. 10 (school logo): kandserg/iStock/Getty Images Plus; p. 10 (TL): Aubrey Hart/Hulton Archive; p. 10 (CR): Michael Stroud/Stringer/Hulton Archive; p. 10 (B/G): clu/E+; p. 10 (BR): Antagain/E+; p. 10 (scroll): Liliboas/E+; p. 11 (TR): tuncaycetin/E+; p. 11 (BR): mphillips007/E+; p. 12 (B): hocus-focus/E+; p. 12 (crown): hudiemm/iStock/Getty Images Plus; p. 12 (B/G): zlisjak/E+; p. 12 (girls): fotostorm/E+; p. 12 (browser): tovovan/iStock/Getty Images Plus; p. 13 (B) & p. 255 (leopard): GlobalP/iStock/Getty Images Plus; p. 14 (C): MissHibiscus/E+; p. 14 (TR): Robert Daly/Caiaimage; p. 14 (L) & p. 165 (Ex 29.3): drbimages/E+; p. 14 (B/G): Yuri_Arcurs/DigitalVision; p. 15 (B) & p. 269 (girl): shironosov/iStock/Getty Images Plus; p. 16 (header): Bloom Productions/Taxi; p. 16 (BR): Martin Novak/Moment; p. 16 (C): Paul Bradbury/OJO Images; p. 17 (B): A-Digit/DigitalVision Vectors; p. 19 (C): mother image/Taxi; p. 19 (B): Andreas Pollok/The Image Bank; p. 19 (T): Michael rasowitz/Photographer's Choice; p. 19 (B/G): monkeybusinessimages/iStock/Getty Images Plus; p. 20 (aquarius), p. 20 (aisces), p. 20 (aries), p. 20 (taurus), p. 20 (gemini), p. 20 (cancer), p. 20 (leo), p. 20 (virgo), p. 20 (libra), p. 20 (scorpio), p. 20 (saggitarius) & p. 20 (capricorn): Tribalium/iStock/Getty Images Plus; p. 20 (B): jarenwicklund/iStock/Getty Images Plus; p. 20 (B/G): orensila/iStock/Getty Images Plus; p. 22 (Selena Gomez): George Pimentel/Getty Images Entertainment; p. 22 (Matt Damon): Steve Granitz/WireImage; p. 22 (Katie Perry): Jason LaVeris/FilmMagic; p. 22 (Ben Affleck): Pascal Le Segretain/Getty Images Entertainment; p. 22 (Rihanna): Nicholas Hunt/BET/Getty Images Entertainment; p. 22 (Taylor Swift): Amanda Edwards/WireImage; p. 22 (B/G): alxpin/iStock/Getty Images Plus; p. 22 (theatre): DigitalVision/Getty Images Plus; p. 23: SolStock/iStock/Getty Images Plus; p. 24 (header): Bruce Yuanyue Bi/Lonely Planet Images; p. 24 (B): Hervé GYSSELS/Photononstop; p. 24 (tree): ma_rish/iStock/Getty Images Plus; p. 24 (C): Tim E White/DigitalVision; p. 26 (robin): Andrew_Howe/Vetta; pp. 26–27: sasimoto/iStock/Getty Images Plus; p. 27 (robin illustration): DEA PICTURE LIBRARY/De Agostini Picture Library; p. 28 (Ex 18.1): Auscape/Universal Images Group; p. 28 (Ex 18.2): Hans Neleman/The Image Bank; p. 28 (Bruce Chatwin): Ulf Andersen/Hulton Archive; p. 28 (Karen Blixen): Keystone-France/Gamma-Keystone; p. 28 (B/G): peepo/E+; p. 28 (photo 1): Nigel Hicks/Dorling Kindersley; p. 28 (photo 2): laughingmango/E+; p. 28 (photo 3): Buena Vista Images/Stone; p. 28 (photo 4): Yun Han Xu/Moment; p. 28 (photo 5): WIN-Initiative/Riser; p. 28 (photo 6): Elena-studio/iStock/Getty Images Plus; p. 28 (photo 7): hadynyah/E+; p. 28 (photo 8): sot/The Image Bank; p. 28 (photo 9): GoodLifeStudio/E+; p. 28 (photo 10): Mark Daffey/Lonely Planet Images; p. 28 (photo 11): Massimiliano Alessandro/EyeEm; p. 28 (photo 12): Danita Delimont/Gallo Images; p. 30 (Italian dishes): Sungmoon Han/EyeEm; p. 30 (catwalk): Antonio de Moraes Barros Filho/WireImage; p. 30 (mountain): Gavin Hellier/robertharding; p. 30 (Ponte Vecchio): Peter Zelei Images/Moment; p. 30 (rugby): Alex Livesey/Stringer/Getty Images Sport; p. 30 (fog): Marco Secchi/Getty Images News; p. 30 (rugby): ADRIAN DENNIS/AFG; p. 31 (hill): alisher9/iStock/Getty Images Plus; p. 31 (bridge), p. 31 (forest) & p. 174 (Ex 5e): bubaone/DigitalVision Vectors; p. 31 (tunnel): ihorzigor/iStock/Getty Images Plus; p. 31 (lake): greyj/iStock/Getty Images Plus; p. 31 (river): kumdinpitak/iStock/Getty Images Plus; p. 31 (road): MicrovOne/iStock/Getty Images Plus; p. 31 (railway): JuliarStudio/iStock/Getty Images Plus; p. 34 (header): Lambert/Archive Photos; p. 34 (B): Dean Mitchell/E+; p. 34 (television): Grafissimo/E+; p. 34 (devices): ahmetemre/iStock/Getty Images Plus; p. 36 (Robert Pattison): Stephane Cardinale - Corbis/Corbis Entertainment; p. 36: mgkaya/e+; p. 36 (B/G): SonerCdem/iStock/Getty Images Plus; p. 37 (Dracula), p. 56 (photo 3) & p. 179 (John Christie): Bettmann; p. 40 (T): Image by Catherine MacBride/Moment; p. 40 (B): Renphoto/Vetta; p. 41 (T): LuminaStock/iStock/Getty Images Plus; p. 41 (B): rez-art/iStock/Getty Images Plus; p. 42 (C): JasonDoiy/E+; p. 42 (BL): Jordan Siemens/The Image Bank; p. 42 (Treadmill): Bulgac/iStock/Getty Images Plus; p. 42 (BL): kali9/E+; p. 43: courtneyk/E+; p. 44: luismmolina/E+; p. 45 (T): Bloomberg; p. 45 (B/G): Godruma/iStock/Getty Images Plus; p. 46 (hockey stick): MileA/iStock/Getty Images Plus; p. 46 (golf clubs): TongRo Images Inc; p. 46 (baseball bat): Coprid/iStock/Getty Images Plus; p. 46 (rugby ball) & p. 66 (Ex 3.A): pepifoto/E+; p. 46 (B/G): enjoynz/DigitalVision Vectors; p. 48 (photo 1): BEN STANSALL/Staff/AFP; p. 48 (photo 2): JONATHAN NACKSTRAND/Stringer/AFP; p. 48 (photo 3): CHRISTOPHE SIMON/Staff/AFP; p. 48 (photo 4): PabloBenitezLope/iStock/Getty Images Plus; p. 49: anouchka/iStock/Getty Images Plus; p. 49 (B/G): Paper Boat Creative/DigitalVision/Getty Images Plus; p. 52 (bank robbers): Patti McConville/The Image Bank; p. 52 (jewellery): American School; p. 52 (cops): Peter Macdiarmid/Staff/Getty Images News; p. 52 (handcuffs): JamesBrey/E+; p. 52 (diamonds): ryasick/E+; p. 52 (header): gorodenkoff/iStock/Getty Images Plus; p. 52 (B): fatihhoca/iStock/Getty Images Plus; p. 53: Freid/Whisenhunt/Photolibrary; p. 54: Jiripravda/iStock/Getty Images Plus; p. 55 (T): Hulton Archive/Stringer; p. 55 (B): FRED TANNEAU/Stringer/AFP; p. 55 (B/G): PytyCzech/iStock/Getty Images Plus; p. 56 (photo 1): Jesse Grant/Stringer/Getty Images Entertainment; p. 56 (thief): bagi1998/E+; p. 56 (film): losw/iStock/Getty Images Plus; p. 58 (T): CBS Photo Archive; p. 58 (B): Jochen Tack/imageBROKER; p. 59 (R) & p. 74 (burn): vgajic/E+; p. 59 (B/G): kyoshino/E+; p. 60 (photo A): peangdao/iStock/Getty Images Plus; p. 60 (header): Andrew_Mayovskyy/iStock/Getty Images Plus; p. 60 (B): Sephirot17/iStock/Getty Images Plu; p. 60 (photo C): Julia Davila-Lampe/Moment; p. 60 (photo B): PicturePartners/iStock/Getty Images Plus; p. 60 (photo D): Michael Kornafel/The Image Bank; pp. 62–63 (B/G): arturbo/E+; p. 62 (leopard): Aditya Singh/Moment; pp. 63, 255 (bower bird): Sylvain Cordier/Photodisc; p. 63 (newt): John Cancalosi/Photolibrary; p. 63 (starlings): Ben Hall/Nature Picture Library/Nature Picture Library; p. 63 (falcon): Bertie Gregory/Nature Picture Library; p. 64 (hurricane): Prairie Pictures/Photolibrary; p. 64 (flood): Majority World/Universal Images Group; p. 64 (drought): cinoby/E+; p. 64 (TL): ssuaphoto/iStock/Getty Images Plus; p. 64 (B/G): AndrewKravchenko/E+; p. 64 (T): Alashi/DigitalVision Vectors; p. 66 (Ex 35.1): Jack Taylor/Stringer/Getty Images News; p. 66 (Ex 35.2): The Washington Post; p. 66 (Ex 35.3): Hans Georg Eiben/Photolibrary; p. 66 (Ex 4.A): cherezoff/iStock/Getty Images Plus; p. 66 (Ex 4.B): Ben Richardson/Photonica; p. 66 (Ex 4.C): subjug/iStock/Getty Images Plus; p. 66 (Ex 3.B): Dave and Les Jacobs/Blend Images; p. 66 (Ex 3.C): Chris Ryan/OJO Images; p. 66 (Ex 5.A): Audhild Ruud/EyeEm; p. 66 (Ex 5.B): Alenka00/iStock/Getty Images Plus; p. 66 (Ex 5.C): Amana Images Inc; p. 66 (Ex 6.A): Rosemary Calvert/Photographer's Choice RF; p. 66 (Ex 6.B): NUMAX3D/iStock/Getty Images Plus; p. 66 (Ex 6.C): Artfully79/iStock/Getty Images Plus; p. 70 (C): Paul Burns/Blend Images; p. 70 (TL): JackF/iStock/Getty Images Plus; p. 70 (CR): Cylonphoto/iStock Editorial/Getty Images Plus; p. 70 (TR): asiseeit/E+; p. 70 (B): dlerick/E+; p. 70 (capsule): FingerMedium/DigitalVision Vectors; p. 70 (B/G): Pixtum/iStock/Getty Images Plus; p. 71: Bobboz/iStock/Getty Images Plus; pp. 72–73 (B/G): Maxiphoto/iStock/Getty Images Plus; p. 72: grinvalds/iStock/Getty Images Plus; p. 73 (swimming): Caiaimage/Paul Bradbury/OJO+; p. 73 (C): wonry/E+; p. 74 (headache) & p. 74 (toothache): AntonioGuillem/iStock/Getty Images Plus; p. 74 (cold): mihailomilovanovic/iStock/Getty Images Plus; p. 74 (finger with blood), p. 165 (Ex 29.4), p. 215 (T) & p. 254 (photo E): Image Source/Stockbyte; p. 74 (flu): Sporrer/Rupp/Cultura; p. 74 (ankle): Fertnig/iStock/Getty Images Plus; p. 74 (knee): Martin Hospach; p. 74 (sore stomach): Science Photo Library; p. 74 (vapour Rub): nattul/iStock/Getty Images Plus; p. 74 (plasters): Andy Crawford/Dorling Kindersley; p. 74 (thermometer): chas53/iStock/Getty Images Plus; p. 74 (tablets): Peter Dazeley/Photographer's Choice; p. 74 (nasal spray): egal/iStock/Getty Images Plus; p. 74 (throat lozenges): subjug/iStock/Getty Images Plus; p. 74 (cough syrup): duckycards/E+; p. 74 (cotton dressing): Paperkites/iStock/Getty Images Plus; p. 74 (bandage): BranislavP/iStock/Getty Images Plus; p. 74 (doctor) & p. 85 (T): sorbetto/DigitalVision Vectors; p. 74 (T): Nik01ay/iStock/Getty Images Plus; p. 74 (bruised knee): LEA PATERSON/SCIENCE PHOTO LIBRARY; p. 74 (ointment): ROBERT BROOK/Science Photo Library; p. 76 (cover photo): karandaev/iStock/Getty Images Plus; p. 76 (B/G): Route55/iStock/Getty Images Plus; p. 76 (B/G): hudiemm/E+; p. 76 (vinegar): Petershort/E+; p. 76 (spaghetti): repinanatoly/iStock/Getty Images Plus; p. 77: Rabbani and Solimene Photography/Getty Images Entertainment; p. 77 (B/G): 94clover/iStock/Getty Images Plus; p. 78 (header): HENNY RAY ABRAMS/Stringer/AFP; p. 78 (photo 2): SCOTT HEPPELL/Stringer/AFP; p. 78 (Obama): Alex Wong/Staff/Getty Images News; p. 78 (BL): Hindustan Times; p. 80 (T): LESLEY MARTIN/Stringer/AFP; p. 80 (B): Richard Drury/Stone; p. 81 (T): Flashpop/DigitalVision; p. 81 (C): Education Images/Universal Images Group; p. 81 (B): Juanmonino/iStock/Getty Images Plus; p. 82 (boy): DGLimages/iStock/Getty Images Plus; p. 84 (EU flag): vojtechvlk/iStock/Getty Images Plus; p. 84 (students): monkeybusinessimages/iStock/Getty Images Plus; p. 84 (flags): gerenme/E+; p. 85 (BR): Photo 12/Universal Images Group; p. 88 (C): duncan1890/iStock/Getty Images Plus; p. 88 (B): SuperStock; p. 88 (T): Lambert/Hulton Archive; p. 88 (header): BananaStock/Getty Images Plus; p. 89 (question mark): Ifness/iStock/Getty Images Plus; p. 90 (T): Foto24/Gallo Images; p. 91 (B) & p. 91 (T): vasabii/iStock/Getty Images Plus; p. 92 (T): Indianapolis Museum of Art/Archive Photos; p. 92 (B): Bryan Chan/Los Angeles Times; p. 94 (record player): snem/iStock/Getty Images Plus; p. 94 (B/G): wragg/E+; p. 94 (cassette recorder): Spiderplay/E+; p. 94 (drier): matty2x4/iStock/Getty Images Plus; p. 94: MarkColeImaging/iStock/Getty Images Plus; p. 95 (T): Photofusion/Universal Images Group; p. 95 (woman): Hulton Archive; p. 96 (Pope Francis): Pacific Press/LightRocket; p. 96 (David Bowie): Jamie McCarthy/Staff/WireImage; p. 96 (newspaper): bgblue/DigitalVision Vectors; p. 96 (B): John Lamb/DigitalVision; p. 96 (header): mediaphotos/E+; p. 96 (laptop): CostinT/iStock/Getty Images Plus; p. 96 (B): Andy445/E+; p. 99 (newspaper stand): Dan Kitwood/Staff/Getty Images News; p. 99 (B): Maica/E+; p. 99 (B/G): liangpv/DigitalVision Vectors; p. 100 (L): DreamPictures/Stone; p. 100 (TR): PLAINVIEW/iStock/Getty Images Plus; p. 100 (C): pressureUA/iStock Editorial/Getty Images Plus; p. 100 (R): Tsidvintsev/iStock/Getty Images Plus; p. 100 (exclamation mark): Chorniy10/iStock/Getty Images Plus; p. 100 (B/G): matdesign24/iStock/Getty Images Plus; p. 102 (TR): NicolasMcComber/iStock/Getty Images Plus; p. 102 (L): wundervisuals/E+; p. 102 (BL): Hollygraphic/iStock/Getty Images Plus; p. 102 (CR): sturti/E+; p. 103: Rawpixel/iStock/Getty Images Plus; p. 130: excape25/DigitalVision Vectors; p. 136: Cultura RM Exclusive/Philip Lee Harvey; p. 138: lushik/DigitalVision Vectors; p. 143: AIMSTOCK/E+; p. 146 (burger): NaCreative/DigitalVision Vectors; p. 147 (T): VICTOR/DigitalVision Vectors; p. 147 (B): simon2579/DigitalVision Vectors; p. 150: Panoramic Images; p. 151: Alain DENANTES/Gamma-Rapho; p. 153: LattaPictures/E+; p. 154: Rakdee/DigitalVision Vectors; p. 161: Michael Loccisano/Getty Images Entertainment; p. 165 (Ex 29.1): bo1982/E+; p. 165 (Ex 29.2): track5/E+; p. 165 (Ex 29.5): SensorSpot/E+; p. 168: VICTOR HABBICK VISIONS/Science Photo Library; p. 170: Ratsanai/DigitalVision Vectors; p. 172: strickke/E+; p. 174 (Ex 5.0): GoodGnom/DigitalVision Vectors; p. 174 (Ex 5.1): jojoo64/iStock/Getty Images Plus; p. 174 (Ex 5.2): bubaone/DigitalVision Vectors; p. 174 (Ex 5.4): Christopher Bradshaw/Hemera/Getty Images Plus; p. 174 (Ex 5d): ryasick/iStock/Getty Images Plus; p. 174 (Ex 5d): davidf/E+; p. 179 (B): Independent News and Media/Hulton Archive; p. 182: Peter Dazeley; p. 184: RobinOlimb/DigitalVision Vectors; p. 187: RomoloTavani/iStock/Getty Images Plus; p. 191: Gonzalo Azumendi/Photolibrary; p. 197: janecampbell21/iStock Editorial/Getty Images Plus; p. 201: ERproductions Ltd/Blend Images; p. 205 (T): Anadolu Agency;

p. 209 (BR): by Paco Calvino (Barcelona, Spain)/Moment; p. 209 (CL): RODGER BOSCH/AFP; p. 209 (BL): DonNichols/iStock/Getty Images Plus; p. 209 (BL): Hemera Technologies/PhotoObjects.net/Getty Images Plus; p. 214: Grady Coppell/Photographer's Choice; p. 215 (bus): ChrisSteer/E+; p. 215 (teapot): Radionphoto/iStock/Getty Images Plus; p. 215 (salt and pepper): gresei/iStock/Getty Images Plus; p. 215 (cutlery): malerapaso/E+; p. 218: WIN-Initiative; p. 222: Alashi/DigitalVision Vectors; p. 223: Alashi/DigitalVision Vectors; p. 227 (B): JohnDWilliams/iStock Editorial/Getty Images Plus; p. 227 (T): travnikovstudio/iStock/Getty Images Plus; p. 230: ANDREYGUDKOV/iStock/Getty Images Plus; p. 231: De Agostini Picture Library; p. 232: Bettmann; p. 233: Bobby Bank/WireImage; p. 234: Culture Club/Hulton Archive; p. 235: John Kobal Foundation/Moviepix; p. 237: Slaven Vlasic/Getty Images Entertainment; p. 238: Hulton Collection; Vatican Pool/Getty Images News; p. 240 (L): cynoclub/iStock/Getty Images Plus; p. 240: GlobalP/iStock/Getty Images Plus; p. 240 (C): FatCamera/E+; p. 240 (R): Caroline von Tuempling/The Image Bank; p. 240 (left moth): Andrs Castro Socolich/EyeEm; p. 240 (right moth): Chan Cheng/EyeEm; p. 241 (fox): GlobalP/iStock/Getty Images Plus; p. 241 (rabbit): chengyuzheng/iStock/Getty Images Plus; p. 241 (mouse): Pakhnyushchyy/iStock/Getty Images Plus; p. 241 (snake): Simon Murrell/Cultura; p. 241 (hawk): Premium/UIG/Universal Images Group; p. 241 (owl): GlobalP/iStock/Getty Images Plus; p. 241 (grasshopper): ithinksky/E+; p. 241 (earth): RapidEye/E+; p. 241 (frog): Studio-Annika/iStock/Getty Images Plus; p. 241 (bird): Cyril Laubscher/Dorling Kindersley; p. 242 (UK map): archymeder/iStock/Getty Images Plus; p. 242 (India map): bgblue/DigitalVision Vectors; p. 242 (B/G): Darragh Hehir/Moment; p. 242 (population): FotografiaBasica/iStock/Getty Images Plus; p. 242 (textiles): valeie/iStock/Getty Images Plus; p. 243 (coal): Michael Betts/Photographer's Choice; p. 243 (CL): Hulton Archive; p. 243 (BL): Print Collector/Hulton Archive; p. 243 (CR): Hulton Archive; p. 243 (BR): Bettmann; p. 244 (village): altrendo travel/Juice Images; p. 244 (city): Juergen Sack/E+; p. 244 (B): Smart/iStock/Getty Images Plus; p. 245 (photo A): Westend61; p. 245 (photo B): Abhinav Mathur/Moment Open; p. 245 (photo C): Universal History Archive/Universal Images Group; p. 245 (photo D): Fratelli Alinari IDEA S.p.A./Corbis Historical; p. 246 (CR): Simone Simone/Moment; p. 246 (C): DEA PICTURE LIBRARY/De Agostini; p. 246 (CL): Simon Montgomery/Moment Open; p. 246 (BL): H. & D. Zielske/LOOK-foto/LOOK; p. 246 (BR): H. & D. Zielske/LOOK-foto/LOOK; p. 247 (CL): Danita Delimont/Gallo Images; p. 247 (BR): John Guidi/robertharding; p. 247 (BC): Zvonimir Atletic/EyeEm; p. 247 (BL): tomwald/iStock/Getty Images Plus; p. 247 (B/G): vm/E+; p. 249 (map): iconeer/DigitalVision Vectors; p. 250: Mondadori Portfolio; p. 250 (TL): Balavan/E+; p. 250 (header): mZwonko/iStock/Getty Images Plus; p. 250 (B): ilyaliren/iStock/Getty Images Plus; p. 250 (B/G): whilerests/iStock/Getty Images Plus; p. 251: catscandotcom/E+; p. 252: Kevin Kane/Stringer/WireImage; p. 252 (B/G): timnewman/E+; p. 253 (T): Talaj/iStock/Getty Images Plus; p. 253: PAUL ELLIS/AFP; p. 254 (photo A): ralucahphotography.ro/Moment Open; p. 254 (photo B): Seb Oliver/Cultura; p. 254 (photo C): Robert Warren/Stone; p. 254 (photo D): Heritage Images/Hulton Archive; p. 254 (B/G): kizilkayaphotos/E+; p. 254 (stamp): VladSt/DigitalVision Vectors; p. 255 (R): artist-unlimited/iStock/Getty Images Plus; p. 255 (L): JurgaR/E+; p. 255 (R): YinYang/E+; p. 256 (R): Pacific Press/LightRocket; p. 257 (T): AFP/Staff; p. 257 (B): Gideon Mendel/Corbis Historical; p. 258 (T): 4X-image/iStock/Getty Images Plus; p. 258 (B/G): llhedgehogll/iStock/Getty Images Plus; p. 259 (T): Paul Morigi/WireImage; p. 260 (R): Yellow Dog Productions; p. 260 (L): KatarzynaBialasiewicz/iStock/Getty Images Plus; p. 261 (T) & p. 267 (B): Image Source/DigitalVision; p. 261 (B): FrankRamspott/DigitalVision Vectors; p. 262 (B): mustafahacalaki/DigitalVision Vectors; p. 263: mifllippo/iStock/Getty Images Plus; p. 264: dolgachov/iStock/Getty Images Plus; p. 265 (B) & p. 266 (B): PeopleImages/DigitalVision; p. 265 (icons): pshonka/iStock/Getty Images Plus; p. 265 (T): fad1986/iStock/Getty Images Plus; p. 266 (T): BrianAJackson/iStock/Getty Images Plus; p. 267 (T): Compassionate Eye Foundation/Jasper White/DigitalVision; p. 267 (BL): zabelin/iStock/Getty Images Plus; p. 268 (B): DNY59/E+; p. 268 (T): Ljupco/iStock/Getty Images Plus; p. 269: olaser/E+; pp. 232–233: Patrick Swan/Design Pics/Perspectives; pp. 236–237: porojnicu/iStock/Getty Images Plus.

p. 56 (photo 2): Everett Collection, Inc./Alamy Stock Photo/Almay; p. 76 (cover photo): GANNA MARTYSHEVA/Shutterstock; p. 82 (village): Vicky Jirayu/Shutterstock; p. 209 (CR): Mark Richardson/Alamy Stock Photo/Alamy; p. 239:Granger Historical Picture Archive/Alamy Stock Photo/Alamy.

Video
All videos are sourced from GettyImages.

Unit 1: 00:03: multifocus/Creatas Video+/Getty Images Plus; 00:11: Teraphim/Creatas Video+/Getty Images Plus; 00:13: SolStock/Creatas Video; 00:15: Thomas Barwick/Image Bank Film; 00:17: gawrav/Creatas Video; 00:21: Madmaxer/Creatas Video+/Getty Images Plus; 00:27: monkeybusinessimages/Creatas Video+/Getty Images Plus; 00:33: Steve Debenport/Creatas Video; 00:43: FatCamera/Vetta; 00:51: TheRabbitHolePictures/Creatas Video+/Getty Images Plus; 00:56: Stephanie Hardt/Verve; 01:09: sylwiab/Creatas Video+/Getty Images Plus; 01:18: Yellow Dog Productions Inc./Image Bank Film; 01:28: hoozone/Vetta; 01:34: bowdenimages/Creatas Video+/Getty Images Plus; 01:42: Andersen Ross/Image Bank Film; 01:51: Georgi-Vasilev/Creatas Video; 01:51: RobinBeckham/Vetta; **Unit 2:** 00:03: Sky News/Film Image Partner; 00:16: Skyworks Places/Image Bank Film; 00:27: ContentWorks/Creatas Video; 00:33: BFI HD Collection/Archive Films: Creative; 00:41: BFI HD Collection/Archive Films: Creative; 00:49: Gregory Christopher Lindsey/Image Bank Film; 00:56: Skyworks Places/Image Bank Film; 01:07: Komplett Media/Image Bank Film; 01:18: Skyworks Places/Image Bank Film; 01:28: Steve Smith/Image Bank Film; 01:41: Blootoad/Creatas Video+/Getty Images Plus; **Unit 3:** 00:03: Peruvian Newsreels - Footage/Archive Films: Editorial; 00:10: Mr. Big Film/one80; 00:15: Grinberg, Paramount, Pathe Newsreels/Sherman Grinberg Library; 00:25: Archive Films/Archive Films: Creative; 00:33: Prelinger/Archive Films: Creative; 00:45: trumzz/Creatas Video+/Getty Images Plus; 00:55: Curious Cumulus Productions/Archive Films: Creative; 01:07: de Lossy/Corbis Video; 01:14: Warner Bros. Studios/Warner Bros. Entertainment; 01:21: Imageways/Archive Films: Creative; 01:29: Videowest Productions/Archive Films: Creative; 01:39: nmlfd/Creatas Video+/Getty Images Plus; 01:52: RobinBeckham/Creatas Video; 01:56: Georgi-Vasilev/Creatas Video; 02:02: Wayne Herron/Creatas Video+/Getty Images Plus; 02:08: Robin Beckham/Creatas Video; **Unit 4:** 00:03: SolStock/Creatas Video; 00:10: gilaxia/Creatas Video; 00:20: Johnce/Creatas Video; 00:28: Steve Debenport/Creatas Video; 00:35: hoozone/Creatas Video; 00:39: hoozone/Creatas Video; 00:42: Simonkr/one80: Signature; 00:45: grafikeray/Creatas Video+/Getty Images Plus; 00:52: kali9/Creatas Video; 00:57: IgorUsachev/Creatas Video+/Getty Images Plus; 01:02: Steve Debenport/Creatas Video; 01:07: Steve Debenport/Creatas Video; 01:12: Sky News/Film Image Partner; 01:17: Steve Debenport/Creatas Video; 01:28: monkeybusinessimages/Creatas Video+/Getty Images Plus; 01:41: Tribune Broadcasting - Elaine Ruiz; 01:51: kali9/Vetta; 01:56: kali9/Vetta; **Unit 5:** 00:03: ITN; 00:08: Jay Feather/Image Bank Film: Signature; 00:16: ITN; 00:22: ITN; 00:34: Hatton Garden Properties Limited/Getty Images Editorial Footage; 00:45: Sky News/Film Image Partner; 00:58: Sky News/Film Image Partner; 01:10: ITN; 01:20: Hatton Garden Properties Limited/Getty Images Editorial Footage; 01:27: monkeybusinessimages/Creatas Video+/Getty Images Plus; 01:38: STEFANOLUNARDI/Creatas Video+/Getty Images Plus; 01:48: ITN; 02:01 & 02:19: Do Diligence Inc./Image Bank Film: Signature; 02:13: Sattaya/Creatas Video; **Unit 6:** 00:03: gmutlu/Creatas Video; 00:08: n-trash/Creatas Video; 00:15: kalarati/Vetta; 00:19: red_moon_rise/Creatas Video; 00:23: SolStock/Creatas Video; 00:26: Nanhatai8/Creatas Video; 00:34: Hal Bergman/Image Bank Film; 00:39: levakovs/Creatas Video; 00:47: Anthony Collins/Image Bank Film; 00:53: Warner Bros. Studios/Warner Bros. Entertainment; 01:03: A&E Television Networks/Image Bank Film; 01:09: Robert Harding Video/Photolibrary Video; 01:17: mastodon41k/Creatas Video; 01:26: Cassidy Inc./Image Bank Film; 01:33: StopInMotion/Image Bank Film; 01:43: piyaset/Creatas Video; 01:49: Hal Bergman/Photodisc; 01:54: haapaiglenn/Vetta; 02:02: Warner Bros. Studios/Warner Bros. Entertainment; 02:09: petekarici/Creatas Video; 02:22: Timothy Hamish Shepherd/Oxford Scientific Video; 02:35: Alen Popov/Creatas Video; **Unit 7:** 00:03: Yellow Dog Productions Inc./Image Bank Film: Signature; 00:07: gabriel__bostan/Vetta; 00:10: Ariel Skelley/Iconica Video: Signature; 00:15: STK Pictures/Image Bank Film: Signature; 00:22: Stephen Marks Inc./Photolibrary Video; 00:31: 10incheslab/Creatas Video; 00:43: Yellow Dog Productions Inc./Image Bank Film: Signature; 00:55: PUZURIN/Creatas Video+/Getty Images Plus; 01:01: Dimitri Otis/Photographer's Choice; 01:06: Peresmeh/Creatas Video; 01:12: manaemedia/Creatas Video+/Getty Images Plus; 01:18: milan2099/Creatas Video; 01:26: WOWstockfootage/Iconica Video: Signature; 01:33: cgtoolbox/Creatas Video; 01:46: mack2happy/Creatas Video; 01:56: STK Pictures/Image Bank Film: Signature; 02:02: eastlight/Creatas Video; **Unit 8:** 00:03: selincevizli/Vetta; 00:14: Bruno Levy - Footage/Getty Images Editorial Footage; 00:17: Photokanok/Creatas Video; 00:20: Sky News/Film Image Partner; 00:24: Mountain Top Films - Footage/Getty Images Editorial Footage; 00:35: Kevin McCullagh - Footage/Getty Images Editorial Footage; 00:46: Sky News/Film Image Partner; 00:59: Sky News/Film Image Partner; 01:08: Lge Inc - Footage/Getty Images Editorial Footage; 01:19: Paul Marotta/Getty Images News; 01:25: Bloomberg; 01:32: monkeybusinessimages/Creatas Video+/Getty Images Plus; 01:39: vision008/Creatas Video+/Getty Images Plus; 01:53: Brian Craig/Getty Images Entertainment Video; 02:04: Sky News/Film Image Partner; 02:12: FedNet; 02:25: Tribune Broadcasting - Fabiola Franco; **Unit 9:** 00:03: ITN; 00:08: DEA/A. DAGLI ORTI/De Agostini Picture Library; 00:13: Onyx Media, Llc - Footage/Archive Films: Editorial; 00:18: NatanaelGinting/Creatas Video+/Getty Images Plus; 00:26: Science Photo Library/Image Bank Film; 00:34: Science Photo Library/Image Bank Film; 00:47: Science Photo Library/Image Bank Film; 01:02: Inok/Creatas Video+/Getty Images Plus; 01:15: nmlfd/Vetta; 01:25: A Luna Blue/Verve+; 01:36: nmlfd/Vetta; 01:51: Brevor/Creatas Video; 01:59: Laurence Dutton/Creatas Video; 02:10: Foto Bureau Nz Limited/DigitalVision; 02:14: Getty Images; **Unit 10:** 00:03: Sky News/Film Image Partner; 00:10: Placebo365/Creatas Video; 00:18: Motortion/Creatas Video+/Getty Images Plus; 00:26: Daniel Sambraus/Photographer's Choice; 00:35: natebowman/Creatas Video+/Getty Images Plus; 00:46: Yellow Dog Productions Inc./Image Bank Film: Signature; 01:01: Stock Footage, Inc./Verve+; 01:09: A&E Television Networks/Archive Films: Creative; 01:22: Petrified Films/Archive Films: Creative; 01:31: Encyclopaedia Britannica Films/Archive Films: Creative; 01:44: Artur Debat/Moment Mobile; 01:48: John Lamb/DigitalVision; 01:52: Monty Rakusen/Cultura; 01:56: gilaxia/Vetta; 02:04: riccardokolp/Creatas Video; 02:14: gmutlu/Creatas Video.

Illustrations by Damiano Groppi.

Music
All music are sourced from GettyImages.

U1: Uncle Carl/SoundExpress; U2: Joe Deninzon/SoundExpress; U3: Jeffrey Reid Baker/SoundExpress; U4: Vytenis Misevicius/SoundExpress; U5: Next Chapter/SoundExpress; U6: Peter Lainson/SoundExpress; U7: Peggy Atwood/SoundExpress; U8: RFM/SoundExpress; U9: Rusuden/SoundExpress; U10: Bradley Sowash/SoundExpress. Changing Language: Thomas Feller/SoundExpress.

Video stills by Lada films.

Video produced by Lada films.

CLIL Modules by Teresa Ting.

The publishers would like to extend a special thank you to the following teachers for the invaluable feedback they have provided during the development of the material:
Claudia Bianchi, Paola Camiciottoli, Giovanna Da Villa, Fiorenza Iori

The authors and publishers would also like to thank the following teachers:
Albertini Katia, Aldegheri Federica, Ariatta Annamaria, Attimonelli Francesca, Avigdor Silvia, Bernascone Rossella, Bertino Mauro, Cara Laura, Coppola Antonietta, Cusinato Mirella, Davino Stefania, Di Marco Cecilia, Fattori Paola, Finzi Mughetto, Fioretta Laura, Giolitti Loredana, Giorgi Claudia, Marchetti Cristina, Meini Valtere, Moscati Franca, Munno Pasquale, Nicolosi Patrizia, Norsa Alessandra, Orlarei Maria Pia, Paoli Anna, Patrizia Cozzini, Pescini Benedetta, Petrelli Patrizia, Piras Gianna, Pisani Antonella, Pluchino Rossana, Pontillo Francesca, Pozzi Ausilia, Prato Maria Teresa, Puccioni Laura, Radini Claudia, Roffi Donatella, Romagnoli Anna Maria, Rossi Antonella, Sale Cinzia, Salvagno Martina, Sollevanti Elena, Sortino Flaviana, Stefanini Laura, Stringa Daniela, Tagliaretti Elena, Tubino Raffaella, Venturi Letizia, Zambito Francesca, Zecchi Antonella

First Published by Cambridge University Press 2018
© Cambridge University Press 2018
cambridge.org/cambridgeenglish

I diritti di elaborazione in qualsiasi forma o opera, di memorizzazione anche digitale su supporti di qualsiasi tipo (inclusi magnetici e ottici), di riproduzione e di adattamento totale o parziale con qualsiasi mezzo (compresi i microfilm e le copie fotostatiche), i diritti di noleggio, di prestito e di traduzione sono riservati per tutti i paesi. L'acquisto della presente copia dell'opera non implica il trasferimento dei suddetti diritti né li esaurisce.

Le fotocopie per uso personale del lettore possono essere effettuate nei limiti del 15% di ciascun volume dietro pagamento alla SIAE del compenso previsto dall'art. 68, commi 4 e 5, della legge 22 aprile 1941 n. 633.

Le fotocopie effettuate per finalità di carattere professionale, economico o commerciale o comunque per uso diverso da quello personale possono essere effettuate a seguito di specifica autorizzazione rilasciata da:

CLEARedi, Centro Licenze e Autorizzazioni per le Riproduzioni Editoriali,
Corso di Porta Romana 108, 20122 Milano

email *autorizzazioni@clearedi.org* e sito web *www.clearedi.org*

L'editore, per quanto di propria spettanza, considera rare le opere fuori dal proprio catalogo editoriale. La fotocopia dei soli esemplari esistenti nelle biblioteche di tali opere è consentita, non essendo concorrenziale all'opera. Non possono considerarsi rare le opere di cui esiste, nel catalogo dell'editore, una successiva edizione, le opere presenti in cataloghi di altri editori o le opere antologiche.

Nel contratto di cessione è esclusa, per biblioteche, istituti di istruzione, musei ed archivi, la facoltà di cui all'art. 71 – ter legge diritto d'autore.

Maggiori informazioni sul sito: *http://www.loescher.it*

Ristampe
11   10   9
2024 2023 2022

ISBN 9781108627719

Nonostante la passione e la competenza delle persone coinvolte nella realizzazione di quest'opera, è possibile che in essa siano riscontrabili errori o imprecisioni. Ce ne scusiamo fin d'ora con i lettori e ringraziamo coloro che, contribuendo al miglioramento dell'opera stessa, vorranno segnalarceli al seguente indirizzo:

Cambridge University Press
Via Vitaliano Donati, 29
10121 Torino, Italy
cupitaly@cambridge.org

Progetto grafico SB: Simona Corniola – Colibrì graphic design, Rapallo
Impaginazione: Simona Corniola – Colibrì graphic design, Rapallo; Fregi e Majuscole s.r.l., Torino
Redazione: Fregi e Majuscole s.r.l., Torino
Copertina: Massimo Principi Adv, Torino
Stampa: Printed in Italy by Rotolito S.p.A.